HOLT CALIFORNIA

Mathematics

Course 1: Numbers to Algebra

Jennie M. Bennett

Edward B. Burger

David J. Chard

Audrey L. Jackson

Paul A. Kennedy

Freddie L. Renfro

Tom W. Roby

Janet K. Scheer

Bert K. Waits

HOLT, RINEHART AND WINSTON

A Harcourt Education Company

Orlando • Austin • New York • San Diego • London

Cover photo: palm trees and buildings, Los Angeles, California;
© J. A. Kraulis/Masterfile

Cover photo: Santa Monica Pier, Los Angeles area, California; © Ron Niebrugge/Alamy

Cover photo: wind turbines, Mojave, California; © Stock Connection Distribution/Alamy

Cover photo: sea otter, Monterey Bay, California; © Robert E. Barber/Alamy

Cover photo: Antelope Valley, California Poppy Reserve; © Macduff Everton/Corbis

ISBN 978-0-03-092315-9

ISBN 0-03-092315-8

5 1421 10 09

California Course 1: Numbers to Algebra
Contents in Brief

Student Handbook

AUTHORS

Jennie M. Bennett, Ed.D. is a mathematics teacher at Hartman Middle School in Houston, Texas. Jennie is past president of the Benjamin Banneker Association, the Second Vice-President of NCSM, and a former board member of NCTM.

Edward B. Burger, Ph.D. is Professor of Mathematics and Chair at Williams College and is the author of numerous articles, books, and videos. He has won several prestigious writing and teaching awards offered by the Mathematical Association of America. Dr. Burger has made numerous television and radio appearances, and has given innumerable mathematical presentations around the world.

David J. Chard, Ph.D., is an Associate Dean of Curriculum and Academic Programs at the University of Oregon. He is the President of the Division for Research at the Council for Exceptional Children, is a member of the International Academy for Research on Learning Disabilities, and is the Principal Investigator on two major research projects for the U.S. Department of Education.

Audrey L. Jackson, M.Ed., is on the Board of Directors for NCTM. She is the Program Coordinator for Leadership Development with the St. Louis, public schools and is a former school administrator for the Parkway School District.

CONSULTING AUTHORS

Lee Haines is an International Baccalaureate Coordinator and Math Academic Coach for San Bernardino City Schools. In 2004, he was awarded the Region 10 California League of Middle Schools Educator of the Year Award.

Robin Scarcella, Ph.D., is the director of the Academic English and English as a Second Language Program at the University of California at Irvine. She has written numerous articles and books about ESL teaching and secondary language acquisition.

Paul A. Kennedy, Ph.D. is a professor in the Department of Mathematics at Colorado State University. Dr. Kennedy is a leader in mathematics education. His research focuses on developing algebraic thinking by using multiple representations and technology. He is the author of numerous publications.

Freddie L. Renfro, MA, has 35 years of experience in Texas education as a classroom teacher and director/coordinator of Mathematics PreK-12 for school districts in the Houston area. She has served as a reviewer and team trainer for Texas Math Institutes and has presented at numerous math workshops.

Tom W. Roby, Ph.D., is Associate Professor of Mathematics and Director of the Quantitative Learning Center at the University of Connecticut. He founded and co-directed the ACCLAIM professional development program. He also chaired the advisory board of the California Mathematics Project, and reviewed content for the California Standards Tests.

Janet K. Scheer, Ph.D., Executive Director of Create A Vision™, is a motivational speaker and provides customized K-12 math staff development. She has taught internationally and domestically at all grade levels.

Bert K. Waits, Ph.D., is a Professor Emeritus of Mathematics at The Ohio State University and co-founder of T^3 (Teachers Teaching with Technology), a national professional development program.

CALIFORNIA ADVISORS

Charlie Bialowas is the Mathematics Curriculum Specialist for the Anaheim Union High School District. He also serves as a mathematics student teacher supervisor for California State University, Fullerton, and was the Math Chairperson at Oxford Academy in Cypress.

Wendy Taub-Hoglund is a Teacher Expert Secondary Math with Los Angeles Unified School District. She has received numerous awards for excellence in teaching, and has coauthored math review books for test preparation.

CALIFORNIA TEACHER ADVISORY PANEL

Kay Barrie
Math Department Chair
Rio Vista MS
Fresno, CA

Youshi Berry
Math Teacher
Emerson MS
Pomona, CA

Charlie Bialowas
Math Curriculum
    Specialist
Anaheim Union HS
    District
Anaheim, CA

**Lorrie Wineberg
Buehler**
Principal
Baldy View Elementary
    School
Upland, CA

Mary Chiaverini
Math Teacher
Plaza Vista MS
Irvine, CA

Dennis Deets
Assistant Principal
AB Miller HS
Fontana, CA

Pauline Embree
Math Department Chair
Rancho San Joaquin MS
Irvine, CA

Sandi Enochs
Math Lead Teacher
Desert Hot Springs HS
Desert Hot Springs, CA

Tricia Gough
Math Department Chair
Emerson MS
Pomona, CA

Lee Haines
IB Coordinator/Math
    Coach
San Bernardino City
    Schools
San Bernardino, CA

Shannon Kelly
Math Teacher
Centennial HS
Corona, CA

Lisa Kernaghan
Math Teacher/
    Administrator
Oak Creek Intermediate
    School
Oakhurst, CA

Mary Ann Kremenliev
Math Teacher
Foothill MS
Walnut Creek, CA

Carole Kuck
Math Department Chair
Jean Farb MS
San Diego, CA

David V. Mattoon
Math Teacher
Potter Junior HS
Fallbrook, CA

Lynette McClintock
Math/Science Teacher
Thompson MS
Murrieta, CA

**Nancy Nazarian-
Carroll**
Math Teacher
Curtiss MS
Carson, CA

John (Jack) P. Nunes
Math Teacher and
    Department Leader
Fern Bacon MS
Sacramento, CA

Suzanne O'Rourke
Math Teacher
Antioch MS
Antioch, CA

Jong Sun Park
Math Teacher
Holmes International MS
Northridge, CA

Barbara Parr
Math Teacher
Emerson MS
Bakersfield, CA

Donna Phair
Math Department Chair
William Hopkins Junior HS
Fremont, CA

Donald R. Price
Math Teacher
Alvarado Intermediate
    School
Irvine, CA

Jennifer Randel
Math/Science Teacher,
    Grade Level Chair
Thompson MS
Murrieta, CA

Wendy Taub-Hoglund
Teacher Expert Secondary
    Math
Los Angeles USD
Los Angeles, CA

Matthew Ting
Math Coach
Peary MS
Gardena, CA

CALIFORNIA REVIEWERS

Youshi Berry
Math Teacher
Emerson MS
Pomona, CA

Charlie Bialowas
Mathematics Curriculum
    Specialist
Anaheim Union HS District
Anaheim, CA

Lorrie Wineberg Buehler
Principal
Baldy View Elementary School
Upland, CA

Mary Chiaverini
Math Department Head
Plaza Vista MS
Irvine, CA

Michael Davoudian
Math Coach
Luther Burbank MS
Burbank, CA

DeAnn DeBey
Math Teacher
Irvine Unified School District
Irvine, CA

Pauline Embree
Math Department Chair
Rancho San Joaquin MS
Irvine, CA

Tricia Gough
Math Department Chair
Emerson MS
Pomona, CA

Lee Haines
IB Coordinator/Math Coach
San Bernardino City Schools
San Bernardino, CA

Lisa Kernaghan
Math Teacher/Administrator
Oak Creek Intermediate School
Oakhurst, CA

David Mattoon
Math Teacher
Potter Junior HS
Fallbrook, CA

Michael Nagaran
Mathematics Coach
Los Angeles Unified School
    District
Los Angeles, CA

Nancy Nazarian-Carroll
Math Teacher
Curtiss MS
Carson, CA

John (Jack) P. Nunes
Math Teacher and
    Department Leader
Fern Bacon MS
Sacramento, CA

Jong Sun Park
Math Teacher
Holmes International MS
Northridge, CA

Raylene Paustain
Teacher on Special Assignment
Clovis Unified School District
Clovis, CA

Donna Phair
Math Department Chair
William Hopkins Junior HS
Fremont, CA

Donald R. Price
Math Teacher
Alvarado Intermediate School
Rowland Heights, CA

Golden T. Quinn
Math Teacher
Audubon MS
Los Angeles, CA

Wendy Taub-Hoglund
Teacher Expert Secondary Math
Los Angeles USD
Los Angeles, CA

CALIFORNIA FIELD TEST PARTICIPANTS

Carmencita Ancora
Dana MS
San Diego, CA

Henry Ashe
Vail Ranch MS
Temecula, CA

Susan Battistv
High Tech MS
San Diego, CA

Donna Campbell
Mesa Intermediate
    School
Palmdale, CA

Todd Cardosa
Encina HS
Sacramento, CA

Lou Catti
Creekside MS
Patterson, CA

Marcie Charlesworth
Excelsior Elementary
    School
Roseville, CA

Peggy Clarke
Temecula MS
Temecula, CA

Sheryl Cleveland
Golden Valley HS
Bakersfield, CA

Joyanna Deutsch
Forty-Niners Academy
East Palo Alto, CA

Andrea Farrow
Margarita MS
Temecula, CA

Ryan Gallagher
High Tech MS
San Diego, CA

Laura Grant
McKinleyville MS
McKinleyville, CA

Sally Haggerty
Martin Luther King MS
Oceanside, CA

V J Hirsch
Lincoln HS
Los Angeles, CA

Mollie Holmgren
Monument MS
Rio Dell, CA

Rayetta Lawson
Kastner Intermediate
    School
Fresno, CA

Tami Llewellyn
Ruth Musser MS
Alta Loma, CA

Lisa Madigan
Helms MS
San Pablo, CA

Eric Manabe
Aptos HS
Aptos, CA

David McKinley
Fort Miller MS
Fresno, CA

Viola Okoro
Franklin HS
Elk Grove, CA

William Olmeda
Lincoln HS
Los Angeles, CA

Breeze Patten
Bella Vista MS
Murrieta, CA

Jeff Perkins
Casa Roble HS
Orangevale, CA

Laurie Pines
Homestead HS
Cupertino, CA

Julie Prater
James L. Day MS
Temecula, CA

Wallace Rayford
Frisbie MS
Rialto, CA

Carey Resch
Leroy F. Greene MS
Sacramento, CA

Katherine Ringer
Heritage Intermediate
    School
Fontana, CA

Wendy Salcedo
Jordan MS
Burbank, CA

Chris Schmidt
Thurgood Marshall MS
San Diego, CA

Mary Ann Sheridan
McKinleyville MS
McKinleyville, CA

Byron Wright
Vail Ranch MS
Temecula, CA

Seunghwan Yom
Abraham Lincoln HS
Los Angeles, CA

Using Your Book to Master the Standards

Holt California Mathematics provides many opportunities for you to master the California Mathematics Content Standards for Grade 6.

Countdown to Mastery

Countdown to Mastery provides practice with the standards every day.

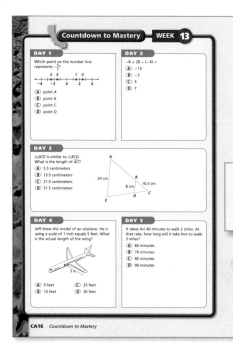

Step 1

✔ **Complete one item each day before you start the lesson.**

There are 24 pages of standards practice. Each page has five questions, one for each day of the week.

California Standards

The California Standards taught in each lesson are listed at the start of the lesson.

Step 2

✔ **Preview the standards before you start the lesson.**

Complete standards are shown. The words in bold tell you which part of the standard is the focus of the lesson.

3-3 Least Common Multiple

California Standards

◆— **NS2.4 Determine the least common multiple** and the greatest common divisor **of whole numbers;** use them to solve problems with fractions (e.g., to find a common denominator to add two fractions or to find the reduced form for a fraction).

Vocabulary
multiple
least common multiple (LCM)

Who uses this? Drivers can use the least common multiple to determine when they need to service their vehicle.

The tires on Kendra's truck should be rotated every 7,500 miles, and the oil filter should be replaced every 5,000 miles. What is the lowest mileage at which both services are due at the same time? To find the answer, you can use *least common multiples.*

A **multiple** of a number is the product of that number and a nonzero whole number. Some multiples of 7,500 and 5,000 are as follows:

7,500: 7,500, 15,000, 22,500, 30,000, 37,500, 45,000, . . .
5,000: 5,000, 10,000, 15,000, 20,000, 25,000, 30,000, . . .

SPIRAL STANDARDS REVIEW

Use the Spiral Standards Review for constant review of standards taught in the current and previous lessons.

Step 3

✓ Keep your skills fresh by practicing the standards daily.

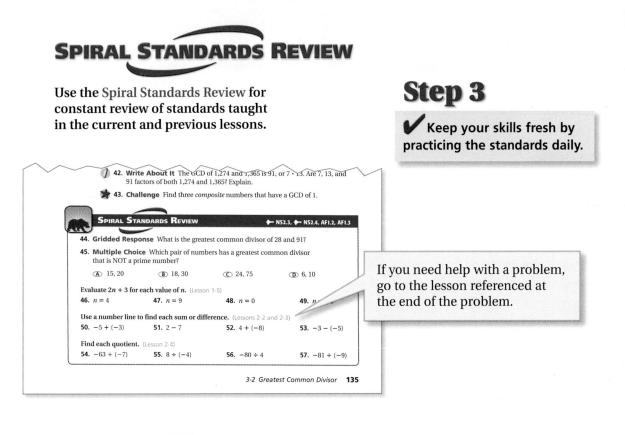

42. Write About It The GCD of 1,274 and 1,365 is 91, or 7 · 13. Are 7, 13, and 91 factors of both 1,274 and 1,365? Explain.

43. Challenge Find three *composite* numbers that have a GCD of 1.

SPIRAL STANDARDS REVIEW ← NS2.3, ← NS2.4, AF1.2, AF1.3

44. Gridded Response What is the greatest common divisor of 28 and 91?

45. Multiple Choice Which pair of numbers has a greatest common divisor that is NOT a prime number?

Ⓐ 15, 20   Ⓑ 18, 30   Ⓒ 24, 75   Ⓓ 6, 10

Evaluate $2n + 3$ for each value of n. (Lesson 1-5)
46. $n = 4$ **47.** $n = 9$ **48.** $n = 0$ **49.** n

Use a number line to find each sum or difference. (Lessons 2-2 and 2-3)
50. $-5 + (-3)$ **51.** $2 - 7$ **52.** $4 + (-8)$ **53.** $-3 - (-5)$

Find each quotient. (Lesson 2-4)
54. $-63 ÷ (-7)$ **55.** $8 ÷ (-4)$ **56.** $-80 ÷ 4$ **57.** $-81 ÷ (-9)$

3-2 Greatest Common Divisor **135**

If you need help with a problem, go to the lesson referenced at the end of the problem.

MASTERING THE STANDARDS

Use the Mastering the Standards for review of standards taught in the current and previous chapters.

Step 4

✓ After finishing each chapter, review your knowledge of the standards.

CHAPTER 3 **MASTERING THE STANDARDS** go.hrw.com Standards Practice Online KEYWORD: MSBCA Practice

Cumulative Assessment, Chapters 1–3

Multiple Choice

1. During a week in January in Cleveland, Ohio, the daily high temperatures were $-4°F$, $-2°F$, $-12°F$, $5°F$, $12°F$, $16°F$, and $20°F$. Which expression can be used to find the difference between the highest temperature of the week and the lowest temperature of the week?
Ⓐ $20 - 2$ Ⓒ $20 - 12$
Ⓑ $20 - (-2)$ Ⓓ $20 - (-12)$

2. Find the greatest common divisor of 16 and 32.
Ⓐ 2   Ⓒ 32
Ⓑ 16   Ⓓ 512

3. The fraction $\frac{2}{5}$ is found between which pair of fractions on a number line?
Ⓐ $\frac{1}{2}$ and $\frac{7}{10}$
Ⓑ $\frac{1}{2}$ and $\frac{7}{10}$
Ⓒ $\frac{3}{10}$ and $\frac{5}{15}$
Ⓓ $\frac{3}{10}$ and $\frac{8}{15}$

4. Maxie earns $210 a week working as a lifeguard. If Maxie gives each of her 3 sisters d dollars after she gets paid, which expression can be used to find the amount of money she has left?
Ⓐ $210 - \frac{d}{3}$
Ⓑ $210 - 3d$
Ⓒ $3(210 - d)$
Ⓓ $(210 - d) ÷ 3$

5. The table shows the thickness of climbing ropes sold at a sporting goods store. What color of rope is the thickest?

Climbing Ropes	
Color	Thickness (in.)
Blue	$\frac{3}{8}$
Green	$\frac{5}{16}$
Red	$\frac{13}{32}$
Yellow	$\frac{1}{4}$

Ⓐ Blue   Ⓒ Red
Ⓑ Green   Ⓓ Yellow

6. Which of the following shows a list of numbers in order from least to greatest?
Ⓐ $-1.05, -2.55, -3.05$
Ⓑ $-2.75, 2\frac{5}{8}, 2.50$
Ⓒ $-0.05, -0.01, 3\frac{1}{4}$
Ⓓ $-1\frac{7}{8}, -1\frac{4}{8}, 1.05$

7. Which expression is equivalent to $5(6 + 2)$?
Ⓐ $5(2 + 6)$ Ⓒ $(5 · 6) + 2$
Ⓑ $6(5 + 2)$ Ⓓ $(5 + 6) · (5 + 2)$

8. What value of x makes the following equation true?
$x - 23 = 42$
Ⓐ 19   Ⓒ 61
Ⓑ 21   Ⓓ 65

16. What is the value of $8^3 ÷ (16 - 12)$?

Short Response

17. The sponsors of the marching band provided 128 sandwiches for a picnic. After the picnic, s sandwiches were left.
a. Write an expression that shows how many sandwiches were handed out.
b. Evaluate your expression for $s = 15$. What does your answer represent?

18. Casey said the solution to the equation $x + 42 = 65$ is 107. Identify the error that Casey made. Explain why this answer is unreasonable.

Extended Response

19. Mary's allowance is based on the amount of time that she spends practicing different activities each week. This week Mary spent 12 hours practicing and earned $12.00.
a. Mary spent the following amounts of time on each activity: $\frac{1}{3}$ practicing flute, $\frac{1}{4}$ studying Spanish, $\frac{1}{3}$ playing soccer, and $\frac{1}{12}$ studying math. Write an equivalent decimal for the amount of time that she spent on each activity. Round to the nearest hundredth, if necessary.
b. For each activity, Mary earned the same fraction of her allowance as the time spent on a particular activity. This week, she was paid $3.60 for math practice. Was this the correct amount? Explain how you know.
c. Order the amount of time that Mary spent practicing each activity from least to greatest.
d. Write a decimal to represent the fraction of time Mary would have spent practicing soccer for 5 hours instead of 4 hours this week.

164 *Chapter 3 Number Theory and Fractions*

Cumulative Assessment, Chapters 1–3 **165**

There are multiple choice, gridded response, short response, and extended response questions to help you check your knowledge of the Grade 6 standards.

COUNTDOWN TO MASTERY

WEEK 1

DAY 1

Miguel recorded the distances that he ran each month. What is the total number of miles that he ran?

Month	May	June	July
Miles	22.5	20.8	25.2

(A) 43.3 miles
(B) 46 miles
(C) 68.5 miles
(D) 69 miles

DAY 2

3,864 ÷ 12 =

(A) 322
(B) 330
(C) 356
(D) 450

DAY 3

$5^2 =$

(A) 5 + 5
(B) 5 • 5
(C) 2 + 2 + 2 + 2 + 2
(D) 2 • 2 • 2 • 2 • 2

DAY 4

10 ÷ 2 • 5 + 4 =

(A) 5
(B) 9
(C) 29
(D) 45

DAY 5

$3(15 - 6) + (18 - 12)^2 =$

(A) 36
(B) 45
(C) 63
(D) 75

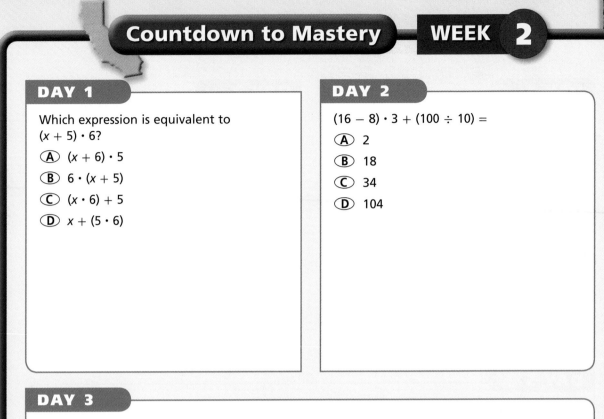

DAY 1

Which expression is equivalent to $(x + 5) \cdot 6$?

Ⓐ $(x + 6) \cdot 5$

Ⓑ $6 \cdot (x + 5)$

Ⓒ $(x \cdot 6) + 5$

Ⓓ $x + (5 \cdot 6)$

DAY 2

$(16 - 8) \cdot 3 + (100 \div 10) =$

Ⓐ 2

Ⓑ 18

Ⓒ 34

Ⓓ 104

DAY 3

The expression $12x + 3$ gives the cost of buying x DVDs from Movie Mania. How much does it cost to buy 3 DVDs from Movie Mania?

Ⓐ $18

Ⓑ $36

Ⓒ $39

Ⓓ $45

DAY 4

Which step should be done first to evaluate the expression $n + 5n \div 2 - 1$ when $n = 4$?

Ⓐ Add 4 and 5.

Ⓑ Subtract 1 from 2.

Ⓒ Multiply 5 by 4.

Ⓓ Divide 2 by 4.

DAY 5

Rebecca is 5 years older than twice Maria's age. If m equals Maria's age, which expression represents Rebecca's age?

Ⓐ $2(m + 5)$

Ⓑ $5 - 2m$

Ⓒ $5m + 2$

Ⓓ $2m + 5$

Countdown to Mastery WEEK 3

DAY 1

Large posters cost $18.95 each, and small posters cost $10.95 each. Which expression gives the total cost in dollars of ℓ large posters and s small posters?

Ⓐ $18.95\ell + 10.95s$

Ⓑ $(18.95 + \ell) + (10.95 + s)$

Ⓒ $18.95\ell - 10.95s$

Ⓓ $\frac{18.95}{\ell} + \frac{10.95}{s}$

DAY 2

$3 + 4 \cdot (2^2 + 21 \div 3) =$

Ⓐ 26

Ⓑ 36

Ⓒ 47

Ⓓ 77

DAY 3

The steps Bernard took to evaluate the expression $3x + 8y$ when $x = 5$ and $y = 7$ are shown below.

$3x + 8y$ when $x = 5$ and $y = 7$
$3 \cdot 5 = 15$
$15 + 8 = 23$
$23 \cdot 7 = 161$

What should Bernard have done differently in order to evaluate the expression?

Ⓐ added 15 to $(8 \cdot 7)$

Ⓑ multiplied 3 by $(5 + 8)$

Ⓒ added $(3 \cdot 5)$ to $(5 + 8)$

Ⓓ multiplied $(3 \cdot 5)$ by $(8 \cdot 7)$

DAY 4

What value of m makes the following equation true?

$$\frac{m}{4} = 12$$

Ⓐ 3

Ⓑ 8

Ⓒ 16

Ⓓ 48

DAY 5

The seats in a theater are arranged in 40 rows, and there are 20 seats in each row. Which equation can be used to determine the total number of seats, t, in the theater?

Ⓐ $t + 20 = 40$

Ⓑ $t - 40 = 20$

Ⓒ $20t = 40$

Ⓓ $\frac{t}{20} = 40$

Countdown to Mastery WEEK 4

DAY 1

After Lana deposited a check for $65, her new account balance was $315. Which equation can she use to find the amount, a, that was in her account before the deposit?

(A) $a + 65 = 315$

(B) $65 - a = 315$

(C) $a - 65 = 315$

(D) $315 + a = 65$

DAY 2

$-3 + 5 =$

(A) -8

(B) -2

(C) 2

(D) 8

DAY 3

What is the value of the expression $2(x^3 - 5)$ when $x = 3$?

(A) 8

(B) 44

(C) 49

(D) 211

DAY 4

What value of x makes the following equation true?

$$15 = x - 12$$

(A) 3

(B) 12

(C) 17

(D) 27

DAY 5

On Monday, the price of a stock decreased by 53 cents per share. On Tuesday, the price increased by 38 cents per share. What was the overall change in the stock price for the two-day period?

(A) -91 cents per share

(B) -15 cents per share

(C) $+15$ cents per share

(D) $+91$ cents per share

Countdown to Mastery WEEK 5

DAY 1

When Kit woke up in the morning, it was −15°C outside. By afternoon, the temperature had risen 20 degrees. What was the afternoon temperature?

Ⓐ −5°C

Ⓑ 5°C

Ⓒ 20°C

Ⓓ 35°C

DAY 2

Each ride at Fun Zone costs $3. Yvonne has $24 to spend on rides. Which equation can Yvonne use to find the greatest number of rides, r, she can go on?

Ⓐ $3r = 24$

Ⓑ $24r = 3$

Ⓒ $\frac{r}{3} = 24$

Ⓓ $\frac{r}{24} = 3$

DAY 3

What value of y makes the following equation true?

$$y + 8 = -5$$

Ⓐ −13

Ⓑ −3

Ⓒ 3

Ⓓ 13

DAY 4

Which of the following expressions is equivalent to $3(m - 4)$?

Ⓐ $3m - 4$

Ⓑ $3(4 - m)$

Ⓒ $3m - 12$

Ⓓ $3 + m - 4$

DAY 5

$-6 \cdot 5 \cdot (-4) =$

Ⓐ −120

Ⓑ −70

Ⓒ 70

Ⓓ 120

Countdown to Mastery WEEK 6

DAY 1

At Monster Music, all CDs cost $12. Lara has a coupon for $8 off her total purchase. If Lara buys n CDs, which expression gives her total cost (not including sales tax)?

Ⓐ $8n - 12$

Ⓑ $12 - 8n$

Ⓒ $8 - 12n$

Ⓓ $12n - 8$

DAY 2

$-12 \div (-6) =$

Ⓐ -6

Ⓑ -2

Ⓒ 2

Ⓓ 6

DAY 3

What value of x makes the following equation true?

$$15 = -3x$$

Ⓐ -12

Ⓑ -5

Ⓒ 5

Ⓓ 18

DAY 4

Which step should be done first when evaluating the expression $3(n + 7) - 14 + 5$ when $n = 2$?

Ⓐ multiplying 3 by 2

Ⓑ adding 2 and 7

Ⓒ subtracting 14 from 7

Ⓓ adding 14 and 5

DAY 5

What is the greatest common divisor of 24 and 36?

Ⓐ 2

Ⓑ 6

Ⓒ 12

Ⓓ 18

DAY 1

A football team gained 7 yards on their first play and then lost 12 yards on their second play. What was the net yardage resulting from the two plays?

(A) −19 yards

(B) −5 yards

(C) 5 yards

(D) 19 yards

DAY 2

What is the least common multiple of 2, 3, and 5?

(A) 20

(B) 30

(C) 60

(D) 120

DAY 3

Miguel has 24 more stamps in his collection than Robert does. Robert has 38 stamps in his collection. Which equation can be used to find the number of stamps, s, in Miguel's collection?

(A) $38 - s = 24$

(B) $38 + s = 24$

(C) $s - 24 = 38$

(D) $s + 24 = 38$

DAY 4

What is the simplest form of the fraction $\frac{18}{30}$?

(A) $\frac{1}{12}$

(B) $\frac{3}{5}$

(C) $\frac{9}{15}$

(D) $\frac{3}{10}$

DAY 5

Which value does NOT make the following statement true?

$$0.028 < \boxed{} < 0.064$$

(A) 0.027

(B) 0.029

(C) 0.043

(D) 0.062

Countdown to Mastery WEEK 8

DAY 1

The table shows the fraction of students in four different classes at Park Street Middle School who take the bus to school. Which class has the greatest fraction of students who take the bus to school?

Class	A	B	C	D
Students Who Take Bus	$\frac{15}{20}$	$\frac{20}{25}$	$\frac{12}{18}$	$\frac{12}{24}$

Ⓐ Class A
Ⓑ Class B
Ⓒ Class C
Ⓓ Class D

DAY 2

$-10 + 16 - (-2) =$

Ⓐ −28
Ⓑ −24
Ⓒ 4
Ⓓ 8

DAY 3

What is the simplest form of the fraction $\frac{40}{48}$?

Ⓐ $\frac{1}{8}$
Ⓑ $\frac{1}{6}$
Ⓒ $\frac{5}{8}$
Ⓓ $\frac{5}{6}$

DAY 4

What value of b makes the following equation true?

$$b + 45 = 90$$

Ⓐ 45
Ⓑ 55
Ⓒ 135
Ⓓ 155

DAY 5

Which of the following decimals is closest to 0?

Ⓐ 0.305
Ⓑ 0.081
Ⓒ 0.10
Ⓓ 0.02

DAY 1

Marc needs $\frac{5}{8}$ pound of blueberries to make a batch of muffins and another $\frac{1}{3}$ pound to make blueberry pancakes. How many pounds of blueberries does Marc need?

(A) $\frac{2}{9}$ pound

(B) $\frac{10}{13}$ pound

(C) $\frac{7}{12}$ pound

(D) $\frac{23}{24}$ pound

DAY 2

What is the product of $\frac{3}{8}$ and $\frac{2}{9}$?

(A) $\frac{1}{12}$

(B) $\frac{5}{17}$

(C) $\frac{43}{72}$

(D) $1\frac{11}{16}$

DAY 3

What is the greatest common divisor of 12, 20, and 36?

(A) 2

(B) 4

(C) 6

(D) 12

DAY 4

Which point shows the location of −3.5 on the number line?

(A) point A

(B) point B

(C) point C

(D) point D

DAY 5

A valley has an elevation of −14 feet, and a nearby hill has an elevation of 720 feet. What is the difference in elevation between the hill and the valley?

(A) 706 feet

(B) 714 feet

(C) 734 feet

(D) 736 feet

DAY 1

Delia has $24\frac{1}{2}$ yards of fabric. She needs $3\frac{1}{2}$ yards of fabric to make a skirt. Which equation can Delia use to find the number of skirts, p, that she can make with the fabric?

(A) $3\frac{1}{2}p = 24\frac{1}{2}$

(B) $24\frac{1}{2}p = 3\frac{1}{2}$

(C) $p \div 3\frac{1}{2} = 24\frac{1}{2}$

(D) $p \div 24\frac{1}{2} = 3\frac{1}{2}$

DAY 2

What is $\frac{1}{3} \div \frac{4}{9}$?

(A) $\frac{4}{27}$

(B) $\frac{3}{4}$

(C) $1\frac{1}{3}$

(D) $6\frac{3}{4}$

DAY 3

How many centimeters are in 4 meters?

(A) 0.4 centimeter

(B) 40 centimeters

(C) 400 centimeters

(D) 4,000 centimeters

DAY 4

$-24 - 8 =$

(A) -32

(B) -16

(C) 16

(D) 32

DAY 5

What is the ratio of the number of stars to the total number of shapes?

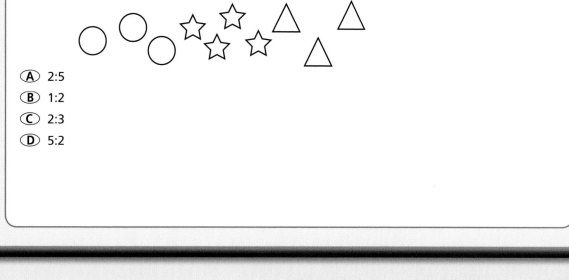

(A) 2:5

(B) 1:2

(C) 2:3

(D) 5:2

DAY 1

Mrs. Reese is taking a trip to visit her sister. If she drives 162 miles in 3 hours, what is her average rate of speed?

(A) 30 miles per hour

(B) 54 miles per hour

(C) 62 miles per hour

(D) 70 miles per hour

DAY 2

Which list of numbers is ordered from *least* to *greatest*?

(A) 0.07, 0.7, $\frac{1}{7}$, $\frac{7}{11}$

(B) 0.07, $\frac{1}{7}$, $\frac{7}{11}$, 0.7

(C) $\frac{1}{7}$, 0.07, $\frac{7}{11}$, 0.7

(D) $\frac{1}{7}$, $\frac{7}{11}$, 0.07, 0.7

DAY 3

Ryan is making $7\frac{1}{2}$ cups of rice to serve at dinner with his friends. If he wants to give $\frac{3}{4}$ cup of rice to each guest, how many people will the rice serve?

(A) 8

(B) 10

(C) 12

(D) 14

DAY 4

Lois made 3 withdrawals of $50 each from her bank account and one deposit of $85 to her bank account. What was the net change in Lois's account balance?

(A) −$65

(B) −$15

(C) +$35

(D) +$235

DAY 5

Olivia read 120 pages of her medical textbook in 4 hours. At this rate, how long will it take her to read 45 pages?

(A) $\frac{2}{3}$ hour

(B) $1\frac{1}{2}$ hours

(C) $2\frac{2}{3}$ hours

(D) 3 hours

DAY 1

How many inches are in 12 feet?

Ⓐ 1 inch

Ⓑ 36 inches

Ⓒ 120 inches

Ⓓ 144 inches

DAY 2

If a car is traveling at a speed of 48 miles per hour, how far can it travel in $2\frac{1}{2}$ hours?

Ⓐ 72 miles

Ⓑ 106 miles

Ⓒ 120 miles

Ⓓ 192 miles

DAY 3

Four shovels of sand are mixed with 5 shovels of gravel to make cement. About how many shovels of gravel are needed for 45 shovels of sand?

Ⓐ 20

Ⓑ 55

Ⓒ 45

Ⓓ 75

DAY 4

A chef can make 36 loaves of bread in 2 hours. At that rate, how long will it take the chef to make 90 loaves of bread?

Ⓐ 5 hours

Ⓑ 6 hours

Ⓒ 8 hours

Ⓓ 10 hours

DAY 5

The rectangles below are similar. What is the length of the smaller rectangle?

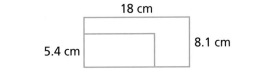

18 cm

5.4 cm

8.1 cm

Ⓐ 6.7 centimeters

Ⓑ 12 centimeters

Ⓒ 14.1 centimeters

Ⓓ 15 centimeters

DAY 1

Which point on the number line represents $-\frac{5}{2}$?

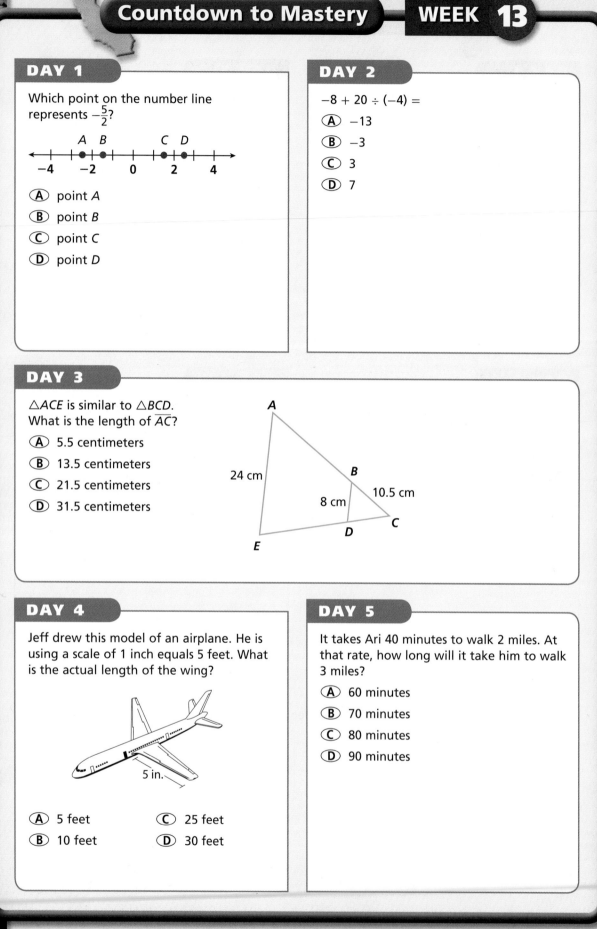

A B   C D

-4   -2   0   2   4

Ⓐ point A

Ⓑ point B

Ⓒ point C

Ⓓ point D

DAY 2

$-8 + 20 \div (-4) =$

Ⓐ −13

Ⓑ −3

Ⓒ 3

Ⓓ 7

DAY 3

$\triangle ACE$ is similar to $\triangle BCD$. What is the length of $\overline{AC}$?

Ⓐ 5.5 centimeters

Ⓑ 13.5 centimeters

Ⓒ 21.5 centimeters

Ⓓ 31.5 centimeters

A

24 cm

B

10.5 cm

8 cm

C

D

E

DAY 4

Jeff drew this model of an airplane. He is using a scale of 1 inch equals 5 feet. What is the actual length of the wing?

5 in.

Ⓐ 5 feet   Ⓒ 25 feet

Ⓑ 10 feet   Ⓓ 30 feet

DAY 5

It takes Ari 40 minutes to walk 2 miles. At that rate, how long will it take him to walk 3 miles?

Ⓐ 60 minutes

Ⓑ 70 minutes

Ⓒ 80 minutes

Ⓓ 90 minutes

Countdown to Mastery WEEK 14

DAY 1

What is the least common multiple of 6 and 10?

Ⓐ 2
Ⓑ 20
Ⓒ 30
Ⓓ 60

DAY 2

At Wilson Middle School, 65% of the 480 students ride the bus to school. How many of the students ride the bus to school?

Ⓐ 74
Ⓑ 135
Ⓒ 268
Ⓓ 312

DAY 3

A faucet is leaking at a rate of 1 gallon of water every 30 minutes. At this rate, how many gallons of water will leak from the faucet in 1 day?

Ⓐ 48 gallons
Ⓑ 30 gallons
Ⓒ 24 gallons
Ⓓ 12 gallons

DAY 4

A map uses a scale of 1 centimeter equals 200 kilometers. On the map, Boston is about 1.5 centimeters from New York. About how far is Boston from New York?

Ⓐ 150 kilometers
Ⓑ 200 kilometers
Ⓒ 300 kilometers
Ⓓ 350 kilometers

DAY 5

How much money does Diego save by buying the shirt on sale?

Ⓐ \$2.00
Ⓑ \$2.50
Ⓒ \$4.00
Ⓓ \$5.00

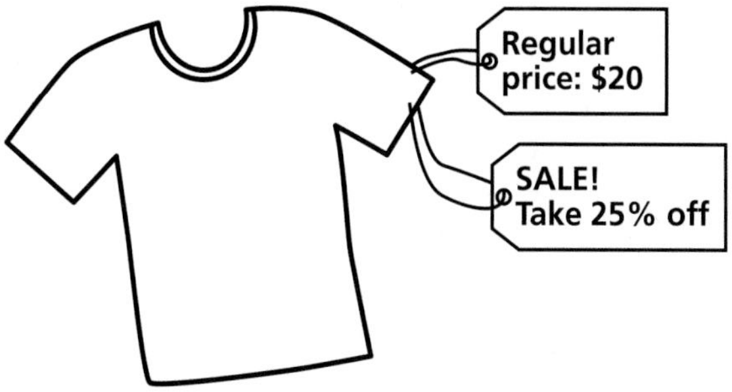

Regular price: $20
SALE! Take 25% off

DAY 1

The picture shows the shirts Teresa owns. What is the ratio of red shirts to blue shirts?

- (A) 3 to 9
- (B) 9 to 6
- (C) 6 to 3
- (D) 6 to 9

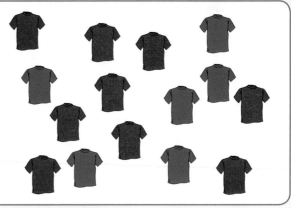

DAY 2

Determine the value of x if $\frac{5}{8} = \frac{x}{48}$.

- (A) 6
- (B) 30
- (C) 35
- (D) 40

DAY 3

What is the median price of these books?

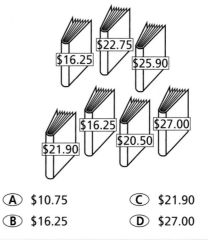

$22.75
$16.25
$25.90
$21.90
$16.25
$20.50
$27.00

- (A) $10.75
- (B) $16.25
- (C) $21.90
- (D) $27.00

DAY 4

What is 36% of 140?

- (A) 10.4
- (B) 25.7
- (C) 38.9
- (D) 50.4

DAY 5

It takes a printer 2.5 minutes to print a 100-page report. At this rate, how long will it take the printer to print a 480-page report?

- (A) 5.2 minutes
- (B) 12.0 minutes
- (C) 19.2 minutes
- (D) 40.0 minutes

DAY 1

Lawrence found the mean and median of this set of numbers.

9, 14, 14, 15

If the number 16 were added to the list, then

(A) the mean would increase.

(B) the mean would decrease.

(C) the median would increase.

(D) the median would decrease.

DAY 2

The regular price of a DVD player is $160. Greg buys the DVD player during a 20%-off sale. How much money does Greg save?

(A) $16

(B) $32

(C) $40

(D) $80

DAY 3

The graph shows the amount Elias saved each month.

Which statement about Elias's savings is valid?

(A) Elias saved at least $30 each month.

(B) Elias saved twice as much in July as in June.

(C) Elias saved $10 more in July than in September.

(D) The greatest amount Elias saved in one month was $40.

DAY 4

To make lavender paint, a painter needs to mix 3 parts white paint with 1 part purple paint. Which proportion could be solved to find n, the number of gallons of purple paint that the painter should mix with 8 gallons of white paint?

(A) $\frac{3}{1} = \frac{8}{n}$

(B) $\frac{3}{n} = \frac{1}{8}$

(C) $\frac{3}{1} = \frac{n}{8}$

(D) $\frac{3}{8} = \frac{n}{1}$

DAY 5

John deposited $200 in an account that earns 2% simple interest. How much interest will the deposit have earned after 5 years?

(A) $2

(B) $4

(C) $20

(D) $40

DAY 1

Determine the value of x if $\frac{6}{8} = \frac{x}{20}$.

Ⓐ 12

Ⓑ 15

Ⓒ 18

Ⓓ 24

DAY 2

If 20% of a number is 8, what is 50% of the number?

Ⓐ 4

Ⓑ 20

Ⓒ 40

Ⓓ 80

DAY 3

Lee wants to take a survey to determine how many of the students at her school can speak Spanish. Which of the following methods is the *best* way for her to choose a random sample of the students at her school?

Ⓐ choosing every 30th name from a school directory

Ⓑ choosing the first 30 students who arrive one morning

Ⓒ choosing 30 students who are sitting together in the cafeteria

Ⓓ choosing the first 30 students to leave school one afternoon

DAY 4

A motorcycle can travel 56 miles per gallon of gasoline. At this rate, how far can the motorcycle travel on 4.5 gallons of gasoline?

Ⓐ 804 miles

Ⓑ 302 miles

Ⓒ 252 miles

Ⓓ 124 miles

DAY 5

The table shows what a town's daily high temperatures were over a 5-day period. If the outlier of 58°F is left out of the data set,

Ⓐ the mean increases more than the median.

Ⓑ the median increases more than the mean.

Ⓒ the mean decreases more than the median.

Ⓓ the median decreases more than the mean.

Day	High Temperature (°F)
Monday	84
Tuesday	82
Wednesday	80
Thursday	79
Friday	58

DAY 1

If 24 apples are needed to make 3 pies, how many apples are needed to make 2 pies?

Ⓐ 8

Ⓑ 12

Ⓒ 14

Ⓓ 16

DAY 2

A bag contains 4 red marbles and 6 blue marbles. If Michelle chooses a marble without looking, what is the probability that it will be blue?

Ⓐ $\frac{1}{6}$

Ⓑ $\frac{2}{5}$

Ⓒ $\frac{3}{5}$

Ⓓ $\frac{2}{3}$

DAY 3

Victor's bill at a restaurant is $8.60. He wants to leave a 15% tip. Which is closest to the amount Victor should leave as a tip?

Ⓐ $1.80

Ⓑ $1.30

Ⓒ $0.90

Ⓓ $0.60

DAY 4

Andrea asked the first 40 people who entered a grocery store about the number of servings of fruit they eat per day. What type of sampling method did Andrea use?

Ⓐ convenience sample

Ⓑ random sample

Ⓒ self-selected sample

Ⓓ systematic sample

DAY 5

Jake rolls a number cube. What is the probability that he rolls a 1 or a 2?

Ⓐ $\frac{1}{6}$

Ⓑ $\frac{1}{4}$

Ⓒ $\frac{1}{3}$

Ⓓ $\frac{1}{2}$

DAY 1

It takes 7 lemons to make 4 servings of lemonade. Kelly is making lemonade for a party. She wants to make 20 servings. How many lemons does she need?

Ⓐ 11

Ⓑ 20

Ⓒ 27

Ⓓ 35

DAY 2

Tyrell chooses a marble at random. Then he replaces the marble and chooses another marble at random. What is the probability that he chooses a green marble and then a yellow marble?

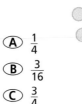

Ⓐ $\frac{1}{4}$

Ⓑ $\frac{3}{16}$

Ⓒ $\frac{3}{4}$

Ⓓ 1

DAY 3

A cow has a mass of 450 kilograms. The cow needs to receive 20 milligrams of a certain drug per kilogram of its body mass. At this rate, how many milligrams of the drug should the cow receive?

Ⓐ 225 milligrams

Ⓑ 900 milligrams

Ⓒ 2,250 milligrams

Ⓓ 9,000 milligrams

DAY 4

Anita wants to determine the favorite sports of students at her school. Which of the following is the *best* way for her to choose a sample that is representative of the students at her school?

Ⓐ surveying the school's coaches

Ⓑ surveying twenty students who ride her bus

Ⓒ surveying two students from each classroom

Ⓓ surveying members of the school's baseball team

DAY 5

Satsuki tosses a coin and spins the spinner shown.
Which set shows *all* of the possible outcomes of the coin toss and the spin?

Ⓐ {(heads, tails), (blue, red)}

Ⓑ {(heads, blue), (tails, red)}

Ⓒ {(heads, blue), (heads, red), (tails, blue), (tails, red)}

Ⓓ {(heads, blue), (heads, red), (heads, tails), (tails, blue), (tails, red), (blue, red)}

DAY 1

Sonya walked 1.6 miles in 30 minutes. At this rate, how long will it take her to walk 8 miles?

Ⓐ 1.5 hours

Ⓑ 2.5 hours

Ⓒ 4 hours

Ⓓ 6 hours

DAY 2

What is the measure of an angle that is supplementary to ∠ABC?

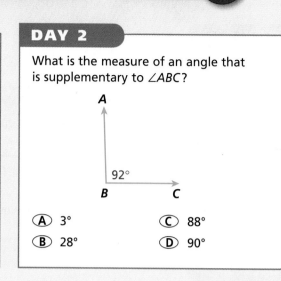

Ⓐ 3°   Ⓒ 88°

Ⓑ 28°   Ⓓ 90°

DAY 3

Which pair of angles are complementary?

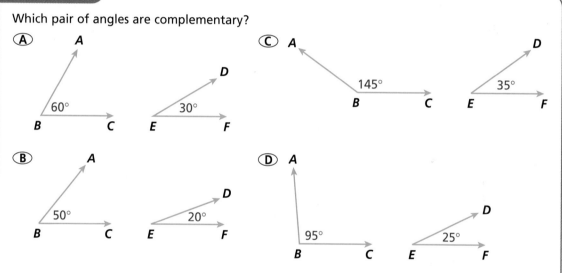

DAY 4

Ravi rolls a number cube. What is the probability that it will *not* land on 6?

Ⓐ $\frac{1}{6}$

Ⓑ $\frac{1}{5}$

Ⓒ $\frac{1}{2}$

Ⓓ $\frac{5}{6}$

DAY 5

Which figure is an obtuse triangle?

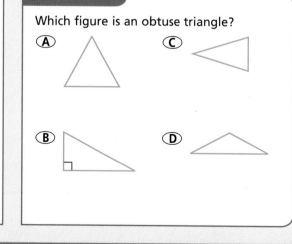

DAY 1

At a cafeteria, students can choose from turkey, tuna, or ham sandwiches on white or wheat bread. Which tree diagram shows *all* the possible choices of one type of bread and one type of meat?

(A)
white — turkey, tuna, ham
wheat — turkey, tuna, ham

(B)
white — wheat
turkey — tuna, ham

(C)
white — turkey, tuna
wheat — ham

(D)
white — turkey, tuna, ham, wheat

DAY 2

At the farmer's market, 6 tomatoes cost $1.50. Miguel wants to buy 15 tomatoes to make sauce. How much will the tomatoes cost?

(A) $3.00

(B) $3.75

(C) $4.50

(D) $5.25

DAY 3

Which is a true statement about the angles shown below?

A, 75°, B, C, E, 15°, D, F

(A) They are congruent.

(B) They are supplementary.

(C) They are complementary.

(D) They are adjacent.

DAY 4

Which set of events are dependent?

(A) tossing a penny and then tossing a quarter

(B) spinning a spinner and then spinning it again

(C) taking a marble from a bag, replacing it, and then taking a second marble from the bag

(D) taking a slip of paper from a hat, setting it aside, and then taking a second slip of paper from the hat

DAY 5

In the figure below, $\overleftrightarrow{JM}$ intersects $\overleftrightarrow{PL}$ at N, and m∠KNL = 50°. What is m∠JNP?

K, L, 50°, J, N, M, P

(A) 30°   (C) 50°

(B) 40°   (D) 60°

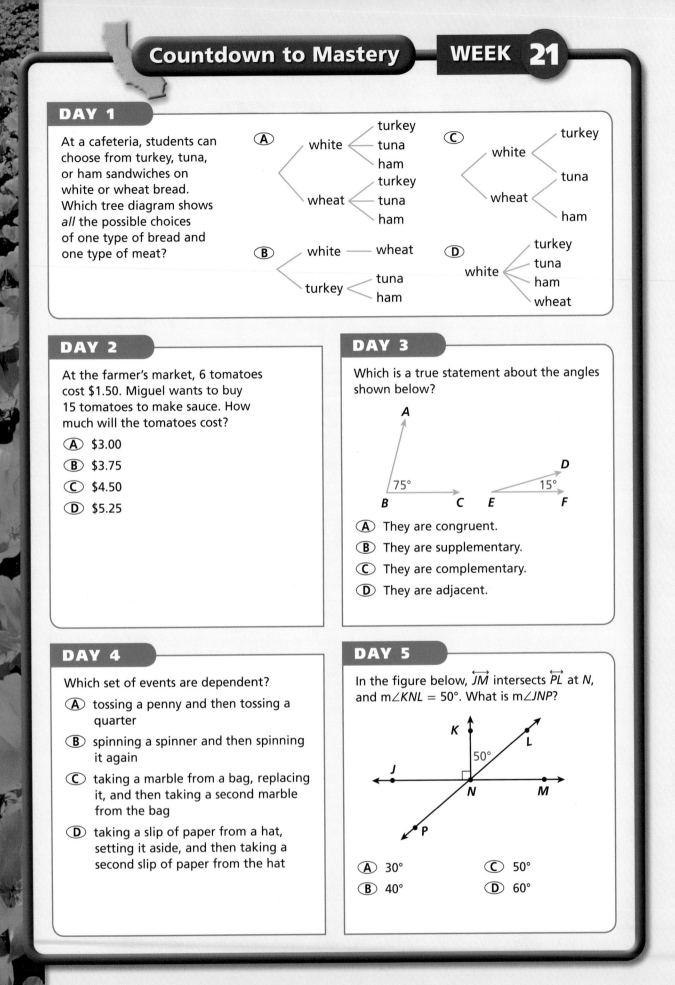

DAY 1

A rectangle with a length of 6 and a width of w is shown below. Which expression represents the perimeter of the rectangle?

Ⓐ $w + 6$

Ⓑ $2w + 12$

Ⓒ $6w$

Ⓓ $12w$

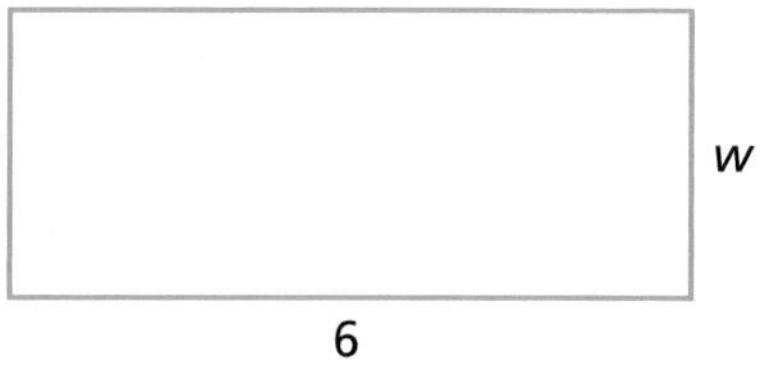

w

6

DAY 2

The table shows the number of paper clips of each color in a box.

Color	Number
Blue	6
Red	7
Silver	15
Gold	12

If Christina chooses a paper clip without looking, what is the probability that it will be gold?

Ⓐ 30%   Ⓒ 42%

Ⓑ 33%   Ⓓ 48%

DAY 3

What is the mean of this set of data?

90, 108, 67, 84, 90, 82, 73, 90

Ⓐ 41

Ⓑ 85.5

Ⓒ 87

Ⓓ 90

DAY 4

What is the measure of $\angle B$ in the triangle below?

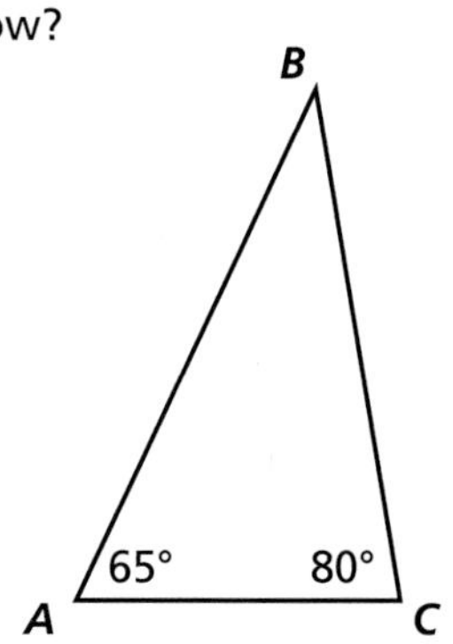

B

65°   80°

A   C

Ⓐ 35°

Ⓑ 40°

Ⓒ 45°

Ⓓ 50°

DAY 5

Which equation could be used to find the circumference of a circle with a diameter of 16 centimeters?

Ⓐ $C = 8\pi$

Ⓑ $C = 16\pi$

Ⓒ $C = \pi \cdot 8^2$

Ⓓ $C = \pi \cdot 16^2$

DAY 1

A can is shaped like a cylinder with a diameter of 3 inches. Which measure is closest to the length that the label must be to wrap all the way around the outside of the can?

3 in.

SOUP

- (A) 4.7 inches
- (B) 7.1 inches
- (C) 9.4 inches
- (D) 18.9 inches

DAY 2

The trapezoid shown below has bases of length 10 inches and 8 inches and an area of A square inches.

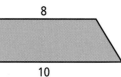
8

10

Which equation could be used to find the height, h, of the trapezoid?

- (A) $A = 9h$
- (B) $A = 18h$
- (C) $A = h + 9$
- (D) $A = h + 18$

DAY 3

A circular rug has a radius of 6 feet. Which expression could be used to find the area of the rug?

6 ft

- (A) $6 \cdot \pi$
- (B) $12 \cdot \pi$
- (C) $6 \cdot 6 \cdot \pi$
- (D) $12 \cdot 12 \cdot \pi$

DAY 4

The tree diagram shows all the possible outcomes of tossing three coins.

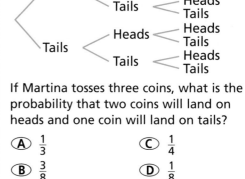
Heads — Heads — Heads, Tails
Heads — Tails — Heads, Tails
Tails — Heads — Heads, Tails
Tails — Tails — Heads, Tails

If Martina tosses three coins, what is the probability that two coins will land on heads and one coin will land on tails?

- (A) $\frac{1}{3}$
- (B) $\frac{3}{8}$
- (C) $\frac{1}{4}$
- (D) $\frac{1}{8}$

DAY 5

A square with a side length of s is inside a rectangle with a length of 8 and a width of 5. Which expression represents the area of the shaded region in terms of s?

- (A) $26 - 4s$
- (B) $40 - 4s$
- (C) $26 - s^2$
- (D) $40 - s^2$

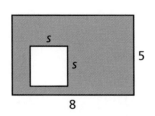
s
s
5
8

DAY 1

A circular flower bed in a park has a diameter of 6 meters. Which equation can be used to find the bed's area, A, in square meters?

Ⓐ $A = 1.5 \cdot \pi$

Ⓑ $A = 3 \cdot \pi$

Ⓒ $A = 1.5^2 \cdot \pi$

Ⓓ $A = 3^2 \cdot \pi$

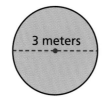

3 meters

DAY 2

A triangle has a height of 12 inches and an area of A square inches. Which equation could be used to find the base, b, of the triangle?

Ⓐ $A = 6b$

Ⓑ $A = 12b$

Ⓒ $A = 6 + b$

Ⓓ $A = 12 + b$

DAY 3

What is the volume of the triangular prism shown below?

20 cm

12 cm

10 cm

Ⓐ 180 cm³

Ⓑ 720 cm³

Ⓒ 1,200 cm³

Ⓓ 2,400 cm³

DAY 4

Which is closest to the volume of the cylinder shown below?

2 m

3 m

Ⓐ 12.6 m³

Ⓑ 18.8 m³

Ⓒ 37.7 m³

Ⓓ 56.5 m³

DAY 5

In the triangle below, $\angle A \cong \angle C$. What is the measure of $\angle B$?

B

70°

A   C

Ⓐ 20°

Ⓑ 40°

Ⓒ 55°

Ⓓ 110°

California
the golden state

California Mathematics Content Standards for Grade 6

Number Sense

1.0 *Students compare and order positive and negative fractions, decimals, and mixed numbers. Students solve problems involving fractions, ratios, proportions, and percentages:*

1.1 Compare and order positive and negative fractions, decimals, and mixed numbers and place them on a number line.

1.2 Interpret and use ratios in different contexts (e.g., batting averages, miles per hour) to show the relative sizes of two quantities, using appropriate notations (a/b, a to b, $a{:}b$).

1.3 Use proportions to solve problems (e.g., determine the value of N if $\frac{4}{7} = \frac{N}{21}$, find the length of a side of a polygon similar to a known polygon). Use cross-multiplication as a method for solving such problems, understanding it as the multiplication of both sides of an equation by a multiplicative inverse.

1.4 Calculate given percentages of quantities and solve problems involving discounts at sales, interest earned, and tips.

2.0 *Students calculate and solve problems involving addition, subtraction, multiplication, and division:*

2.1 Solve problems involving addition, subtraction, multiplication, and division of positive fractions and explain why a particular operation was used for a given situation.

2.2 Explain the meaning of multiplication and division of positive fractions and perform the calculations (e.g., $\frac{5}{8} \div \frac{15}{16} = \frac{5}{8} \times \frac{16}{15} = \frac{2}{3}$).

2.3 Solve addition, subtraction, multiplication, and division problems, including those arising in concrete situations, that use positive and negative integers and combinations of these operations.

The state
bird is the
California Quail

The Poppy is
the state flower

**California Mathematics
Content Standards
for Grade 6**

2.4 Determine the least common multiple and the greatest common divisor of whole numbers; use them to solve problems with fractions (e.g., to find a common denominator to add two fractions or to find the reduced form for a fraction).

Algebra and Functions

1.0 *Students write verbal expressions and sentences as algebraic expressions and equations; they evaluate algebraic expressions, solve simple linear equations, and graph and interpret their results:*

1.1 Write and solve one-step linear equations in one variable.

1.2 Write and evaluate an algebraic expression for a given situation, using up to three variables.

1.3 Apply algebraic order of operations and the commutative, associative, and distributive properties to evaluate expressions; and justify each step in the process.

1.4 Solve problems manually by using the correct order of operations or by using a scientific calculator.

2.0 *Students analyze and use tables, graphs, and rules to solve problems involving rates and proportions:*

2.1 Convert one unit of measurement to another (e.g., from feet to miles, from centimeters to inches).

2.2 Demonstrate an understanding that rate is a measure of one quantity per unit value of another quantity.

2.3 Solve problems involving rates, average speed, distance, and time.

3.0 *Students investigate geometric patterns and describe them algebraically:*

3.1 Use variables in expressions describing geometric quantities (e.g., $P = 2w + 2l$, $A = \frac{1}{2}bh$, $C = \pi d$—the formulas for the perimeter of a rectangle, the area of a triangle, and the circumference of a circle, respectively).

3.2 Express in symbolic form simple relationships arising from geometry.

Measurement and Geometry

1.0 *Students deepen their understanding of the measurement of plane and solid shapes and use this understanding to solve problems:*

1.1 Understand the concept of a constant such as π; know the formulas for the circumference and area of a circle.

1.2 Know common estimates of π $(3.14; \frac{22}{7})$ and use these values to estimate and calculate the circumference and the area of circles; compare with actual measurements.

1.3 Know and use the formulas for the volume of triangular prisms and cylinders (area of base × height); compare these formulas and explain the similarity between them and the formula for the volume of a rectangular solid.

Continued

CA29

2.0 *Students identify and describe the properties of two-dimensional figures:*

2.1 Identify angles as vertical, adjacent, complementary, or supplementary and provide descriptions of these terms.

2.2 Use the properties of complementary and supplementary angles and the sum of the angles of a triangle to solve problems involving an unknown angle.

2.3 Draw quadrilaterals and triangles from given information about them (e.g., a quadrilateral having equal sides but no right angles, a right isosceles triangle).

Statistics, Data Analysis, and Probability

1.0 *Students compute and analyze statistical measurements for data sets:*

1.1 Compute the range, mean, median, and mode of data sets.

1.2 Understand how additional data added to data sets may affect these computations.

1.3 Understand how the inclusion or exclusion of outliers affects these computations.

1.4 Know why a specific measure of central tendency (mean, median) provides the most useful information in a given context.

Bay Bridge

Algebraic Reasoning

CHAPTER 1

go.hrw.com
Online Resources
KEYWORD: MS8CA TOC

Table of Contents

Tools for Success

Reading Math 5, 10, 34
Writing Math 9, 13, 17, 23, 27, 31, 37, 43, 46, 50, 53
Vocabulary 3, 10, 14, 20, 24, 34, 40, 58

Know-It Notebook Chapter 1
Homework Help Online 8, 12, 16, 22, 26, 30, 36, 42, 45, 49, 52
Student Help 10, 15, 34, 47, 48

MASTERING THE STANDARDS

Countdown to Mastery Weeks 1, 2, 3
Spiral Standards Review 9, 13, 17, 23, 27, 31, 37, 43, 46, 50, 53
Ready to Go On? 32, 54
Mastering the Standards 64

Integers

Tools for Success

Reading Math 71
Writing Math 69, 73, 79, 91, 97, 103, 107, 111
Vocabulary 67, 70, 94, 100, 108, 118

Know-It Notebook Chapter 2
Homework Help Online 72, 78, 84, 90, 96, 102, 106, 110
Student Help 70, 71, 77, 82, 88, 94, 100, 104

MASTERING THE STANDARDS

Countdown to Mastery Weeks 3, 4, 5, 6
Spiral Standards Review 73, 79, 85, 91, 97, 103, 107, 111
Ready to Go On? 98, 114
Mastering the Standards 122

Number Theory and Fractions

go.hrw.com
Online Resources
KEYWORD: MS8CA TOC

Tools for Success

Reading Math 132, 147

Writing Math 127, 128, 131, 135, 139, 145, 149, 153

Vocabulary 125, 128, 132, 136, 142, 146, 150, 158

Know-It Notebook Chapter 3

Homework Help Online 130, 134, 138, 144, 148, 152

Student Help 128, 132, 142, 143, 147, 150, 151

MASTERING THE STANDARDS

Countdown to Mastery Weeks 6, 7

Spiral Standards Review 131, 135, 139, 145, 149, 153

Ready to Go On? 140, 154

Mastering the Standards 164

Operations with Rational Numbers

Tools for Success

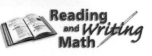

MASTERING THE
STANDARDS

Reading Math 211
Writing Math 173, 179, 183, 191, 194, 199, 205, 213, 217
Vocabulary 167, 192, 222

Know-It Notebook Chapter 4
Homework Help Online 172, 178, 182, 190, 194, 198, 204, 208, 212, 216
Student Help 170, 171, 176, 177, 180, 188, 196, 197, 202, 206, 207, 211, 214

Countdown to Mastery Weeks 7, 8, 9, 10
Spiral Standards Review 173, 179, 183, 191, 195, 199, 205, 209, 213, 217
Ready to Go On? 184, 200, 218
Mastering the Standards 226

Proportional Relationships

go.hrw.com
Online Resources
KEYWORD: MS8CA TOC

Tools for Success

Reading Math 240, 259

Writing Math 231, 239, 243, 248, 252, 258, 261, 265, 268

Vocabulary 229, 232, 236, 240, 244, 258, 262, 266, 274

Know-It Notebook Chapter 5

Homework Help Online 234, 238, 242, 247, 251, 260, 264, 268

Student Help 233, 236, 240, 241, 244, 258, 259, 266

MASTERING THE STANDARDS

Countdown to Mastery Weeks 10, 11, 12

Spiral Standards Review 235, 239, 243, 248, 252, 261, 265, 269

Ready to Go On? 254, 270

Mastering the Standards 280

CHAPTER 6

Percents

go.hrw.com
Online Resources
KEYWORD: MS8CA TOC

Tools for Success

 **Reading and Writing Math**

Reading Math 286

Writing Math 288, 291, 295, 301, 305, 315

Vocabulary 283, 286, 308, 312, 320

 Study Skills

Know-It Notebook Chapter 6

Homework Help Online 287, 290, 294, 300, 304, 310, 314

Student Help 286, 289, 292, 298, 303

 **MASTERING THE STANDARDS**

Countdown to Mastery Weeks 12, 13, 14

Spiral Standards Review 288, 291, 295, 301, 305, 311, 315

Ready to Go On? 306, 316

Mastering the Standards 324

CHAPTER 7

Collecting, Displaying, and Analyzing Data

go.hrw.com
Online Resources
KEYWORD: MS8CA TOC

Tools for Success

Reading and Writing Math

Reading Math 329
Writing Math 338, 341, 345, 351, 357, 360, 365
Vocabulary 327, 331, 335, 342, 354, 358, 362, 370

Study Skills

Know-It Notebook Chapter 7
Homework Help Online 333, 337, 340, 344, 350, 356, 359, 364
Student Help 336, 343, 355

Countdown to Mastery Weeks 14, 15, 16, 17
Spiral Standards Review 334, 338, 341, 345, 351, 357, 360, 365
Ready to Go On? 352, 366
Mastering the Standards 376

CHAPTER

8

go.hrw.com
Online Resources
KEYWORD: MS8CA TOC

Probability

ARE YOU READY? 379

Unpacking the Standards 380

Understanding Probability

SDAP3.3   **8-1**   Introduction to Probability 382

SDAP3.2   **8-2**   Experimental Probability 386

SDAP3.3   **8-3**   Theoretical Probability 390

SDAP3.1   **8-4**   Sample Spaces 394

SDAP3.2   **LAB**   Experimental and Theoretical Probability 398

  READY TO GO ON? QUIZ 400

  Focus on Problem Solving: Understanding the Problem. . 401

Using Probability

SDAP3.4   **8-5**   Disjoint Events 402

SDAP3.5   **8-6**   Independent and Dependent Events..................... 406

SDAP3.2   **8-7**   Making Predictions 410

  READY TO GO ON? QUIZ 414

  CONCEPT CONNECTION 415

Reading and Writing Math............................ 381

Game Time: Probability Brain Teasers................. 416

It's in the Bag! CD Spinner 417

Study Guide: Review 418

Chapter Test 421

Tools for Success

Reading and Writing **Math**

Reading Math 381, 402

Writing Math 385, 386, 393, 397, 405, 409, 413

Vocabulary 379, 382, 386, 390, 394, 402, 406, 410, 418

Study Skills

Know-It Notebook Chapter 8

Homework Help Online 384, 388, 392, 396, 404, 408, 412

Student Help 386, 391, 402, 407, 410

MASTERING THE STANDARDS

Countdown to Mastery Weeks 17, 18, 19

Spiral Standards Review 385, 389, 393, 397, 405, 409, 413

Ready to Go On? 400, 414

Mastering the Standards 422

Geometric Figures

Tools for Success

Reading and Writing Math

Reading Math 429, 432, 433, 448, 467

Writing Math 427, 431, 435, 439, 443, 455, 461, 465, 469

Vocabulary 425, 428, 432, 436, 448, 452, 462, 466, 474

Study Skills

Know-It Notebook Chapter 9

Homework Help Online 430, 434, 438, 442, 450, 454, 460, 464, 468

Student Help 428, 429, 432, 433, 437, 441, 448, 449, 460, 462, 466, 467

MASTERING THE STANDARDS

Countdown to Mastery Weeks 19, 20, 21

Spiral Standards Review 431, 435, 439, 443, 451, 455, 461, 465, 469

Ready to Go On? 446, 470

Mastering the Standards 480

CHAPTER 10

Measurement and Geometry

Tools for Success

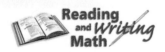

Reading Math 485, 497, 503
Writing Math 489, 495, 500, 505, 509, 513, 521, 527, 531, 537
Vocabulary 483, 486, 492, 497, 510, 518, 524, 534, 542

Know-It Notebook Chapter 10
Homework Help Online 488, 494, 499, 504, 508, 512, 520, 526, 530, 536
Student Help 493, 497, 503, 506, 510, 511, 518, 519, 524, 525, 529, 535

Countdown to Mastery Weeks 21, 22, 23, 24
Spiral Standards Review 489, 495, 500, 505, 509, 513, 521, 527, 531, 537
Ready to Go On? 514, 538
Mastering the Standards 546

go.hrw.com
Online Resources
KEYWORD: MS8CA TOC

Tools for Success

Reading and Writing Math

Reading Math 573
Writing Math 561, 565, 569, 573, 579, 583, 587
Vocabulary 549, 558, 572, 592

Study Skills

Know-It Notebook Chapter 11
Homework Help Online 556, 560, 564, 568, 574, 578, 582, 586
Student Help 554, 558, 559, 562, 573, 577, 584

MASTERING THE STANDARDS

Spiral Standards Review 557, 561, 565, 569, 575, 579, 583, 587
Ready to Go On? 570, 588
Mastering the Standards 598

Focus on Problem Solving

The Problem Solving Plan

In order to be a good problem solver, you first need a good problem-solving plan. A plan or strategy will help you to understand the problem, to work through a solution, and to check that your answer makes sense. The plan used in this book is detailed below.

UNDERSTAND the Problem

- **What are you asked to find?**   Restate the problem in your own words.
- **What information is given?**   Identify the important facts in the problem.
- **What information do you need?**   Determine which facts are needed to solve the problem.
- **Is all the information given?**   Determine whether all the facts are given.

Make a PLAN

- **Have you ever solved a similar problem?**   Think about other problems like this that you successfully solved.
- **What strategy or strategies can you use?**   Determine a strategy that you can use and how you will use it.

SOLVE

- **Follow your plan.**   Show the steps in your solution. Write your answer as a complete sentence.

LOOK BACK

- **Have you answered the question?**   Be sure that you answered the question that is being asked.
- **Is your answer reasonable?**   Your answer should make sense in the context of the problem.
- **Is there another strategy you could use?**   Solving the problem using another strategy is a good way to check your work.
- **Did you learn anything while solving this problem that could help you solve similar problems in the future?**   Try to remember the problems you have solved and the strategies you used to solve them.

PROBLEM SOLVING

Using the Problem Solving Plan

In a game at an amusement park, players throw 3 darts at a target to score points and win prizes. If each dart lands within the target area, how many different total scores are possible?

UNDERSTAND the Problem

Identify the important information.

- A player throws three darts at the target.
- Each dart can score 2 points, 5 points, or 10 points.

The answer will be the number of different scores a player could earn.

Make a PLAN

You can **make an organized list** to determine all possible outcomes and score totals. List the value of each dart and the point total for all three darts.

SOLVE

You can organize your list by the number of darts that land in the center. All three darts could hit the center circle. Or, two darts could hit the center circle and the third could hit a different circle. One dart could hit the center circle, or no darts could hit the center circle.

3 Darts Hit Center	2 Darts Hit Center	1 Dart Hits Center	0 Darts Hit Center
10 + 10 + 10 = 30	10 + 10 + 5 = 25	10 + 5 + 5 = 25	5 + 5 + 5 = 15
	10 + 10 + 2 = 22	10 + 5 + 2 = 17	5 + 5 + 2 = 12
		10 + 2 + 2 = 14	5 + 2 + 2 = 9
			2 + 2 + 2 = 6

Count the different outcomes. There are 10 possible scores.

LOOK BACK

You could have listed outcomes in random order, but because your list is organized, you can be sure that you have not missed any possibilities. Check to be sure that every score is different.

Using Your Book for Success

Holt California Mathematics has many features designed to help you learn and study math. Becoming familiar with these features will prepare you for greater success.

Learn

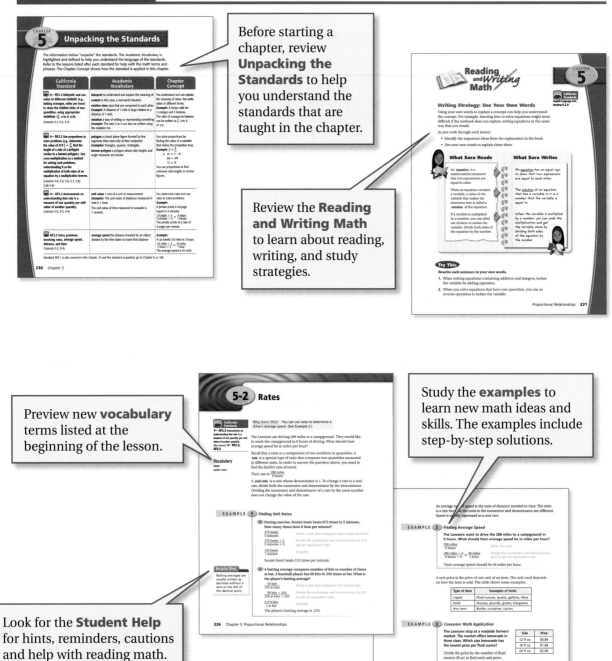

Before starting a chapter, review **Unpacking the Standards** to help you understand the standards that are taught in the chapter.

Review the **Reading and Writing Math** to learn about reading, writing, and study strategies.

Preview new **vocabulary** terms listed at the beginning of the lesson.

Look for the **Student Help** for hints, reminders, cautions and help with reading math.

Study the **examples** to learn new math ideas and skills. The examples include step-by-step solutions.

Practice

Look back at examples from the lesson to help with the **Guided Practice** and **Independent Practice** exercises.

Use the internet for **Homework Help Online**.

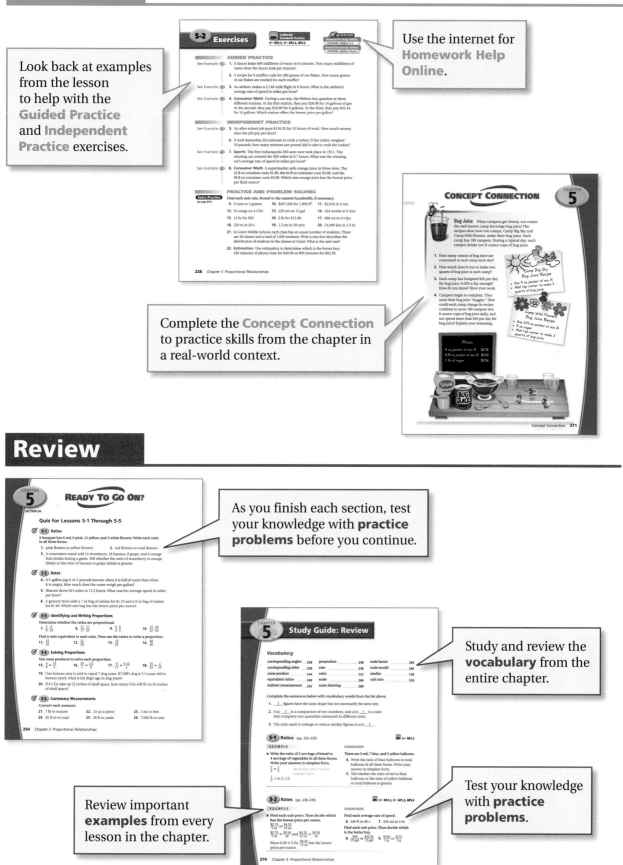

Complete the **Concept Connection** to practice skills from the chapter in a real-world context.

Review

As you finish each section, test your knowledge with **practice problems** before you continue.

Study and review the **vocabulary** from the entire chapter.

Test your knowledge with **practice problems**.

Review important **examples** from every lesson in the chapter.

Scavenger Hunt

Holt California Mathematics is your resource to help you succeed. Use this scavenger hunt to discover some of the many tools Holt provides to help you be an independent learner.

On a separate sheet of paper, fill in the blanks to answer each question below. In each answer, one letter will be in a yellow box. When you have answered every question, use the letters to fill in the blank at the bottom of the page.

1. What is the first **vocabulary** term in the Study Guide: Preview for chapter 10?
■■■■

2. What is the tenth **vocabulary** term in the Study Guide: Review for chapter 2?
■■■■■■■■■

3. What game is featured in chapter 1 **Game Time**?
■■■■■■■ ■■■■■

4. What keyword should you enter for **Parent Resources Online** for the exercises for Lesson 9–1 (p. 430)?
■■■■■ ■■■■■■

5. What project is outlined in chapter 4 **It's in the Bag**?
■■■■■■■■■ ■■■■ ■■■■■■

6. What is the first word of the first question in chapter 7 **Mastering the Standards**?
■■■■■

7. What is the first Academic Vocabulary word in Chapter 3 **Unpacking the Standards**?
■■■■■■■

8. The chapter 5 **Strategies for Success** gives strategies for what kind of test item?
■■■■■■■ ■■■■■■■

Math Humor

Why did the chicken add its opposite to itself? To get to the other side of the...
■■■■■■■

Math Builders

The Math Builders on the following pages present important standards using a step-by-step, layered approach.

Proportion Builder 🐻🔑 NS1.0, 🔑 NS1.2, 🔑 NS1.3

Overlays that show multiple representations of a proportion and how they are related

Use with Lessons 5-3, 6-4, and 8-7.

Volume Builder 🐻 MG1.3

Overlays that show how to find the volume of a rectangular prism and a triangular prism

Use with Lessons 10-8 and 10-9.

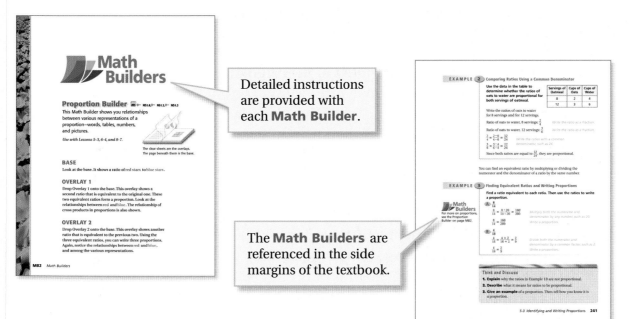

Detailed instructions are provided with each **Math Builder**.

The **Math Builders** are referenced in the side margins of the textbook.

Math Builders

Proportion Builder  NS1.0, NS1.2, NS1.3

This Math Builder shows you relationships between various representations of a proportion—words, tables, numbers, and pictures.

Use with Lessons 5-3, 6-4, and 8-7.

The clear sheets are the overlays.
The page beneath them is the base.

BASE

Look at the base. It shows a ratio of red stars to blue stars.

OVERLAY 1

Drop Overlay 1 onto the base. This overlay shows a second ratio that is equivalent to the original one. These two equivalent ratios form a proportion. Look at the relationships between red and blue. The relationship of cross products in proportions is also shown.

OVERLAY 2

Drop Overlay 2 onto the base. This overlay shows another ratio that is equivalent to the previous two. Using the three equivalent ratios, you can write three proportions. Again, notice the relationships between red and blue, and among the various representations.

Total Red	1
Total Blue	2

The ratio of red to blue is $\dfrac{1}{2}$

Math Builders

Volume Builder  MG1.3

This Math Builder shows you how to find the volume of a rectangular or triangular prism by using models.

Use with Lessons 10-8 and 10-9.

The clear sheets are the overlays.
The page beneath them is the base.

BASE

Look at the base. It shows a rectangular prism and a triangular prism. This page shows how to find the area of the base B of each prism. (Since h represents the height of the triangular prism and its base is a right triangle, use $B = \frac{1}{2} \ell w$ instead of $B = \frac{1}{2} bh$.)

OVERLAY 1

Drop Overlay 1 onto the base. The page shows you how many unit cubes you need to fill one layer of each prism.

OVERLAY 2

Drop Overlay 2 onto the base. The page shows you how to find the total number of unit cubes you need to completely fill each prism or find the volume.

BASE: Volume of a Prism

Area of the Base

• **First find the area of the base B.**

Rectangular Prism

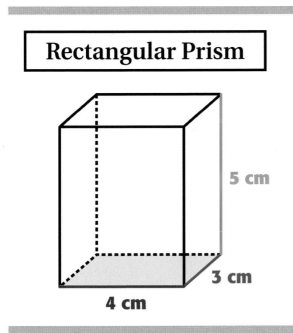

5 cm

3 cm

4 cm

$$B = \ell w$$
$$= (4)(3)$$
$$= 12$$

The area of the base is 12 cm^2.

Triangular Prism

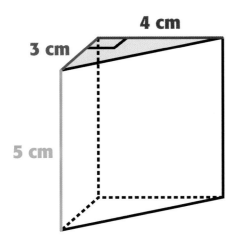

4 cm

3 cm

5 cm

$$B = \frac{1}{2}\ell w$$
$$= \frac{1}{2}(4)(3)$$
$$= 6$$

The area of the base is 6 cm^2.

Algebraic Reasoning

CONCEPT CONNECTION

go.hrw.com
Chapter Project Online
KEYWORD: MS8CA Ch1

Yosemite National Park was created by Congress in 1890. An algebraic expression can model the current age of the park.

Yosemite National Park

ARE YOU READY?

✓ Vocabulary

Choose the best term from the list to complete each sentence.

1. The operation that gives the quotient of two numbers is ___?___.

2. The ___?___ of the digit 3 in 4,903,672 is thousands.

3. The operation that gives the product of two numbers is ___?___.

4. In the equation $15 \div 3 = 5$, the ___?___ is 5.

division

multiplication

place value

product

quotient

Complete these exercises to review skills you will need for this chapter.

✓ Find Place Value

Give the place value of the digit 4 in each number.

5. 4,092
6. 608,241
7. 7,040,000
8. 4,556,890,100
9. 3,408,289
10. 34,506,123
11. 500,986,402
12. 3,540,277,009

✓ Use Repeated Multiplication

Find each product.

13. $2 \cdot 2 \cdot 2$
14. $9 \cdot 9 \cdot 9 \cdot 9$
15. $14 \cdot 14 \cdot 14$
16. $10 \cdot 10 \cdot 10 \cdot 10$
17. $3 \cdot 3 \cdot 5 \cdot 5$
18. $2 \cdot 2 \cdot 5 \cdot 7$
19. $3 \cdot 3 \cdot 11 \cdot 11$
20. $5 \cdot 10 \cdot 10 \cdot 10$

✓ Division Facts

Find each quotient.

21. $49 \div 7$
22. $54 \div 9$
23. $96 \div 12$
24. $88 \div 8$
25. $42 \div 6$
26. $65 \div 5$
27. $39 \div 3$
28. $121 \div 11$

✓ Whole Number Operations

Add, subtract, multiply, or divide.

29. $\begin{array}{r} 425 \\ + 12 \\ \hline \end{array}$
30. $\begin{array}{r} 619 \\ + 254 \\ \hline \end{array}$
31. $\begin{array}{r} 62 \\ - 47 \\ \hline \end{array}$
32. $\begin{array}{r} 373 \\ + 86 \\ \hline \end{array}$

33. $\begin{array}{r} 62 \\ \times 42 \\ \hline \end{array}$
34. $\begin{array}{r} 122 \\ \times 15 \\ \hline \end{array}$
35. $7\overline{)623}$
36. $24\overline{)149}$

Unpacking the Standards

The information below "unpacks" the standards. The Academic Vocabulary is highlighted and defined to help you understand the language of the standards. Refer to the lessons listed after each standard for help with the math terms and phrases. The Chapter Concept shows how the standard is applied in this chapter.

California Standard	Academic Vocabulary	Chapter Concept
AF1.1 Write and solve one-step linear equations in one variable. (Lessons 1-8, 1-9, 1-10, 1-11) (Lab 1-8)	**solve** find the value or values of an unknown quantity that make one side of an equation equal to the other side (make the equation true) *Example:* $2 \cdot \square = 6$ $2 \cdot 3 = 6$ **variable** a **symbol**, usually a letter, used to show an amount that can change *Example:* x	You write an equation that describes a situation. You find the value of a variable that makes an equation true. *Example:* $2x = 6$ $2(3) = 6$ The value that makes $2x = 6$ true is **3**.
AF1.2 Write and evaluate an algebraic expression for a given situation, using up to three variables. (Lessons 1-5, 1-6)	**expression** a mathematical phrase that includes **numbers**, **operations**, and/or variables *Example:* $4x + 3$ **algebraic** an expression is algebraic if it includes at least one variable *Example:* $4x + 3$ **evaluate** find the value of an algebraic expression	You find the value of an expression containing variables when you are given the values of its variables. *Example:* $4x$ for $x = 2$ $4x$ $4(2)$ 8
AF1.3 Apply algebraic order of operations and the commutative, associative, and distributive properties to evaluate expressions; and justify each step in the process. (Lessons 1-3, 1-4, 1-5) (Lab 1-3)	**property** a characteristic of numbers, operations, or equations *Example:* One property of addition is that you can add numbers in any order without changing the sum. **justify** give a reason for	You use mathematical properties to find the value of expressions. You give reasons for each step when you find the value of expressions.
AF1.4 Solve problems manually by using the correct order of operations or by using a scientific calculator. (Lesson 1-3) (Lab 1-3)	**manually** by hand **operations** include addition, subtraction, multiplication, and division **scientific calculator** a calculator that does more than basic arithmetic operations, but cannot make graphs	You find the value of expressions by performing basic arithmetic operations in a certain order. *Example:* $10 + 4 \cdot 3$ Multiply. $10 + 12$ Then add. 22

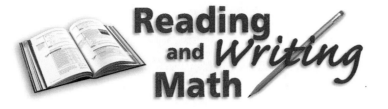

Reading and Writing Math

Reading Strategy: Use Your Book for Success

Understanding how your textbook is organized will help you locate and use helpful information.

As you read through an example problem, pay attention to the **margin notes**, such as Reading Math notes, Writing Math notes, Helpful Hints, and Caution notes. These notes will help you understand concepts and avoid common mistakes.

Reading Math
Read -4^3 as "-4 to the 3rd power or -4 cubed".

Writing Math
A repeating decima can be written with a bar over the digits

Helpful Hint
In Example 1A, parentheses are no needed because

Caution!
An open circle means that the corresponding value

The **glossary** is found in the back of your textbook. Use it to find definitions and examples of unfamiliar words or properties.

The **index** is located at the end of your textbook. Use it to find the page where a particular concept is taught.

The **Skills Bank** is found in the back of your textbook. These pages review concepts from previous math courses.

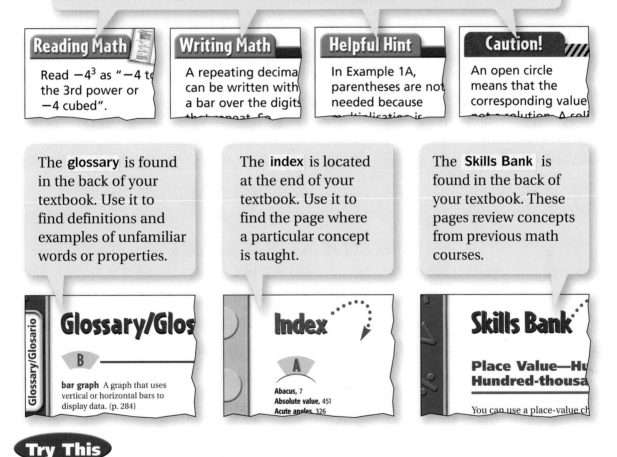

Glossary/Glos

Glossary/Glosario

B

bar graph A graph that uses vertical or horizontal bars to display data. (p. 284)

Index

A

Abacus, 7
Absolute value, 451
Acute angles, 326

Skills Bank

Place Value—Hu Hundred-thousa

You can use a place-value ch

Try This

Use your textbook for the following problems.

1. Use the index to find the page where *exponent* is defined.

2. Use the glossary to find the definition of each term: *order of operations, numerical expression, equation.*

3. Where can you review how to multiply whole numbers?

4. On what page can you find answers to exercises in Chapter 1?

1-1

Numbers and Patterns

California Standards

Preparation for AF2.0

Students analyze and use tables, graphs, **and rules to solve problems** involving rates and proportions.

<u>Why learn this?</u> You can use a pattern to find out how many football teams are in each round of playoffs.

The pattern in the table shows that the number of teams in each round of playoffs is half the number of teams in the previous round.

Football Playoffs				
Round	1	2	3	4
Number of Teams	64	32	16	8

EXAMPLE **1** **Identifying and Extending Number Patterns**

Reasoning

Identify a possible pattern. Use your pattern to write the next three numbers.

A 64, 32, 16, 8, ▨, ▨, ▨, . . .

$$64 \quad 32 \quad 16 \quad 8 \quad ▨ \quad ▨ \quad ▨$$
$$\div 2 \quad \div 2 \quad \div 2 \quad \div 2 \quad \div 2 \quad \div 2$$

A pattern is to divide each number by 2 to get the next number.

$8 \div 2 = 4$ $\qquad$ $4 \div 2 = 2$ $\qquad$ $2 \div 2 = 1$

The next three numbers will be 4, 2, and 1.

B 51, 44, 37, 30, ▨, ▨, ▨, . . .

$$51 \quad 44 \quad 37 \quad 30 \quad ▨ \quad ▨ \quad ▨$$
$$-7 \quad -7 \quad -7 \quad -7 \quad -7 \quad -7$$

A pattern is to subtract 7 from each number to get the next number.

$30 - 7 = 23$ $\qquad$ $23 - 7 = 16$ $\qquad$ $16 - 7 = 9$

The next three numbers will be 23, 16, and 9.

C 2, 3, 5, 8, 12, ▨, ▨, ▨, . . .

$$2 \quad 3 \quad 5 \quad 8 \quad 12 \quad ▨ \quad ▨ \quad ▨$$
$$+1 \quad +2 \quad +3 \quad +4 \quad +5 \quad +6 \quad +7$$

A pattern is to add one more than you did the time before.

$12 + 5 = 17$ $\qquad$ $17 + 6 = 23$ $\qquad$ $23 + 7 = 30$

The next three numbers will be 17, 23, and 30.

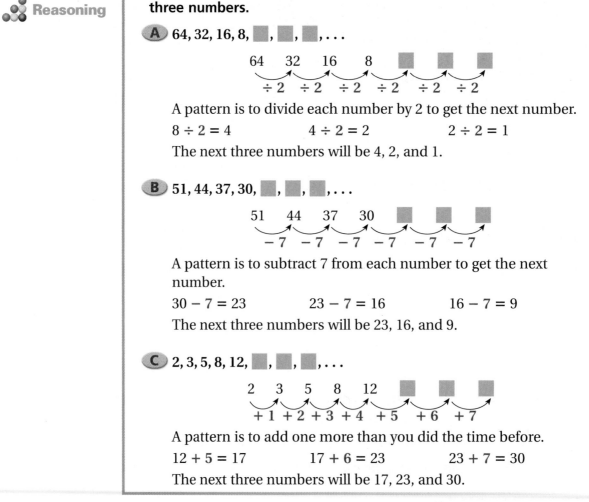

EXAMPLE 2 Identifying and Extending Geometric Patterns

Identify a possible pattern. Use your pattern to draw the next three figures.

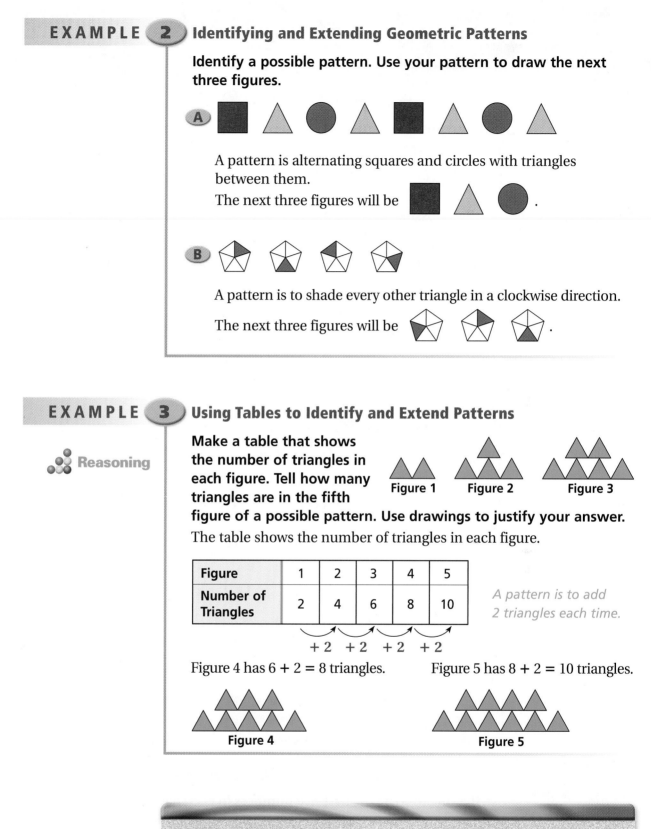

A

A pattern is alternating squares and circles with triangles between them.

The next three figures will be ▪ ▲ ● .

B

A pattern is to shade every other triangle in a clockwise direction.

The next three figures will be ⬠ ⬠ ⬠ .

EXAMPLE 3 Using Tables to Identify and Extend Patterns

Reasoning

Make a table that shows the number of triangles in each figure. Tell how many triangles are in the fifth figure of a possible pattern. Use drawings to justify your answer.

Figure 1   Figure 2   Figure 3

The table shows the number of triangles in each figure.

Figure	1	2	3	4	5
Number of Triangles	2	4	6	8	10

+2 +2 +2 +2

A pattern is to add 2 triangles each time.

Figure 4 has 6 + 2 = 8 triangles.   Figure 5 has 8 + 2 = 10 triangles.

Figure 4   Figure 5

Think and Discuss

1. Describe two different number patterns that begin with 3, 6, . . .

2. Tell when it would be useful to make a table to help you identify and extend a pattern.

1-1 Exercises

California Standards Practice
Preparation for AF2.0

go.hrw.com
Homework Help Online
KEYWORD: MS8CA 1-1
Parent Resources Online
KEYWORD: MS8CA Parent

GUIDED PRACTICE

See Example ① Identify a possible pattern. Use your pattern to write the next three numbers.

1. 6, 14, 22, 30, ▪, ▪, ▪, . . .

2. 1, 3, 9, 27, ▪, ▪, ▪, . . .

3. 59, 50, 41, 32, ▪, ▪, ▪, . . .

4. 8, 9, 11, 14, ▪, ▪, ▪, . . .

See Example ② Identify a possible pattern. Use your pattern to draw the next three figures.

5.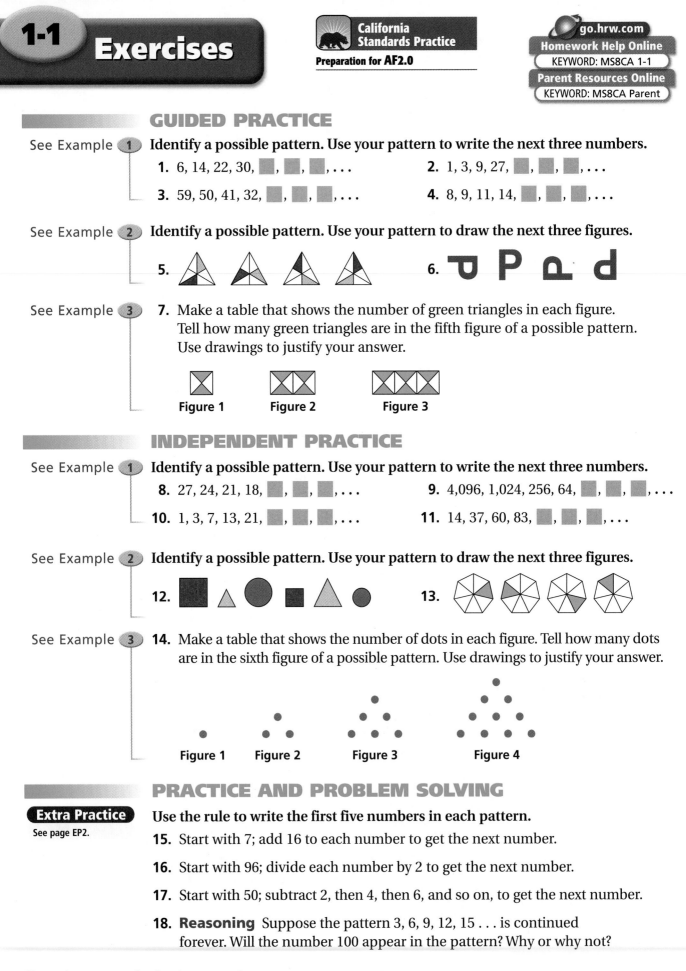

6. ℧ ⅁ Ρ ⅁

See Example ③ **7.** Make a table that shows the number of green triangles in each figure. Tell how many green triangles are in the fifth figure of a possible pattern. Use drawings to justify your answer.

Figure 1   Figure 2   Figure 3

INDEPENDENT PRACTICE

See Example ① Identify a possible pattern. Use your pattern to write the next three numbers.

8. 27, 24, 21, 18, ▪, ▪, ▪, . . .

9. 4,096, 1,024, 256, 64, ▪, ▪, ▪, . . .

10. 1, 3, 7, 13, 21, ▪, ▪, ▪, . . .

11. 14, 37, 60, 83, ▪, ▪, ▪, . . .

See Example ② Identify a possible pattern. Use your pattern to draw the next three figures.

12. ■ △ ● ■ △ ●

13.

See Example ③ **14.** Make a table that shows the number of dots in each figure. Tell how many dots are in the sixth figure of a possible pattern. Use drawings to justify your answer.

Figure 1   Figure 2   Figure 3   Figure 4

PRACTICE AND PROBLEM SOLVING

Extra Practice
See page EP2.

Use the rule to write the first five numbers in each pattern.

15. Start with 7; add 16 to each number to get the next number.

16. Start with 96; divide each number by 2 to get the next number.

17. Start with 50; subtract 2, then 4, then 6, and so on, to get the next number.

18. **Reasoning** Suppose the pattern 3, 6, 9, 12, 15 . . . is continued forever. Will the number 100 appear in the pattern? Why or why not?

Identify a possible pattern. Use your pattern to find the missing numbers.

19. 3, 12, ▨, 192, 768, ▨, ▨, . . .

20. 61, 55, ▨, 43, ▨, ▨, 25, . . .

21. ▨, ▨, 19, 27, 35, ▨, 51, . . .

22. 2, ▨, 8, ▨, 32, 64, ▨, . . .

23. Health The table shows the target heart rate during exercise for athletes of different ages. Assuming the pattern continues, what is the target heart rate for a 40-year-old athlete? a 65-year-old athlete?

Target Heart Rate	
Age	Heart Rate (beats per minute)
20	150
25	146
30	142
35	138

Draw the next three figures in each pattern.

24. ▷1 , ▷5 , ◁9 , ▽13 , ▷17 , △21 , . . .

25. ●4 , ■5 , △7 , ●10 , ■14 , △19 , ●25 , . . .

26. Social Studies In the ancient Mayan civilization, people used a number system based on bars and dots. Several numbers are shown below. Look for a pattern and write the number 18 in the Mayan system.

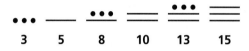

| 3 | 5 | 8 | 10 | 13 | 15 |

27. What's the Error? A student was asked to write the next three numbers in the pattern 96, 48, 24, 12, ... The student's response was 6, 2, 1. Describe and correct the student's error.

28. Write About It A school chess club meets every Tuesday during the month of March. March 1 falls on a Sunday. Explain how to use a number pattern to find all the dates when the club meets.

29. Challenge Find the 83rd number in the pattern 5, 10, 15, 20, 25, ...

30. Multiple Choice Which rule best describes the pattern 2, 6, 18, 54, 162, . . . ?

ⓐ Add 4.   ⓑ Add 12.   ⓒ Multiply by 3.   ⓓ Multiply by 4.

31. Short Response What could be the next number in the pattern 9, 11, 15, 21, 29, 39, . . .? Explain how you determined your answer.

Round each number to the nearest hundred thousand. (Previous course)

32. 4,224,315   **33.** 12,483,028   **34.** 8,072,339

Find each quotient. (Previous course)

35. 3,068 ÷ 26   **36.** 8,680 ÷ 35   **37.** 51,408 ÷ 136

 **Exponents**

California Standards

Preparation for **AF1.4** Solve problems manually by using the correct order of **operations** or by using a scientific calculator.

Also covered: **Preparation for AF1.3**

Vocabulary
power
exponent
base

Who uses this? Scientists can use exponents to determine the number of DNA molecules in a sample.

A DNA molecule makes a copy of itself that is identical to the original.

The molecules continue to split so that the two become four, the four become eight, and so on.

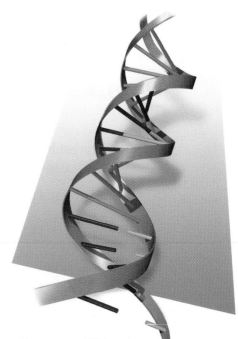

The structure of DNA can be compared to a twisted ladder.

Each time DNA copies itself, the number of molecules doubles. After four copies, the number of molecules is $2 \cdot 2 \cdot 2 \cdot 2 = 16$.

This multiplication can also be written as a **power**, using a *base* and an *exponent*. The **exponent** tells how many times to use the **base** as a factor.

$$2 \cdot 2 \cdot 2 \cdot 2 = 2^4 = 16$$

Exponent ← 2^4

Base →

EXAMPLE 1 **Evaluating Powers**

Find each value.

A 5^2

$5^2 = 5 \cdot 5$ *Use 5 as a factor 2 times.*

$\quad = 25$

B 2^6

$2^6 = 2 \cdot 2 \cdot 2 \cdot 2 \cdot 2 \cdot 2$ *Use 2 as a factor 6 times.*

$\quad = 64$

C 25^1 *Any number to the first power is equal*

$25^1 = 25$ *to that number.*

Reading Math

Read 5^2 as "5 to the second power" or "5 squared." Read 2^6 as "2 to the sixth power."

To express a whole number as a power, write the number as the product of equal factors. Then write the product using the base and an exponent. For example, $10{,}000 = 10 \cdot 10 \cdot 10 \cdot 10 = 10^4$.

EXAMPLE 2 **Expressing Whole Numbers as Powers**

Write each number using an exponent and the given base.

A 49, base 7

$49 = 7 \cdot 7$ *7 is used as a factor 2 times.*

$\quad = 7^2$

B 81, base 3

$81 = 3 \cdot 3 \cdot 3 \cdot 3$ *3 is used as a factor 4 times.*

$\quad = 3^4$

EXAMPLE 3 *Earth Science Application*

Most earthquakes occur along faults. The San Andreas Fault in California is approximately 800 miles long.

The Richter scale measures an earthquake's strength, or magnitude. Each category in the table is 10 times stronger than the next lower category. For example, a large earthquake is 10 times stronger than a moderate earthquake. How many times stronger is a great earthquake than a moderate one?

Earthquake Strength	
Category	Magnitude
Moderate	5
Large	6
Major	7
Great	8

An earthquake with a magnitude of 6 is 10 times stronger than one with a magnitude of 5.

An earthquake with a magnitude of 7 is 10 times stronger than one with a magnitude of 6.

An earthquake with a magnitude of 8 is 10 times stronger than one with a magnitude of 7.

$$10 \cdot 10 \cdot 10 = 10^3 = 1{,}000$$

A great earthquake is 1,000 times stronger than a moderate one.

Think and Discuss

1. Describe a relationship between 3^5 and 3^6.

2. Tell which power of 8 is equal to 2^6. Explain.

3. Explain why any number to the first power is equal to that number.

1-2 Exercises

California Standards Practice
Preparation for **AF1.3** and **AF1.4**

go.hrw.com
Homework Help Online
KEYWORD: MS8CA 1-2
Parent Resources Online
KEYWORD: MS8CA Parent

GUIDED PRACTICE

See Example **1** **Find each value.**

1. 2^5 **2.** 3^3 **3.** 6^2 **4.** 9^1 **5.** 10^6

See Example **2** **Write each number using an exponent and the given base.**

6. 25, base 5   **7.** 16, base 4   **8.** 27, base 3   **9.** 100, base 10

See Example **3** **10. Earth Science** On the Richter scale, a great earthquake is 10 times stronger than a major one, and a major one is 10 times stronger than a large one. How many times stronger is a great earthquake than a large one?

INDEPENDENT PRACTICE

See Example **1** **Find each value.**

11. 11^2 **12.** 3^5 **13.** 8^3 **14.** 4^3 **15.** 3^4

16. 2^4 **17.** 5^1 **18.** 2^3 **19.** 5^3 **20.** 30^1

See Example **2** **Write each number using an exponent and the given base.**

21. 81, base 9   **22.** 4, base 4   **23.** 64, base 4

24. 7, base 7   **25.** 32, base 2   **26.** 128, base 2

27. 1,600, base 40   **28.** 2,500, base 50   **29.** 100,000, base 10

See Example **3** **30.** In a game, a contestant had a starting score of one point. He tripled his score every turn for four turns. Write his score after four turns as a power. Then find his score.

PRACTICE AND PROBLEM SOLVING

Extra Practice
See page EP2.

Give two ways to represent each number using powers.

31. 81   **32.** 16   **33.** 64   **34.** 729   **35.** 625

Compare. Write <, >, or =.

36. 4^2 ▤ 15   **37.** 2^3 ▤ 3^2 **38.** 64 ▤ 4^3 **39.** 8^3 ▤ 7^4

40. 10,000 ▤ 10^5 **41.** 6^5 ▤ 3,000   **42.** 9^3 ▤ 3^6 **43.** 5^4 ▤ 7^3

44. To find the volume of a cube, find the third power of the length of an edge of the cube. What is the volume of a cube that is 6 inches long on an edge?

45. Reasoning Domingo decided to save $0.03 the first day and to triple the amount he saves each day. How much will he save on the seventh day?

46. Science A newborn panda cub weighs an average of 4 ounces. How many ounces might a one-year-old panda weigh if its weight doubles 8 times in one year?

47. Social Studies If the populations of the cities in the table double every 10 years, what will their populations be in 2034?

City	Population (2004)
Yuma, AZ	86,070
Phoenix, AZ	1,421,298

48. Critical Thinking Is 2^5 greater than or less than 3^3? Explain your answer.

49. Hobbies Malia is making a quilt with a pattern of rings. In the center ring, she uses four stars. In each of the next three rings, she uses three times as many stars as in the one before. How many stars does she use in the fourth ring? Write the answer using a power and find its value.

Order each set of numbers from least to greatest.

50. $29, 2^3, 6^2, 16, 3^5$

51. $4^3, 33, 6^2, 5^3, 10^1$

52. $7^2, 2^4, 80, 10^2, 1^8$

53. $2, 1^8, 3^4, 16^1, 0$

54. $5^2, 21, 11^2, 13^1, 1^9$

55. $2^5, 3^3, 9, 5^2, 8^1$

56. Science The cells of some kinds of bacteria divide every 30 minutes. If you begin with a single cell, how many cells will there be after 1 hour? 2 hours? 3 hours?

57. What's the Error? A student wrote 64 as 8 · 2. How did the student apply exponents incorrectly?

58. Write About It Explain why $6^3 \neq 3^6$.

59. Challenge What is the length of the edge of a cube if its volume is 1,000 cubic meters?

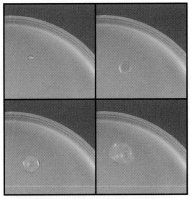

Bacteria divide by pinching in two. This process is called binary fission.

60. Multiple Choice What is the value of 4^6?

(A) 24 (B) 1,024 (C) 4,096 (D) 16,384

61. Multiple Choice Which of the following is NOT equal to 64?

(A) 6^4 (B) 4^3 (C) 2^6 (D) 8^2

62. Gridded Response Simplify $2^3 + 3^2$.

63. Money The students at a middle school raised $612 by having a garage sale, $102 by having a car wash, and $294 by having a concert. The money will be divided equally among 12 charities. How much will each charity receive? (Previous course)

Identify a possible pattern. Use your pattern to write the next three numbers. (Lesson 1-1)

64. $100, 91, 82, 73, 64, \ldots$

65. $17, 19, 22, 26, 31, \ldots$

66. $2, 6, 18, 54, 162, \ldots$

1-3 Order of Operations

California Standards

AF1.4 Solve problems manually by using the correct order of operations or by using a scientific calculator.
Also covered: **AF1.3**

Why learn this? You put on your socks *before* you put on your shoes. In mathematics, as in life, some tasks must be done in a certain order.

Vocabulary
numerical expression
order of operations

A **numerical expression** is made up of numbers and operations. When simplifying a numerical expression, rules must be followed so that everyone gets the same answer. That is why mathematicians have agreed upon the **order of operations**.

ORDER OF OPERATIONS

1. Perform operations within grouping symbols.
2. Evaluate powers.
3. Multiply and divide in order from left to right.
4. Add and subtract in order from left to right.

EXAMPLE 1 Using the Order of Operations

Simplify each expression. Use the order of operations to justify your work.

Reasoning

A $27 - 18 \div 6$

$27 - 18 \div 6$ *Divide.*

$27 - 3$ *Subtract.*

24

B $36 - 18 \div 2 \cdot 3 + 8$

$36 - 18 \div 2 \cdot 3 + 8$ *Divide and multiply from left to right.*

$36 - 9 \cdot 3 + 8$

$36 - 27 + 8$ *Subtract and add from left to right.*

$9 + 8$

17

C $5 + 6^2 \cdot 10$

$5 + 6^2 \cdot 10$ *Evaluate the power.*

$5 + 36 \cdot 10$ *Multiply.*

$5 + 360$ *Add.*

365

EXAMPLE 2 Using the Order of Operations with Grouping Symbols

Reasoning

Simplify each expression.

A $36 - (2 \cdot 6) \div 3$

$36 - (2 \cdot 6) \div 3$ *Perform the operation in parentheses.*

$36 - 12 \div 3$ *Divide.*

$36 - 4$ *Subtract.*

32

B $[(4 + 12 \div 4) - 2]^3$

$[(4 + 12 \div 4) - 2]^3$ *The parentheses are inside the brackets,*

$[(4 + 3) - 2]^3$ *so perform the operations inside the*

$[7 - 2]^3$ *parentheses first.*

5^3

125

Helpful Hint

When an expression has a set of grouping symbols within a second set of grouping symbols, begin with the innermost set.

EXAMPLE 3 *Career Application*

Maria works part-time in a law office, where she earns $20 per hour. The table shows the number of hours she worked last week. Simplify the expression (6 + 5 · 3) · 20 to find out how much money Maria earned last week.

Day	Hours
Monday	6
Tuesday	5
Wednesday	5
Thursday	5

$(6 + 5 \cdot 3) \cdot 20$ *Perform the operations in parentheses.*

$(6 + 15) \cdot 20$ *Add.*

$21 \cdot 20$ *Multiply.*

420

Maria earned $420 last week.

Think and Discuss

1. Apply the order of operations to determine if the expressions $3 + 4^2$ and $(3 + 4)^2$ have the same value.

2. Give the correct order of operations for simplifying $(5 + 3 \cdot 20) \div 13 + 3^2$.

3. Determine where grouping symbols should be inserted in the expression $3 + 9 - 4 \cdot 2$ so that its value is 13.

California Standards Practice

AF1.3, AF1.4

go.hrw.com
Homework Help Online
KEYWORD: MS8CA 1-3
Parent Resources Online
KEYWORD: MS8CA Parent

GUIDED PRACTICE

See Example 1   Simplify each expression. Use the order of operations to justify your work.

1. $43 + 16 \div 4$ **2.** $28 - 4 \cdot 3 \div 6 + 4$ **3.** $25 - 4^2 \div 8$

See Example 2   **4.** $26 - (7 \cdot 3) + 2$ **5.** $(3^2 + 11) \div 5$ **6.** $32 + 6(4 - 2^2) + 8$

See Example 3   **7. Career** Caleb earns \$10 per hour. He worked 4 hours on Monday, Wednesday, and Friday. He worked 8 hours on Tuesday and Thursday. Simplify the expression $(3 \cdot 4 + 2 \cdot 8) \cdot 10$ to find out how much Caleb earned in all.

INDEPENDENT PRACTICE

See Example 1   Simplify each expression. Use the order of operations to justify your work.

8. $3 + 7 \cdot 5 - 1$ **9.** $5 \cdot 9 - 3$ **10.** $3 - 2 + 6 \cdot 2^2$

See Example 2   **11.** $(3 \cdot 3 - 3)^2 \div 3 + 3$ **12.** $2^5 - (4 \cdot 5 + 3)$ **13.** $(3 \div 3) + 3 \cdot (3^3 - 3)$

14. $4^3 \div 8 - 2$ **15.** $(8 - 2)^2 \cdot (8 - 1)^2 \div 3$ **16.** $9{,}234 \div [3 \cdot 3(1 + 8^3)]$

See Example 3   **17. Consumer Math** Maki paid a \$14 basic fee plus \$25 a day to rent a car. Simplify the expression $14 + 5 \cdot 25$ to find out how much it cost her to rent the car for 5 days.

18. Consumer Math Enrico spent \$20 per square yard for carpet and \$35 for a carpet pad. Simplify the expression $35 + 20(16)$ to find out how much Enrico spent to carpet a room with an area of 16 square yards.

PRACTICE AND PROBLEM SOLVING

Extra Practice
See page EP2.

Simplify each expression. Use the order of operations to justify your work.

19. $90 - 36 \times 2$ **20.** $16 + 14 \div 2 - 7$ **21.** $64 \div 2^2 + 4$

22. $10 \times (18 - 2) + 7$ **23.** $(9 - 4)^2 - 12 \times 2$ **24.** $[1 + (2 + 5)^2] \times 2$

Compare. Write $<$, $>$, or $=$.

25. $8 \cdot 3 - 2 \; \blacksquare \; 8 \cdot (3 - 2)$ **26.** $(6 + 10) \div 2 \; \blacksquare \; 6 + 10 \div 2$

27. $12 \div 3 \cdot 4 \; \blacksquare \; 12 \div (3 \cdot 4)$ **28.** $18 + 6 - 2 \; \blacksquare \; 18 + (6 - 2)$

29. $[6(8 - 3) + 2] \; \blacksquare \; 6(8 - 3) + 2$ **30.** $(18 - 14) \div (2 + 2) \; \blacksquare \; 18 - 14 \div 2 + 2$

Reasoning Insert grouping symbols to make each statement true.

31. $4 \cdot 8 - 3 = 20$ **32.** $5 + 9 - 3 \div 2 = 8$ **33.** $12 - 2^2 \div 5 = 20$

34. $4 \cdot 2 + 6 = 32$ **35.** $4 + 6 - 3 \div 7 = 1$ **36.** $9 \cdot 8 - 6 \div 3 = 6$

37. Bertha earned \$8.00 per hour for 4 hours babysitting and \$10.00 per hour for 5 hours painting a room. Simplify the expression $8 \cdot 4 + 10 \cdot 5$ to find out how much Bertha earned in all.

38. **Consumer Math** Mike bought a painting for $512. He sold it at an antique auction for 4 times the amount that he paid for it, and then he purchased another painting with half of the profit that he made. Simplify the expression $(512 \cdot 4 - 512) \div 2$ to find how much Mike paid for the second painting.

39. **Multi-Step** Anelise bought four shirts and two pairs of jeans. She paid $6 in sales tax.

   a. Write an expression that shows how much she spent on shirts.
   b. Write an expression that shows how much she spent on jeans.
   c. Write and simplify an expression to show how much she spent on clothes, including sales tax.

40. **Choose a Strategy** There are four children in a family. The sum of the squares of the ages of the three youngest children equals the square of the age of the oldest child. How old are the children?

   Ⓐ 1, 4, 8, 9   Ⓑ 1, 3, 6, 12   Ⓒ 4, 5, 8, 10   Ⓓ 2, 3, 8, 16

41. **Write About It** Describe the order in which you would perform the operations to find the correct value of $[(2 + 4)^2 - 2 \cdot 3] \div 6$.

42. **Challenge** Use the numbers 3, 5, 6, 2, 54, and 5 in that order to write an expression that has a value of 100.

43. **Multiple Choice** Which operation should be performed first to simplify the expression $18 - 1 \cdot 9 \div 3 + 8$?

   Ⓐ Addition   Ⓑ Subtraction   Ⓒ Multiplication   Ⓓ Division

44. **Multiple Choice** Which expression does NOT simplify to 81?

   Ⓐ $9 \cdot (4 + 5)$ Ⓑ $7 + 16 \cdot 4 + 10$ Ⓒ $3 \cdot 25 + 2$ Ⓓ $10^2 - 4 \cdot 5 + 1$

45. **Multiple Choice** Quinton bought 2 pairs of jeans for $30 each and 3 pairs of socks for $5 each. Which expression can be simplified to determine the total amount Quinton paid for the jeans and socks?

   Ⓐ $2 \cdot 3(30 + 5)$ Ⓑ $(2 + 3) \cdot (30 + 5)$ Ⓒ $2 \cdot (30 + 5) \cdot 3$ Ⓓ $2 \cdot 30 + 3 \cdot 5$

Identify a possible pattern. Use your pattern to write the next three numbers. (Lesson 1-1)

46. 56, 60, 64, 68, 72, . . .   **47.** 5, 10, 20, 40, 80, . . .   **48.** 70, 63, 56, 49, 42, . . .

Find each value. (Lesson 1-2)

49. 8^6 **50.** 9^3 **51.** 4^5 **52.** 3^3 **53.** 7^1

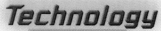

Explore Order of Operations

go.hrw.com
Lab Resources Online
KEYWORD: MS8CA Lab1

California Standards

AF1.4 Solve problems manually by using the correct order of operations or by using a scientific calculator.
Also covered: **AF1.3**

REMEMBER

The order of operations
1. Perform operations within grouping symbols.
2. Evaluate powers.
3. Multiply and divide in order from left to right.
4. Add and subtract in order from left to right.

Activity 1

❶ Simplify $6 + 4 \cdot 2$ using paper and pencil. Use the order of operations.

$6 + 4 \cdot 2$
$6 + 8$ *Multiply.*
14 *Add.*

❷ Simplify the expression using a scientific calculator.

Scientific calculators automatically perform the order of operations. However, some other types of calculators do not.

If the calculator performed the addition before the multiplication, the answer displayed on the screen would have been 20 instead of 14.

Think and Discuss

1. In what order would a scientific calculator perform the operations if you used it to simplify the expression $64 \div 8 - 2 \cdot 4$?

2. Is $4 + 5 \cdot 6$ equivalent to $5 \cdot 6 + 4$? Explain.

Try This

Simplify each expression with pencil and paper. Check your answers with a scientific calculator.

1. $20 - 3 \cdot 5$ **2.** $15 \cdot 6 + 13$ **3.** $2 + 7 \cdot 5 \cdot 4$ **4.** $50 \div 10 \cdot 2$ **5.** $90 \div 3 - 30$

Use a scientific calculator to simplify each expression.

6. $56 \cdot 113 \div 8 - 247$ **7.** $336 \cdot 42 + 17 \cdot 218$ **8.** $2{,}462 - 352 \div 11 \cdot 24$

Many calculators have an x^2 key that allows you to find the square of a number. On calculators that do not have this key, or to use exponents other than 2, you can use the caret key, ∧ . For example, to evaluate 3^5, press 3 ∧ 5, and then press ENTER .

To enter grouping symbols on a calculator, use the (and) keys.

Activity 2

❶ Simplify $4 \cdot 2^3$ using paper and pencil. Then check your answer with a scientific calculator.

First simplify the expression using paper and pencil.

$4 \cdot 2^3$
$4 \cdot 8$ *Evaluate the power.*
32 *Multiply.*

Then simplify $4 \cdot 2^3$ using a scientific calculator.

Scientific calculators automatically evaluate the power first. If you want to perform the multiplication first, you must put that operation inside parentheses.

❷ Simplify $[(3 + 7) \cdot 2]^2$ using paper and pencil. Then check your answer with a scientific calculator.

$[(3 + 7) \cdot 2]^2$
$[10 \cdot 2]^2$ *Perform the operation in parentheses.*
20^2 *Perform the operation in brackets.*
400 *Evaluate the power.*

Then simplify $[(3 + 7) \cdot 2]^2$ using a scientific calculator. Enter both sets of grouping symbols by using the parentheses keys. Notice that both methods give the same answer.

❸ Use a scientific calculator to simplify $\dfrac{(2 + 5 \cdot 4)^3}{4^2}$.

Think and Discuss

1. Is $2 + 5 \cdot 4^3 + 4^2$ equivalent to $(2 + 5 \cdot 4^3) + 4^2$? Explain.

Try This

Simplify each expression with pencil and paper. Check your answers with a scientific calculator.

1. $3 \cdot 2^3 + 5$ 2. $3 \cdot (2^3 + 5)$ 3. $(3 \cdot 2)^2$ 4. $3 \cdot 2^2$ 5. $2^{(3 \cdot 2)}$

Use a scientific calculator to simplify each expression. Round your answers to the nearest hundredth.

6. $(2.1 + 5.6 \cdot 4^3) \div 6^4$ 7. $[(2.1 + 5.6) \cdot 4^3] \div 6^4$ 8. $[(8.6 - 1.5) \div 2^3] \div 5^2$

1-4 Properties of Numbers

California Standards

AF1.3 Apply algebraic order of operations and **the commutative, associative, and distributive properties to evaluate expressions; and justify each step in the process.**

Vocabulary
Commutative Property
Associative Property
Identity Property
Distributive Property

Who uses this? Architects can use properties of numbers to find the area of floor plans. (See Exercise 41.)

COMMUTATIVE PROPERTY		
Words	**Numbers**	**Algebra**
You can add numbers in any order and multiply numbers in any order.	$3 + 8 = 8 + 3$ $5 \cdot 7 = 7 \cdot 5$	$a + b = b + a$ $ab = ba$

ASSOCIATIVE PROPERTY		
Words	**Numbers**	**Algebra**
When you add or multiply, you can group the numbers together in any combination.	$(4 + 5) + 1 = 4 + (5 + 1)$ $(9 \cdot 2) \cdot 6 = 9 \cdot (2 \cdot 6)$	$(a + b) + c = a + (b + c)$ $(a \cdot b) \cdot c = a \cdot (b \cdot c)$

IDENTITY PROPERTY		
Words	**Numbers**	**Algebra**
The sum of 0 and any number is the number. The product of 1 and any number is the number.	$4 + 0 = 4$ $8 \cdot 1 = 8$	$a + 0 = a$ $a \cdot 1 = a$

EXAMPLE 1 **Identifying Properties of Addition and Multiplication**

Tell which property is represented.

A $2 + (7 + 8) = (2 + 7) + 8$

$2 + (7 + 8) = (2 + 7) + 8$ *The numbers are regrouped.*
Associative Property

B $25 \cdot 1 = 25$

$25 \cdot 1 = 25$ *One of the factors is 1.*
Identity Property

C $xy = yx$

$xy = yx$ *The order of the variables is switched.*
Commutative Property

You can use properties and mental math to rearrange or regroup numbers into combinations that are easier to work with.

 EXAMPLE 2 **Using Properties to Simplify Expressions**

Simplify each expression. Justify each step.

A $12 + 19 + 18$

$$12 + 19 + 18 = 19 + 12 + 18 \qquad \textit{Commutative Property}$$
$$= 19 + (12 + 18) \qquad \textit{Associative Property}$$
$$= 19 + 30 \qquad \textit{Add.}$$
$$= 49$$

B $25 \cdot 13 \cdot 4$

$$25 \cdot 13 \cdot 4 = 25 \cdot 4 \cdot 13 \qquad \textit{Commutative Property}$$
$$= (25 \cdot 4) \cdot 13 \qquad \textit{Associative Property}$$
$$= 100 \cdot 13 \qquad \textit{Multiply.}$$
$$= 1{,}300$$

DISTRIBUTIVE PROPERTY		
Numbers	$6 \cdot (9 + 14) = 6 \cdot 9 + 6 \cdot 14$	$8 \cdot (5 - 2) = 8 \cdot 5 - 8 \cdot 2$
Algebra	$a \cdot (b + c) = ab + ac$	$a \cdot (b - c) = ab - ac$

You can use the Distributive Property to multiply numbers mentally by breaking apart one of the numbers and writing it as a sum or difference.

EXAMPLE 3 **Using the Distributive Property to Multiply Mentally**

Use the Distributive Property to find 7(29).

Method 1

$$7(29) = 7(20 + 9) \qquad \textit{Rewrite 29.}$$
$$= (7 \cdot 20) + (7 \cdot 9) \qquad \textit{Use the Distributive Property.}$$
$$= 140 + 63 \qquad \textit{Multiply.}$$
$$= 203 \qquad \textit{Simplify.}$$

Method 2

$$7(29) = 7(30 - 1)$$
$$= (7 \cdot 30) - (7 \cdot 1)$$
$$= 210 - 7$$
$$= 203$$

Think and Discuss

1. Describe two different ways to simplify the expression $7 \cdot (3 + 9)$.

2. Explain how the Distributive Property can help you find $6 \cdot 102$ using mental math.

GUIDED PRACTICE

See Example 1 Tell which property is represented.

1. $1 + (6 + 7) = (1 + 6) + 7$ **2.** $1 \cdot 10 = 10$ **3.** $3 \cdot 5 = 5 \cdot 3$

4. $6 + 0 = 6$ **5.** $4 \cdot (4 \cdot 2) = (4 \cdot 4) \cdot 2$ **6.** $x + y = y + x$

See Example 2 Simplify each expression. Justify each step.

7. $8 + 23 + 2$ **8.** $2 \cdot (17 \cdot 5)$ **9.** $(25 \cdot 11) \cdot 4$

10. $17 + 29 + 3$ **11.** $16 + (17 + 14)$ **12.** $5 \cdot 19 \cdot 20$

See Example 3 Use the Distributive Property to find each product.

13. $2(19)$ **14.** $5(31)$ **15.** $(22)2$

16. $(13)6$ **17.** $8(26)$ **18.** $(34)6$

INDEPENDENT PRACTICE

See Example 1 Tell which property is represented.

19. $1 + 0 = 1$ **20.** $xyz = x \cdot (yz)$ **21.** $9 + (9 + 0) = (9 + 9) + 0$

22. $11 + 25 = 25 + 11$ **23.** $7 \cdot 1 = 7$ **24.** $(16 \cdot 4) \cdot 2 = (4 \cdot 16) \cdot 2$

See Example 2 Simplify each expression. Justify each step.

25. $50 \cdot 16 \cdot 2$ **26.** $9 + 34 + 1$ **27.** $4 \cdot (25 \cdot 9)$

28. $27 + 28 + 3$ **29.** $20 + (63 + 80)$ **30.** $25 + 17 + 75$

See Example 3 Use the Distributive Property to find each product.

31. $9(15)$ **32.** $(14)5$ **33.** $3(58)$

34. $10(42)$ **35.** $(23)4$ **36.** $(16)5$

PRACTICE AND PROBLEM SOLVING

Extra Practice
See page EP2.

Write an example of each property using whole numbers.

37. Commutative Property **38.** Identity Property

39. Associative Property **40.** Distributive Property

41. Architecture The figure shows the floor plan for a studio loft. To find the area of the loft, the architect multiplies the length and the width: $(14 + 8) \cdot 10$. Use the Distributive Property to find the area of the loft.

10 ft

14 ft   8 ft

Simplify each expression. Justify each step.

42. $32 + 26 + 43$ **43.** $50 \cdot 45 \cdot 4$ **44.** $5 + 16 + 25$ **45.** $35 \cdot 25 \cdot 20$

Complete each equation. Then tell which property is represented.

46. $5 + 16 = 16 + \blacksquare$

47. $15 \cdot 1 = \blacksquare$

48. $\blacksquare \cdot (4 + 7) = 3 \cdot 4 + 3 \cdot 7$

49. $20 + \blacksquare = 20$

50. $2 \cdot \blacksquare \cdot 9 = (2 \cdot 13) \cdot 9$

51. $8 + (\blacksquare + 4) = (8 + 8) + 4$

52. $2 \cdot (6 + 1) = 2 \cdot \blacksquare + 2 \cdot 1$

53. $(12 - 9) \cdot \blacksquare = 12 \cdot 2 - 9 \cdot 2$

54. Sports Janice wants to know the total number of games won by the Denver Nuggets basketball team over the three seasons shown in the table. What expression should she simplify? Explain how she can use mental math and the properties of this lesson to simplify the expression.

Denver Nuggets		
Season	Won	Lost
2001–02	27	55
2002–03	17	65
2003–04	43	39

55. What's the Error? A student simplified the expression $6 \cdot (9 + 12)$ as shown. What is the student's error?

$$6 \cdot (9 + 12) = 6 \cdot 9 + 12$$
$$= 54 + 12$$
$$= 66$$

56. Write About It Do you think there is a Commutative Property of Division? Give an example to explain your answer.

57. Challenge Use the Distributive Property to simplify $\frac{1}{6} \cdot (36 + \frac{1}{2})$.

58. Multiple Choice Which expression is equivalent to $(24 + 8) + 12$?

Ⓐ $(24 - 8) - 12$

Ⓒ $(24 + 12) + (8 + 12)$

Ⓑ $24 + (8 + 12)$

Ⓓ $(24 \cdot 12) + (8 \cdot 12)$

59. Multiple Choice Which number completes the equation $12 \cdot (20 + 6) = 12 \cdot 20 + \blacksquare \cdot 6$?

Ⓐ 1   Ⓑ 6   Ⓒ 12   Ⓓ 20

60. Short Response Show how to use the Distributive Property to simplify the expression $8(27)$.

Compare. Write $<$, $>$, or $=$. (Lesson 1-2)

61. $7^2 \blacksquare 50$

62. $10^3 \blacksquare 300$

63. $9^2 \blacksquare 6^3$

64. $2^4 \blacksquare 4^2$

Simplify each expression. (Lesson 1-3)

65. $25 + 5 - (6^2 - 7)$

66. $3^3 - (6 + 3)$

67. $(4^2 + 5) \div 7$

68. $(5 - 3)^2 \div (3^2 - 7)$

1-5 Evaluating Algebraic Expressions

California Standards

AF1.2 Write and **evaluate** an algebraic expression for a given situation, using up to three variables.

Also covered: **AF1.3**

Vocabulary
variable
constant
algebraic expression
evaluate

Why learn this? You can use an algebraic expression to determine the year in which a person was a certain age.

The actor and director Ron Howard was born in 1954.

You can use a letter such as *a* to represent Ron Howard's age. When he turns *a* years old, the year will be

$$1954 + a.$$

The letter *a* has a value that can change, or vary. When a letter represents a number that can vary, it is called a **variable**. The year 1954 is a **constant** because the number cannot change.

An **algebraic expression** is an expression that contains at least one variable. For example, $1954 + a$ is an algebraic expression.

Age	Year born + age = year at age	
16	1954 + 16	1970
18	1954 + 18	1972
21	1954 + 21	1975
36	1954 + 36	1990
a	1954 + *a*	

To **evaluate** an algebraic expression, substitute a number for the variable.

EXAMPLE 1 Evaluating Algebraic Expressions

The expression $s + 7$ represents Nancy's age when her sister is *s* years old. Evaluate the expression for each value of *s*, and tell what the value of the expression means.

A $s = 3$ $s + 7$

         $3 + 7$ *Substitute 3 for s.*

          10 *Add.*

When her sister is 3 years old, Nancy is 10 years old.

B $s = 5$ $s + 7$

         $5 + 7$ *Substitute 5 for s.*

          12 *Add.*

When her sister is 5 years old, Nancy is 12 years old.

Multiplication and division of variables can be written in several ways, as shown in the table.

When evaluating expressions, use the order of operations.

Multiplication		Division	
$7t$	$7 \cdot t$	$\dfrac{q}{2}$	$q/2$
$7(t)$	$7 \times t$	$q \div 2$	
ab	$a \cdot b$	$\dfrac{s}{r}$	s/r
$a(b)$	$a \times b$	$s \div r$	

EXAMPLE **2** **Evaluating Expressions Involving Order of Operations**

Evaluate each expression for the given value of the variable.

A $3x - 2$ for $x = 5$

$3(5) - 2$	*Substitute 5 for x.*
$15 - 2$	*Multiply.*
13	*Subtract*

B $n \div 2 + n$ for $n = 4$

$4 \div 2 + 4$	*Substitute 4 for n.*
$2 + 4$	*Divide.*
6	*Add.*

C $6y^2 + 2y$ for $y = 2$

$6(2)^2 + 2(2)$	*Substitute 2 for y.*
$6(4) + 2(2)$	*Evaluate the power.*
$24 + 4$	*Multiply.*
28	*Add.*

EXAMPLE **3** **Evaluating Expressions with More Than One Variable**

Evaluate $\dfrac{3}{n} + 2m - p$ for $n = 3$, $m = 4$, and $p = 6$.

$\dfrac{3}{3} + 2(4) - 6$	*Substitute 3 for n, 4 for m, and 6 for p.*
$1 + 8 - 6$	*Divide and multiply from left to right.*
3	*Add and subtract from left to right.*

Think and Discuss

1. Write each expression another way. **a.** $12x$ **b.** $\dfrac{4}{y}$ **c.** $\dfrac{3xy}{2}$

2. Explain the difference between a variable and a constant.

California Standards Practice
AF1.2, AF1.3

go.hrw.com
Homework Help Online
KEYWORD: MS8CA 1-5
Parent Resources Online
KEYWORD: MS8CA Parent

GUIDED PRACTICE

See Example ① The expression $12d$ represents the number of eggs in d dozen. Evaluate the expression for each value of d, and tell what the value of the expression means.

1. $d = 3$ **2.** $d = 2$ **3.** $d = 11$

See Example ② Evaluate each expression for the given value of the variable.

4. $2x - 3$ for $x = 4$ **5.** $n \div 3 + n$ for $n = 6$ **6.** $5y^2 + 3y$ for $y = 2$

See Example ③ Evaluate each expression for the given values of the variables.

7. $\dfrac{8}{n} + 3m$ for $n = 2$ and $m = 5$ **8.** $5a - 3b + 5$ for $a = 4$ and $b = 3$

INDEPENDENT PRACTICE

See Example ① The expression $\dfrac{q}{4}$ represents the number of dollars equal to q quarters. Evaluate the expression for each value of q, and tell what the value of the expression means.

9. $q = 16$ **10.** $q = 36$ **11.** $q = 64$

See Example ② Evaluate each expression for the given value of the variable.

12. $5y - 1$ for $y = 3$ **13.** $10b - 9$ for $b = 2$ **14.** $p \div 7 + p$ for $p = 14$

15. $n \div 5 + n$ for $n = 20$ **16.** $3x^2 + 2x$ for $x = 10$ **17.** $3c^2 - 5c$ for $c = 3$

See Example ③ Evaluate each expression for the given values of the variables.

18. $\dfrac{12}{n} + 7m$ for $n = 6$ and $m = 4$ **19.** $7p - 2t + 3$ for $p = 6$ and $t = 2$

20. $x - \dfrac{y}{4} + 20z$ for $x = 9$, $y = 4$, and $z = 5$

PRACTICE AND PROBLEM SOLVING

Extra Practice
See page EP3.

Evaluate each expression for the given values of the variables. Justify each step.

21. $22p \div 11 + p$ for $p = 3$ **22.** $q + q^2 + q \div 2$ for $q = 4$

23. $\dfrac{16}{k} + 7h$ for $k = 8$ and $h = 2$ **24.** $f \div 3 + f$ for $f = 18$

25. $3t \div 3 + t$ for $t = 13$ **26.** $9 + 3p - 5t + 3$ for $p = 2$ and $t = 1$

27. $3m + \dfrac{y}{5} - b$ for $m = 2$, $y = 35$, and $b = 7$

28. The expression $60m$ gives the number of seconds in m minutes. Evaluate $60m$ for $m = 7$. How many seconds are there in 7 minutes?

29. **Money** Betsy has n quarters. You can use the expression $0.25n$ to find the total value of her coins in dollars. What is the value of 18 quarters?

30. Recreation Yosemite National Park was created by Congress in 1890. The expression $x - 1890$ models the current age of the park in years, where x is the present year. What is the current age of the park?

31. Science The graph shows the changes of state for water.

    a. What is the boiling point of water in degrees Celsius?

    b. Use the expression $1.8c + 32$ to find the boiling point of water in degrees Fahrenheit.

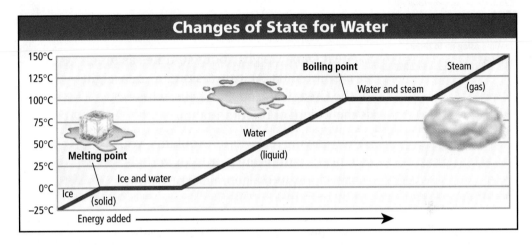

32. What's the Error? A student was asked to identify the variable in the expression $72x + 8$. The student answered $72x$. What was the student's error?

33. Write About It Explain why letters such as x, p, and n used in algebraic expressions are called variables. Use examples to illustrate your response.

34. Challenge Evaluate the expression $\dfrac{x + y}{y - x}$ for $x = 6$ and $y = 8$.

35. Multiple Choice Which expression does NOT equal 15?

    Ⓐ $3t$ for $t = 5$ Ⓑ $3 + t$ for $t = 12$ Ⓒ $t \div 3$ for $t = 60$ Ⓓ $t - 10$ for $t = 25$

36. Multiple Choice A group of 11 students go rock climbing at a local gym. It costs $12 per student plus $4 for each shoe rental. If only 8 students rent shoes, what is the total cost for the group to go climbing? Use the expression $12x + 4y$, where x represents the total number of students and y represents the number of students who rent shoes.

    Ⓐ $132   Ⓑ $140   Ⓒ $164   Ⓓ $176

Simplify each expression. (Lesson 1-3)

37. $6^2 - 28 + 5$ **38.** $15 \cdot 2 + 64 \div 8$ **39.** $17 + 6^2 \cdot 2$ **40.** $28 \div 4 \cdot 7 + 20$

Use the Distributive Property to find each product. (Lesson 1-4)

41. $5(16)$ **42.** $(17)4$ **43.** $7(23)$ **44.** $(29)3$

1-6 Writing Algebraic Expressions

California Standards

AF1.2 Write and evaluate **an algebraic expression for a given situation, using up to three variables.**

Why learn this? You can write an expression to show the relationship between the weights of dogs.

A Great Dane weighs about 40 times as much as a Chihuahua. An expression for the weight of the Great Dane could be $40c$, where c is the weight of the Chihuahua.

When solving real-world problems, you will need to translate words, or verbal expressions, into algebraic expressions.

Operation	Verbal Expressions	Algebraic Expression
✚	• add 3 to a number • a number plus 3 • the sum of a number and 3 • 3 more than a number • a number increased by 3	$n + 3$
▬	• subtract 12 from a number • a number minus 12 • the difference of a number and 12 • 12 less than a number • a number decreased by 12 • take away 12 from a number • a number less 12	$x - 12$
✖	• 2 times a number • 2 multiplied by a number • the product of 2 and a number	$2m$ or $2 \cdot m$
➗	• 6 divided into a number • a number divided by 6 • the quotient of a number and 6	$a \div 6$ or $\frac{a}{6}$

EXAMPLE 1 **Translating Verbal Expressions into Algebraic Expressions**

Write each phrase as an algebraic expression.

A the product of 20 and t
product means "multiply"
$20t$

B 24 less than a number
less than means "subtract from"
$n - 24$

Write each phrase as an algebraic expression.

C 4 times the sum of a number and 2

4 times the sum of a number and 2

4 · $(n + 2)$

$4(n + 2)$

EXAMPLE 2 **Translating Real-World Problems into Algebraic Expressions**

A Jed reads p pages each day of a 200-page book. Write an algebraic expression for how many days it will take Jed to read the book. Then evaluate the expression for $p = 25$, and tell what the value of the expression means.

You need to *separate* the total number of pages *into equal parts*. This involves division.

$$\frac{\text{total number of pages}}{\text{pages read each day}} = \frac{200}{p}$$

$\frac{200}{p}$ *Write the expression.*

$\frac{200}{25}$ *Substitute 25 for p.*

8   *Divide.*

It will take Jed 8 days to read the book if he reads 25 pages each day.

B Adult tickets to a concert cost $24, teen tickets cost $20, and child tickets cost $16. Write an algebraic expression to show how much it costs for a adult tickets, t teen tickets, and c child tickets. Then evaluate the expression for $a = 3$, $t = 1$, and $c = 2$, and tell what the value of the expression means.

Multiply to *put equal parts together.*

Cost of adult tickets: $24a$ Cost of teen tickets: $20t$

Cost of child tickets: $16c$

Add to *put parts together.*

Total cost: $24a + 20t + 16c$

$24a + 20t + 16c$ *Write the expression.*

$24(3) + 20(1) + 16(2)$ *Substitute 3 for a, 1 for t, and 2 for c.*

$72 + 20 + 32$ *Multiply from left to right.*

124 *Add.*

The cost of 3 adult, 1 teen, and 2 child tickets is $124.

Think and Discuss

1. Write three different verbal expressions that can be represented by $2 - y$.

California
Standards Practice
AF1.2

go.hrw.com
Homework Help Online
KEYWORD: MS8CA 1-6
Parent Resources Online
KEYWORD: MS8CA Parent

GUIDED PRACTICE

See Example ① Write each phrase as an algebraic expression.

1. the product of 7 and p

2. 3 less than a number

3. 12 divided into a number

4. 3 times the sum of a number and 5

See Example ② **5.** A used bookstore is selling American comics for $2 each and Japanese comics for $3 each. Write an algebraic expression to show the total cost of a American comics and j Japanese comics. Then evaluate the expression for $a = 4$ and $j = 2$, and tell what the value of the expression means.

INDEPENDENT PRACTICE

See Example ① Write each phrase as an algebraic expression.

6. the sum of 5 and a number

7. 2 less than a number

8. the quotient of a number and 8

9. 9 times a number

10. 10 less than the product of a number and 3

See Example ② **11.** A roller coaster carries r passengers, and a Ferris wheel carries f passengers. Write an algebraic expression to show how many more passengers are riding on the roller coaster than on the Ferris wheel. Then evaluate the expression for $r = 42$ and $f = 36$, and tell what the value of the expression means.

PRACTICE AND PROBLEM SOLVING

Extra Practice
See page EP3.

Write each phrase as an algebraic expression.

12. m plus the product of 6 and n

13. the quotient of 23 and u minus t

14. 14 less than the quantity k times 6

15. 2 times the sum of y and 5

16. the quotient of 100 and the quantity 6 plus w

17. 35 multiplied by the quantity r less 45

18. Multi-Step An ice machine can produce 17 pounds of ice in one hour.

   a. Write an algebraic expression to describe the number of pounds of ice produced in n hours.

   b. How many pounds of ice can the machine produce in 4 hours?

19. Hobbies Karen makes beaded jewelry. She uses 3 beads for a ring, 8 beads for a pin, and 15 beads for a bracelet. Write an algebraic expression to show the total number of beads she will need for r rings, p pins, and b bracelets.

Science

Up to 25 follicle mite nymphs can hatch in a single hair follicle.

Write a verbal expression for each algebraic expression.

20. $h + 3$ **21.** $90 \div y$ **22.** $s - 405$ **23.** $16t$

24. $5(a - 8)$ **25.** $4p - 10$ **26.** $(r + 1) \div 14$ **27.** $\frac{m}{15} + 3$

28. **Science** Tiny and harmless, follicle mites live in our eyebrows and eyelashes. They are relatives of spiders. So like spiders, they have eight legs. Write an algebraic expression for the number of legs in m mites.

Nutrition The table shows the estimated number of grams of carbohydrates commonly found in various types of foods.

29. Write an algebraic expression for the number of grams of carbohydrates in y pieces of fruit and 1 cup of skim milk.

30. How many grams of carbohydrates are in a sandwich made from t ounces of lean meat and 2 slices of bread?

Food	Carbohydrates
1 c skim milk	12 g
1 piece of fruit	15 g
1 slice of bread	15 g
1 oz lean meat	0 g

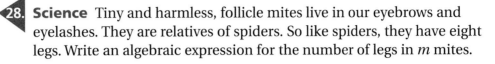

31. **What's the Question?** Al has twice as many baseball cards as Frank and four times as many football cards as Joe. The expression $2x + 4y$ can be used to show the total number of baseball and football cards Al has. If the answer is y, then what is the question?

32. **Write About It** If you are asked to compare two numbers, what two operations might you use? Why?

33. **Challenge** On June 7, 2006, one U.S. dollar was equivalent to $1.116 in Canadian money. Write an algebraic expression for the number of U.S. dollars you could get for n Canadian dollars.

SPIRAL STANDARDS REVIEW AF1.2, AF1.3, AF1.4

34. **Multiple Choice** Which verbal expression does NOT represent $9 - x$?

Ⓐ x less than nine

Ⓑ x decreased by nine

Ⓒ subtract x from nine

Ⓓ the difference of nine and x

35. **Short Response** A room at the Oak Creek Inn costs $104 per night for two people. There is a $19 charge for each extra person. Write an algebraic expression that shows the cost for a family of four staying at the inn for x nights. Then evaluate your expression for 3 nights.

Simplify each expression. (Lesson 1-3)

36. $6 + 4 \div 2$ **37.** $9 \cdot 1 - 4$ **38.** $5^2 - 3$ **39.** $24 \div 3 + 3^3$

40. Evaluate $b - a^2$ for $a = 2$ and $b = 9$. (Lesson 1-5)

Quiz for Lessons 1-1 Through 1-6

1-1 Numbers and Patterns

Identify a possible pattern. Use your pattern to write the next three numbers or figures.

1. 8, 15, 22, 29, . . . **2.** 79, 66, 53, 40, . . .

3.

1-2 Exponents

Find each value.

4. 8^4 **5.** 7^3 **6.** 4^5 **7.** 6^2

8. The number of bacteria in a sample doubles every hour. How many bacteria cells will there be after 8 hours if there is one cell at the beginning? Write your answer as a power.

1-3 Order of Operations

Simplify each expression.

9. $8 - 14 \div (9 - 2)$ **10.** $54 - 6 \cdot 3 + 4^2$ **11.** $4 - 24 \div 2^3$ **12.** $4(3 + 2)^2 - 9$

13. Toshio paid $50 to join a health club plus $24 per month. Simplify the expression $50 + 24 \cdot 12$ to find out how much Toshio paid to use the health club for one year.

1-4 Properties of Numbers

Simplify each expression. Justify each step.

14. $29 + 50 + 21$ **15.** $5 \cdot 18 \cdot 20$ **16.** $34 + 62 + 36$ **17.** $3 \cdot 11 \cdot 20$

1-5 Evaluating Algebraic Expressions

Evaluate each expression for the given values of the variable.

18. $7(x + 4)$ for $x = 5$ **19.** $11 - n \div 3$ for $n = 6$ **20.** $p + 6t^2$ for $p = 11$ and $t = 3$

1-6 Writing Algebraic Expressions

Write each phrase as an algebraic expression.

21. the quotient of a number and 15 **22.** a number decreased by 13

23. 10 times the difference of p and 2 **24.** 3 plus the product of a number and 8

25. A long-distance phone company charges a $2.95 monthly fee plus $0.14 for each minute. Write an algebraic expression to show the cost of calling for t minutes in one month.

Focus on Problem Solving

California Standards

MR1.1 Analyze problems by identifying relationships, distinguishing relevant from irrelevant information, identifying missing information, sequencing and prioritizing information, and observing patterns.
Also covered: **NS2.0, MR2.4**

Solve

• **Choose an operation: multiplication or division**

To solve a word problem, you must determine which mathematical operation you can use to find the answer. One way of doing this is to determine the action the problem is asking you to take. If you are putting equal parts together, then you need to multiply. If you are separating something into equal parts, then you need to divide.

Decide what action each problem is asking you to take, and tell whether you must multiply or divide. Then explain your decision.

1 Judy plays the flute in the band. She practices for 3 hours every week. Judy practices only half as long as Angie, who plays the clarinet. How long does Angie practice playing the clarinet each week?

2 Each year, members of the band and choir are invited to join the bell ensemble for the winter performance. There are 18 bells in the bell ensemble. This year, each student has 3 bells to play. How many students are in the bell ensemble this year?

3 For every percussion instrument in the band, there are 4 wind instruments. If there are 48 wind instruments in the band, how many percussion instruments are there?

4 A group of 4 people singing together in harmony is called a quartet. At a state competition for high school choir students, 8 quartets from different schools competed. How many students competed in the quartet competition?

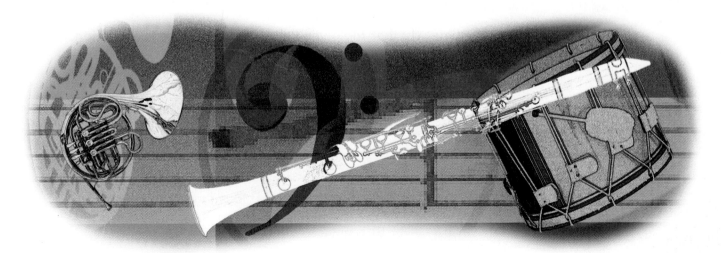

1-7 Equations and Their Solutions

California Standards

Preparation for ➡ **AF1.1**
Write and solve one-step linear equations in one variable.

Vocabulary
equation
solution

Why learn this? You can use an equation to determine whether two measurements are equal. (See Example 2.)

An **equation** is a mathematical statement that two quantities are equal. You can think of a correct equation as a balanced scale.

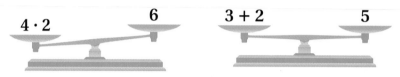

Equations may contain variables. If a value for a variable makes an equation true, that value is a **solution** of the equation. You can test a value to see if it is a solution of an equation by substituting the value for the variable.

Reading Math

The symbol ≠ means "is not equal to."

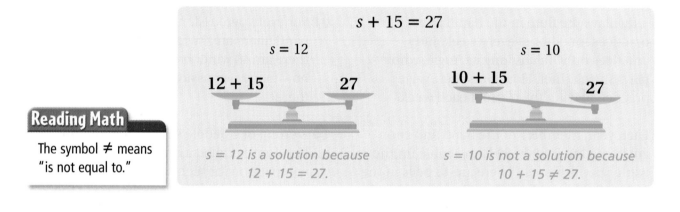

$$s + 15 = 27$$

$s = 12$

$12 + 15$ 27

$s = 12$ is a solution because $12 + 15 = 27$.

$s = 10$

$10 + 15$ 27

$s = 10$ is not a solution because $10 + 15 \neq 27$.

EXAMPLE **1** **Determining Solutions of Equations**

Determine whether the given value of the variable is a solution.

A $a + 23 = 82$ for $a = 61$

$$a + 23 = 82$$
$$61 + 23 \overset{?}{=} 82 \qquad \textit{Substitute 61 for a.}$$
$$84 \overset{?}{=} 82 \qquad \textit{Add.}$$

84 82

Since $84 \neq 82$, 61 is not a solution to $a + 23 = 82$.

Determine whether the given value of the variable is a solution.

B $60 \div c = 6$ for $c = 10$

$$60 \div c = 6$$
$$60 \div 10 \overset{?}{=} 6 \qquad \textit{Substitute 10 for c.}$$
$$6 \overset{?}{=} 6 \qquad \textit{Divide.}$$

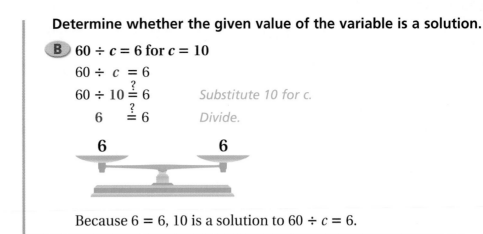

$$6 \qquad\qquad 6$$

Because $6 = 6$, 10 is a solution to $60 \div c = 6$.

You can use equations to check whether measurements given in different units are equal.

For example, there are 12 inches in one foot. If you have a measurement in feet, multiply by 12 to find the measurement in inches: $12 \cdot \text{feet} = \text{inches}$, or $12f = i$.

If you have one measurement in feet and another in inches, check whether the two numbers make the equation $12f = i$ true.

EXAMPLE 2 *Science Application*

One science book states that a manatee can grow to be 13 feet long. According to another book, a manatee may grow to 156 inches. Determine if these two measurements are equal.

$$12f = i$$
$$12 \cdot 13 \overset{?}{=} 156 \qquad \textit{Substitute.}$$
$$156 \overset{?}{=} 156 \qquad \textit{Multiply.}$$

Because $156 = 156$, 13 feet is equal to 156 inches.

Think and Discuss

1. Tell which of the following is the solution to $y \div 2 = 9$: $y = 14$, $y = 16$, or $y = 18$. How do you know?

2. Give an example of an equation with a solution of 15.

GUIDED PRACTICE

See Example ① **Determine whether the given value of the variable is a solution.**

1. $c + 23 = 48$ for $c = 35$ **2.** $z + 31 = 73$ for $z = 42$

3. $96 = 130 - d$ for $d = 34$ **4.** $85 = 194 - a$ for $a = 105$

5. $75 \div y = 5$ for $y = 15$ **6.** $78 \div n = 13$ for $n = 5$

See Example ② **7. Social Studies** An almanac states that the Minnehaha Waterfall in Minnesota is 53 feet tall. A tour guide said the Minnehaha Waterfall is 636 inches tall. Determine if these two measurements are equal.

INDEPENDENT PRACTICE

See Example ① **Determine whether the given value of the variable is a solution.**

8. $w + 19 = 49$ for $w = 30$ **9.** $d + 27 = 81$ for $d = 44$

10. $g + 34 = 91$ for $g = 67$ **11.** $k + 16 = 55$ for $k = 39$

12. $101 = 150 - h$ for $h = 49$ **13.** $89 = 111 - m$ for $m = 32$

14. $116 = 144 - q$ for $q = 38$ **15.** $92 = 120 - t$ for $t = 28$

16. $80 \div b = 20$ for $b = 4$ **17.** $91 \div x = 7$ for $x = 12$

18. $55 \div j = 5$ for $j = 10$ **19.** $49 \div r = 7$ for $r = 7$

See Example ② **20. Money** Kent earns $6 per hour at his after-school job. One week, he worked 12 hours and received a paycheck for $66. Determine if Kent was paid the correct amount of money. (*Hint:* $6 · hours = total pay)

21. Measurement The Eiffel Tower in Paris, France, is 300 meters tall. A student claims that it is 300,000 centimeters tall. Determine if these two measurements are equal. (*Hint:* 1 m = 100 cm)

PRACTICE AND PROBLEM SOLVING

Extra Practice
See page EP3.

Determine whether the given value of the variable is a solution.

22. $93 = 48 + u$ for $u = 35$ **23.** $112 = 14 \times f$ for $f = 8$

24. $13 = m \div 8$ for $m = 104$ **25.** $79 = z - 23$ for $z = 112$

26. $64 = l - 34$ for $l = 98$ **27.** $105 = p \times 7$ for $p = 14$

28. $94 \div s = 26$ for $s = 3$ **29.** $v + 79 = 167$ for $v = 88$

30. $m + 36 = 54$ for $m = 18$ **31.** $x - 35 = 96$ for $x = 112$

32. $12y = 84$ for $y = 7$ **33.** $7x = 56$ for $x = 8$

34. Estimation A large pizza has 8 slices. Determine if 6 large pizzas will be enough to feed 24 people, if each person eats 2 to 3 slices of pizza.

35. Multi-Step Rebecca has 17 one-dollar bills. Courtney has 350 nickels. Do the two girls have the same amount of money? (*Hint*: First find how many nickels are in a dollar.)

Replace each ▪ with a number that makes the equation correct.

36. $4 + 1 = \blacksquare + 2$

37. $2 + \blacksquare = 6 + 2$

38. $\blacksquare - 5 = 9 - 2$

39. $5(4) = 10(\blacksquare)$

40. $3 + 6 = \blacksquare - 4$

41. $12 \div 4 = 9 \div \blacksquare$

42. Critical Thinking Linda is building a rectangular playhouse. The width is x feet. The length is $x + 3$ feet. The distance around the base of the playhouse is 36 feet. Is 8 the value of x? Explain.

43. Reasoning What should replace the question mark to keep the scale balanced?

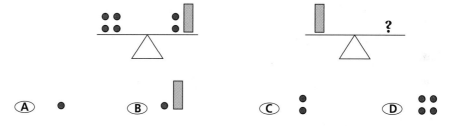

44. Write About It Explain how to determine if a value is a solution to an equation.

45. Challenge Is $n = 4$ a solution for $n^2 + 79 = 88$? Explain.

SPIRAL STANDARDS REVIEW ⬅ **AF1.1, AF1.2, AF1.3**

46. Multiple Choice For which equation is $b = 8$ a solution?

Ⓐ $13 - b = 8$ Ⓑ $8 + b = 21$ Ⓒ $b - 13 = 21$ Ⓓ $b + 13 = 21$

47. Multiple Choice When Paul gets 53 more postcards, he will have 82 cards in his collection. Solve the equation $n + 53 = 82$ to find how many postcards Paul has in his collection now.

Ⓐ 135 Ⓑ 125 Ⓒ 29 Ⓓ 27

Simplify each expression. Justify each step. (Lesson 1-4)

48. $25 \cdot 22 \cdot 4$

49. $84 + (23 + 16)$

50. $28 + 33 + 7$

51. A bus can carry 55 passengers. Write an algebraic expression for the number of buses needed to carry p passengers. (Lesson 1-6)

52. Velvet ribbon costs \$3 per yard, and silk ribbon costs \$4 per yard. Write an algebraic expression for the total cost of v yards of velvet ribbon and s yards of silk ribbon. (Lesson 1-6)

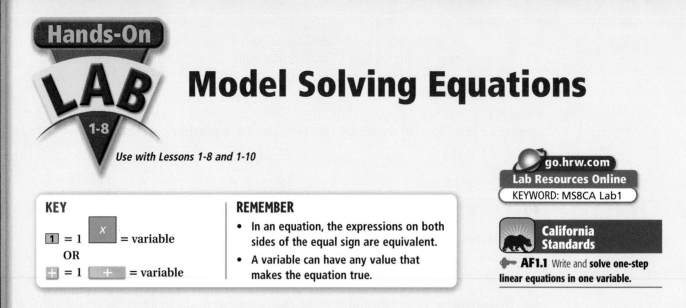

Model Solving Equations

Use with Lessons 1-8 and 1-10

go.hrw.com
Lab Resources Online
KEYWORD: MS8CA Lab1

California Standards

◆ **AF1.1** Write and **solve one-step linear equations in one variable.**

KEY

$\boxed{1} = 1$ $\boxed{x} = $ variable
OR
$\boxed{+} = 1$ $\boxed{+} = $ variable

REMEMBER

- In an equation, the expressions on both sides of the equal sign are equivalent.
- A variable can have any value that makes the equation true.

You can use balance scales and algebra tiles to model and solve equations.

Activity

1 Use a balance scale to model and solve the equation $3 + x = 11$.

a. On the left side of the scale, place 3 unit weights and one variable weight. On the right side, place 11 unit weights. This models $3 + x = 11$.

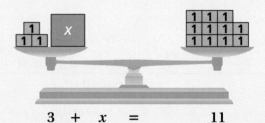

$$3 + x = 11$$

b. Remove 3 of the unit weights from each side of the scale to leave the variable weight by itself on one side.

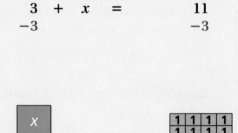

$$3 + x = 11$$
$$-3 \qquad\qquad -3$$

c. Count the remaining unit weights on the right side of the scale. This number represents the solution of the equation.

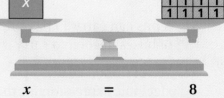

$$x = 8$$

The model shows that if $3 + x = 11$, then $x = 8$.

2 Use algebra tiles to model and solve the equation $3y = 15$.

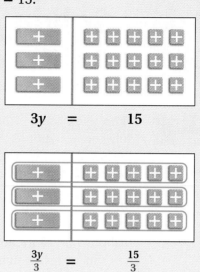

a. On the left side of the mat, place 3 variable tiles. On the right side, place 15 unit tiles. This models $3y = 15$.

$$3y \quad = \quad 15$$

b. Since there are 3 variable tiles, divide the tiles on each side of the mat into 3 equal groups.

$$\frac{3y}{3} \quad = \quad \frac{15}{3}$$

c. Count the number of unit tiles in one of the groups. This number represents the solution of the equation.

$$y \quad = \quad 5$$

The model shows that if $3y = 15$, then $y = 5$.

To check your solutions, substitute the variable in each equation with your solution. If the resulting equation is true, your solution is correct.

$3 + x = 11$ $\qquad\qquad\qquad$ $3y = 15$

$3 + 8 \stackrel{?}{=} 11$ $\qquad\qquad\qquad$ $3 \cdot 5 \stackrel{?}{=} 15$

$11 \stackrel{?}{=} 11$ ✔ $\qquad\qquad\qquad$ $15 \stackrel{?}{=} 15$ ✔

Think and Discuss

1. What operation did you use to solve the equation $3 + x = 11$ in **1**? What operation did you use to solve $3y = 15$ in **2**?

2. Compare using a balance scale and weights with using a mat and algebra tiles. Which method of modeling equations is more helpful to you? Explain.

Try This

Use a balance scale or algebra tiles to model and solve each equation.

1. $4x = 16$ $\qquad$ 2. $3 + 5 = n$ $\qquad$ 3. $5r = 15$ $\qquad$ 4. $n + 7 = 12$

5. $y + 6 = 13$ $\qquad$ 6. $8 = 2r$ $\qquad$ 7. $9 = 7 + w$ $\qquad$ 8. $18 = 6p$

California Standards

← **AF1.1** Write and solve one-step linear equations in one variable.

Vocabulary
inverse operations

Who uses this? Surfers can solve an equation to find the best length for a surfboard based on their height.

Some surfers recommend that the length of a beginner's surfboard be 14 inches greater than the surfer's height. If a surfboard is 82 inches, how tall should the surfer be to ride it?

Let *h* stand for the surfer's height. You can use the equation $h + 14 = 82$.

The equation $h + 14 = 82$ can be represented as a balanced scale.

To find the value of h, you need h by itself on one side of a balanced scale.

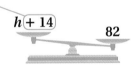

To get h by itself, first take away 14 from the left side of the scale. Now the scale is unbalanced.

To rebalance the scale, take away 14 from the other side.

Taking away 14 from both sides of the scale is the same as subtracting 14 from both sides of the equation.

$$\begin{aligned} h + 14 &= 82 \\ -14 &-14 \\ \hline h &= 68 \end{aligned}$$

A surfer using an 82-inch surfboard should be 68 inches tall.

Subtracting a number is the *inverse,* or opposite, of adding that number. **Inverse operations** are operations that undo each other. If an equation contains addition, solve it by subtracting from both sides to "undo" the addition.

EXAMPLE 1 Solving Equations by Subtracting

Solve each equation. Check your answers.

A $x + 62 = 93$

$$
\begin{aligned}
x + 62 &= 93 \\
-\,62 \quad &\, -62 \\
\hline
x &= 31
\end{aligned}
$$

62 is added to x.
Subtract 62 from both sides to undo the addition.

Check $x + 62 = 93$

$$31 + 62 \overset{?}{=} 93$$
$$93 \overset{?}{=} 93 \; ✔$$

Substitute 31 for x in the equation.
31 is the solution.

B $81 = 17 + y$

$$
\begin{aligned}
81 &= 17 + y \\
-\,17 \quad & \, -17 \\
\hline
64 &= y
\end{aligned}
$$

17 is added to y.
Subtract 17 from both sides to undo the addition.

Check $81 = 17 + y$

$$81 \overset{?}{=} 17 + 64$$
$$81 \overset{?}{=} 81 \; ✔$$

Substitute 64 for y in the equation.
64 is the solution.

EXAMPLE 2 *Social Studies Application*

Dyersberg, Newton, and St. Thomas are located along Ventura Highway, as shown on the map. Find the distance d between Newton and Dyersberg.

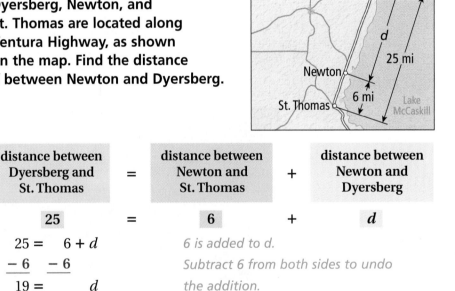

distance between Dyersberg and St. Thomas		distance between Newton and St. Thomas		distance between Newton and Dyersberg
25	=	6	+	d

$$
\begin{aligned}
25 &= 6 + d \\
-\,6 \quad & \, -6 \\
\hline
19 &= d
\end{aligned}
$$

6 is added to d.
Subtract 6 from both sides to undo the addition.

The distance between Newton and Dyersberg is 19 miles.

Think and Discuss

1. Tell whether the solution of $c + 4 = 21$ will be less than 21 or greater than 21. Explain.

2. Describe how you could check your answer in Example 2.

California Standards Practice
🐻 AF1.1

go.hrw.com
Homework Help Online
KEYWORD: MS8CA 1-8
Parent Resources Online
KEYWORD: MS8CA Parent

GUIDED PRACTICE

See Example ① Solve each equation. Check your answers.

1. $x + 54 = 90$ **2.** $49 = 12 + y$ **3.** $n + 27 = 46$

4. $22 + t = 91$ **5.** $31 = p + 13$ **6.** $c + 38 = 54$

See Example ② **7.** Lou, Michael, and Georgette live on Mulberry Street, as shown on the map. Lou lives 10 blocks from Georgette. Georgette lives 4 blocks from Michael. How many blocks b does Michael live from Lou?

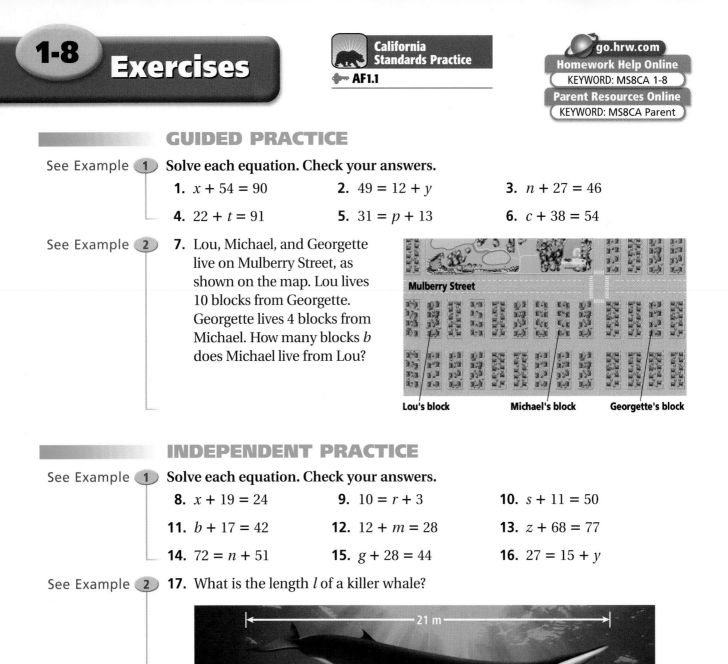

Mulberry Street

Lou's block   Michael's block   Georgette's block

INDEPENDENT PRACTICE

See Example ① Solve each equation. Check your answers.

8. $x + 19 = 24$ **9.** $10 = r + 3$ **10.** $s + 11 = 50$

11. $b + 17 = 42$ **12.** $12 + m = 28$ **13.** $z + 68 = 77$

14. $72 = n + 51$ **15.** $g + 28 = 44$ **16.** $27 = 15 + y$

See Example ② **17.** What is the length l of a killer whale?

21 m

Fin whale

Gray whale

Killer whale

15 m   ?

PRACTICE AND PROBLEM SOLVING

Extra Practice
See page EP3.

Solve each equation.

18. $x + 12 = 16$ **19.** $n + 32 = 39$ **20.** $23 + q = 34$

21. $52 + y = 71$ **22.** $73 = c + 35$ **23.** $93 = h + 15$

24. $125 = n + 85$ **25.** $87 = b + 18$ **26.** $12 + y = 50$

27. $t + 17 = 43$ **28.** $k + 9 = 56$ **29.** $25 + m = 47$

Write an equation for each statement.

30. The number of eggs e increased by 3 equals 14.

31. The number of new photos taken p added to 20 equals 36.

32. **Science** Temperature can be measured in degrees Fahrenheit, degrees Celsius, or kelvins. To convert from degrees Celsius to kelvins, add 273 to the Celsius temperature. Complete the table.

	Kelvins (K)	°C + 273 = K	Celsius (°C)
Water Freezes	273	°C + 273 = 273	▨
Body Temperature	310	▨	▨
Water Boils	373	▨	▨

Popular items like the ball and the mood rings above are made of heat-sensitive materials. Changes in temperature cause these materials to change color.

33. **History** In 1520, the explorer Ferdinand Magellan tried to measure the depth of the ocean. He weighted a 370 m rope and lowered it into the ocean. This rope was not long enough to reach the ocean floor. Suppose the depth at this location was 1,250 m. How much longer would Magellan's rope have to have been to reach the ocean floor?

34. **Reasoning** Use data from your science book to write a problem that can be solved using an equation that contains addition. Solve your problem.

35. **Write About It** Why is adding a number the inverse of subtracting that number?

36. **Challenge** In the magic square at right, each row, column, and diagonal has the same sum. Find the values of x, y, and z.

7	61	x
y	37	1
31	z	67

SPIRAL STANDARDS REVIEW   🗝 **AF1.1, AF1.2, AF1.3**

37. **Multiple Choice** Pauline hit 6 more home runs than Danielle. Pauline hit 18 home runs. How many home runs did Danielle hit?

Ⓐ 3   Ⓑ 12   Ⓒ 18   Ⓓ 24

38. **Multiple Choice** Which is the solution to the equation $79 + r = 118$?

Ⓐ $r = 39$ Ⓑ $r = 52$ Ⓒ $r = 79$ Ⓓ $r = 197$

Evaluate the expression $9y - 3$ for each given value of the variable. (Lesson 1-5)

39. $y = 2$ **40.** $y = 6$ **41.** $y = 10$ **42.** $y = 18$

Write each phrase as an algebraic expression. (Lesson 1-6)

43. 7 less than t

44. the product of m and 5

45. 12 minus the sum of x and 10

46. 8 more than the quotient of b and 10

47. the product of 24 and the quantity w plus 7

1-9 Solving Equations by Adding

Kennedy was President
from 1961 to 1963.

California Standards

🔑 **AF1.1** Write and solve one-step linear equations in one variable.

Why learn this? You can solve an equation that contains subtraction to determine someone's age.

When John F. Kennedy became president of the United States, he was 43 years old. He was 8 years younger than Abraham Lincoln was when Lincoln became president. How old was Lincoln when he became president?

Lincoln was President
from 1861 to 1865.

Let *a* represent Abraham Lincoln's age.

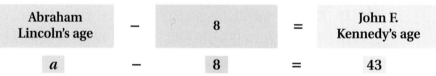

Abraham Lincoln's age	−	8	=	John F. Kennedy's age
a	−	8	=	43

Remember that adding a number is the inverse of subtracting that number. When an equation contains subtraction, use addition to "undo" the subtraction. Add the same amount to both sides of the equation.

$$\begin{array}{rcl} a - 8 &=& 43 \\ \underline{+\,8} && \underline{+\,8} \\ a &=& 51 \end{array}$$

Abraham Lincoln was 51 years old when he became president.

EXAMPLE **1** **Solving Equations by Adding**

A Solve $p - 2 = 5$. Check your answer.

$$\begin{array}{rcl} p - 2 &=& 5 \\ \underline{+\,2} && \underline{+\,2} \\ p &=& 7 \end{array}$$

2 is subtracted from p.
Add 2 to both sides to undo the subtraction.

Check $p - 2 = 5$

$7 - 2 \overset{?}{=} 5$ *Substitute 7 for p in the equation.*

$5 \overset{?}{=} 5$ ✔   *7 is the solution.*

B Solve $40 = x - 11$. Check your answer.

$$40 = x - 11$$
$$\underline{+\ 11 \qquad\ \ +\ 11}$$
$$51 = x$$

11 is subtracted from x.

Add 11 to both sides to undo the subtraction.

Check $40 = x - 11$

$$40 \overset{?}{=} 51 - 11$$

Substitute 51 for x in the equation.

$$40 \overset{?}{=} 40 ✔$$

51 is the solution.

C Solve $x - 56 = 19$. Check your answer.

$$x - 56 = 19$$
$$\underline{+\ 56 \qquad +\ 56}$$
$$x \qquad = \qquad 75$$

56 is subtracted from x.

Add 56 to both sides to undo the subtraction.

Check $x - 56 = 19$

$$75 - 56 \overset{?}{=} 19$$

Substitute 75 for x in the equation.

$$19 \overset{?}{=} 19 ✔$$

75 is the solution.

Think and Discuss

1. Tell whether the solution of $b - 14 = 9$ will be less than 9 or greater than 9. Explain.

2. Explain how you know what number to add to both sides of an equation containing subtraction.

1-9 Exercises

California Standards Practice

🔑 AF1.1

go.hrw.com
Homework Help Online
KEYWORD: MS8CA 1-9
Parent Resources Online
KEYWORD: MS8CA Parent

GUIDED PRACTICE

See Example **1**   Solve each equation. Check your answers.

1. $p - 8 = 9$ **2.** $3 = x - 16$ **3.** $a - 13 = 18$

4. $15 = y - 7$ **5.** $n - 24 = 9$ **6.** $39 = d - 2$

INDEPENDENT PRACTICE

See Example **1**   Solve each equation. Check your answers.

7. $y - 18 = 7$ **8.** $8 = n - 5$ **9.** $a - 34 = 4$

10. $c - 21 = 45$ **11.** $a - 40 = 57$ **12.** $31 = x - 14$

13. $28 = p - 5$ **14.** $z - 42 = 7$ **15.** $s - 19 = 12$

PRACTICE AND PROBLEM SOLVING

Extra Practice
See page EP3.

Solve each equation.

16. $r - 57 = 7$

17. $11 = x - 25$

18. $8 = y - 96$

19. $a - 6 = 15$

20. $q - 14 = 22$

21. $f - 12 = 2$

22. $18 = j - 19$

23. $109 = r - 45$

24. $d - 8 = 29$

25. $g - 71 = 72$

26. $p - 13 = 111$

27. $13 = m - 5$

California LINK
Geography

Mt. Shasta is a volcano in the Cascade Range of northern California. The last known eruption of the volcano was in 1786.

28. Geography Mt. Rainier, in Washington, has a higher elevation than Mt. Shasta. The difference between their elevations is 248 feet. What is the elevation of Mt. Rainier? Write an equation and solve.

29. Social Studies In 2004, the population of New York City was 5 million less than the population of Shanghai, China. The population of New York City was 8 million. Solve the equation $8 = s - 5$ to find the population of Shanghai.

U.S. Mountains

Height (ft)

14,200 — 14,196
14,160 — 14,162 14,153
14,120
14,080 — 14,070
14,040
14,000
0

Yale (CO) Shasta (CA) Sill (CA) Augusta (AK)

30. Write About It Suppose $n - 15$ is a whole number. What do you know about the value of n? Explain.

31. What's the Error? Look at the student paper at right. What did the student do wrong? What is the correct answer?

$51 = n - 17$
$\underline{-17 \qquad -17}$
$34 = n$ ✗

32. Challenge Write "the difference between n and 16 is 5" as an algebraic equation. Then find the solution.

SPIRAL STANDARDS REVIEW
🔑 AF1.1, AF1.3, AF1.4

33. Multiple Choice Which is a solution to the equation $j - 39 = 93$?

Ⓐ $j = 54$ Ⓑ $j = 66$ Ⓒ $j = 93$ Ⓓ $j = 132$

34. Short Response When 17 is subtracted from a number, the result is 64. Write an equation that can be used to find the original number. Then find the original number.

Simplify each expression. Use the order of operations to justify your work. (Lesson 1-3)

35. $81 - 4 \times 3 + 18 \div (6 + 3)$

36. $17 \times (5 - 3) + 16 \div 8$

37. $3^2 - (15 - 8) + 4 \times 5$

Solve each equation. (Lesson 1-8)

38. $a + 3 = 18$

39. $y + 7 = 45$

40. $x + 16 = 71$

41. $87 = b + 31$

California Standards

AF1.1 Write and solve one-step linear equations in one variable.

Who uses this? Biologists can solve equations that contain multiplication to learn about animal populations.

Nine-banded armadillos are always born in groups of 4. If you count 32 babies, what is the number of mother armadillos?

Let m represent the number of mother armadillos. There will be m equal groups of 4. You can use the equation $4m = 32$.

Dividing by a number is the inverse of multiplying by that number. To solve an equation that contains multiplication, use division to "undo" the multiplication.

Caution!

$4m$ means "$4 \times m$."

$$4m = 32$$
$$\frac{4m}{4} = \frac{32}{4}$$
$$m = 8$$

There are 8 mother armadillos.

EXAMPLE 1 Solving Equations by Dividing

Solve each equation. Check your answers.

A $3x = 12$

$3x = 12$ *x is multiplied by 3.*

$\dfrac{3x}{3} = \dfrac{12}{3}$ *Divide both sides by 3 to undo the multiplication.*

$x = 4$

Check $3x = 12$

$3(4) \overset{?}{=} 12$ *Substitute 4 for x in the equation.*

$12 \overset{?}{=} 12$ ✔   *4 is the solution.*

B $8 = 4w$

$8 = 4w$ *w is multiplied by 4.*

$\dfrac{8}{4} = \dfrac{4w}{4}$ *Divide both sides by 4 to undo the multiplication.*

$2 = w$

Check $8 = 4w$

$8 \overset{?}{=} 4(2)$ *Substitute 2 for w in the equation.*

$8 \overset{?}{=} 8$ ✔   *2 is the solution.*

EXAMPLE 2

PROBLEM SOLVING APPLICATION

The area of a rectangle is 36 square inches. Its length is 9 inches. What is its width w?

1 Understand the Problem

The **answer** will be the width of the rectangle in inches.

List the **important information:**

- The area of the rectangle is 36 square inches.
- The length of the rectangle is 9 inches.

Draw a diagram to represent this information.

2 Make a Plan

Reasoning

You can write and solve an equation using the formula for area. To find the area of a rectangle, multiply its length by its width.

$$A = \ell w$$
$$36 = 9w$$

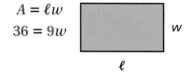

Remember!

For a rectangle, area = length × width.

3 Solve

$36 = 9w$ *w is multiplied by 9.*

$\dfrac{36}{9} = \dfrac{9w}{9}$ *Divide both sides by 9 to undo the multiplication.*

$4 = w$

So the width of the rectangle is 4 inches.

4 Look Back

Arrange 36 identical squares in a rectangle. The length is 9, so line up the squares in rows of 9. You can make 4 rows of 9, so the width of the rectangle is 4.

Think and Discuss

1. Tell what number you would use to divide both sides of the equation $15x = 60$.

2. Tell whether the solution of $10c = 90$ will be less than 90 or greater than 90. Explain.

California Standards Practice
🔑 AF1.1

go.hrw.com
Homework Help Online
KEYWORD: MS8CA 1-10
Parent Resources Online
KEYWORD: MS8CA Parent

GUIDED PRACTICE

See Example **1** — Solve each equation. Check your answers.

1. $7x = 21$ **2.** $27 = 3w$ **3.** $90 = 10a$

4. $56 = 7b$ **5.** $3c = 33$ **6.** $12 = 2n$

See Example **2**

7. The area of a rectangular deck is 675 square feet. The deck's width is 15 feet. What is its length ℓ?

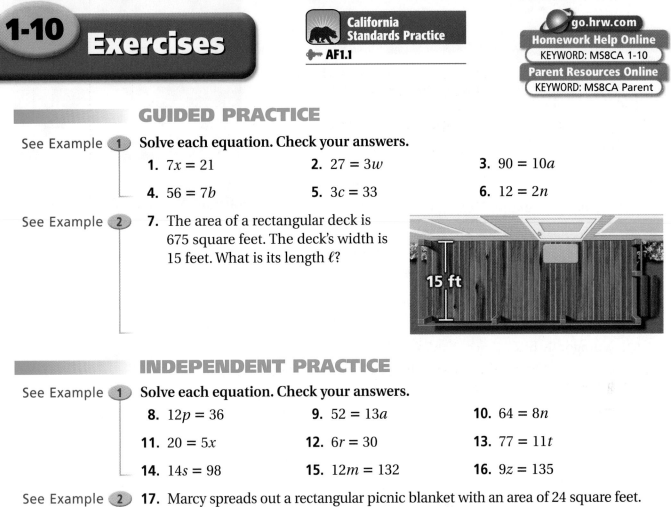
15 ft

INDEPENDENT PRACTICE

See Example **1** — Solve each equation. Check your answers.

8. $12p = 36$ **9.** $52 = 13a$ **10.** $64 = 8n$

11. $20 = 5x$ **12.** $6r = 30$ **13.** $77 = 11t$

14. $14s = 98$ **15.** $12m = 132$ **16.** $9z = 135$

See Example **2**

17. Marcy spreads out a rectangular picnic blanket with an area of 24 square feet. Its width is 4 feet. What is its length ℓ?

PRACTICE AND PROBLEM SOLVING

Extra Practice
See page EP3.

Solve each equation.

18. $5y = 35$ **19.** $18 = 2y$ **20.** $54 = 9y$ **21.** $15y = 120$

22. $4y = 0$ **23.** $22y = 440$ **24.** $3y = 63$ **25.** $z - 6 = 34$

26. $6y = 114$ **27.** $161 = 7y$ **28.** $135 = 3y$ **29.** $y - 15 = 3$

30. $81 = 9y$ **31.** $4 + y = 12$ **32.** $7y = 21$ **33.** $a + 12 = 26$

34. $10x = 120$ **35.** $36 = 12x$ **36.** $s - 2 = 7$ **37.** $15 + t = 21$

38. Estimation Colorado is almost a perfect rectangle on a map. Its border from east to west is about 387 mi, and its area is about 104,247 mi². Estimate the length of Colorado's border from north to south. (Area = length × width)

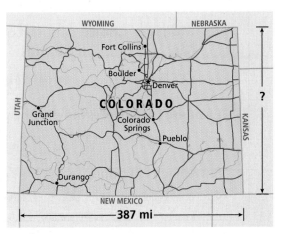

WYOMING   NEBRASKA
Fort Collins
Boulder
Denver
UTAH   COLORADO   KANSAS
Grand Junction   Colorado Springs
Pueblo
Durango
NEW MEXICO
387 mi
?

Arthropods make up the largest group of animals on Earth. They include insects, spiders, crabs, and centipedes. Arthropods have segmented bodies. In centipedes and millipedes, all of the segments are identical.

A horsefly magnified to twelve times its actual size

39. Centipedes have 2 legs per segment. They can have from 30 to 354 legs. Find a range for the number of segments a centipede can have.

40. Millipedes have 4 legs per segment. The record number of legs on a millipede is 752. How many segments did this millipede have?

Many arthropods have compound eyes. Compound eyes are made up of tiny bundles of identical light-sensitive cells.

41. A dragonfly has 7 times as many light-sensitive cells as a housefly. How many of these cells does a housefly have?

42. Find how many times more light-sensitive cells a dragonfly has than a butterfly.

43. **Write About It** A trapdoor spider can pull with a force that is 140 times its own weight. What other information would you need to find the spider's weight? Explain.

44. ⭐ **Challenge** There are about 6 billion humans in the world. Scientists estimate that there are a billion billion arthropods in the world. About how many times larger is the arthropod population than the human population?

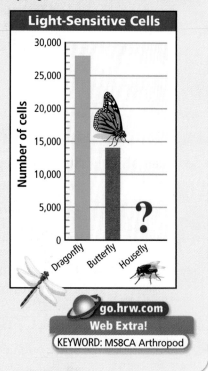

Light-Sensitive Cells

go.hrw.com
Web Extra!
KEYWORD: MS8CA Arthropod

SPIRAL STANDARDS REVIEW   🔑 AF1.1, AF1.2, AF1.3

45. **Multiple Choice** Solve the equation $25x = 175$.

 Ⓐ $x = 5$ Ⓑ $x = 6$ Ⓒ $x = 7$ Ⓓ $x = 8$

46. **Multiple Choice** The area of a rectangle is 42 square inches. Its width is 6 inches. What is its length?

 Ⓐ 5 inches   Ⓑ 7 inches   Ⓒ 9 inches   Ⓓ 11 inches

Evaluate each expression for the given value of the variables. (Lesson 1-5)

47. $3r + 6p$ for $r = 11$ and $p = 6$ 48. $x^2 - 5(y + 4)$ for $x = 7$ and $y = 2$

Solve each equation. (Lessons 1-8 and 1-9)

49. $b + 53 = 95$ 50. $a - 100 = 340$ 51. $n - 24 = 188$ 52. $w + 20 = 95$

California Standards

AF1.1 Write and solve one-step linear equations in one variable.

Who uses this? Divers can use equations that contain division to determine water pressure at a certain depth.

Japanese pearl divers go as deep as 165 feet underwater. At this depth, the pressure is much greater than at the water's surface. Water pressure can be described using equations containing division.

Multiplying by a number is the inverse of dividing by that number. When an equation contains division, use multiplication to "undo" the division.

EXAMPLE 1 Solving Equations by Multiplying

Solve each equation. Check your answers.

A $\dfrac{y}{5} = 4$

$\dfrac{y}{5} = 4$ *y is divided by 5.*

$5 \cdot \dfrac{y}{5} = 5 \cdot 4$ *Multiply both sides by 5 to undo the division.*

$y = 20$

Check

$\dfrac{y}{5} = 4$

$\dfrac{20}{5} \overset{?}{=} 4$ *Substitute 20 for y in the equation.*

$4 \overset{?}{=} 4$ ✔   *20 is the solution.*

B $12 = \dfrac{z}{4}$

$12 = \dfrac{z}{4}$ *z is divided by 4.*

$4 \cdot 12 = 4 \cdot \dfrac{z}{4}$ *Multiply both sides by 4 to undo the division.*

$48 = z$

Check

$12 = \dfrac{z}{4}$

$12 \overset{?}{=} \dfrac{48}{4}$ *Substitute 48 for z in the equation.*

$12 \overset{?}{=} 12$ ✔   *48 is the solution.*

EXAMPLE 2

Science Application

Pressure is the amount of force exerted on an area. Pressure can be measured in pounds per square inch, or psi.

The pressure at the surface of the water is half the pressure at 30 ft underwater.

$$\text{pressure at surface} = \frac{\text{pressure at 30 ft underwater}}{2}$$

The pressure at the surface is 15 psi. What is the water pressure at 30 ft underwater?

Let p represent the pressure at 30 ft underwater.

$$15 = \frac{p}{2}$$ *Substitute 15 for pressure at the surface. p is divided by 2.*

$$2 \cdot 15 = 2 \cdot \frac{p}{2}$$ *Multiply both sides by 2 to undo the division.*

$$30 = p$$

The water pressure at 30 ft underwater is 30 psi.

Think and Discuss

1. **Tell** whether the solution of $\frac{c}{10} = 70$ will be less than 70 or greater than 70. Explain.

2. **Describe** how you would check your answer to Example 2.

3. **Explain** why $13 \cdot \frac{x}{13} = x$.

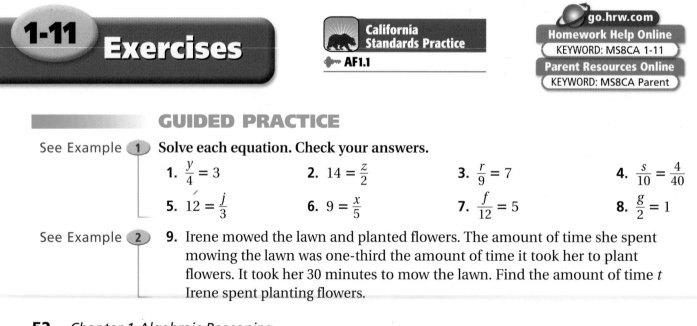

1-11 Exercises

California Standards Practice
AF1.1

go.hrw.com
Homework Help Online
KEYWORD: MS8CA 1-11
Parent Resources Online
KEYWORD: MS8CA Parent

GUIDED PRACTICE

See Example 1   Solve each equation. Check your answers.

1. $\frac{y}{4} = 3$

2. $14 = \frac{z}{2}$

3. $\frac{r}{9} = 7$

4. $\frac{s}{10} = \frac{4}{40}$

5. $12 = \frac{j}{3}$

6. $9 = \frac{x}{5}$

7. $\frac{f}{12} = 5$

8. $\frac{g}{2} = 1$

See Example 2   9. Irene mowed the lawn and planted flowers. The amount of time she spent mowing the lawn was one-third the amount of time it took her to plant flowers. It took her 30 minutes to mow the lawn. Find the amount of time t Irene spent planting flowers.

See Example **1** Solve each equation. Check your answers.

10. $\dfrac{d}{3} = 12$ **11.** $\dfrac{c}{2} = 13$ **12.** $7 = \dfrac{m}{7}$ **13.** $\dfrac{g}{7} = 14$

14. $6 = \dfrac{f}{4}$ **15.** $\dfrac{x}{12} = 12$ **16.** $\dfrac{j}{20} = 10$ **17.** $9 = \dfrac{r}{9}$

See Example **2** **18.** The area of Danielle's garden is one-twelfth the area of her entire yard. The area of the garden is 10 square feet. Find the area a of the yard.

PRACTICE AND PROBLEM SOLVING

Extra Practice
See page EP3.

Find the value of c in each equation.

19. $\dfrac{c}{12} = 8$ **20.** $4 = \dfrac{c}{9}$ **21.** $\dfrac{c}{15} = 11$ **22.** $c + 21 = 40$

23. $14 = \dfrac{c}{5}$ **24.** $\dfrac{c}{4} = 12$ **25.** $\dfrac{c}{4} = 15$ **26.** $5c = 120$

27. Multi-Step The Empire State Building is 381 m tall. At the Grand Canyon's widest point, 76 Empire State Buildings would fit end to end. Write and solve an equation to find the width of the Grand Canyon at this point.

28. Earth Science You can estimate the distance of a thunderstorm in kilometers by counting the number of seconds between the lightning flash and the thunder and then dividing this number by 3. If a storm is 5 km away, how many seconds will you count between the lightning flash and the thunder?

29. Reasoning Write a problem about money that can be solved with an equation that contains division.

30. Write About It Use a numerical example to explain how multiplication and division by the same number undo each other.

31. Challenge A number halved and then halved again is equal to 2. What was the original number?

SPIRAL STANDARDS REVIEW

AF1.1

32. Multiple Choice Carl has n action figures in his collection. He wants to place them in 6 bins with 12 figures in each bin. Solve the equation $\dfrac{n}{6} = 12$ to determine the number of action figures Carl has.

Ⓐ $n = 2$ Ⓑ $n = 6$ Ⓒ $n = 18$ Ⓓ $n = 72$

33. Multiple Choice Which equation does NOT have $k = 28$ as a solution?

Ⓐ $\dfrac{k}{14} = 2$ Ⓑ $\dfrac{k}{7} = 4$ Ⓒ $\dfrac{k}{28} = 1$ Ⓓ $\dfrac{k}{6} = 12$

Solve each equation. (Lesson 1-9)

34. $t - 14 = 20$ **35.** $b - 7 = 6$ **36.** $y - 25 = 17$ **37.** $m - 6 = 68$

Solve each equation. (Lesson 1-10)

38. $4r = 52$ **39.** $8k = 128$ **40.** $81 = 9p$ **41.** $119 = 17q$

READY TO GO ON?

Quiz for Lessons 1-7 Through 1-11

✓ 1-7 Equations and Their Solutions

Determine whether the given value of the variable is a solution.

1. $c - 13 = 54$ for $c = 67$ **2.** $5r = 65$ for $r = 15$ **3.** $48 \div x = 6$ for $x = 8$

4. Brady buys 2 notebooks and should get $3 back in change. The cashier gives him 12 quarters. Determine if Brady was given the correct amount of change.

✓ 1-8 Solving Equations by Subtracting

Solve each equation. Check your answers.

5. $p + 51 = 76$ **6.** $107 = 19 + j$ **7.** $45 = s + 27$

8. A large section of the original Great Wall of China is now in ruins. As measured today, the length of the wall is about 6,350 kilometers. When the length of the section now in ruins is included, the length of the wall is about 6,850 kilometers. Write and solve an equation to find the approximate length of the section of the Great Wall that is now in ruins.

✓ 1-9 Solving Equations by Adding

Solve each equation. Check your answers.

9. $k - 5 = 17$ **10.** $150 = p - 30$ **11.** $n - 24 = 72$

12. A roller coaster in New Jersey is taller than a roller coaster in Ohio. The difference between their heights is 36 feet. The roller coaster in Ohio is 420 feet high. Write and solve an equation to find the height of the roller coaster in New Jersey.

✓ 1-10 Solving Equations by Dividing

Solve each equation. Check your answers.

13. $6f = 18$ **14.** $105 = 5d$ **15.** $11x = 99$

16. Taryn buys 8 identical glasses. Her total is $48 before tax. Write and solve an equation to find out how much Taryn pays per glass.

✓ 1-11 Solving Equations by Multiplying

Solve each equation. Check your answers.

17. $10 = \frac{j}{9}$ **18.** $5 = \frac{t}{6}$ **19.** $\frac{r}{15} = 3$

20. Paula is baking peach pies for a bake sale. Each pie requires 2 pounds of peaches. She bakes 6 pies. Write and solve an equation to find how many pounds of peaches Paula had to buy.

Have a Heart Chuck's family decides to begin a fitness program. Their doctor encourages each family member to determine his or her maximum heart rate and then exercise at a lower rate.

1. The table shows the recommended maximum heart rate for people of various ages. Describe the pattern in the table. Then find the maximum heart rate for Chuck's father, who is 45 years old.

2. There is another way to find a person's maximum heart rate. The sum of the maximum heart rate, h, and the person's age, a, should be 220. Write an equation that relates h and a.

3. Chuck's mother used the equation from problem 2 to determine that her maximum heart rate is 174 beats per minute. How old is Chuck's mother?

Maximum Heart Rate	
Age	Rate (beats per minute)
10	210
15	205
20	200
25	195
30	190
35	185

4. Chuck's mother counts the number of heartbeats in 10 seconds and multiplies by 6 to find her heart rate. Write and solve an equation to find the number of times her heart beats in 10 seconds when she is at her maximum heart rate.

5. The family doctor recommends warming up before exercise. The expression $110 - a \div 2$ gives a warm-up heart rate based on a person's age, a. Find the warm-up heart rate for Chuck's mother.

Game Time

Jumping Beans

You will need a grid that is 4 squares by 6 squares. Each square must be large enough to contain a bean. Mark off a 3-square by 3-square section of the grid. Place nine beans in the nine spaces, as shown below.

You must move all nine beans to the nine marked-off squares in the fewest number of moves.

Follow the rules below to move the beans.

1 You may move one space to any empty square in any direction.

2 You may jump over another bean in any direction to an empty square.

3 You may jump over one bean at a time as many times as you like.

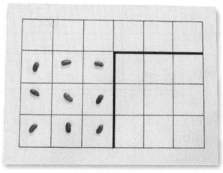 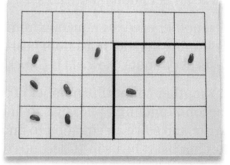

Moving all the beans in ten moves is not too difficult, but can you do it in nine moves?

Trading Spaces

The purpose of the game is to replace the red counters with the yellow counters, and the yellow counters with the red counters, in the fewest moves possible. The counters must be moved one at a time in an L-shape. No two counters may occupy the same square.

A complete copy of the rules and a game board are available online.

go.hrw.com
Game Time Extra
KEYWORD: MS8CA Games

Materials
- file folder
- 3 small pockets
- card stock
- scissors
- glue stick
- markers

It's in the Bag!

PROJECT **Tri-Sided Equations**

Use a colorful file folder to prepare a three-sided review of algebra!

Directions

❶ Close the file folder. Fold one side down to the folded edge. Turn the folder over and fold the other side down to the folded edge. **Figure A**

❷ Open the folder. It will be divided into four sections. On the top section, cut off $\frac{1}{4}$ inch from each edge. On the bottom section, make a 1 inch diagonal slit in the top left corner and in the top right corner. **Figure B**

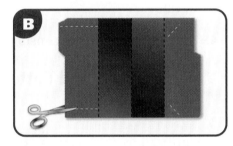

❸ Fold the folder so that the corners of the smaller top section fit into the slits. This will create your three-sided holder for notes. **Figure C**

❹ Write the definition of an equation on one side of your note holder. Write the order of operations on another side. Write examples of expressions on the third side.

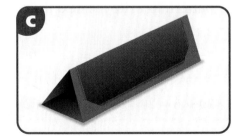

Taking Note of the Math

Glue a small pocket made from construction paper or card stock onto each side of your note holder. On rectangular slips of card stock, write problems that demonstrate your knowledge of equations, order of operations, and expressions. Store the note cards in the appropriate pockets.

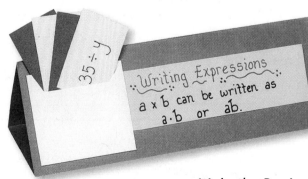

Study Guide: Review

Vocabulary

algebraic
expression 24

Associative Property 20

base 10

Commutative
Property 20

constant 24

Distributive Property 21

equation 34

evaluate 24

exponent 10

Identity Property 20

inverse operations 40

numerical
expression 14

order of operations 14

power 10

solution 34

variable 24

Complete the sentences below with vocabulary words from the list above.

1. The __?__ tells how many times to use the __?__ as a factor.

2. A(n) __?__ is a mathematical phrase made up of numbers and operations.

3. A(n) __?__ is a mathematical statement that two expressions are equal in value.

4. A(n) __?__ consists of constants, variables, and operations.

1-1 Numbers and Patterns (pp. 6–9)

 Preparation for AF2.0

EXAMPLE

- Identify a possible pattern. Use your pattern to write the next three numbers.

  2, 8, 14, 20, . . .

  $2 + 6 = 8$ $8 + 6 = 14$ $14 + 6 = 20$

  A possible pattern is to add 6 each time.

  $20 + 6 = 26$ $26 + 6 = 32$ $32 + 6 = 38$

EXERCISES

Identify a possible pattern. Use your pattern to write the next three numbers.

5. 6, 10, 14, 18, . . .   **6.** 15, 35, 55, 75, . . .

7. 7, 14, 21, 28, . . .   **8.** 8, 40, 200, 1,000, . . .

9. 41, 37, 33, 29, . . .   **10.** 68, 61, 54, 47, . . .

1-2 Exponents (pp. 10–13)

 Preparation for AF1.3 and AF1.4

EXAMPLE

- Find the value of 4^3.

  $4^3 = 4 \cdot 4 \cdot 4 = 64$

EXERCISES

Find each value.

11. 9^2 **12.** 10^1 **13.** 2^7

14. 1^7 **15.** 11^2 **16.** 3^3

1-3 Order of Operations (pp. 14–17)

AF1.3, AF1.4

EXAMPLE

■ Simplify $(18 + 6) \cdot 5$.

$(18 + 6) \cdot 5 = 24 \cdot 5 = 120$

EXERCISES

Simplify each expression.

17. $2 + (9 - 6) \div 3$ **18.** $12 \cdot 3^2 - 5$

19. $11 + 2 \cdot 5 - (9 + 7)$ **20.** $75 \div 5^2 + 8^2$

1-4 Properties of Numbers (pp. 20–23)

AF1.3

EXAMPLE

■ Tell which property is represented.

$(10 \cdot 13) \cdot 28 = 10 \cdot (13 \cdot 28)$
Associative Property

EXERCISES

Tell which property is represented.

21. $42 + 17 = 17 + 42$

22. $6 \cdot (x - 5) = 6 \cdot x - 6 \cdot 5$

1-5 Evaluating Algebraic Expressions (pp. 24–27)

AF1.2, AF1.3

EXAMPLE

■ Evaluate $5a - 6b + 7$ for $a = 4$ and $b = 3$.

$5a - 6b + 7$
$5(4) - 6(3) + 7$
$20 - 18 + 7$
9

EXERCISES

Evaluate each expression for the given values of the variables.

23. $4x - 5$ for $x = 6$

24. $8y^3 + 3y$ for $y = 4$

25. $\frac{n}{5} + 6m - 3$ for $n = 5$ and $m = 2$

1-6 Writing Algebraic Expressions (pp. 28–31)

AF1.2

EXAMPLE

■ Write as an algebraic expression.

5 times the sum of a number and 6
$5(n + 6)$

EXERCISES

Write as an algebraic expression.

26. 4 divided by the sum of a number and 12

27. 2 times the difference of t and 11

1-7 Equations and Their Solutions (pp. 34–37)

Preparation for AF1.1

EXAMPLE

■ Determine whether the given value of the variable is a solution.

$f + 14 = 50$ for $f = 34$
$34 + 14 \overset{?}{=} 50$ *Substitute 34 for f.*
$48 \neq 50$ *Add.*
34 is not a solution.

EXERCISES

Determine whether the given value of each variable is a solution.

28. $28 + n = 39$ for $n = 11$

29. $12t = 74$ for $t = 6$

30. $y - 53 = 27$ for $y = 80$

1-8 Solving Equations by Subtracting (pp. 40–43)

■ AF1.1

EXAMPLE

■ Solve the equation $x + 18 = 31$.

$$
\begin{aligned}
x + 18 &= 31 \\
-18 \quad & \quad -18 \\
x \quad\quad &= 13
\end{aligned}
$$

18 is added to x.
Subtract 18 from both sides to undo the addition.

EXERCISES

Solve each equation.

31. $4 + x = 10$ **32.** $n + 10 = 24$

33. $c + 71 = 100$ **34.** $y + 16 = 22$

35. $44 = p + 17$ **36.** $94 + w = 103$

37. $23 + b = 34$ **38.** $56 = n + 12$

39. $39 = 23 + p$ **40.** $d + 28 = 85$

1-9 Solving Equations by Adding (pp. 44–46)

■ AF1.1

EXAMPLE

■ Solve the equation $c - 7 = 16$.

$$
\begin{aligned}
c - 7 &= 16 \\
+7 \quad & \quad +7 \\
c \quad &= 23
\end{aligned}
$$

7 is subtracted from c.
Add 7 to each side to undo the subtraction.

EXERCISES

Solve each equation.

41. $28 = k - 17$ **42.** $d - 8 = 1$

43. $p - 55 = 8$ **44.** $n - 31 = 36$

45. $3 = r - 11$ **46.** $97 = w - 47$

47. $12 = h - 48$ **48.** $9 = p - 158$

1-10 Solving Equations by Dividing (pp. 47–50)

■ AF1.1

EXAMPLE

■ Solve the equation $6x = 36$.

$$
\begin{aligned}
6x &= 36 \\
\frac{6x}{6} &= \frac{36}{6} \\
x &= 6
\end{aligned}
$$

x is multiplied by 6.

Divide both sides by 6 to undo the multiplication.

EXERCISES

Solve each equation.

49. $5v = 40$ **50.** $27 = 3y$

51. $12c = 84$ **52.** $18n = 36$

53. $72 = 9s$ **54.** $11t = 110$

55. $7a = 56$ **56.** $8y = 64$

1-11 Solving Equations by Multiplying (pp. 51–53)

■ AF1.1

EXAMPLE

■ Solve the equation $\frac{k}{4} = 8$.

$$
\begin{aligned}
\frac{k}{4} &= 8 \\
4 \cdot \frac{k}{4} &= 4 \cdot 8 \\
k &= 32
\end{aligned}
$$

k is divided by 4.

Multiply both sides by 4 to undo the division.

EXERCISES

Solve each equation.

57. $\frac{r}{7} = 6$ **58.** $\frac{t}{5} = 3$

59. $6 = \frac{y}{3}$ **60.** $12 = \frac{n}{6}$

61. $\frac{z}{13} = 4$ **62.** $20 = \frac{b}{5}$

63. $\frac{n}{11} = 7$ **64.** $10 = \frac{p}{9}$

CHAPTER TEST

Identify a possible pattern. Use your pattern to write the next three numbers.

1. 24, 32, 40, 48, . . .   **2.** 6, 18, 54, 162, . . .   **3.** 64, 58, 52, 46, . . .   **4.** 13, 30, 47, 64, . . .

Find each value.

5. 6^2 **6.** 7^5 **7.** 8^6 **8.** 3^5

Simplify each expression.

9. $18 \cdot 3 \div 3^3$ **10.** $36 + 16 - 50$ **11.** $149 - (2^8 - 200)$ **12.** $(4 \div 2) \cdot 9 + 11$

Simplify each expression. Justify each step.

13. $91 + 63 + 9$ **14.** $38 + (12 + 157)$ **15.** $200 \cdot 14 \cdot 5$

Evaluate each expression for the given values of the variables.

16. $4a + 6b + 7$ for $a = 2$ and $b = 3$ **17.** $7y^2 + 7y$ for $y = 3$

18. $4m + n(26 - p)$ for $m = 10$, $n = 6$, and $p = 4$

Write each phrase as an algebraic expression.

19. a number increased by 12   **20.** the quotient of a number and 7

21. 5 less than the product of 7 and s **22.** the difference between 3 times x and 4

23. There are more reptile species than amphibian species. There are 3,100 living species of amphibians. Write an expression to show how many more reptile species there are than amphibian species.

Solve each equation.

24. $x + 9 = 19$ **25.** $21 = y - 20$ **26.** $m - 54 = 72$ **27.** $136 = y + 114$

28. $16 = \dfrac{y}{3}$ **29.** $102 = 17y$ **30.** $\dfrac{r}{7} = 1,400$ **31.** $6x = 42$

32. An Olympic skater bought a pair of skate blades and a pair of skate boots for a total of $1,016. The blades cost $442. Write and solve an equation to find the cost of the boots.

33. The male Siberian tiger at a zoo is heavier than the male Bengal tiger. The difference in their weights is 140 pounds. The Bengal tiger weighs 480 pounds. Write and solve an equation to find the weight of the Siberian tiger.

34. A caterer charged $15 per person for a banquet. The total charge was $1,530. Write and solve an equation to find the number of people who attended.

35. A scientist is studying corn plants. She divides the plants into 6 equal groups, with 28 plants in each group. Write and solve an equation to find the total number of plants.

Multiple Choice: Eliminate Answer Choices

With some multiple-choice test items, you can use mental math or number sense to quickly eliminate some of the answer choices before you begin solving the problem.

EXAMPLE 1

Which is the solution to the equation $x + 7 = 15$?

x = ❤❤❤ ❤❤❤❤
❤❤ = ❤❤❤❤
❤❤ ❤❤❤❤

  Ⓐ $x = 22$ Ⓑ $x = 15$ Ⓒ $x = 8$ Ⓓ $x = 7$

READ the question. Then try to **eliminate** some of the answer choices.

Use number sense:

Since $x + 7 = 15$, 15 must be greater than x, or x must be less than 15. Since 22 and 15 are not less than 15, you can eliminate answer choices A and B.

The correct answer choice is C.

EXAMPLE 2

What is the value of the expression $18x + 6$ for $x = 5$?

  Ⓐ 90   Ⓑ 96   Ⓒ 191   Ⓓ 198

LOOK at the choices. Then try to **eliminate** some of the answer choices.

Use mental math:

Estimate the value of the expression. Round 18 to 20 to make the multiplication easier.

    $20x + 6$
    $20(5) + 6$ *Substitute 5 for x.*
      106 *Multiply. Then add.*

Because you rounded up, the value of the expression should be less than 106. You can eliminate choices C and D because they are too large.

The correct answer choice is B.

Before you work a test question, use mental math to help you decide if there are answer choices that you can eliminate right away.

Read each test item and answer the questions that follow.

Item A
During the August back-to-school sale, 2 pairs of shoes cost $34, a shirt costs $15, and a pair of pants costs $27. Janet bought 2 pairs of shoes, 4 shirts, and 4 pairs of pants and then paid an additional $7 for tax. Which expression shows the total that Janet spent?

Ⓐ $34 + 4(15 + 27)$

Ⓑ $34 + 4(15 + 27) + 7$

Ⓒ $4(34 + 15 + 27) + 7$

Ⓓ $34 + 15 + 4 \cdot 27$

1. Can any of the answer choices be eliminated immediately? If so, which choices and why?

2. Describe how you can determine the correct answer from the remaining choices.

Item B
Anthony saved $1 from his first paycheck, $2 from his second paycheck, then $4, $8, and so on. How much money did Anthony save from his tenth paycheck?

Ⓐ $10 Ⓒ $512

Ⓑ $16 Ⓓ $1,023

3. Are there any answer choices you can eliminate immediately? If so, which choices and why?

4. What common error was made in finding answer choice A?

Item C
Craig has three weeks to read an 850-page book. Which equation can be used to find the number of pages Craig has to read each day?

Ⓐ $\frac{x}{3} = 850$ Ⓒ $3x = 850$

Ⓑ $21x = 850$ Ⓓ $\frac{x}{21} = 850$

5. Describe how to use number sense to eliminate at least one answer choice.

6. What common error was made in finding answer choice D?

Item D
What value of t makes the following equation true?

$$22t = 132$$

Ⓐ 6 Ⓒ 154

Ⓑ 110 Ⓓ 2,904

7. Which choices can be eliminated by using number sense? Explain.

8. What common error was made in finding answer choice D?

9. Describe how you could check your answer to this problem.

Item E
What is the value of the expression $(1 + 2)^2 + 14 \div 2 + 5$?

Ⓐ 0 Ⓒ 17

Ⓑ 11 Ⓓ 21

10. Use mental math to quickly eliminate one answer choice. Explain your choice.

11. What common error was made in finding answer choice B?

12. What common error was made in finding answer choice C?

MASTERING THE STANDARDS

Cumulative Assessment, Chapter 1

Multiple Choice

1. Which expression has a value of 74 when $x = 10$, $y = 8$, and $z = 12$?

Ⓐ $4xyz$
Ⓒ $2xz - 3y$
Ⓑ $x + 5y + 2z$
Ⓓ $6xyz + 8$

2. What is the value of the expression $16 - 2^3$?

Ⓐ 8
Ⓒ 14
Ⓑ 10
Ⓓ 42

3. A contractor charges $22 to install one miniblind. How much does the contractor charge to install m miniblinds?

Ⓐ $22m$
Ⓒ $22 + m$
Ⓑ $\frac{m}{22}$
Ⓓ $\frac{22}{m}$

4. Which of the following is an example of the Commutative Property?

Ⓐ $20 + 10 = 2(10 + 5)$
Ⓑ $20 + 10 = 10 + 20$
Ⓒ $5 + (20 + 10) = (5 + 20) + 10$
Ⓓ $20 + 0 = 20$

5. Which expression is equivalent to $16(200 + 18)$?

Ⓐ $16 + (200 \cdot 18)$
Ⓑ $16(200) + 16(18)$
Ⓒ $200(16 + 18)$
Ⓓ $16(200) + 18(200)$

6. What is the solution to the equation $810 = x - 625$?

Ⓐ $x = 185$
Ⓒ $x = 845$
Ⓑ $x = 215$
Ⓓ $x = 1{,}435$

7. Damaris buys 4 tubes of watercolor paint and 2 large tubes of oil paint. Which expression can be used to determine the total cost of Damaris's paint?

Paint Sale Prices	
Item	**Price per Tube**
Watercolor	$7.00
Acrylic	$3.00
Oil (small)	$9.00
Oil (large)	$13.00

Ⓐ $(4 + 2) \cdot (7 + 13)$
Ⓒ $4 + 7 \cdot 2 + 13$
Ⓑ $(4 \cdot 2) + (7 \cdot 13)$
Ⓓ $4 \cdot 7 + 2 \cdot 13$

8. To make a beaded necklace, Kris needs 88 beads. If Kris has 1,056 beads, how many necklaces can she make?

Ⓐ 968
Ⓒ 264
Ⓑ 12
Ⓓ 8

9. What rule best describes the pattern?

$$3, 12, 21, 30, 39, \ldots$$

Ⓐ Add 4.
Ⓑ Add 9.
Ⓒ Multiply by 4.
Ⓓ Multiply by 9.

10. Marc spends $78 for n shirts. Which expression can be used to represent the cost of one shirt?

Ⓐ $\frac{n}{78}$
Ⓒ $\frac{78}{n}$
Ⓑ $78n$
Ⓓ $78 + n$

11. Which situation best matches the expression $0.29x + 2$?

　Ⓐ A taxi company charges a $2.00 flat fee plus $0.29 for every mile.

　Ⓑ Jimmy ran 0.29 miles, stopped to rest, and then ran 2 more miles.

　Ⓒ There are 0.29 grams of calcium in 2 servings of Hearty Health Cereal.

　Ⓓ Amy bought 2 pieces of gum for $0.29 each.

12. Which of the following should be performed first to simplify this expression?

$$16 \cdot 2 + (20 \div 5) - 3^2 \div 3 + 1$$

　Ⓐ $3^2 \div 3$

　Ⓑ $20 \div 5$

　Ⓒ $16 \cdot 2$

　Ⓓ $3 + 1$

 When you read a word problem, cross out any information that is not needed to solve the problem.

Gridded Response

13. If $x = 15$ and $y = 5$, what is the value of $\frac{2x}{y} + 3y$?

14. What value of r makes the following equation true?
$$15r = 180$$

15. An airplane has seats for 198 passengers. If each row seats 6 people, how many rows are on the plane?

16. What is the value of the expression $3^2 \times (2 + 3 \times 4) - 5$?

17. What is the solution to the equation $10 + s = 42$?

18. What is the sum of 4 and the product of 9 and 5?

Short Response

19. Luke can swim 25 laps in one hour. Write an algebraic expression to show how many laps Luke can swim in h hours. How many hours will it take Luke to swim 100 laps?

20. An aerobics instructor teaches a 45-minute class at 9:30 A.M., three times a week. She dedicates 12 minutes during each class to stretching. The rest of the class consists of aerobic dance. How many minutes of each class does the instructor spend teaching aerobic dance? Write and solve an equation to explain how you found your answer.

21. Ike and Joe ran the same distance but took different routes. Ike ran 3 blocks east and 7 blocks south. Joe ran 4 blocks west and then turned north. How far north did Joe run? Show your work.

Extended Response

22. The Raiders and the Hornets are buying new uniforms for their baseball teams. Each team member will receive a new cap, a jersey, and a pair of pants.

Uniform Costs		
	Raiders	Hornets
Cap	$15	$15
Jersey	$75	$70
Pants	$60	$70

　a. Let r represent the number of Raiders team members, and let h represent the number of Hornets team members. For each team, write an expression that gives the total cost of the team's uniforms.

　b. If the Raiders and the Hornets both have 12 team members, how much will each team spend on uniforms? Which team will spend the most, and by how much? Show your work.

CHAPTER 2

Integers

CONCEPT CONNECTION

go.hrw.com
Chapter Project Online
KEYWORD: MS8CA Ch2

Negative integers can describe elevations below sea level. The lowest elevation of Badwater basin in California is −282 feet.

Badwater salt pan
Death Valley, California

ARE YOU READY?

✓ Vocabulary

Choose the best term from the list to complete each sentence.

1. To __?__ a number on a number line, mark and label the point that corresponds to that number.

2. The expression $1 < 3 < 5$ tells the __?__ of these three numbers on a number line.

3. A(n) __?__ is a mathematical statement showing two things are equal.

4. Each number in the set 0, 1, 2, 3, 4, 5, 6, 7, . . . is a(n) __?__.

5. To __?__ an equation, find a value that makes it true.

whole number

expression

graph

solve

equation

order

Complete these exercises to review skills you will need for this chapter.

✓ Order of Operations

Simplify.

6. $7 + 9 - 5 \cdot 2$

7. $12 \cdot 3 - 4 \cdot 5$

8. $115 - 15 \cdot 3 + 9(8 - 2)$

9. $20 \cdot 5 \cdot 2(7 + 1) \div 4$

10. $300 + 6(5 - 3) - 11$

11. $14 - 13 + 9 \cdot 2$

✓ Compare Whole Numbers

Write $<$, $>$, or $=$ to compare the numbers.

12. 9 ▓ 2

13. 4 ▓ 5

14. 8 ▓ 1

15. 3 ▓ 3

16. 412 ▓ 214

17. 1,076 ▓ 1,074

18. 502 ▓ 520

19. 9,123 ▓ 9,001

✓ Evaluate Expressions

Evaluate each expression.

20. $x + 5$ for $x = 18$

21. $9y$ for $y = 13$

22. $\frac{z}{6}$ for $z = 96$

23. $w - 9$ for $w = 13$

✓ Use Inverse Operations to Solve Equations

Solve.

24. $n + 3 = 10$

25. $x - 4 = 16$

26. $9p = 63$

27. $\frac{t}{5} = 80$

28. $x - 3 = 14$

29. $\frac{q}{3} = 21$

30. $9 + r = 91$

31. $15p = 45$

Unpacking the Standards

The information below "unpacks" the standards. The Academic Vocabulary is highlighted and defined to help you understand the language of the standards. Refer to the lessons listed after each standard for help with the math terms and phrases. The Chapter Concept shows how the standard is applied in this chapter.

California Standard	Academic Vocabulary	Chapter Concept
NS2.3 Solve addition, subtraction, multiplication, and division problems, including those arising in concrete situations, that use positive and negative integers and combinations of these operations. (Lessons 2-2, 2-3, 2-4, 2-5, 2-8) (Labs 2-2, 2-3, 2-4, 2-5)	**arising** happening **concrete situations** situations from everyday life *Example:* The temperature rises from $-12°F$ to $15°F$, and you want to know how many degrees the temperature rose. This is a problem involving a concrete situation. **combination** in this case, a group of two or more *Example:* The expression $2 + 8 \div 2$ includes a combination of the operations addition and division.	You add, subtract, multiply, and divide integers to solve problems. *Example:* $-5 + (-4)$ The sum of -5 and -4 is negative because both -5 and -4 are negative. $-5 + (-4) = -9$ *Example:* $-9 \cdot 4$ The product of -9 and 4 is negative because the signs of the factors are different. $-9 \cdot 4 = -36$
AF1.0 Students write verbal expressions and sentences as algebraic expressions and equations; they evaluate algebraic expressions, solve simple linear equations, and **graph and interpret their results.** (Lesson 2-8)	**interpret** explain the meaning or importance of **results** in this case, the answer to a problem	You determine solutions to linear equations and then graph the solutions on the coordinate plane. *Example:* The table shows some of the solutions of the linear equation $y = x + 1$. | x	-4	-2	0	2	4
---	---	---	---	---	---
y	-3	-1	1	3	5	 The graph of the linear equation $y = x + 1$ is shown below.

Standards AF1.1, AF1.2, and AF1.3 are also covered in this chapter. To see these standards unpacked, go to Chapter 1, p. 4.

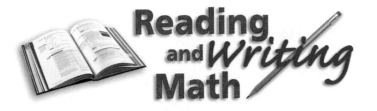

Reading and Writing Math

Writing Strategy: Translate Between Words and Math

To translate words into algebraic expressions, read the problem to determine what actions are taking place.

Example

At FunZone the cost to play laser tag is $8 per game. The cost to play miniature golf is $5 per game. The one-time admission fee to the park is $3. Jonna wants to play both laser tag and miniature golf. Write an algebraic expression to find the total amount Jonna would pay to play ℓ laser tag games and m golf games at FunZone.

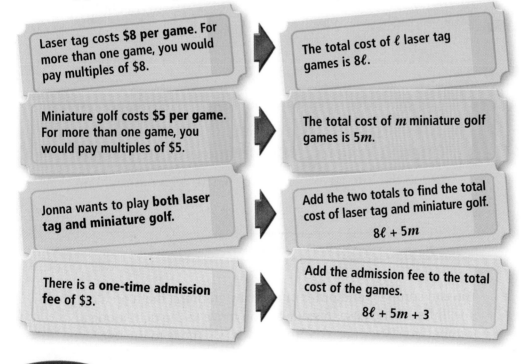

Laser tag costs **$8 per game.** For more than one game, you would pay multiples of $8.

→ The total cost of ℓ laser tag games is 8ℓ.

Miniature golf costs **$5 per game.** For more than one game, you would pay multiples of $5.

→ The total cost of m miniature golf games is $5m$.

Jonna wants to play **both laser tag and miniature golf.**

→ Add the two totals to find the total cost of laser tag and miniature golf.
$8\ell + 5m$

There is a **one-time admission fee of $3.**

→ Add the admission fee to the total cost of the games.
$8\ell + 5m + 3$

Try This

Write an algebraic expression that describes the situation. Explain why you chose each operation in the expression.

1. Fred has f crackers, and Gary has g crackers. Fred and Gary each eat 3 crackers. How many total crackers are left?

2. School supplies are half-price at Bargain Mart this week. The original prices were $2 per package of pens and $4 per notebook. Cally buys 1 package of pens and n notebooks. How much does Cally spend?

2-1 Introduction to Integers

California Standards

Preparation for ☞ **NS1.1** Compare and order positive and negative fractions, decimals, and mixed numbers and place them on a number line.

Vocabulary
opposite
integer
absolute value

Remember!

The whole numbers are the counting numbers and zero: 0, 1, 2, 3, ...

Why learn this? You can use negative integers to describe elevations below sea level.

The **opposite** of a number is the same distance from 0 on a number line as the original number, but on the other side of 0. Zero is its own opposite.

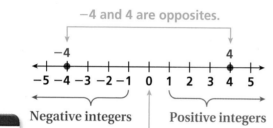

−4 and 4 are opposites.

Negative integers   Positive integers

0 is neither positive nor negative.

Dr. Sylvia Earle holds the world record for the deepest solo dive to an elevation of −1,250 feet.

The **integers** are the set of whole numbers and their opposites.

EXAMPLE 1 Graphing Integers and Their Opposites on a Number Line

Graph the integer −3 and its opposite on a number line.

3 units   3 units

−5 −4 −3 −2 −1 0 1 2 3 4 5   *The opposite of −3 is 3.*

You can compare and order integers by graphing them on a number line. Integers increase in value as you move to the right along a number line. They decrease in value as you move to the left.

EXAMPLE 2 Comparing Integers Using a Number Line

Remember!

The symbol < means "is less than," and the symbol > means "is greater than."

Compare the integers. Use < or >.

A 2 ▨ −2

−4 −3 −2 −1 0 1 2 3 4

2 is farther to the right than −2, so 2 > −2.

Compare the integers. Use < or >.

B $-10 \quad \blacksquare \quad -7$

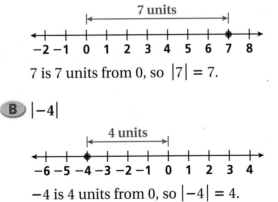

−10 is farther to the left than −7, so $-10 < -7$.

EXAMPLE 3 **Ordering Integers Using a Number Line**

Use a number line to order the integers −2, 5, −4, 1, −1, and 0 from least to greatest.

Graph the integers on a number line. Then read them from left to right.

The numbers in order from least to greatest are −4, −2, −1, 0, 1, and 5.

A number's **absolute value** is its distance from 0 on a number line. Since distance can never be negative, absolute values are never negative. They are always positive or zero.

EXAMPLE 4 **Finding Absolute Value**

Use a number line to find each absolute value.

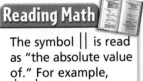

Reading Math

The symbol $|\ |$ is read as "the absolute value of." For example, $|-3|$ means "the absolute value of −3."

A $|7|$

7 is 7 units from 0, so $|7| = 7$.

B $|-4|$

−4 is 4 units from 0, so $|-4| = 4$.

Think and Discuss

1. Tell which number is greater: −4,500 or −10,000.

2. Name the greatest negative integer and the least nonnegative integer. Then compare the absolute values of these integers.

California
Standards Practice
Preparation for ⊶ NS1.1

go.hrw.com
Homework Help Online
KEYWORD: MS8CA 2-1
Parent Resources Online
KEYWORD: MS8CA Parent

GUIDED PRACTICE

See Example ① Graph each integer and its opposite on a number line.

1. 2 **2.** -9 **3.** -1 **4.** 6

See Example ② Compare the integers. Use $<$ or $>$.

5. 5 ▓ -5 **6.** -9 ▓ -18 **7.** -21 ▓ -17 **8.** -12 ▓ 12

See Example ③ Use a number line to order the integers from least to greatest.

9. $6, -3, -1, -5, 4$ **10.** $8, -2, 7, 1, -8$ **11.** $-6, -4, 3, 0, 1$

See Example ④ Use a number line to find each absolute value.

12. $|-2|$ **13.** $|8|$ **14.** $|-7|$ **15.** $|-10|$

INDEPENDENT PRACTICE

See Example ① Graph each integer and its opposite on a number line.

16. -4 **17.** 10 **18.** -12 **19.** 7

See Example ② Compare the integers. Use $<$ or $>$.

20. -14 ▓ -7 **21.** 9 ▓ -9 **22.** -12 ▓ 12 **23.** -31 ▓ -27

See Example ③ Use a number line to order the integers from least to greatest.

24. $-3, 2, -5, -6, 5$ **25.** $-7, -9, -2, 0, -5$ **26.** $3, -6, 9, -1, -2$

See Example ④ Use a number line to find each absolute value.

27. $|-16|$ **28.** $|12|$ **29.** $|-20|$ **30.** $|15|$

PRACTICE AND PROBLEM SOLVING

Extra Practice
See page EP4.

Compare. Write $<$, $>$, or $=$.

31. -25 ▓ 25 **32.** 18 ▓ -55 **33.** $|-21|$ ▓ 21 **34.** -9 ▓ -27

35. 34 ▓ $|34|$ **36.** 64 ▓ $|-75|$ **37.** $|-3|$ ▓ $|3|$ **38.** -100 ▓ -82

39. Earth Science The table shows the average temperatures in Vostok, Antarctica from March to October. List the months in order from coldest to warmest.

Month	Mar	Apr	May	Jun	Jul	Aug	Sep	Oct
Temperature (°F)	-72	-84	-86	-85	-88	-90	-87	-71

40. What is the opposite of $|32|$? **41.** What is the opposite of $|-29|$?

42. Business A company reported a net loss of $2,000,000 during its first year. In its second year it reported a profit of $5,000,000. Write each amount as an integer.

43. Reasoning Give an example in which a negative number has a greater absolute value than a positive number.

44. Social Studies Lines of latitude are imaginary lines that circle the globe in an east-west direction. They measure distances north and south of the equator. The equator represents 0° latitude.

a. What latitude is opposite of 30° north latitude?

b. How do these latitudes' distances from the equator compare?

Sports The graph shows how participation in several sports changed between 1999 and 2000 in the United States.

45. By about what percent did participation in racquetball increase or decrease?

46. By about what percent did participation in wall climbing increase or decrease?

47. What's the Error? At 9 A.M. the outside temperature was −3°F. By noon, the temperature was −12°F. A newscaster said that it was getting warmer outside. Why is this incorrect?

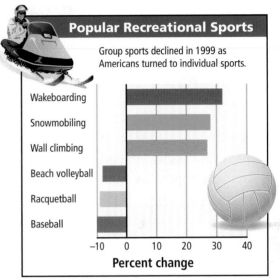

Popular Recreational Sports

Group sports declined in 1999 as Americans turned to individual sports.

Wakeboarding
Snowmobiling
Wall climbing
Beach volleyball
Racquetball
Baseball

−10 0 10 20 30 40

Percent change

Source: *USA Today,* July 6, 2001

48. Write About It Explain how to compare two integers.

49. Challenge What values can x have if $|x| = 11$?

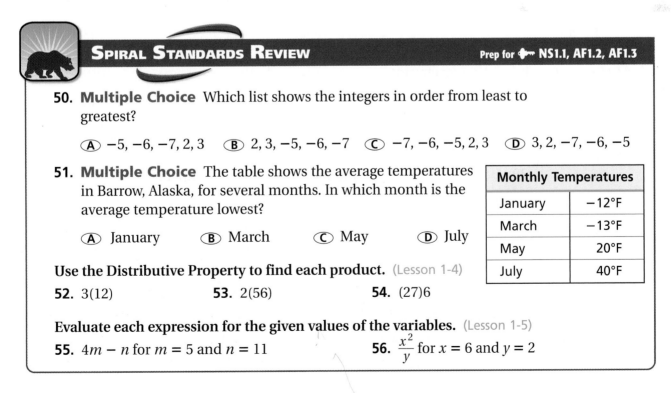

SPIRAL STANDARDS REVIEW
Prep for NS1.1, AF1.2, AF1.3

50. Multiple Choice Which list shows the integers in order from least to greatest?

Ⓐ −5, −6, −7, 2, 3　　Ⓑ 2, 3, −5, −6, −7　　Ⓒ −7, −6, −5, 2, 3　　Ⓓ 3, 2, −7, −6, −5

51. Multiple Choice The table shows the average temperatures in Barrow, Alaska, for several months. In which month is the average temperature lowest?

Ⓐ January　　Ⓑ March　　Ⓒ May　　Ⓓ July

Monthly Temperatures	
January	−12°F
March	−13°F
May	20°F
July	40°F

Use the Distributive Property to find each product. (Lesson 1-4)

52. 3(12)　　　　**53.** 2(56)　　　　**54.** (27)6

Evaluate each expression for the given values of the variables. (Lesson 1-5)

55. $4m - n$ for $m = 5$ and $n = 11$　　　　**56.** $\dfrac{x^2}{y}$ for $x = 6$ and $y = 2$

Model Integer Addition

go.hrw.com
Lab Resources Online
KEYWORD: MS8CA Lab2

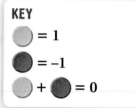

KEY
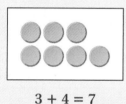
= 1
= –1
+ = 0

REMEMBER
• Adding or subtracting zero does not change the value of an expression.

California Standards

NS2.3 Solve addition, subtraction, multiplication, and division **problems,** including those arising in concrete situations, **that use positive and negative integers** and combinations of these operations.

You can model integer addition by using integer chips. Yellow chips represent positive numbers and red chips represent negative numbers.

Activity

When you model adding numbers with the same sign, you can count the total number of chips to find the sum.

The total number of positive chips is 7.

3 + 4 = 7

The total number of negative chips is 7.

−3 + (−4) = −7

1 Use integer chips to find each sum.

a. 2 + 4   **b.** −2 + (−4)   **c.** 6 + 3   **d.** −5 + (−4)

When you model adding numbers with different signs, you cannot count the chips to find their sum.

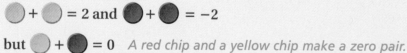
+ = 2 and + = −2

but + = 0   *A red chip and a yellow chip make a zero pair.*

When you model adding a positive and a negative number, you need to remove all of the zero pairs that you can find—that is, all pairs of 1 red chip and 1 yellow chip. These pairs have a value of zero, so they do not affect the sum.

$3 + (-4) = $ ▮

You cannot just count the colored chips to find their sum.

Before you count the chips, you need to remove all of the zero pairs.

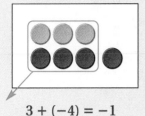

When you remove the zero pairs, there is one red chip left. So the sum of the chips is −1.

$3 + (-4) = -1$

2 Use integer chips to find each sum.

a. $4 + (-6)$ **b.** $-5 + 2$ **c.** $7 + (-3)$ **d.** $-6 + 3$

Think and Discuss

1. Will $8 + (-3)$ and $-3 + 8$ give the same answer? Why or why not?

2. If you have more red chips than yellow chips in a group, is the sum of the chips positive or negative?

3. If you have more yellow chips than red chips in a group, is the sum of the chips positive or negative?

4. Make a rule for the sign of the answer when negative and positive integers are added. Give examples.

Try This

Use integer chips to find each sum.

1. $4 + (-7)$ **2.** $-5 + (-4)$ **3.** $-5 + 1$ **4.** $6 + (-4)$

Write the addition problems modeled below.

5.

6.

7.

8.

2-2 Adding Integers

California Standards

← **NS2.3 Solve addition,** subtraction, multiplication, and division **problems, including those arising in concrete situations, that use positive and negative integers** and combinations of these operations. *Also covered:* **AF1.2**

Who uses this? Club leaders can add integers to determine whether the club has enough money for a trip.

Income items are positive, and expenses are negative. By adding all your income and expenses, you can find your total profit or loss.

One way to add integers is by using a number line.

Club Ledger
Estimated Income and Expenses

Description	Amount
Car wash supplies	–$25.00
Car wash earnings	$300.00
Bake sale supplies	–$50.00
Bake sale earnings	$250.00

EXAMPLE 1 **Modeling Integer Addition**

Reasoning

Use a number line to find each sum.

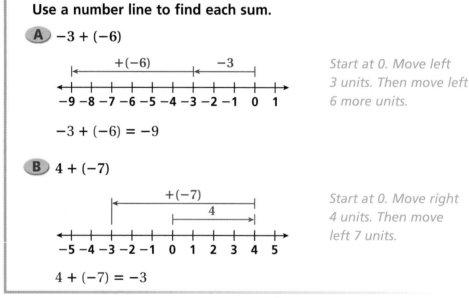

A $-3 + (-6)$

Start at 0. Move left 3 units. Then move left 6 more units.

$-3 + (-6) = -9$

B $4 + (-7)$

Start at 0. Move right 4 units. Then move left 7 units.

$4 + (-7) = -3$

You can also use absolute value to add integers.

Adding Integers

To add two integers with the same sign, find the sum of their absolute values. Use the sign of the two integers.

To add two integers with different signs, find the difference of their absolute values. Use the sign of the integer with the greater absolute value.

EXAMPLE 2 **Adding Integers Using Absolute Values**

Find each sum.

Reasoning

A $-7 + (-4)$

The signs are the **same**. Find the **sum** of the absolute values.

| $-7 + (-4)$ | *Think: 7 + 4 = 11.* |
| -11 | *Use the sign of the two integers.* |

Helpful Hint

When adding integers, think: If the signs are the *same*, find the *sum*. If the signs are *different,* find the *difference.*

B $-8 + 6$

The signs are **different**. Find the **difference** of the absolute values.

| $-8 + 6$ | *Think: 8 − 6 = 2.* |
| -2 | *Use the sign of the integer with the greater absolute value.* |

EXAMPLE 3 **Evaluating Expressions with Integers**

Evaluate $a + b$ for $a = 6$ and $b = -10$.

$a + b$	
$6 + (-10)$	*Substitute 6 for a and −10 for b.*
	*The signs are **different**. Think: 10 − 6 = 4.*
-4	*Use the sign of the integer with the greater absolute value (**negative**).*

EXAMPLE 4 *Banking Application*

The Debate Club's income from a car wash was $300, including tips. Supply expenses were $25. Use integer addition to find the club's total profit or loss.

$300 + (-25)$	*Use negative for the expenses.*
$300 - 25$	*Find the difference of the absolute values.*
275	*The answer is positive.*

The club earned $275.

Think and Discuss

1. **Explain** whether $-7 + 2$ is the same as $7 + (-2)$.

2. **Use** the Commutative Property to write an expression that is equivalent to $3 + (-5)$.

2-2 Exercises

California Standards Practice
NS2.3, AF1.2

go.hrw.com
Homework Help Online
KEYWORD: MS8CA 2-2
Parent Resources Online
KEYWORD: MS8CA Parent

GUIDED PRACTICE

See Example ① **Use a number line to find each sum.**

1. $9 + 3$ **2.** $-4 + (-2)$ **3.** $7 + (-9)$ **4.** $-3 + 6$

See Example ② **Find each sum.**

5. $7 + 8$ **6.** $-1 + (-12)$ **7.** $-25 + 10$ **8.** $31 + (-20)$

See Example ③ **Evaluate $a + b$ for the given values.**

9. $a = 5, b = -17$ **10.** $a = 8, b = -8$ **11.** $a = -4, b = -16$

See Example ④ **12. Sports** A football team gains 8 yards on one play and then loses 13 yards on the next. Use integer addition to find the team's total yardage.

INDEPENDENT PRACTICE

See Example ① **Use a number line to find each sum.**

13. $-16 + 7$ **14.** $-5 + (-1)$ **15.** $4 + 9$ **16.** $-7 + 8$

17. $10 + (-3)$ **18.** $-20 + 2$ **19.** $-12 + (-5)$ **20.** $-9 + 6$

See Example ② **Find each sum.**

21. $-13 + (-6)$ **22.** $14 + 25$ **23.** $-22 + 6$ **24.** $35 + (-50)$

25. $-81 + (-7)$ **26.** $28 + (-3)$ **27.** $-70 + 15$ **28.** $-18 + (-62)$

See Example ③ **Evaluate $c + d$ for the given values.**

29. $c = 6, d = -20$ **30.** $c = -8, d = -21$ **31.** $c = -45, d = 32$

See Example ④ **32.** The temperature dropped 17°F in 6 hours. The final temperature was −3°F. Use integer addition to find the starting temperature.

PRACTICE AND PROBLEM SOLVING

Extra Practice
See page EP4.

Find each sum.

33. $-8 + (-5)$ **34.** $14 + (-7)$ **35.** $-41 + 15$

36. $-22 + (-18) + 22$ **37.** $27 + (-29) + 16$ **38.** $-30 + 71 + (-70)$

Compare. Write <, >, or =.

39. $-23 + 18$ ▨ -41 **40.** $59 + (-59)$ ▨ 0 **41.** $31 + (-20)$ ▨ 9

42. $-24 + (-24)$ ▨ 48 **43.** $25 + (-70)$ ▨ -95 **44.** $16 + (-40)$ ▨ -24

45. Personal Finance Cody made deposits of $45, $18, and $27 into his checking account. He then wrote checks for $21 and $93. Write an expression to show the change in Cody's account. Then simplify the expression.

Recreation

The Appalachian Trail extends about 2,160 miles from Maine to Georgia. It takes about 5 to 7 months to hike the entire trail.

Evaluate each expression for $w = -12$, $x = 10$, and $y = -7$.

46. $7 + y$ **47.** $-4 + w$ **48.** $w + y$ **49.** $x + y$ **50.** $w + x$

51. Recreation Hikers along the Appalachian Trail camped overnight at Horns Pond, at an elevation of 3,100 ft. Then they hiked along the ridge of the Bigelow Mountains to West Peak, which is one of Maine's highest peaks. Use the diagram to determine the elevation of West Peak.

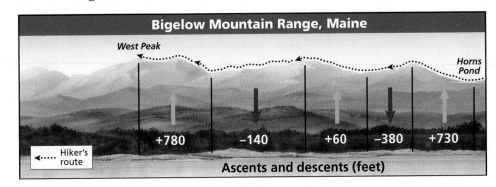

Bigelow Mountain Range, Maine

West Peak

Horns Pond

+780   −140   +60   −380   +730

Hiker's route

Ascents and descents (feet)

52. Reasoning Hector and Luis are playing a game. In the game, each player starts with 0 points, and the player with the most points at the end wins. Hector gains 5 points, loses 3, loses 2, and then gains 3. Luis loses 5 points, gains 1, gains 5, and then loses 3. Determine the final scores by modeling the problem on a number line. Then tell who wins the game and by how much.

53. What's the Question? The temperature was −8°F at 6 A.M. and rose 15°F by 9 A.M. The answer is 7°F. What is the question?

54. Write About It Compare the method used to add integers with the same sign and the method used to add integers with different signs.

55. Challenge A business had losses of $225 million, $75 million, and $375 million and profits of $15 million and $125 million. How much was its overall profit or loss?

SPIRAL STANDARDS REVIEW   NS2.3, AF1.1, AF1.4

56. Multiple Choice What is $25 + (-46)$?

Ⓐ −71   Ⓑ −21   Ⓒ 21   Ⓓ 71

57. Multiple Choice Which expression has the greatest value?

Ⓐ $-4 + 8$ Ⓑ $-2 + (-3)$ Ⓒ $1 + 2$ Ⓓ $4 + (-6)$

Simplify each expression. (Lesson 1-3)

58. $2 + 5 \cdot 2 - 3$ **59.** $3^3 - (6 \cdot 4) + 1$ **60.** $30 - 5 \cdot (3 + 2)$ **61.** $15 - 3 \cdot 2^2 + 1$

62. On Saturday, an art museum collected $20,412 in ticket sales. Tickets to the museum cost $6 each. Write and solve an equation to determine how many museum tickets were sold on Saturday. (Lesson 1-10)

Model Integer Subtraction

Use with Lesson 2-3

go.hrw.com
Lab Resources Online
KEYWORD: MS8CA Lab2

KEY	**REMEMBER**
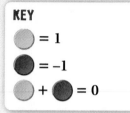 = 1 = −1 + = 0	• Adding or subtracting zero does not change the value of an expression.

California Standards

NS2.3 Solve addition, **subtraction**, multiplication, and division **problems,** including those arising in concrete situations, **that use positive and negative integers** and combinations of these operations.

You can model integer subtraction by using integer chips.

Activity

These groups of chips show three different ways of modeling 2.

1 Show two other ways of modeling 2.

These groups of chips show two different ways of modeling −2.

2 Show two other ways of modeling −2.

You can model subtraction problems involving two integers with the same sign by taking away chips.

$8 - 3 = 5$

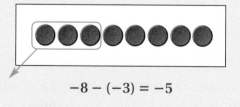

$-8 - (-3) = -5$

3 Use integer chips to find each difference.

a. $6 - 5$ **b.** $-6 - (-5)$ **c.** $10 - 7$ **d.** $-7 - (-4)$

80 Chapter 2 Integers

To model subtraction problems involving two integers with different signs, such as −6 − 3, you will need to add zero pairs before you can take chips away.

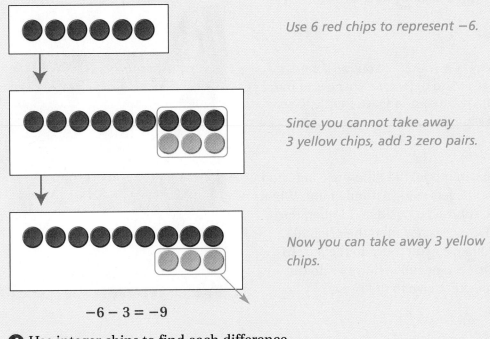

Use 6 red chips to represent −6.

Since you cannot take away 3 yellow chips, add 3 zero pairs.

Now you can take away 3 yellow chips.

−6 − 3 = −9

4 Use integer chips to find each difference.

a. −6 − 5   **b.** 5 − (−6)   **c.** 4 − 7   **d.** −2 − (−3)

Think and Discuss

1. How could you model the expression 0 − 5?

2. When you add zero pairs to model subtraction using chips, does it matter how many zero pairs you add?

3. Would 2 − 3 have the same answer as 3 − 2? Why or why not?

4. Make a rule for the sign of the answer when a positive integer is subtracted from a negative integer. Give examples.

Try This

Use integer chips to find each difference.

1. 4 − 2   **2.** −4 − (−2)   **3.** −2 − (−3)

4. 3 − 4   **5.** 2 − 3   **6.** 0 − 3

7. 5 − 3   **8.** −3 − (−5)   **9.** 6 − (−4)

2-3 Subtracting Integers

California Standards

NS2.3 Solve addition, **subtraction**, multiplication, and division **problems, including those arising in concrete situations, that use positive and negative integers** and combinations of these operations.
Also covered: **AF1.2**

Why learn this? You can subtract integers to determine changes in the temperature of a space shuttle. (See Example 4.)

You can model the difference between two integers using a number line. When you subtract a positive number, the difference is *less* than the original number, so you move to the *left*. To subtract a negative number do the opposite: move to the *right*.

EXAMPLE 1 · Modeling Integer Subtraction

Reasoning

Use a number line to find each difference.

A 3 − 8

$$3 - 8 = -5$$

Start at 0.
Move right 3 units.
To subtract 8,
move to the left 8 units.

Helpful Hint

If the number being subtracted is less than the number it is subtracted from, the answer will be positive. If the number being subtracted is greater, the answer will be negative.

B −4 − 2

$$-4 - 2 = -6$$

Start at 0.
Move left 4 units.
To subtract 2,
move to the left 2 units.

C 2 − (−3)

$$2 - (-3) = 5$$

Start at 0.
Move right 2 units.
To subtract −3,
move to the right 3 units.

You can also subtract an integer by adding its opposite. You can then use the rules for addition of integers.

82 Chapter 2 Integers

EXAMPLE **2** **Subtracting Integers by Adding the Opposite**

Find each difference.

A $5 - 9$

$5 - 9 = 5 + (-9)$ *Add the opposite of 9.*
$\quad\quad = -4$

B $-9 - (-2)$

$-9 - (-2) = -9 + 2$ *Add the opposite of −2.*
$\quad\quad\quad = -7$

C $-4 - 3$

$-4 - 3 = -4 + (-3)$ *Add the opposite of 3.*
$\quad\quad\quad = -7$

EXAMPLE **3** **Evaluating Expressions with Integers**

Evaluate $a - b$ for each set of values.

A $a = -6, b = 7$

$a - b$
$-6 - 7 = -6 + (-7)$ *Substitute for a and b. Add the opposite*
$\quad\quad\quad = -13$ *of 7.*

B $a = 14, b = -9$

$a - b$
$14 - (-9) = 14 + 9$ *Substitute for a and b. Add the opposite*
$\quad\quad\quad = 23$ *of −9.*

EXAMPLE **4** *Temperature Application*

During flight, the space shuttle may be exposed to temperatures as low as −250°F and as high as 3,000°F. Find the difference between the temperatures the space shuttle must endure.

$3,000 - (-250)$
$3,000 + 250 = 3,250$ *Add the opposite of −250.*

The difference in temperatures the shuttle must endure is 3,250°F.

Think and Discuss

1. Suppose you subtract one negative integer from another. Will your answer be greater than or less than the number you started with?

2. Tell whether you can reverse the order of integers when subtracting and still get the same answer. Why or why not?

2-3 **Exercises**

California
Standards Practice
🔑 NS2.3, AF1.2

go.hrw.com
Homework Help Online
KEYWORD: MS8CA 2-3
Parent Resources Online
KEYWORD: MS8CA Parent

GUIDED PRACTICE

See Example ① **Use a number line to find each difference.**

1. $4 - 7$ **2.** $-6 - 5$ **3.** $2 - (-4)$ **4.** $-8 - (-2)$

See Example ② **Find each difference.**

5. $6 - 10$ **6.** $-3 - (-8)$ **7.** $-1 - 9$ **8.** $-12 - (-2)$

See Example ③ **Evaluate $a - b$ for each set of values.**

9. $a = 5, b = -2$ **10.** $a = -8, b = 6$ **11.** $a = 4, b = 18$

See Example ④ **12.** In 1980, in Great Falls, Montana, the temperature rose from $-32°F$ to $15°F$ in seven minutes. How much did the temperature increase?

INDEPENDENT PRACTICE

See Example ① **Use a number line to find each difference.**

13. $7 - 12$ **14.** $-5 - (-9)$ **15.** $2 - (-6)$ **16.** $7 - (-8)$

17. $9 - (-3)$ **18.** $-4 - 10$ **19.** $8 - (-8)$ **20.** $-3 - (-3)$

See Example ② **Find each difference.**

21. $-22 - (-5)$ **22.** $-4 - 21$ **23.** $27 - 19$ **24.** $-10 - (-7)$

25. $30 - (-20)$ **26.** $-15 - 15$ **27.** $12 - (-6)$ **28.** $194 - (-272)$

See Example ③ **Evaluate $a - b$ for each set of values.**

29. $a = 9, b = -7$ **30.** $a = -11, b = 2$ **31.** $a = -2, b = 3$

32. $a = 8, b = 19$ **33.** $a = -10, b = 10$ **34.** $a = -4, b = -15$

See Example ④ **35.** The lowest elevation in California is -282 feet, and the highest elevation is 14,505 feet. How much higher is the highest point than the lowest point?

PRACTICE AND PROBLEM SOLVING

Extra Practice
See page EP4.

Simplify.

36. $2 - 8$ **37.** $-360 - 118$ **38.** $15 - 12 - 8$

39. $6 + (-5) - 3$ **40.** $1 - 8 + (-6)$ **41.** $4 - (-7) - 9$

42. $(2 - 3) - (5 - 6)$ **43.** $5 - (-8) - (-3)$ **44.** $10 - 12 + 2$

Evaluate each expression for $m = -5, n = 8,$ and $p = -14$.

45. $m - n + p$ **46.** $n - m - p$ **47.** $p - m - n$ **48.** $m + n - p$

49. Reasoning What could be the next three numbers in the pattern $7, 3, -1, -5, -9 \ldots$? Write a rule that describes your pattern.

50. The temperature of Mercury, the planet closest to the Sun, can be as high as 873°F. The temperature of Pluto is about −393°F. What is the difference between these temperatures?

51. One side of Mercury always faces the Sun. The temperature on this side can reach 873°F. The temperature on the other side can be as low as −361°F. What is the difference between the two temperatures?

Maat Mons volcano on Venus
Source: NASA (computer-generated from the *Magellan* probe)

52. Earth's moon rotates relative to the Sun about once a month. The side facing the Sun at a given time can be as hot as 224°F. The side away from the Sun can be as cold as −307°F. What is the difference between these temperatures?

53. The highest recorded temperature on Earth is 136°F. The lowest is −129°F. What is the difference between these temperatures?

Use the graph for Exercises 54 and 55.

54. How much deeper is the deepest canyon on Mars than the deepest canyon on Venus?

55. ⭐**Challenge** What is the difference between Earth's highest mountain and its deepest ocean canyon? What is the difference between Mars' highest mountain and its deepest canyon? Which difference is greater? How much greater is it?

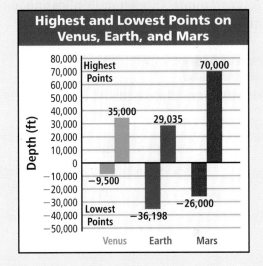

Highest and Lowest Points on Venus, Earth, and Mars

SPIRAL STANDARDS REVIEW ⟜ NS2.3, AF1.2, AF1.3

56. Multiple Choice Which expression does NOT have a value of −3?

Ⓐ $-2 - 1$ Ⓑ $10 - 13$ Ⓒ $5 - (-8)$ Ⓓ $-4 - (-1)$

57. Extended Response If $m = -2$ and $n = 4$, which expression has the least absolute value: $m + n$, $n - m$, or $m - n$? Explain your answer.

Evaluate each expression for the given values of the variables. (Lesson 1-5)

58. $3x - 5$ for $x = 2$ **59.** $2n^2 + n$ for $n = 1$ **60.** $4y^2 - 3y$ for $y = 2$

61. $4a + 7$ for $a = 3$ **62.** $x^2 + 9$ for $x = 1$ **63.** $5z + z^2$ for $z = 3$

64. Sports In three plays, a football team gained 10 yards, lost 22 yards, and gained 15 yards. Use integer addition to find the team's total yardage for the three plays. (Lesson 2-2)

Model Integer Multiplication and Division

Use with Lesson 2-4

go.hrw.com
Lab Resources Online
KEYWORD: MS8CA Lab2

California Standards

NS2.3 Solve addition, subtraction, multiplication, and division problems, including those arising in concrete situations, that use positive and negative integers and combinations of these operations.

KEY

⬜ = 1

⚫ = −1

REMEMBER

- The Commutative Property states that two numbers can be multiplied in any order without changing the product.
- Multiplication is repeated addition.
- Multiplying by a number is the inverse operation of dividing by that number.

You can model integer multiplication and division by using integer chips.

Activity 1

Use integer chips to model $3 \cdot (-5)$.

Think: $3 \cdot (-5)$ means 3 groups of −5.

Arrange 3 groups of 5 red chips.
There are a total of 15 red chips.

$$3 \cdot (-5) = -15$$

1 Use integer chips to find each product.

   a. $2 \cdot (-2)$ **b.** $3 \cdot (-6)$ **c.** $5 \cdot (-4)$ **d.** $6 \cdot (-3)$

Use integer chips to model $-4 \cdot 2$.

Using the Commutative Property, you can write $-4 \cdot 2$ as $2 \cdot (-4)$.

Think: $2 \cdot (-4)$ means 2 groups of −4.

Arrange 2 groups of 4 red chips.
There are a total of 8 red chips.

$$-4 \cdot 2 = -8$$

2 Use integer chips to find each product.

   a. $-6 \cdot 5$ **b.** $-4 \cdot 6$ **c.** $-3 \cdot 4$ **d.** $-2 \cdot 3$

1. What is the sign of the product when you multiply two positive numbers? a negative and a positive number?

2. If −12 were the answer to a multiplication problem, list all of the possible pairs of factors that are integers.

Try This

Use integer chips to find each product.

1. 4 · (−5)　　　　**2.** −3 · 2　　　　**3.** 1 · (−6)　　　　**4.** −5 · 2

5. On days that Kathy has swimming lessons, she spends $2.00 of her allowance on snacks. Last week, Kathy had swimming lessons on Monday, Wednesday, and Friday. How much of her allowance did Kathy spend on snacks last week? Use integer chips to model the situation and solve the problem.

Activity 2

Use integer chips to model −15 ÷ 3.

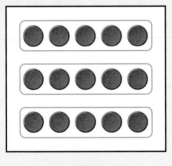

Think: −15 is separated into 3 equal groups.

Arrange 15 red chips into 3 equal groups.

There are 5 red chips in each group.

−15 ÷ 3 = −5

1 Use integer chips to find each quotient.

a. −20 ÷ 5　　　　**b.** −18 ÷ 6　　　　**c.** −12 ÷ 4　　　　**d.** −24 ÷ 8

Think and Discuss

1. What is the sign of the answer when you divide a negative integer by a positive integer?

2. How are multiplication and division of integers related?

Try This

Use integer chips to find each quotient.

1. −21 ÷ 7　　　　**2.** −12 ÷ 4　　　　**3.** −8 ÷ 2　　　　**4.** −10 ÷ 5

5. Ty spent $18.00 of his allowance at the arcade. He hit baseballs, played pinball, and played video games. Each of these activities cost the same amount at the arcade. How much did each activity cost? Use integer chips to model the situation and solve the problem.

2-4 Multiplying and Dividing Integers

California Standards

NS2.3 Solve addition, subtraction, multiplication, and division problems, including those arising in concrete situations, that use positive and negative integers and combinations of these operations.
Also covered: **AF1.4**

Why learn this? You can multiply integers to determine whether a football team made a first down. (See Example 4).

You can think of multiplication as repeated addition.

$$3 \cdot 2 = 2 + 2 + 2 = 6$$

$$3 \cdot (-2) = (-2) + (-2) + (-2) = -6$$

EXAMPLE 1 Multiplying Integers Using Repeated Addition

Reasoning

Use a number line to find each product.

A $3 \cdot (-3)$

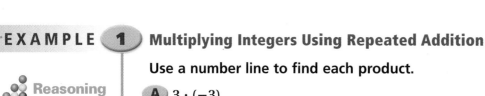

Think: Start at 0.
Add −3 three times.

$$3 \cdot (-3) = -9$$

B $-4 \cdot 2$

$$-4 \cdot 2 = 2 \cdot (-4)$$

Use the Commutative Property.

Think: Start at 0.
Add −4 two times.

$$-4 \cdot 2 = -8$$

Remember!

Inverse operations "undo" each other. Multiplying by a number is the inverse operation of dividing by that number.

See Lesson 1-8, p. 40.

Example 1 and the patterns below suggest that when the signs of two integers are different, their product or quotient is negative. The patterns also suggest that the product or quotient of two negative integers is positive.

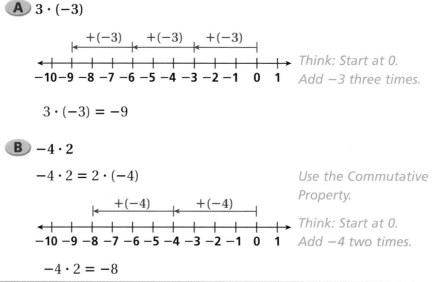

$$-3 \cdot \quad 2 = -6$$
$$-3 \cdot \quad 1 = -3$$
$$-3 \cdot \quad 0 = \quad 0$$
$$-3 \cdot (-1) = \quad 3$$
$$-3 \cdot (-2) = \quad 6$$

$$-6 \div (-3) = \quad 2$$
$$-3 \div (-3) = \quad 1$$
$$0 \div (-3) = \quad 0$$
$$3 \div (-3) = -1$$
$$6 \div (-3) = -2$$

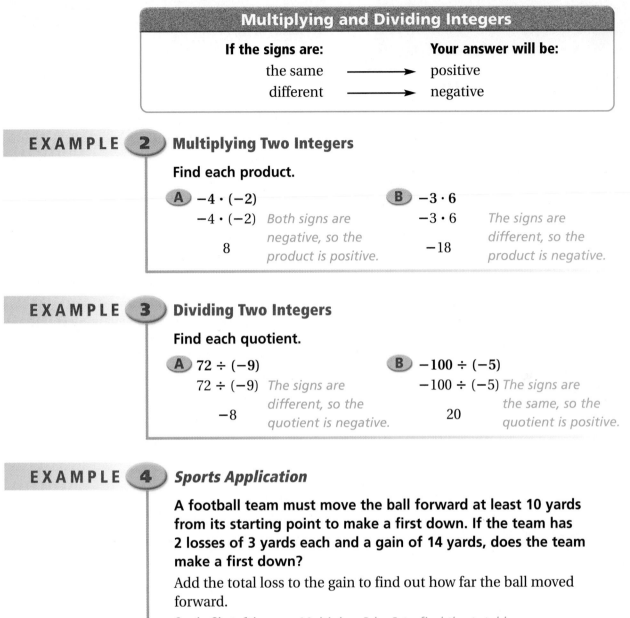

Multiplying and Dividing Integers

If the signs are:		Your answer will be:
the same	$\longrightarrow$	positive
different	$\longrightarrow$	negative

EXAMPLE 2 **Multiplying Two Integers**

Find each product.

A $-4 \cdot (-2)$

$-4 \cdot (-2)$ *Both signs are negative, so the product is positive.*

8

B $-3 \cdot 6$

$-3 \cdot 6$ *The signs are different, so the product is negative.*

-18

EXAMPLE 3 **Dividing Two Integers**

Find each quotient.

A $72 \div (-9)$

$72 \div (-9)$ *The signs are different, so the quotient is negative.*

-8

B $-100 \div (-5)$

$-100 \div (-5)$ *The signs are the same, so the quotient is positive.*

20

EXAMPLE 4 ***Sports Application***

A football team must move the ball forward at least 10 yards from its starting point to make a first down. If the team has 2 losses of 3 yards each and a gain of 14 yards, does the team make a first down?

Add the total loss to the gain to find out how far the ball moved forward.

$2 \cdot (-3) + 14$ *Multiply −3 by 2 to find the total loss; then add the gain of 14.*

$-6 + 14$ *Use the order of operations. Multiply first.*

8 *Then add.*

The team moved the ball forward 8 yards, so it did not make a first down.

Think and Discuss

1. List at least four different multiplication examples that have 24 as their product. Use both positive and negative integers.

2. Explain how the signs of two integers affect their products and quotients.

California
Standards Practice
NS2.3, AF1.3, AF1.4

go.hrw.com
Homework Help Online
KEYWORD: MS8CA 2-4
Parent Resources Online
KEYWORD: MS8CA Parent

GUIDED PRACTICE

See Example **1** Use a number line to find each product.

1. $5 \cdot (-3)$ **2.** $5 \cdot (-2)$ **3.** $-3 \cdot 5$ **4.** $-4 \cdot 6$

See Example **2** Find each product.

5. $-5 \cdot (-3)$ **6.** $-2 \cdot 5$ **7.** $3 \cdot (-5)$ **8.** $-7 \cdot (-4)$

See Example **3** Find each quotient.

9. $32 \div (-4)$ **10.** $-18 \div 3$ **11.** $-20 \div (-5)$ **12.** $49 \div (-7)$

13. $-63 \div (-9)$ **14.** $-50 \div 10$ **15.** $63 \div (-9)$ **16.** $-45 \div (-5)$

See Example **4** **17.** In January, Angelina made one deposit of $90 to her savings account and made 3 withdrawals of $40 each. What was the total change in the amount of money in Angelina's account in January?

INDEPENDENT PRACTICE

See Example **1** Use a number line to find each product.

18. $2 \cdot (-1)$ **19.** $-5 \cdot 2$ **20.** $-4 \cdot 2$ **21.** $3 \cdot (-4)$

See Example **2** Find each product.

22. $4 \cdot (-6)$ **23.** $-6 \cdot (-8)$ **24.** $-8 \cdot 4$ **25.** $-5 \cdot (-7)$

See Example **3** Find each quotient.

26. $48 \div (-6)$ **27.** $-35 \div (-5)$ **28.** $-16 \div 4$ **29.** $-64 \div 8$

30. $-42 \div (-7)$ **31.** $81 \div (-9)$ **32.** $-77 \div 11$ **33.** $27 \div (-3)$

See Example **4** **34.** A bus had 27 passengers. At each of the next 4 stops on the route, 3 passengers got off the bus. At the fifth stop, 7 passengers got on the bus. How many passengers were on the bus after the fifth stop?

PRACTICE AND PROBLEM SOLVING

Extra Practice
See page EP4.

Find each product or quotient.

35. $-4 \cdot 10$ **36.** $-3 \cdot (-9)$ **37.** $-45 \div 15$ **38.** $-3 \cdot 4 \cdot (-1)$

39. $-500 \div (-10)$ **40.** $5 \cdot (-4) \cdot (-2)$ **41.** $225 \div (-75)$ **42.** $-2 \cdot (-5) \cdot 9$

Evaluate each expression for $a = -5$, $b = 6$, and $c = -12$.

43. $-2c + b$ **44.** $4a - b$ **45.** $ab + c$ **46.** $ac \div b$

47. Earth Science A scuba diver is swimming at a depth of -12 feet in the Flower Garden Banks National Marine Sanctuary. She dives down to a coral reef that is at five times this depth. What is the depth of the coral reef?

Simplify each expression. Justify your steps using the Commutative, Associative, and Distributive Properties when necessary.

48. $(-3)^2$ **49.** $-2(-2 + 1)$ **50.** $8 + (-5)^3 + 7$ **51.** $(-1)^5 \cdot (9 + 3)$

52. $29 - (-7) - 3$ **53.** $-4 \cdot 14 \cdot (-25)$ **54.** $25 - (-2) \cdot 4^2$ **55.** $8 - (6 \div (-2))$

56. Earth Science The table shows the depths of major caves in the United States. Approximately how many times deeper is Jewel Cave than Kartchner Caverns?

Personal Finance Does each person end up with more or less money than he started with? By how much?

Depths of Major U.S. Caves	
Cave	Depth (ft)
Carlsbad Caverns	−1,022
Caverns of Sonora	−150
Ellison's Cave	−1,000
Jewel Cave	−696
Kartchner Caverns	−137
Mammoth Cave	−379

Source: NSS U.S.A. Long Cave List, Caves over one mile long as of 10/18/2001

57. Kevin spends $24 a day for 3 days.

58. Devin earns $15 a day for 5 days.

59. Evan spends $20 a day for 3 days. Then he earns $18 a day for 4 days.

60. What's the Error? A student writes, "The quotient of an integer divided by an integer of the opposite sign has the sign of the integer with the greater absolute value." What is the student's error?

61. Write About It Explain how to find the product and the quotient of two integers.

62. Challenge Use > or < to compare $-2 \cdot (-1) \cdot 4 \cdot 2 \cdot (-3)$ and $-1 + (-2) + 4 + (-25) + (-10)$.

SPIRAL STANDARDS REVIEW NS2.3, AF1.2

63. Multiple Choice Which of the expressions are equal to −20?

I $-2 \cdot 10$ **II** $-40 \div (-2)$ **III** $-5 \cdot (-2)^2$ **IV** $-4 \cdot 2 - 12$

Ⓐ I only   Ⓑ I and II   Ⓒ I, III, and IV   Ⓓ I, II, III, IV

64. Multiple Choice Which expression has a value that is greater than the value of $-25 \div (-5)$?

Ⓐ $36 \div (-6)$ Ⓑ $-100 \div 10$ Ⓒ $-50 \div (-10)$ Ⓓ $-45 \div (-5)$

Write each phrase as an algebraic expression. (Lesson 1-6)

65. the sum of a number and 6

66. the product of −3 and a number

67. 4 less than twice a number

68. 5 more than a number divided by 3

Find each difference. (Lesson 2-3)

69. $3 - (-2)$ **70.** $-5 - 6$ **71.** $6 - 8$ **72.** $2 - (-7)$

Model Integer Equations

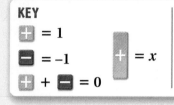

Use with Lesson 2-5

go.hrw.com
Lab Resources Online
KEYWORD: MS8CA Lab2

KEY

$\boxed{+} = 1$

$\boxed{-} = -1$

$\boxed{+} + \boxed{-} = 0$

$\boxed{} = x$

REMEMBER

• Adding or subtracting zero does not change the value of an expression.

California Standards

AF1.1 Write and **solve one-step linear equations in one variable.**
Also covered: **NS2.3**

You can use algebra tiles to model and solve equations.

Activity

To solve the equation $x + 2 = 3$, you need to get x alone on one side of the equal sign. You can add or remove tiles as long as you add the same amount or remove the same amount on both sides.

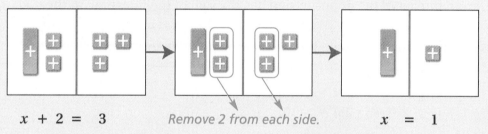

$x + 2 = 3$ *Remove 2 from each side.* $x = 1$

1 Use algebra tiles to model and solve each equation.

    a. $x + 3 = 5$ **b.** $x + 4 = 9$ **c.** $x + 5 = 8$ **d.** $x + 6 = 6$

The equation $x + 6 = 4$ is more difficult to model because there are not enough tiles on the right side of the mat to remove 6 from each side.

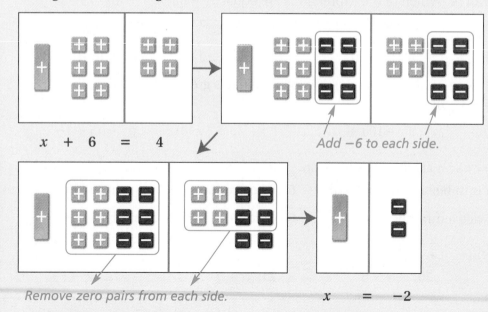

$x + 6 = 4$ *Add −6 to each side.*

Remove zero pairs from each side. $x = -2$

❷ Use algebra tiles to model and solve each equation.

a. $x + 5 = 3$ **b.** $x + 4 = 2$ **c.** $x + 7 = -3$ **d.** $x + 6 = -2$

When modeling an equation that involves subtraction, such as $x - 6 = 2$, you can rewrite the equation as an addition equation. For example, the equation $x - 6 = 2$ can be rewritten as $x + (-6) = 2$.

Modeling equations that involve addition of negative numbers is similar to modeling equations that involve addition of positive numbers.

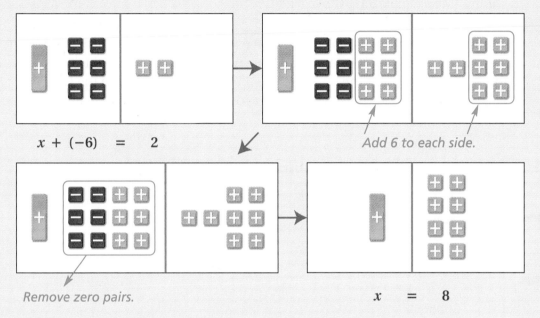

❸ Use algebra tiles to model and solve each equation.

a. $x - 4 = 3$ **b.** $x - 2 = 8$ **c.** $x - 5 = -5$ **d.** $x - 7 = 0$

Think and Discuss

1. When you remove tiles, what operation are you modeling? When you add tiles, what operation are you modeling?

2. How can you use the original model to check your solution?

3. To model $x - 6 = 2$, you must rewrite the equation as $x + (-6) = 2$. Why are you allowed to do this?

Try This

Use algebra tiles to model and solve each equation.

1. $x + 7 = 10$ **2.** $x - 5 = -8$ **3.** $x + (-5) = -4$ **4.** $x - 2 = 1$

5. $x + 4 = 8$ **6.** $x + 3 = -2$ **7.** $x + (-1) = 9$ **8.** $x - 7 = -6$

2-5 Solving Equations Containing Integers

California Standards

AF1.1 Write and solve one-step linear equations in one variable.

Also covered: **NS2.3**

Vocabulary
additive inverse

Who uses this? Business managers can solve equations with integers to determine a company's profit. (See Example 3.)

To solve integer equations such as $-3 + y = -5$ you must isolate the variable on one side of the equation. One way to isolate the variable in this equation is to add the opposite of -3 to both sides. Because the sum of a number and its opposite is 0, the opposite of a number is also known as the **additive inverse** of the number.

E X A M P L E **1** **Solving Addition and Subtraction Equations**

Helpful Hint

$3 + (-3) = 0$
3 is the opposite, or additive inverse, of -3.

Solve each equation. Check your answer.

A $\quad -3 + y = -5$

$$-3 + y = -5$$
$$\underline{+\ 3 \qquad\quad +\ 3} \qquad \textit{Add 3 to both sides.}$$
$$y = -2$$

Check

$$-3 + y = -5$$
$$-3 + (-2) \overset{?}{=} -5 \qquad \textit{Substitute –2 for y in the original equation.}$$
$$-5 \overset{?}{=} -5 ✔ \qquad \textit{True. –2 is the solution to } -3 + y = -5.$$

B $\quad n + 3 = -10$

$$n + 3 = \quad -10$$
$$\underline{+\ (-3) \qquad +\ (-3)} \qquad \textit{Add –3 to both sides.}$$
$$n = \quad -13$$

Check

$$n + 3 = -10$$
$$-13 + 3 \overset{?}{=} -10 \qquad \textit{Substitute –13 for n in the original equation.}$$
$$-10 \overset{?}{=} -10 ✔ \qquad \textit{True. –13 is the solution to } n + 3 = -10.$$

C $\quad x - 8 = -32$

$$x - 8 = -32$$
$$\underline{+\ 8 \qquad +\ 8} \qquad \textit{Add 8 to both sides.}$$
$$x = -24$$

Check

$$x - 8 = -32$$
$$-24 - 8 \overset{?}{=} -32 \qquad \textit{Substitute –24 for x in the original equation.}$$
$$-32 \overset{?}{=} -32 ✔ \qquad \textit{True. –24 is the solution to } x - 8 = -32.$$

EXAMPLE 2 **Solving Multiplication and Division Equations**

Solve each equation. Check your answer.

Reasoning

A $\dfrac{a}{-3} = 9$

$$\dfrac{a}{-3} = 9$$

$$(-3)\left(\dfrac{a}{-3}\right) = (-3)9 \qquad \text{Multiply both sides by } -3.$$

$$a = -27$$

Check $\quad \dfrac{a}{-3} = 9$

$$\dfrac{-27}{-3} \overset{?}{=} 9 \qquad \text{Substitute } -27 \text{ for } a.$$

$$9 \overset{?}{=} 9 \checkmark \qquad \text{True. } -27 \text{ is the solution.}$$

B $-120 = 6x$

$$-120 = 6x$$

$$\dfrac{-120}{6} = \dfrac{6x}{6} \qquad \text{Divide both sides by 6.}$$

$$-20 = x$$

Check $\quad -120 = 6x$

$$-120 \overset{?}{=} 6(-20) \qquad \text{Substitute } -20 \text{ for } x.$$

$$-120 \overset{?}{=} -120 \checkmark \qquad \text{True. } -20 \text{ is the solution.}$$

EXAMPLE 3 *Business Application*

A shoe manufacturer made a profit of $800 million. This amount is $200 million more than last year's profit. What was last year's profit?

Let p represent last year's profit (in millions of dollars).

This year's profit	is	$200 million	more than	last year's profit.
800	=	200	+	p

$$800 = 200 + p$$
$$\underline{-\,200 \quad -\,200}$$
$$600 = p \qquad \text{Last year's profit was \$600 million.}$$

Think and Discuss

1. Tell what value of n makes $-n + 32$ equal to zero.

2. Explain why you would or would not multiply both sides of an equation by 0 to solve it.

2-5 **Exercises**

California
Standards Practice
NS2.3, AF1.1

go.hrw.com
Homework Help Online
KEYWORD: MS8CA 2-5
Parent Resources Online
KEYWORD: MS8CA Parent

GUIDED PRACTICE

See Example ① Solve each equation. Check your answer.

1. $w - 6 = -2$ **2.** $x + 5 = -7$ **3.** $k = -18 + 11$

See Example ② **4.** $\dfrac{n}{-4} = 2$ **5.** $-240 = 8y$ **6.** $-5a = 300$

See Example ③ **7. Business** Last year, a chain of electronics stores had a loss of $45 million. This year the loss is $12 million more than last year's loss. What is this year's loss?

INDEPENDENT PRACTICE

See Example ① Solve each equation. Check your answer.

8. $b - 7 = -16$ **9.** $k + 6 = 3$ **10.** $s + 2 = -4$

11. $v + 14 = 10$ **12.** $c + 8 = -20$ **13.** $a - 25 = -5$

See Example ② **14.** $9c = -99$ **15.** $\dfrac{t}{8} = -4$ **16.** $-16 = 2z$

17. $\dfrac{n}{-5} = -30$ **18.** $200 = -25p$ **19.** $\dfrac{l}{-12} = 12$

See Example ③ **20.** The temperature in Nome, Alaska, was $-50°F$. This was $18°F$ less than the temperature in Anchorage, Alaska, on the same day. What was the temperature in Anchorage?

PRACTICE AND PROBLEM SOLVING

Extra Practice
See page EP5.

Solve each equation. Check your answer.

21. $9y = 900$ **22.** $d - 15 = 45$ **23.** $j + 56 = -7$

24. $\dfrac{s}{-20} = 7$ **25.** $-85 = -5c$ **26.** $v - 39 = -16$

27. $11y = -121$ **28.** $\dfrac{n}{36} = 9$ **29.** $w + 41 = 0$

30. $\dfrac{r}{238} = 8$ **31.** $-23 = x + 35$ **32.** $0 = -15m$

33. $4x = 2 + 14$ **34.** $c + c + c = 6$ **35.** $t - 3 = 4 + 2$

36. Geometry The three angles of a triangle have equal measures. The sum of their measures is $180°$. What is the measure of each angle?

37. Sports Herb has 42 days to prepare for a cross-country race. During his training, he will run a total of 126 miles. If Herb runs the same distance every day, how many miles will he run each day?

38. Multi-Step Jared bought one share of stock for $225.
  a. He sold the stock for a profit of $55. What was the selling price of the stock?
  b. The price of the stock dropped $40 the day after Jared sold it. At what price would Jared have sold it if he had waited until then?

Translate each sentence into an equation. Then solve the equation.

39. The sum of -13 and a number p is 8.

40. A number x divided by 4 is -7.

41. 9 less than a number t is -22.

42. Science On the Kelvin temperature scale, pure water boils at 373 K. The difference between the boiling point and the freezing point of water on this scale is 100 K. What is the freezing point of water?

Recreation The graph shows the most popular travel destinations over the 2001 Labor Day weekend. Use the graph for Exercises 43 and 44.

43. Which destination was 5 times more popular than theme or amusement parks?

44. According to the graph, the mountains were as popular as state or national parks and what other destination combined?

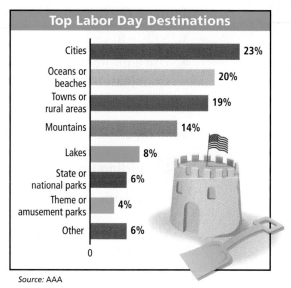

Source: AAA

45. Reasoning Matthew (M) earns $23 less a week than his sister Allie (A). Their combined salaries are $93. How much does each of them earn per week?

Ⓐ A: $35; M: $12   Ⓑ A: $35; M: $58   Ⓒ A: $58; M: $35

46. Write About It Explain how to solve an equation containing integers.

47. Challenge Write an equation that includes the variable p and the numbers 5, 3, and 31 so that the solution is $p = 16$.

48. Multiple Choice Solve $-15m = 60$.

Ⓐ $m = -4$ Ⓑ $m = 5$ Ⓒ $m = 45$ Ⓓ $m = 75$

49. Multiple Choice For which equation does $x = 2$?

Ⓐ $-3x = 6$ Ⓑ $x + 3 = -5$ Ⓒ $x + x = 4$ Ⓓ $\frac{x}{4} = -8$

Simplify each expression. (Lesson 1-3)

50. $4(-2 + 5) + (-10)$

51. $3^2 + 16 \div (-4) - 20$

52. $-15 \div 3 + 12 \cdot 4 - 1$

53. $[2 + (10 - 20)] \div (-2)$

Find each product or quotient. (Lesson 2-4)

54. $-5 \cdot (-6)$ **55.** $25 \div (-5)$ **56.** $22 \cdot (-3)$ **57.** $-42 \div 3$

READY TO GO ON?

Quiz for Lessons 2-1 Through 2-5

2-1 Integers

Compare the integers. Use < or > .

1. 5 ☐ −8

2. −2 ☐ −6

3. −4 ☐ 3

4. Use a number line to order the integers −7, 3, 6, −1, 0, 5, −4, and 7 from least to greatest.

Use a number line to find each absolute value.

5. |−23|

6. |17|

7. |−10|

2-2 Adding Integers

Find each sum.

8. −6 + 3

9. 5 + (−9)

10. −7 + (−11)

Evaluate $p + t$ for the given values.

11. $p = 5, t = −18$

12. $p = −4, t = −13$

13. $p = −37, t = 39$

2-3 Subtracting Integers

Find each difference.

14. −21 − (−7)

15. 9 − (−11)

16. 6 − 17

17. When Cai traveled from New Orleans, Louisiana, to the Ozark Mountains in Arkansas, the elevation changed from 7 ft below sea level to 2,314 ft above sea level. How much did the elevation increase?

2-4 Multiplying and Dividing Integers

Find each product or quotient.

18. −7 · 3

19. 30 ÷ (−15)

20. −5 · (−9)

21. After reaching the top of a cliff, a rock climber descended the rock face using a 65 ft rope. The distance to the base of the cliff was 585 ft. How many rope lengths did it take the climber to complete her descent?

2-5 Solving Equations Containing Integers

Solve each equation. Check your answer.

22. $3x = 30$

23. $k − 25 = 50$

24. $y + 16 = −8$

25. This year, 72 students completed projects for the science fair. This was 23 more students than last year. How many students completed projects for the science fair last year?

Focus on Problem Solving

California Standards

MR1.1 Analyze problems by identifying relationships, **distinguishing relevant from irrelevant information, identifying missing information,** sequencing and prioritizing information, and observing patterns.

Also covered: **AF1.1**

Understand the Problem

- Identify too much or too little information

Problems often give too much or too little information. You must decide whether you have enough information to work the problem.

Read the problem and identify the facts that are given. Can you use any of these facts to arrive at an answer? Are there facts in the problem that are not necessary to find the answer? These questions can help you determine whether you have too much or too little information.

If you cannot solve the problem with the information given, decide what information you need. Then read the problem again to be sure you haven't missed the information in the problem.

Copy each problem. Circle the important facts. Underline any facts that you do not need to answer the question. If there is not enough information, list the additional information you need.

1. The reticulated python is one of the longest snakes in the world. One was found in Indonesia in 1912 that was 33 feet long. At birth, a reticulated python is 2 feet long. Suppose an adult python is 29 feet long. Let f represent the number of feet the python grew since birth. What is the value of f?

2. The largest flying flag in the world is 7,410 square feet and weighs 180 pounds. There are a total of 13 horizontal stripes on it. Let h represent the height of each stripe. What is the value of h?

3. The elevation of Mt. McKinley is 20,320 ft. People who climb Mt. McKinley are flown to a base camp located at 7,200 ft. From there, they begin a climb that may last 20 days or longer. Let d represent the change in elevation from the base camp to the summit of Mt. McKinley. What is the value of d?

4. Let c represent the cost of a particular computer in 1981. Six years later, in 1987, the price of the computer had increased to $3,600. What is the value of c?

2-6 The Coordinate Plane

California Standards

Preparation for AF1.0 Students write verbal expressions and sentences as algebraic expressions and equations; they evaluate algebraic expressions, solve simple linear equations, and **graph and interpret their results.**

Why learn this? You can use a coordinate system to find locations on a map. (See Exercises 49–54.)

A **coordinate plane** is formed by two number lines in a plane that intersect at right angles. The point of intersection is the zero on each number line.

- The two number lines are called the **axes**.

- The horizontal axis is called the **x-axis**.

- The vertical axis is called the **y-axis**.

- The two axes divide the coordinate plane into four **quadrants**.

- The point where the axes intersect is called the **origin**.

Vocabulary
coordinate plane
axes
x-axis
y-axis
quadrants
origin
coordinates
x-coordinate
y-coordinate

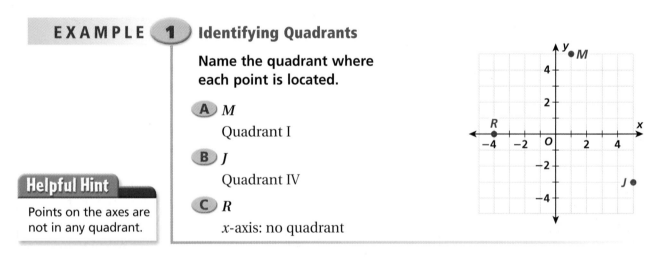

EXAMPLE 1 Identifying Quadrants

Name the quadrant where each point is located.

A *M*

Quadrant I

B *J*

Quadrant IV

C *R*

x-axis: no quadrant

Helpful Hint

Points on the axes are not in any quadrant.

An ordered pair gives the location of a point on a coordinate plane. The first number tells how far to move right (positive) or left (negative) from the origin. The second number tells how far to move up (positive) or down (negative).

The numbers in an ordered pair are called **coordinates**. The first number is called the *x*-**coordinate**. The second number is called the *y*-**coordinate**. The ordered pair for the origin is (0, 0).

EXAMPLE 2 **Locating Points on a Coordinate Plane**

Give the coordinates of each point.

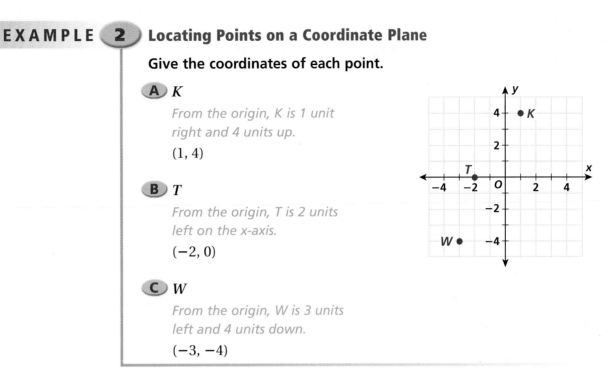

A *K*

From the origin, K is 1 unit right and 4 units up.

(1, 4)

B *T*

From the origin, T is 2 units left on the x-axis.

(−2, 0)

C *W*

From the origin, W is 3 units left and 4 units down.

(−3, −4)

EXAMPLE 3 **Graphing Points on a Coordinate Plane**

Graph each point on a coordinate plane.

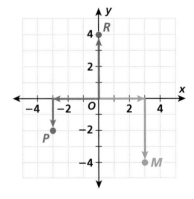

A *P*(−3, −2)

From the origin, move 3 units left and 2 units down.

B *R*(0, 4)

From the origin, move 4 units up.

C *M*(3, −4)

From the origin, move 3 units right and 4 units down.

Think and Discuss

1. Tell which number in an ordered pair indicates how far to move left or right from the origin and which number indicates how far to move up or down.

2. Describe how graphing the point (5, 4) is similar to graphing the point (5, −4). How is it different?

3. Tell why it is important to start at the origin when you are graphing points.

California
Standards Practice

Preparation for AF1.0

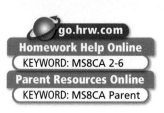

go.hrw.com
Homework Help Online
KEYWORD: MS8CA 2-6
Parent Resources Online
KEYWORD: MS8CA Parent

GUIDED PRACTICE

Use the coordinate plane for Exercises 1–6.

See Example ① Name the quadrant where each point is located.

1. *T*   **2.** *U*   **3.** *B*

See Example ② Give the coordinates of each point.

4. *A*   **5.** *B*   **6.** *U*

See Example ③ Graph each point on a coordinate plane.

7. *E*(4, 2)   **8.** *F*(−1, −4)   **9.** *G*(0, 2)

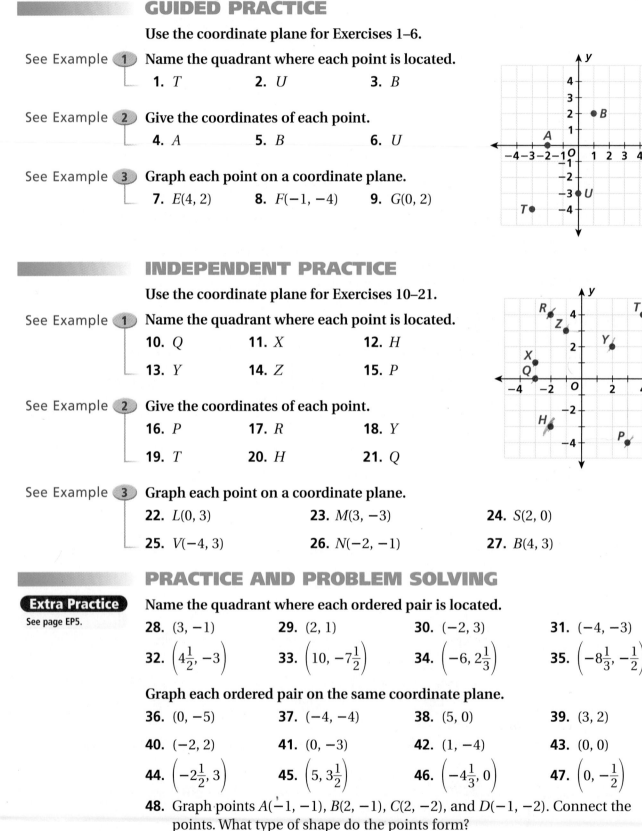

INDEPENDENT PRACTICE

Use the coordinate plane for Exercises 10–21.

See Example ① Name the quadrant where each point is located.

10. *Q*   **11.** *X*   **12.** *H*

13. *Y*   **14.** *Z*   **15.** *P*

See Example ② Give the coordinates of each point.

16. *P*   **17.** *R*   **18.** *Y*

19. *T*   **20.** *H*   **21.** *Q*

See Example ③ Graph each point on a coordinate plane.

22. *L*(0, 3)   **23.** *M*(3, −3)   **24.** *S*(2, 0)

25. *V*(−4, 3)   **26.** *N*(−2, −1)   **27.** *B*(4, 3)

PRACTICE AND PROBLEM SOLVING

Extra Practice
See page EP5.

Name the quadrant where each ordered pair is located.

28. (3, −1)   **29.** (2, 1)   **30.** (−2, 3)   **31.** (−4, −3)

32. $\left(4\frac{1}{2}, -3\right)$ **33.** $\left(10, -7\frac{1}{2}\right)$ **34.** $\left(-6, 2\frac{1}{3}\right)$ **35.** $\left(-8\frac{1}{3}, -\frac{1}{2}\right)$

Graph each ordered pair on the same coordinate plane.

36. (0, −5)   **37.** (−4, −4)   **38.** (5, 0)   **39.** (3, 2)

40. (−2, 2)   **41.** (0, −3)   **42.** (1, −4)   **43.** (0, 0)

44. $\left(-2\frac{1}{2}, 3\right)$ **45.** $\left(5, 3\frac{1}{2}\right)$ **46.** $\left(-4\frac{1}{3}, 0\right)$ **47.** $\left(0, -\frac{1}{2}\right)$

48. Graph points *A*(−1, −1), *B*(2, −1), *C*(2, −2), and *D*(−1, −2). Connect the points. What type of shape do the points form?

We use a coordinate system on Earth to find exact locations. The *equator* is like the *x*-axis, and the *prime meridian* is like the *y*-axis.

The lines that run east-west are *lines of latitude*. They are measured in degrees north and south of the equator.

The lines that run north-south are *lines of longitude*. They are measured in degrees east and west of the prime meridian.

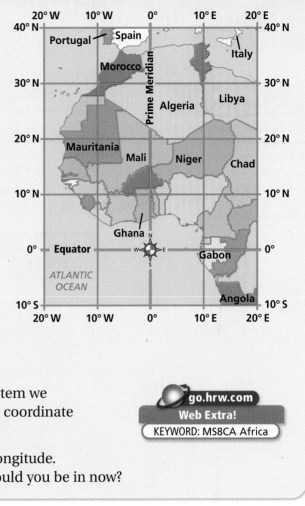

49. In what country is the location 0° latitude, 10° E longitude?

50. Give the coordinates of a location in Algeria.

51. Name two countries that lie along the 30° N line of latitude.

52. Where would you be if you were located at 10° S latitude, 10° W longitude?

53. **Write About It** How is the coordinate system we use to locate places on Earth different from the coordinate plane? How is it similar?

go.hrw.com
Web Extra!
KEYWORD: MS8CA Africa

54. **Challenge** Begin at 10° S latitude, 20° E longitude. Travel 40° north and 20° west. What country would you be in now?

SPIRAL STANDARDS REVIEW
NS2.3, Prep for AF1.0, AF1.1

55. Multiple Choice In which quadrant is the point (−1, 2) located?

(A) Quadrant I   (B) Quadrant II   (C) Quadrant III   (D) Quadrant IV

56. Multiple Choice Which of the following coordinates is the farthest to the right of the origin on a coordinate plane?

(A) (−19, 7)   (B) (0, 12)   (C) (4, 15)   (D) (7, 0)

Find each sum or difference. (Lessons 2-2 and 2-3)

57. $-47 + 93$ **58.** $22 - (-19)$ **59.** $-58 - (-36)$ **60.** $26 + (-35)$

Solve each equation. Check your answer. (Lesson 2-5)

61. $x - 42 = -8$ **62.** $n + 49 = -63$ **63.** $12m = -72$ **64.** $\frac{y}{16} = -8$

![bear] **California Standards**

Preparation for AF1.0 Students write verbal expressions and sentences as algebraic expressions and equations; they evaluate algebraic expressions, solve simple linear equations, and **graph and interpret their results.**

Who uses this? Directors can use equations in two variables to determine how many feet of film they will need to shoot a movie.

Most movies shown in theaters are shot using film. The table shows the relationship between the duration of a movie in minutes and the length of the film in feet. Look for a pattern in the table.

Duration of Movie (min)	Length of Film Needed (ft)	
1	90	$90(1) = 90$
2	180	$90(2) = 180$
3	270	$90(3) = 270$

The length of film in feet is 90 times the duration of a movie in minutes. An *equation in two variables* can represent this relationship.

Length in feet is 90 times duration in minutes.

$$y = 90 \cdot x$$

An equation in two variables can be used to make predictions. For example, a director can use the equation $y = 90x$ to determine how many feet of film are needed for a 110-minute movie.

$y = 90x$

$y = 90(110) = 9{,}900$ *Substitute 110 for x.*

The director would need 9,900 feet of film for a 110-minute movie.

E X A M P L E **1**   **Writing Equations from Tables**

Write an equation in two variables that gives the values in the table. Use your equation to find the value of *y* for the indicated value of *x*.

x	3	4	5	6	7	10
y	7	8	9	10	11	▪

Helpful Hint

When all the *y*-values are greater than the corresponding *x*-values, try using addition or multiplication of a positive integer in your equation.

y is 4 more than x.   *Compare x and y to find a pattern.*

$y = x + 4$ *Use the pattern to write an equation.*

$y = 10 + 4$ *Substitute 10 for x.*

$y = 14$ *Use your equation to find y when x = 10.*

You can write equations in two variables for relationships that are described in words.

EXAMPLE 2 **Translating Words into Math**

Write an equation for the relationship. Tell what each variable you use represents.

The length of a rectangle is 5 times its width.

ℓ = length of rectangle   *Choose variables for the equation.*

w = width of rectangle

$\ell = 5w$ *Write an equation.*

EXAMPLE 3 **PROBLEM SOLVING APPLICATION**

Reasoning

Car washers tracked the number of cars they washed and the total amount of money they earned. They charged the same price for each car they washed. They earned $60 for 20 cars, $66 for 22 cars, and $81 for 27 cars. Write an equation for the relationship.

1 **Understand the Problem**

The **answer** will be an equation that describes the relationship between the number of cars washed and the money earned.

2 **Make a Plan**

You can make a table to display the data.

3 **Solve**

Let c be the number of cars. Let m be the amount of money earned.

c	20	22	27
m	60	66	81

m is equal to 3 times c.   *Compare c and m.*

$m = 3c$ *Write an equation.*

4 **Look Back**

Substitute the c and m values in the table to check that they are solutions of the equation $m = 3c$.

$m = 3c$ (20, 60) $m = 3c$ (22, 66) $m = 3c$ (27, 81)

$60 \stackrel{?}{=} 3 \cdot 20$ $66 \stackrel{?}{=} 3 \cdot 22$ $81 \stackrel{?}{=} 3 \cdot 27$

$60 \stackrel{?}{=} 60$ ✔ $66 \stackrel{?}{=} 66$ ✔ $81 \stackrel{?}{=} 81$ ✔

Think and Discuss

1. Explain how you find the y-value when the x-value is 20 for the equation $y = 5x$.

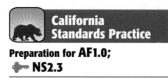

GUIDED PRACTICE

See Example 1 Write an equation in two variables that gives the values in each table. Use your equation to find the value of *y* for the indicated value of *x*.

1.

x	1	2	3	6	9
y	7	8	9	12	■

2.

x	3	4	5	6	10
y	15	20	25	30	■

See Example 2 Write an equation for the relationship. Tell what each variable you use represents.

3. Jen is 6 years younger than her brother.

See Example 3 **4.** Brenda sells balloon bouquets. She charges the same price for each balloon in a bouquet. The cost of a bouquet with 6 balloons is $3, with 9 balloons is $4.50, and with 12 balloons is $6. Write an equation for the relationship.

INDEPENDENT PRACTICE

See Example 1 Write an equation in two variables that gives the values in each table. Use your equation to find the value of *y* for the indicated value of *x*.

5.

x	0	1	2	5	7
y	0	4	8	20	■

6.

x	4	5	6	7	12
y	0	1	2	3	■

See Example 2 Write an equation for the relationship. Tell what each variable you use represents.

7. The cost of a case of bottled juices is $2 less than the cost of twelve individual bottles.

8. The population of New York is twice as large as the population of Michigan.

See Example 3 **9.** Oliver is playing a video game. He earns the same number of points for each prize he captures. He earned 1,050 points for 7 prizes and 2,850 points for 19 prizes. Write an equation for the relationship.

PRACTICE AND PROBLEM SOLVING

Extra Practice
See page EP5.

Write an equation in two variables that gives the values in each table, and then find the missing terms.

10.

x	−1	0	1	2	5	7
y	■	3.4	4.4	5.4	■	10.4

11.

x	2	3	5	9	11	14
y	−8	−12	−20	−36	−44	■

12.

x	20	24	28	32	36	40
y	−5	−6	−7	■	−9	−10

13.

x	−5	−3	−1	0	1	3
y	−10	−6	■	0	2	■

14. Multi-Step The height of a triangle is 5 centimeters more than twice the length of its base. Write an equation relating the height of the triangle to the length of its base. Find the height when the base is 20 centimeters long.

Write an equation for each relationship. Define the variables that you use.

15.

16.

17. **Multi-Step** Georgia earns $6.50 per hour at a part-time job. She wants to buy a sweater that costs $58.50. Write an equation relating the number of hours she works to the amount of money she earns. Find how many hours Georgia needs to work to buy the sweater.

Use the table for Exercises 18–20.

18. **Graphic Design** Margo is designing a Web page displaying similar rectangles. Use the table to write an equation relating the width of a rectangle to the length of a rectangle. Find the length of a rectangle on Margo's Web page that has a width of 250 pixels.

Width (pixels)	Length (pixels)
30	90
40	120
50	150
60	180

19. **What's the Error?** Margo predicted that the length of a rectangle with a width of 100 pixels would be 160 pixels. Explain the error she made. Then find the correct length.

20. **Write About It** Explain how to write an equation for the data in the table.

21. **Challenge** Write an equation that would give the same y-values as $y = 3x - 2$ for $x = 1$ and $x = 2$.

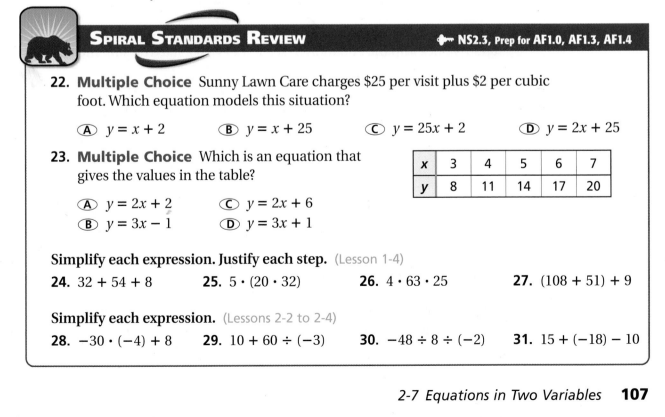

SPIRAL STANDARDS REVIEW ← NS2.3, Prep for AF1.0, AF1.3, AF1.4

22. **Multiple Choice** Sunny Lawn Care charges $25 per visit plus $2 per cubic foot. Which equation models this situation?

    Ⓐ $y = x + 2$ Ⓑ $y = x + 25$ Ⓒ $y = 25x + 2$ Ⓓ $y = 2x + 25$

23. **Multiple Choice** Which is an equation that gives the values in the table?

x	3	4	5	6	7
y	8	11	14	17	20

    Ⓐ $y = 2x + 2$ Ⓒ $y = 2x + 6$
    Ⓑ $y = 3x - 1$ Ⓓ $y = 3x + 1$

Simplify each expression. Justify each step. (Lesson 1-4)

24. $32 + 54 + 8$ 25. $5 \cdot (20 \cdot 32)$ 26. $4 \cdot 63 \cdot 25$ 27. $(108 + 51) + 9$

Simplify each expression. (Lessons 2-2 to 2-4)

28. $-30 \cdot (-4) + 8$ 29. $10 + 60 \div (-3)$ 30. $-48 \div 8 \div (-2)$ 31. $15 + (-18) - 10$

2-8 Graphing Equations

 **California Standards**

AF1.0 Students write verbal expressions and sentences as algebraic expressions and equations; they **evaluate algebraic expressions,** solve simple linear equations, **and graph and interpret their results.**
Also covered: 🔑 **NS2.3**

Vocabulary
linear equation

Why learn this? You can use equations to determine the cost of ordering items online.

Christa is ordering CDs online. Each CD costs $16, and the shipping charge is $6 for the whole order. The total cost y depends on the number of CDs x. This relationship is described by the equation $y = 16x + 6$.

To find solutions of an equation with two variables, first choose a replacement value for one variable and then find the value of the other variable.

EXAMPLE 1 Finding Solutions of Equations with Two Variables

Use the given *x*-values to write solutions of the equation $y = 16x + 6$ as ordered pairs.

Make a table by using the given values for x to find values for y.

x	$16x + 6$	y
1	16(1) + 6	22
2	16(2) + 6	38
3	16(3) + 6	54

(x, y) *Write these solutions as*
$(1, 22)$ *ordered pairs.*
$(2, 38)$
$(3, 54)$

Check if an ordered pair is a solution of an equation by putting the x and y values into the equation to see if they make it a true statement.

EXAMPLE 2 Checking Solutions of Equations with Two Variables

Determine whether each ordered pair is a solution to the given equation.

Ⓐ $(8, 16); y = 2x$

$y = 2x$ *Write the equation.*
$16 \stackrel{?}{=} 2(8)$ *Substitute 8 for x and 16 for y.*
$16 \stackrel{?}{=} 16$ ✔

So $(8, 16)$ is a solution of $y = 2x$.

Ⓑ $(4, 1); y = x - 5$

$y = x - 5$ *Write the equation.*
$1 \stackrel{?}{=} 4 - 5$ *Substitute 4 for x and 1 for y.*
$1 \neq -1$ ✘

So $(4, 1)$ is not a solution of $y = x - 5$.

---

108 *Chapter 2 Integers*

You can also graph the solutions of an equation on a coordinate plane. When you graph the ordered pairs given by some equations, they form a straight line. For this reason, these equations are called **linear equations** .

EXAMPLE 3 **Reading Solutions on Graphs**

Use the graph of the linear equation to find the value of *y* for the given value of *x*.

$x = 1$

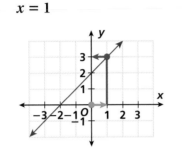

Start at the origin and move 1 unit right. Move up until you reach the graph. Move left to find the y-value on the y-axis.

When $x = 1$, $y = 3$. The ordered pair is (1, 3).

EXAMPLE 4 **Graphing Linear Equations**

Graph the equation *y* = 2*x* + 1.

Make a table. Substitute different values for x.

Write the solutions as ordered pairs.

x	2x + 1	y
−1	2(−1) + 1	−1
0	2(0) + 1	1
1	2(1) + 1	3

(x, y)

(−1, −1)

(0, 1)

(1, 3)

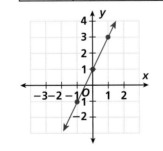

Graph the ordered pairs on a coordinate plane. Draw a line through the points to represent all the values of x you could have chosen and the corresponding values of y.

Think and Discuss

1. Explain why the points in Example 4 are not the only points on the graph. Name two points that you did not plot.

2. Tell whether the equation $y = 10x - 5$ is a linear equation.

2-8 **Exercises**

California Standards Practice
NS2.3, AF1.0

go.hrw.com
Homework Help Online
KEYWORD: MS8CA 2-8
Parent Resources Online
KEYWORD: MS8CA Parent

GUIDED PRACTICE

See Example **1** Use the given x-values to write solutions of each equation as ordered pairs.

1. $y = 6x + 2$ for $x = 1, 2, 3, 4$ **2.** $y = -2x$ for $x = 1, 2, 3, 4$

See Example **2** Determine whether each ordered pair is a solution to the given equation.

3. $(2, 12)$; $y = 4x$ **4.** $(5, 9)$; $y = 2x - 1$

See Example **3** Use the graph of the linear equation to find the value of y for each given value of x.

5. $x = 1$ **6.** $x = 0$ **7.** $x = -1$

See Example **4** Graph each equation.

8. $y = x + 3$ **9.** $y = 3x - 1$ **10.** $y = -2x + 3$

INDEPENDENT PRACTICE

See Example **1** Use the given x-values to write solutions of each equation as ordered pairs.

11. $y = -4x + 1$ for $x = 1, 2, 3, 4$ **12.** $y = 5x - 5$ for $x = 1, 2, 3, 4$

See Example **2** Determine whether each ordered pair is a solution to the given equation.

13. $(3, -10)$; $y = -6x + 8$ **14.** $(-8, 1)$; $y = 7x - 15$

See Example **3** Use the graph of the linear equation to find the value of y for each given value of x.

15. $x = -2$ **16.** $x = 1$ **17.** $x = -3$

18. $x = 0$ **19.** $x = -1$ **20.** $x = 2$

See Example **4** Graph each equation.

21. $y = 4x + 1$ **22.** $y = -x - 2$ **23.** $y = x - 2$

24. $y = -2x - 4$ **25.** $y = 3x - 2$ **26.** $y = -x$

PRACTICE AND PROBLEM SOLVING

Extra Practice
See page EP5.

Complete each table, and then use the table to graph the equation.

27. $y = x - 2$

x	−1	0	1	2
y				

28. $y = 2x - 4$

x	−1	0	1	2
y				

29. Which of the ordered pairs below is not a solution of $y = 4x + 9$?

$(1, 14)$, $(0, 9)$, $(-1, 5)$, $(-2, 1)$, $(2, 17)$

Temperature can be expressed according to different scales. The Kelvin scale is divided into units called kelvins, and the Celsius scale is divided into degrees Celsius.

The table shows several temperatures recorded in degrees Celsius and their equivalent measures in kelvins.

30. Write an equation in two variables that gives the values in the table. Define the variables that you use.

31. Graph your equation.

32. **Reasoning** Use your graph to find the value of y when x is 0.

Equivalent Temperatures	
Celsius (°C)	Kelvin (K)
−100	173
−50	223
0	273
50	323
100	373

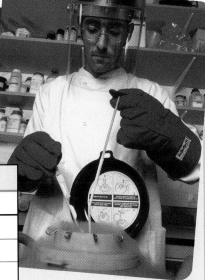

A technician preserves brain cells in this tank of liquid nitrogen, which is at −196°C, for later research.

33. Use your equation to find the equivalent Kelvin temperature for –54°C.

34. Use your equation to find the equivalent Celsius temperature for 77 kelvins.

go.hrw.com
Web Extra!
KEYWORD: MS8CA Temp

35. **What's the Question?** The answer is −273°C. What is the question?

36. **Write About It** Explain how to use your equation to determine whether 75°C is equivalent to 345 kelvins. Then determine whether the temperatures are equivalent.

37. **Challenge** How many ordered-pair solutions exist for the equation you wrote in Exercise 30?

SPIRAL STANDARDS REVIEW
NS2.3, AF1.0, AF1.1

38. **Multiple Choice** Which of the ordered pairs is NOT a solution of $y = -5x + 10$?

   (A) $(-20, 6)$ (B) $(5, -15)$ (C) $(4, -10)$ (D) $(2, 0)$

39. **Multiple Choice** The equation $y = 12x$ shows the number of inches y in x feet. Which ordered pair is on the graph of the equation?

   (A) $(-2, 24)$ (B) $(1, 13)$ (C) $(4, 48)$ (D) $(12, 1)$

40. Komali hiked from an elevation of 420 feet to an elevation of −26 feet. What was Komali's change in elevation? (Lesson 2-3)

Solve each equation. Check your answers. (Lesson 2-5)

41. $\left(\dfrac{y}{-10}\right) = 12$ 42. $p + 25 = -4$ 43. $j - 3 = -15$ 44. $5m = -20$

Explore Linear and Nonlinear Relationships

Use with Lesson 2-8

go.hrw.com
Lab Resources Online
KEYWORD: MS8CA Lab2

You can learn about linear and nonlinear relationships by looking at patterns.

California Standards

Extension of AF1.0 Students write verbal expressions and sentences as algebraic expressions and equations; they evaluate algebraic expressions, solve simple linear equations, and **graph and interpret their results.**

Activity

1 This model shows stage 1 to stage 3 of a pattern.

  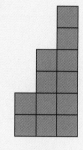

Stage 1   Stage 2   Stage 3

a. Use square tiles or graph paper to model stages 4, 5, and 6.

b. Record each stage and the perimeter of each figure in a table.

c. Graph the ordered pairs (x, y) from the table on a coordinate plane.

Stage (x)	Perimeter (y)
1	6
2	12
3	18
4	24
5	30
6	36

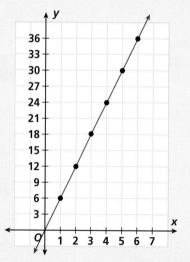

If you connected the points you graphed, you would draw a straight line. This shows that the relationship between the stage and the perimeter of the figure is linear. The equation for this line is $y = 6x$.

2 This table shows several ordered pairs in a relationship.

x	y
1	1
4	2
9	3
16	4
25	5
36	6

a. Describe the relationship between the *x*-values and
   y-values in the table.

b. Graph the ordered pairs (*x*, *y*) from the table on a
   coordinate plane.

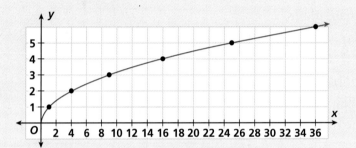

If you connect the graphed points, you draw a curve. This shows
that the relationship is nonlinear because the points do not lie
on a straight line.

Think and Discuss

1. Explain what pattern you see in the *y*-values of the ordered pairs
from the graph above.

Try This

**Use the *x*-values 1, 2, 3, and 4 to find ordered pairs for each equation.
Then graph the equation. Tell whether the relationship between *x* and *y*
is linear or nonlinear.**

1. $y = 2 + x$ **2.** $y = 4x$ **3.** $y = x^3$

4. $y = x + 4$ **5.** $y = x(2 + x)$ **6.** $y = x + x$

7. $y = 2x$ **8.** $y = x^2$ **9.** $y = 3 + 2x$

READY TO GO ON?

Quiz for Lessons 2-6 Through 2-8

 2-6 **The Coordinate Plane**

Use the coordinate plane for problems 1–8.

Name the quadrant where each point is located.

1. A **2.** Y **3.** J **4.** C

Give the coordinates of each point.

5. H **6.** I **7.** W **8.** B

Graph each point on a coordinate plane.

9. $N(-5, -2)$ **10.** $S(0, 4)$ **11.** $R(-2, 6)$ **12.** $M(2, 2)$

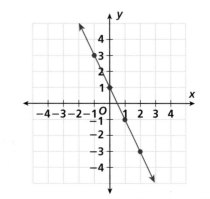

2-7 **Equations in Two Variables**

Write an equation in two variables that gives the values in each table. Use your equation to find the value of y for each indicated value of x.

13.

x	2	3	4	5	8
y	7	8	9	10	▨

14.

x	1	4	5	6	8
y	▨	16	20	24	32

For problems 15 and 16, write an equation for the relationship. Tell what each variable you use represents.

15. The number of plates is 5 less than 3 times the number of cups.

16. The time Rodney spends running is 10 minutes more than twice the time he spends stretching.

2-8 **Graphing Equations**

Use the given x-values to write solutions of each equation as ordered pairs.

17. $y = 4x + 6$ for $x = 1, 2, 3, 4$ **18.** $y = 10x - 7$ for $x = 2, 3, 4, 5$

Use the graph of the linear equation at right to find the value of y for each given value of x.

19. $x = 3$ **20.** $x = 0$

21. $x = -1$ **22.** $x = -2$

Graph each equation.

23. $y = x + 5$ **24.** $y = 3x + 2$ **25.** $y = -2x$

CONCEPT CONNECTION

It's All Mine Underground mines make it possible to reach coal deposits deep beneath the earth. The headframe is the only part of the mine that is visible above the ground. It contains the machinery that lowers miners into the shaft and carries the coal back to the surface. The diagram shows a typical mining operation.

1. What is the total distance the coal travels as it goes from level C to the top of the headframe?

2. How far do miners travel in the elevator as they descend from level A to level B? from level B to level C?

3. A miner takes an elevator from Level C to Level A. How many feet does the miner rise?

4. A new level is added to the mine. It is three times as deep as level A. What is the depth of the new level? Where is it located in relation to the other levels?

5. In 3 hours, each miner produces 18 tons of coal. In 5 hours, each miner produces 30 tons of coal. In 8 hours, each miner produces 48 tons of coal. Make a table and write an equation for the relationship.

6. Use your equation to find the number of tons of coal that each miner produces in a 40-hour work week.

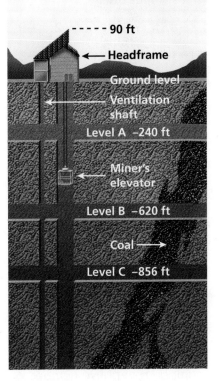

90 ft
← Headframe
Ground level
Ventilation shaft
Level A –240 ft
Miner's elevator
Level B –620 ft
Coal →
Level C –856 ft

Game Time

A Math Riddle

What coin doubles in value when half is subtracted?

To find the answer, graph each set of points. Connect each pair of points with a straight line.

1. $(-8, 3) (-6, 3)$ **2.** $(-9, 1) (-7, 5)$ **3.** $(-7, 5) (-5, 1)$ **4.** $(-3, 1) (-3, 5)$

5. $(-1, 1) (-1, 5)$ **6.** $(-3, 3) (-1, 3)$ **7.** $(1, 1) (3, 5)$ **8.** $(3, 5) (5, 1)$

9. $(2, 3) (4, 3)$ **10.** $(6, 1) (6, 5)$ **11.** $(6, 1) (8, 1)$ **12.** $(9, 1) (9, 5)$

13. $(9, 5) (11, 5)$ **14.** $(9, 3) (11, 3)$ **15.** $(-9, -5) (-9, -1)$ **16.** $(-9, -1) (-7, -3)$

17. $(-7, -3) (-9, -5)$ **18.** $(-6, -1) (-6, -5)$ **19.** $(-6, -5) (-4, -5)$ **20.** $(-4, -5) (-4, -1)$

21. $(-4, -1) (-6, -1)$ **22.** $(-3, -1) (-3, -5)$ **23.** $(-3, -5) (-1, -5)$ **24.** $(1, -1) (1, -5)$

25. $(1, -5) (3, -5)$ **26.** $(4, -5) (6, -1)$ **27.** $(6, -1) (8, -5)$ **28.** $(5, -3) (7, -3)$

29. $(9, -5) (9, -1)$ **30.** $(9, -1) (11, -3)$ **31.** $(11, -3) (9, -3)$ **32.** $(9, -3) (11, -5)$

Zero Sum

Each card contains either a positive number, a negative number, or 0. The dealer deals three cards to each player. On your turn, you may exchange one or two of your cards for new ones, or you may keep your three original cards. After everyone has had a turn, the player whose sum is closest to 0 wins the round and receives everyone's cards. The dealer deals a new round and the game continues until the dealer runs out of cards. The winner is the player with the most cards at the end of the game.

go.hrw.com
Game Time Extra
KEYWORD: MS8CA Games

A complete copy of the rules and game pieces are available online.

Materials
- business-size envelope
- ruler
- scissors
- tape
- hole punch
- chenille stem
- adding-machine tape

PROJECT Positive-Negative Pull-Out

Pull questions and answers out of the bag to check your knowledge of integers.

Directions

❶ Seal the envelope. Then cut it in half.

❷ Hold the envelope with the opening at the top. Lightly draw lines $\frac{3}{4}$ inch from the bottom and from each side. Fold the envelope back and forth along these lines until the envelope is flexible and easy to work with. **Figure A**

❸ Put your hand into the envelope and push out the sides and bottom to form a bag. There will be two triangular points at the bottom of the bag. Tape these to the bottom so that the bag sits flat. **Figure B**

❹ Make a 2-inch slit on the front of the bag about an inch from the bottom. Punch two holes at the top of each side of the bag and insert half of a chenille stem to make handles. **Figure C**

Taking Note of the Math

Starting at the end of the adding-machine tape, write a question about integers, and then write the answer. After you have written several questions and answers, roll up the tape, place it in the bag, and pull the end through the slit.

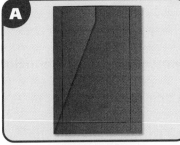
A

B

C

Study Guide: Review

Vocabulary

absolute value 71

additive inverse 94

axes 100

coordinate plane 100

coordinates 100

integer 70

linear equation 108

opposite 70

origin 100

quadrants 100

x-axis 100

x-coordinate 100

y-axis 100

y-coordinate 100

Complete the sentences below with vocabulary words from the list above.

1. In the ordered pair (7, 5), 7 is the ___?___ and 5 is the ___?___.

2. The axes separate the ___?___ into four ___?___.

2-1 Introduction to Integers (pp. 70–73)

Prep for NS1.1

EXAMPLE

■ Use a number line to order the integers from least to greatest.

3, 4, −2, 1, −3

−3, −2, 1, 3, 4

EXERCISES

Compare the integers. Use < or >.

3. −8 ▨ −15   **4.** −7 ▨ 7

5. −10 ▨ −4   **6.** 4 ▨ −8

Use a number line to order the integers from least to greatest.

7. −6, 4, 0, −2, 5   **8.** 8, −3, 2, −8, 1

Use a number line to find each absolute value.

9. $|0|$ **10.** $|−17|$ **11.** $|6|$

2-2 Adding Integers (pp. 76–79)

NS2.3, AF1.2

EXAMPLE

■ Find the sum.

−7 + (−11)

−7 + (−11)   *The signs are the same.*

−18

EXERCISES

Find each sum.

12. −8 + 5   **13.** 7 + (−6)

14. −16 + (−40)   **15.** −9 + 18

16. −2 + 16   **17.** 12 + (−18)

18. 24 + (−13)   **19.** −47 + 62

2-3 Subtracting Integers (pp. 82–85)

 NS2.3, AF1.2

EXAMPLES

Find each difference.

- $-5 - (-3)$
  $-5 + 3$ *Add the opposite of −3.*
  -2

- $12 - 15$
  $12 + (-15)$ *Add the opposite of 15.*
  -3

- Evaluate $a - b$ for $a = -8$ and $b = 9$.
  $a - b$
  $-8 - 9$ *Substitute.*
  $-8 + (-9)$ *Add the opposite.*
  -17

EXERCISES

Find each difference.

20. $8 - 2$ **21.** $10 - 19$

22. $-6 - (-5)$ **23.** $-5 - 4$

24. $-27 - 15$ **25.** $18 - (-6)$

26. $-30 - (-8)$ **27.** $7 - 12$

28. $-18 - 20$ **29.** $9 - (-14)$

Evaluate $a - b$ for each set of values.

30. $a = -6, b = 10$ **31.** $a = 17, b = 21$

32. $a = 4, b = -2$ **33.** $a = -9, b = -8$

34. $a = -1, b = 1$ **35.** $a = 8, b = -3$

2-4 Multiplying and Dividing Integers (pp. 88–91)

NS2.3, AF1.4

EXAMPLES

Find each product or quotient.

- $12 \cdot (-3)$ *The signs are different, so*
  -36 *the product is negative.*

- $-16 \div (-4)$ *The signs are the same, so*
  4 *the quotient is positive.*

- $48 \div (-8)$ *The signs are different, so*
  -6 *the quotient is negative.*

EXERCISES

Find each product or quotient.

36. $5 \cdot (-10)$ **37.** $-27 \div (-9)$

38. $-2 \cdot (-8)$ **39.** $-40 \div 20$

40. $-3 \cdot 4$ **41.** $45 \div (-15)$

42. $12 \cdot (-8)$ **43.** $24 \div (-6)$

44. $-10 \cdot (-7)$ **45.** $-48 \div (-3)$

46. $-14 \cdot 5$ **47.** $-84 \div 4$

2-5 Solving Equations Containing Integers (pp. 94–97)

NS2.3, AF1.1

EXAMPLES

Solve.

- $n + 8 = -10$
  $\underline{+(-8) \quad +(-8)}$ *Add −8 to both sides.*
  $n = -18$

- $x - 12 = 4$
  $\underline{+12 \quad +12}$ *Add 12 to both sides.*
  $x = 16$

- $-10 = -2f$
  $\dfrac{-10}{-2} = \dfrac{-2f}{-2}$ *Divide both sides by −2.*
  $5 = f$

EXERCISES

Solve.

48. $7y = 70$ **49.** $d - 8 = 6$

50. $j + 23 = -3$ **51.** $\dfrac{n}{36} = 2$

52. $-26 = -2c$ **53.** $28 = -7m$

54. $-15 = \dfrac{y}{7}$ **55.** $g - 12 = -31$

56. $-13 + p = 8$ **57.** $-8 + f = 8$

58. $n + 12 = -5$ **59.** $-5x = 60$

60. $\dfrac{b}{4} = -1$ **61.** $d - 16 = -48$

62. $-7 + c = 15$ **63.** $y - (-3) = 10$

2-6 The Coordinate Plane (pp. 100–103)

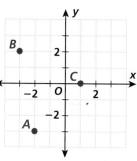

EXAMPLE

- **Give the coordinates of A and name the quadrant where it is located.**

  A is in the fourth quadrant. Its coordinates are $(2, -3)$.

EXERCISES

Give the coordinates of each point.

64. A **65.** C

Name the quadrant where each point is located.

66. A **67.** B

2-7 Equations in Two Variables (pp. 104–107)

EXAMPLE

- **Write an equation in two variables that gives the values in the table. Use your equation to find the value of y for the indicated value of x.**

x	2	3	4	5	6	12
y	6	9	12	15	18	

y is 3 times x.   *Find a pattern.*

$y = 3x$ *Write an equation.*

$y = 3(12)$ *Substitute 12 for x.*

$y = 36$

EXERCISES

Write an equation in two variables that gives the values in each table. Use your equation to find the value of y for each indicated value of x.

68.

x	2	3	4	5	6	8
y	8	9	10	11	12	

Write an equation to describe the relationship. Tell what each variable you use represents.

69. The length of a rectangle is 4 times its width.

70. A mother's age is 27 years more than her daughter's age.

2-8 Graphing Equations (pp. 108–111)

EXAMPLE

- **Graph the equation $y = 3x + 4$.**

  Make a table.   *Write as ordered pairs.*

x	3x + 4	y
−2	3(−2) + 4	−2
−1	3(−1) + 4	1
0	3(0) + 4	4

(x, y)

$(-2, -2)$

$(-1, 1)$

$(0, 4)$

Graph the ordered pairs on a coordinate plane.

EXERCISES

Use the given x-values to write solutions of each equation as ordered pairs.

71. $y = 2x - 5$ for $x = 1, 2, 3, 4$

72. $y = x + 7$ for $x = 1, 2, 3, 4$

Determine whether each ordered pair is a solution to the given equation.

73. $(3, 12)$; $y = 5x - 3$ **74.** $(6, 14)$; $y = x + 7$

Use a number line to order the integers from least to greatest.

1. $-4, 3, -2, 0, 1$

2. $7, -6, 5, -8, -3$

Use a number line to find each absolute value.

3. $|11|$

4. $|-5|$

5. $|-74|$

6. $|-1|$

Find each sum, difference, product, or quotient.

7. $-7 + (-3)$

8. $-6 - 3$

9. $17 - (-9) - 8$

10. $102 + (-97) + 3$

11. $-3 \cdot 20$

12. $-36 \div 12$

13. $-400 \div (-10)$

14. $-5 \cdot (-2) \cdot 9$

15. On Monday, the high temperature was $14°F$ and the low temperature was $-6°F$. What was the difference between the high and low temperatures?

16. Mr. Ellis owns 54 shares of stock in a sporting goods company. The price of the stock decreased by \$2 per share. What was the total change in the value of Mr. Ellis's stock?

Solve.

17. $w - 4 = -6$

18. $x + 5 = -5$

19. $-6a = 60$

20. $\dfrac{n}{-4} = 12$

21. Kathryn's tennis team has won 52 matches. Her team has won 9 more matches than Rebecca's team. How many matches has Rebecca's team won this season?

Graph each point on a coordinate plane.

22. $A(2, 3)$

23. $B(3, -2)$

24. $C(-1, 3)$

25. $D\left(-1, 2\tfrac{1}{2}\right)$

26. $E(0, 1)$

Write an equation in two variables that gives the values in each table. Use your equation to find the value of y for each indicated value of x.

27.

x	2	3	4	5	6	7
y		8	9	10	11	12

28.

x	1	2	3	4	5	9
y	8	16	24	32	40	

Write an equation for the relationship. Tell what each variable you use represents.

29. The number of buttons on the jacket is 4 more than the number of zippers.

30. The length of a parallelogram is 2 in. more than twice the height.

Use the given x-values to write solutions of each equation as ordered pairs. Then graph each equation.

31. $y = 5x - 3$ for $x = 1, 2, 3, 4$

32. $y = 2x - 3$ for $x = 0, 1, 2, 3$

Cumulative Assessment, Chapters 1–2

Multiple Choice

1. Which is an algebraic expression for the product of 15 and x?

   Ⓐ $15 - x$ Ⓒ $x + 15$

   Ⓑ $15x$ Ⓓ $15 \div x$

2. Zane biked 23 miles this week. This is 8 miles more than he biked the week before. Solve the equation $x + 8 = 23$ to find how many miles Zane biked last week.

   Ⓐ 15 miles   Ⓒ 31 miles

   Ⓑ 23 miles   Ⓓ 33 miles

3. For which equation is $x = -10$ the solution?

   Ⓐ $x - 4 = -6$

   Ⓑ $x - 8 = 2$

   Ⓒ $x + (-7) = 3$

   Ⓓ $x + 18 = 8$

4. Which expression is equivalent to $5 + (8 + 17)$?

   Ⓐ $5(8 + 17)$

   Ⓑ $5 - (8 - 17)$

   Ⓒ $8 + (5 + 17)$

   Ⓓ $(5 + 8) + (5 + 17)$

5. What is the value of the expression $35 - 4^3 \div 8$?

   Ⓐ 3   Ⓒ 21

   Ⓑ 9   Ⓓ 27

6. Which problem situation matches the equation below?

   $$x + 55 = 92$$

   Ⓐ Liam has 55 tiles but needs a total of 92 to complete a project. How many more tiles does Liam need?

   Ⓑ Cher spent $55 at the market and has only $92 left. How much did Cher start with?

   Ⓒ Byron drove 55 miles each day for 92 days. How many total miles did he drive?

   Ⓓ For every 55 students who buy "spirit wear," the boosters donate $92. How many students have bought spirit wear so far?

7. Yancy buys 3 shirts for $15 each and 2 pairs of shorts for $19 each. Which expression can be used to determine the total cost of Yancy's purchases?

   Ⓐ $3 + 15 \cdot 2 + 19$

   Ⓑ $3 \cdot 15 + 2 \cdot 19$

   Ⓒ $(3 + 2) \cdot (15 + 19)$

   Ⓓ $(3 + 15) \cdot (2 + 19)$

8. Ryan's score in a round of golf was +6 strokes. Akashi's score was 9 strokes less than Ryan's score. What was Akashi's score?

   Ⓐ -15 Ⓒ 3

   Ⓑ -3 Ⓓ 15

9. Nicole is 15 years old. She is 3 years younger than her sister Jan. Solve the equation $j - 3 = 15$ to find Jan's age.

Ⓐ 18 years   Ⓒ 12 years

Ⓑ 17 years   Ⓓ 5 years

10. Reggie saved $587 in one year. He used $211 of his savings to buy a used saxophone. Which equation can be used to find s, the amount of savings Reggie has left?

Ⓐ $s + 211 = 587$

Ⓑ $s - 211 = 587$

Ⓒ $s + 587 = 211$

Ⓓ $s - 587 = 211$

11. Which expression has a value of -12?

Ⓐ $5 + 2^3 - 18$

Ⓑ $-4 + 2 \cdot 4$

Ⓒ $(-2 + 6) \cdot (-3)$

Ⓓ $(7 - 9) \cdot (-6)$

12. Which operation should you perform first when simplifying the expression $(4 \cdot 4 - 6)^2 \cdot 5 - 1$?

Ⓐ Multiply 4 by 4.

Ⓑ Subtract 6 from 4.

Ⓒ Square 6.

Ⓓ Subtract 1 from 5.

 Substitute the values given in the answers into an equation to see which value makes the equation true.

Gridded Response

13. What is the value of $5^2 - (18 \div 6) \times 7$?

14. What is the value of the expression $5n - p^2 + 6q$ for $n = 12$, $p = 3$, and $q = 4$?

15. What is the solution to the equation $8a = 48$?

Short Response

16. Every week Brandi runs 7 more miles than her sister Jamie.

a. Write an expression for the number of miles that Brandi runs each week. Identify the variable.

b. Evaluate your expression to find the number of miles Brandi runs when Jamie runs 5 miles.

17. A vacation tour costs $450. Additional outings cost $25 each. The table shows the total cost to go on additional outings.

Outings	1	2	3	n
Total Cost ($)	475	500	525	

Write an expression for the cost of n outings. Use the expression to find how much it costs to go on 5 outings.

Extended Response

18. Chrissy and Kathie are sisters. Chrissy was born on Kathie's birthday and is exactly 8 years younger. Chrissy celebrated her 16th birthday on December 8, 2005.

a. Complete the table to show the ages of the sisters in the years 2005, 2008, and 2011.

Year	Kathie's Age	Chrissy's Age
2005		
2008		
2011		

b. Write an equation that could be used to find Kathie's age in 2011. Identify the variable in the equation.

c. Solve the equation. Show your work. Compare your answer to the value in the table. Are the two solutions the same? Explain your answer.

Number Theory and Fractions

CONCEPT CONNECTION

go.hrw.com
Chapter Project Online
KEYWORD: MS8CA Ch3

Fields on flower farms are often divided into sections. Farmers can use number theory to determine the number of rows they will need for each section.

Flower farm,
Lompoc, California

ARE YOU READY?

✓ Vocabulary

Choose the best term from the list to complete each sentence.

1. To find the sum of two numbers, you should ___?___.

2. Fractions are written as a ___?___ over a ___?___.

3. In the equation $4 \cdot 3 = 12$, 12 is the ___?___.

4. The ___?___ of 18 and 10 is 8.

5. The numbers 18, 27, and 72 are ___?___ of 9.

add
denominator
difference
multiples
numerator
product
quotient

Complete these exercises to review skills you will need for this chapter.

✓ Write and Read Decimals

Write each decimal in word form.

6. 0.5   7. 2.78   8. 0.125

9. 12.8   10. 125.49   11. 8.024

✓ Multiples

List the first four multiples of each number.

12. 6   13. 8   14. 5   15. 12

16. 7   17. 20   18. 14   19. 9

✓ Factors

Find all the whole-number factors of each number.

20. 8   21. 12   22. 24   23. 30

24. 45   25. 52   26. 75   27. 150

✓ Locate Points on a Number Line

Name the point on the number line that corresponds to each given value.

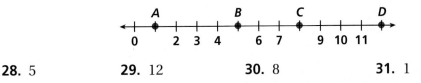

28. 5   29. 12   30. 8   31. 1

Unpacking the Standards

The information below "unpacks" the standards. The Academic Vocabulary is highlighted and defined to help you understand the language of the standards. Refer to the lessons listed after each standard for help with the math terms and phrases. The Chapter Concept shows how the standard is applied in this chapter.

California Standard	Academic Vocabulary	Chapter Concept
NS1.1 Compare and order positive and negative fractions, decimals, and mixed numbers and place them on a number line. (Lesson 3-6)	**compare** tell whether a number is less than, greater than, or equal to another number *Example:* 2 is less than 6. **order** arrange a set of numbers from least to greatest value or from greatest to least value *Example:* The numbers 24, 32, −6, and 0 in order from least to greatest are −6, 0, 24, and 32.	You compare numbers by deciding which number has the greater or lesser value. You can do this by placing the numbers on a number line. The number that is farther to the left on a number line is the lesser value. ***Examples:*** $\frac{1}{2} < \frac{3}{4}$ $-0.4 > -0.6$ You order fractions, decimals, and mixed numbers from least to greatest. ***Example:*** $-\frac{3}{4} < -0.5 < \frac{1}{2} < 1\frac{3}{4}$
NS2.4: Determine the least common multiple and the greatest common divisor of whole numbers; use them to solve problems with fractions (e.g., to find a common denominator to add two fractions or to find the reduced form for a fraction). (Lessons 3-2 to 3-6)	**common** a characteristic shared by two or more numbers or objects **multiple** the product of a number and any nonzero whole number *Example:* 8 is a multiple of 2 because 2 · 4 = 8. **divisor** the number you are dividing by in a division problem; in this case, a whole number that can be divided into another number without leaving a remainder *Example:* 4 is a divisor of 8 because 8 ÷ 4 = 2. **e.g.** abbreviation that stands for the Latin phrase *exempli gratia,* which means "for example"	You find the least common multiple of two numbers. ***Example:*** The multiples of 3 are 3, 6, 9, 12, **15**, 18, 21, 24, 27, **30**, …. The multiples of 5 are 5, 10, **15**, 20, 25, **30**, 35, …. **15** is the least common multiple of 3 and 5. You find the greatest common divisor of two numbers. ***Example:*** The divisors of 18 are **1**, **2**, **3**, **6**, 9, and 18. The divisors of 24 are **1**, **2**, **3**, 4, **6**, 8, 12, and 24. **6** is the greatest common divisor of 18 and 24.

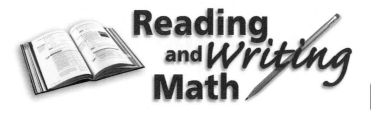

Reading and Writing Math

California Standards

English-Language Arts
Writing 6.2.2

Writing Strategy:
Write a Persuasive Argument

A persuasive argument or explanation should include the following:

• The problem restated in your own words

• A short response

• Reasoning to support the response

• A summary statement

Example

Tell whether you can reverse the order of integers when subtracting and still get the same answer. Why or why not?

Step 1 **Identify the goal.**

Determine whether reversing the order of integers when subtracting affects the answer, and explain why or why not.

Step 2 **Provide a short response.**

You cannot reverse the order of integers when subtracting and still get the same answer. Subtraction is not commutative.

Step 3 **Provide reasoning or an example to support your response.**

$-7 - (-3) = -7 + 3 = -4$ *Subtract two integers as an example.*

$-3 - (-7) = -3 + 7 = 4$ *Then reverse the order of the integers and subtract.*

The example shows that you do not necessarily get the same answer if you reverse the order of integers when subtracting.

Step 4 **Summarize your argument.**

When subtracting integers, the order of the integers is important. Changing the order will usually change the answer.

Try This

Write a persuasive argument by using the method above.

1. Tell whether you can reverse the order of integers when multiplying and still get the same answer. Why or why not?

2. If you subtract a positive integer from a negative integer, will your answer be greater than or less than the negative integer? Explain.

Prime Factorization

California Standards

Preparation for ◄— NS2.4
Determine the least common multiple and the greatest common divisor of whole numbers; use them to solve problems with fractions (e.g., to find a common denominator to add two fractions or to find the reduced form for a fraction).

Who uses this? Computer programmers use large prime numbers to develop safe methods of sending information over the Internet.

Nayan Hajratwala received a $50,000 award for discovering a prime number with more than one million digits.

Vocabulary
prime number
composite number
prime factorization

A **prime number** is a whole number greater than 1 that has exactly two positive factors, 1 and itself. Three is a prime number because its only positive factors are 1 and 3.

A **composite number** is a whole number that has more than two positive factors. Six is a composite number because it has more than two positive factors—1, 2, 3, and 6. The number 1 has exactly one positive factor and is neither prime nor composite.

EXAMPLE 1 **Identifying Prime and Composite Numbers**

Tell whether each number is prime or composite.

A 19
  The positive factors of 19 are 1 and 19.
  So 19 is prime.

B 20
  The positive factors of 20 are 1, 2, 4, 5, 10, and 20.
  So 20 is composite.

A composite number can be written as the product of its prime factors. This is called the **prime factorization** of the number. You can use a factor tree to find the prime factors of a composite number.

EXAMPLE 2 **Using a Factor Tree to Find Prime Factorization**

Write the prime factorization of each number.

Writing Math

You can write prime factorizations by using exponents. The exponent tells how many times to use the base as a factor.

A 36

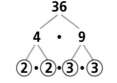

Write 36 as the product of two positive factors.

Continue factoring until all factors are prime.

The prime factorization of 36 is $2 \cdot 2 \cdot 3 \cdot 3$, or $2^2 \cdot 3^2$.

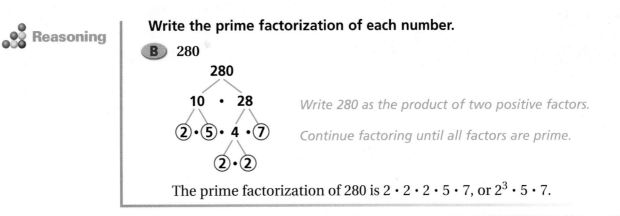

Reasoning

Write the prime factorization of each number.

B 280

$$280$$
$$10 \cdot 28$$
$$②\cdot⑤\cdot 4 \cdot ⑦$$
$$②\cdot②$$

Write 280 as the product of two positive factors.

Continue factoring until all factors are prime.

The prime factorization of 280 is $2 \cdot 2 \cdot 2 \cdot 5 \cdot 7$, or $2^3 \cdot 5 \cdot 7$.

You can also use a step diagram to find the prime factorization of a number. At each step, divide by a prime factor. Continue dividing until the quotient is 1.

EXAMPLE 3 Using a Step Diagram to Find Prime Factorization

Reasoning

Write the prime factorization of each number.

A 252

```
2 | 252
  2 | 126
    3 | 63
      3 | 21
        7 | 7
            1
```

Divide 252 by 2. Write the quotient below 252. Keep dividing by a prime factor.

Stop when the quotient is 1.

The prime factorization of 252 is $2 \cdot 2 \cdot 3 \cdot 3 \cdot 7$, or $2^2 \cdot 3^2 \cdot 7$.

B 495

```
3 | 495
  3 | 165
    5 | 55
     11 | 11
            1
```

Divide 495 by 3. Keep dividing by a prime factor.

Stop when the quotient is 1.

The prime factorization of 495 is $3 \cdot 3 \cdot 5 \cdot 11$, or $3^2 \cdot 5 \cdot 11$.

There is only one prime factorization for any given composite number. Example 3B began by dividing 495 by 3, the smallest prime factor of 495. Beginning with any prime factor of 495 gives the same result.

```
5 | 495        11 | 495
  3 | 99          3 | 45
    3 | 33          5 | 15
     11 | 11          3 | 3
            1              1
```

Think and Discuss

1. Explain how to decide whether 47 is prime.

2. Compare prime numbers and composite numbers.

California Standards Practice
Preparation for ➤ NS2.4

GUIDED PRACTICE

See Example **1** Tell whether each number is prime or composite.

1. 7 **2.** 15 **3.** 49 **4.** 12

See Example **2** Write the prime factorization of each number.

5. 16 **6.** 54 **7.** 81 **8.** 105

16
4 · 4
? · ? · ? · ?

54
6 · 9
? · ? · ? · ?

81
9 · ?
? · ? · ? · ?

105
5 · ?
? · ? · ?

9. 18 **10.** 26 **11.** 45 **12.** 80

See Example **3** **13.** 250 **14.** 190 **15.** 100 **16.** 360

17. 639 **18.** 414 **19.** 1,000 **20.** 140

INDEPENDENT PRACTICE

See Example **1** Tell whether each number is prime or composite.

21. 31 **22.** 18 **23.** 67 **24.** 8

25. 77 **26.** 5 **27.** 9 **28.** 113

See Example **2** Write the prime factorization of each number.

29. 68 **30.** 75 **31.** 120 **32.** 150

33. 135 **34.** 48 **35.** 154 **36.** 210

37. 800 **38.** 310 **39.** 625 **40.** 2,000

See Example **3** **41.** 315 **42.** 728 **43.** 189 **44.** 396

45. 242 **46.** 700 **47.** 187 **48.** 884

49. 1,225 **50.** 288 **51.** 360 **52.** 1,152

PRACTICE AND PROBLEM SOLVING

Extra Practice
See page EP6.

Complete the prime factorization for each composite number.

53. $180 = 2^2 \cdot \blacksquare \cdot 5$ **54.** $462 = 2 \cdot 3 \cdot 7 \cdot \blacksquare$ **55.** $1{,}575 = 3^2 \cdot \blacksquare \cdot 7$

56. $117 = 3^2 \cdot \blacksquare$ **57.** $144 = \blacksquare \cdot 3^2$ **58.** $13{,}000 = 2^3 \cdot \blacksquare \cdot 13$

59. Critical Thinking Use three different factor trees to find the prime factors of 30. What is the same about each factor tree? What is different?

60. Critical Thinking If the prime factors of a number are all the prime numbers less than 10 and no factor is repeated, what is the number?

61. Reasoning A number n is a prime factor of 28 and 63. What is the number?

62. A rectangular area on a farm has side lengths that are factors of 308. One of the side lengths is a prime number. Which of the areas in the diagram have the correct dimensions?

Barn
19 ft × 22 ft

Pig pen
14 ft × 22 ft

Sheep pen
11 ft × 28 ft

Garden
4 ft × 77 ft

Chicken coop
7 ft × 44 ft

63. Business Eric is catering a party for 152 people. He wants to seat the same number of people at each table. He also wants more than 2 people but fewer than 10 people at a table. How many people can he seat at each table?

64. Write a Problem Using the information in the table, write a problem using prime factorization that includes the number of calories per serving of the melons.

65. Write About It Describe how to use factor trees to find the prime factorization of a number.

66. Challenge Find the smallest number that is divisible by 2, 3, 4, 5, 6, 7, 8, 9, and 10.

Fruit	Calories per Serving	
Cantaloupe	66	
Watermelon	15	
Honeydew	42	

67. Multiple Choice Which is the prime factorization of 75?

Ⓐ $3^2 \cdot 5$ Ⓑ $3 \cdot 5^2$ Ⓒ $3^2 \cdot 5^2$ Ⓓ $3 \cdot 5^3$

68. Multiple Choice The expression $2 \cdot 3^3 \cdot 5^2$ is the prime factorization of which number?

Ⓐ 84   Ⓑ 180   Ⓒ 450   Ⓓ 1,350

69. Short Response Create two different factor trees for 120. Then write the prime factorization for 120.

Simplify each expression. (Lesson 1-3)

70. $-5 + 2^2 - 2$ **71.** $2^2 \cdot (-3) + 12$ **72.** $4 \cdot 5^2$ **73.** $3 + 2^3 - 12$

Solve each equation. Check your answer. (Lesson 2-5)

74. $3x = -6$ **75.** $y - 4 = -3$ **76.** $z + 4 = 3 - 5$ **77.** $0 = -4x$

Greatest Common Divisor

California Standards

⚷ **NS2.4 Determine** the least common multiple and **the greatest common divisor of whole numbers;** use them to solve problems with fractions (e.g., to find a common denominator to add two fractions or to find the reduced form for a fraction).

Vocabulary
greatest common divisor (GCD)

Who uses this? Party planners can use the greatest common divisor to find the number of matching centerpieces they can make. (See Example 3.)

The **greatest common divisor (GCD)** of two or more whole numbers is the greatest whole number that divides evenly into each number.

One way to find the GCD of two or more numbers is to list all the factors of each number. The GCD is the greatest factor that appears in all the lists.

EXAMPLE 1 **Using a List to Find the GCD**

Find the greatest common divisor (GCD) of 24, 36, and 48.

Factors of 24: 1, 2, 3, 4, 6, 8, ⑫, 24

Factors of 36: 1, 2, 3, 4, 6, 9, ⑫, 18, 36

Factors of 48: 1, 2, 3, 4, 6, 8, ⑫, 16, 24, 48

The GCD is 12.

List all the factors of each number.

Circle the greatest factor that is in all the lists.

A second way to find the GCD is to use prime factorization.

EXAMPLE 2 **Using Prime Factorization to Find the GCD**

Find the greatest common divisor (GCD).

A 60, 45

$60 = 2 \cdot 2 \cdot ③ \cdot ⑤$

$45 = ③ \cdot 3 \cdot ⑤$

$3 \cdot 5 = 15$

The GCD is 15.

Write the prime factorization of each number and circle the common prime factors.

Multiply the common prime factors.

B 504, 132, 96, 60

$504 = ②\cdot②\cdot 2 \cdot ③\cdot 3 \cdot 7$

$132 = ②\cdot②\cdot ③\cdot 11$

$96 = ②\cdot②\cdot 2 \cdot 2 \cdot 2 \cdot ③$

$60 = ②\cdot②\cdot ③\cdot 5$

$2 \cdot 2 \cdot 3 = 12$

The GCD is 12.

Write the prime factorization of each number and circle the common prime factors.

Multiply the common prime factors.

Reading Math

The greatest common divisor (GCD) is also known as the greatest common factor (GCF).

EXAMPLE 3

PROBLEM SOLVING

 Reasoning

PROBLEM SOLVING APPLICATION

Sasha and David are making centerpieces for the Fall Festival. They have 50 small pumpkins and 30 ears of corn. What is the greatest number of matching centerpieces they can make using all of the pumpkins and corn?

1 Understand the Problem

Rewrite the question as a statement.

• Find the greatest number of centerpieces they can make.

List the **important information:**

• There are 50 pumpkins.

• There are 30 ears of corn.

• Each centerpiece must have the same number of pumpkins and the same number of ears of corn.

The **answer** will be the GCD of 50 and 30.

2 Make a Plan

You can write the prime factorizations of 50 and 30 to find the GCD.

3 Solve

$50 = ②\cdot⑤\cdot 5$
$30 = ②\cdot 3 \cdot⑤$ *Multiply the prime factors that are*
$2 \cdot 5 = 10$ *common to both 50 and 30.*

Sasha and David can make 10 centerpieces.

4 Look Back

If Sasha and David make 10 centerpieces, each one will have 5 pumpkins and 3 ears of corn, with nothing left over.

Think and Discuss

1. Tell what the letters GCD stand for and explain what the GCD of two numbers is.

2. Discuss whether the GCD of two numbers could be a prime number.

3. Explain whether every factor of the GCD of two numbers is also a factor of each number. Give an example.

3-2 **Exercises**

California Standards Practice
🔑 NS2.4

go.hrw.com
Homework Help Online
KEYWORD: MS8CA 3-2
Parent Resources Online
KEYWORD: MS8CA Parent

GUIDED PRACTICE

See Example **1** Find the greatest common divisor (GCD).

1. 30, 42   **2.** 36, 45   **3.** 24, 36, 60, 84

See Example **2** **4.** 60, 231   **5.** 12, 28   **6.** 20, 40, 50, 120

See Example **3** **7.** The Math Club members are preparing identical welcome kits for the sixth-graders. They have 60 pencils and 48 memo pads. What is the greatest number of kits they can prepare using all of the pencils and memo pads?

INDEPENDENT PRACTICE

See Example **1** Find the greatest common divisor (GCD).

8. 60, 126   **9.** 12, 36   **10.** 75, 90

11. 22, 121   **12.** 28, 42   **13.** 38, 76

See Example **2** **14.** 28, 60   **15.** 54, 80   **16.** 30, 45, 60, 105

17. 26, 52   **18.** 11, 44, 77   **19.** 18, 27, 36, 48

See Example **3** **20.** Hetty is making identical gift baskets for the Senior Citizens Center. She has 39 small soap bars and 26 small bottles of lotion. What is the greatest number of baskets she can make using all of the soap bars and bottles of lotion?

PRACTICE AND PROBLEM SOLVING

Extra Practice
See page EP6.

Find the greatest common divisor (GCD).

21. 5, 7   **22.** 12, 15   **23.** 4, 6

24. 9, 11   **25.** 22, 44, 66   **26.** 77, 121

27. 80, 120   **28.** 20, 28   **29.** 2, 3, 4, 5, 7

30. 4, 6, 10, 22   **31.** 14, 21, 35, 70   **32.** 6, 10, 11, 14

33. 6, 15, 33, 48   **34.** 18, 45, 63, 81   **35.** 13, 39, 52, 78

36. Critical Thinking Which pair of numbers has a GCD that is a prime number, 48 and 90 or 105 and 56?

37. Museum employees are preparing an exhibit of ancient coins. They have 49 copper coins and 35 silver coins to arrange on shelves. Each shelf will have the same number of copper coins and the same number of silver coins. How many shelves will the employees need for this exhibit?

38. Multi-Step A flower farmer has 480 red tulips and 540 yellow tulips to plant in a field. He wants to plant only one color of tulip per row. What is the greatest number of tulips the farmer can plant in each row if each row has the same number of tulips? How many rows of red tulips and how many rows of yellow tulips will there be?

39. School Some of the students in the Math Club signed up to bring food and drinks to a party.

   a. If each club member gets the same amount of each item at the party, how many students are in the Math Club?

   b. How many carrots, pizza slices, cans of juice, and apples can each club member have at the party?

40. Art A gallery is displaying a collection of 12 sculptures and 20 paintings by local artists. The exhibit is arranged into as many sections as possible so that each section has the same number of sculptures and the same number of paintings. How many sections are in the exhibit?

41. **What's the Error?** A student used these factor trees to find the GCD of 50 and 70. The student decided that the GCD is 5. Explain the student's error and give the correct GCD.

42. Write About It The GCD of 1,274 and 1,365 is 91, or 7 · 13. Are 7, 13, and 91 factors of both 1,274 and 1,365? Explain.

43. Challenge Find three *composite* numbers that have a GCD of 1.

SPIRAL STANDARDS REVIEW   ⬩ NS2.3, ⬩ NS2.4, AF1.2, AF1.3

44. Gridded Response What is the greatest common divisor of 28 and 91?

45. Multiple Choice Which pair of numbers has a greatest common divisor that is NOT a prime number?

   (A) 15, 20   (B) 18, 30   (C) 24, 75   (D) 6, 10

Evaluate $2n + 3$ for each value of n. (Lesson 1-5)

46. $n = 4$ **47.** $n = 9$ **48.** $n = 0$ **49.** $n = -5$

Use a number line to find each sum or difference. (Lessons 2-2 and 2-3)

50. $-5 + (-3)$ **51.** $2 - 7$ **52.** $4 + (-8)$ **53.** $-3 - (-5)$

Find each quotient. (Lesson 2-4)

54. $-63 \div (-7)$ **55.** $8 \div (-4)$ **56.** $-80 \div 4$ **57.** $-81 \div (-9)$

3-3 Least Common Multiple

California Standards

↝ **NS2.4 Determine the least common multiple** and the greatest common divisor **of whole numbers;** use them to solve problems with fractions (e.g., to find a common denominator to add two fractions or to find the reduced form for a fraction).

Vocabulary
multiple
least common
  multiple (LCM)

Who uses this? Drivers can use the least common multiple to determine when they need to service their vehicle.

The tires on Kendra's truck should be rotated every 7,500 miles, and the oil filter should be replaced every 5,000 miles. What is the lowest mileage at which both services are due at the same time? To find the answer, you can use *least common multiples*.

A **multiple** of a number is the product of that number and a nonzero whole number. Some multiples of 7,500 and 5,000 are as follows:

7,500: 7,500, **15,000**, 22,500, **30,000**, 37,500, 45,000, . . .
5,000: 5,000, 10,000, **15,000**, 20,000, 25,000, **30,000**, . . .

A common multiple of two or more numbers is a number that is a multiple of each of the given numbers. So **15,000** and **30,000** are common multiples of 7,500 and 5,000.

The **least common multiple (LCM)** of two or more numbers is the common multiple with the least value. The LCM of 7,500 and 5,000 is **15,000**. This is the lowest mileage at which both services are due at the same time.

EXAMPLE **1** **Using a List to Find the LCM**

Find the least common multiple (LCM).

A 3, 5

Multiples of 3: 3, 6, 9, 12, ⑮, 18   *List multiples of each number.*
Multiples of 5: 5, 10, ⑮, 20, 25   *Find the least value that*
                                            is in both lists.
The LCM is 15.

B 4, 6, 12

Multiples of 4: 4, 8, ⑫, 16, 20, 24, 28   *List multiples of each number.*
Multiples of 6: 6, ⑫, 18, 24, 30   *Find the least value that*
Multiples of 12: ⑫, 24, 36, 48   *is in all the lists.*
The LCM is 12.

Sometimes, listing the multiples of numbers is not the easiest way to find the LCM. For example, the LCM of 78 and 110 is 4,290. You would have to list 55 multiples of 78 and 39 multiples of 110 to reach 4,290!

EXAMPLE 2 Using Prime Factorization to Find the LCM

Find the least common multiple (LCM).

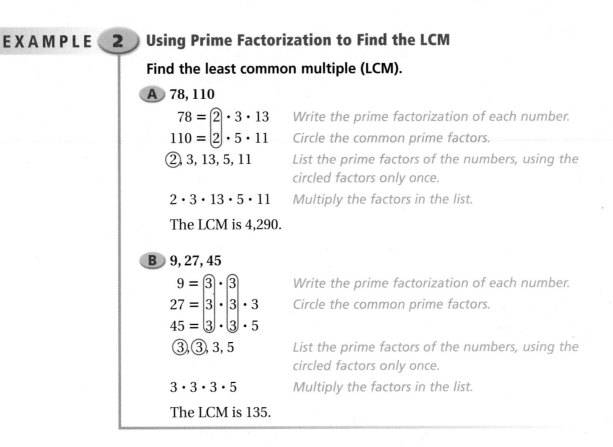

A 78, 110

$78 = ②\cdot 3\cdot 13$ *Write the prime factorization of each number.*
$110 = ②\cdot 5\cdot 11$ *Circle the common prime factors.*

②, 3, 13, 5, 11   *List the prime factors of the numbers, using the circled factors only once.*

$2\cdot 3\cdot 13\cdot 5\cdot 11$ *Multiply the factors in the list.*

The LCM is 4,290.

B 9, 27, 45

$9 = ③\cdot ③$ *Write the prime factorization of each number.*
$27 = ③\cdot ③\cdot 3$ *Circle the common prime factors.*
$45 = ③\cdot ③\cdot 5$

③, ③, 3, 5   *List the prime factors of the numbers, using the circled factors only once.*

$3\cdot 3\cdot 3\cdot 5$ *Multiply the factors in the list.*

The LCM is 135.

EXAMPLE 3 *Recreation Application*

Charla and her little brother are walking laps on a track. Charla walks one lap every 4 minutes, and her brother walks one lap every 6 minutes. They start together. In how many minutes will they be together at the starting line again?

Find the LCM of 4 and 6.

$4 = ②\cdot 2$
$6 = ②\cdot 3$

The LCM is ②$\cdot 2\cdot 3 = 12$.

They will be together at the starting line in 12 minutes.

Think and Discuss

1. Tell what the letters LCM stand for and explain what the LCM of two numbers is.

2. Describe a way to remember the difference between GCD and LCM.

3. List four common multiples of 6 and 9 that are not the LCM.

California Standards Practice
NS2.4

go.hrw.com
Homework Help Online
KEYWORD: MS8CA 3-3
Parent Resources Online
KEYWORD: MS8CA Parent

GUIDED PRACTICE

See Example 1   **Find the least common multiple (LCM).**

1. 4, 7   **2.** 14, 21, 28   **3.** 4, 8, 12, 16

See Example 2   **4.** 30, 48   **5.** 3, 9, 15   **6.** 10, 40, 50

See Example 3   **7.** Jerry and his dad are walking around the track. Jerry completes one lap every 8 minutes. His dad completes one lap every 6 minutes. They start together. In how many minutes will they be together at the starting line again?

INDEPENDENT PRACTICE

See Example 1   **Find the least common multiple (LCM).**

8. 6, 9   **9.** 8, 12   **10.** 15, 20

11. 6, 14   **12.** 18, 27   **13.** 6, 12, 24

See Example 2   **14.** 6, 27   **15.** 16, 20   **16.** 12, 15, 22

17. 10, 15, 18, 20   **18.** 11, 22, 44   **19.** 8, 12, 18, 20

See Example 3   **20. Recreation** On her bicycle, Anna circles the block every 4 minutes. Her brother, on his scooter, circles the block every 10 minutes. They start out together. In how many minutes will they meet again at the starting point?

21. Rod helped his mom plant a vegetable garden. Rod planted a row every 30 minutes, and his mom planted a row every 20 minutes. If they started together, how long will it be before they both finish a row at the same time?

PRACTICE AND PROBLEM SOLVING

Extra Practice
See page EP6.

Find the least common multiple (LCM).

22. 3, 7   **23.** 4, 6   **24.** 9, 12

25. 22, 44, 66   **26.** 80, 120   **27.** 10, 18

28. 3, 5, 7   **29.** 3, 6, 12   **30.** 5, 7, 9

31. 24, 36, 48   **32.** 2, 3, 4, 5   **33.** 14, 21, 35, 70

34. Jack mows the lawn every three weeks and washes the car every two weeks. If he does both today, how many days will pass before he does them both on the same day again?

35. Reasoning Is it possible for two numbers to have the same LCM and GCD? Explain.

36. Multi-Step Milli jogs every day, bikes every 3 days, and swims once a week. She does all three activities on October 3. On what date will she next perform all three activities?

The Mayan, the Chinese, and the standard western calendar are all based on cycles.

37. The main Mayan calendar, or *tzolkin*, was 260 days long. It had two independent cycles, a 13-day cycle and a 20-day cycle. At the beginning of the calendar, both cycles are at day 1. Will both cycles be at day 1 at the same time again before the 260 days are over? If so, when?

38. The Chinese calendar has 12 months of 30 days each and 6-day weeks. The Chinese New Year begins on the first day of a month and the first day of a week. Will the first day of a month and the first day of a week occur again at the same time before the 360-day year is over? If so, when? Explain your answer.

39. ✎ **Write About It** The Julian Date calendar assigns each day a unique number. It begins on day 0 and adds 1 for each new day. So JD 2266296, or October 12, 1492, is 2,266,296 days from the beginning of the calendar. What are some advantages of using the Julian Date calendar? What are some advantages of using calendars that are based on cycles?

40. ★ **Challenge** The Mayan Long Count calendar used the naming system at right. Assuming the calendar began on JD 584285, express JD 2266296 in terms of the Mayan Long Count calendar. Start by finding the number of pictun that had passed up to that date.

Mayan Long Count Calendar
1 Pictun = 20 Baktun = 2,880,000 days
1 Baktun = 20 Katun = 144,000 days
1 Katun = 20 Tun = 7,200 days
1 Tun = 18 Winal = 360 days
1 Winal = 20 Kin = 20 days
1 Kin = 1 day

SPIRAL STANDARDS REVIEW ⟵ NS2.3, ⟵ NS2.4, ⟵ AF1.1

41. Multiple Choice Which is the least common multiple of 4 and 10?

Ⓐ 2   Ⓑ 10   Ⓒ 20   Ⓓ 40

42. Multiple Choice Which pair of numbers has a least common multiple of 150?

Ⓐ 10, 15   Ⓑ 150, 300   Ⓒ 2, 300   Ⓓ 15, 50

Solve each equation. (Lesson 2-5)

43. $x + 12 = -6$ **44.** $-11 = x - 4$ **45.** $-24 = x + 8$ **46.** $-8x = 40$

Find the greatest common divisor (GCD). (Lesson 3-2)

47. 12, 28   **48.** 16, 24   **49.** 15, 75   **50.** 28, 70

Quiz for Lessons 3-1 Through 3-3

☑ **3-1** **Prime Factorization**

Complete each factor tree to find the prime factorization.

1.   24
    6 • 4
    ? • ? • ? • ?

2.   140
    14 • 10
    ? • ? • ? • ?

3.   45
    3 • ?
    3 • ? • ?

4.   42
    ? • ?
    3 • 7 • ?

Write the prime factorization of each number.

5. 96

6. 125

7. 99

8. 105

9. 324

10. 500

☑ **3-2** **Greatest Common Divisor**

Find the greatest common divisor (GCD).

11. 66, 96

12. 18, 27, 45

13. 16, 28, 44

14. 14, 28, 56

15. 85, 102

16. 76, 95

17. 52, 91, 104

18. 30, 75, 90

19. 118, 116

20. Yasmin and Jon have volunteered to prepare snacks for the first-grade field trip. They have 63 carrot sticks and 105 strawberries. What is the greatest number of identical snacks they can prepare using all of the carrot sticks and strawberries?

☑ **3-3** **Least Common Multiple**

Find the least common multiple (LCM).

21. 35, 40

22. 8, 25

23. 64, 72

24. 12, 20

25. 21, 33

26. 6, 30

27. 20, 42

28. 9, 13

29. 14, 18

30. Eddie goes jogging every other day, lifts weights every third day, and swims every fourth day. If Eddie begins all three activities on Monday, how many days will it be before he does all three activities on the same day again?

31. Sean and his mom start running around a 1-mile track at the same time. Sean runs 1 mile every 8 minutes. His mom runs 1 mile every 10 minutes. In how many minutes will they be together at the starting line again?

Focus on Problem Solving

California Standards

MR2.1 Use estimation to verify the reasonableness of calculated results.

Also covered: NS2.0, MR2.5

Look Back

• **Check that your answer is reasonable**

In some situations, such as when you are looking for an estimate or completing a multiple-choice question, check to see whether a solution or answer is reasonably accurate. One way to do this is by rounding the numbers to the nearest multiple of 10 or 100, depending on how large the numbers are. Sometimes it is useful to round one number up and another down.

Read each problem, and determine whether the given answer is too high, is too low, or appears to be correct. Explain your reasoning.

1 The cheerleading team is preparing to host a spaghetti dinner as a fund-raising project. They have set up and decorated 54 tables in the gymnasium. Each table can seat 8 people. How many people can be seated at the spaghetti dinner?

Answer: 432 people

2 The cheerleaders need to raise $4,260 to attend a cheerleader camp. How much money must they charge each person if they are expecting 400 people at the spaghetti dinner?

Answer: $4

3 To help out the fund-raising project, local restaurants have offered $25 gift certificates to give as door prizes. One gift certificate will be given for each door prize, and there will be six door prizes in all. What is the total value of all of the gift certificates given by the restaurants?

Answer: $250

4 The total cost of hosting the spaghetti dinner will be about $270. If the cheerleaders make $3,280 in ticket sales, how much money will they have after paying for the spaghetti dinner?

Answer: $3,000

5 Eighteen cheerleaders and two coaches plan to attend the camp. If each person will have an equal share of the $4,260 expense money, how much money will each person have?

Answer: $562

3-4 Equivalent Fractions and Mixed Numbers

California Standards

🔑 **NS2.4** Determine the least common multiple and **the greatest common divisor of whole numbers; use them to solve problems with fractions** (e.g., to find a common denominator to add two fractions or **to find the reduced form for a fraction**).

Also covered: 🔑 **NS1.1**

Vocabulary
equivalent fractions
improper fraction
mixed number

Who uses this? In recipes, the amounts of ingredients are often given as fractions. Knowing how fractions relate to each other can be helpful when you cook. (See Exercise 65.)

Different fractions can name the same number.

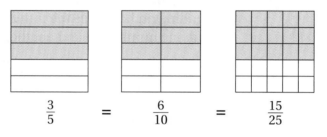

$$\frac{3}{5} \qquad = \qquad \frac{6}{10} \qquad = \qquad \frac{15}{25}$$

In the diagram, $\frac{3}{5} = \frac{6}{10} = \frac{15}{25}$. These are called **equivalent fractions** because they are different expressions for the same nonzero number.

To create fractions equivalent to a given fraction, multiply or divide the numerator and denominator by the same number.

EXAMPLE 1 **Finding Equivalent Fractions**

Find two fractions equivalent to $\frac{14}{16}$.

Remember!

A fraction with the same numerator and denominator, such as $\frac{2}{2}$, is equal to 1.

$\frac{14}{16} = \frac{14 \cdot 2}{16 \cdot 2} = \frac{28}{32}$ *Multiply the numerator and denominator by 2.*

$\frac{14}{16} = \frac{14 \div 2}{16 \div 2} = \frac{7}{8}$ *Divide the numerator and denominator by 2.*

The fractions $\frac{7}{8}$, $\frac{14}{16}$, and $\frac{28}{32}$ in Example 1 are equivalent, but only $\frac{7}{8}$ is in simplest form. A fraction is in simplest form when the greatest common divisor of its numerator and denominator is 1.

EXAMPLE 2 **Writing Fractions in Simplest Form**

Write the fraction $\frac{24}{36}$ in simplest form.

Find the GCD of 24 and 36.

$24 = 2 \cdot 2 \cdot 2 \cdot 3$ *The GCD is $12 = 2 \cdot 2 \cdot 3$.*

$36 = 2 \cdot 2 \cdot 3 \cdot 3$

$\frac{24}{36} = \frac{24 \div 12}{36 \div 12} = \frac{2}{3}$ *Divide the numerator and denominator by 12.*

To determine if two fractions are equivalent, simplify the fractions.

EXAMPLE **3** **Determining Whether Fractions Are Equivalent**

Determine whether the fractions in each pair are equivalent.

A $\frac{6}{8}$ and $\frac{9}{12}$

Simplify both fractions and compare.

$$\frac{6}{8} = \frac{6 \div 2}{8 \div 2} = \frac{3}{4} \qquad\qquad \frac{9}{12} = \frac{9 \div 3}{12 \div 3} = \frac{3}{4}$$

$\frac{6}{8}$ and $\frac{9}{12}$ are equivalent because both are equal to $\frac{3}{4}$.

B $\frac{18}{15}$ and $\frac{25}{20}$

Simply both fractions and compare.

$$\frac{18}{15} = \frac{18 \div 3}{15 \div 3} = \frac{6}{5} \qquad\qquad \frac{25}{20} = \frac{25 \div 5}{20 \div 5} = \frac{5}{4}$$

$\frac{18}{15}$ and $\frac{25}{20}$ are *not* equivalent because their simplest forms are not equal.

$\frac{8}{5}$ is an **improper fraction**. Its numerator is greater than its denominator.

$$\frac{8}{5} = 1\frac{3}{5}$$

$1\frac{3}{5}$ is a **mixed number**. It contains both a whole number and a fraction.

EXAMPLE **4** **Converting Between Improper Fractions and Mixed Numbers**

Remember!

$$\begin{array}{r} \text{Quotient} \longrightarrow 5 \\ 4\overline{)21} \\ -20 \\ \text{Remainder} \longrightarrow 1 \end{array}$$

See Skills Bank p. SB6.

A Write $\frac{21}{4}$ as a mixed number.

First divide the numerator by the denominator.

$$\frac{21}{4} = 5\frac{1}{4} \quad \textit{Use the quotient and remainder to write the mixed number.}$$

B Write $4\frac{2}{3}$ as an improper fraction.

First multiply the denominator and whole number, and then add the numerator.

$$4\frac{2}{3} = \frac{3 \cdot 4 + 2}{3} = \frac{14}{3} \quad \textit{Use the result to write the improper fraction.}$$

Think and Discuss

1. Explain a process for finding common denominators.

2. Describe how to convert between improper fractions and mixed numbers.

3-4 **Exercises**

California Standards Practice
🔑 NS1.1, 🔑 NS2.4

go.hrw.com
Homework Help Online
KEYWORD: MS8CA 3-4
Parent Resources Online
KEYWORD: MS8CA Parent

GUIDED PRACTICE

See Example ① Find two fractions equivalent to the given fraction.

1. $\frac{21}{42}$ **2.** $\frac{33}{55}$ **3.** $\frac{10}{12}$ **4.** $\frac{15}{40}$

See Example ② Write each fraction in simplest form.

5. $\frac{13}{26}$ **6.** $\frac{54}{72}$ **7.** $\frac{12}{15}$ **8.** $\frac{36}{42}$

See Example ③ Determine whether the fractions in each pair are equivalent.

9. $\frac{3}{9}$ and $\frac{6}{8}$ **10.** $\frac{10}{12}$ and $\frac{20}{24}$ **11.** $\frac{8}{6}$ and $\frac{20}{15}$ **12.** $\frac{15}{8}$ and $\frac{19}{12}$

See Example ④ Write each as a mixed number.

13. $\frac{15}{4}$ **14.** $\frac{22}{5}$ **15.** $\frac{17}{13}$ **16.** $\frac{14}{3}$

Write each as an improper fraction.

17. $6\frac{1}{5}$ **18.** $1\frac{11}{12}$ **19.** $7\frac{3}{5}$ **20.** $2\frac{7}{16}$

INDEPENDENT PRACTICE

See Example ① Find two fractions equivalent to the given fraction.

21. $\frac{18}{20}$ **22.** $\frac{25}{50}$ **23.** $\frac{9}{15}$ **24.** $\frac{42}{70}$

See Example ② Write each fraction in simplest form.

25. $\frac{63}{81}$ **26.** $\frac{14}{21}$ **27.** $\frac{34}{48}$ **28.** $\frac{100}{250}$

See Example ③ Determine whether the fractions in each pair are equivalent.

29. $\frac{5}{10}$ and $\frac{14}{28}$ **30.** $\frac{15}{20}$ and $\frac{20}{24}$ **31.** $\frac{125}{100}$ and $\frac{40}{32}$ **32.** $\frac{10}{5}$ and $\frac{18}{8}$

33. $\frac{2}{3}$ and $\frac{12}{18}$ **34.** $\frac{8}{12}$ and $\frac{24}{36}$ **35.** $\frac{54}{99}$ and $\frac{84}{132}$ **36.** $\frac{25}{15}$ and $\frac{175}{75}$

See Example ④ Write each as a mixed number.

37. $\frac{19}{3}$ **38.** $\frac{13}{9}$ **39.** $\frac{81}{11}$ **40.** $\frac{71}{8}$

Write each as an improper fraction.

41. $25\frac{3}{5}$ **42.** $4\frac{7}{16}$ **43.** $9\frac{2}{3}$ **44.** $4\frac{16}{31}$

PRACTICE AND PROBLEM SOLVING

Extra Practice
See page EP7.

45. Personal Finance Every month, Adrian pays for his own long-distance calls made on the family phone. Last month, 15 of the 60 minutes of long-distance charges were Adrian's, and he paid $2.50 of the $12 long-distance bill. Did Adrian pay his fair share? Explain.

Food

A single bread company can make as many as 1,217 loaves of bread each minute.

Write a fraction equivalent to the given number.

46. 8　　　**47.** $6\frac{1}{2}$　　**48.** $2\frac{2}{3}$　　**49.** $\frac{8}{21}$　　**50.** $9\frac{8}{11}$

51. $\frac{55}{10}$　　**52.** 101　　**53.** $6\frac{15}{21}$　　**54.** $\frac{475}{75}$　　**55.** $11\frac{23}{50}$

Find the equivalent pair of fractions in each set.

56. $\frac{6}{15}, \frac{21}{35}, \frac{3}{5}$　　**57.** $\frac{7}{12}, \frac{12}{20}, \frac{6}{10}$　　**58.** $\frac{2}{3}, \frac{12}{15}, \frac{20}{30}, \frac{15}{24}$　　**59.** $\frac{7}{4}, \frac{9}{5}, \frac{32}{20}, \frac{72}{40}$

There are 12 inches in 1 foot. Write a mixed number to represent each measurement in feet. (Example: 14 inches $= 1\frac{2}{12}$ feet or $1\frac{1}{6}$ feet)

60. 25 inches　　**61.** 100 inches　　**62.** 362 inches　　**63.** 42 inches

64. A dollar bill is $15\frac{7}{10}$ centimeters long and $6\frac{13}{20}$ centimeters wide. Write each number as an improper fraction.

65. **Food** A bakery uses $37\frac{1}{2}$ cups of flour to make 25 loaves of bread each day. Write a fraction that shows how many $\frac{1}{4}$ cups of flour are used to make bread each day at the bakery.

66. **Reasoning** Cal made the graph at right. Use the graph to write a problem involving fractions.

67. **Write About It** Draw a diagram to show how you can use division to write $\frac{25}{3}$ as a mixed number. Explain your diagram.

68. **Challenge** Kenichi spent $\frac{2}{5}$ of his $100 birthday check on clothes. How much did Kenichi's new clothes cost?

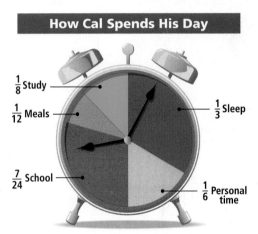

How Cal Spends His Day

$\frac{1}{8}$ Study
$\frac{1}{12}$ Meals
$\frac{7}{24}$ School
$\frac{1}{3}$ Sleep
$\frac{1}{6}$ Personal time

69. **Multiple Choice** Which improper fraction is NOT equivalent to $2\frac{1}{2}$?

(A) $\frac{5}{2}$　　(B) $\frac{10}{4}$　　(C) $\frac{20}{6}$　　(D) $\frac{25}{10}$

70. **Multiple Choice** Which fraction is equivalent to $\frac{5}{6}$?

(A) $\frac{20}{24}$　　(B) $\frac{10}{18}$　　(C) $\frac{6}{7}$　　(D) $\frac{6}{5}$

71. **Short Response** Maria sold 16 of her 28 paintings at a fair. Write the fraction that she sold in simplest form. Explain how you determined your answer.

Solve each equation. Check your answer. (Lessons 1-8 to 1-11)

72. $5b = 25$　　**73.** $6 + y = 18$　　**74.** $k - 57 = 119$　　**75.** $\frac{z}{4} = 20$

Find the least common multiple (LCM). (Lesson 3-3)

76. 2, 3, 4　　**77.** 9, 15　　**78.** 15, 20　　**79.** 3, 7, 8

Equivalent Fractions and Decimals

California Standards

Preparation for ◆— **NS1.1**

Compare and order positive and negative **fractions, decimals, and mixed numbers** and place them on a number line.

Also covered: ◆— **NS2.4**

Why learn this? You can determine a baseball player's batting average by writing a fraction as a decimal.

In baseball, a player's batting average compares the number of hits with the number of times the player has been at bat.

Lance Berkman had 172 hits in the 2004 season.

Vocabulary
terminating decimal
repeating decimal

Player	Hits	At Bats	Hits / At Bats	Batting Average (thousandths)
Lance Berkman	172	544	$\frac{172}{544}$	$172 \div 544 \approx 0.316$
Alex Rodriguez	172	601	$\frac{172}{601}$	$172 \div 601 \approx 0.286$

To convert a fraction to a decimal, divide the numerator by the denominator.

EXAMPLE 1 **Writing Fractions as Decimals**

Reasoning

Write each fraction as a decimal. Round to the nearest hundredth, if necessary.

A $\frac{3}{4}$

$$\begin{array}{r} 0.75 \\ 4\overline{)3.00} \\ -28 \\ \hline 20 \\ -20 \\ \hline 0 \end{array}$$

$$\frac{3}{4} = 0.75$$

B $\frac{6}{5}$

$$\begin{array}{r} 1.2 \\ 5\overline{)6.0} \\ -5 \\ \hline 10 \\ -10 \\ \hline 0 \end{array}$$

$$\frac{6}{5} = 1.2$$

C $\frac{1}{3}$

$$\begin{array}{r} 0.333\ldots \\ 3\overline{)1.000} \\ -9 \\ \hline 10 \\ -9 \\ \hline 10 \\ -9 \\ \hline 1 \end{array}$$

$$\frac{1}{3} = 0.333\ldots$$
$$\approx 0.33$$

The decimals 0.75 and 1.2 in Example 1 are **terminating decimals** because the decimals come to an end. The decimal 0.333... is a **repeating decimal** because it includes a group of one or more digits (where all digits are not zero) that repeats forever. You can also write a repeating decimal with a bar over the repeating part.

$$0.333\ldots = 0.\overline{3} \qquad 0.8333\ldots = 0.8\overline{3} \qquad 0.727272\ldots = 0.\overline{72}$$

You can use place value to write some fractions as decimals.

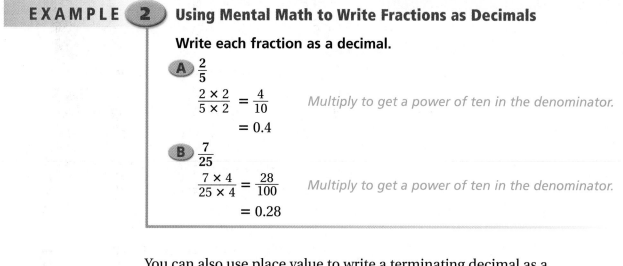

EXAMPLE 2 **Using Mental Math to Write Fractions as Decimals**

Write each fraction as a decimal.

A $\frac{2}{5}$

$\frac{2 \times 2}{5 \times 2} = \frac{4}{10}$ *Multiply to get a power of ten in the denominator.*

$= 0.4$

B $\frac{7}{25}$

$\frac{7 \times 4}{25 \times 4} = \frac{28}{100}$ *Multiply to get a power of ten in the denominator.*

$= 0.28$

You can also use place value to write a terminating decimal as a fraction. Use the place value of the last digit to the right of the decimal point as the denominator of the fraction.

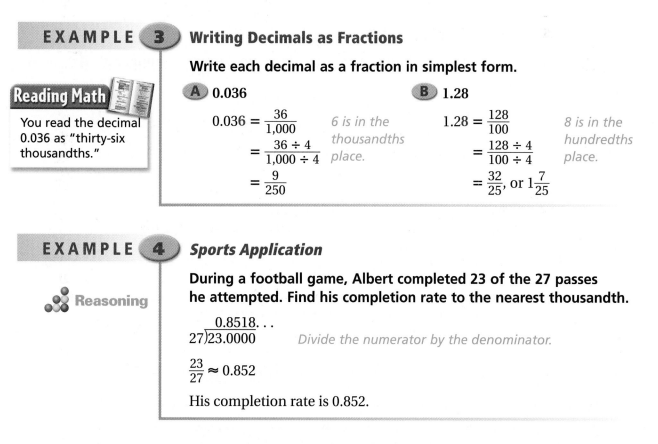

EXAMPLE 3 **Writing Decimals as Fractions**

Write each decimal as a fraction in simplest form.

Reading Math

You read the decimal 0.036 as "thirty-six thousandths."

A 0.036

$0.036 = \frac{36}{1,000}$ *6 is in the thousandths place.*

$= \frac{36 \div 4}{1,000 \div 4}$

$= \frac{9}{250}$

B 1.28

$1.28 = \frac{128}{100}$ *8 is in the hundredths place.*

$= \frac{128 \div 4}{100 \div 4}$

$= \frac{32}{25}$, or $1\frac{7}{25}$

EXAMPLE 4 **Sports Application**

Reasoning

During a football game, Albert completed 23 of the 27 passes he attempted. Find his completion rate to the nearest thousandth.

$$\begin{array}{r} 0.8518... \\ 27\overline{)23.0000} \end{array}$$ *Divide the numerator by the denominator.*

$\frac{23}{27} \approx 0.852$

His completion rate is 0.852.

Think and Discuss

1. Tell how to write a fraction as a decimal.

2. Explain how to use place value to convert 0.2048 to a fraction.

California
Standards Practice
Preparation for ◆ NS1.1;
◆ NS1.1, ◆ NS2.4

go.hrw.com
Homework Help Online
KEYWORD: MS8CA 3-5
Parent Resources Online
KEYWORD: MS8CA Parent

GUIDED PRACTICE

See Example ① Write each fraction as a decimal. Round to the nearest hundredth, if necessary.

1. $\frac{4}{7}$ **2.** $\frac{21}{8}$ **3.** $\frac{11}{6}$ **4.** $\frac{7}{9}$

See Example ② Write each fraction as a decimal.

5. $\frac{3}{25}$ **6.** $\frac{7}{10}$ **7.** $\frac{1}{20}$ **8.** $\frac{3}{5}$

See Example ③ Write each decimal as a fraction in simplest form.

9. 0.008 **10.** −0.6 **11.** −2.05 **12.** 3.75

See Example ④ **13. Sports** After sweeping the Baltimore Orioles at home in 2001, the Seattle Mariners had a record of 103 wins out of 143 games played. Find the Mariners' winning rate. Write your answer as a decimal rounded to the nearest thousandth.

INDEPENDENT PRACTICE

See Example ① Write each fraction as a decimal. Round to the nearest hundredth, if necessary.

14. $\frac{9}{10}$ **15.** $\frac{32}{5}$ **16.** $\frac{18}{25}$ **17.** $\frac{7}{8}$

18. $\frac{16}{11}$ **19.** $\frac{500}{500}$ **20.** $\frac{17}{3}$ **21.** $\frac{23}{12}$

See Example ② Write each fraction as a decimal.

22. $\frac{5}{4}$ **23.** $\frac{4}{5}$ **24.** $\frac{15}{25}$ **25.** $\frac{11}{20}$

See Example ③ Write each decimal as a fraction in simplest form.

26. 0.45 **27.** 0.01 **28.** −0.25 **29.** −0.08

30. 1.8 **31.** 15.25 **32.** 5.09 **33.** 8.375

See Example ④ **34. School** On a test, Caleb answered 73 out of 86 questions correctly. What portion of his answers was correct? Write your answer as a decimal rounded to the nearest thousandth.

PRACTICE AND PROBLEM SOLVING

Extra Practice
See page EP7.

Give two numbers equivalent to each fraction or decimal.

35. $8\frac{3}{4}$ **36.** 0.66 **37.** 5.05 **38.** $\frac{8}{25}$

39. 15.35 **40.** $8\frac{3}{8}$ **41.** $4\frac{3}{1,000}$ **42.** $3\frac{1}{3}$

Determine whether the numbers in each pair are equivalent.

43. $\frac{3}{4}$ and 0.75 **44.** $\frac{7}{20}$ and 0.45 **45.** $\frac{11}{21}$ and 0.55 **46.** 0.8 and $\frac{4}{5}$

47. 0.275 and $\frac{11}{40}$ **48.** $1\frac{21}{25}$ and 1.72 **49.** 0.74 and $\frac{16}{25}$ **50.** 0.35 and $\frac{7}{20}$

Use the table for Exercises 51 and 52.

XYZ Stock Values (October 2001)				
Date	Open	High	Low	Close
Oct 16	17.89	18.05	17.5	17.8
Oct 17	18.01	18.04	17.15	17.95
Oct 18	17.84	18.55	17.81	18.20

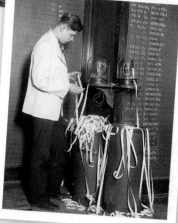

Traders watch the stock prices change from the floor of a stock exchange.

51. Write the highest value of stock XYZ for each day as a mixed number in simplest form.

52. Multi-Step On which date did the price of stock XYZ fall by $\frac{3}{50}$ of a dollar between the open and close of the day?

53. 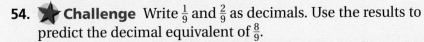 **Write About It** Until recently, prices of stocks were expressed as mixed numbers, such as $24\frac{15}{32}$ dollars. The denominators of such fractions were multiples of 2, such as 2, 4, 6, 8, and so forth. Today, the prices are expressed as decimals to the nearest hundredth, such as 32.35 dollars.

  a. What are some advantages of using decimals instead of fractions?

  b. The old ticker-tape machine punched stock prices onto a tape. Perhaps because fractions could not be shown using the machine, the prices were punched as decimals. Write some decimal equivalents of fractions that the machine might print.

Before the days of computer technology, ticker-tape machines were used to punch the stock prices onto paper strands.

54. ⭐ **Challenge** Write $\frac{1}{9}$ and $\frac{2}{9}$ as decimals. Use the results to predict the decimal equivalent of $\frac{8}{9}$.

go.hrw.com
Web Extra!
KEYWORD: MS8CA Stock

SPIRAL STANDARDS REVIEW ◆— NS1.1, ◆— NS2.4, ◆— AF1.1

55. Multiple Choice Which is NOT equivalent to 0.35?

    Ⓐ $\frac{35}{100}$ Ⓑ $\frac{7}{20}$ Ⓒ $\frac{14}{40}$ Ⓓ $\frac{25}{80}$

56. Gridded Response Write $\frac{6}{17}$ as a decimal rounded to the nearest hundredth.

Solve each equation. Check your answers. (Lesson 1-11)

57. $\frac{x}{6} = 36$ **58.** $8 = \frac{m}{4}$ **59.** $\frac{t}{15} = 5$

Write each fraction in simplest form. (Lesson 3-4)

60. $\frac{42}{48}$ **61.** $\frac{70}{90}$ **62.** $\frac{30}{45}$ **63.** $\frac{66}{72}$

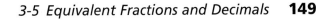

Comparing and Ordering Rational Numbers

California Standards

◆━ **NS1.1** Compare and order positive and negative fractions, decimals, and mixed numbers and place them on a number line.
Also covered: ◆━ **NS2.4**

Vocabulary
rational number

Who uses this? Astronomers use rational numbers to compare the densities of planets. (See Exercise 39.)

Which is greater, $\frac{7}{9}$ or $\frac{2}{9}$? To compare fractions with the same denominator, just compare the numerators.

$$\frac{7}{9} > \frac{2}{9} \text{ because } 7 > 2.$$

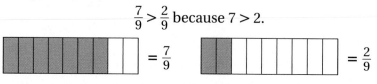

$= \frac{7}{9}$ $= \frac{2}{9}$

One way to compare fractions with unlike denominators is to use models. For example, the models show that $\frac{3}{8} < \frac{1}{2}$.

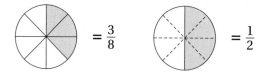

$= \frac{3}{8}$ $= \frac{1}{2}$

Another way to compare fractions with unlike denominators is to first write equivalent fractions with common denominators. Then compare the numerators.

EXAMPLE 1 **Comparing Fractions**

Compare the fractions. Write < or >.

A $\frac{5}{6} \blacksquare \frac{7}{10}$

The LCM of the denominators 6 and 10 is 30.

$$\frac{5}{6} = \frac{5 \cdot 5}{6 \cdot 5} = \frac{25}{30}$$ *Write equivalent fractions with 30 as the denominator.*

$$\frac{7}{10} = \frac{7 \cdot 3}{10 \cdot 3} = \frac{21}{30}$$

$$\frac{25}{30} > \frac{21}{30}, \text{ and so } \frac{5}{6} > \frac{7}{10}.$$ *Compare the numerators.*

B $-\frac{3}{5} \blacksquare -\frac{5}{9}$

Both fractions can be written with a denominator of 45.

$$-\frac{3}{5} = \frac{-3 \cdot 9}{5 \cdot 9} = \frac{-27}{45}$$ *Write equivalent fractions with 45 as the denominator. Put the negative signs in the numerators.*

$$-\frac{5}{9} = \frac{-5 \cdot 5}{9 \cdot 5} = \frac{-25}{45}$$

$$\frac{-27}{45} < \frac{-25}{45}, \text{ and so } -\frac{3}{5} < -\frac{5}{9}.$$

Helpful Hint

A fraction less than 0, such as $-\frac{3}{5}$, can be written as $-\frac{3}{5}$, $\frac{-3}{5}$, or $\frac{3}{-5}$.

To compare decimals, line up the decimal points and compare digits from left to right until you find the place where the digits are different.

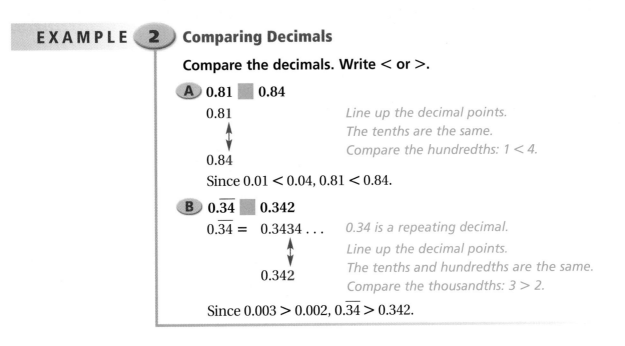

EXAMPLE 2 Comparing Decimals

Compare the decimals. Write < or >.

A 0.81 ▩ 0.84

0.81

0.84

Line up the decimal points.
The tenths are the same.
Compare the hundredths: 1 < 4.

Since 0.01 < 0.04, 0.81 < 0.84.

B $0.\overline{34}$ ▩ 0.342

$0.\overline{34} = 0.3434\ldots$

0.342

$0.\overline{34}$ is a repeating decimal.
Line up the decimal points.
The tenths and hundredths are the same.
Compare the thousandths: 3 > 2.

Since 0.003 > 0.002, $0.\overline{34}$ > 0.342.

A **rational number** is a number that can be written as a fraction or quotient of integers with a nonzero denominator. When rational numbers are written in a variety of forms, you can compare the numbers by writing them all in the same form.

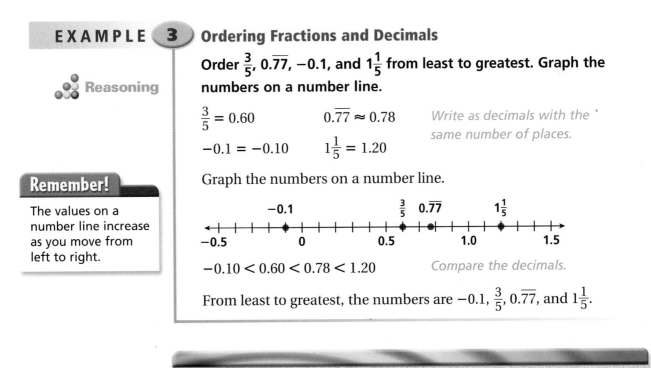

EXAMPLE 3 Ordering Fractions and Decimals

Reasoning

Order $\frac{3}{5}$, $0.\overline{77}$, −0.1, and $1\frac{1}{5}$ from least to greatest. Graph the numbers on a number line.

$\frac{3}{5} = 0.60$ $0.\overline{77} \approx 0.78$

$-0.1 = -0.10$ $1\frac{1}{5} = 1.20$

Write as decimals with the same number of places.

Graph the numbers on a number line.

Remember!

The values on a number line increase as you move from left to right.

$-0.10 < 0.60 < 0.78 < 1.20$ *Compare the decimals.*

From least to greatest, the numbers are -0.1, $\frac{3}{5}$, $0.\overline{77}$, and $1\frac{1}{5}$.

Think and Discuss

1. Tell how to compare two fractions with different denominators.

3-6 Exercises

California Standards Practice
🐻 NS1.1

go.hrw.com
Homework Help Online
KEYWORD: MS8CA 3-6
Parent Resources Online
KEYWORD: MS8CA Parent

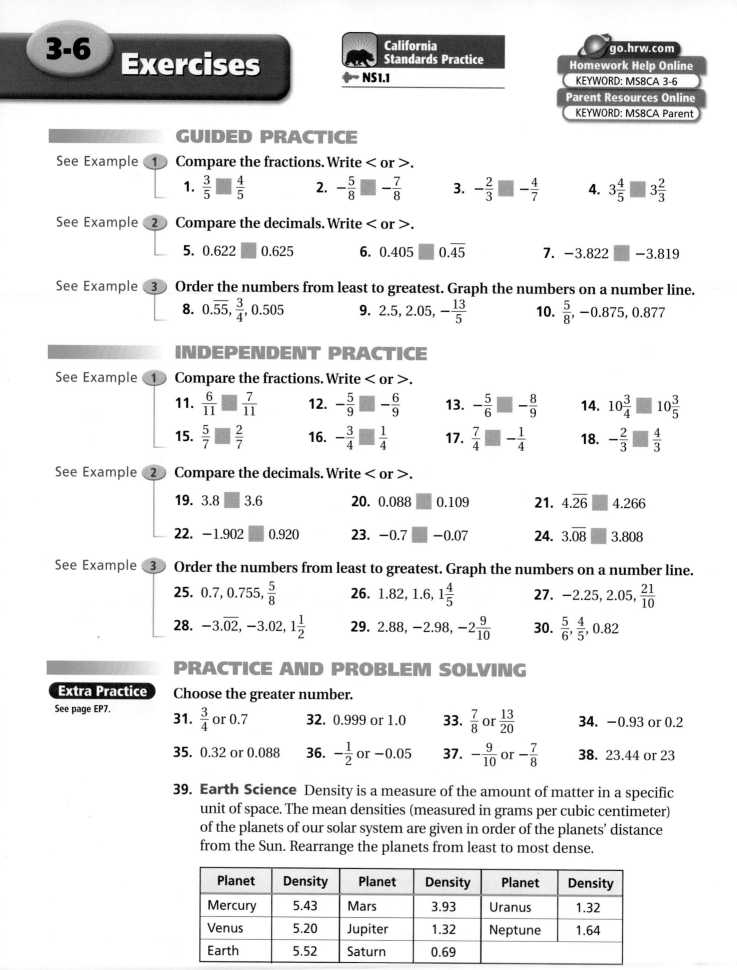

GUIDED PRACTICE

See Example **1** Compare the fractions. Write < or >.

1. $\frac{3}{5} \ \blacksquare \ \frac{4}{5}$
2. $-\frac{5}{8} \ \blacksquare \ -\frac{7}{8}$
3. $-\frac{2}{3} \ \blacksquare \ -\frac{4}{7}$
4. $3\frac{4}{5} \ \blacksquare \ 3\frac{2}{3}$

See Example **2** Compare the decimals. Write < or >.

5. $0.622 \ \blacksquare \ 0.625$
6. $0.405 \ \blacksquare \ 0.\overline{45}$
7. $-3.822 \ \blacksquare \ -3.819$

See Example **3** Order the numbers from least to greatest. Graph the numbers on a number line.

8. $0.\overline{55}, \frac{3}{4}, 0.505$
9. $2.5, 2.05, -\frac{13}{5}$
10. $\frac{5}{8}, -0.875, 0.877$

INDEPENDENT PRACTICE

See Example **1** Compare the fractions. Write < or >.

11. $\frac{6}{11} \ \blacksquare \ \frac{7}{11}$
12. $-\frac{5}{9} \ \blacksquare \ -\frac{6}{9}$
13. $-\frac{5}{6} \ \blacksquare \ -\frac{8}{9}$
14. $10\frac{3}{4} \ \blacksquare \ 10\frac{3}{5}$
15. $\frac{5}{7} \ \blacksquare \ \frac{2}{7}$
16. $-\frac{3}{4} \ \blacksquare \ \frac{1}{4}$
17. $\frac{7}{4} \ \blacksquare \ -\frac{1}{4}$
18. $-\frac{2}{3} \ \blacksquare \ \frac{4}{3}$

See Example **2** Compare the decimals. Write < or >.

19. $3.8 \ \blacksquare \ 3.6$
20. $0.088 \ \blacksquare \ 0.109$
21. $4.\overline{26} \ \blacksquare \ 4.266$
22. $-1.902 \ \blacksquare \ 0.920$
23. $-0.7 \ \blacksquare \ -0.07$
24. $3.\overline{08} \ \blacksquare \ 3.808$

See Example **3** Order the numbers from least to greatest. Graph the numbers on a number line.

25. $0.7, 0.755, \frac{5}{8}$
26. $1.82, 1.6, 1\frac{4}{5}$
27. $-2.25, 2.05, \frac{21}{10}$
28. $-3.\overline{02}, -3.02, 1\frac{1}{2}$
29. $2.88, -2.98, -2\frac{9}{10}$
30. $\frac{5}{6}, \frac{4}{5}, 0.82$

PRACTICE AND PROBLEM SOLVING

Extra Practice
See page EP7.

Choose the greater number.

31. $\frac{3}{4}$ or 0.7
32. 0.999 or 1.0
33. $\frac{7}{8}$ or $\frac{13}{20}$
34. -0.93 or 0.2
35. 0.32 or 0.088
36. $-\frac{1}{2}$ or -0.05
37. $-\frac{9}{10}$ or $-\frac{7}{8}$
38. 23.44 or 23

39. **Earth Science** Density is a measure of the amount of matter in a specific unit of space. The mean densities (measured in grams per cubic centimeter) of the planets of our solar system are given in order of the planets' distance from the Sun. Rearrange the planets from least to most dense.

Planet	Density	Planet	Density	Planet	Density
Mercury	5.43	Mars	3.93	Uranus	1.32
Venus	5.20	Jupiter	1.32	Neptune	1.64
Earth	5.52	Saturn	0.69		

40. **Multi-Step** Twenty-four karat gold is considered pure.

    a. Angie's necklace is 22-karat gold. What is its purity as a fraction?

    b. Luke's ring is 0.75 gold. Whose jewelry contains a greater fraction of gold?

41. **Science** Sloths are tree-dwelling animals that live in South and Central America. They sleep about $\frac{3}{4}$ of a 24-hour day. Humans sleep an average of 8 hours each day. Which sleep the most each day, sloths or humans?

42. **Ecology** Of Ty's total household water use, $\frac{5}{9}$ is for bathing, toilet flushing, and laundry. How does his water use for these purposes compare with that shown in the graph?

Average Daily Household Use of Water

$\frac{3}{5}$ Bathing, toilet flushing, laundry

$\frac{8}{25}$ Lawn watering, car washing, pool maintenance

$\frac{2}{25}$ Drinking, cooking, washing dishes, running garbage disposal

43. **Reasoning** How can you compare $\frac{3}{10}$ and $\frac{3}{11}$ without finding a common denominator? Explain.

44. **What's the Error?** A recipe for a large cake called for $4\frac{1}{2}$ cups of flour. The chef added 10 one-half cupfuls of flour to the mixture. What was the chef's error?

45. **Write About It** Explain how to compare a mixed number with a decimal.

46. **Challenge** Scientists estimate that Earth is approximately 4.6 billion years old. We are currently in what is called the Phanerozoic eon, which has made up about $\frac{7}{60}$ of the time that Earth has existed. The first eon, called the Hadean, made up approximately 0.175 of the time Earth has existed. Which eon represents the most time?

SPIRAL STANDARDS REVIEW

NS1.1, NS2.3, AF1.2

47. **Multiple Choice** Which number is closest to 0?

    Ⓐ 0.34   Ⓑ $-\frac{1}{3}$ Ⓒ -0.31 Ⓓ $\frac{3}{10}$

48. **Multiple Choice** Which shows the order of the animals from fastest to slowest?

    Ⓐ Spider, tortoise, snail, sloth

    Ⓑ Snail, sloth, tortoise, spider

    Ⓒ Tortoise, spider, snail, sloth

    Ⓓ Spider, tortoise, sloth, snail

Maximum Speed (mi/h)				
Animal	Snail	Tortoise	Spider	Sloth
Speed	0.03	0.17	1.17	0.15

Write each phrase as an algebraic expression. (Lesson 1-6)

49. 6 more than the product of 5 and x

50. 4 less than the sum of t and 16

Simplify. (Lessons 2-2 and 2-3)

51. $-13 + 51$ 52. $142 - (-27)$ 53. $-118 - (-57)$ 54. $-27 + 84$

READY TO GO ON?

Quiz for Lessons 3-4 Through 3-6

☑ **3-4** **Equivalent Fractions and Mixed Numbers**

Determine whether the fractions in each pair are equivalent.

1. $\frac{3}{4}$ and $\frac{2}{3}$

2. $\frac{3}{12}$ and $\frac{4}{16}$

3. $\frac{7}{25}$ and $\frac{6}{20}$

4. $\frac{5}{9}$ and $\frac{25}{45}$

5. There are $2\frac{54}{100}$ centimeters in an inch. When asked to write this value as an improper fraction, Aimee wrote $\frac{127}{50}$. Was she correct? Explain.

☑ **3-5** **Equivalent Fractions and Decimals**

Write each fraction as a decimal. Round to the nearest hundredth, if necessary.

6. $\frac{7}{10}$

7. $\frac{5}{8}$

8. $\frac{2}{3}$

9. $\frac{14}{15}$

Write each decimal as a fraction in simplest form.

10. 0.22

11. -0.135

12. -4.06

13. 0.07

14. In one 30-gram serving of snack crackers, there are 24 grams of carbohydrates. What fraction of a serving is made up of carbohydrates? Write your answer as a fraction and as a decimal.

15. During a softball game, Sara threw 70 pitches. Of those pitches, 29 were strikes. What portion of the pitches that Sara threw were strikes? Write your answer as a decimal rounded to the nearest thousandth.

☑ **3-6** **Comparing and Ordering Rational Numbers**

Compare the fractions. Write < or >.

16. $\frac{3}{7}$ ▦ $\frac{2}{4}$

17. $-\frac{1}{8}$ ▦ $-\frac{2}{11}$

18. $\frac{5}{4}$ ▦ $\frac{4}{5}$

19. $-1\frac{2}{3}$ ▦ $\frac{1}{2}$

Compare the decimals. Write < or >.

20. 0.521 ▦ 0.524

21. 2.05 ▦ -2.50

22. 3.001 ▦ 3.010

23. -0.26 ▦ -0.626

Order the numbers from least to greatest. Graph the numbers on a number line.

24. $\frac{3}{7}$, -0.372, $-\frac{2}{3}$, 0.5

25. $2\frac{9}{11}$, $\frac{4}{5}$, 2.91, 0.9

26. -5.36, 2.36, $-5\frac{1}{3}$, $-2\frac{3}{6}$

27. 8.75, $\frac{7}{8}$, 0.8, $\frac{8}{7}$

28. Rafael measured the rainfall at his house for 3 days. On Sunday, it rained $\frac{2}{5}$ in. On Monday, it rained $\frac{5}{8}$ in. On Wednesday, it rained 0.57 in. List the days in order from the least to the greatest amount of rainfall.

CONCEPT CONNECTION

A Party with Palm Trees

Jamal and Sarah are planning an end-of-year party for the Spanish Club. They want it to have a tropical theme.

1. There will be 16 girls and 12 boys at the party. Jamal wants to set up the tables so that every table has the same number of girls and the same number of boys. How many tables will there be? How many girls and boys will be at each table?

2. Sarah finds three recipes for fruit punch. She wants to choose the recipe that calls for the greatest amount of pineapple juice per serving. Which recipe should she choose? Explain.

3. Sarah's recipe makes 1.25 cups of punch per serving. Each punch glass holds up to $1\frac{5}{8}$ cups of liquid. If one serving is poured into a glass, will there be enough space left in the glass for ice? Explain.

4. Jamal wants to give out sunglasses and key chains as party favors. Sunglasses come in packages of 6, and key chains come in packages of 8. Jamal wants to buy the same number of sunglasses as key chains. What is the least number of packages of each type of favor that he should buy? Explain.

Thirst Quencher One Serving

$\frac{2}{3}$ cup	Orange juice
$\frac{1}{3}$ cup	Cranberry juice
$\frac{2}{3}$ cup	Pineapple juice

Sea Breeze One Serving

$\frac{1}{4}$ cup	Orange juice
$\frac{1}{4}$ cup	Cranberry juice
$\frac{3}{4}$ cup	Pineapple juice

Tropical Mist One Serving

0.75 cup	Orange juice
0.25 cup	Cranberry juice
0.5 cup	Pineapple juice

Magic Squares

A magic square is a grid with numbers, such that the numbers in each row, column, and diagonal have the same "magic" sum. Test the square at right to see an example of this.

You can use a magic square to do some amazing calculations. Cover a block of four squares (2 × 2) with a piece of paper. There is a way you can find the sum of these squares without looking at them. Try to find it. (*Hint:* What number in the magic square can you subtract from the magic sum to give you the sum of the numbers in the block? Where is that number located?)

Here's the answer: To find the sum of any block of four numbers, take 65 (the magic sum) and subtract from it the number that is diagonally two squares away from a corner of the block.

18	10	22	14	1
12	4	16	8	25
6	23	15	2	19
5	17	9	21	13
24	11	3	20	7

$65 - 21 = 44$

18	10	22	14	1
12	4	16	8	25
6	23	15	2	19
5	17	9	21	13
24	11	3	20	7

$65 - 1 = 64$

The number you subtract must fall on an extension of a diagonal of the block. For each block that you choose, there will be only one direction you can go.

Try to create a 3 × 3 magic square with the numbers 1–9.

Modified Tic-Tac-Toe

The board has a row of nine squares numbered 1 through 9. Players take turns selecting squares. The goal of the game is for a player to select squares such that any three of the player's squares add up to 15. The game can also be played with a board numbered 1 through 16 and a sum goal of 34.

A complete copy of the rules and a game board are available online.

go.hrw.com
Game Time Extra
KEYWORD: MS8CA Games

Materials
- 3 sheets of decorative paper ($8\frac{1}{2}$ in. by $8\frac{1}{2}$ in.)
- scissors
- clear tape
- markers

It's in the Bag!

PROJECT ## Flipping Over Number Theory and Fractions

Create your own flip-flop-fold book and use it to write definitions, sample problems, and practice exercises.

Directions

1. Stack the sheets of decorative paper. Fold the stack into quarters and then unfold it. Use scissors to make a slit from the edge of the stack to the center of the stack along the left-hand crease. **Figure A**

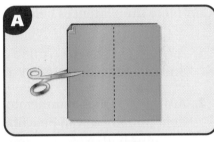

2. Place the stack in front of you with the slit on the left side. Fold the top left square over to the right side of the stack. **Figure B**

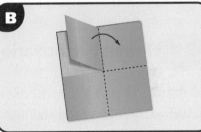

3. Now fold down the top two squares from the top right corner. Along the slit, tape the bottom left square to the top left square. **Figure C**

4. Continue folding around the stack, always in a clockwise direction. When you get to the second layer, tape the slit in the same place as before.

Taking Note of the Math

Unfold your completed booklet. This time, as you flip the pages, add definitions, sample problems, practice exercises, or any other notes you need to help you study the material in the chapter.

CHAPTER 3
FLIPPING OVER
NUMBER THEORY
AND FRACTIONS

Study Guide: Review

Vocabulary

composite number **128**

equivalent fractions ... **142**

greatest common divisor (GCD) **132**

improper fraction **143**

least common multiple (LCM) **136**

mixed number **143**

multiple **136**

prime factorization **128**

prime number **128**

rational number **151**

repeating decimal **146**

terminating decimal ... **146**

Complete the sentences below with vocabulary words from the list above.

1. A(n) ___?___ can be written as the ratio of one integer to another and can be represented by a repeating or ___?___.

2. A(n) ___?___ has a numerator that is greater than its denominator; it can be written as a(n) ___?___, which contains both a whole number and a fraction.

3-1 Prime Factorization (pp. 128–131)

Prep for ⟜ NS2.4

EXAMPLE

■ Write the prime factorization of 28.

```
     28
    /  \
   4  · ⑦
  / \
 ② · ②
```

The prime factorization is $2 \cdot 2 \cdot 7$, or $2^2 \cdot 7$.

EXERCISES

Write the prime factorization of each number.

3. 88   **4.** 27   **5.** 162

6. 65   **7.** 94   **8.** 110

9. 81   **10.** 99   **11.** 76

12. 97   **13.** 55   **14.** 46

3-2 Greatest Common Divisor (pp. 132–135)

⟜ NS2.4

EXAMPLE

■ Find the greatest common divisor (GCD) of 32 and 12.

$32 = ②\cdot②\cdot 2 \cdot 2 \cdot 2$ *Circle the common*
$12 = ②\cdot②\cdot 3$ *prime factors.*
$2 \cdot 2 = 4$ *Multiply the common*
The GCD is 4.   *prime factors.*

EXERCISES

Find the greatest common divisor (GCD).

15. 120, 210   **16.** 81, 132

17. 36, 60   **18.** 50, 75, 125

19. 36, 60, 96   **20.** 220, 440, 880

3-3 Least Common Multiple (pp. 136–139) ← NS2.4

EXAMPLES

■ **Find the least common multiple (LCM) of 8 and 10.**

Multiples of 8: 8, 16, 24, 32, ⑩
Multiples of 10: 10, 20, 30, ⑩
The LCM is 40.

■ **Find the least common multiple (LCM) of 6, 14, and 20.**

$6 = ②\cdot 3$ *Circle the common*
$14 = ②\cdot 7$ *prime factors.*
$20 = ②\cdot 2 \cdot 5$

2, 3, 7, 2, 5   *List the prime factors, using the circled factors only once.*

$2 \cdot 3 \cdot 7 \cdot 2 \cdot 5$ *Multiply the factors in*
The LCM is 420.   *the list.*

EXERCISES

Find the least common multiple (LCM).

21. 5, 12   **22.** 4, 32

23. 3, 27   **24.** 15, 18

25. 6, 12   **26.** 5, 7, 9

27. 3, 5, 10   **28.** 6, 8, 16

29. 3, 9, 27   **30.** 4, 12, 30

31. 25, 45   **32.** 12, 22, 30

33. Ethan washes dishes every 4 days and weeds the garden every 10 days. If he did both chores today, how many days will pass before he does them both on the same day again?

3-4 Equivalent Fractions and Mixed Numbers (pp. 142–145) 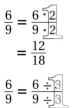 ← NS1.1, ← NS2.4

EXAMPLES

■ **Find two fractions equivalent to $\frac{6}{9}$.**

$\frac{6}{9} = \frac{6 \cdot 2}{9 \cdot 2}$ *Multiply the numerator and denominator by 2.*

$= \frac{12}{18}$

$\frac{6}{9} = \frac{6 \div 3}{9 \div 3}$ *Divide the numerator and denominator by 3.*

$= \frac{2}{3}$

■ **Write the fraction $\frac{12}{60}$ in simplest form.**

Find the GCD of 12 and 60.

$12 = ②\cdot ②\cdot ③$ *The GCD is 12 = 2 · 2 · 3.*
$60 = ②\cdot ②\cdot ③\cdot 5$

$\frac{12}{60} = \frac{12 \div 12}{60 \div 12}$ *Divide the numerator and denominator by 12.*

$= \frac{1}{5}$

■ **Write $5\frac{2}{3}$ as an improper fraction.**

$5\frac{2}{3} = \frac{3 \cdot 5 + 2}{3} = \frac{17}{3}$

■ **Write $\frac{17}{4}$ as a mixed number.**

$\frac{17}{4} = 4\frac{1}{4}$ *Divide the numerator by the denominator.*

EXERCISES

Find two fractions equivalent to the given fraction.

34. $\frac{4}{6}$ **35.** $\frac{4}{5}$ **36.** $\frac{3}{12}$

37. $\frac{16}{18}$ **38.** $\frac{21}{24}$ **39.** $\frac{48}{63}$

Write each fraction in simplest form.

40. $\frac{14}{16}$ **41.** $\frac{9}{30}$ **42.** $\frac{8}{10}$

43. $\frac{20}{100}$ **44.** $\frac{15}{35}$ **45.** $\frac{36}{54}$

Write each as an improper fraction.

46. $4\frac{1}{5}$ **47.** $3\frac{1}{6}$ **48.** $10\frac{3}{4}$

49. $3\frac{7}{9}$ **50.** $2\frac{5}{12}$ **51.** $5\frac{2}{7}$

Write each as a mixed number.

52. $\frac{10}{3}$ **53.** $\frac{5}{2}$ **54.** $\frac{17}{7}$

55. $\frac{23}{6}$ **56.** $\frac{17}{5}$ **57.** $\frac{41}{8}$

3-5 Equivalent Fractions and Decimals (pp. 146–149)   Prep for ← NS1.1, ← NS2.4

EXAMPLES

■ Write 0.75 as a fraction in simplest form.

$0.75 = \frac{75}{100}$ *5 is in the hundredths place.*

$= \frac{75 \div 25}{100 \div 25}$

$= \frac{3}{4}$

■ Write $\frac{6}{5}$ as a decimal.

$$\begin{array}{r} 1.2 \\ 5\overline{)6.0} \\ \underline{-5} \\ 10 \\ \underline{-10} \\ 0 \end{array}$$ *Divide the numerator by the denominator.*

$\frac{6}{5} = 1.2$

EXERCISES

Write each decimal as a fraction in simplest form.

58. 0.25   **59.** −0.004

60. 0.05   **61.** 0.37

62. −0.48   **63.** 0.08

Write each fraction as a decimal. Round to the nearest hundredth, if necessary

64. $\frac{7}{2}$ **65.** $\frac{3}{5}$

66. $\frac{2}{3}$ **67.** $\frac{7}{8}$

68. $-\frac{1}{16}$ **69.** $\frac{7}{9}$

70. Sarita spelled 70 out of 75 words correctly. What portion of the words did she spell correctly? Write your answer as a decimal rounded to the nearest hundredth.

3-6 Comparing and Ordering Rational Numbers (pp. 150–153)   ← NS1.1, ← NS2.4

EXAMPLES

■ Compare. Write < or >.

$-\frac{3}{4} \;\blacksquare\; -\frac{2}{3}$

$-\frac{3}{4} \cdot \frac{3}{3} \;\blacksquare\; -\frac{2}{3} \cdot \frac{4}{4}$ *Write as fractions with common denominators.*

$-\frac{9}{12} < -\frac{8}{12}$

■ Order -0.3, 0.1, $-\frac{1}{3}$, and $\frac{3}{10}$ from least to greatest. Graph the numbers on a number line.

$-0.3 = -0.30$ *Write as decimals with the*
$0.1 = 0.10$ *same number of places.*
$-\frac{1}{3} \approx -0.33$
$\frac{3}{10} = 0.30$

$-0.33 < -0.30 < 0.10 < 0.30$

From least to greatest, the numbers are $-\frac{1}{3}$, -0.3, 0.1, and $\frac{3}{10}$.

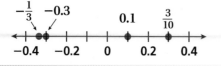

EXERCISES

Compare the fractions. Write < or > .

71. $\frac{4}{5} \;\blacksquare\; \frac{81}{100}$ **72.** $\frac{11}{50} \;\blacksquare\; \frac{3}{20}$

73. $-\frac{3}{5} \;\blacksquare\; -\frac{3}{2}$ **74.** $1\frac{1}{8} \;\blacksquare\; 1\frac{2}{9}$

75. $\frac{7}{9} \;\blacksquare\; \frac{2}{3}$ **76.** $-\frac{3}{12} \;\blacksquare\; -\frac{1}{3}$

Compare the decimals. Write < or>.

77. 0.04 ▮ 0.39   **78.** −0.25 ▮ −0.29

79. 0.185 ▮ 0.24   **80.** −0.14 ▮ −0.145

Order the numbers from least to greatest. Graph the numbers on a number line.

81. $\frac{6}{13}$, 0.58, −0.55, $\frac{1}{2}$

82. 1.45, $1\frac{2}{5}$, 1.5, $\frac{13}{10}$

83. $-\frac{14}{5}$, $-2\frac{1}{2}$, −2.09, −0.2

84. 0.8, $-\frac{8}{9}$, $\frac{7}{8}$, −0.7

CHAPTER TEST

Write the prime factorization of each number.

1. 30　　　　　　**2.** 66　　　　　　**3.** 78　　　　　　**4.** 110

Find the greatest common divisor (GCD).

5. 18, 27, 45　　**6.** 16, 28, 44　　**7.** 14, 28, 56　　**8.** 24, 36, 64

9. Reggie is designing displays for a music store. He has 36 CDs, 12 CD players, and 8 CD cases. What is the greatest number of identical displays Reggie can make if he uses all of the CDs, players, and cases?

Find the least common multiple (LCM).

10. 24, 36, 64　　**11.** 24, 72, 144　　**12.** 12, 15, 36　　**13.** 9, 16, 25

14. A teacher is buying school supplies. Pencils come in boxes of 10, pens come in boxes of 12, and rulers come in boxes of 6. What is the least number of each type of box the teacher can buy to have an equal number of pens, pencils, and rulers?

Determine whether the fractions in each pair are equivalent.

15. $\frac{6}{12}$ and $\frac{13}{26}$　　**16.** $\frac{17}{20}$ and $\frac{20}{24}$　　**17.** $\frac{30}{24}$ and $\frac{35}{28}$　　**18.** $\frac{5}{3}$ and $\frac{8}{5}$

Write each fraction as a decimal. Round to the nearest hundredth, if necessary.

19. $\frac{3}{50}$　　　　**20.** $\frac{25}{10}$　　　　**21.** $\frac{7}{9}$　　　　**22.** $\frac{9}{20}$

Write each decimal as a fraction in simplest form.

23. 0.2　　　　**24.** 0.85　　　　**25.** 3.15　　　　**26.** 0.004

27. The Drama Club has 52 members. Of these members, 18 are in the seventh grade. What fraction of the Drama Club is made up of seventh-graders? Write your answer as a fraction and a decimal. Round the decimal to the nearest thousandth.

Compare. Write < or >.

28. $\frac{2}{3}$ ▦ 0.62　　**29.** 1.5 ▦ $1\frac{6}{20}$　　**30.** $-\frac{9}{7}$ ▦ -1　　**31.** $\frac{11}{5}$ ▦ $1\frac{2}{3}$

Order the numbers from least to greatest. Graph the numbers on a number line.

32. $\frac{9}{4}$, 2.04, $2\frac{1}{6}$, 2.15　　　　**33.** -0.7, $-\frac{3}{5}$, -0.75, $-\frac{5}{8}$

34. Last week, Padma went hiking on 3 trails. One trail measured $3\frac{3}{8}$ miles, one measured 3.3 miles, and one measured $3\frac{1}{4}$ miles. List the distances Padma hiked in order from least to greatest.

STRATEGIES FOR SUCCESS

Short Response: Write Short Responses

Short-response test items require a solution to the problem and the reasoning or work used to get that solution. Short-response test items are often scored according to a 2-point scoring rubric. A sample scoring rubric is provided below.

EXAMPLE

Short Response Dario needs $1\frac{1}{3}$ pounds of turkey for a recipe. At the grocery store, there are three packages of turkey that are marked 1.42 pounds, 1.03 pounds, and 1.15 pounds. Which package is closest to the amount that Dario needs? Explain how you determined your answer.

2-point response:

> Write the number of pounds Dario needs as a decimal.
>
> $1\frac{1}{3} \approx 1.33$
>
> Graph on a number line the weight of each package and the weight of turkey that Dario needs.
>
>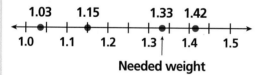
>
> The number line shows that the package weighing 1.42 pounds is closest to the amount that Dario needs.

Scoring Rubric

2 points: The student correctly answers the question, shows all work, and provides a complete and correct explanation.

1 point: The student correctly answers the question but does not show all work or does not provide a complete explanation; or the student makes minor errors resulting in an incorrect solution but shows all work and provides a complete explanation.

0 points: The student gives an incorrect answer and shows no work or explanation, or the student gives no response.

1-point response:

> $1.03 < 1.15 < 1\frac{1}{3} < 1.42$
> Dario should choose the package that weighs 1.42 pounds.

The student correctly solved the problem but did not show all of his or her work or did not provide an explanation.

0-point response:

> 1.15 pounds

The student gave an incorrect answer and did not show any work or give an explanation.

Never leave a short-response test item blank. Showing your work and providing a reasonable explanation will result in at least some credit.

Read each test item and answer the questions that follow by using the scoring rubric.

Item A
Short Response Write two equations that each have a solution of 12. You cannot use the same mathematical operation for both equations. Explain how to solve both equations.

Student's Answer

One equation that has a solution of 12 is $\frac{x}{6} = 2$. To solve this equation, I must undo the division by multiplying by 6 on both sides.

$$\frac{x}{6} = 2$$

$$6 \cdot \left(\frac{x}{6}\right) = 6 \cdot 2$$

$$x = 12$$

Another equation with a solution of 12 is $x - 8 = 20$.

To solve this equation, I must add the opposite of 8 to both sides.

$$x - 8 = 20$$
$$\underline{-8 = -8}$$
$$x = 12$$

1. The student's answer will not receive full credit. Find the error in the student's answer.

2. Rewrite the student's answer so that it receives full credit.

Item B
Short Response June is 8 years older than her cousin Liv. Write an expression to find June's age. Identify the variable and list three possible solutions showing the ages of June and Liv.

Student's Answer

Let x = Liv's age. Since June is 8 years older, the expression $x + 8$ can be used to find June's age.

Three possible solutions for Liv and June follow:

$x = 3$, $3 + 8 = 11$; Liv: 3, June: 11
$x = 8$, $8 + 8 = 16$; Liv: 8, June: 16
$x = 11$, $11 + 8 = 19$; Liv: 11, June: 19

3. What score should the student's answer receive? Explain your reasoning.

4. What additional information, if any, should the student's answer include in order to receive full credit?

Item C
Short Response Jin feeds her pet snake once every 10 days and cleans its cage once every 14 days. If she does both tasks today, how many days will pass before she does both tasks on the same day again? Explain how you determined your answer.

Student's Answer

$2 \cdot 5 \cdot 7 = 70$

It will be 70 days before Jin does both tasks on the same day again.

5. How would you score the student's response? Explain.

6. Rewrite the response so that it receives full credit.

MASTERING THE STANDARDS

Cumulative Assessment, Chapters 1–3

Multiple Choice

1. During a week in January in Cleveland, Ohio, the daily high temperatures were −4°F, −2°F, −12°F, 5°F, 12°F, 16°F, and 20°F. Which expression can be used to find the difference between the highest temperature of the week and the lowest temperature of the week?

   Ⓐ 20 − 2   Ⓒ 20 − 12
   Ⓑ 20 − (−2)   Ⓓ 20 − (−12)

2. Find the greatest common divisor of 16 and 32.

   Ⓐ 2   Ⓒ 32
   Ⓑ 16   Ⓓ 512

3. The fraction $\frac{3}{5}$ is found between which pair of fractions on a number line?

   Ⓐ $\frac{1}{2}$ and $\frac{2}{10}$

   Ⓑ $\frac{1}{2}$ and $\frac{7}{10}$

   Ⓒ $\frac{3}{10}$ and $\frac{5}{15}$

   Ⓓ $\frac{3}{10}$ and $\frac{8}{15}$

4. Maxie earns $210 a week working as a lifeguard. If Maxie gives each of her 3 sisters d dollars after she gets paid, which expression can be used to find the amount of money she has left?

   Ⓐ $210 - \frac{d}{3}$

   Ⓑ $210 - 3d$

   Ⓒ $3(210 - d)$

   Ⓓ $(210 - d) \div 3$

5. The table shows the thickness of climbing ropes sold at a sporting goods store. What color of rope is the thickest?

Climbing Ropes	
Color	**Thickness (in.)**
Blue	$\frac{3}{8}$
Green	$\frac{5}{16}$
Red	$\frac{13}{32}$
Yellow	$\frac{1}{4}$

   Ⓐ Blue   Ⓒ Red
   Ⓑ Green   Ⓓ Yellow

6. Which of the following shows a list of numbers in order from least to greatest?

   Ⓐ −1.05, −2.55, −3.05

   Ⓑ −2.75, $2\frac{5}{6}$, 2.50

   Ⓒ −0.05, −0.01, $3\frac{1}{4}$

   Ⓓ $-1\frac{2}{8}$, $-1\frac{4}{8}$, 1.05

7. Which expression is equivalent to 5(6 + 2)?

   Ⓐ 5(2 + 6)   Ⓒ (5 · 6) + 2
   Ⓑ 6(5 + 2)   Ⓓ (5 + 6) · (5 + 2)

8. What value of x makes the following equation true?

   $$x - 23 = 42$$

   Ⓐ 19   Ⓒ 61
   Ⓑ 21   Ⓓ 65

9. To get to the next level in a video game, Jorge must find 48 treasures. So far, he has found 16 of the treasures. What fraction of the treasures has Jorge found?

(A) $\frac{1}{32}$　　　(C) $\frac{1}{4}$

(B) $\frac{1}{16}$　　　(D) $\frac{1}{3}$

10. Simplify the expression $(-5)^2 - 3 \cdot 4$.

(A) -112　　　(C) 13

(B) -37　　　(D) 88

11. Evaluate $a - b$ for $a = -5$ and $b = 3$.

(A) -8　　　(C) 2

(B) -2　　　(D) 8

 You may not be able to enter negative numbers into some types of grids. If you get a negative value to a gridded response question, you may have made an error. Check your work!

Gridded Response

12. On Friday, the high temperature was 37°F warmer than the low temperature. If the low temperature was −6°F, what was the high temperature, in degrees Fahrenheit?

13. Solve for x and y in each equation. Grid the sum of x and y.

$$x + 6 = -4 \qquad -3y = -39$$

14. Garrett dusts his bedroom every four days and sweeps his bedroom every three days. If he does both today, how many days will pass before he does them both on the same day again?

15. What is the least common multiple of 15 and 12?

16. What is the value of $8^3 \div (16 - 12)$?

Short Response

17. The sponsors of the marching band provided 128 sandwiches for a picnic. After the picnic, s sandwiches were left.

 a. Write an expression that shows how many sandwiches were handed out.

 b. Evaluate your expression for $s = 15$. What does your answer represent?

18. Casey said the solution to the equation $x + 42 = 65$ is 107. Identify the error that Casey made. Explain why this answer is unreasonable.

Extended Response

19. Mary's allowance is based on the amount of time that she spends practicing different activities each week. This week Mary spent 12 hours practicing and earned $12.00.

 a. Mary spent the following amounts of time on each activity: $\frac{1}{5}$ practicing flute, $\frac{1}{6}$ studying Spanish, $\frac{1}{3}$ playing soccer, and $\frac{3}{10}$ studying math. Write an equivalent decimal for the amount of time that she spent on each activity. Round to the nearest hundredth, if necessary.

 b. For each activity, Mary earned the same fraction of her allowance as the time spent on a particular activity. This week, she was paid $3.60 for math practice. Was this the correct amount? Explain how you know.

 c. Order the amount of time that Mary spent practicing each activity from least to greatest.

 d. Write a decimal to represent the fraction of time Mary would have spent practicing soccer for 5 hours instead of 4 hours this week.

Operations with Rational Numbers

CONCEPT CONNECTION

go.hrw.com
Chapter Project Online
KEYWORD: MS8CA Ch4

By using operations with fractions, you can determine the total weight of gold found by a miner.
Gold Mining
California

ARE YOU READY?

☑ Vocabulary

Choose the best term from the list to complete each sentence.

1. A(n) __?__ is a number that is written using the base-ten place value system.

2. An example of a(n) __?__ is $\frac{14}{5}$.

3. A(n) __?__ is a number that represents a part of a whole.

decimal

fraction

improper fraction

mixed number

simplest form

Complete these exercises to review the skills you will need for this chapter.

☑ Simplify Fractions

Write each fraction in simplest form.

4. $\frac{24}{40}$ 5. $\frac{64}{84}$ 6. $\frac{66}{78}$ 7. $\frac{64}{192}$

8. $\frac{21}{35}$ 9. $\frac{11}{99}$ 10. $\frac{16}{36}$ 11. $\frac{20}{30}$

☑ Write Mixed Numbers as Fractions

Write each mixed number as an improper fraction.

12. $7\frac{1}{2}$ 13. $2\frac{5}{6}$ 14. $1\frac{14}{15}$ 15. $3\frac{2}{11}$

16. $3\frac{7}{8}$ 17. $8\frac{4}{9}$ 18. $4\frac{1}{7}$ 19. $5\frac{9}{10}$

☑ Write Fractions as Mixed Numbers

Write each improper fraction as a mixed number.

20. $\frac{23}{6}$ 21. $\frac{17}{3}$ 22. $\frac{29}{7}$ 23. $\frac{39}{4}$

24. $\frac{48}{5}$ 25. $\frac{82}{9}$ 26. $\frac{69}{4}$ 27. $\frac{35}{8}$

☑ Add, Subtract, Multiply, or Divide Integers

Find each sum, difference, product, or quotient.

28. $-11 + (-24)$ 29. $-11 - 7$ 30. $-4 \cdot (-10)$

31. $-22 \div (-11)$ 32. $23 + (-30)$ 33. $-33 - 74$

34. $-62 \cdot (-34)$ 35. $84 \div (-12)$ 36. $-26 - 18$

Unpacking the Standards

The information below "unpacks" the standards. The Academic Vocabulary is highlighted and defined to help you understand the language of the standards. Refer to the lessons listed after each standard for help with the math terms and phrases. The Chapter Concept shows how the standard is applied in this chapter.

California Standard	Academic Vocabulary	Chapter Concept
NS2.1 Solve problems involving addition, subtraction, multiplication, and division of positive fractions and explain why a particular operation was used for a given situation. (Lessons 4-2, 4-3, 4-4, 4-5, 4-6) (Labs 4-2, 4-4)	**operations** include addition, subtraction, multiplication, and division	You add, subtract, multiply, and divide to solve problems with fractions. **Example:** $\frac{1}{5} + \frac{2}{5}$ Add the numerators and keep the common denominator. $\frac{1}{5} + \frac{2}{5} = \frac{3}{5}$ **Example:** $2\frac{1}{10} + 3\frac{6}{10}$ Add the whole numbers and add the fractions. $2\frac{1}{10} + 3\frac{6}{10} = 5\frac{7}{10}$
NS2.2 Explain the meaning of multiplication and division of positive fractions and perform the calculations (e.g., $\frac{5}{8} \div \frac{15}{16} = \frac{5}{8} \cdot \frac{16}{15} = \frac{2}{3}$). (Lessons 4-4, 4-5, 4-6) (Lab 4-4)	**perform** do **calculations** the steps of doing the operations in a problem	You understand multiplying and dividing fractions. **Example:** $\frac{1}{2} \times \frac{3}{4}$ Multiply the numerators and multiply the denominators. $\frac{1}{2} \times \frac{3}{4} = \frac{3}{8}$
AF2.1 Convert one unit of measurement to another (e.g., from feet to miles, from centimeters to inches). (Lesson 4-9)	**convert** change from one form to another **unit of measurement** a quantity used for measuring **Examples:** A **meter** is a unit of **length**. A **kilogram** is a unit of **mass**. A **second** is a unit of **time**.	You change measurements from one type of unit to another. **Example:** 1 meter is equal to 100 centimeters, so 4 meters is equal to 400 centimeters. **Example:** 1 kilogram is equal to 1,000 grams, so 2,000 grams is equal to 2 kilograms.

Standards ← NS2.4 and ← AF1.1 are also covered in this chapter. To see these standards unpacked, go to Chapter 3, p. 126 (← NS2.4) and Chapter 1, p. 4 (← AF1.1).

Reading and Writing Math

California Standards
English-Language Arts
Reading 6.2.4

Study Strategy: Use Your Notes Effectively

Taking notes helps you understand and remember information from your textbook and lessons in class. Listed below are some steps for effectively using your notes before and after class.

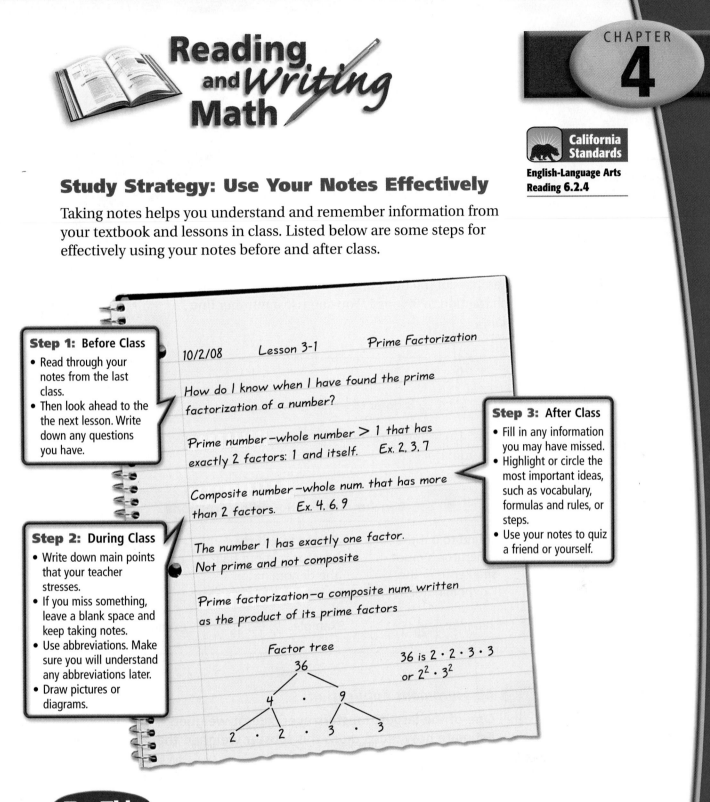

Step 1: Before Class
- Read through your notes from the last class.
- Then look ahead to the the next lesson. Write down any questions you have.

Step 2: During Class
- Write down main points that your teacher stresses.
- If you miss something, leave a blank space and keep taking notes.
- Use abbreviations. Make sure you will understand any abbreviations later.
- Draw pictures or diagrams.

Step 3: After Class
- Fill in any information you may have missed.
- Highlight or circle the most important ideas, such as vocabulary, formulas and rules, or steps.
- Use your notes to quiz a friend or yourself.

10/2/08   Lesson 3-1   Prime Factorization

How do I know when I have found the prime factorization of a number?

Prime number—whole number > 1 that has exactly 2 factors: 1 and itself.   Ex. 2, 3, 7

Composite number—whole num. that has more than 2 factors.   Ex. 4, 6, 9

The number 1 has exactly one factor. Not prime and not composite

Prime factorization—a composite num. written as the product of its prime factors

Factor tree
36
4 · 9
2 · 2 · 3 · 3

36 is 2 · 2 · 3 · 3 or $2^2 \cdot 3^2$

Try This

1. Look at the next lesson in your textbook. Think about how the new information relates to previous lessons. Write down any questions you have.

2. With a classmate, compare the notes you took during the last class. Are there differences in the main points that you each recorded? Then brainstorm two ways you can improve your note-taking skills.

4-1 Estimating with Fractions

California Standards

Preparation for **NS2.1** Solve problems involving addition, subtraction, multiplication, and division of positive fractions and explain why a particular operation was used for a given situation.

Why learn this? You can estimate with fractions to compare measurements, such as the weights of lobsters.

Sometimes, when solving problems, you may not need an exact answer. To estimate sums and differences of fractions and mixed numbers, round each fraction to 0, $\frac{1}{2}$, or 1. You can use a number line to help.

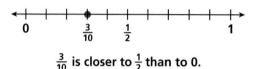

$\frac{3}{10}$ is closer to $\frac{1}{2}$ than to 0.

You can also round a fraction by comparing its numerator with its denominator.

Benchmarks for Rounding Fractions		
Round to **0** if the numerator is much smaller than the denominator.	Round to $\frac{1}{2}$ if the numerator is about half the denominator.	Round to **1** if the numerator is nearly equal to the denominator.
Examples: $\frac{1}{9}, \frac{3}{20}, \frac{2}{11}$	Examples: $\frac{2}{5}, \frac{5}{12}, \frac{7}{13}$	Examples: $\frac{8}{9}, \frac{23}{25}, \frac{97}{100}$

EXAMPLE 1 Measurement Application

One of the largest lobsters ever caught weighed $44\frac{3}{8}$ lb. Estimate how much more this lobster weighed than an average 3 lb lobster.

Think: How much more is $44\frac{3}{8}$ than 3? Use subtraction to find how much more.

$44\frac{3}{8} - 3$

$44\frac{3}{8} \longrightarrow 44\frac{1}{2}$ *Round the mixed number.*

$44\frac{1}{2} - 3 = 41\frac{1}{2}$ *Subtract.*

The $44\frac{3}{8}$-lb lobster weighed about $41\frac{1}{2}$ lb more than an average lobster.

Helpful Hint

Round $\frac{1}{4}$ to $\frac{1}{2}$, round $\frac{1}{3}$ to $\frac{1}{2}$, and round $\frac{3}{4}$ to 1.

EXAMPLE **2** **Estimating Sums and Differences**

Estimate each sum or difference.

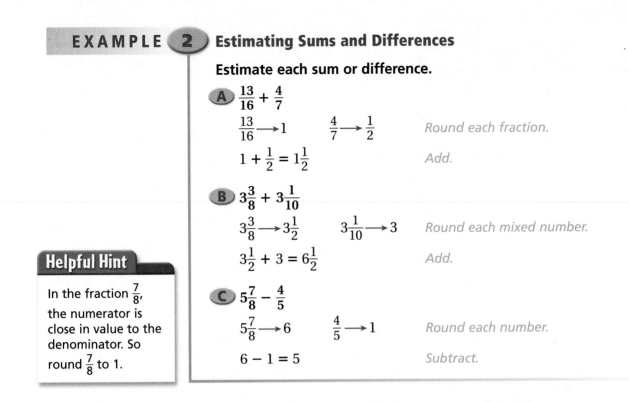

A $\frac{13}{16} + \frac{4}{7}$

$\frac{13}{16} \longrightarrow 1$ $\frac{4}{7} \longrightarrow \frac{1}{2}$ *Round each fraction.*

$1 + \frac{1}{2} = 1\frac{1}{2}$ *Add.*

B $3\frac{3}{8} + 3\frac{1}{10}$

$3\frac{3}{8} \longrightarrow 3\frac{1}{2}$ $3\frac{1}{10} \longrightarrow 3$ *Round each mixed number.*

$3\frac{1}{2} + 3 = 6\frac{1}{2}$ *Add.*

C $5\frac{7}{8} - \frac{4}{5}$

$5\frac{7}{8} \longrightarrow 6$ $\frac{4}{5} \longrightarrow 1$ *Round each number.*

$6 - 1 = 5$ *Subtract.*

> **Helpful Hint**
>
> In the fraction $\frac{7}{8}$, the numerator is close in value to the denominator. So round $\frac{7}{8}$ to 1.

You can estimate products and quotients of mixed numbers by rounding to the nearest whole number. If the fraction in a mixed number is greater than or equal to $\frac{1}{2}$, round the mixed number up to the next whole number. If the fraction is less than $\frac{1}{2}$, round down to a whole number by dropping the fraction.

EXAMPLE **3** **Estimating Products and Quotients**

Estimate each product or quotient.

A $4\frac{2}{7} \cdot 6\frac{9}{10}$

$4\frac{2}{7} \longrightarrow 4$ $6\frac{9}{10} \longrightarrow 7$ *Round each mixed number to the nearest whole number.*

$4 \cdot 7 = 28$ *Multiply.*

B $11\frac{3}{4} \div 2\frac{1}{5}$

$11\frac{3}{4} \longrightarrow 12$ $2\frac{1}{5} \longrightarrow 2$ *Round each mixed number to the nearest whole number.*

$12 \div 2 = 6$ *Divide.*

Think and Discuss

1. Demonstrate how to round $\frac{5}{12}$ and $5\frac{1}{5}$.

2. Explain how you know that $25\frac{5}{8} \cdot 5\frac{1}{10} > 125$.

California
Standards Practice
Preparation for NS2.1

go.hrw.com
Homework Help Online
KEYWORD: MS8CA 4-1
Parent Resources Online
KEYWORD: MS8CA Parent

GUIDED PRACTICE

See Example 1

1. The length of a large SUV is $18\frac{9}{10}$ feet, and the length of a small SUV is $15\frac{1}{8}$ feet. Estimate how much longer the large SUV is than the small SUV.

See Example 2

Estimate each sum or difference.

2. $\frac{5}{6} + \frac{5}{12}$ **3.** $\frac{15}{16} - \frac{4}{5}$ **4.** $2\frac{1}{6} + 3\frac{6}{11}$ **5.** $5\frac{1}{7} - 2\frac{7}{9}$

See Example 3

Estimate each product or quotient.

6. $1\frac{3}{25} \cdot 9\frac{6}{7}$ **7.** $21\frac{2}{7} \div 7\frac{1}{3}$ **8.** $31\frac{7}{8} \div 4\frac{1}{5}$ **9.** $12\frac{2}{5} \cdot 3\frac{6}{9}$

INDEPENDENT PRACTICE

See Example 1

10. Measurement Sarah's bedroom is $14\frac{5}{6}$ feet long and $12\frac{1}{4}$ feet wide. Estimate the difference between the length and width of Sarah's bedroom.

See Example 2

Estimate each sum or difference.

11. $\frac{4}{9} + \frac{3}{5}$ **12.** $2\frac{5}{9} + 1\frac{7}{8}$ **13.** $8\frac{3}{4} - 6$ **14.** $6\frac{1}{3} - \frac{5}{6}$

15. $\frac{7}{8} - \frac{2}{5}$ **16.** $15\frac{1}{7} - 10\frac{8}{9}$ **17.** $8\frac{7}{15} + 2\frac{7}{8}$ **18.** $\frac{4}{5} + 7\frac{1}{8}$

See Example 3

Estimate each product or quotient.

19. $23\frac{5}{7} \div 3\frac{6}{9}$ **20.** $10\frac{2}{5} \div 4\frac{5}{8}$ **21.** $2\frac{1}{8} \cdot 14\frac{5}{6}$ **22.** $7\frac{9}{10} \cdot 11\frac{3}{4}$

23. $5\frac{3}{5} \div 2\frac{2}{3}$ **24.** $12\frac{4}{6} \cdot 3\frac{2}{7}$ **25.** $8\frac{1}{4} \div 1\frac{7}{8}$ **26.** $15\frac{12}{15} \cdot 1\frac{5}{7}$

PRACTICE AND PROBLEM SOLVING

Extra Practice
See page EP8.

Estimate each sum, difference, product, or quotient.

27. $\frac{7}{9} - \frac{3}{8}$ **28.** $\frac{3}{5} + \frac{6}{7}$ **29.** $2\frac{5}{7} \cdot 8\frac{3}{11}$ **30.** $16\frac{7}{20} \div 3\frac{8}{9}$

31. $1\frac{3}{5} \cdot 4\frac{6}{13}$ **32.** $5\frac{3}{5} - 4\frac{1}{6}$ **33.** $3\frac{7}{8} + \frac{2}{15}$ **34.** $19\frac{5}{7} \div 5\frac{2}{5}$

35. $\frac{3}{8} + 3\frac{5}{7} + 6\frac{7}{8}$ **36.** $8\frac{4}{5} + 6\frac{1}{12} + 3\frac{2}{5}$ **37.** $14\frac{2}{3} + 1\frac{7}{9} - 11\frac{14}{29}$

38. Kevin has $3\frac{3}{4}$ pounds of pecans and $6\frac{2}{3}$ pounds of walnuts. About how many more pounds of walnuts than pecans does Kevin have?

39. Business On October 19, 1987, the stock market fell 508 points. A company's stock began the day at $\$70\frac{1}{8}$ and finished at $\$56\frac{1}{4}$. Approximately how far did the company's stock price fall during the day?

40. Recreation Monica and Paul hiked $5\frac{3}{8}$ miles on Saturday and $4\frac{9}{10}$ miles on Sunday. Estimate the number of miles Monica and Paul hiked.

41. Critical Thinking If you round a divisor down, is the quotient going to be less than or greater than the actual quotient? Explain.

Science The diagram shows the wingspans of different species of birds. Use the diagram for Exercises 42 and 43.

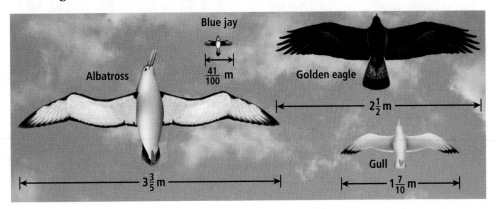

42. Approximately how much longer is the wingspan of an albatross than the wingspan of a gull?

43. Approximately how much longer is the wingspan of a golden eagle than the wingspan of a blue jay?

44. **Reasoning** Using mixed numbers, write a problem in which an estimate is enough to solve the problem.

45. **Write About It** How is estimating fractions or mixed numbers similar to rounding whole numbers?

46. **Challenge** Suppose you had bought 10 shares of stock on October 16, 1987, for $73 per share and sold them at the end of the day on October 19, 1987, for $56\frac{1}{4}$ per share. Approximately how much money would you have lost?

SPIRAL STANDARDS REVIEW   NS2.1, ✦ NS2.3, ✦ AF1.1

47. **Multiple Choice** For which of the following would 2 be the best estimate?

Ⓐ $8\frac{7}{9} \cdot 4\frac{2}{5}$ Ⓑ $4\frac{1}{5} \div 2\frac{5}{9}$ Ⓒ $8\frac{7}{9} \cdot 2\frac{1}{5}$ Ⓓ $8\frac{1}{9} \div 4\frac{2}{5}$

48. **Multiple Choice** The table shows the distance Maria biked each day last week.

Day	Mon	Tue	Wed	Thu	Fri	Sat	Sun
Distance (mi)	$12\frac{3}{8}$	$9\frac{11}{15}$	$3\frac{1}{4}$	$8\frac{1}{2}$	0	$4\frac{3}{4}$	$5\frac{2}{5}$

Which is the best estimate for the total distance Maria biked last week?

Ⓐ 40 mi   Ⓑ 44 mi   Ⓒ 48 mi   Ⓓ 52 mi

Solve each equation. Check your answer. (Lessons 1-8 to 1-11)

49. $x + 16 = 43$ 50. $y - 32 = 14$ 51. $5m = 65$ 52. $\frac{n}{3} = 18$

Find each product or quotient. (Lesson 2-4)

53. $20 \cdot (-5)$ 54. $-72 \div (-9)$ 55. $-16 \cdot (-8)$ 56. $-36 \div 3$

Model Fraction Addition and Subtraction

Use with Lesson 4-2

Fraction bars can be used to model addition and subtraction of fractions.

California Standards

NS2.1 Solve problems involving addition, subtraction, multiplication, and division **of positive fractions** and explain why a particular operation was used for a given situation.

Activity

You can use fraction bars to find $\frac{3}{8} + \frac{2}{8}$.

Use fraction bars to represent both fractions. Place the fraction bars side by side.

| $\frac{1}{8}$ | $\frac{1}{8}$ | $\frac{1}{8}$ | $\frac{1}{8}$ | $\frac{1}{8}$ |

$$\frac{3}{8} + \frac{2}{8} = \frac{5}{8}$$

1 Use fraction bars to find each sum.

a. $\frac{1}{3} + \frac{1}{3}$ b. $\frac{2}{4} + \frac{1}{4}$ c. $\frac{3}{12} + \frac{2}{12}$ d. $\frac{1}{5} + \frac{2}{5}$

You can use fraction bars to find $\frac{1}{3} + \frac{1}{4}$.

Use fraction bars to represent both fractions. Place the fraction bars side by side. Which kind of fraction bar placed side by side will fit below $\frac{1}{3}$ and $\frac{1}{4}$? (*Hint:* What is the LCM of 3 and 4?)

$\frac{1}{3}$			$\frac{1}{4}$	
$\frac{1}{12}$	$\frac{1}{12}$	$\frac{1}{12}$	$\frac{1}{12}$	$\frac{1}{12}$ $\frac{1}{12}$ $\frac{1}{12}$

$$\frac{1}{3} + \frac{1}{4} = \frac{7}{12}$$

2 Use fraction bars to find each sum.

a. $\frac{1}{2} + \frac{1}{3}$ b. $\frac{1}{2} + \frac{1}{4}$ c. $\frac{1}{3} + \frac{1}{6}$ d. $\frac{1}{4} + \frac{1}{6}$

You can use fraction bars to find $\frac{1}{3} + \frac{5}{6}$.

Use fraction bars to represent both fractions. Place the fraction bars side by side. Which kind of fraction bar placed side by side will fit below $\frac{1}{3}$ and $\frac{5}{6}$? (*Hint:* What is the LCM of 3 and 6?)

$$\frac{1}{3} + \frac{5}{6} = \frac{7}{6}$$

When the sum is an improper fraction, you can use the 1 bar along with fraction bars to find the mixed-number equivalent.

$$\frac{7}{6} = 1\frac{1}{6}$$

❸ Use fraction bars to find each sum.

a. $\frac{3}{4} + \frac{3}{4}$ b. $\frac{2}{3} + \frac{1}{2}$ c. $\frac{5}{6} + \frac{1}{4}$ d. $\frac{3}{8} + \frac{3}{4}$

You can use fraction bars to find $\frac{2}{3} - \frac{1}{2}$.

Place a $\frac{1}{2}$ bar beneath bars that show $\frac{2}{3}$, and find which fraction fills in the remaining space.

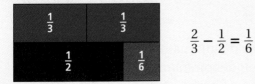

$$\frac{2}{3} - \frac{1}{2} = \frac{1}{6}$$

❹ Use fraction bars to find each difference.

a. $\frac{2}{3} - \frac{1}{3}$ b. $\frac{1}{4} - \frac{1}{6}$ c. $\frac{1}{2} - \frac{1}{3}$ d. $\frac{3}{4} - \frac{2}{3}$

Think and Discuss

1. Model and solve $\frac{3}{4} - \frac{1}{6}$. Explain your steps.

2. Two students solved $\frac{1}{4} + \frac{1}{3}$ in different ways. One got $\frac{7}{12}$ for the answer, and the other got $\frac{2}{7}$. Use models to show which student is correct.

3. Find three different ways to model $\frac{1}{2} + \frac{1}{4}$.

Try This

Use fraction bars to find each sum or difference.

1. $\frac{1}{2} + \frac{1}{2}$ 2. $\frac{2}{3} + \frac{1}{6}$ 3. $\frac{1}{4} + \frac{1}{6}$ 4. $\frac{1}{3} + \frac{7}{12}$

5. $\frac{5}{12} - \frac{1}{3}$ 6. $\frac{1}{2} - \frac{1}{4}$ 7. $\frac{3}{4} - \frac{1}{6}$ 8. $\frac{2}{3} - \frac{1}{4}$

9. You ate $\frac{1}{4}$ of a pizza for lunch and $\frac{5}{8}$ of the pizza for dinner. How much of the pizza did you eat in all?

10. It is $\frac{5}{6}$ mile from your home to the library. After walking $\frac{3}{4}$ mile, you stop to visit a friend on your way to the library. How much farther must you walk to reach the library?

4-2 Adding and Subtracting Fractions

California Standards

NS2.1 Solve problems involving addition, subtraction, multiplication, and division **of positive fractions and explain why a particular operation was used for a given situation.**

Also covered: **NS2.4**

Why learn this? You can add fractions to determine how much of Earth's surface is covered by oceans. (See Example 3.)

To add and subtract fractions with like denominators, add or subtract the numerators and keep the common denominator.

EXAMPLE 1 **Adding and Subtracting Fractions with Like Denominators**

Add or subtract. Write each answer in simplest form.

A $\dfrac{3}{10} + \dfrac{1}{10}$

$\dfrac{3}{10} + \dfrac{1}{10} = \dfrac{3+1}{10}$ *Add the numerators and keep the common denominator.*

$= \dfrac{4}{10} = \dfrac{2}{5}$ *Simplify.*

B $\dfrac{7}{9} - \dfrac{4}{9}$

$\dfrac{7}{9} - \dfrac{4}{9} = \dfrac{7-4}{9}$ *Subtract the numerators and keep the common denominator.*

$= \dfrac{3}{9} = \dfrac{1}{3}$ *Simplify.*

To add or subtract fractions with different denominators, you must rewrite the fractions with a common denominator.

Helpful Hint

The LCM of two denominators is the least common denominator (LCD) of the fractions.

Two Ways to Find a Common Denominator
Method 1: Multiply the denominators.
Method 2: Find the LCM (least common multiple) of the denominators.

176 *Chapter 4 Operations with Rational Numbers*

EXAMPLE **2** **Adding and Subtracting Fractions with Unlike Denominators**

Add or subtract. Write each answer in simplest form.

A $\dfrac{5}{8} - \dfrac{1}{10}$

$\dfrac{5}{8} - \dfrac{1}{10} = \dfrac{5 \cdot 10}{8 \cdot 10} - \dfrac{1 \cdot 8}{10 \cdot 8}$ *Use Method 1: Multiply the denominators.*

$= \dfrac{50}{80} - \dfrac{8}{80}$ *Write equivalent fractions using a common denominator.*

$= \dfrac{42}{80} = \dfrac{21}{40}$ *Subtract. Then simplify.*

B $\dfrac{3}{8} + \dfrac{5}{12}$

$\dfrac{3}{8} + \dfrac{5}{12} = \dfrac{3 \cdot 3}{8 \cdot 3} + \dfrac{5 \cdot 2}{12 \cdot 2}$ *Use Method 2: The LCM of the denominators is 24.*

$= \dfrac{9}{24} + \dfrac{10}{24}$ *Write equivalent fractions using a common denominator.*

$= \dfrac{19}{24}$ *Add.*

C $\dfrac{2}{3} + \dfrac{5}{8}$

$\dfrac{2}{3} + \dfrac{5}{8} = \dfrac{2 \cdot 8}{3 \cdot 8} + \dfrac{5 \cdot 3}{8 \cdot 3}$ *Use Method 2: The LCM of the denominators is 24.*

$= \dfrac{16}{24} + \dfrac{15}{24}$ *Write equivalent fractions using a common denominator.*

$= \dfrac{31}{24} = 1\dfrac{7}{24}$ *Add. Then simplify.*

Helpful Hint

When you add and subtract fractions, you will get the same answer no matter which method you use to find a common denominator.

EXAMPLE **3** *Earth Science Application*

The Pacific Ocean covers about $\frac{1}{3}$ of Earth's surface, and the Atlantic Ocean covers about $\frac{1}{5}$ of Earth's surface. Find the fraction of Earth's surface covered by both oceans.

Think: How much is $\frac{1}{3}$ combined with $\frac{1}{5}$? Use addition to put parts together.

$\dfrac{1}{3} + \dfrac{1}{5} = \dfrac{1 \cdot 5}{3 \cdot 5} + \dfrac{1 \cdot 3}{5 \cdot 3}$ *Use Method 1: Multiply the denominators.*

$= \dfrac{5}{15} + \dfrac{3}{15}$ *Write equivalent fractions.*

$= \dfrac{8}{15}$ *Add.*

Together, the Pacific Ocean and Atlantic Ocean cover about $\frac{8}{15}$ of Earth's surface.

Think and Discuss

1. Describe the process for subtracting fractions with different denominators.

4-2 Adding and Subtracting Fractions   **177**

4-2 **Exercises**

California Standards Practice
🔑 **NS1.1, NS2.1,** 🔑 **NS2.4**

go.hrw.com
Homework Help Online
KEYWORD: MS8CA 4-2
Parent Resources Online
KEYWORD: MS8CA Parent

GUIDED PRACTICE

See Example ① Add or subtract. Write each answer in simplest form.

1. $\dfrac{2}{3} - \dfrac{1}{3}$ **2.** $\dfrac{1}{12} + \dfrac{1}{12}$ **3.** $\dfrac{16}{21} - \dfrac{7}{21}$ **4.** $\dfrac{4}{17} + \dfrac{11}{17}$

See Example ② **5.** $\dfrac{1}{6} + \dfrac{1}{3}$ **6.** $\dfrac{9}{10} - \dfrac{3}{4}$ **7.** $\dfrac{2}{3} + \dfrac{1}{8}$ **8.** $\dfrac{5}{8} - \dfrac{3}{10}$

See Example ③ **9.** Parker spends $\dfrac{1}{4}$ of his earnings on rent and $\dfrac{1}{6}$ on entertainment. How much more of his earnings does Parker spend on rent than on entertainment?

INDEPENDENT PRACTICE

See Example ① Add or subtract. Write each answer in simplest form.

10. $\dfrac{2}{3} + \dfrac{1}{3}$ **11.** $\dfrac{3}{20} + \dfrac{7}{20}$ **12.** $\dfrac{5}{8} + \dfrac{7}{8}$ **13.** $\dfrac{6}{15} + \dfrac{3}{15}$

14. $\dfrac{7}{12} - \dfrac{5}{12}$ **15.** $\dfrac{5}{6} - \dfrac{1}{6}$ **16.** $\dfrac{8}{9} - \dfrac{5}{9}$ **17.** $\dfrac{9}{25} - \dfrac{4}{25}$

See Example ② **18.** $\dfrac{1}{5} + \dfrac{2}{3}$ **19.** $\dfrac{1}{6} + \dfrac{1}{12}$ **20.** $\dfrac{5}{6} + \dfrac{3}{4}$ **21.** $\dfrac{1}{2} + \dfrac{2}{8}$

22. $\dfrac{21}{24} - \dfrac{1}{2}$ **23.** $\dfrac{11}{12} - \dfrac{3}{4}$ **24.** $\dfrac{1}{2} - \dfrac{2}{7}$ **25.** $\dfrac{7}{10} - \dfrac{1}{6}$

See Example ③ **26.** Seana picked $\dfrac{3}{4}$ quart of blackberries. She ate $\dfrac{1}{12}$ quart. How much was left?

27. Armando lives $\dfrac{2}{3}$ mi from his school. If he has walked $\dfrac{1}{2}$ mi already this morning, how much farther must he walk to get to his school?

PRACTICE AND PROBLEM SOLVING

Extra Practice
See page EP8.

Find each sum or difference. Write your answer in simplest form.

28. $\dfrac{4}{5} + \dfrac{6}{7}$ **29.** $\dfrac{5}{6} - \dfrac{1}{9}$ **30.** $\dfrac{3}{4} - \dfrac{1}{2}$ **31.** $\dfrac{2}{3} + \dfrac{2}{15}$

32. $\dfrac{5}{7} + \dfrac{1}{3}$ **33.** $\dfrac{7}{12} - \dfrac{1}{2}$ **34.** $\dfrac{3}{4} + \dfrac{2}{5}$ **35.** $\dfrac{9}{14} - \dfrac{1}{7}$

36. $\dfrac{7}{8} + \dfrac{2}{3} + \dfrac{5}{6}$ **37.** $\dfrac{3}{5} + \dfrac{3}{4} - \dfrac{1}{10}$ **38.** $\dfrac{3}{10} + \dfrac{5}{8} + \dfrac{1}{5}$ **39.** $\dfrac{2}{5} - \dfrac{1}{6} + \dfrac{7}{10}$

40. $\dfrac{3}{8} + \dfrac{2}{7} - \dfrac{1}{2}$ **41.** $\dfrac{1}{3} + \dfrac{3}{7} - \dfrac{1}{9}$ **42.** $\dfrac{2}{9} - \dfrac{7}{18} + \dfrac{1}{6}$ **43.** $\dfrac{2}{15} + \dfrac{4}{9} + \dfrac{1}{3}$

44. $\dfrac{9}{35} + \dfrac{4}{7} - \dfrac{5}{14}$ **45.** $\dfrac{1}{3} - \dfrac{5}{7} + \dfrac{8}{21}$ **46.** $\dfrac{2}{9} - \dfrac{1}{12} + \dfrac{7}{18}$ **47.** $\dfrac{4}{5} + \dfrac{5}{8} - \dfrac{2}{3}$

48. Cooking One fruit salad recipe calls for $\dfrac{1}{2}$ cup of sugar. Another recipe calls for 2 tablespoons of sugar. Since 1 tablespoon is $\dfrac{1}{16}$ cup, how much more sugar does the first recipe require?

49. It took Earl $\dfrac{1}{2}$ hour to do his science homework and $\dfrac{1}{3}$ hour to do his math homework. How long did Earl work on homework?

50. Music In music written in $\dfrac{4}{4}$ time, a half note lasts for $\dfrac{1}{2}$ measure and an eighth note lasts for $\dfrac{1}{8}$ measure. In terms of a musical measure, what is the difference in the duration of the two notes?

Fitness Four friends had a competition to see how far they could walk while spinning a hoop around their waists. The table shows how far each friend walked. Use the table for Exercises 51–53.

Person	Distance (mi)
Rosalyn	$\frac{1}{8}$
Cai	$\frac{3}{4}$
Lauren	$\frac{2}{3}$
Janna	$\frac{7}{10}$

51. How much farther did Lauren walk than Rosalyn?

52. What is the combined distance that Cai and Rosalyn walked?

53. Who walked farther, Janna or Cai?

54. Measurement A shrew weighs $\frac{3}{16}$ lb. A hamster weighs $\frac{1}{4}$ lb.

    a. How many more pounds does a hamster weigh than a shrew?

    b. There are 16 oz in 1 lb. How many more ounces does the hamster weigh than the shrew?

55. Multi-Step To make $\frac{3}{4}$ lb of mixed nuts, how many pounds of cashews would you add to $\frac{1}{8}$ lb of almonds and $\frac{1}{4}$ lb of peanuts?

Shrew

Hamster

56. Reasoning Use facts you find in a newspaper or magazine to write a problem that can be solved using addition or subtraction of fractions. Explain how you know whether addition or subtraction could be used to solve your problem.

57. Write About It Explain the steps you use to add or subtract fractions that have different denominators.

58. Challenge The sum of two fractions is 1. If one fraction is $\frac{3}{8}$ greater than the other, what are the two fractions?

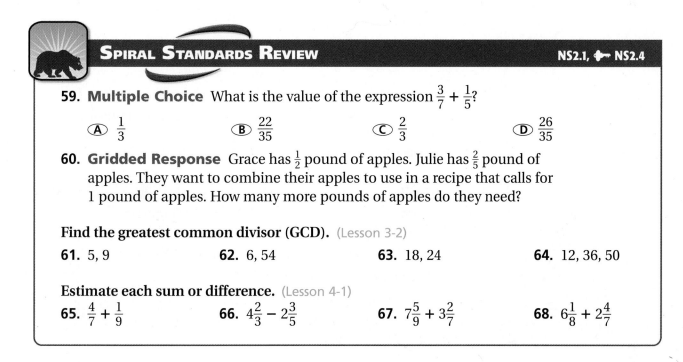

SPIRAL STANDARDS REVIEW   NS2.1, ← NS2.4

59. Multiple Choice What is the value of the expression $\frac{3}{7} + \frac{1}{5}$?

  Ⓐ $\frac{1}{3}$ Ⓑ $\frac{22}{35}$ Ⓒ $\frac{2}{3}$ Ⓓ $\frac{26}{35}$

60. Gridded Response Grace has $\frac{1}{2}$ pound of apples. Julie has $\frac{2}{5}$ pound of apples. They want to combine their apples to use in a recipe that calls for 1 pound of apples. How many more pounds of apples do they need?

Find the greatest common divisor (GCD). (Lesson 3-2)

61. 5, 9   **62.** 6, 54   **63.** 18, 24   **64.** 12, 36, 50

Estimate each sum or difference. (Lesson 4-1)

65. $\frac{4}{7} + \frac{1}{9}$ **66.** $4\frac{2}{3} - 2\frac{3}{5}$ **67.** $7\frac{5}{9} + 3\frac{2}{7}$ **68.** $6\frac{1}{8} + 2\frac{4}{7}$

Adding and Subtracting Mixed Numbers

California Standards

NS2.1 Solve problems involving **addition, subtraction,** multiplication, and division **of positive fractions** and explain why a particular operation was used for a given situation.

Also covered: 🔑 **NS2.4**

Why learn this? You can add mixed numbers to find the lengths of different types of beetles. (See Example 3.)

Giant green fruit beetle

A mixed number can be written as the sum of an integer and a fraction.

$$3\frac{4}{5} = 3 + \frac{4}{5}$$

To add mixed numbers, add the integers and then add the fractions.

Giraffe beetle

EXAMPLE 1 Adding Mixed Numbers

Add. Write each answer in simplest form.

Ⓐ $3\frac{4}{5} + 4\frac{2}{5}$

$3\frac{4}{5} + 4\frac{2}{5} = 7 + \frac{6}{5}$ *Add the integers, and then add the fractions.*

$= 7 + 1\frac{1}{5}$ *Rewrite the improper fraction as a mixed number.*

$= 8\frac{1}{5}$ *Add.*

Ⓑ $1\frac{2}{15} + 7\frac{1}{6}$

$1\frac{2}{15} + 7\frac{1}{6} = 1\frac{4}{30} + 7\frac{5}{30}$ *Find a common denominator.*

$= 8 + \frac{9}{30}$ *Add the integers, and then add the fractions.*

$= 8\frac{9}{30} = 8\frac{3}{10}$ *Add. Then simplify.*

Sometimes, when you subtract mixed numbers, the fraction portion of the first number is less than the fraction portion of the second number. In these cases, you must regroup before subtracting.

Remember!

Any fraction in which the numerator and denominator are the same nonzero number is equal to 1.

REGROUPING MIXED NUMBERS	
Words	**Numbers**
Regroup.	$7\frac{1}{8} = 6 + 1 + \frac{1}{8}$
Rewrite 1 as a fraction with a common denominator.	$= 6 + \frac{8}{8} + \frac{1}{8}$
Add.	$= 6\frac{9}{8}$

EXAMPLE 2 **Subtracting Mixed Numbers**

Subtract. Write each answer in simplest form.

A $10\frac{7}{9} - 4\frac{2}{9}$

$$10\frac{7}{9} - 4\frac{2}{9} = 6\frac{5}{9}$$ *Subtract the integers, and then subtract the fractions.*

B $12\frac{7}{8} - 5\frac{17}{24}$

$$12\frac{7}{8} - 5\frac{17}{24} = 12\frac{21}{24} - 5\frac{17}{24}$$ *Find a common denominator.*

$$= 7\frac{4}{24}$$ *Subtract the integers, and then subtract the fractions.*

$$= 7\frac{1}{6}$$ *Simplify.*

C $72\frac{3}{5} - 63\frac{4}{5}$

$$72\frac{3}{5} - 63\frac{4}{5} = 71\frac{8}{5} - 63\frac{4}{5}$$ *Regroup. $72\frac{3}{5} = 71 + \frac{5}{5} + \frac{3}{5}$*

$$= 8\frac{4}{5}$$ *Subtract the integers, and then subtract the fractions.*

EXAMPLE 3 *Measurement Application*

The giraffe beetle can grow about $6\frac{2}{5}$ centimeters longer than the giant green fruit beetle can. The giant green fruit beetle can grow up to $1\frac{1}{5}$ centimeters long. What is the maximum length of the giraffe beetle?

Think: What is $6\frac{2}{5}$ cm longer than $1\frac{1}{5}$ cm? Use addition to put two measurements together.

$$6\frac{2}{5} + 1\frac{1}{5} = 7 + \frac{3}{5}$$ *Add the integers, and then add the fractions.*

$$= 7\frac{3}{5}$$ *Add.*

The maximum length of the giraffe beetle is $7\frac{3}{5}$ centimeters.

Estimate $6\frac{1}{2} + 1 = 7\frac{1}{2}$ *Round $6\frac{2}{5}$ to $6\frac{1}{2}$ and $1\frac{1}{5}$ to 1.*

$7\frac{3}{5}$ is close to $7\frac{1}{2}$, so the answer is reasonable.

Think and Discuss

1. **Describe** the process for subtracting mixed numbers.

2. **Explain** whether $2\frac{3}{5} + 1\frac{3}{5} = 3\frac{6}{5}$ is correct. Is there another way to write the answer?

3. **Demonstrate** how to regroup to simplify $6\frac{2}{5} - 4\frac{3}{5}$.

Exercises

California
Standards Practice
NS1.1, NS2.1, NS2.4

go.hrw.com
Homework Help Online
KEYWORD: MS8CA 4-3
Parent Resources Online
KEYWORD: MS8CA Parent

GUIDED PRACTICE

See Example 1 Add. Write each answer in simplest form.

1. $3\frac{2}{5} + 4\frac{1}{5}$ 2. $2\frac{7}{8} + 3\frac{3}{4}$ 3. $1\frac{8}{9} + 4\frac{4}{9}$ 4. $5\frac{1}{2} + 2\frac{1}{4}$

See Example 2 Subtract. Write each answer in simplest form.

5. $6\frac{2}{3} - 5\frac{1}{3}$ 6. $8\frac{1}{6} - 2\frac{5}{6}$ 7. $3\frac{2}{3} - 2\frac{3}{4}$ 8. $7\frac{5}{8} - 3\frac{2}{5}$

See Example 3 9. **Measurement** Chrystelle's mother is $1\frac{2}{3}$ ft taller than Chrystelle. If Chrystelle is $3\frac{1}{2}$ ft tall, how tall is her mother?

INDEPENDENT PRACTICE

See Example 1 Add. Write each answer in simplest form.

10. $6\frac{1}{4} + 8\frac{3}{4}$ 11. $3\frac{3}{5} + 7\frac{4}{5}$ 12. $3\frac{5}{6} + 1\frac{5}{6}$ 13. $2\frac{3}{5} + 4\frac{1}{3}$

14. $2\frac{3}{10} + 4\frac{1}{2}$ 15. $6\frac{1}{8} + 8\frac{9}{10}$ 16. $6\frac{1}{6} + 5\frac{3}{10}$ 17. $1\frac{2}{5} + 9\frac{1}{4}$

See Example 2 Subtract. Write each answer in simplest form.

18. $2\frac{1}{14} - 1\frac{3}{14}$ 19. $4\frac{5}{12} - 1\frac{7}{12}$ 20. $8 - 2\frac{3}{4}$ 21. $7\frac{3}{4} - 5\frac{2}{3}$

22. $8\frac{3}{4} - 6\frac{2}{5}$ 23. $3\frac{1}{3} - 2\frac{5}{8}$ 24. $4\frac{2}{5} - 3\frac{1}{2}$ 25. $11 - 6\frac{5}{9}$

See Example 3 26. **Sports** The track at Daytona International Speedway is $\frac{24}{25}$ mi longer than the track at Atlanta Motor Speedway. If the track at Atlanta is $1\frac{27}{50}$ mi long, how long is the track at Daytona?

PRACTICE AND PROBLEM SOLVING

Extra Practice
See page EP8.

Add or subtract. Write each answer in simplest form.

27. $7\frac{1}{3} + 8\frac{1}{5}$ 28. $14\frac{3}{5} - 8\frac{1}{2}$ 29. $9\frac{1}{6} + 4\frac{6}{9}$ 30. $21\frac{8}{12} - 3\frac{1}{2}$

31. $3\frac{5}{8} + 2\frac{7}{12}$ 32. $25\frac{1}{3} + 3\frac{5}{6}$ 33. $1\frac{7}{9} - \frac{17}{18}$ 34. $3\frac{1}{2} + 5\frac{1}{4}$

35. $1\frac{7}{15} + 2\frac{7}{10}$ 36. $12\frac{4}{6} - \frac{2}{5}$ 37. $4\frac{2}{3} + 1\frac{7}{8} + 3\frac{1}{2}$ 38. $5\frac{1}{6} + 8\frac{2}{3} - 9\frac{1}{2}$

Compare. Write <, >, or =.

39. $12\frac{1}{4} - 10\frac{3}{4}$ ▇ $5\frac{1}{2} - 3\frac{7}{10}$ 40. $4\frac{1}{2} + 3\frac{4}{5}$ ▇ $4\frac{5}{7} + 3\frac{1}{2}$

41. $13\frac{3}{4} - 2\frac{3}{8}$ ▇ $5\frac{5}{6} + 4\frac{2}{9}$ 42. $4\frac{1}{3} - 2\frac{1}{4}$ ▇ $3\frac{1}{4} - 1\frac{1}{6}$

43. **History** During the California Gold Rush, a miner discovers 4 nuggets that separately weigh $\frac{1}{4}$ ounce, $1\frac{1}{4}$ ounces, $1\frac{1}{2}$ ounces, and $\frac{3}{4}$ ounce. What is the total weight of the nuggets?

Travel The table shows the distances in miles between four cities. To find the distance between two cities, locate the square where the row for one city and the column for the other city intersect.

	Atherton	Baily	Charleston	Dixon
Atherton	✕	$40\frac{2}{3}$	$100\frac{5}{6}$	$16\frac{1}{2}$
Baily	$40\frac{2}{3}$	✕	$210\frac{3}{8}$	$30\frac{2}{3}$
Charleston	$100\frac{5}{6}$	$210\frac{3}{8}$	✕	$98\frac{3}{4}$
Dixon	$16\frac{1}{2}$	$30\frac{2}{3}$	$98\frac{3}{4}$	✕

44. How much farther is it from Charleston to Dixon than from Atherton to Baily?

45. If you drove from Charleston to Atherton and then from Atherton to Dixon, how far would you drive?

46. Agriculture In 2003, the United States imported $\frac{97}{100}$ of its tulip bulbs from the Netherlands and $\frac{1}{50}$ of its tulip bulbs from New Zealand. What fraction more of tulip imports came from the Netherlands?

47. Recreation Kathy wants to hike to Candle Lake. The waterfall trail is $1\frac{2}{3}$ miles long, and the meadow trail is $1\frac{5}{6}$ miles long. Which route is shorter and by how much? Explain how you decided which operation to use to solve this problem.

48. Choose a Strategy Spiro needs to draw a 6-inch-long line. He does not have a ruler, but he has sheets of notebook paper that are $8\frac{1}{2}$ in. wide and 11 in. long. Describe how Spiro can use the notebook paper to measure 6 in.

49. Write About It Explain why it is sometimes necessary to regroup a mixed number when subtracting.

50. Challenge Todd had d pounds of nails. He sold $3\frac{1}{2}$ pounds on Monday and $5\frac{2}{3}$ pounds on Tuesday. Write an expression to show how many pounds he had left and then simplify it.

SPIRAL STANDARDS REVIEW

NS2.1, ➡ NS2.3, ➡ NS2.4

51. Multiple Choice Which expression is NOT equal to $2\frac{7}{8}$?

Ⓐ $1\frac{1}{2} + 1\frac{3}{8}$ Ⓑ $5\frac{15}{16} - 3\frac{1}{16}$ Ⓒ $6 - 3\frac{1}{8}$ Ⓓ $1\frac{1}{8} + 1\frac{1}{4}$

52. Short Response Where Maddie lives, there is a $5\frac{1}{2}$-cent state sales tax, a $1\frac{3}{4}$-cent county sales tax, and a $\frac{3}{4}$-cent city sales tax. The total sales tax is the sum of the state, county, and city sales taxes. What is the total sales tax where Maddie lives? Show your work.

Find each sum. (Lesson 2-2)

53. $-3 + 9$ **54.** $6 + (-15)$ **55.** $-4 + (-8)$ **56.** $-11 + 5$

Find each sum or difference. Write your answer in simplest form. (Lesson 4-2)

57. $\frac{2}{5} + \frac{7}{20}$ **58.** $\frac{3}{7} - \frac{1}{3}$ **59.** $\frac{3}{4} + \frac{7}{18}$ **60.** $\frac{4}{5} - \frac{1}{3}$

Quiz for Lessons 4-1 Through 4-3

☑ **4-1** **Estimating with Fractions**

1. Stacy's new mug is $4\frac{3}{4}$ inches tall, and her old mug is $3\frac{1}{8}$ inches tall. About how much taller is her new mug?

Estimate each sum or difference.

2. $\frac{3}{4} - \frac{2}{9}$ 3. $\frac{2}{7} + 5\frac{6}{11}$ 4. $\frac{7}{15} - \frac{3}{5}$ 5. $4\frac{9}{10} + 4\frac{1}{7}$

Estimate each product or quotient.

6. $4\frac{9}{15} \cdot 3\frac{1}{4}$ 7. $9\frac{7}{9} \div 4\frac{3}{5}$ 8. $8\frac{2}{3} \cdot 3\frac{3}{7}$ 9. $15\frac{1}{2} \div 3\frac{5}{9}$

☑ **4-2** **Adding and Subtracting Fractions**

Add or subtract. Write each answer in simplest form.

10. $\frac{5}{8} + \frac{1}{8}$ 11. $\frac{14}{15} - \frac{11}{15}$ 12. $\frac{6}{9} - \frac{1}{3}$ 13. $\frac{2}{3} - \frac{5}{8}$

14. $\frac{1}{4} + \frac{1}{6}$ 15. $\frac{5}{8} - \frac{1}{2}$ 16. $\frac{7}{8} + \frac{5}{6}$ 17. $\frac{5}{12} - \frac{1}{3}$

18. Inés added $\frac{2}{3}$ cup of dried apples and $\frac{1}{2}$ cup of dried blueberries to a container of yogurt. How many cups of dried fruit did Inés add to the yogurt?

19. The distance from Gabriel's house to his school is $\frac{7}{10}$ mile. The distance from his house to the library is $\frac{1}{4}$ mile. How much closer is Gabriel's house to the library than to his school?

☑ **4-3** **Adding and Subtracting Mixed Numbers**

Add or subtract. Write each answer in simplest form.

20. $6\frac{1}{9} + 2\frac{2}{9}$ 21. $1\frac{3}{6} + 7\frac{2}{3}$ 22. $5\frac{5}{8} - 3\frac{1}{8}$ 23. $8\frac{1}{12} - 3\frac{1}{4}$

24. $4\frac{2}{5} - 2\frac{4}{5}$ 25. $9\frac{1}{12} - 6\frac{1}{2}$ 26. $3\frac{1}{5} + 7\frac{1}{3}$ 27. $11\frac{1}{2} + 8\frac{7}{8}$

28. A stone carving in a museum weighs $35\frac{1}{2}$ pounds. A wood carving in the museum weighs $26\frac{3}{4}$ pounds less than the stone carving. How much does the wood carving weigh?

29. A mother giraffe is $13\frac{7}{10}$ ft tall. She is $5\frac{1}{2}$ ft taller than her young giraffe. How tall is the young giraffe?

30. Rachel ran $\frac{7}{8}$ mile on Monday, $1\frac{1}{4}$ miles on Tuesday, and $2\frac{1}{2}$ miles on Wednesday. How many miles did Rachel run in all?

Focus on Problem Solving

California Standards

MR1.1 Analyze problems by identifying relationships, distinguishing relevant from irrelevant information, identifying missing information, **sequencing and prioritizing information,** and observing patterns.
Also covered: **NS2.0, MR1.3**

Understand the Problem

- Sequence and prioritize information

When you are reading a math problem, putting events in order, or in *sequence,* can help you understand the problem better. It helps to *prioritize* the information when you put it in order. To prioritize, you decide which of the information in your list is most important. The most important information has highest priority.

Use the information in the list or table to answer each question.

1 The list shows everything that Roderick has to do on Saturday. He starts the day without any money.

a. Which two activities on Roderick's list must be done before any of the other activities? Do these two activities have higher or lower priority?

b. Is there more than one way that he can order his activities? Explain.

c. List the order in which Roderick's activities could occur on Saturday.

> **Saturday Activities**
> - Attend birthday party at 4 P.M.
> - Buy gift – either a CD for $18 or a computer game for $25.
> - Get haircut at 2 P.M.; pay $16.
> - Mow Mrs. Mayberry's lawn before 10 A.M.; earn $15.
> - Mow Mr. Boyar's lawn and trim hedge anytime after 10 A.M.; earn $25.

2 Tara and her family will visit Ocean World Park from 9:30 to 4:00. They want to see the waterskiing show at 10:00. Each show in the park is 50 minutes long. The time they choose to eat lunch will depend on the schedule they choose for seeing the shows.

a. Which of the information given in the paragraph above has the highest priority? Which has the lowest priority?

b. List the order in which they can see all of the shows, including the time they will see each.

c. When should they plan to have lunch? Explain your reasoning.

Show Times at Ocean World Park	
9:00, 12:00	Underwater acrobats
9:00, 3:00	Whale acts
10:00, 2:00	Dolphin acts
10:00, 1:00	Waterskiing
11:00, 4:00	Aquarium tour

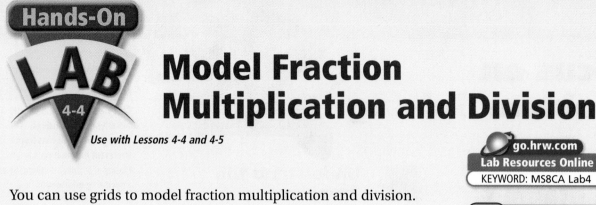

Model Fraction Multiplication and Division

Use with Lessons 4-4 and 4-5

go.hrw.com
Lab Resources Online
KEYWORD: MS8CA Lab4

You can use grids to model fraction multiplication and division.

California Standards

NS2.2 Explain the meaning of multiplication and division of positive fractions and perform the calculations (e.g., $\frac{5}{8} \div \frac{15}{16} = \frac{5}{8} \times \frac{16}{15} = \frac{2}{3}$).
Also covered: **NS2.1**

Activity 1

Use a grid to model $\frac{3}{4} \cdot \frac{1}{2}$.

Think of $\frac{3}{4} \cdot \frac{1}{2}$ as $\frac{3}{4}$ of $\frac{1}{2}$.

1 Model $\frac{1}{2}$ by shading half of a grid.

Divide the grid into 2 columns. Shade 1 column to show $\frac{1}{2}$.

2 Use a different color to shade $\frac{3}{4}$ of the same grid.

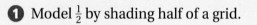

Divide the grid into 4 rows. Shade 3 rows to show $\frac{3}{4}$.

3 Determine what fraction of the grid is shaded with both colors.

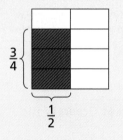

There are 8 equal parts, and 3 of the parts are shaded with both colors. The fraction shaded with both colors is $\frac{3}{8}$.

$$\frac{3}{4} \cdot \frac{1}{2} = \frac{3}{8}$$

The section of the grid shaded with both colors shows 3 parts of $\frac{1}{2}$ when $\frac{1}{2}$ is divided into 4 equal parts. In other words, the grid shows $\frac{3}{4}$ of $\frac{1}{2}$, or $\frac{3}{4} \cdot \frac{1}{2}$.

Think and Discuss

1. Are $\frac{2}{3} \cdot \frac{1}{5}$ and $\frac{1}{5} \cdot \frac{2}{3}$ modeled the same way? Explain.

2. When you multiply a positive fraction by a positive fraction, the product is less than either factor. Why?

Use a grid to find each product. Explain how your grid shows the product.

1. $\frac{1}{2} \cdot \frac{1}{2}$ **2.** $\frac{3}{4} \cdot \frac{2}{3}$ **3.** $\frac{5}{8} \cdot \frac{1}{3}$ **4.** $\frac{2}{5} \cdot \frac{5}{6}$

Activity 2

Use grids to model $4\frac{1}{3} \div \frac{2}{3}$.

Divide 5 grids into thirds. Shade 4 grids and $\frac{1}{3}$ of a fifth grid to represent $4\frac{1}{3}$.

Think: How many groups of $\frac{2}{3}$ are in $4\frac{1}{3}$?

Divide the shaded grids into equal groups of 2.

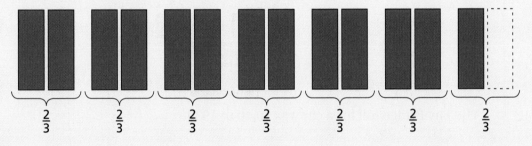

$\frac{2}{3}$ $\frac{2}{3}$ $\frac{2}{3}$ $\frac{2}{3}$ $\frac{2}{3}$ $\frac{2}{3}$ $\frac{2}{3}$

There are 6 groups of $\frac{2}{3}$, with $\frac{1}{3}$ left over. This piece is $\frac{1}{2}$ of a group of $\frac{2}{3}$.

Thus there are $6 + \frac{1}{2}$ groups of $\frac{2}{3}$ in $4\frac{1}{3}$.

$4\frac{1}{3} \div \frac{2}{3} = 6\frac{1}{2}$

Think and Discuss

1. Are $\frac{3}{4} \div \frac{1}{6}$ and $\frac{1}{6} \div \frac{3}{4}$ modeled the same way? Explain.

2. When you divide positive fractions less than 1, is the quotient greater than or less than the dividend? Explain.

Try This

Use grids to find each quotient. Explain how your grid shows the quotient.

1. $\frac{7}{12} \div \frac{1}{6}$ **2.** $\frac{4}{5} \div \frac{3}{10}$ **3.** $\frac{2}{3} \div \frac{4}{9}$ **4.** $3\frac{2}{5} \div \frac{3}{5}$

Multiplying Fractions and Mixed Numbers

California Standards

NS2.1 Solve problems involving addition, subtraction, **multiplication**, and division of positive fractions and explain why a particular operation was used for a given situation.

Also covered: **NS2.2**, ➡ **NS2.4**

Why learn this? You can multiply by fractions to determine the change over time in bridge tolls.

Recall that multiplication can be written as repeated addition. For example, $3 \cdot 5 = 5 + 5 + 5 = 15$. You can use repeated addition to multiply a whole number by a fraction.

E X A M P L E **1** *Transportation Application*

In 2005, the San Francisco–Oakland Bay Bridge toll for a car was $3.00. In 1939, the toll was $\frac{2}{15}$ of the toll in 2005. What was the toll in 1939?

Think: How much is $\frac{2}{15}$ of 3? Use multiplication to find a fraction of a number.

$$3 \cdot \frac{2}{15} = \frac{2}{15} + \frac{2}{15} + \frac{2}{15}$$

$$= \frac{6}{15}$$

$$= \frac{2}{5} = 0.40$$

The Bay Bridge toll for a car was $0.40 in 1939.

MULTIPLYING FRACTIONS

Words	Numbers	Algebra
Multiply the numerators to find the product's numerator. Multiply the denominators to find the product's denominator.	$\frac{1}{3} \cdot \frac{2}{5} = \frac{1 \cdot 2}{3 \cdot 5} = \frac{2}{15}$	$\frac{a}{b} \cdot \frac{c}{d} = \frac{ac}{bd}$ where $b \neq 0$ and $d \neq 0$

E X A M P L E **2** **Multiplying Fractions**

Helpful Hint

Use the GCD of a numerator and denominator to simplify before multiplying.

Multiply. Write each answer in simplest form.

A) $15 \cdot \frac{2}{3}$

$$15 \cdot \frac{2}{3} = \frac{15}{1} \cdot \frac{2}{3}$$ *Write 15 as a fraction.*

$$= \frac{\overset{5}{\cancel{15}}}{1} \cdot \frac{2}{\cancel{3}_{1}}$$ *Divide a numerator and denominator by their GCD, 3.*

$$= \frac{10}{1} = 10$$ *Multiply numerators. Multiply denominators.*

Multiply. Write each answer in simplest form.

B $\dfrac{2}{5} \cdot \dfrac{6}{7}$

$\dfrac{2}{5} \cdot \dfrac{6}{7} = \dfrac{2 \cdot 6}{5 \cdot 7}$ *Multiply numerators. Multiply denominators.*

$\qquad\quad = \dfrac{12}{35}$

C $\dfrac{1}{4} \cdot \dfrac{4}{5}$

$\dfrac{1}{4} \cdot \dfrac{4}{5} = \dfrac{1}{\cancel{4}} \cdot \dfrac{\cancel{4}^{\,1}}{5}$ *Divide a numerator and denominator by their GCD, 4.*

$\qquad\quad = \dfrac{1}{5}$ *Multiply numerators. Multiply denominators.*

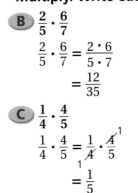

EXAMPLE 3   **Multiplying Mixed Numbers**

Multiply. Write each answer in simplest form.

A $8 \cdot 2\dfrac{3}{4}$

$8 \cdot 2\dfrac{3}{4} = \dfrac{8}{1} \cdot \dfrac{11}{4}$ *Write mixed numbers as improper fractions.*

$\qquad\quad = \dfrac{\cancel{8}^{\,2}}{1} \cdot \dfrac{11}{\cancel{4}_{\,1}}$ *Divide a numerator and denominator by their GCD, 4.*

$\qquad\quad = \dfrac{22}{1} = 22$ *Multiply numerators. Multiply denominators.*

B $\dfrac{1}{3} \cdot 4\dfrac{1}{2}$

$\dfrac{1}{3} \cdot 4\dfrac{1}{2} = \dfrac{1}{3} \cdot \dfrac{9}{2}$ *Write the mixed number as an improper fraction.*

$\qquad\quad = \dfrac{1}{\cancel{3}_{\,1}} \cdot \dfrac{\cancel{9}^{\,3}}{2}$ *Divide a numerator and denominator by their GCD, 3.*

$\qquad\quad = \dfrac{3}{2} \text{ or } 1\dfrac{1}{2}$ *Multiply numerators. Multiply denominators.*

C $3\dfrac{3}{5} \cdot 1\dfrac{1}{12}$

$3\dfrac{3}{5} \cdot 1\dfrac{1}{12} = \dfrac{18}{5} \cdot \dfrac{13}{12}$ *Write mixed numbers as improper fractions.*

$\qquad\quad = \dfrac{\cancel{18}^{\,3}}{5} \cdot \dfrac{13}{\cancel{12}_{\,2}}$ *Divide a numerator and denominator by their GCD, 6.*

$\qquad\quad = \dfrac{39}{10} \text{ or } 3\dfrac{9}{10}$ *Multiply numerators. Multiply denominators.*

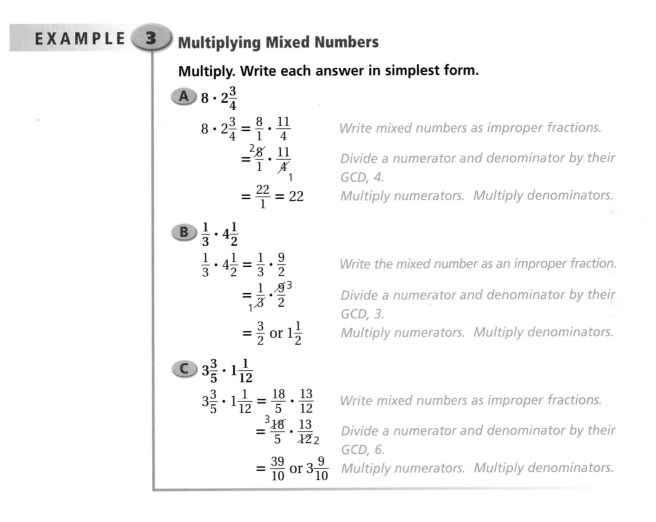

Think and Discuss

1. Describe how to multiply a mixed number and a fraction.

2. Explain why $\dfrac{1}{2} \cdot \dfrac{1}{3} \cdot \dfrac{1}{4} = \dfrac{1}{24}$ is or is not correct.

3. Explain why $3 \cdot \dfrac{2}{15}$ can be written as $\dfrac{2}{15} + \dfrac{2}{15} + \dfrac{2}{15}$.

4-4 **Exercises**

California Standards Practice
NS2.1, NS2.2, 🔑 NS2.4

go.hrw.com
Homework Help Online
KEYWORD: MS8CA 4-4
Parent Resources Online
KEYWORD: MS8CA Parent

GUIDED PRACTICE

See Example ① **1.** On average, people spend $\frac{1}{4}$ of the time they sleep in a dream state. If Maxwell slept 10 hours last night, how much time did he spend dreaming? Write your answer in simplest form.

See Example ② **Multiply. Write each answer in simplest form.**

2. $8 \cdot \frac{3}{4}$ **3.** $\frac{2}{3} \cdot \frac{3}{5}$ **4.** $\frac{1}{4} \cdot \frac{2}{3}$ **5.** $\frac{3}{5} \cdot 15$

See Example ③ **6.** $4 \cdot 3\frac{1}{2}$ **7.** $\frac{4}{9} \cdot 5\frac{2}{5}$ **8.** $1\frac{1}{2} \cdot 1\frac{5}{9}$ **9.** $2\frac{6}{7} \cdot 7$

INDEPENDENT PRACTICE

See Example ① **10.** Sherry spent 4 hours exercising last week. If $\frac{5}{6}$ of the time was spent jogging, how much time did she spend jogging? Write your answer in simplest form.

11. Measurement A bread recipe calls for $\frac{1}{3}$ teaspoon of salt for 1 batch. Doreen wants to bake 5 batches of bread. How much salt does she need? Write your answer in simplest form.

See Example ② **Multiply. Write each answer in simplest form.**

12. $5 \cdot \frac{1}{8}$ **13.** $4 \cdot \frac{1}{8}$ **14.** $3 \cdot \frac{5}{8}$ **15.** $6 \cdot \frac{2}{3}$

16. $\frac{2}{5} \cdot \frac{5}{7}$ **17.** $\frac{3}{8} \cdot \frac{2}{3}$ **18.** $\frac{1}{2} \cdot \frac{4}{9}$ **19.** $\frac{5}{6} \cdot \frac{2}{3}$

See Example ③ **20.** $7\frac{1}{2} \cdot 2\frac{2}{5}$ **21.** $6 \cdot 7\frac{2}{5}$ **22.** $2\frac{4}{7} \cdot \frac{1}{6}$ **23.** $2\frac{5}{8} \cdot 6\frac{2}{3}$

24. $\frac{2}{3} \cdot 2\frac{1}{4}$ **25.** $1\frac{1}{2} \cdot 1\frac{5}{9}$ **26.** $7 \cdot 5\frac{1}{8}$ **27.** $3\frac{3}{4} \cdot 2\frac{1}{5}$

PRACTICE AND PROBLEM SOLVING

Extra Practice
See page EP8.

Multiply. Write each answer in simplest form.

28. $\frac{5}{8} \cdot \frac{4}{5}$ **29.** $4\frac{3}{7} \cdot \frac{5}{6}$ **30.** $\frac{2}{3} \cdot 6$ **31.** $2 \cdot \frac{1}{6}$

32. $\frac{1}{8} \cdot 5$ **33.** $\frac{3}{4} \cdot \frac{2}{9}$ **34.** $4\frac{2}{3} \cdot 2\frac{4}{7}$ **35.** $\frac{4}{9} \cdot \frac{3}{16}$

36. $3\frac{1}{2} \cdot 5$ **37.** $\frac{1}{2} \cdot \frac{2}{3} \cdot \frac{3}{5}$ **38.** $\frac{6}{7} \cdot 5$ **39.** $1\frac{1}{2} \cdot \frac{3}{5} \cdot \frac{7}{9}$

40. $\frac{2}{3} \cdot 1\frac{1}{2} \cdot \frac{2}{3}$ **41.** $\frac{8}{9} \cdot \frac{3}{11} \cdot \frac{33}{40}$ **42.** $\frac{1}{6} \cdot 6 \cdot 8\frac{2}{3}$ **43.** $\frac{8}{9} \cdot 1\frac{1}{8}$

Reasoning Complete each multiplication sentence.

44. $\frac{1}{2} \cdot \frac{\blacksquare}{8} = \frac{3}{16}$ **45.** $\frac{2}{3} \cdot \frac{\blacksquare}{4} = \frac{1}{2}$ **46.** $\frac{\blacksquare}{3} \cdot \frac{5}{8} = \frac{5}{12}$ **47.** $\frac{3}{5} \cdot \frac{\blacksquare}{7} = \frac{3}{7}$

48. $\frac{5}{6} \cdot \frac{3}{\blacksquare} = \frac{1}{4}$ **49.** $\frac{4}{\blacksquare} \cdot \frac{4}{5} = \frac{8}{15}$ **50.** $\frac{2}{3} \cdot \frac{9}{\blacksquare} = \frac{3}{11}$ **51.** $\frac{\blacksquare}{15} \cdot \frac{3}{5} = \frac{1}{25}$

52. Measurement A standard paper clip is $1\frac{1}{4}$ in. long. If you laid 75 paper clips end to end, how long would the line of paper clips be?

53. **Science** The weight of an object on the moon is $\frac{1}{6}$ its weight on Earth. If a bowling ball weighs $12\frac{1}{2}$ pounds on Earth, how much would it weigh on the moon? Explain how you decided which operation to use to solve this problem.

54. In a survey, 200 students were asked what most influenced them to buy their latest CD. The results are shown in the circle graph.

    a. How many students said radio most influenced them?

    b. How many more students were influenced by radio than by a music video channel?

    c. How many said a friend or relative influenced them or they heard the CD in a store?

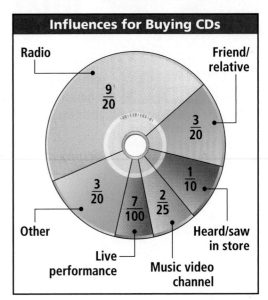

Influences for Buying CDs

55. The Mississippi River flows at a rate of 2 miles per hour. If Eduardo floats down the river in a boat for $5\frac{2}{3}$ hours, how far will he travel?

56. **Choose a Strategy** What is the product of $\frac{1}{2} \cdot \frac{2}{3} \cdot \frac{3}{4} \cdot \frac{4}{5}$?

    Ⓐ $\frac{1}{5}$ Ⓑ 5   Ⓒ $\frac{1}{20}$ Ⓓ $\frac{3}{5}$

57. **Write About It** Explain what it means to multiply $\frac{1}{4}$ by $\frac{2}{3}$. Use a model in your explanation.

58. **Challenge** Write three multiplication problems to show that the product of two fractions can be less than, equal to, or greater than 1.

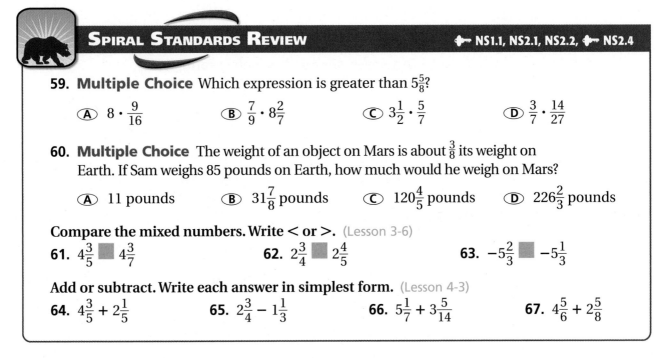

59. **Multiple Choice** Which expression is greater than $5\frac{5}{8}$?

    Ⓐ $8 \cdot \frac{9}{16}$ Ⓑ $\frac{7}{9} \cdot 8\frac{2}{7}$ Ⓒ $3\frac{1}{2} \cdot \frac{5}{7}$ Ⓓ $\frac{3}{7} \cdot \frac{14}{27}$

60. **Multiple Choice** The weight of an object on Mars is about $\frac{3}{8}$ its weight on Earth. If Sam weighs 85 pounds on Earth, how much would he weigh on Mars?

    Ⓐ 11 pounds   Ⓑ $31\frac{7}{8}$ pounds   Ⓒ $120\frac{4}{5}$ pounds   Ⓓ $226\frac{2}{3}$ pounds

Compare the mixed numbers. Write < or >. (Lesson 3-6)

61. $4\frac{3}{5} \ \blacksquare \ 4\frac{3}{7}$ 62. $2\frac{3}{4} \ \blacksquare \ 2\frac{4}{5}$ 63. $-5\frac{2}{3} \ \blacksquare \ -5\frac{1}{3}$

Add or subtract. Write each answer in simplest form. (Lesson 4-3)

64. $4\frac{3}{5} + 2\frac{1}{5}$ 65. $2\frac{3}{4} - 1\frac{1}{3}$ 66. $5\frac{1}{7} + 3\frac{5}{14}$ 67. $4\frac{5}{6} + 2\frac{5}{8}$

4-5 Dividing Fractions and Mixed Numbers

California Standards

NS2.1 Solve problems involving addition, subtraction, **multiplication**, and division of positive fractions and explain why a particular operation was used for a given situation.

Also covered: **NS2.2**, ⚷ **NS2.4**

Who uses this? Industrial artists divide fractions and mixed numbers when working with measurements. (See Exercises 47–51.)

Reciprocals can help you divide by fractions. Two numbers are **reciprocals** or **multiplicative inverses** if their product is 1. The reciprocal of $\frac{1}{3}$ is 3 because

$$\frac{1}{3} \cdot 3 = \frac{1}{3} \cdot \frac{3}{1} = \frac{3}{3} = 1.$$

Dividing by a number is the same as multiplying by its reciprocal.

Vocabulary
reciprocal
multiplicative inverse

— Reciprocals —

$$6 \div 3 = 2 \qquad 6 \cdot \frac{1}{3} = 2$$

— Same answer —

You can use this rule to divide by fractions.

DIVIDING FRACTIONS		
Words	**Numbers**	**Algebra**
To divide by a fraction, find its reciprocal and then multiply.	$\frac{1}{2} \div \frac{3}{5} = \frac{1}{2} \cdot \frac{5}{3} = \frac{5}{6}$	$\frac{a}{b} \div \frac{c}{d} = \frac{a}{b} \cdot \frac{d}{c}$ where $b, c, d \neq 0$

EXAMPLE 1 Dividing Fractions

Divide. Write each answer in simplest form.

A $\frac{2}{3} \div \frac{1}{5}$

$\frac{2}{3} \div \frac{1}{5} = \frac{2}{3} \cdot \frac{5}{1}$ *Multiply by the reciprocal of $\frac{1}{5}$.*

$= \frac{2 \cdot 5}{3 \cdot 1}$

$= \frac{10}{3}$ or $3\frac{1}{3}$

B $\frac{3}{5} \div 6$

$\frac{3}{5} \div 6 = \frac{3}{5} \cdot \frac{1}{6}$ *Multiply by the reciprocal of 6.*

$= \frac{\overset{1}{3}}{5} \cdot \frac{1}{\underset{2}{6}}$ *Simplify.*

$= \frac{1}{10}$

EXAMPLE 2 **Dividing Mixed Numbers**

Divide. Write each answer in simplest form.

A $4\frac{1}{3} \div 2\frac{1}{2}$

$4\frac{1}{3} \div 2\frac{1}{2} = \frac{13}{3} \div \frac{5}{2}$ *Write mixed numbers as improper fractions.*

$= \frac{13}{3} \cdot \frac{2}{5}$ *Multiply by the reciprocal of $\frac{5}{2}$.*

$= \frac{26}{15}$ or $1\frac{11}{15}$

B $\frac{5}{6} \div 7\frac{1}{7}$

$\frac{5}{6} \div 7\frac{1}{7} = \frac{5}{6} \div \frac{50}{7}$ *Write $7\frac{1}{7}$ as an improper fraction.*

$= \frac{5}{6} \cdot \frac{7}{50}$ *Multiply by the reciprocal of $\frac{50}{7}$.*

$= \frac{\overset{1}{5}}{6} \cdot \frac{7}{\underset{10}{50}}$ *Simplify.*

$= \frac{7}{60}$

EXAMPLE 3 **Social Studies Application**

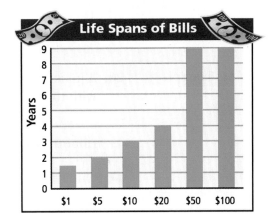

Life Spans of Bills

Reasoning

Use the bar graph to determine how many times longer a $100 bill is expected to stay in circulation than a $1 bill.

The life span of a $1 bill is $1\frac{1}{2}$ years. The life span of a $100 bill is 9 years.

Think: How many $1\frac{1}{2}$'s are there in 9? Use division.

$9 \div 1\frac{1}{2} = \frac{9}{1} \div \frac{3}{2}$ *Write both numbers as improper fractions.*

$= \frac{9}{1} \cdot \frac{2}{3}$ *Multiply by the reciprocal of $\frac{3}{2}$.*

$= \frac{\overset{3}{9}}{1} \cdot \frac{2}{\underset{1}{3}}$ *Simplify.*

$= \frac{6}{1}$ or 6

A $100 bill is expected to stay in circulation 6 times longer than a $1 bill.

Think and Discuss

1. Explain whether finding half of a number is the same as dividing a number by $\frac{1}{2}$.

California Standards Practice
NS2.1, NS2.2, ← NS2.4

go.hrw.com
Homework Help Online
KEYWORD: MS8CA 4-5
Parent Resources Online
KEYWORD: MS8CA Parent

GUIDED PRACTICE

See Example **1** Divide. Write each answer in simplest form.

1. $6 \div \frac{1}{3}$ **2.** $\frac{3}{5} \div \frac{3}{4}$ **3.** $\frac{3}{4} \div 8$ **4.** $\frac{5}{9} \div \frac{2}{5}$

See Example **2**   **5.** $\frac{5}{6} \div 3\frac{1}{3}$ **6.** $5\frac{5}{8} \div 4\frac{1}{2}$ **7.** $10\frac{4}{5} \div 5\frac{2}{5}$ **8.** $2\frac{1}{10} \div \frac{3}{5}$

See Example **3**   **9.** Kareem has $12\frac{1}{2}$ yards of material. A cape for a play takes $3\frac{5}{6}$ yards. How many capes can Kareem make with the material?

INDEPENDENT PRACTICE

See Example **1** Divide. Write each answer in simplest form.

10. $2 \div \frac{7}{8}$ **11.** $10 \div \frac{5}{9}$ **12.** $\frac{3}{4} \div \frac{6}{7}$ **13.** $\frac{7}{8} \div \frac{1}{5}$

14. $\frac{8}{9} \div \frac{1}{4}$ **15.** $\frac{4}{9} \div 12$ **16.** $\frac{9}{10} \div 6$ **17.** $16 \div \frac{2}{5}$

See Example **2**   **18.** $\frac{7}{11} \div 4\frac{1}{5}$ **19.** $\frac{3}{4} \div 2\frac{1}{10}$ **20.** $22\frac{1}{2} \div 4\frac{2}{7}$ **21.** $10\frac{1}{2} \div \frac{3}{4}$

22. $3\frac{5}{7} \div 9\frac{1}{7}$ **23.** $14\frac{2}{3} \div 1\frac{1}{6}$ **24.** $7\frac{7}{10} \div 2\frac{2}{5}$ **25.** $8\frac{2}{5} \div \frac{7}{8}$

See Example **3**   **26.** A juicer holds $43\frac{3}{4}$ pints of juice. How many $2\frac{1}{2}$-pint bottles can be filled with that much juice?

27. Measurement How many $24\frac{1}{2}$ in. pieces of ribbon can be cut from a roll of ribbon that is 147 in. long?

PRACTICE AND PROBLEM SOLVING

Extra Practice
See page EP8.

Evaluate. Write each answer in simplest form.

28. $6\frac{2}{3} \div \frac{7}{9}$ **29.** $9 \div 1\frac{2}{3}$ **30.** $\frac{2}{3} \div \frac{8}{9}$ **31.** $1\frac{7}{11} \div \frac{9}{11}$

32. $\frac{1}{2} \div 4\frac{3}{4}$ **33.** $\frac{4}{21} \div 3\frac{1}{2}$ **34.** $4\frac{1}{2} \div 3\frac{1}{2}$ **35.** $1\frac{3}{5} \div 2\frac{1}{2}$

36. $\frac{7}{8} \div 2\frac{1}{10}$ **37.** $1\frac{3}{5} \div \left(2\frac{2}{9}\right)$ **38.** $\left(\frac{1}{2} + \frac{2}{3}\right) \div 1\frac{1}{2}$ **39.** $\left(2\frac{3}{4} + 3\frac{2}{3}\right) \div \frac{11}{18}$

40. $2\frac{2}{3} \div \left(\frac{1}{5} \cdot \frac{2}{3}\right)$ **41.** $\frac{4}{5} \cdot \frac{3}{8} \div \frac{9}{10}$ **42.** $\frac{12}{13} \cdot \frac{13}{18} \div 1\frac{1}{2}$ **43.** $\frac{3}{7} \div \frac{15}{28} \div \frac{4}{5}$

44. Three friends will be driving to an amusement park that is $226\frac{4}{5}$ mi from their town. If each friend drives the same distance, how far will each drive? Explain how you decided which operation to use to solve this problem.

45. Multi-Step How many $\frac{1}{4}$ lb hamburger patties can be made from a $10\frac{1}{4}$ lb package and an $11\frac{1}{2}$ lb package of ground meat?

46. Write About It Explain what it means to divide $\frac{2}{3}$ by $\frac{1}{3}$. Use a model in your explanation.

47. **Multi-Step** The students in Mr. Park's woodworking class are making birdhouses. The plans call for the side pieces of the birdhouses to be $7\frac{1}{4}$ inches long. If Mr. Park has 6 boards that are $50\frac{3}{4}$ inches long, how many side pieces can be cut?

48. For his drafting class, Manuel is drawing plans for a bookcase. He wants his drawing to be $\frac{1}{4}$ the actual size of the bookcase. If the bookcase will be $3\frac{2}{3}$ feet wide, how wide will Manuel's drawing be?

49. The table shows the total number of hours that the students in each of Mrs. Anwar's 5 industrial arts classes took to complete their final projects. If the third-period class has 17 students, how many hours did each student in that class work on average?

Period	Hours
1st	$200\frac{1}{2}$
2nd	$179\frac{2}{5}$
3rd	$199\frac{3}{4}$
5th	$190\frac{3}{4}$
6th	$180\frac{1}{4}$

50. **Critical Thinking** Brandy is stamping circles from a strip of aluminum. If each circle is $1\frac{1}{4}$ inches in diameter, how many circles can she get from an $8\frac{3}{4}$-inch by $1\frac{1}{4}$-inch strip of aluminum?

51. ⭐**Challenge** Alexandra is cutting wood stencils to spell her first name with capital letters. Her first step is to cut a square of wood that is $3\frac{1}{2}$ in. long on a side for each letter in her name. Will Alexandra be able to make all of the letters of her name from a single piece of wood that is $7\frac{1}{2}$ in. wide and 18 in. long? Explain your answer.

SPIRAL STANDARDS REVIEW

NS2.1, NS2.2, ⚠ NS2.4

52. **Multiple Choice** Which expression is NOT equivalent to $2\frac{2}{3} \div 1\frac{5}{8}$?

Ⓐ $\frac{8}{3} \cdot \frac{8}{13}$ Ⓑ $2\frac{2}{3} \div \frac{13}{8}$ Ⓒ $\frac{8}{3} \div \frac{13}{8}$ Ⓓ $\frac{8}{3} \cdot 1\frac{5}{8}$

53. **Multiple Choice** What is the value of the expression $\frac{3}{5} \cdot \frac{1}{6} \div \frac{2}{5}$?

Ⓐ $\frac{1}{25}$ Ⓑ $\frac{1}{4}$ Ⓒ $\frac{15}{22}$ Ⓓ 25

54. **Gridded Response** Each cat at the animal shelter gets $\frac{3}{4}$ c of food every day. If Alysse has $16\frac{1}{2}$ c of cat food, how many cats can she feed?

Find the least common multiple (LCM). (Lesson 3-3)

55. 2, 15 56. 6, 8 57. 4, 6, 18 58. 3, 4, 8

Multiply. Write each answer in simplest form. (Lesson 4-4)

59. $\frac{2}{15} \cdot \frac{5}{8}$ 60. $1\frac{7}{20} \cdot 6$ 61. $1\frac{2}{7} \cdot 2\frac{3}{4}$ 62. $\frac{1}{8} \cdot 6 \cdot 2\frac{5}{9}$

Solving Equations Containing Fractions

California Standards

AF1.1 Write and solve one-step linear equations in one variable.

Also covered: **NS2.1, NS2.2, NS2.4**

Who uses this? Jewelers can solve equations containing fractions to determine the amounts of certain metals in gold jewelry. (See Example 3.)

The goal when solving equations that contain fractions is the same as when working with other kinds of numbers—to get the variable by itself on one side of the equation.

E X A M P L E 1 **Solving Equations by Adding or Subtracting**

Reasoning

Solve. Write each answer in simplest form.

A $x - \frac{1}{5} = \frac{3}{5}$

$$x - \frac{1}{5} = \frac{3}{5}$$

$$x - \frac{1}{5} + \frac{1}{5} = \frac{3}{5} + \frac{1}{5}$$ *Since $\frac{1}{5}$ is subtracted from x, add $\frac{1}{5}$ to both sides.*

$$x = \frac{4}{5}$$ *Simplify.*

B $\frac{5}{12} + y = \frac{2}{3}$

$$\frac{5}{12} + y = \frac{2}{3}$$

$$\frac{5}{12} + y - \frac{5}{12} = \frac{2}{3} - \frac{5}{12}$$ *Since $\frac{5}{12}$ is added to y, subtract $\frac{5}{12}$ from both sides.*

$$y = \frac{8}{12} - \frac{5}{12}$$ *Find a common denominator.*

$$y = \frac{3}{12} = \frac{1}{4}$$ *Subtract. Then simplify.*

C $\frac{7}{18} + u = \frac{14}{27}$

$$\frac{7}{18} + u = \frac{14}{27}$$

$$\frac{7}{18} + u - \frac{7}{18} = \frac{14}{27} - \frac{7}{18}$$ *Since $\frac{7}{18}$ is added to u, subtract $\frac{7}{18}$ from both sides.*

$$u = \frac{28}{54} - \frac{21}{54}$$ *Find a common denominator.*

$$u = \frac{7}{54}$$ *Subtract.*

Check $\frac{7}{18} + u = \frac{14}{27}$

$$\frac{7}{18} + \frac{7}{54} \stackrel{?}{=} \frac{14}{27}$$ *Substitute $\frac{7}{54}$ for u.*

$$\frac{21}{54} + \frac{7}{54} \stackrel{?}{=} \frac{28}{54}$$ *Find a common denominator.*

$$\frac{28}{54} = \frac{28}{54} \quad \checkmark$$ *Add.*

Remember!

You can check that a value is a solution to an equation by substituting the value for the variable. *See Lesson 1-7, p. 34.*

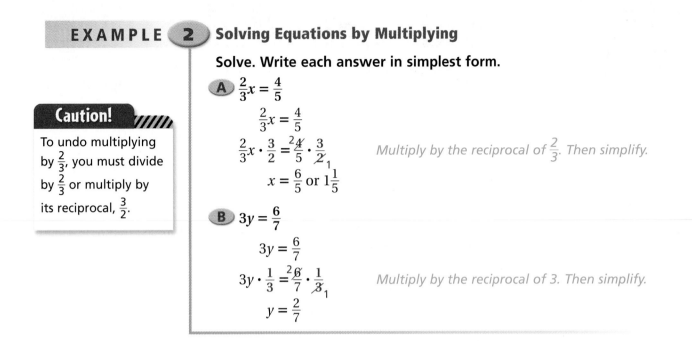

EXAMPLE 2 Solving Equations by Multiplying

Solve. Write each answer in simplest form.

A $\frac{2}{3}x = \frac{4}{5}$

$$\frac{2}{3}x = \frac{4}{5}$$

$$\frac{2}{3}x \cdot \frac{3}{2} = \frac{2\cancel{4}}{5} \cdot \frac{3}{\cancel{2}_1}$$ *Multiply by the reciprocal of $\frac{2}{3}$. Then simplify.*

$$x = \frac{6}{5} \text{ or } 1\frac{1}{5}$$

B $3y = \frac{6}{7}$

$$3y = \frac{6}{7}$$

$$3y \cdot \frac{1}{3} = \frac{2\cancel{6}}{7} \cdot \frac{1}{\cancel{3}_1}$$ *Multiply by the reciprocal of 3. Then simplify.*

$$y = \frac{2}{7}$$

Caution!

To undo multiplying by $\frac{2}{3}$, you must divide by $\frac{2}{3}$ or multiply by its reciprocal, $\frac{3}{2}$.

EXAMPLE 3 *Science Application*

Pink gold is made of pure gold, silver, and copper. There is $\frac{11}{20}$ more pure gold than copper in pink gold. If pink gold is $\frac{3}{4}$ pure gold, what portion of pink gold is copper?

Let c represent the amount of copper in pink gold.

$$c + \frac{11}{20} = \frac{3}{4}$$ *Write an equation.*

$$c + \frac{11}{20} - \frac{11}{20} = \frac{3}{4} - \frac{11}{20}$$ *Since $\frac{11}{20}$ is added to c, subtract $\frac{11}{20}$ from both sides.*

$$c = \frac{15}{20} - \frac{11}{20}$$ *Find a common denominator.*

$$c = \frac{4}{20}$$ *Subtract.*

$$c = \frac{1}{5}$$ *Simplify.*

Pink gold is $\frac{1}{5}$ copper.

Think and Discuss

1. Show the first step you would use to solve $m + 3\frac{5}{8} = 12\frac{1}{2}$.

2. Describe how to decide whether $\frac{2}{3}$ is a solution of $\frac{7}{8}y = \frac{3}{5}$.

3. Explain why solving $\frac{2}{5}c = \frac{8}{9}$ by multiplying both sides by $\frac{5}{2}$ is the same as solving it by dividing both sides by $\frac{2}{5}$.

4-6 **Exercises**

California Standards Practice
NS2.1, NS2.2, ⟜ NS2.4, ⟜ AF1.1

go.hrw.com
Homework Help Online
KEYWORD: MS8CA 4-6
Parent Resources Online
KEYWORD: MS8CA Parent

GUIDED PRACTICE

See Example **1** Solve. Write each answer in simplest form.

1. $a - \frac{1}{2} = \frac{1}{4}$ **2.** $m + \frac{1}{6} = \frac{5}{6}$ **3.** $p - \frac{2}{3} = \frac{5}{6}$

See Example **2**   **4.** $\frac{1}{5}x = 8$ **5.** $\frac{2}{3}r = \frac{3}{5}$ **6.** $3w = \frac{3}{7}$

See Example **3**   **7.** Kara has $\frac{3}{8}$ cup less oatmeal than she needs for a cookie recipe. If she has $\frac{3}{4}$ cup of oatmeal, how much oatmeal does she need?

INDEPENDENT PRACTICE

See Example **1** Solve. Write each answer in simplest form.

8. $n - \frac{1}{5} = \frac{3}{5}$ **9.** $t - \frac{3}{8} = \frac{1}{4}$ **10.** $s - \frac{7}{24} = \frac{1}{3}$

11. $x + \frac{2}{3} = 2\frac{7}{8}$ **12.** $h + \frac{7}{10} = \frac{7}{10}$ **13.** $y + \frac{5}{6} = \frac{19}{20}$

See Example **2**   **14.** $\frac{1}{5}x = 4$ **15.** $\frac{1}{4}w = \frac{1}{8}$ **16.** $5y = \frac{3}{10}$

17. $6z = \frac{1}{2}$ **18.** $\frac{5}{8}x = \frac{2}{5}$ **19.** $\frac{5}{8}n = 1\frac{1}{5}$

See Example **3**   **20. Earth Science** Carbon-14 has a half-life of 5,730 years. After 17,190 years, $\frac{1}{8}$ of the carbon-14 in a sample will be left. If 5 grams of carbon-14 are left after 17,190 years, how much was in the original sample?

PRACTICE AND PROBLEM SOLVING

Extra Practice
See page EP8.

Solve. Write each answer in simplest form.

21. $\frac{4}{5}t = \frac{1}{5}$ **22.** $m - \frac{1}{2} = \frac{2}{3}$ **23.** $\frac{1}{8}w = \frac{3}{4}$

24. $\frac{8}{9} + t = \frac{17}{18}$ **25.** $\frac{5}{3}x = 1$ **26.** $j + \frac{5}{8} = \frac{11}{16}$

27. $\frac{4}{3}n = 3\frac{1}{5}$ **28.** $z + \frac{1}{6} = 3\frac{9}{15}$ **29.** $\frac{3}{4}y = \frac{3}{8}$

30. $\frac{5}{26} + m = \frac{7}{13}$ **31.** $\frac{1}{11} + r = \frac{8}{77}$ **32.** $y - \frac{3}{4} = \frac{9}{20}$

33. $h - \frac{3}{8} = \frac{11}{24}$ **34.** $\frac{5}{36}t = \frac{5}{16}$ **35.** $\frac{8}{13}v = \frac{6}{13}$

36. $4\frac{6}{7} + p = 5\frac{1}{4}$ **37.** $d - 5\frac{1}{8} = 9\frac{3}{10}$ **38.** $6\frac{8}{21}k = 13\frac{1}{3}$

39. Food Each person in Finland drinks an average of $24\frac{1}{4}$ lb of coffee per year. This is $13\frac{1}{16}$ lb more than the average person in Italy consumes. On average, how much coffee does an Italian drink each year?

40. Weather Yuma, Arizona, receives $102\frac{1}{100}$ fewer inches of rain each year than Quillayute, Washington, which receives $105\frac{9}{50}$ inches per year. (*Source: National Weather Service*). How much rain does Yuma get in one year?

41. Science Scientists have discovered $1\frac{1}{2}$ million species of animals. This is estimated to be $\frac{1}{10}$ the total number of species thought to exist. About how many species do scientists think exist?

42. History The circle graph shows the birthplaces of the United States' presidents who were in office between 1789 and 1845.

a. If six of the presidents represented in the graph were born in Virginia, how many presidents are represented in the graph?

b. Based on your answer to **a**, how many of the presidents were born in Massachusetts?

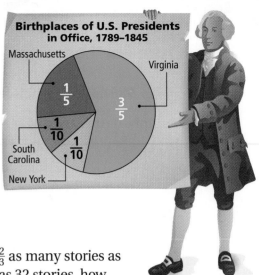

Birthplaces of U.S. Presidents in Office, 1789–1845

Massachusetts $\frac{1}{5}$
Virginia $\frac{3}{5}$
$\frac{1}{10}$
South Carolina $\frac{1}{10}$
New York

43. Architecture An office building has $\frac{2}{3}$ as many stories as a bank building. If the office building has 32 stories, how many stories does the bank building have?

44. Multi-Step This week, Jennifer had $\frac{2}{15}$ of her allowance left over after she put $\frac{1}{5}$ of it into her savings account and used part of it to buy her lunch each day. What fraction of her allowance did she spend on lunches?

45. What's the Error? A student solved $\frac{3}{5}x = \frac{2}{3}$ and got $x = \frac{2}{5}$. Find the error.

46. Write About It Solve $3\frac{1}{3}z = 1\frac{1}{2}$. Explain why you need to write mixed numbers as improper fractions when multiplying and dividing.

47. Challenge Solve $\frac{3}{5}w = 0.9$. Write your answer as a fraction and as a decimal.

SPIRAL STANDARDS REVIEW ⬥ NS1.1, NS2.1, NS2.2, ⬥ NS2.4, ⬥ AF1.1

48. Multiple Choice Which value of y is the solution to the equation $y - \frac{7}{8} = \frac{3}{5}$?

Ⓐ $y = \frac{11}{40}$ Ⓑ $y = \frac{10}{13}$ Ⓒ $y = 1\frac{19}{40}$ Ⓓ $y = 2$

49. Multiple Choice Which equation has the solution $x = \frac{2}{5}$?

Ⓐ $\frac{2}{5}x = 1$ Ⓑ $\frac{3}{4}x = \frac{6}{20}$ Ⓒ $\frac{4}{7} + x = \frac{2}{3}$ Ⓓ $x - 3\frac{5}{7} = 3\frac{1}{2}$

Order the numbers from least to greatest. (Lesson 3-6)

50. $-0.61, -\frac{3}{5}, -\frac{4}{3}, -1.25$ **51.** $3.25, 3\frac{2}{10}, 3, 3.02$ **52.** $\frac{1}{2}, -0.2, -\frac{7}{10}, 0.04$

Divide. Write each answer in simplest form. (Lesson 4-5)

53. $\frac{2}{5} \div \frac{7}{12}$ **54.** $5 \div \frac{3}{4}$ **55.** $3\frac{1}{2} \div 2\frac{5}{8}$

READY TO GO ON?

Quiz for Lessons 4-4 Through 4-6

✓ **4-4** **Multiplying Fractions and Mixed Numbers**

Multiply. Write each answer in simplest form.

1. $12 \cdot \frac{5}{6}$ 2. $\frac{5}{14} \cdot \frac{7}{10}$ 3. $8\frac{4}{5} \cdot \frac{10}{11}$ 4. $10\frac{5}{12} \cdot 1\frac{3}{5}$

5. $5\frac{2}{5} \cdot 3$ 6. $4\frac{2}{7} \cdot 3\frac{4}{15}$ 7. $1\frac{1}{17} \cdot 5\frac{2}{3}$ 8. $3\frac{1}{11} \cdot 10\frac{1}{2}$

9. During the first day of a recycle drive, the seventh grade collected $23\frac{1}{2}$ pounds of aluminum cans. The sixth grade collected $\frac{3}{4}$ as many pounds as the seventh grade. How many pounds of aluminum cans did the sixth grade collect?

10. A recipe calls for $1\frac{1}{3}$ cups flour. Tom is making $2\frac{1}{2}$ times the recipe for his family reunion. How much flour does he need? Write your answer in simplest form.

✓ **4-5** **Dividing Fractions and Mixed Numbers**

Divide. Write each answer in simplest form.

11. $\frac{1}{6} \div \frac{5}{6}$ 12. $\frac{2}{3} \div 4$ 13. $5\frac{3}{5} \div \frac{4}{5}$ 14. $4\frac{2}{7} \div 1\frac{1}{5}$

15. $2\frac{3}{4} \div 6$ 16. $9 \div \frac{2}{3}$ 17. $5\frac{4}{5} \div \frac{1}{10}$ 18. $5 \div 2\frac{1}{7}$

19. Marcus feeds his dog $1\frac{3}{4}$ pounds of food each day. How many days can he feed his dog if he has a 42-pound bag of dog food?

20. Nina has $9\frac{3}{7}$ yards of material. She needs $1\frac{4}{7}$ yards to make a pillow case. How many pillow cases can Nina make with the material?

✓ **4-6** **Solving Equations Containing Fractions**

Solve. Write each answer in simplest form.

21. $x - \frac{2}{3} = \frac{2}{15}$ 22. $\frac{4}{9} = 2q$ 23. $\frac{1}{6}m = \frac{1}{9}$ 24. $\frac{1}{6} + p = \frac{5}{8}$

25. $x - 2\frac{1}{2} = 8\frac{5}{8}$ 26. $\frac{3}{5}n = \frac{4}{5}$ 27. $\frac{1}{7}m = \frac{2}{3}$ 28. $5\frac{4}{5} + x = 19$

29. Adrian used $\frac{4}{5}$ of his supply of clay to make a statue. If the statue weighed 68 pounds, how much did Adrian's original supply of clay weigh?

30. A recipe for Uncle Frank's homemade hush puppies calls for $\frac{1}{8}$ teaspoon of cayenne pepper. The recipe calls for 6 times as much salt as it does cayenne pepper. How much salt does Uncle Frank's recipe require?

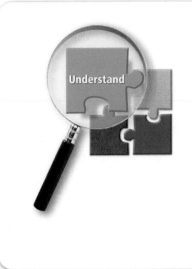

California Standards

NS2.1 Solve problems involving addition, **subtraction, multiplication, and division of positive fractions** and explain why a particular operation was used for a given situation.
Also covered: **MR1.1**

Understand the Problem

• Write the problem in your own words

One way to understand a problem better is to write it in your own words. Before you do this, you may need to read it over several times, perhaps aloud so that you can hear yourself say the words.

When you write a problem in your own words, try to make the problem simpler. Use smaller words and shorter sentences. Leave out any extra information, but make sure to include all the information you need to answer the question.

Write each problem in your own words. Check that you have included all the information you need to answer the question.

1 Martin is making muffins for his class bake sale. The recipe calls for $2\frac{1}{3}$ cups of flour, but Martin's only measuring cup holds $\frac{1}{3}$ cup. How many times should he fill his measuring cups?

2 Mariko sold an old book to a used bookstore. She had hoped to sell it for $0.80, but the store gave her $\frac{3}{4}$ of a dollar. What is the difference between the two amounts?

3 Koalas of eastern Australia feed mostly on eucalyptus leaves. They select certain trees over others to find the $1\frac{1}{4}$ pounds of food they need each day. Suppose a koala has eaten $1\frac{1}{8}$ pounds of food. Has the koala eaten enough food for the day?

4 The first day of the Tour de France is called the prologue. Each of the days after that is called a stage, and each stage covers a different distance. The total distance covered in the race is about 3,600 km. If a cyclist has completed $\frac{1}{3}$ of the race, how many kilometers has he ridden?

Adding, Subtracting, and Multiplying Decimals

California Standards

Extension of ⊷ NS2.3
Solve addition, subtraction, **multiplication,** and division problems, including those arising in concrete situations, that use **positive and negative integers** and combinations of these operations.

Why learn this? You can use operations with decimals to compare temperatures.

One of the coolest summers on record in the Midwest was in 1992. The average summertime temperature that year was 66.8°F. Normally, the average temperature is 4°F higher than it was in 1992.

To find the normal average summertime temperature in the Midwest, you can add 66.8°F and 4°F.

$$
\begin{array}{r}
\mathbf{66.8} \\
\mathbf{+\ 4.0} \\
\hline
\mathbf{70.8}
\end{array}
$$

Use zero as a placeholder so that both numbers have the same number of digits after their decimal points.

Add each column just as you would add integers.

Line up the decimal points.

The normal average summertime temperature in the Midwest is 70.8°F.

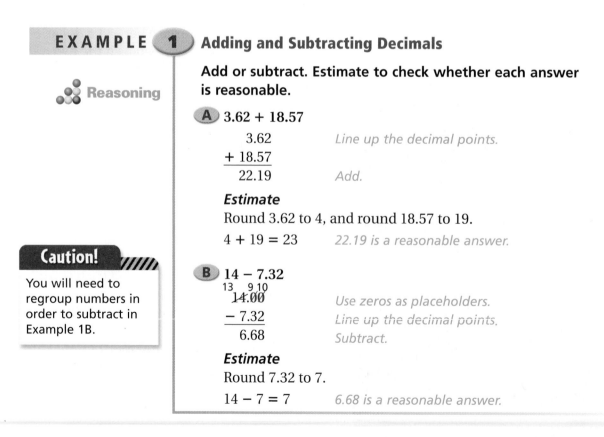

EXAMPLE 1 Adding and Subtracting Decimals

Reasoning

Add or subtract. Estimate to check whether each answer is reasonable.

A 3.62 + 18.57

$$
\begin{array}{r}
3.62 \\
+\ 18.57 \\
\hline
22.19
\end{array}
$$

Line up the decimal points.

Add.

Estimate
Round 3.62 to 4, and round 18.57 to 19.
4 + 19 = 23   *22.19 is a reasonable answer.*

Caution!

You will need to regroup numbers in order to subtract in Example 1B.

B 14 − 7.32

$$
\begin{array}{r}
\overset{13\ \ \ 9\ 10}{\cancel{14.00}} \\
-\ 7.32 \\
\hline
6.68
\end{array}
$$

Use zeros as placeholders.
Line up the decimal points.
Subtract.

Estimate
Round 7.32 to 7.
14 − 7 = 7   *6.68 is a reasonable answer.*

To multiply decimals, multiply as you would with integers, and then place the decimal point. The product should have the same number of decimal places as the sum of the decimal places in the factors.

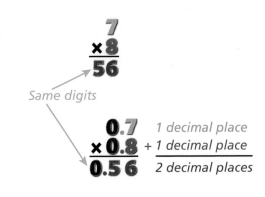

$$\begin{array}{r} 7 \\ \times\, 8 \\ \hline 56 \end{array}$$

Same digits

$$\begin{array}{r} 0.7 \\ \times\, 0.8 \\ \hline 0.56 \end{array}$$ 1 decimal place
+ 1 decimal place
2 decimal places

EXAMPLE 2   **Multiplying Decimals**

●● Reasoning

Multiply. Estimate to check whether each answer is reasonable.

Ⓐ $0.04 \cdot 2$

$$\begin{array}{r} 0.04 \\ \times\, 2 \\ \hline 0.08 \end{array}$$
   2 decimal places
   0 decimal places
   0 + 2 = 2 decimal places

Estimate
$0 \cdot 2 = 0$ *0.08 is a reasonable answer.*

Ⓑ $-2.78 \cdot 0.8$

$$\begin{array}{r} -2.78 \\ \times\, 0.8 \\ \hline -2.224 \end{array}$$
   2 decimal places
   1 decimal place
   2 + 1 = 3 decimal places

Estimate
$-3 \cdot 1 = -3$ *-2.224 is a reasonable answer.*

EXAMPLE 3   *Earth Science Application*

On average, 0.36 kg of carbon dioxide is added to the atmosphere for each mile a single car is driven. How many kilograms of carbon dioxide are added for each mile the 132 million cars in the United States are driven?

$$\begin{array}{r} 132 \\ \times\, 0.36 \\ \hline 792 \\ 3960 \\ \hline 47.52 \end{array}$$
   0 decimal places
   2 decimal places

    0 + 2 = 2 decimal places

Approximately 47.52 million (47,520,000) kilograms of carbon dioxide are added to the atmosphere for each mile driven.

Think and Discuss

1. Describe how you can check an answer when adding and subtracting decimals.

2. Explain whether the multiplication $2.1 \cdot 3.3 = 69.3$ is correct.

4-7 Exercises

California Standards Practice
Extension of NS2.3;
SDAP2.5

go.hrw.com
Homework Help Online
KEYWORD: MS8CA 4-7
Parent Resources Online
KEYWORD: MS8CA Parent

GUIDED PRACTICE

See Example 1 — Add or subtract. Estimate to check whether each answer is reasonable.

1. $5.37 + 16.45$ **2.** $7 + 5.826$ **3.** $7.89 - 5.91$ **4.** $4.97 - 3.2$

See Example 2 — Multiply. Estimate to check whether each answer is reasonable.

5. $3 \cdot 0.2$ **6.** $2.6 \cdot 0.4$ **7.** $1.5 \cdot (-0.21)$ **8.** $-0.4 \cdot 1.17$

See Example 3 — **9.** If Carla is able to drive her car 24.03 miles on one gallon of gas, how far could she drive on 13.93 gallons of gas?

INDEPENDENT PRACTICE

See Example 1 — Add or subtract. Estimate to check whether each answer is reasonable.

10. $7.82 + 31.23$ **11.** $5.98 + 12.99$ **12.** $4.917 + 12$ **13.** $10.022 + 0.11$

14. $5.45 - 3.21$ **15.** $15.39 - 2.6$ **16.** $21.04 - 4.99$ **17.** $5 - 0.53$

See Example 2 — Multiply. Estimate to check whether each answer is reasonable.

18. $2.4 \cdot 3.2$ **19.** $2.8 \cdot 1.6$ **20.** $5.3 \cdot 4.6$ **21.** $4.02 \cdot 0.7$

22. $-5.14 \cdot 0.03$ **23.** $1.04 \cdot (-8.9)$ **24.** $4.31 \cdot (-9.5)$ **25.** $-6.1 \cdot (-1.01)$

See Example 3 — **26.** Nicholas bicycled 15.8 kilometers each day for 18 days last month. How many kilometers did he bicycle last month?

27. While walking, Lara averaged 3.63 miles per hour. How far did she walk in 1.5 hours?

PRACTICE AND PROBLEM SOLVING

Extra Practice
See page EP9.

Add or subtract. Estimate to check whether each answer is reasonable.

28. $7.238 - 6.9$ **29.** $9.043 - 4.16$ **30.** $2.09 + 15.271$

31. $5.23 + 9.1$ **32.** $123 + 2.55$ **33.** $5.29 - 3.37$

Multiply. Estimate to check whether each answer is reasonable.

34. $-325.9 \cdot 1.5$ **35.** $14.7 \cdot 0.13$ **36.** $-28.5 \cdot (-1.07)$

37. $-7.02 \cdot (-0.05)$ **38.** $1.104 \cdot (-0.7)$ **39.** $0.072 \cdot 0.12$

40. Multi-Step Students at Hill Middle School plan to run a total of 2,462 mi, which is the distance from Los Angeles to New York City. So far, the sixth grade has run 273.5 mi, the seventh grade has run 275.8 mi, and the eighth grade has run 270.2 mi. How many more miles must the students run to reach their goal?

41. Critical Thinking Why must you line up the decimal points when adding and subtracting decimals?

42. **Reasoning** The graph shows the results of a survey about river recreation activities.

a. A report claimed that about 3 times as many people enjoyed canoeing in 1999–2000 than in 1994–1995. According to the graph, is this claim reasonable? Explain.

b. Suppose a future survey shows that 6 times as many people enjoyed kayaking in 2009–2010 than in 1999–2000. About how many people reported that they enjoyed kayaking in 2009–2010?

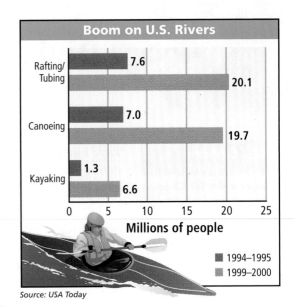

Boom on U.S. Rivers

Rafting/Tubing 7.6 20.1
Canoeing 7.0 19.7
Kayaking 1.3 6.6

Millions of people

■ 1994–1995
■ 1999–2000

Source: USA Today

43. **Science** To float in water, an object must have a density of less than 1 gram per milliliter. The density of a fresh egg is about 1.2 grams per milliliter. If the density of a spoiled egg is about 0.3 grams per milliliter less than that of a fresh egg, what is the density of a spoiled egg? How can you use water to tell whether an egg is spoiled?

44. **What's the Question?** In a collection, each rock sample has a mass of 4.35 kilograms. There are a dozen rocks in the collection. If the answer is 52.2 kilograms, what is the question?

45. **Write About It** How do the products 4.3 · 0.56 and 0.43 · 5.6 compare? Explain.

46. **Challenge** Find the missing number. $5.11 + 6.9 - 15.3 + \boxed{} = 20$

47. **Multiple Choice** In the 1900 Olympic Games, the 200-meter dash was won in 22.20 seconds. In 2000, the 200-meter dash was won in 20.09 seconds. How many seconds faster was the winning time in the 2000 Olympics?

Ⓐ 1.10 seconds   Ⓑ 2.11 seconds   Ⓒ 2.29 seconds   Ⓓ 4.83 seconds

48. **Gridded Response** Julia walked 1.8 mi each day from Monday through Friday. On Saturday, she walked 2.3 mi. How many miles did she walk in all?

Solve each equation. Check your answer. (Lesson 2-5)

49. $x - 8 = -22$ 50. $-3y = -45$ 51. $\frac{z}{2} = -8$ 52. $29 = -10 + p$

Solve. Write each answer in simplest form. (Lesson 4-6)

53. $n - \frac{2}{7} = \frac{1}{2}$ 54. $x + \frac{2}{3} = \frac{3}{4}$ 55. $\frac{1}{4}m = \frac{1}{2}$ 56. $\frac{5}{8}x = 1$

Dividing Decimals

Why learn this? You can divide decimals to determine how far a car can travel per gallon of gasoline. (See Example 3.)

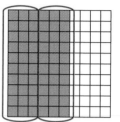

You can use a grid to model $0.6 \div 0.3$. Circle groups of 0.3 and count the number of groups. There are 2 groups of 0.3 in 0.6, so $0.6 \div 0.3 = 2$.

When you divide two numbers, you can multiply *both numbers* by the same power of ten without changing the final answer.

Multiply both 0.6 and 0.3 by 10: **0.6 · 10 = 6** and **0.3 · 10 = 3**

$$0.6 \div 0.3 = 2 \quad \text{and} \quad 6 \div 3 = 2$$

By multiplying both numbers by the same power of ten, you can make the divisor an integer. Dividing by an integer is much easier than dividing by a decimal.

EXAMPLE 1 **Dividing Decimals by Decimals**

Divide.

Helpful Hint

Multiply both numbers by the least power of ten that will make the divisor an integer.

See Skills Bank, p. SB5.

A $4.32 \div 3.6$

$$3.6\overline{)4.3\,2}$$

$$\begin{array}{r} 1.2 \\ 36\overline{)43.2} \\ -36 \\ \hline 7\,2 \\ -7\,2 \\ \hline 0 \end{array}$$

Multiply both numbers by 10 to make the divisor an integer.

Divide as with whole numbers.

B $12.95 \div (-1.25)$

$$1.25\overline{)12.95}$$

$$\begin{array}{r} 10.36 \\ 125\overline{)1,295.00} \\ -1\,25 \\ \hline 45\,0 \\ -37\,5 \\ \hline 7\,50 \\ -7\,50 \\ \hline 0 \end{array}$$

Multiply both numbers by 100 to make the divisor an integer.

Use zeros as placeholders. Divide as with whole numbers.

$$12.95 \div (-1.25) = -10.36$$

The signs are different.

EXAMPLE **2** **Dividing Integers by Decimals**

Divide. Estimate to check whether each answer is reasonable.

Reasoning

A 9 ÷ 1.25

$$1.25\overline{)9.00}$$

Multiply both numbers by 100 to make the divisor an integer.

$$\begin{array}{r} 7.2 \\ 125\overline{)900.0} \\ -875 \\ \hline 25\ 0 \\ -25\ 0 \\ \hline 0 \end{array}$$

Use zero as a placeholder. Divide as with whole numbers.

Estimate 9 ÷ 1 = 9

7.2 is a reasonable answer.

B −12 ÷ (−1.6)

$$1.6\overline{)12.0}$$

Multiply both numbers by 10 to make the divisor an integer.

$$\begin{array}{r} 7.5 \\ 16\overline{)120.0} \\ -112 \\ \hline 8\ 0 \\ -8\ 0 \\ \hline 0 \end{array}$$

Divide as with whole numbers.

−12 ÷ (−1.6) = 7.5

The signs are the same.

Estimate −12 ÷ (−2) = 6

7.5 is a reasonable answer.

EXAMPLE **3** *Transportation Application*

If Sandy used 15.45 gallons of gas to drive her car 370.8 miles, how many miles per gallon did she get?

$$15.45\overline{)370.80}$$

Multiply both numbers by 100 to make the divisor an integer.

$$\begin{array}{r} 24 \\ 1{,}545\overline{)37{,}080} \\ -30\ 90 \\ \hline 6\ 180 \\ -6\ 180 \\ \hline 0 \end{array}$$

Divide as with whole numbers.

Sandy got 24 miles per gallon.

> **Helpful Hint**
>
> To calculate miles per gallon, divide the number of miles driven by the number of gallons of gas used.

Think and Discuss

1. **Explain** whether 4.27 ÷ 0.7 is the same as 427 ÷ 7.

2. **Explain** how to divide an integer by a decimal.

Exercises

California Standards Practice
Extension of ✛ NS2.3;
AF1.3, AF1.4

go.hrw.com
Homework Help Online
KEYWORD: MS8CA 4-8
Parent Resources Online
KEYWORD: MS8CA Parent

GUIDED PRACTICE

See Example ① **Divide.**

1. $3.78 \div 4.2$ **2.** $13.3 \div (-0.38)$ **3.** $14.49 \div 3.15$

4. $1.06 \div 0.2$ **5.** $-9.76 \div 3.05$ **6.** $263.16 \div (-21.5)$

See Example ② **Divide. Estimate to check whether each answer is reasonable.**

7. $3 \div 1.2$ **8.** $84 \div 2.4$ **9.** $36 \div (-2.25)$

10. $24 \div (-1.2)$ **11.** $-18 \div 3.75$ **12.** $189 \div 8.4$

See Example ③ **13. Transportation** Samuel used 14.35 gallons of gas to drive his car 401.8 miles. How many miles per gallon did he get?

INDEPENDENT PRACTICE

See Example ① **Divide.**

14. $81.27 \div 0.03$ **15.** $-0.408 \div 3.4$ **16.** $38.5 \div (-5.5)$

17. $-1.12 \div 0.08$ **18.** $27.82 \div 2.6$ **19.** $14.7 \div 3.5$

See Example ② **Divide. Estimate to check whether each answer is reasonable.**

20. $35 \div (-2.5)$ **21.** $361 \div 7.6$ **22.** $63 \div (-4.2)$

23. $5 \div 1.25$ **24.** $14 \div 2.5$ **25.** $-78 \div 1.6$

See Example ③ **26. Transportation** Lonnie used 26.75 gallons of gas to drive his truck 508.25 miles. How many miles per gallon did he get?

27. Mitchell walked 8.5 laps in 20.4 minutes. If he walked each lap at the same pace, how long did it take him to walk one full lap?

PRACTICE AND PROBLEM SOLVING

Extra Practice
See page EP9.

Divide. Estimate to check whether each answer is reasonable.

28. $-24 \div 0.32$ **29.** $153 \div 6.8$ **30.** $-2.58 \div (-4.3)$

31. $4.12 \div (-10.3)$ **32.** $-17.85 \div 17$ **33.** $64 \div 2.56$

Simplify each expression.

34. $4.2 + (11.5 \div 4.6) + 5.8$ **35.** $2 \cdot (6.8 \div 3.4) \cdot 5$

36. $(6.4 \div 2.56) - 1.2 + 2.5$ **37.** $11.7 \div (0.7 + 0.6) \cdot 2$

38. $4 \cdot (0.6 + 0.78) \cdot 0.25$ **39.** $(1.6 \div 3.2) \cdot (4.2 + 8.6)$

40. Reasoning A car loan totaling $13,456.44 is to be paid off in 36 equal monthly payments. Lin Yao can afford no more than $350 per month. Can she afford the loan? Explain.

A glacier in Col Ferret, a pass in the Swiss Alps

41. Glaciers form when snow accumulates faster than it melts and thus becomes compacted into ice under the weight of more snow. Once the ice reaches a thickness of about 18 m, it begins to flow. If ice were to accumulate at a rate of 0.0072 m per year, how long would it take to start flowing?

42. An alpine glacier is estimated to be flowing at a rate of 4.75 m per day. At this rate, how long will it take for a marker placed on the glacier by a researcher to move 1,140 m?

43. If the Muir Glacier in Glacier Bay, Alaska, retreats at an average speed of 0.73 m per year, how long will it take to retreat a total of 7.9 m? Round your answer to the nearest year.

44. Multi-Step The table shows the thickness of a glacier as measured at five different points using radar. What is the average thickness of the glacier?

45. The Harvard Glacier in Alaska is advancing at a rate of about 0.055 m per day. At this rate, how long will it take the glacier to advance 20 m? Round your answer to the nearest hundredth.

46. ⭐ **Challenge** Hinman Glacier, on Mount Hinman, in Washington State, had an area of 1.3 km^2 in 1958. The glacier has lost an average of 0.06875 km^2 of area each year. Based on this rate, in what year was the total area 0.2 km^2?

Location	Thickness (m)
A	180.23
B	160.5
C	210.19
D	260
E	200.22

go.hrw.com
Web Extra!
KEYWORD: MS8CA Ice

SPIRAL STANDARDS REVIEW   NS2.1, AF1.3, AF1.4

47. Multiple Choice Simplify $4.42 \div 2.6 + 4.6$.

   Ⓐ 6.3   Ⓑ 2.9   Ⓒ 1.4   Ⓓ 0.6

48. Multiple Choice A deli is selling 5 sandwiches for $5.55, including tax. A school spent $83.25 on roast beef sandwiches for its 25 football players. How many sandwiches did each player get?

   Ⓐ 1   Ⓑ 2   Ⓒ 3   Ⓓ 5

Simplify each expression. (Lesson 1-3)

49. $2 + 6 \cdot 2$ **50.** $3^2 - 8 \cdot 0$ **51.** $(2 - 1)^5 + 3 \cdot 2^2$

52. A monarch butterfly has a wingspan of $3\frac{3}{8}$ in., and a common blue butterfly has a wingspan of $1\frac{3}{16}$ in. How much greater is the wingspan of the monarch butterfly than that of the common blue butterfly? (Lesson 4-3)

4-9 Metric Measurements

California Standards

AF2.1 Convert one unit of measurement to another (e.g., from feet to miles, from centimeters to inches).

Why learn this? Metric measurements are used throughout the world to describe and compare objects, such as the mass of rocks. (See Example 2.)

You can use the following benchmarks to help you understand millimeters, grams, and other metric units.

	Metric Unit	Benchmark
Length	Millimeter (mm)	Thickness of a dime
	Centimeter (cm)	Width of your little finger
	Meter (m)	Width of a doorway
	Kilometer (km)	Length of 10 football fields
Mass	Milligram (mg)	Mass of a grain of sand
	Gram (g)	Mass of a small paperclip
	Kilogram (kg)	Mass of a textbook
Capacity	Milliliter (mL)	Amount of liquid in an eyedropper
	Liter (L)	Amount of water in a large water bottle
	Kiloliter (kL)	Capacity of 2 large refrigerators

EXAMPLE 1 Choosing the Appropriate Metric Unit

Choose the most appropriate metric unit for each measurement. Justify your answer.

A The length of a car

Meters—the length of a car is similar to the width of several doorways.

B The mass of a skateboard

Kilograms—the mass of a skateboard is similar to the mass of several textbooks.

C The recommended dose of a cough syrup

Milliliters—one dose of cough syrup is similar to the amount of liquid in several eyedroppers.

Reading Math

Prefixes:
Milli- means
"thousandth"
Centi- means
"hundredth"
Kilo- means
"thousand"

The prefixes of metric units correlate to place values in the base-10 number system. The table shows how metric units are based on powers of 10.

1,000	100	10	1	0.1	0.01	0.001
Thousands	Hundreds	Tens	Ones	Tenths	Hundredths	Thousandths
Kilo-	*Hecto-*	*Deca-*	Base unit	*Deci-*	*Centi-*	*Milli-*

You can convert units within the metric system by multiplying or dividing by powers of 10. To convert to a smaller unit, you must multiply. To convert to a larger unit, you must divide.

EXAMPLE 2 **Converting Metric Units**

Convert each measure.

A **510 cm to meters**

510 cm = (510 ÷ 100) m   *100 cm = 1 m, so divide by 100.*
        = 5.1 m   *Move the decimal point 2 places left: 5.10.*

B **2.3 L to milliliters**

2.3 L = (2.3 × 1,000) mL   *1 L = 1,000 mL, so multiply by 1,000.*
      = 2,300 mL   *Move the decimal point 3 places right: 2.300.*

EXAMPLE 3 **Using Unit Conversion to Make Comparisons**

⬤⬤ Reasoning

Mai and Brian are measuring the mass of rocks in their Earth Science class. Mai's rock has a mass of 480 g. Brian's rock has a mass of 0.05 kg. Whose rock has the greater mass?

You can convert the mass of Mai's rock to kilograms.

480 g = (480 ÷ 1,000) kg   *1,000 g = 1 kg, so divide by 1,000.*
      = 0.48 kg   *Move the decimal point 3 places left: 480.*

Since 0.48 kg > 0.05 kg, Mai's rock has the greater mass.

Check

Use number sense. There are 1,000 grams in a kilogram, so the mass of Mai's rock is about half a kilogram, or 0.5 kg. This is much greater than 0.05 kg, the mass of Brian's rock, so the answer is reasonable.

Think and Discuss

1. Tell how the metric system relates to the base-10 number system.

2. Explain why it makes sense to multiply by a whole number when you convert to a smaller unit.

4-9 Metric Measurements **211**

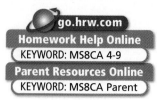

GUIDED PRACTICE

See Example ① **Choose the most appropriate metric unit for each measurement. Justify your answer.**

1. The mass of a pumpkin

2. The amount of water in a pond

3. The length of an eagle's beak

4. The mass of a penny

See Example ② **Convert each measure.**

5. 12 kg to grams

6. 4.3 m to centimeters

7. 0.7 mm to centimeters

8. 3,200 mL to liters

See Example ③ 9. On Sunday, Li ran 0.8 km. On Monday, she ran 7,200 m. On which day did Li run farther? Use estimation to explain why your answer makes sense.

INDEPENDENT PRACTICE

See Example ① **Choose the most appropriate metric unit for each measurement. Justify your answer.**

10. The capacity of a teacup

11. The mass of 10 grains of salt

12. The height of a palm tree

13. The distance between your eyes

See Example ② **Convert each measure.**

14. 0.067 L to milliliters

15. 1.4 m to kilometers

16. 900 mg to grams

17. 355 cm to millimeters

See Example ③ 18. Carmen pours 75 mL of water into a beaker. Nick pours 0.75 L of water into a different beaker. Who has the greater amount of water? Use estimation to explain why your answer makes sense.

PRACTICE AND PROBLEM SOLVING

Extra Practice
See page EP9.

Convert each measure.

19. 1.995 m = ▓ cm

20. 0.00004 kg = ▓ g

21. 2,050 kL = ▓ L

22. 0.002 mL = ▓ L

23. 3.7 mm = ▓ cm

24. 61.8 g = ▓ mg

Compare. Write <, >, or =.

25. 0.1 cm ▓ 1 mm

26. 25 g ▓ 3,000 mg

27. 340 mg ▓ 0.4 g

28. 0.05 kL ▓ 5 L

29. 0.3 mL ▓ 0.005 L

30. 1.3 kg ▓ 1,300 g

31. **Art** The *Mona Lisa* by Leonardo da Vinci is 77 cm tall. *Starry Night* by Vincent Van Gogh is 0.73 m tall. Which is the taller painting? How much taller is it?

Write each set of measures in order from least to greatest.

32. 0.005 kL; 4.1 L; 6,300 mL

33. 1.5 m; 1,200 mm; 130 cm

34. 4,000 mg; 50 kg; 70 g

35. 9.03 g; 0.0008 kg; 1,000 mg

36. Measurement Use a ruler to measure the line segment at right in centimeters. Then give the length of the segment in millimeters and meters.

Science

Bats consume up to 25% of their mass at each feeding.

Science The table gives information about several species of Vesper, or Evening, bats. Use the table for Exercises 37 and 38.

37. Which bat has the greatest mass?

38. Which bat has a longer wingspread, the Red Bat or the Big Brown Bat? How much longer is its wingspread?

U.S. Vesper Bats		
Name	Wingspread	Mass
Red Bat	0.3 m	10.9 g
Silver-Haired Bat	28.7 cm	8,500 mg
Big Brown Bat	317 mm	0.01 kg

39. Critical Thinking One milliliter of water has a mass of 1 gram. What is the mass of a liter of water?

40. What's the Error? A student converted 45 grams to milligrams as shown below. Explain the student's error.

$$45 \text{ g} = (45 \div 1,000) \text{ mg} = 0.045 \text{ mg}$$

41. Write About It Explain how to decide whether milligrams, grams, or kilograms are the most appropriate unit for measuring the mass of an object.

42. Challenge A decimeter is $\frac{1}{10}$ of a meter. Explain how to convert millimeters to decimeters.

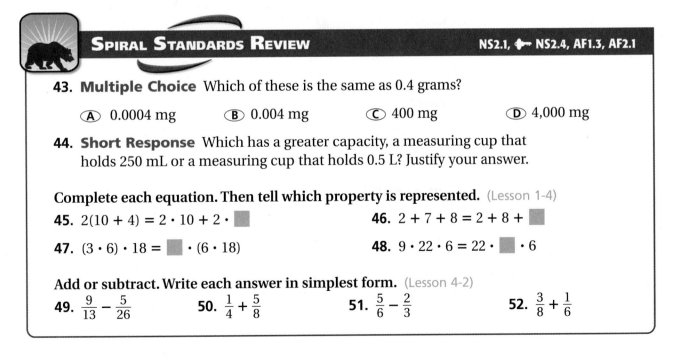

SPIRAL STANDARDS REVIEW   NS2.1, ← NS2.4, AF1.3, AF2.1

43. Multiple Choice Which of these is the same as 0.4 grams?

(A) 0.0004 mg   (B) 0.004 mg   (C) 400 mg   (D) 4,000 mg

44. Short Response Which has a greater capacity, a measuring cup that holds 250 mL or a measuring cup that holds 0.5 L? Justify your answer.

Complete each equation. Then tell which property is represented. (Lesson 1-4)

45. $2(10 + 4) = 2 \cdot 10 + 2 \cdot$ ▓

46. $2 + 7 + 8 = 2 + 8 +$ ▓

47. $(3 \cdot 6) \cdot 18 =$ ▓ $\cdot (6 \cdot 18)$

48. $9 \cdot 22 \cdot 6 = 22 \cdot$ ▓ $\cdot 6$

Add or subtract. Write each answer in simplest form. (Lesson 4-2)

49. $\frac{9}{13} - \frac{5}{26}$ **50.** $\frac{1}{4} + \frac{5}{8}$ **51.** $\frac{5}{6} - \frac{2}{3}$ **52.** $\frac{3}{8} + \frac{1}{6}$

Solving Equations Containing Decimals

California Standards

🔑 **AF1.1** Write and solve one-step linear equations in one variable.

Why learn this? You can use equations with decimals to determine finishing times in races.

The slowest time in a 40-yard dash was 3.84 seconds slower than the fastest time of 7.2 seconds. You can write an equation to represent this situation. The slowest time s minus 3.84 is equal to the fastest time of 7.2 seconds.

$$s - 3.84 = 7.2$$

EXAMPLE 1 Solving Equations by Adding or Subtracting

Remember!

You can solve an equation by performing the same operation on both sides of the equation to isolate the variable.

See Lesson 1-8, p. 40

Solve.

A $s - 3.84 = 7.2$

$$
\begin{array}{r}
s - 3.84 = 7.20 \\
\underline{+\ 3.84 \quad +\ 3.84} \\
s = 11.04
\end{array}
$$

Since 3.84 is subtracted from s, add 3.84 to both sides.

B $y + 20.51 = 26$

$$
\begin{array}{r}
y + 20.51 = 26.\overset{5\ 9\ 10}{\cancel{00}} \\
\underline{-\ 20.51 \quad -\ 20.51} \\
y = 5.49
\end{array}
$$

Since 20.51 is added to y, subtract 20.51 from both sides.

EXAMPLE 2 Solving Equations by Multiplying or Dividing

Solve.

A $\dfrac{w}{3.9} = 1.2$

$$\frac{w}{3.9} = 1.2$$

$$\frac{w}{3.9} \cdot 3.9 = 1.2 \cdot 3.9$$

$$w = 4.68$$

Since w is divided by 3.9, multiply both sides by 3.9.

B $4 = 1.6c$

$$4 = 1.6c$$

$$\frac{4}{1.6} = \frac{1.6c}{1.6}$$

$$\frac{4}{1.6} = c$$

$$2.5 = c$$

Since c is multiplied by 1.6, divide both sides by 1.6.
Think: $4 \div 1.6 = 40 \div 16$.

EXAMPLE **3** **PROBLEM SOLVING APPLICATION**

 **Reasoning**

Yancey wants to buy a new snowboard that costs $396.00. If she earns $8.25 per hour at work, how many hours must she work to earn enough money to buy the snowboard?

1. Understand the Problem

Rewrite the question as a statement.
• Find the number of hours Yancey must work to earn $396.00.

List the **important information**:
• Yancey earns $8.25 per hour.
• Yancey needs $396.00 to buy a snowboard.

2. Make a Plan

Yancey's pay is equal to her hourly pay times the number of hours she works. Since you know how much money she needs to earn, you can write an equation with h being the number of hours.

$$8.25h = 396$$

3. Solve

$$8.25h = 396$$

$$\frac{8.25h}{8.25} = \frac{396}{8.25}$$ *Since h is multiplied by 8.25, divide both sides by 8.25.*

$$h = 48$$

Yancey must work 48 hours.

4. Look Back

You can round 8.25 to 8 and 396 to 400 to estimate how many hours Yancey needs to work.

$$400 \div 8 = 50$$

So 48 hours is a reasonable answer.

Think and Discuss

1. Describe how to solve the equation $-1.25 + x = 1.25$. Then solve.

2. Explain how you can tell if 1.01 is a solution of $10s = -10.1$ without solving the equation.

4-10 **Exercises**

California Standards Practice
🔑 **NS1.1,** 🔑 **AF1.1**

go.hrw.com
Homework Help Online
KEYWORD: MS8CA 4-10
Parent Resources Online
KEYWORD: MS8CA Parent

GUIDED PRACTICE

See Example ① Solve.

1. $w - 5.8 = 1.2$

2. $x + 9.15 = 17$

3. $k + 3.91 = 28$

4. $n - 1.35 = 19.9$

See Example ② **5.** $\dfrac{b}{1.4} = 3.6$

6. $\dfrac{x}{0.8} = 7.2$

7. $3.1t = 27.9$

8. $7.5 = 5y$

See Example ③ **9. Consumer Math** Jeff bought a sandwich and a salad for lunch. His total bill was $7.10. The salad cost $2.85. How much did the sandwich cost?

INDEPENDENT PRACTICE

See Example ① Solve.

10. $v + 0.84 = 6$

11. $c - 32.56 = 12$

12. $d - 14.25 = 23.9$

13. $3.52 + a = 8.6$

14. $w - 9.01 = 12.6$

15. $p - 30.34 = 22.87$

See Example ② **16.** $3.2c = 8$

17. $72 = 4.5z$

18. $21.8x = -124.26$

19. $\dfrac{w}{2.8} = 4.2$

20. $\dfrac{m}{0.19} = 12$

21. $\dfrac{a}{21.23} = -3.5$

See Example ③ **22.** At the fair, 25 food tickets cost $31.25. What is the cost of each ticket?

23. To climb the rock wall at the fair, you must have 5 ride tickets. If each ticket costs $1.50, how much does it cost to climb the rock wall?

PRACTICE AND PROBLEM SOLVING

Extra Practice
See page EP9.

Solve.

24. $1.2y = -1.44$

25. $\dfrac{n}{8.2} = -0.6$

26. $w - 4.1 = 5$

27. $r + 0.48 = 1.2$

28. $x - 5.2 = 7.3$

29. $1.05 = -7m$

30. $a + 0.81 = 6.3$

31. $60k = 54$

32. $\dfrac{h}{-7.1} = 0.62$

33. $\dfrac{t}{-0.18} = -5.2$

34. $7.9 = d - 12.7$

35. $v - 1.8 = 3.8$

36. $-k = 287.658$

37. $-n = -12.254$

38. $0.64f = 12.8$

39. $15.217 = 4.11 + j$

40. $2.1 = p - 9.3$

41. $27.3 = 54.6g$

42. The Drama Club at Smith Valley Middle School is selling mugs in order to raise money for costumes. If each mug costs $4.75, how many mugs must members sell to make $570.00?

43. Consumer Math Gregory bought a computer desk at a thrift store for $38. The regular price of a similar desk at a furniture store is 4.5 times as much. What is the regular price of the desk at the furniture store?

44. Science Pennies minted, or created, before 1982 are made mostly of copper and have a density of 8.85 grams per cubic centimeter. The density of pennies made after 1982 is 1.71 grams per cubic centimeter less. What is the density of pennies minted today?

45. Social Studies The table shows the most common European ancestral origins of Americans (in millions), according to a Census 2000 supplementary survey. In addition, 19.6 million people stated that their ancestry was "American."

Ancestral Origins of Americans	
European Ancestry	**Number (millions)**
English	28.3
French	9.8
German	46.5
Irish	33.1
Italian	15.9
Polish	9.1
Scottish	5.4

   a. How many people claimed ancestry from the countries listed, according to the survey?

   b. If the data were placed in order from greatest to least, between which two nationalities would "American" ancestry be placed?

46. What's the Error? A student's solution to the equation $m + 0.63 = 5$ was $m = 5.63$. What is the error? What is the correct solution?

47. Write About It Compare the process of solving equations containing integers with the process of solving equations containing decimals.

48. Challenge Solve the equation $-2.8 + (b - 1.7) = -0.6 \cdot 9.4$.

SPIRAL STANDARDS REVIEW   ↙ AF1.1, AF1.2, AF1.3, AF1.4

49. Multiple Choice What is the solution to the equation $x - 4.55 = 6.32$?

   Ⓐ $x = -1.39$ Ⓑ $x = 1.77$ Ⓒ $x = 10.87$ Ⓓ $x = 28.76$

50. Multiple Choice The pep squad is selling tickets for a raffle. The tickets are $0.25 each or 5 for $1.00. Julie bought a pack of 5 tickets. Which equation can be used to find how much Julie paid per ticket?

   Ⓐ $5x = 0.25$ Ⓑ $0.25x = 1.00$ Ⓒ $5x = 1.00$ Ⓓ $1.00x = 0.25$

51. Extended Response Write a word problem that the equation $6.25x = 125$ can be used to solve. Solve the problem and explain what the solution means.

Evaluate each expression for the given value of the variable. (Lesson 1-5)

52. $2x - 4x$ for $x = 5$ **53.** $n^2 + 6n$ for $n = 7$ **54.** $\frac{p}{4} + 3p$ for $p = 8$

Simplify each expression. (Lesson 4-8)

55. $6.3 \div 2.1 - 1.5$ **56.** $4 \cdot 5.1 \div 2 + 3.6$ **57.** $(1.6 + 3.8) \div 1.8$

58. $(5.4 + 3.6) \div 0.9$ **59.** $4.5 \div 0.6 \cdot 1.2$ **60.** $5.8 + 3.2 \div 6.4$

READY TO GO ON?

Quiz for Lessons 4-7 Through 4-10

✓ **4-7** **Adding, Subtracting, and Multiplying Decimals**

Add or subtract.

1. $4.73 + 29.68$ **2.** $6.89 + 29.4$ **3.** $23.58 - 8.36$ **4.** $15 - 9.44$

5. $17 + 8.37$ **6.** $6.2 - 0.45$ **7.** $0.35 + 10.4$ **8.** $17.8 - 6.92$

Multiply.

9. $3.4 \cdot 9.6$ **10.** $-2.66 \cdot 0.9$ **11.** $-7 \cdot (-0.06)$ **12.** $6.94 \cdot (-24)$

13. $12.67 \cdot 15$ **14.** $15.2 \cdot 2.4$ **15.** $-5.4 \cdot 0.03$ **16.** $-265 \cdot (-0.04)$

17. Cami can run 7.02 miles per hour. How many miles can she run in 1.75 hours? Round your answer to the nearest hundredth.

✓ **4-8** **Dividing Decimals**

Divide.

18. $10.8 \div (-4)$ **19.** $6.5 \div 2$ **20.** $-45.6 \div 12$ **21.** $-99.36 \div (-4)$

22. $10.4 \div (-0.8)$ **23.** $18 \div 2.4$ **24.** $-3.3 \div 0.11$ **25.** $-36 \div (-0.9)$

26. Cynthia ran 17.5 laps in 38.5 minutes. If she ran each lap at the same pace, how long did it take her to run one full lap?

✓ **4-9** **Metric Measurements**

Convert each measure.

27. 17.3 kg to grams   **28.** 540 mL to liters   **29.** 0.46 cm to millimeters

30. Cat ran in the 400-meter dash and the 800-meter run. Hilo ran in the 2-kilometer cross-country race. All together, who ran the farthest, Cat or Hilo?

✓ **4-10** **Solving Equations Containing Decimals**

Solve.

31. $3.4 + n = 8$ **32.** $x - 1.75 = 19$ **33.** $-3.5 = -5x$ **34.** $10.1 = \frac{s}{8}$

35. Pablo earns \$5.50 per hour. His friend Raymond earns 1.2 times as much. How much does Raymond earn per hour?

36. Emma bought a scrapbook and a pair of scissors for a total of \$22.15. If the scissors cost \$3.24, how much did the scrapbook cost?

Something's Fishy! Maria and Victor are setting up a 20-gallon aquarium. They want to choose fish for the aquarium using the rule "1 inch of fish per gallon of water." This means that the total length of the fish in their tank should be no more than 20 inches.

1. Maria considers getting one of each fish shown in the table. Estimate the total length of the fish. Could she add more fish? Explain.

2. Victor would like to have a neon tetra and a guppy in the tank. What is the total length of the two fish?

3. What is the total length of the remaining fish that Victor could add to the tank? Explain.

4. Is there enough room left for Victor to add 4 clown barbs to the tank? Why or why not?

5. Maria and Victor decide to fill the tank with neon tetras only. Write and solve an equation to find out how many neon tetras they can put in the tank.

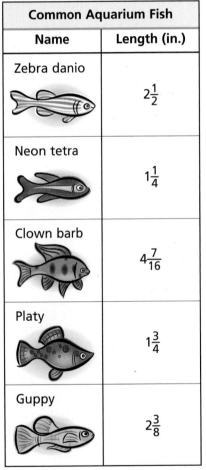

Common Aquarium Fish	
Name	**Length (in.)**
Zebra danio	$2\frac{1}{2}$
Neon tetra	$1\frac{1}{4}$
Clown barb	$4\frac{7}{16}$
Platy	$1\frac{3}{4}$
Guppy	$2\frac{3}{8}$

Game Time

Fraction Riddles

1 What is the value of one-half of two-thirds of three-fourths of four-fifths of five-sixths of six-sevenths of seven-eighths of eight-ninths of nine-tenths of one thousand?

2 What could be the next fraction in the pattern below?
$$\frac{1}{12}, \frac{1}{6}, \frac{1}{4}, \frac{1}{3}, \cdots$$

3 I am a three-digit number. My hundreds digit is one-third of my tens digit. My tens digit is one-third of my ones digit. What number am I?

4 A *splorg* costs three-fourths of a dollar plus three-fourths of a *splorg*. How much does a *splorg* cost?

5 How many cubic inches of dirt are in a hole that measures $\frac{1}{3}$ feet by $\frac{1}{4}$ feet by $\frac{1}{2}$ feet?

Fraction Bingo

The object is to be the first player to cover five squares in a row horizontally, vertically, or diagonally.

One person is the caller. On each of the caller's cards, there is an expression containing fractions. When the caller draws a card, he or she reads the expression aloud for the players.

The players must find the value of the expression. If a square on the player's card has that value or a fraction equivalent to that value, they cover the square.

The first player to cover five squares in a row is the winner. Take turns being the caller. A variation can be played in which the winner is the first person to cover all their squares.

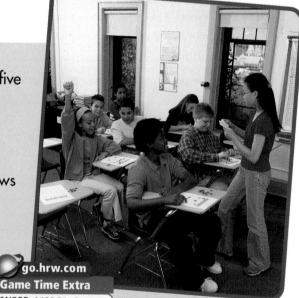

go.hrw.com
Game Time Extra
KEYWORD: MS8CA Games

A complete copy of the rules and game pieces are available online.

Materials
- file folder
- ruler
- pencil
- scissors
- markers

It's in the Bag!

PROJECT **Operation Slide Through**

Slide notes through the frame to review key concepts about operations with rational numbers.

Directions

❶ Keep the file folder closed throughout the project. Cut off a $3\frac{1}{2}$-inch strip from the bottom of the folder. Trim the remaining folder so that is has no tabs and measures 8 inches by 8 inches. **Figure A**

❷ Cut out a thin notch about 4 inches long along the middle of the folded edge. **Figure B**

❸ Cut a $3\frac{3}{4}$-inch slit about 2 inches to the right of the notch. Make another slit, also $3\frac{3}{4}$ inches long, about 3 inches to the right of the first slit. **Figure C**

❹ Weave the $3\frac{1}{2}$-inch strip of the folder into the notch, through the first slit, and into the second slit. **Figure D**

Taking Note of the Math

As you pull the strip through the frame, divide the strip into several sections. Use each section to record vocabulary and practice problems from the chapter.

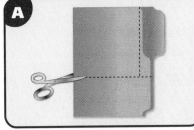

A

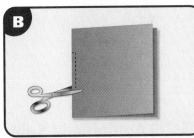

B

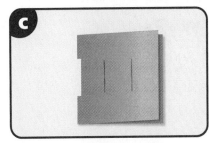

C

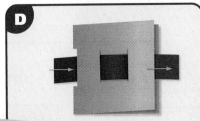

D

CHAPTER 4

OPERATIONS WITH RATIONAL NUMBERS

Vocabulary

multiplicative inverse 192   reciprocal 192

4-1 Estimating with Fractions (pp. 170–173)

Prep for **NS2.1**

EXAMPLE

■ Estimate.

$7\frac{3}{4} - 4\frac{1}{3}$

$7\frac{3}{4} \longrightarrow 8 \qquad 4\frac{1}{3} \longrightarrow 4\frac{1}{2}$

$8 - 4\frac{1}{2} = 3\frac{1}{2}$

$11\frac{7}{12} \div 3\frac{2}{5}$

$11\frac{7}{12} \longrightarrow 12 \quad 3\frac{2}{5} \longrightarrow 3$

$12 \div 3 = 4$

EXERCISES

Estimate each sum, difference, product, or quotient.

1. $11\frac{1}{7} + 12\frac{3}{4}$ 2. $13\frac{10}{17} - 5\frac{5}{7}$

3. $9\frac{7}{8} - 7\frac{1}{13}$ 4. $11\frac{8}{9} - 11\frac{1}{20}$

5. $5\frac{13}{20} \cdot 4\frac{1}{2}$ 6. $6\frac{1}{4} \div 1\frac{5}{8}$

7. Sara ran $2\frac{1}{3}$ laps on Monday and $7\frac{3}{4}$ laps on Friday. About how many more laps did Sara run on Friday?

4-2 Adding and Subtracting Fractions (pp. 176–179)

NS2.1, **NS2.4**

EXAMPLE

■ Add.

$\frac{1}{3} + \frac{2}{5} = \frac{5}{15} + \frac{6}{15}$ *Write equivalent*
                                    fractions using a
$\qquad = \frac{11}{15}$ *common denominator.*

EXERCISES

Add or subtract. Write each answer in simplest form.

8. $\frac{3}{4} - \frac{1}{3}$ 9. $\frac{1}{4} + \frac{3}{5}$

10. $\frac{4}{11} + \frac{4}{44}$ 11. $\frac{4}{9} - \frac{1}{3}$

12. $\frac{5}{8} + \frac{7}{12}$ 13. $\frac{9}{16} - \frac{2}{5}$

4-3 Adding and Subtracting Mixed Numbers (pp. 180–183)

NS2.1, **NS2.4**

EXAMPLE

■ Add.

$1\frac{1}{3} + 2\frac{1}{2} = 1\frac{2}{6} + 2\frac{3}{6}$ *Add the integers,*
                                        and then add the
$\qquad = 3 + \frac{5}{6}$ *fractions.*

$\qquad = 3\frac{5}{6}$

EXERCISES

Add or subtract. Write each answer in simplest form.

14. $3\frac{7}{8} + 2\frac{1}{3}$ 15. $2\frac{1}{4} + 1\frac{1}{12}$

16. $8\frac{1}{2} - 2\frac{1}{4}$ 17. $11\frac{3}{4} - 10\frac{1}{3}$

18. $4\frac{3}{10} + 6\frac{11}{12}$ 19. $7 - 5\frac{1}{3}$

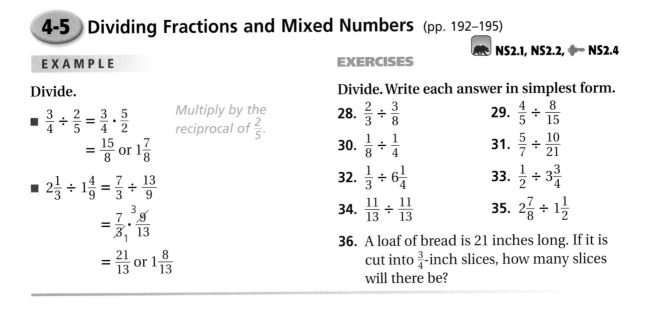

4-4 Multiplying Fractions and Mixed Numbers (pp. 188–191)

NS2.1, NS2.2, NS2.4

EXAMPLE

Multiply. Write the answer in simplest form.

■ $\dfrac{2}{9} \cdot \dfrac{3}{4} = \dfrac{\overset{1}{\cancel{2}}}{\cancel{9}_3} \cdot \dfrac{\overset{1}{\cancel{3}}}{\cancel{4}_2}$ *Multiply numerators.*
Multiply denominators.

     $= \dfrac{1}{6}$

■ $4\dfrac{1}{2} \cdot 5\dfrac{3}{4} = \dfrac{9}{2} \cdot \dfrac{23}{4}$

     $= \dfrac{207}{8}$ or $25\dfrac{7}{8}$

EXERCISES

Multiply. Write each answer in simplest form.

20. $\dfrac{1}{8} \cdot \dfrac{2}{9}$ **21.** $\dfrac{5}{12} \cdot \dfrac{4}{7}$

22. $\dfrac{11}{24} \cdot \dfrac{6}{11}$ **23.** $\dfrac{3}{25} \cdot \dfrac{5}{18}$

24. $1\dfrac{2}{3} \cdot 4\dfrac{1}{2}$ **25.** $\dfrac{4}{5} \cdot 2\dfrac{3}{10}$

26. $4\dfrac{6}{7} \cdot 3\dfrac{5}{9}$ **27.** $3\dfrac{4}{7} \cdot 1\dfrac{3}{4}$

4-5 Dividing Fractions and Mixed Numbers (pp. 192–195)

NS2.1, NS2.2, NS2.4

EXAMPLE

Divide.

■ $\dfrac{3}{4} \div \dfrac{2}{5} = \dfrac{3}{4} \cdot \dfrac{5}{2}$ *Multiply by the reciprocal of $\dfrac{2}{5}$.*

     $= \dfrac{15}{8}$ or $1\dfrac{7}{8}$

■ $2\dfrac{1}{3} \div 1\dfrac{4}{9} = \dfrac{7}{3} \div \dfrac{13}{9}$

     $= \dfrac{7}{\cancel{3}_1} \cdot \dfrac{\overset{3}{\cancel{9}}}{13}$

     $= \dfrac{21}{13}$ or $1\dfrac{8}{13}$

EXERCISES

Divide. Write each answer in simplest form.

28. $\dfrac{2}{3} \div \dfrac{3}{8}$ **29.** $\dfrac{4}{5} \div \dfrac{8}{15}$

30. $\dfrac{1}{8} \div \dfrac{1}{4}$ **31.** $\dfrac{5}{7} \div \dfrac{10}{21}$

32. $\dfrac{1}{3} \div 6\dfrac{1}{4}$ **33.** $\dfrac{1}{2} \div 3\dfrac{3}{4}$

34. $\dfrac{11}{13} \div \dfrac{11}{13}$ **35.** $2\dfrac{7}{8} \div 1\dfrac{1}{2}$

36. A loaf of bread is 21 inches long. If it is cut into $\dfrac{3}{4}$-inch slices, how many slices will there be?

4-6 Solving Equations Containing Fractions (pp. 196–199)

NS2.1, NS2.2, NS2.4, AF1.1

EXAMPLE

Solve. Write the answer in simplest form.

■ $t + \dfrac{2}{3} = \dfrac{3}{4}$

  $t + \dfrac{2}{3} - \dfrac{2}{3} = \dfrac{3}{4} - \dfrac{2}{3}$ *Subtract $\dfrac{2}{3}$ from both sides.*

     $t = \dfrac{9}{12} - \dfrac{8}{12}$ *Find a common denominator.*

     $t = \dfrac{1}{12}$

■ $\dfrac{1}{4}x = \dfrac{1}{6}$

  $\dfrac{4}{1} \cdot \dfrac{1}{4}x = \dfrac{1}{6} \cdot \dfrac{4}{1}$ *Multiply by the reciprocal of $\dfrac{1}{4}$.*

     $x = \dfrac{4}{6} = \dfrac{2}{3}$

EXERCISES

Solve. Write each answer in simplest form.

37. $\dfrac{1}{5}x = \dfrac{1}{3}$ **38.** $\dfrac{1}{3} + y = \dfrac{2}{5}$

39. $\dfrac{1}{6}x = \dfrac{2}{7}$ **40.** $\dfrac{2}{7} + x = \dfrac{3}{4}$

41. $m - \dfrac{1}{3} = \dfrac{4}{5}$ **42.** $p + \dfrac{1}{12} = \dfrac{1}{10}$

43. $y - \dfrac{3}{4} = \dfrac{2}{7}$ **44.** $\dfrac{2}{15}c = \dfrac{2}{5}$

45. A chef had $2\dfrac{1}{2}$ cups of olive oil and used $\dfrac{3}{4}$ cup for a recipe. How many cups of olive oil are left?

4-7 Adding, Subtracting, and Multiplying Decimals (pp. 202–205)

 Ext. of NS2.3

EXAMPLE

■ Add.

5.67 + 22.44

   5.67   *Line up the decimal points.*

+ 22.44

  28.11   *Add.*

■ Multiply.

1.44 · 0.6

  1.44   *2 decimal places*

× 0.6   *1 decimal place*

0.864   *2 + 1 = 3 decimal places*

EXERCISES

Add or subtract.

46. 4.99 + 22.89   **47.** 6.7 + 44.5

48. 18.09 − 11.87   **49.** 47 + 5.902

50. 23 − 8.905   **51.** 4.68 + 31.2

Multiply.

52. 7 · 0.5   **53.** −4.3 · 9

54. 4.55 · 8.9   **55.** 7.88 · 7.65

56. 63.4 · 1.22   **57.** −9.9 · 1.9

4-8 Dividing Decimals (pp. 206–209)

Ext. of NS2.3

EXAMPLE

■ Divide.

0.96 ÷ 1.6   *Multiply both numbers by*

$\dfrac{0.6}{16)\overline{9.6}}$ *10 to make the divisor an*

  −9 6   *integer.*

     0

EXERCISES

Divide.

58. 7.65 ÷ 1.7   **59.** 9.483 ÷ (−8.7)

60. 126.28 ÷ (−8.2)   **61.** 2.5 ÷ (−0.005)

62. 9 ÷ 4.5   **63.** 13 ÷ 3.25

4-9 Metric Measurements (pp. 210–213)

AF2.1

EXAMPLE

■ Convert 63 m to centimeters.

63 m = (63 × 100) cm   *100 cm = 1 m*

     = 6,300 cm

EXERCISES

Convert each measure.

64. 18 L to mL   **65.** 720 mg to g

66. 5.3 km to m   **67.** 0.6 cm to mm

4-10 Solving Equations Containing Decimals (pp. 214–217)

AF1.1

EXAMPLE

■ Solve.

$n − 4.77 = 8.60$

$\underline{+ 4.77 + 4.77}$ *Add to isolate n.*

$n = 13.37$

EXERCISES

Solve.

68. $x + 30 = 40.44$ **69.** $\dfrac{s}{1.07} = 100$

70. $0.8n = 0.0056$ **71.** $k − 8 = 0.64$

72. $3.65 = e − 1.4$ **73.** $\dfrac{w}{−0.2} = 15.4$

CHAPTER TEST

Estimate each sum, difference, product, or quotient.

1. $\frac{3}{4} + \frac{3}{8}$
2. $5\frac{7}{8} - 3\frac{1}{4}$
3. $6\frac{5}{7} \cdot 2\frac{2}{9}$
4. $8\frac{1}{5} \div 3\frac{9}{10}$

Add or subtract. Write each answer in simplest form.

5. $\frac{3}{10} + \frac{2}{5}$
6. $\frac{7}{8} - \frac{11}{16}$
7. $7\frac{1}{3} + 5\frac{11}{12}$
8. $9 - 3\frac{2}{5}$

Multiply or divide. Write each answer in simplest form.

9. $5 \cdot 4\frac{1}{3}$
10. $2\frac{7}{10} \cdot 2\frac{2}{3}$
11. $\frac{3}{10} \div \frac{4}{5}$
12. $2\frac{1}{5} \div 1\frac{5}{6}$

13. A recipe calls for $4\frac{4}{5}$ tbsp of butter. Nasim is making $3\frac{1}{3}$ times the recipe for his soccer team. How much butter does he need? Write your answer in simplest form.

14. Brianna has $11\frac{2}{3}$ cups of milk. She needs $1\frac{1}{6}$ cups of milk to make a pot of hot cocoa. How many pots of hot cocoa can Brianna make?

Solve. Write each answer in simplest form.

15. $\frac{1}{5}a = \frac{1}{8}$
16. $\frac{1}{4}c = 980$
17. $w - \frac{7}{9} = \frac{2}{3}$
18. $z - \frac{5}{13} = \frac{6}{7}$

19. Alan finished his homework in $1\frac{1}{2}$ hours. It took Jimmy $\frac{3}{4}$ of an hour longer than Alan to finish his homework. How long did it take Jimmy to finish his homework?

20. Mya played in two softball games one afternoon. The first game lasted 42 min. The second game lasted $1\frac{2}{3}$ times longer than the first game. How long did Mya's second game last?

Add or subtract.

21. $3.086 + 6.152$
22. $5.91 + 12.8$
23. $3.1 - 2.076$
24. $14.75 - 6.926$

Multiply or divide.

25. $3.25 \cdot 24$
26. $-3.79 \cdot 0.9$
27. $3.2 \div 16$
28. $3.57 \div (-0.7)$

Convert each measure.

29. 180 mL to liters
30. 7.8 m to centimeters
31. 23.4 kg to grams

32. Jesse is 1,460 millimeters tall. Her sister is 168 centimeters tall, and her brother is 1.56 meters tall. Who is the tallest?

Solve.

33. $w - 5.3 = 7.6$
34. $4.9 = c + 3.7$
35. $b \div 1.8 = 2.1$
36. $4.3h = 81.7$

37. All sweaters in a store are on sale for the same price. The total cost of 3 sweaters is $63.12. How much does each sweater cost?

Cumulative Assessment, Chapters 1–4

Multiple Choice

1. A cell phone company charges $0.05 per text message. Which expression represents the cost of t text messages?

(A) $0.05t$ (C) $0.05 - t$

(B) $0.05 + t$ (D) $0.05 \div t$

2. Ahmed had $75 in his bank account on Sunday. The table shows his account activity for each day last week. What was the balance in Ahmed's account on Friday?

Day	Deposit	Withdrawal
Monday	$25	none
Tuesday	none	−$108
Wednesday	$65	none
Thursday	$32	none
Friday	none	−$101

(A) −$86   (C) $0

(B) −$12   (D) $96

3. Natasha is designing a doghouse. She wants the front of the doghouse to be $3\frac{1}{2}$ feet wide, and she wants the side of the doghouse to be $2\frac{3}{4}$ feet wider than the front. Which expression can be used to find the length of the side of the doghouse?

(A) $3\frac{1}{2} + 2\frac{3}{4}$ (C) $3\frac{1}{2} \cdot 2\frac{3}{4}$

(B) $3\frac{1}{2} - 2\frac{3}{4}$ (D) $3\frac{1}{2} \div 2\frac{3}{4}$

4. What is the value of $5\frac{2}{3} \div \frac{3}{9}$?

(A) 17 (C) 10

(B) $\frac{17}{9}$ (D) $5\frac{1}{3}$

5. Mrs. Herold has $5\frac{1}{4}$ yards of material to make two dresses. The larger dress requires $3\frac{3}{4}$ yards of material. Which equation can be used to find t, the number of yards of material remaining to make the smaller dress?

(A) $3\frac{3}{4} - t = 5\frac{1}{4}$ (C) $3\frac{3}{4} \div t = 5\frac{1}{4}$

(B) $3\frac{3}{4} \cdot t = 5\frac{1}{4}$ (D) $3\frac{3}{4} + t = 5\frac{1}{4}$

6. On a quiz show, a player receives 10 points for each correct answer and loses 5 points for each incorrect answer. What is Janice's total score if she has 16 correct answers and 9 incorrect answers?

(A) 94 (C) 151

(B) 115 (D) 205

7. Daisy the bulldog weighs $45\frac{13}{16}$ pounds. Henry the beagle weighs $21\frac{3}{4}$ pounds. How many more pounds does Daisy weigh than Henry?

(A) $23\frac{15}{16}$ pounds   (C) $24\frac{1}{16}$ pounds

(B) $24\frac{5}{6}$ pounds   (D) $67\frac{9}{16}$ pounds

8. What is the value of the expression $6x - y$ for $x = -2$ and $y = 10$?

(A) -22 (C) 2

(B) -2 (D) 22

9. Joel threw a shot put $24\frac{2}{9}$ yards. Jamil threw the shot put $33\frac{10}{11}$ yards. Estimate how much farther Jamil threw the shot put than Joel did.

(A) 8 yards   (C) 12 yards

(B) 10 yards   (D) 15 yards

10. Which model best represents the expression $\frac{3}{4} \times \frac{1}{2}$?

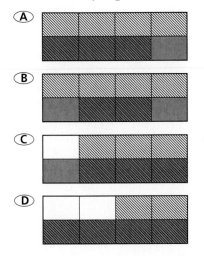

Ⓐ

Ⓑ

Ⓒ

Ⓓ

11. The table shows the different types of pets owned by the 15 students in Mrs. Sizer's Spanish class. What fraction of the students listed own a dog?

Type of Pet	Number of Students
Cat	5
Dog	9
Hamster	1

Ⓐ $\frac{3}{5}$ Ⓒ $\frac{1}{15}$

Ⓑ $\frac{1}{5}$ Ⓓ $\frac{1}{9}$

Gridded Response

12. In 2004, the expression $5.85x$ could be used to determine the amount in dollars a worker earned for working x hours at minimum wage. How many dollars would a worker have earned in 2004 for working 2.4 hours at minimum wage?

13. Solve the equation $\frac{5}{12}x = \frac{1}{4}$ for x.

14. What is the value of the expression $2(3) + (-4) - 8 + 3^2$?

Short Response

15. Louise is staying on the 22nd floor of a hotel. Her mother is staying on the 43rd floor. Louise wants to visit her mother, but the elevator is temporarily out of service. Write and solve an equation to find the number of floors that Louise must climb if she takes the stairs.

16. Mari bought 3 packages of colored paper. She used $\frac{3}{4}$ of a package to make greeting cards and used $1\frac{1}{6}$ packages for an art project. She gave $\frac{2}{3}$ of a package to her brother. How much colored paper does Mari have left? Show the steps you used to find the answer.

17. A building proposal calls for 6 acres of land to be divided into $\frac{3}{4}$-acre lots. How many lots can be made? Explain your answer.

Extended Response

18. A high school is hosting a triple-jump competition. In this event, athletes make three leaps in a row to try to cover the greatest distance.

  a. Tony's first two jumps were $11\frac{2}{3}$ ft and $11\frac{1}{2}$ ft. His total distance was 44 ft. Write and solve an equation to find the length of his final jump.

  b. Candice's three jumps were all the same length. Her total distance was 38 ft. What was the length of each of her jumps?

  c. The lengths of Davis's jumps were 11.6 ft, $11\frac{1}{4}$ ft, and $11\frac{2}{3}$ ft. Plot these lengths on a number line. What was the farthest distance he jumped? How much farther was this distance than the shortest distance Davis jumped?

Proportional Relationships

CONCEPT CONNECTION

go.hrw.com
Chapter Project Online
KEYWORD: MS8CA Ch5

You can use ratios and proportions to describe the relationship between this binoculars-shaped building and an actual pair of binoculars.

Main Street
Venice, California

ARE YOU READY?

✓ Vocabulary

Choose the best term from the list to complete each sentence.

1. A(n) __?__ is a number in the form $\frac{a}{b}$, where $b \neq 0$.

2. A closed figure with three sides is called a(n) __?__.

3. Two fractions are __?__ if they represent the same number.

4. One way to compare two fractions is to first find a(n) __?__.

common denominator

equivalent

fraction

quadrilateral

triangle

Complete these exercises to review skills you will need for this chapter.

✓ Write Equivalent Fractions

Find two fractions that are equivalent to each fraction.

5. $\frac{2}{5}$ 6. $\frac{7}{11}$ 7. $\frac{25}{100}$ 8. $\frac{4}{6}$

9. $\frac{5}{17}$ 10. $\frac{15}{23}$ 11. $\frac{24}{78}$ 12. $\frac{150}{325}$

✓ Compare Fractions

Compare. Write < or >.

13. $\frac{5}{6}$ ▧ $\frac{2}{3}$ 14. $\frac{3}{8}$ ▧ $\frac{2}{5}$ 15. $\frac{6}{11}$ ▧ $\frac{1}{4}$ 16. $\frac{5}{8}$ ▧ $\frac{11}{12}$

17. $\frac{8}{9}$ ▧ $\frac{12}{13}$ 18. $\frac{5}{11}$ ▧ $\frac{7}{21}$ 19. $\frac{4}{10}$ ▧ $\frac{3}{7}$ 20. $\frac{3}{4}$ ▧ $\frac{2}{9}$

✓ Solve Multiplication Equations

Solve each equation.

21. $3x = 12$ 22. $15t = 75$ 23. $2y = 14$ 24. $7m = 84$

25. $25c = 125$ 26. $16f = 320$ 27. $11n = 121$ 28. $53y = 318$

✓ Multiply Fractions

Solve. Write each answer in simplest form.

29. $\frac{2}{3} \cdot \frac{5}{7}$ 30. $\frac{12}{16} \cdot \frac{3}{9}$ 31. $\frac{4}{9} \cdot \frac{18}{24}$ 32. $\frac{1}{56} \cdot \frac{50}{200}$

33. $\frac{1}{5} \cdot \frac{5}{9}$ 34. $\frac{7}{8} \cdot \frac{4}{3}$ 35. $\frac{25}{100} \cdot \frac{30}{90}$ 36. $\frac{46}{91} \cdot \frac{3}{6}$

Unpacking the Standards

The information below "unpacks" the standards. The Academic Vocabulary is highlighted and defined to help you understand the language of the standards. Refer to the lessons listed after each standard for help with the math terms and phrases. The Chapter Concept shows how the standard is applied in this chapter.

California Standard	Academic Vocabulary	Chapter Concept
NS1.2 Interpret and use ratios in different contexts (e.g., batting averages, miles per hour) to show the relative sizes of two quantities, using appropriate notations ($\frac{a}{b}$, *a* to *b*, *a:b*). (Lessons 5-1, 5-2, 5-3)	**interpret** to understand and explain the meaning of **context** in this case, a real-world situation **relative sizes** sizes that are compared to each other *Example:* A distance of 1 mile is large relative to a distance of 1 inch. **notation** a way of writing or representing something *Example:* The ratio 3 to 4 can also be written using the notation 3:4.	You understand and can explain the meaning of ratios. You write ratios in different forms. *Example:* A recipe calls for 2 oranges and 3 lemons. The ratio of **oranges** to **lemons** can be written as $\frac{2}{3}$, **2 to 3**, or **2:3**.
NS1.3 Use proportions to solve problems (e.g., determine the value of *N* if $\frac{4}{7}=\frac{N}{21}$, find the length of a side of a polygon similar to a known polygon). Use cross-multiplication as a method for solving such problems, understanding it as the multiplication of both sides of an equation by a multiplicative inverse. (Lessons 5-4, 5-5, 5-6, 5-7, 5-8) (Lab 5-6)	**polygon** a closed plane figure formed by line segments that meet only at their endpoints *Examples:* triangles, squares, rectangles **known polygon** a polygon whose side lengths and angle measures are known	You solve proportions by finding the value of a variable that makes the proportion true. *Example:* $\frac{4}{7}=\frac{N}{21}$ $4 \cdot 21 = 7 \cdot N$ $84 = 7N$ $12 = N$ You use proportions to find unknown side lengths in similar figures.
AF2.2 Demonstrate an understanding that rate is a measure of one quantity per unit value of another quantity. (Lessons 5-2, 5-3, 5-4)	**unit value** 1 unit of a unit of measurement *Examples:* The unit value of distances measured in **feet** is **1 foot**. The unit value of time measured in **seconds** is **1 second.**	You determine rates and use rates to solve problems. *Example:* A printer prints a 20-page report in 5 minutes. $\frac{20 \text{ pages} \div 5}{5 \text{ minutes} \div 5} = \frac{4 \text{ pages}}{1 \text{ minute}}$ The printer prints at a rate of 4 pages per minute.
AF2.3 Solve problems involving rates, average speed, distance, and time. (Lessons 5-2, 5-4)	**average speed** the distance traveled by an object divided by the time taken to travel that distance	*Example:* A car travels 135 miles in 3 hours. $\frac{135 \text{ miles} \div 3}{3 \text{ hours} \div 3} = \frac{45 \text{ miles}}{1 \text{ hour}}$ The average speed is 45 mi/h.

Standard AF2.1 is also covered in this chapter. To see this standard unpacked, go to Chapter 4, p. 168.

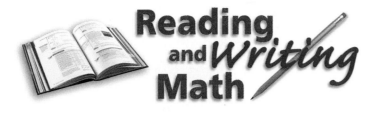

California Standards
English-Language Arts
Reading 6.2.4

Writing Strategy: Use Your Own Words

Using your own words to explain a concept can help you understand the concept. For example, learning how to solve equations might seem difficult if the textbook does not explain solving equations in the same way that you would.

As you work through each lesson:

• Identify the important ideas from the explanation in the book.

• Use your own words to explain these ideas.

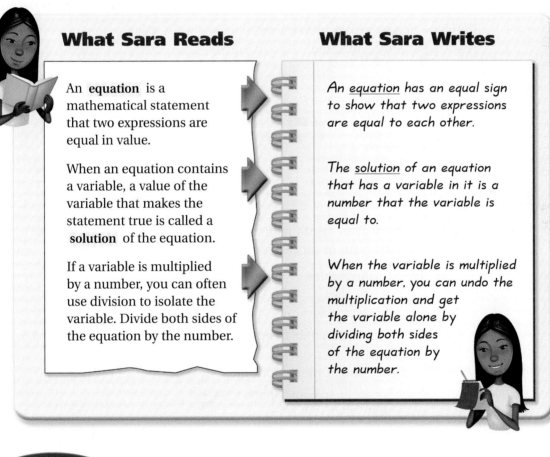

What Sara Reads

An **equation** is a mathematical statement that two expressions are equal in value.

When an equation contains a variable, a value of the variable that makes the statement true is called a **solution** of the equation.

If a variable is multiplied by a number, you can often use division to isolate the variable. Divide both sides of the equation by the number.

What Sara Writes

An equation has an equal sign to show that two expressions are equal to each other.

The solution of an equation that has a variable in it is a number that the variable is equal to.

When the variable is multiplied by a number, you can undo the multiplication and get the variable alone by dividing both sides of the equation by the number.

Try This

Rewrite each sentence in your own words.

1. When solving equations containing addition and integers, isolate the variable by adding opposites.

2. When you solve equations that have one operation, you use an inverse operation to isolate the variable.

 **Ratios**

California Standards

◆— **NS1.2 Interpret and use ratios in different contexts** (e.g., batting averages, miles per hour) **to show the relative sizes of two quantities, using appropriate notations** ($\frac{a}{b}$, *a* to *b*, *a:b*).

Vocabulary
ratio

Who uses this? Basketball players can use ratios to compare the number of baskets they make to the number they attempt.

In basketball practice, Kathlene made 17 baskets in 25 attempts. She compared the number of baskets she made to the total number of attempts she made by using the *ratio* $\frac{17}{25}$. A **ratio** is a comparison of two numbers or quantities.

Kathlene can write her ratio of baskets made to attempts in three different ways.

EXAMPLE 1 **Writing Ratios**

A basket of fruit contains 6 apples, 4 bananas, and 3 oranges. Write each ratio in all three forms.

A bananas to apples

$$\frac{\text{number of bananas}}{\text{number of apples}} = \frac{4}{6} \qquad \textit{There are 4 bananas and 6 apples.}$$

The ratio of bananas to apples can be written as $\frac{4}{6}$, 4 to 6, or 4:6.

B bananas and apples to oranges

$$\frac{\text{number of bananas and apples}}{\text{number of oranges}} = \frac{4+6}{3} = \frac{10}{3}$$

The ratio of bananas and apples to oranges can be written as $\frac{10}{3}$, 10 to 3, or 10:3.

C oranges to total pieces of fruit

$$\frac{\text{number of oranges}}{\text{number of total pieces of fruit}} = \frac{3}{6+4+3} = \frac{3}{13}$$

The ratio of oranges to total pieces of fruit can be written as $\frac{3}{13}$, 3 to 13, or 3:13.

Sometimes a ratio can be simplified. To simplify a ratio, first write it in fraction form and then simplify the fraction.

EXAMPLE 2 **Writing Ratios in Simplest Form**

Remember!

A fraction is in simplest form when the GCD of the numerator and denominator is 1.

See Lesson 3-4, p. 142

At Franklin Middle School, there are 252 students in the sixth grade and 9 sixth-grade teachers. Write the ratio of students to teachers in simplest form.

$$\frac{\text{students}}{\text{teachers}} = \frac{252}{9}$$ *Write the ratio as a fraction.*

$$= \frac{252 \div 9}{9 \div 9}$$ *Simplify.*

$$= \frac{28}{1}$$ *For every 28 students, there is 1 teacher.*

The ratio of students to teachers is 28 to 1.

To compare ratios, write them as fractions with common denominators. Then compare the numerators.

EXAMPLE 3 **Comparing Ratios**

Reasoning

Tell whether the wallet size photo or the portrait size photo has the greater ratio of width to length.

	Width (in.)	Length (in.)
Wallet	3.5	5
Personal	4	6
Desk	5	7
Portrait	8	10

Wallet: $$\frac{\text{width (in.)}}{\text{length (in.)}} = \frac{3.5}{5}$$ *Write the ratios as fractions with common denominators.*

Portrait: $$\frac{\text{width (in.)}}{\text{length (in.)}} = \frac{8}{10} = \frac{4}{5}$$

Because $4 > 3.5$ and the denominators are the same, the portrait size photo has the greater ratio of width to length.

Think and Discuss

1. **Explain** why you think the ratio $\frac{10}{3}$ in Example 1B is not written as a mixed number.

2. **Tell** how to simplify a ratio.

3. **Explain** how to compare two ratios.

California
Standards Practice
⚷ NS1.2

go.hrw.com
Homework Help Online
KEYWORD: MS8CA 5-1
Parent Resources Online
KEYWORD: MS8CA Parent

GUIDED PRACTICE

See Example ① Sun-Li has 10 blue marbles, 3 red marbles, and 17 white marbles. Write each ratio in all three forms.

1. blue marbles to red marbles   **2.** red marbles to total marbles

See Example ② **3.** In a 40-gallon aquarium, there are 21 neon tetras and 7 zebra danio fish. Write the ratio of neon tetras to zebra danio fish in simplest form.

See Example ③ **4.** Tell whose DVD collection has the greater ratio of comedy movies to adventure movies.

	Joseph	Yolanda
Comedy	5	7
Adventure	3	5

INDEPENDENT PRACTICE

See Example ① A soccer league has 25 sixth-graders, 30 seventh-graders, and 15 eighth-graders. Write each ratio in all three forms.

5. 6th-graders to 7th-graders   **6.** 6th-graders to total students

7. 7th-graders to 8th-graders   **8.** 7th- and 8th-graders to 6th-graders

See Example ② **9.** Thirty-six people auditioned for a play, and 9 people got roles. Write the ratio in simplest form of the number of people who auditioned to the number of people who got roles.

See Example ③ **10.** Tell whose bag of nut mix has the greater ratio of peanuts to total nuts.

	Dina	Don
Almonds	6	11
Cashews	8	7
Peanuts	10	18

PRACTICE AND PROBLEM SOLVING

Extra Practice
See page EP10.

Use the table for Exercises 11–13.

11. Tell whether group 1 or group 2 has the greater ratio of the number of people for an open-campus lunch to the number of people with no opinion.

Opinions on Open-Campus Lunch			
	Group 1	Group 2	Group 3
For	9	10	12
Against	14	16	16
No Opinion	5	6	8

12. Which group has the least ratio of the number of people against an open-campus lunch to the total number of survey responses?

13. **Estimation** For each group, is the ratio of the number of people for an open-campus lunch to the number of people against it less than or greater than $\frac{1}{2}$?

The pressure of water at different depths can be measured in *atmospheres,* or atm. The water pressure on a scuba diver increases as the diver descends below the surface. Use the table for Exercises 14–20.

Write each ratio in all three forms.

14. pressure at −33 ft to pressure at surface

15. pressure at −66 ft to pressure at surface

16. pressure at −99 ft to pressure at surface

17. pressure at −66 ft to pressure at −33 ft

18. pressure at −99 ft to pressure at −66 ft

19. Tell whether the ratio of pressure at −66 ft to pressure at −33 ft is greater than or less than the ratio of pressure at −99 ft to pressure at −66 ft.

20. ⭐ **Challenge** The ratio of the beginning pressure and the new pressure when a scuba diver goes from −33 ft to −66 ft is less than the ratio of pressures when the diver goes from the surface to −33 ft. The ratio of pressures is even less when the diver goes from −66 ft to −99 ft. Explain why this is true.

Pressure Experienced by Diver	
Depth (ft)	Pressure (atm)
0	1
−33	2
−66	3
−99	4

go.hrw.com
Web Extra!
KEYWORD: MS8CA Pressure

SPIRAL STANDARDS REVIEW

🔑 NS1.2, NS2.1, NS2.2, 🏋 AF1.1

21. Multiple Choice Johnson Middle School has 125 sixth-graders, 150 seventh-graders, and 100 eighth-graders. Which statement is NOT true?

(A) The ratio of sixth-graders to seventh-graders is 5 to 6.

(B) The ratio of eighth-graders to seventh-graders is 3:2.

(C) The ratio of sixth-graders to students in all three grades is 1:3.

(D) The ratio of eighth-graders to students in all three grades is 4 to 15.

22. Short Response A pancake recipe calls for 4 cups of pancake mix for every 3 cups of milk. A biscuit recipe calls for 2 cups of biscuit mix for every 1 cup of milk. Which recipe has a greater ratio of mix to milk? Explain.

Solve. (Lesson 4-10)

23. $1.23 + x = 5.47$ **24.** $3.8y = 27.36$ **25.** $v − 3.8 = 4.7$

26. How many $2\frac{1}{2}$-yard pieces can be cut from $17\frac{1}{2}$ yards of string? (Lesson 4-5)

5-2 Rates

California Standards

↞ **AF2.2** Demonstrate an understanding that rate is a measure of one quantity per unit value of another quantity. *Also covered:* ↞ **NS1.2, AF2.3**

Vocabulary
rate
unit rate

Why learn this? You can use rates to determine a driver's average speed. (See Example 2.)

The Lawsons are driving 288 miles to a campground. They would like to reach the campground in 6 hours of driving. What should their average speed be in miles per hour?

Recall that a ratio is a comparison of two numbers or quantities. A **rate** is a special type of ratio that compares two quantities measured in different units. In order to answer the question above, you need to find the family's rate of travel.

Their rate is $\frac{288 \text{ miles}}{6 \text{ hours}}$.

A **unit rate** is a rate whose denominator is 1. To change a rate to a unit rate, divide both the numerator and denominator by the denominator. Dividing the numerator and denominator of a rate by the same number does not change the value of the rate.

EXAMPLE **1** **Finding Unit Rates**

A During exercise, Sonia's heart beats 675 times in 5 minutes. How many times does it beat per minute?

$\frac{675 \text{ beats}}{5 \text{ minutes}}$ *Write a rate that compares heart beats and time.*

$\frac{675 \text{ beats} \div 5}{5 \text{ minutes} \div 5}$ *Divide the numerator and denominator by 5 to get an equivalent rate.*

$\frac{135 \text{ beats}}{1 \text{ minute}}$ *Simplify.*

Sonia's heart beats 135 times per minute.

Helpful Hint

Batting averages are usually written as decimals without a zero to the left of the decimal point.

B A batting average compares number of hits to number of times at bat. A baseball player has 69 hits in 250 times at bat. What is the player's batting average?

$\frac{69 \text{ hits}}{250 \text{ at bats}}$ *Write a rate that compares hits and at bats.*

$\frac{69 \text{ hits} \div 250}{250 \text{ at bats} \div 250}$ *Divide the numerator and denominator by 250 to get an equivalent rate.*

$\frac{0.276 \text{ hits}}{1 \text{ at bat}}$ *Simplify.*

The player's batting average is .276.

An average rate of speed is the ratio of distance traveled to time. The ratio is a rate because the units in the numerator and denominator are different. Speed is usually expressed as a unit rate.

EXAMPLE 2 **Finding Average Speed**

The Lawsons want to drive the 288 miles to a campground in 6 hours. What should their average speed be in miles per hour?

$\dfrac{288 \text{ miles}}{6 \text{ hours}}$ *Write the rate.*

$\dfrac{288 \text{ miles} \div 6}{6 \text{ hours} \div 6} = \dfrac{48 \text{ miles}}{1 \text{ hour}}$ *Divide the numerator and denominator by 6 to get an equivalent rate.*

Their average speed should be 48 miles per hour.

A unit price is the price of one unit of an item. The unit used depends on how the item is sold. The table shows some examples.

Type of Item	Examples of Units
Liquid	Fluid ounces, quarts, gallons, liters
Solid	Ounces, pounds, grams, kilograms
Any item	Bottle, container, carton

EXAMPLE 3 *Consumer Math Application*

The Lawsons stop at a roadside farmers' market. The market offers lemonade in three sizes. Which size lemonade has the lowest price per fluid ounce?

Size	Price
12 fl oz	$0.89
18 fl oz	$1.69
24 fl oz	$2.09

Divide the price by the number of fluid ounces (fl oz) to find each unit price.

$\dfrac{\$0.89}{12 \text{ fl oz}} \approx \dfrac{\$0.07}{\text{fl oz}}$ $\dfrac{\$1.69}{18 \text{ fl oz}} \approx \dfrac{\$0.09}{\text{fl oz}}$ $\dfrac{\$2.09}{24 \text{ fl oz}} \approx \dfrac{\$0.09}{\text{fl oz}}$

Since $\$0.07 < \$0.09$, the 12 fl oz lemonade has the lowest price per fluid ounce.

Think and Discuss

1. Explain how you can tell whether an expression represents a unit rate.

2. Suppose a store offers cereal with a price of $2.40 per box. Another store offers cereal with a price of $2.88 per box. Before determining which is the better buy, what variables must you consider?

California Standards Practice

🔑 NS1.2, 🔑 AF2.2, AF2.3

go.hrw.com
Homework Help Online
KEYWORD: MS8CA 5-2
Parent Resources Online
KEYWORD: MS8CA Parent

GUIDED PRACTICE

See Example ①
1. A faucet leaks 668 milliliters of water in 8 minutes. How many milliliters of water does the faucet leak per minute?

2. A recipe for 6 muffins calls for 360 grams of oat flakes. How many grams of oat flakes are needed for each muffin?

See Example ②
3. An airliner makes a 2,748-mile flight in 6 hours. What is the airliner's average rate of speed in miles per hour?

See Example ③
4. **Consumer Math** During a car trip, the Webers buy gasoline at three different stations. At the first station, they pay $28.98 for 14 gallons of gas. At the second, they pay $18.99 for 9 gallons. At the third, they pay $33.44 for 16 gallons. Which station offers the lowest price per gallon?

INDEPENDENT PRACTICE

See Example ①
5. An after-school job pays $116.25 for 15 hours of work. How much money does the job pay per hour?

6. It took Samantha 324 minutes to cook a turkey. If the turkey weighed 18 pounds, how many minutes per pound did it take to cook the turkey?

See Example ②
7. **Sports** The first Indianapolis 500 auto race took place in 1911. The winning car covered the 500 miles in 6.7 hours. What was the winning car's average rate of speed in miles per hour?

See Example ③
8. **Consumer Math** A supermarket sells orange juice in three sizes. The 32 fl oz container costs $1.99, the 64 fl oz container costs $3.69, and the 96 fl oz container costs $5.85. Which size orange juice has the lowest price per fluid ounce?

PRACTICE AND PROBLEM SOLVING

Extra Practice
See page EP10.

Find each unit rate. Round to the nearest hundredth, if necessary.

9. 9 runs in 3 games

10. $207,000 for 1,800 ft^2

11. $2,010 in 6 mo

12. 52 songs on 4 CDs

13. 226 mi on 12 gal

14. 324 words in 6 min

15. 12 hr for $69

16. 6 lb for $12.96

17. 488 mi in 4 trips

18. 220 m in 20 s

19. 1.5 mi in 39 min

20. 24,000 km in 1.5 hr

21. In Grant Middle School, each class has an equal number of students. There are 38 classes and a total of 1,026 students. Write a rate that describes the distribution of students in the classes at Grant. What is the unit rate?

22. **Estimation** Use estimation to determine which is the better buy: 450 minutes of phone time for $49.99 or 800 minutes for $62.99.

Find each unit price. Then decide which is the better buy.

23. $\dfrac{\$2.52}{42 \text{ oz}}$ or $\dfrac{\$3.64}{52 \text{ oz}}$

24. $\dfrac{\$28.40}{8 \text{ yd}}$ or $\dfrac{\$55.50}{15 \text{ yd}}$

25. $\dfrac{\$8.28}{0.3 \text{ m}}$ or $\dfrac{\$13.00}{0.4 \text{ m}}$

26. Sports In the 2004 Summer Olympics, Justin Gatlin won the 100-meter race in 9.85 seconds. Shawn Crawford won the 200-meter race in 19.79 seconds. Which runner ran at a faster average rate?

27. Social Studies The population density of a country is the average number of people per unit of area. Write the population densities of the countries in the table as unit rates. Round your answers to the nearest person per square mile. Then rank the countries from least to greatest population density.

Country	Population	Land Area (mi²)
France	60,424,213	210,669
Germany	82,424,609	134,836
Poland	38,626,349	117,555

28. Reasoning A store sells paper towels in packs of 6 and packs of 8. Use this information to write a problem about comparing unit rates.

29. Write About It Michael Jordan has the highest scoring average in NBA history. He played in 1,072 games and scored 32,292 points. Explain how to find a unit rate to describe his scoring average. What is the unit rate?

30. Challenge Mike fills his car's gas tank with 20 gallons of regular gas at $2.87 per gallon. His car averages 25 miles per gallon. Serena fills her car's tank with 15 gallons of premium gas at $3.16 per gallon. Her car averages 30 miles per gallon. Compare the drivers' unit costs of driving one mile.

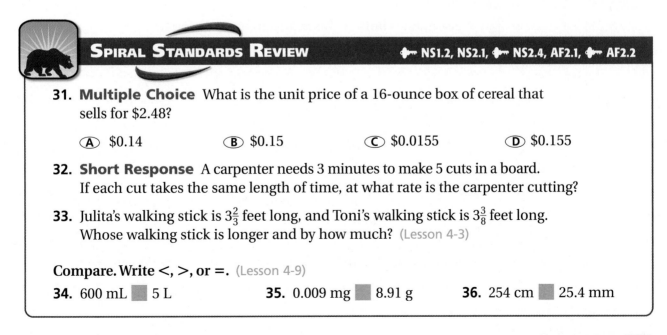

31. Multiple Choice What is the unit price of a 16-ounce box of cereal that sells for $2.48?

   Ⓐ $0.14   Ⓑ $0.15   Ⓒ $0.0155   Ⓓ $0.155

32. Short Response A carpenter needs 3 minutes to make 5 cuts in a board. If each cut takes the same length of time, at what rate is the carpenter cutting?

33. Julita's walking stick is $3\frac{2}{3}$ feet long, and Toni's walking stick is $3\frac{3}{8}$ feet long. Whose walking stick is longer and by how much? (Lesson 4-3)

Compare. Write <, >, or =. (Lesson 4-9)

34. 600 mL ▦ 5 L

35. 0.009 mg ▦ 8.91 g

36. 254 cm ▦ 25.4 mm

Identifying and Writing Proportions

🔑 **NS1.2 Interpret and use ratios in different contexts** (e.g., batting averages, miles per hour) **to show the relative sizes of two quantities, using appropriate notations** ($\frac{a}{b}$, *a* to *b*, *a:b*).

Vocabulary
equivalent ratios
proportion

Why learn this? You can determine whether two ratios of length to width are equivalent.

Students are measuring the width w and the length ℓ of their heads. The ratio of ℓ to w is 10 inches to 6 inches for Jean and 25 centimeters to 15 centimeters for Pat.

Calipers have adjustable arms that are used to measure the thickness of objects.

These ratios can be written as the fractions $\frac{10}{6}$ and $\frac{25}{15}$. Since both ratios simplify to $\frac{5}{3}$, they are equivalent. **Equivalent ratios** are ratios that name the same comparison.

An equation stating that two ratios are equivalent is called a **proportion**. The equation, or proportion, below states that the ratios $\frac{10}{6}$ and $\frac{25}{15}$ are equivalent.

Reading Math

If two ratios are equivalent, they are said to be *proportional* to each other, or *in proportion*.

$$\frac{10}{6} = \frac{25}{15}$$

EXAMPLE 1 **Comparing Ratios in Simplest Form**

Determine whether the ratios are proportional.

A $\frac{2}{7}, \frac{6}{21}$

$\frac{2}{7}$ *$\frac{2}{7}$ is already in simplest form.*

$\frac{6}{21} = \frac{6 \div 3}{21 \div 3} = \frac{2}{7}$ *Simplify $\frac{6}{21}$.*

Since $\frac{2}{7} = \frac{2}{7}$, the ratios are proportional.

B $\frac{8}{24}, \frac{6}{20}$

$\frac{8}{24} = \frac{8 \div 8}{24 \div 8} = \frac{1}{3}$ *Simplify $\frac{8}{24}$.*

$\frac{6}{20} = \frac{6 \div 2}{20 \div 2} = \frac{3}{10}$ *Simplify $\frac{6}{20}$.*

Since $\frac{1}{3} \neq \frac{3}{10}$, the ratios are *not* proportional.

EXAMPLE **2** **Comparing Ratios Using a Common Denominator**

Use the data in the table to determine whether the ratios of oats to water are proportional for both servings of oatmeal.

Servings of Oatmeal	Cups of Oats	Cups of Water
8	2	4
12	3	6

Write the ratios of oats to water for 8 servings and for 12 servings.

Ratio of oats to water, 8 servings: $\frac{2}{4}$ *Write the ratio as a fraction.*

Ratio of oats to water, 12 servings: $\frac{3}{6}$ *Write the ratio as a fraction.*

$\frac{2}{4} = \frac{2 \cdot 6}{4 \cdot 6} = \frac{12}{24}$ *Write the ratios with a common*

$\frac{3}{6} = \frac{3 \cdot 4}{6 \cdot 4} = \frac{12}{24}$ *denominator, such as 24.*

Since both ratios are equal to $\frac{12}{24}$, they are proportional.

You can find an equivalent ratio by multiplying or dividing the numerator and the denominator of a ratio by the same number.

EXAMPLE **3** **Finding Equivalent Ratios and Writing Proportions**

Find a ratio equivalent to each ratio. Then use the ratios to write a proportion.

For more on proportions, see the Proportion Builder on page MB2.

A $\frac{8}{14}$

$\frac{8}{14} = \frac{8 \cdot 20}{14 \cdot 20} = \frac{160}{280}$ *Multiply both the numerator and denominator by any number, such as 20.*

$\frac{8}{14} = \frac{160}{280}$ *Write a proportion.*

B $\frac{4}{18}$

$\frac{4}{18} = \frac{4 \div 2}{18 \div 2} = \frac{2}{9}$ *Divide both the numerator and denominator by a common factor, such as 2.*

$\frac{4}{18} = \frac{2}{9}$ *Write a proportion.*

Think and Discuss

1. Explain why the ratios in Example 1B are not proportional.

2. Describe what it means for ratios to be proportional.

3. Give an example of a proportion. Then tell how you know it is a proportion.

Exercises

California Standards Practice
NS1.2, AF2.2

go.hrw.com
Homework Help Online
KEYWORD: MS8CA 5-3
Parent Resources Online
KEYWORD: MS8CA Parent

GUIDED PRACTICE

See Example 1 Determine whether the ratios are proportional.

1. $\frac{2}{3}, \frac{4}{6}$ **2.** $\frac{5}{10}, \frac{8}{18}$ **3.** $\frac{9}{12}, \frac{15}{20}$ **4.** $\frac{3}{4}, \frac{8}{12}$

See Example 2 **5.** $\frac{10}{12}, \frac{15}{18}$ **6.** $\frac{6}{9}, \frac{8}{12}$ **7.** $\frac{3}{4}, \frac{5}{6}$ **8.** $\frac{4}{6}, \frac{6}{9}$

See Example 3 Find a ratio equivalent to each ratio. Then use the ratios to write a proportion.

9. $\frac{1}{3}$ **10.** $\frac{9}{21}$ **11.** $\frac{8}{3}$ **12.** $\frac{10}{4}$

INDEPENDENT PRACTICE

See Example 1 Determine whether the ratios are proportional.

13. $\frac{5}{8}, \frac{7}{14}$ **14.** $\frac{8}{24}, \frac{10}{30}$ **15.** $\frac{18}{20}, \frac{81}{180}$ **16.** $\frac{15}{20}, \frac{27}{35}$

See Example 2 **17.** $\frac{2}{3}, \frac{4}{9}$ **18.** $\frac{18}{12}, \frac{15}{10}$ **19.** $\frac{7}{8}, \frac{14}{24}$ **20.** $\frac{18}{54}, \frac{10}{30}$

See Example 3 Find a ratio equivalent to each ratio. Then use the ratios to write a proportion.

21. $\frac{5}{9}$ **22.** $\frac{27}{60}$ **23.** $\frac{6}{15}$ **24.** $\frac{121}{99}$

25. $\frac{11}{13}$ **26.** $\frac{5}{22}$ **27.** $\frac{78}{104}$ **28.** $\frac{27}{72}$

PRACTICE AND PROBLEM SOLVING

Extra Practice
See page EP10.

Complete each table of equivalent ratios.

29.

angelfish	4	8		20
tiger fish		6	18	

30.

squares	2	4	6	8
circles		16		

Find two ratios equivalent to each given ratio.

31. 3 to 7 **32.** 6:2 **33.** $\frac{5}{12}$ **34.** 8:4

35. 6 to 9 **36.** $\frac{10}{50}$ **37.** 10:4 **38.** 1 to 10

39. Ecology If you recycle one aluminum can, you save enough energy to run a TV for four hours.

    a. Write the ratio of cans to hours.

    b. Marti's class recycled enough aluminum cans to run a TV for 2,080 hours. Did the class recycle 545 cans? Justify your answer using equivalent ratios.

40. Reasoning The ratio of girls to boys riding a bus is 15:12. If the driver drops off the same number of girls as boys at the next stop, does the ratio of girls to boys remain 15:12? Explain.

41. **Critical Thinking** Write all possible proportions using only the numbers 1, 2, and 4.

42. **School** Last year in Kerry's school, the ratio of students to teachers was 22:1. Write an equivalent ratio to show how many students and teachers there could have been at Kerry's school.

43. **Science** Students in a biology class surveyed four ponds to determine whether salamanders and frogs were inhabiting the area.

Pond	Number of Salamanders	Number of Frogs
Cypress Pond	8	5
Mill Pond	15	10
Clear Pond	3	2
Gill Pond	2	7

 a. What was the ratio of salamanders to frogs in Cypress Pond?

 b. In which two ponds was the ratio of salamanders to frogs the same?

44. Marcus earned $230 for 40 hours of work. Phillip earned $192 for 32 hours of work. Are these pay rates proportional? Explain.

45. **What's the Error?** A student wrote the proportion $\frac{13}{20} = \frac{26}{60}$. What did the student do wrong?

46. **Write About It** Explain two different ways to determine if two ratios are proportional.

47. **Challenge** A skydiver jumps out of an airplane. After 0.8 second, she has fallen 100 feet. After 3.1 seconds, she has fallen 500 feet. Is the rate (in feet per second) at which she falls the first 100 feet proportional to the rate at which she falls the next 400 feet? Explain.

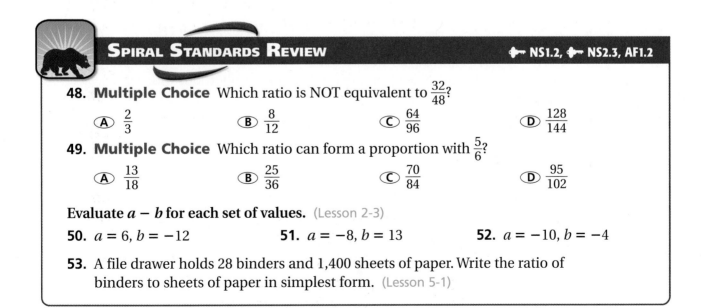

48. **Multiple Choice** Which ratio is NOT equivalent to $\frac{32}{48}$?

 Ⓐ $\frac{2}{3}$ Ⓑ $\frac{8}{12}$ Ⓒ $\frac{64}{96}$ Ⓓ $\frac{128}{144}$

49. **Multiple Choice** Which ratio can form a proportion with $\frac{5}{6}$?

 Ⓐ $\frac{13}{18}$ Ⓑ $\frac{25}{36}$ Ⓒ $\frac{70}{84}$ Ⓓ $\frac{95}{102}$

Evaluate $a - b$ for each set of values. (Lesson 2-3)

50. $a = 6, b = -12$ 51. $a = -8, b = 13$ 52. $a = -10, b = -4$

53. A file drawer holds 28 binders and 1,400 sheets of paper. Write the ratio of binders to sheets of paper in simplest form. (Lesson 5-1)

5-4 Solving Proportions

California Standards

← **NS1.3** Use proportions to solve problems (e.g., determine the value of *N* if $\frac{4}{7} = \frac{N}{21}$, find the length of a side of a polygon similar to a known polygon). **Use cross-multiplication as a method for solving such problems, understanding it as the multiplication of both sides of an equation by a multiplicative inverse.**

Also covered: ← **AF2.2, AF2.3**

Vocabulary
cross product

Remember!

A number multiplied by its multiplicative inverse is equal to 1. *See Lesson 4-5, p. 192.*

Who uses this? Bicyclists can solve proportions to find out how long it will take them to finish a race. (See Example 2.)

For two ratios, the product of the numerator in one ratio and the denominator in the other is a **cross product**.

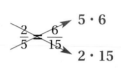

If two ratios form a proportion, then the cross products are equal.

$$\frac{a}{b} = \frac{c}{d}$$ *Write a proportion, where a, b, c, and d are not equal to 0.*

$$\frac{a}{b} \cdot \frac{d}{c} = \frac{\overset{1}{\cancel{c}}}{\cancel{d}} \cdot \frac{\overset{1}{\cancel{d}}}{\cancel{c}}$$ *Multiply each side by $\frac{d}{c}$, the multiplicative inverse of $\frac{c}{d}$.*

$$\frac{a \cdot d}{b \cdot c} = 1$$ *Simplify each side. $\frac{c}{d} \cdot \frac{d}{c} = 1$*

$$a \cdot d = b \cdot c$$ *The fraction $\frac{a \cdot d}{b \cdot c}$ is equal to 1, so the numerator must equal the denominator*

CROSS PRODUCT RULE		
Words	**Numbers**	**Algebra**
In a proportion, the cross-products are equal.	$\frac{2}{5} = \frac{6}{15}$ $2 \cdot 15 = 5 \cdot 6$ $30 = 30$	If $\frac{a}{b} = \frac{c}{d}$, where $b \neq 0$ and $d \neq 0$, then $a \cdot d = b \cdot c$.

You can use the cross product rule to solve proportions with variables.

EXAMPLE **1** **Solving Proportions Using Cross Products**

Use cross products to solve the proportion $\frac{p}{6} = \frac{10}{3}$.

$$\frac{p}{6} = \frac{10}{3}$$

$$p \cdot 3 = 6 \cdot 10$$ *The cross products are equal.*

$$3p = 60$$ *Multiply.*

$$\frac{3p}{3} = \frac{60}{3}$$ *Divide each side by 3.*

$$p = 20$$

It is important to set up proportions correctly. Each ratio must compare corresponding quantities in the same order. Suppose a boat travels 16 miles in 4 hours and 8 miles in x hours at the same speed. Either of these proportions could represent this situation.

$$\underset{\text{Trip 1}}{\boxed{\frac{16\ \text{mi}}{4\ \text{hr}}}} = \underset{\text{Trip 2}}{\boxed{\frac{8\ \text{mi}}{x\ \text{hr}}}}$$

$$\frac{\boxed{16\ \text{mi}} \qquad \boxed{4\ \text{hr}}}{\boxed{8\ \text{mi}} \qquad \boxed{x\ \text{hr}}} \quad \begin{array}{l} \longleftarrow \text{Trip 1} \\ \longleftarrow \text{Trip 2} \end{array}$$

EXAMPLE 2 *Sports Application*

The graph shows the time and distance Sunee rode her bike during training. She plans to enter a 54-mile race. If Sunee rides at the same rate she rode during training, how long will it take her to finish the race?

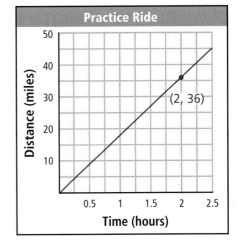

Practice Ride

The labeled point on the graph shows that Sunee rode 36 miles in 2 hours. Let t represent the time in hours it will take Sunee to finish the race.

Method 1 Set up a proportion in which each ratio compares distance to the time needed to ride that distance.

$$\frac{36\ \text{mi}}{2\ \text{hr}} = \frac{54\ \text{mi}}{t\ \text{hr}} \quad \begin{array}{l} \longleftarrow \textit{Distance} \\ \longleftarrow \textit{Time} \end{array}$$

$36 \cdot t = 2 \cdot 54$ *The cross products are equal.*

$36t = 108$ *Multiply.*

$\dfrac{36t}{36} = \dfrac{108}{36}$ *Divide each side by 36.*

$t = 3$

Method 2 Set up a proportion in which one ratio compares distance and one ratio compares time.

$$\frac{36\ \text{mi}}{54\ \text{mi}} = \frac{2\ \text{hr}}{t\ \text{hr}} \quad \begin{array}{l} \longleftarrow \textit{Training} \\ \longleftarrow \textit{Race} \end{array}$$

$36 \cdot t = 54 \cdot 2$ *The cross products are equal.*

$36t = 108$ *Multiply.*

$\dfrac{36t}{36} = \dfrac{108}{36}$ *Divide each side by 36.*

$t = 3$

Both methods show that it will take Sunee 3 hours to finish the race if she rides at her training rate.

EXAMPLE 3 **PROBLEM SOLVING APPLICATION**

Reasoning

Density is the ratio of a substance's mass to its volume. The density of ice is 0.92 g/mL. What is the mass of 3 mL of ice?

1 Understand the Problem

Rewrite the question as a statement.
- Find the mass, in grams, of 3 mL of ice.

List the **important information:**
- density = $\dfrac{\text{mass (g)}}{\text{volume (mL)}}$

- density of ice = $\dfrac{0.92 \text{ g}}{1 \text{ mL}}$

2 Make a Plan

Set up a proportion using the given information. Let m represent the mass of 3 mL of ice.

$$\dfrac{0.92 \text{ g}}{1 \text{ mL}} = \dfrac{m}{3 \text{ mL}} \quad \begin{array}{l} \leftarrow \text{ mass} \\ \leftarrow \text{ volume} \end{array}$$

3 Solve

Solve the proportion.

$\dfrac{0.92}{1} = \dfrac{m}{3}$ ⠀⠀⠀⠀*Write the proportion.*

$1 \cdot m = 0.92 \cdot 3$ ⠀⠀*The cross products are equal.*

$m = 2.76$ ⠀⠀⠀⠀⠀*Multiply.*

The mass of 3 mL of ice is 2.76 g.

4 Look Back

Since the density of ice is 0.92 g/mL, each milliliter of ice has a mass of a little less than 1 g. So 3 mL of ice should have a mass of a little less than 3 g. Since 2.76 is a little less than 3, the answer is reasonable.

Think and Discuss

1. Explain how the term *cross product* can help you remember how to solve a proportion.

2. Describe the error in these steps: $\frac{2}{3} = \frac{x}{12}$; $2x = 36$; $x = 18$.

3. Show how to use cross products to decide whether the ratios 6:45 and 2:15 are proportional.

California Standards Practice
↞ NS1.3, ↞ AF2.2, AF2.3

go.hrw.com
Homework Help Online
KEYWORD: MS8CA 5-4
Parent Resources Online
KEYWORD: MS8CA Parent

GUIDED PRACTICE

See Example 1 Use cross products to solve each proportion.

1. $\dfrac{6}{10} = \dfrac{36}{x}$ 2. $\dfrac{4}{7} = \dfrac{5}{p}$ 3. $\dfrac{12.3}{m} = \dfrac{75}{100}$ 4. $\dfrac{t}{42} = \dfrac{1.5}{3}$

See Example 2 5. The graph shows the time and distance that a horse ran around a track. If the horse runs at that same speed, how long will it take the horse to run 1.5 miles?

See Example 3 6. A stack of 2,450 one-dollar bills weighs 5 pounds. How much does a stack of 1,470 one-dollar bills weigh?

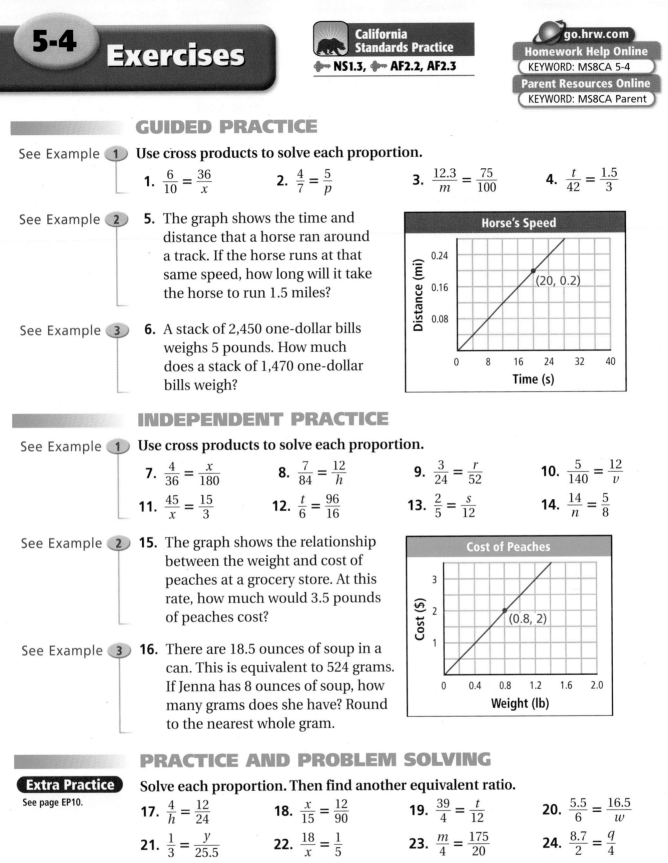

Horse's Speed

Distance (mi) — 0.08, 0.16, 0.24

(20, 0.2)

Time (s) — 0, 8, 16, 24, 32, 40

INDEPENDENT PRACTICE

See Example 1 Use cross products to solve each proportion.

7. $\dfrac{4}{36} = \dfrac{x}{180}$ 8. $\dfrac{7}{84} = \dfrac{12}{h}$ 9. $\dfrac{3}{24} = \dfrac{r}{52}$ 10. $\dfrac{5}{140} = \dfrac{12}{v}$

11. $\dfrac{45}{x} = \dfrac{15}{3}$ 12. $\dfrac{t}{6} = \dfrac{96}{16}$ 13. $\dfrac{2}{5} = \dfrac{s}{12}$ 14. $\dfrac{14}{n} = \dfrac{5}{8}$

See Example 2 15. The graph shows the relationship between the weight and cost of peaches at a grocery store. At this rate, how much would 3.5 pounds of peaches cost?

See Example 3 16. There are 18.5 ounces of soup in a can. This is equivalent to 524 grams. If Jenna has 8 ounces of soup, how many grams does she have? Round to the nearest whole gram.

Cost of Peaches

Cost ($) — 1, 2, 3

(0.8, 2)

Weight (lb) — 0, 0.4, 0.8, 1.2, 1.6, 2.0

PRACTICE AND PROBLEM SOLVING

Extra Practice
See page EP10.

Solve each proportion. Then find another equivalent ratio.

17. $\dfrac{4}{h} = \dfrac{12}{24}$ 18. $\dfrac{x}{15} = \dfrac{12}{90}$ 19. $\dfrac{39}{4} = \dfrac{t}{12}$ 20. $\dfrac{5.5}{6} = \dfrac{16.5}{w}$

21. $\dfrac{1}{3} = \dfrac{y}{25.5}$ 22. $\dfrac{18}{x} = \dfrac{1}{5}$ 23. $\dfrac{m}{4} = \dfrac{175}{20}$ 24. $\dfrac{8.7}{2} = \dfrac{q}{4}$

25. Sandra drove 126.2 miles in 2 hours at a constant speed. Use a proportion to find how long it would take her to drive 189.3 miles at the same speed.

26. **Multi-Step** In June, a camp has 325 campers and 26 counselors. In July, 265 campers leave and 215 new campers arrive. How many counselors does the camp need in July to keep an equivalent ratio of campers to counselors?

27. **Science** On Monday a marine biologist took a random sample of 50 fish from a pond and tagged them. On Tuesday she took a new sample of 100 fish. Among them were 4 fish that had been tagged on Monday.

  a. What comparison does the ratio $\frac{4}{100}$ represent?

  b. What is the ratio of the number of fish tagged on Monday to n, the estimated total number of fish in the pond?

  c. Use a proportion to estimate the number of fish in the pond.

28. **Chemistry** The table shows the type and number of atoms in one molecule of citric acid. Use a proportion to find the number of oxygen atoms in 15 molecules of citric acid.

Composition of Citric Acid	
Type of Atom	Number of Atoms
Carbon	6
Hydrogen	8
Oxygen	7

29. **Earth Science** You can find your distance from a thunderstorm by counting the number of seconds between a lightning flash and the thunder. For example, if the time difference is 21 s, then the storm is 7 km away. How far away is a storm if the time difference is 9 s?

30. **Reasoning** Use a multiplicative inverse to show that the cross product rule is true for the proportion $\frac{r}{6} = \frac{s}{5}$.

31. **What's the Question?** There are 20 grams of protein in 3 ounces of sautéed fish. If the answer is 9 ounces, what is the question?

32. **Write About It** Give an example from your own life that can be described using a ratio. Then tell how a proportion can give you additional information.

33. **Challenge** Determine whether the proportion $\frac{a}{b} = \frac{c}{d}$ is equivalent to the proportion $\frac{a}{d} = \frac{c}{b}$, where $b \neq 0$ and $d \neq 0$. Use the cross product rule to explain your answer.

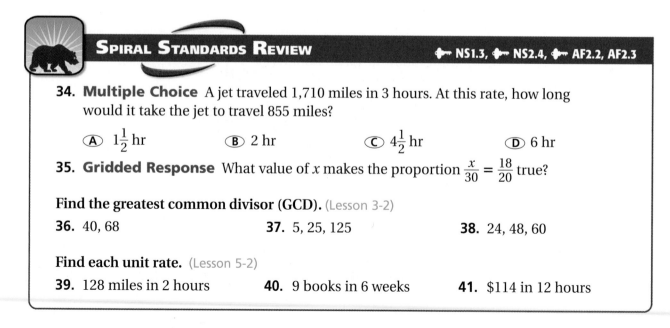

34. **Multiple Choice** A jet traveled 1,710 miles in 3 hours. At this rate, how long would it take the jet to travel 855 miles?

  Ⓐ $1\frac{1}{2}$ hr   Ⓑ 2 hr   Ⓒ $4\frac{1}{2}$ hr   Ⓓ 6 hr

35. **Gridded Response** What value of x makes the proportion $\frac{x}{30} = \frac{18}{20}$ true?

Find the greatest common divisor (GCD). (Lesson 3-2)

36. 40, 68   37. 5, 25, 125   38. 24, 48, 60

Find each unit rate. (Lesson 5-2)

39. 128 miles in 2 hours   40. 9 books in 6 weeks   41. $114 in 12 hours

5-5 Customary Measurements

California Standards

AF2.1 Convert one unit of measurement to another (e.g., from feet to miles, from centimeters to inches).

Also covered: ☞ **NS1.3**

Why learn this? You can use customary measurements to describe lengths, weights, and capacity.

Just 2 fluid ounces of a king cobra's venom is enough to kill a 2-ton elephant. You can use the following benchmarks to help you understand fluid ounces, tons, and other customary units of measure.

	Customary Unit	Benchmark
Length	Inch (in.)	Length of a small paper clip
	Foot (ft)	Length of a standard sheet of paper
	Mile (mi)	Length of about 18 football fields
Weight	Ounce (oz)	Weight of a slice of bread
	Pound (lb)	Weight of 3 apples
	Ton	Weight of a buffalo
Capacity	Fluid ounce (fl oz)	Amount of water in 2 tablespoons
	Cup (c)	Capacity of a standard measuring cup
	Gallon (gal)	Capacity of a large milk jug

EXAMPLE 1 **Choosing the Appropriate Customary Unit**

Choose the most appropriate customary unit for each measurement. Justify your answer.

A the length of a rug

Feet—the length of a rug is similar to the length of several sheets of paper.

B the weight of a magazine

Ounces—the weight of a magazine is similar to the weight of several slices of bread.

C the capacity of an aquarium

Gallons—the capacity of an aquarium is similar to the capacity of several large milk jugs.

The following table shows some common equivalent customary units. You can use equivalent measures to convert units of measure.

Length	Weight	Capacity
12 inches (in.) = 1 foot (ft) 3 feet = 1 yard (yd) 5,280 feet = 1 mile (mi)	16 ounces (oz) = 1 pound (lb) 2,000 pounds = 1 ton	8 fluid ounces (fl oz) = 1 cup (c) 2 cups = 1 pint (pt) 2 pints = 1 quart (qt) 4 quarts = 1 gallon (gal)

EXAMPLE 2 Converting Customary Units

Convert 19 c to fluid ounces.

Method 1: Use a proportion.

Write a proportion using a ratio of equivalent measures.

$$\frac{\text{fluid ounces} \rightarrow}{\text{cups} \rightarrow} \frac{8}{1} = \frac{x}{19}$$

$$8 \cdot 19 = 1 \cdot x$$

$$152 = x$$

Method 2: Multiply by 1.

Multiply by a ratio equal to 1, and cancel the units.

$$19 \text{ c} = \frac{19 \cancel{c}}{1} \times \frac{8 \text{ fl oz}}{1 \cancel{c}}$$

$$= \frac{19 \cdot 8 \text{ fl oz}}{1}$$

$$= 152 \text{ fl oz}$$

Nineteen cups is equal to 152 fluid ounces.

EXAMPLE 3 Converting Between Metric and Customary Units

Reasoning

One inch is about 2.54 centimeters. A bookmark has a length of 18 centimeters. What is the length of the bookmark in inches, rounded to the nearest inch?

$$\frac{\text{inches} \rightarrow}{\text{centimeters} \rightarrow} \frac{1}{2.54} = \frac{x}{18}$$ *Write a proportion using 1 in. ≈ 2.54 cm.*

$$1 \cdot 18 = 2.54 \cdot x$$ *The cross products are equal.*

$$18 = 2.54x$$ *Multiply.*

$$\frac{18}{2.54} = \frac{2.54x}{2.54}$$ *Divide each side by 2.54.*

$$7 \approx x$$ *Round to the nearest whole number.*

The bookmark is about 7 inches long.

Think and Discuss

1. **Describe** an object that you would weigh in ounces.

2. **Explain** how to convert yards to feet and feet to yards.

5-5 Exercises

California Standards Practice
NS1.3, AF2.1

go.hrw.com
Homework Help Online
KEYWORD: MS8CA 5-5
Parent Resources Online
KEYWORD: MS8CA Parent

GUIDED PRACTICE

See Example **1** Choose the most appropriate customary unit for each measurement. Justify your answer.

1. the width of a sidewalk

2. the amount of water in a pool

3. the weight of a truck

4. the distance across Lake Erie

See Example **2** Convert each measure.

5. 12 gal to quarts

6. 8 mi to feet

7. 72 oz to pounds

8. 3.5 c to fluid ounces

See Example **3** **9.** One gallon is about 3.79 liters. A car has a 55-liter gas tank. What is the capacity of the tank in gallons, rounded to the nearest tenth of a gallon?

INDEPENDENT PRACTICE

See Example **1** Choose the most appropriate customary unit for each measurement. Justify your answer.

10. the weight of a watermelon

11. the wingspan of a sparrow

12. the capacity of a soup bowl

13. the height of an office building

See Example **2** Convert each measure.

14. 28 pt to quarts

15. 15,840 ft to miles

16. 5.4 tons to pounds

17. $6\frac{1}{4}$ ft to inches

See Example **3** **18.** A 1-pound weight has a mass of about 0.45 kilogram. What is the mass in kilograms of a sculpture that weighs 570 pounds? Round to the nearest tenth of a kilogram.

PRACTICE AND PROBLEM SOLVING

Extra Practice
See page EP11.

Compare. Write <, >, or =.

19. 6 yd ▨ 12 ft

20. 80 oz ▨ 5 lb

21. 18 in. ▨ 3 ft

22. 5 tons ▨ 12,000 lb

23. 8 gal ▨ 30 qt

24. 6.5 c ▨ 52 fl oz

25. 10,000 ft ▨ 2 mi

26. 20 pt ▨ 40 c

27. 1 gal ▨ 18 c

28. **Literature** The novel *Twenty Thousand Leagues Under the Sea* was written by Jules Verne in 1873. One league is approximately 3.45 miles. How many miles are in 20,000 leagues?

29. **Earth Science** One meter is about 3.28 feet. The average depth of the Pacific Ocean is 12,925 feet. How deep is this in meters, rounded to the nearest meter?

In 2005, the Grand Champion pumpkin at California's Half Moon Bay Art and Pumpkin Festival weighed 1,229 pounds.

Order each set of measures from least to greatest.

30. 8 ft; 2 yd; 60 in.

31. 5 qt; 2 gal; 12 pt; 8 c

32. $\frac{1}{2}$ ton; 8,000 oz; 430 lb

33. 2.5 mi; 12,000 ft; 5,000 yd

34. 63 fl oz; 7 c; 1.5 qt

35. 9.5 yd; 32.5 ft; 380 in.

36. Agriculture In one year, the United States produced nearly 895 million pounds of pumpkins. How many ounces were produced by the state with the lowest production shown in the table?

U.S. Pumpkin Production	
State	Pumpkins (million pounds)
California	180
Illinois	364
New York	114
Pennsylvania	109

37. Multi-Step A marathon is a race that is 26 miles 385 yards long. What is the length of a marathon in yards?

38. In 1998, a 2,505-gallon ice cream float was made in Atlanta, Georgia. How many 1-pint servings did the float contain?

39. Reasoning Explain why it makes sense to divide when you convert a measurement to a larger unit.

40. What's the Error? A student converted 480 ft to inches as follows. What did the student do wrong? What is the correct answer?

$$\frac{1 \text{ ft}}{12 \text{ in.}} = \frac{x}{480 \text{ ft}}$$

41. Write About It Explain how to convert 1.2 tons to ounces.

42. Challenge A dollar bill is 6.125 in. long. A radio station gives away a prize consisting of a mile-long string of dollar bills. What is the approximate value of the prize?

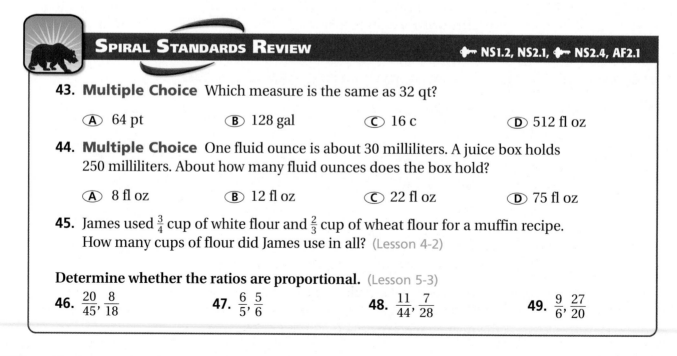

SPIRAL STANDARDS REVIEW NS1.2, NS2.1, NS2.4, AF2.1

43. Multiple Choice Which measure is the same as 32 qt?

(A) 64 pt   (B) 128 gal   (C) 16 c   (D) 512 fl oz

44. Multiple Choice One fluid ounce is about 30 milliliters. A juice box holds 250 milliliters. About how many fluid ounces does the box hold?

(A) 8 fl oz   (B) 12 fl oz   (C) 22 fl oz   (D) 75 fl oz

45. James used $\frac{3}{4}$ cup of white flour and $\frac{2}{3}$ cup of wheat flour for a muffin recipe. How many cups of flour did James use in all? (Lesson 4-2)

Determine whether the ratios are proportional. (Lesson 5-3)

46. $\frac{20}{45}, \frac{8}{18}$ **47.** $\frac{6}{5}, \frac{5}{6}$ **48.** $\frac{11}{44}, \frac{7}{28}$ **49.** $\frac{9}{6}, \frac{27}{20}$

Generate Formulas to Convert Units

Use with Lesson 5-5

California Standards Practice

Extension of AF2.1 Convert one unit of measurement to another (e.g., from feet to miles, from centimeters to inches).

go.hrw.com
Lab Resources Online
KEYWORD: MS8CA Lab5

Activity

Publishers, editors, and graphic designers measure lengths in *picas*. Measure each of the following line segments to the nearest inch, and record your results in the table.

Segment	Length (in.)	Length (picas)	Ratio of Picas to Inches
1		6	
2		12	
3		24	
4		30	
5		36	

① _____

② _____

③ _____

④ _____

⑤ _____

Think and Discuss

1. Make a conjecture about the relationship between picas and inches.

2. Use your conjecture to write a formula relating inches n to picas p.

3. How many picas wide is a sheet of paper that is $8\frac{1}{2}$ in. wide?

Try This

Using inches for *x*-coordinates and picas for *y*-coordinates, write ordered pairs for the data in the table. Then plot the points and draw a graph.

1. What shape is the graph?

2. Use the graph to find the number of picas that is equal to 3 inches.

3. Use the graph to find the number of inches that is equal to 27 picas.

4. A designer is laying out a page in a magazine. The dimensions of a photo are 18 picas by 15 picas. She doubles the dimensions of the photo. What are the new dimensions of the photo in inches?

READY TO GO ON?

Quiz for Lessons 5-1 Through 5-5

 **5-1 Ratios**

A bouquet has 6 red, 8 pink, 12 yellow, and 2 white flowers. Write each ratio in all three forms.

1. pink flowers to yellow flowers

2. red flowers to total flowers

3. A concession stand sold 14 strawberry, 18 banana, 8 grape, and 6 orange fruit drinks during a game. Tell whether the ratio of strawberry to orange drinks or the ratio of banana to grape drinks is greater.

5-2 Rates

4. A 5-gallon jug is 41.5 pounds heavier when it is full of water than when it is empty. How much does the water weigh per gallon?

5. Shaunti drove 621 miles in 11.5 hours. What was her average speed in miles per hour?

6. A grocery store sells a 7 oz bag of raisins for $1.10 and a 9 oz bag of raisins for $1.46. Which size bag has the lowest price per ounce?

5-3 Identifying and Writing Proportions

Determine whether the ratios are proportional.

7. $\frac{3}{8}, \frac{9}{24}$

8. $\frac{11}{17}, \frac{17}{23}$

9. $\frac{3}{4}, \frac{8}{9}$

10. $\frac{15}{22}, \frac{45}{66}$

Find a ratio equivalent to each ratio. Then use the ratios to write a proportion.

11. $\frac{10}{16}$

12. $\frac{21}{28}$

13. $\frac{12}{25}$

14. $\frac{40}{48}$

5-4 Solving Proportions

Use cross products to solve each proportion.

15. $\frac{n}{8} = \frac{15}{4}$

16. $\frac{20}{t} = \frac{2.5}{6}$

17. $\frac{6}{11} = \frac{0.12}{z}$

18. $\frac{15}{24} = \frac{x}{10}$

19. One human year is said to equal 7 dog years. If Cliff's dog is 5.5 years old in human years, what is his dog's age in dog years?

20. If 8 CDs take up $3\frac{1}{4}$ inches of shelf space, how many CDs will fit on 65 inches of shelf space?

5-5 Customary Measurements

Convert each measure.

21. 7 lb to ounces

22. 15 qt to pints

23. 3 mi to feet

24. 20 fl oz to cups

25. 39 ft to yards

26. 7,000 lb to tons

Focus on Problem Solving

Plan

California Standards

MR3.2 Note the method of **deriving the solution** and demonstrate a conceptual understanding of the derivation by solving similar problems.

Also covered: **NS1.3, MR1.1, MR2.4**

Make a Plan

• **Choose a problem-solving strategy**

The following are strategies that you might choose to help you solve a problem:

- Make a table
- Find a pattern
- Make an organized list
- Work backward
- Write an equation
- Draw a diagram
- Guess and check
- Solve a simpler problem
- Make a model

Tell which strategy from the list above you would use to solve each problem. Explain your choice.

1 A recipe for blueberry muffins calls for 1 cup of milk and 1.5 cups of blueberries. Ashley wants to make more muffins than the recipe yields. In Ashley's muffin batter, there are 4.5 cups of blueberries. If she is using the recipe as a guide, how many cups of milk will she need?

2 The length of a rectangle is 8 cm, and its width is 5 cm less than its length. A larger rectangle with dimensions that are proportional to those of the first has a length of 24 cm. What is the width of the larger rectangle?

3 Each of four brothers gets an allowance for doing chores at home each week. The amount of money each boy receives depends on his age. Jeremy is 13 years old, and he gets $12.75. His 11-year-old brother gets $11.25, and his 9-year-old brother gets $9.75. Determine a possible relationship between the boys' ages and their allowances, and use it to determine how much money Jeremy's 7-year-old brother gets.

4 According to an article in a medical journal, a healthful diet should include a ratio of 2.5 servings of meat to 4 servings of vegetables. If you eat 7 servings of meat per week, how many servings of vegetables should you eat?

Make Similar Figures

Use with Lesson 5-6

go.hrw.com

Lab Resources Online

KEYWORD: MS8CA Lab5

Similar figures are figures that have the same shape but not necessarily the same size. You can make similar figures by increasing or decreasing both dimensions of a rectangle while keeping the ratios of the side lengths proportional. Modeling similar figures using square tiles can help you solve proportions.

California Standards

NS1.3 Use proportions to solve problems (e.g., determine the value of N if $\frac{4}{7} = \frac{N}{21}$, find the length of a side of a polygon similar to a known polygon). Use cross-multiplication as a method for solving such problems, understanding it as the multiplication of both sides of an equation by a multiplicative inverse.

Activity

A rectangle made of square tiles measures 5 tiles long and 2 tiles wide. What is the length of a similar rectangle whose width is 6 tiles?

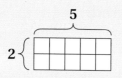

Use tiles to make a 5 × 2 rectangle.

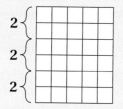

Add tiles to increase the width of the rectangle to 6 tiles.

Notice that there are now 3 sets of 2 tiles along the width of the rectangle because 2 × 3 = 6.

The width of the new rectangle is three times greater than the width of the original rectangle. To keep the ratios of the side measures proportional, the length must also be three times greater than the length of the original rectangle.

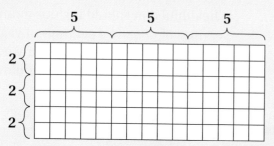

5 × 3 = 15

Add tiles to increase the length of the rectangle to 15 tiles.

The length of the similar rectangle is 15 tiles.

To check your answer, you can use ratios.

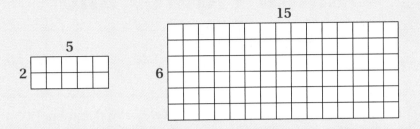

$\dfrac{2}{6} \overset{?}{=} \dfrac{5}{15}$ *Write ratios using the corresponding side lengths.*

$\dfrac{1}{3} \overset{?}{=} \dfrac{1}{3}$ ✔   *Simplify each ratio.*

1 Use square tiles to model similar figures with the given dimensions. Then find the missing dimension of each similar rectangle.

    a. The original rectangle is 4 tiles wide by 3 tiles long. The similar rectangle is 8 tiles wide by x tiles long.

    b. The original rectangle is 8 tiles wide by 10 tiles long. The similar rectangle is x tiles wide by 15 tiles long.

    c. The original rectangle is 3 tiles wide by 7 tiles long. The similar rectangle is 9 tiles wide by x tiles long.

Think and Discuss

    1. Sarah wants to increase the size of her rectangular backyard patio. Why must she change both dimensions of the patio to create a patio similar to the original?

    2. In a backyard, a plot of land that is 5 yd × 8 yd is used to grow tomatoes. The homeowner wants to decrease this plot to 4 yd × 6 yd. Will the new plot be similar to the original? Why or why not?

Try This

    1. A rectangle is 3 feet long and 7 feet wide. What is the width of a similar rectangle whose length is 9 feet?

    2. A rectangle is 6 feet long and 12 feet wide. What is the length of a similar rectangle whose width is 4 feet?

Use square tiles to model similar rectangles to solve each proportion.

3. $\dfrac{4}{5} = \dfrac{8}{x}$ **4.** $\dfrac{5}{9} = \dfrac{h}{18}$ **5.** $\dfrac{2}{y} = \dfrac{6}{18}$ **6.** $\dfrac{1}{t} = \dfrac{4}{16}$

7. $\dfrac{2}{3} = \dfrac{8}{m}$ **8.** $\dfrac{9}{12} = \dfrac{p}{4}$ **9.** $\dfrac{6}{r} = \dfrac{9}{15}$ **10.** $\dfrac{k}{12} = \dfrac{7}{6}$

5-6 Similar Figures and Proportions

California Standards

Preparation for ⬥ **NS1.3**
Use proportions to solve problems (e.g., determine the value of N if $\frac{4}{7} = \frac{N}{21}$, find the length of a side of a polygon similar to a known polygon). Use cross-multiplication as a method for solving such problems, understanding it as the multiplication of both sides of an equation by a multiplicative inverse.

Vocabulary
similar
corresponding sides
corresponding angles

Why learn this? You can use proportions to determine whether two photographs are similar. (See Exercise 10.)

Similar figures have the same shape but not necessarily the same size. The symbol ~ means "is similar to."

Corresponding angles of two or more figures are in the same relative position. **Corresponding sides** of two or more figures are between corresponding angles.

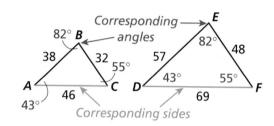

Corresponding angles

Corresponding sides

SIMILAR FIGURES

Two figures are similar if

- the measures of their corresponding angles are equal.

- the ratios of the lengths of their corresponding sides are proportional.

EXAMPLE 1 Determining Whether Two Triangles Are Similar

Reasoning

Writing Math

When naming similar figures, list the letters of the corresponding angles in the same order. In Example 1, $\triangle DEF \sim \triangle QRS$.

Tell whether the triangles are similar.

The corresponding angles of the figures have equal measures.
$\overline{DE}$ corresponds to $\overline{QR}$.
$\overline{EF}$ corresponds to $\overline{RS}$.
$\overline{DF}$ corresponds to $\overline{QS}$.

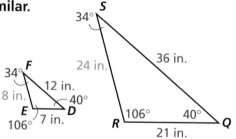

$$\frac{DE}{QR} \stackrel{?}{=} \frac{EF}{RS} \stackrel{?}{=} \frac{DF}{QS} \qquad \textit{Write ratios using the corresponding sides.}$$

$$\frac{7}{21} \stackrel{?}{=} \frac{8}{24} \stackrel{?}{=} \frac{12}{36} \qquad \textit{Substitute the lengths of the sides.}$$

$$\frac{1}{3} = \frac{1}{3} = \frac{1}{3} \qquad \textit{Simplify each ratio.}$$

Since the measures of the corresponding angles are equal and the ratios of the corresponding sides are equivalent, the triangles are similar.

For triangles, if the corresponding side lengths are all proportional, then the corresponding angles *must* have equal measures. For figures that have four or more sides, if the corresponding side lengths are all proportional, then the corresponding angles *may or may not* have equal angle measures.

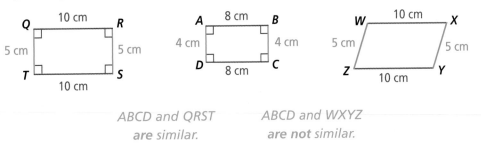

ABCD and QRST
are similar.

ABCD and WXYZ
are not similar.

EXAMPLE **2** **Determining Whether Two Four-Sided Figures Are Similar**

Tell whether the figures are similar.

Reasoning

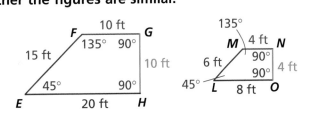

Reading Math

A side of a figure can be named by its endpoints, with a bar above.

$\overline{AB}$

Without the bar, the letters indicate the *length* of the side.

The corresponding angles of the figures have equal measures. Write each set of corresponding sides as a ratio.

$\dfrac{EF}{LM}$ $\overline{EF}$ corresponds to $\overline{LM}$. $\dfrac{FG}{MN}$ $\overline{FG}$ corresponds to $\overline{MN}$.

$\dfrac{GH}{NO}$ $\overline{GH}$ corresponds to $\overline{NO}$. $\dfrac{EH}{LO}$ $\overline{EH}$ corresponds to $\overline{LO}$.

Determine whether the ratios of the lengths of the corresponding sides are proportional.

$\dfrac{EF}{LM} \overset{?}{=} \dfrac{FG}{MN} \overset{?}{=} \dfrac{GH}{NO} \overset{?}{=} \dfrac{EH}{LO}$ *Write ratios using the corresponding sides.*

$\dfrac{15}{6} \overset{?}{=} \dfrac{10}{4} \overset{?}{=} \dfrac{10}{4} \overset{?}{=} \dfrac{20}{8}$ *Substitute the lengths of the sides.*

$\dfrac{5}{2} = \dfrac{5}{2} = \dfrac{5}{2} = \dfrac{5}{2}$ *Write the ratios with common denominators.*

Since the measures of the corresponding angles are equal and the ratios of the corresponding sides are equivalent, $EFGH \sim LMNO$.

Think and Discuss

1. Identify the corresponding angles of $\triangle JKL$ and $\triangle UTS$.

2. Explain whether all rectangles are similar. Give specific examples to justify your answer.

California
Standards Practice
Preparation for ← NS1.3

go.hrw.com
Homework Help Online
KEYWORD: MS8CA 5-6
Parent Resources Online
KEYWORD: MS8CA Parent

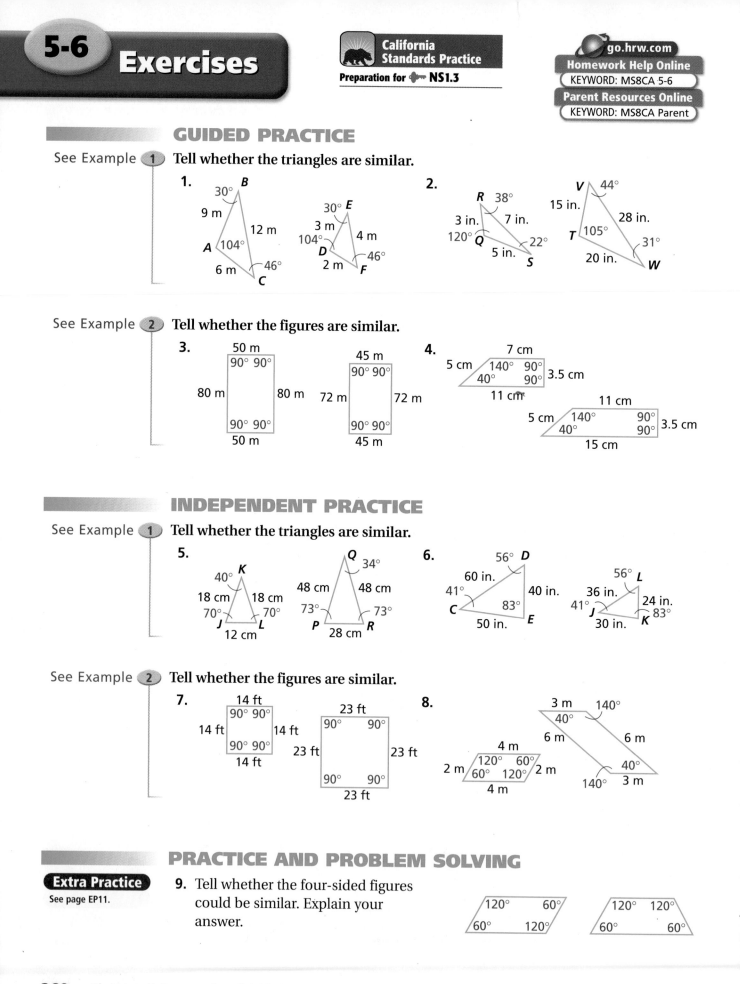

GUIDED PRACTICE

See Example 1 **Tell whether the triangles are similar.**

1.

2.

See Example 2 **Tell whether the figures are similar.**

3.

4.

INDEPENDENT PRACTICE

See Example 1 **Tell whether the triangles are similar.**

5.

6.

See Example 2 **Tell whether the figures are similar.**

7.

8.

PRACTICE AND PROBLEM SOLVING

Extra Practice
See page EP11.

9. Tell whether the four-sided figures
could be similar. Explain your
answer.

10. Kia wants similar prints in small and large sizes of a favorite photo. The photo lab sells prints in these sizes: 3 in. × 5 in., 4 in. × 6 in., 8 in. × 18 in., 9 in. × 20 in., and 16 in. × 24 in. Which could she order to get similar prints?

Tell whether the triangles are similar.

11.

12.

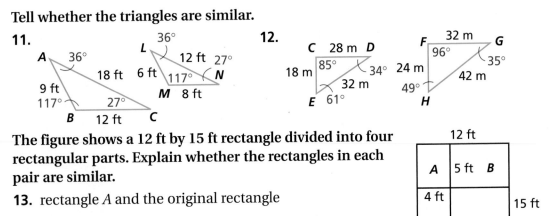

The figure shows a 12 ft by 15 ft rectangle divided into four rectangular parts. Explain whether the rectangles in each pair are similar.

13. rectangle *A* and the original rectangle

14. rectangle *C* and rectangle *B*

15. the original rectangle and rectangle *D*

Reasoning For Exercises 16–19, justify your answers using words or drawings.

16. Are all squares similar?

17. Are all 5-sided figures similar?

18. Are all rectangles similar?

19. Are all 6-sided figures similar?

20. Choose a Strategy What number gives the same result when multiplied by 6 as it does when 6 is added to it?

21. Write About It Tell how to decide whether two figures are similar.

22. Challenge Two triangles are similar. The ratio of the lengths of the corresponding sides is $\frac{5}{4}$. If the length of one side of the larger triangle is 40 feet, what is the length of the corresponding side of the smaller triangle?

23. Multiple Choice Luis wants to make a deck that is similar to one that is 10 feet long and 8 feet wide. If Luis's deck must be 18 feet long, what must its width be?

(A) 20 feet   (B) 16 feet   (C) 14.4 feet   (D) 22.5 feet

24. Short Response If a real dollar bill measures 2.61 in. by 6.14 in. and a play dollar bill measures 3.61 in. by 7.14 in., is the play money similar to the real money? Explain your answer.

Multiply. Write each answer in simplest form. (Lesson 4-4)

25. $\frac{3}{4} \cdot 14$

26. $2\frac{1}{8} \cdot 5$

27. $\frac{1}{4} \cdot 1\frac{7}{8} \cdot 3\frac{1}{5}$

28. Tell whether 5:3 or 12:7 is a greater ratio. (Lesson 5-1)

California Standards

<del></del> **NS1.3 Use proportions to solve problems (e.g.,** determine the value of N if $\frac{4}{7} = \frac{N}{21}$, **find the length of a side of a polygon similar to a known polygon). Use cross-multiplication as a method for solving such problems,** understanding it as the multiplication of both sides of an equation by a multiplicative inverse.

Vocabulary
indirect measurement

Why learn this? You can use similar figures to determine the heights of totem poles and other tall objects.

Native Americans of the Northwest, such as the Tlingit tribe of Alaska, carved totem poles out of tree trunks. These poles, sometimes painted with bright colors, could stand up to 80 feet tall.

Measuring the heights of tall objects, like some totem poles, cannot be done by using a ruler or yardstick. Instead, you can use *indirect measurement.*

Indirect measurement is a method of using proportions to find an unknown length or distance in similar figures.

EXAMPLE **1** **Finding Unknown Lengths in Similar Figures**

△*ABC* ~ △*JKL*. Find the unknown length.

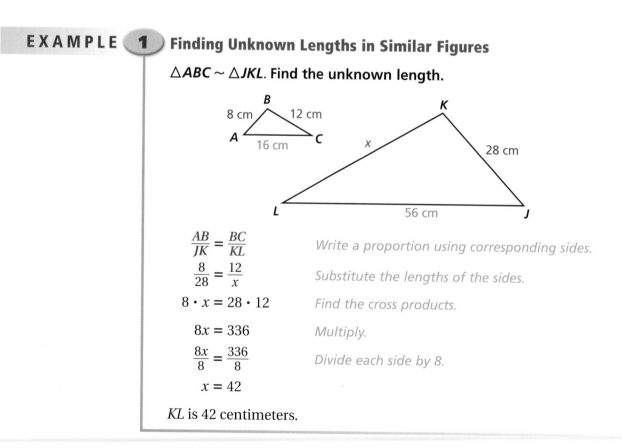

$$\frac{AB}{JK} = \frac{BC}{KL}$$ *Write a proportion using corresponding sides.*

$$\frac{8}{28} = \frac{12}{x}$$ *Substitute the lengths of the sides.*

$$8 \cdot x = 28 \cdot 12$$ *Find the cross products.*

$$8x = 336$$ *Multiply.*

$$\frac{8x}{8} = \frac{336}{8}$$ *Divide each side by 8.*

$$x = 42$$

KL is 42 centimeters.

EXAMPLE 2 Measurement Application

A volleyball court is a rectangle that is similar in shape to an Olympic-sized pool. Find the width of the pool.

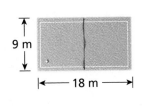

9 m

18 m

?

50 m

Let w = the width of the pool.

$$\frac{18}{50} = \frac{9}{w}$$ *Write a proportion using corresponding side lengths.*

$$18 \cdot w = 50 \cdot 9$$ *Find the cross products.*

$$18w = 450$$ *Multiply.*

$$\frac{18w}{18} = \frac{450}{18}$$ *Divide each side by 18.*

$$w = 25$$

The pool is 25 meters wide.

EXAMPLE 3 Estimating with Indirect Measurement

Estimate the height of the birdhouse in Chantal's yard, shown at right.

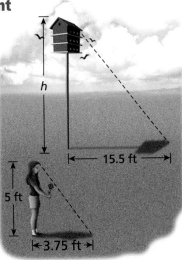

h

15.5 ft

5 ft

3.75 ft

$$\frac{h}{5} = \frac{15.5}{3.75}$$ *Write a proportion.*

$$\frac{h}{5} \approx \frac{16}{4}$$ *Use compatible numbers to estimate.*

$$\frac{h}{5} \approx 4$$ *Simplify.*

$$5 \cdot \frac{h}{5} \approx 5 \cdot 4$$ *Multiply each side by 5.*

$$h \approx 20$$

The birdhouse is about 20 feet tall.

Think and Discuss

1. Write another proportion that could be used to find the value of x in Example 1.

2. Name two objects that it would make sense to measure using indirect measurement.

5-7 **Exercises**

California Standards Practice
🔑 NS1.3

go.hrw.com
Homework Help Online
KEYWORD: MS8CA 5-7
Parent Resources Online
KEYWORD: MS8CA Parent

GUIDED PRACTICE

See Example ① △XYZ ~ △PQR in each pair. Find the unknown lengths.

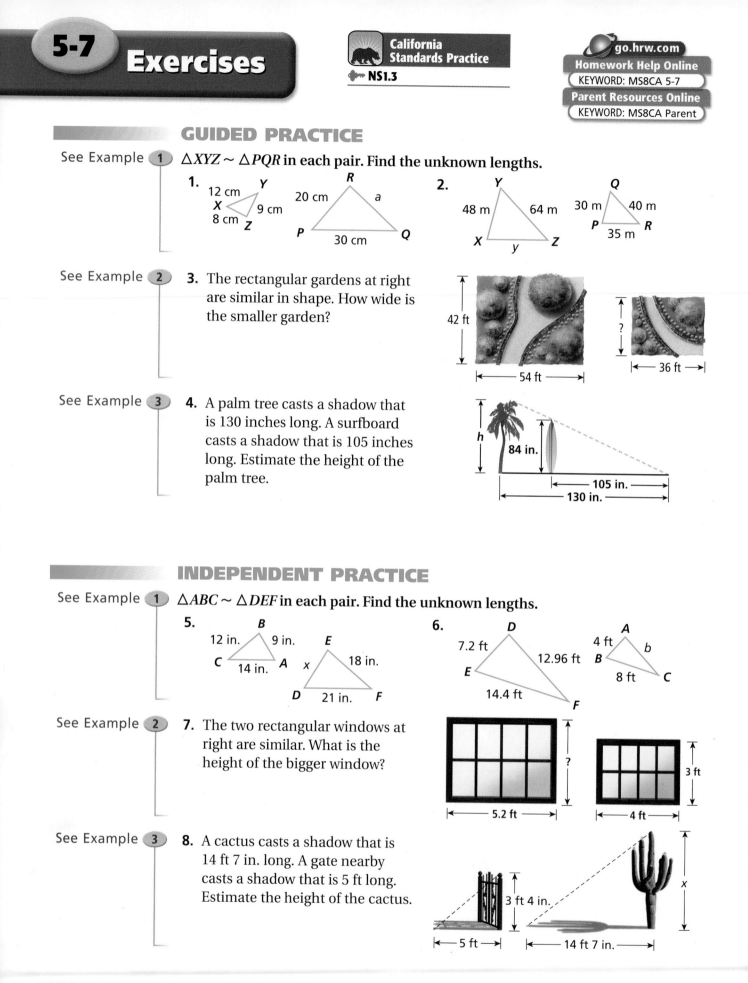

1.

2.

See Example ② 3. The rectangular gardens at right are similar in shape. How wide is the smaller garden?

See Example ③ 4. A palm tree casts a shadow that is 130 inches long. A surfboard casts a shadow that is 105 inches long. Estimate the height of the palm tree.

INDEPENDENT PRACTICE

See Example ① △ABC ~ △DEF in each pair. Find the unknown lengths.

5.

6.

See Example ② 7. The two rectangular windows at right are similar. What is the height of the bigger window?

See Example ③ 8. A cactus casts a shadow that is 14 ft 7 in. long. A gate nearby casts a shadow that is 5 ft long. Estimate the height of the cactus.

PRACTICE AND PROBLEM SOLVING

Extra Practice

See page EP11.

9. A building with a height of 14 m casts a shadow that is 16 m long while a taller building casts a 24 m long shadow. What is the height of the taller building?

10. Two common envelope sizes are $3\frac{1}{2}$ in. × $6\frac{1}{2}$ in. and 4 in. × $9\frac{1}{2}$ in. Are these envelopes similar? Explain.

11. Art An art class is painting a mural composed of brightly colored geometric shapes. The class has decided that all the right triangles in the design will be similar to the right triangle that will be painted fire red. Find the measures of the right triangles in the table. Round your answers to the nearest tenth.

Triangle Color	Length (in.)	Height (in.)
Fire Red	12	16
Blazing Orange	7	
Grape Purple		4
Dynamite Blue	15	

12. Reasoning Write a problem that can be solved using indirect measurement.

13. Write About It Assume you know the side lengths of one triangle and the length of one side of a second similar triangle. Explain how to use the properties of similar figures to find the unknown lengths in the second triangle.

14. Challenge $\triangle ABE \sim \triangle ACD$. What is the value of y in the diagram?

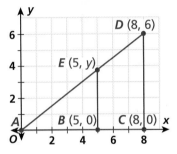

---

15. Multiple Choice Find the unknown length in the similar figures.

(A) 10 cm   (C) 15 cm

(B) 12 cm   (D) 18 cm

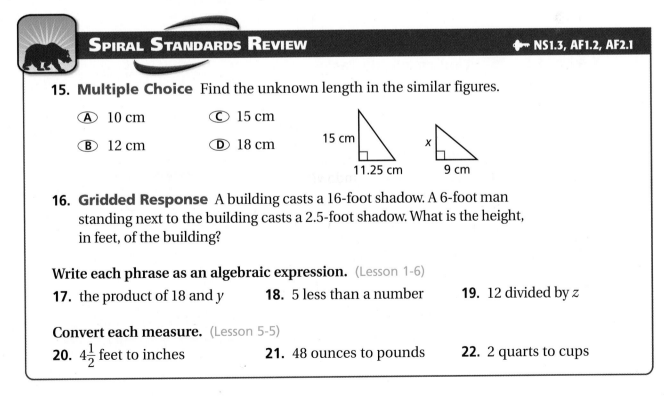

16. Gridded Response A building casts a 16-foot shadow. A 6-foot man standing next to the building casts a 2.5-foot shadow. What is the height, in feet, of the building?

Write each phrase as an algebraic expression. (Lesson 1-6)

17. the product of 18 and y **18.** 5 less than a number   **19.** 12 divided by z

Convert each measure. (Lesson 5-5)

20. $4\frac{1}{2}$ feet to inches   **21.** 48 ounces to pounds   **22.** 2 quarts to cups

5-8 Scale Drawings and Scale Models

California Standards

← **NS1.3 Use proportions to solve problems** (e.g., determine the value of N if $\frac{4}{7} = \frac{N}{21}$, find the length of a side of a polygon similar to a known polygon). **Use cross-multiplication as a method for solving such problems,** understanding it as the multiplication of both sides of an equation by an multiplicative inverse.

Vocabulary
scale model
scale factor
scale
scale drawing

Who uses this? Model builders use scale factors to create realistic models.

This HO gauge model train is a *scale model* of a historic train. A **scale model** is a proportional three-dimensional model of an object. Its dimensions are related to the dimensions of the actual object by a ratio called the **scale factor**. The HO scale factor is $\frac{1}{87}$. This means that each dimension of the model is $\frac{1}{87}$ of the corresponding dimension of the actual train.

A **scale** is the ratio between two sets of measurements. Scales can use the same units or different units. The photograph shows a *scale drawing* of the model train. A **scale drawing** is a proportional two-dimensional drawing of an object. Both scale drawings and scale models can be smaller or larger than the objects they represent.

EXAMPLE 1 **Finding a Scale Factor**

 **Reasoning**

Identify the scale factor.

	Race Car	Model
Length (in.)	132	11
Height (in.)	66	5.5

You can use the lengths *or* heights to find the scale factor.

$\dfrac{\text{model length}}{\text{race car length}} = \dfrac{11}{132} = \dfrac{1}{12}$ *Write a ratio. Then simplify.*

$\dfrac{\text{model height}}{\text{race car height}} = \dfrac{5.5}{66} = \dfrac{1}{12}$

The scale factor is $\frac{1}{12}$. This is reasonable because $\frac{1}{10}$ the length of the race car is 13.2 in. The length of the model is 11 in., which is less than 13.2 in., and $\frac{1}{12}$ is less than $\frac{1}{10}$.

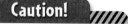 **Caution!**

A scale factor is always the ratio of the model's dimensions to the actual object's dimensions.

EXAMPLE 2 Using Scale Factors to Find Unknown Lengths

A photograph of Vincent van Gogh's painting *Still Life with Irises Against a Yellow Background* has dimensions 6.13 cm and 4.90 cm. The scale factor is $\frac{1}{15}$. Find the size of the actual painting, to the nearest tenth of a centimeter.

$$Think: \frac{\text{photo}}{\text{painting}} = \frac{1}{15}$$

$\frac{6.13}{\ell} = \frac{1}{15}$ *Write a proportion to find the length ℓ.*

$\ell = 6.13 \cdot 15$ *Find the cross products.*

$\ell = 92.0 \text{ cm}$ *Multiply and round to the nearest tenth.*

$\frac{4.90}{w} = \frac{1}{15}$ *Write a proportion to find the width w.*

$w = 4.90 \cdot 15$ *Find the cross products.*

$w = 73.5 \text{ cm}$ *Multiply and round to the nearest tenth.*

The painting is 92.0 cm long and 73.5 cm wide.

EXAMPLE 3 *Measurement Application*

On a map of Florida, the distance between Hialeah and Tampa is 10.5 cm. What is the actual distance *d* between the cities if the map scale is 3 cm = 80 mi?

$$Think: \frac{\text{map distance}}{\text{actual distance}} = \frac{3}{80}$$

$\frac{3}{80} = \frac{10.5}{d}$ *Write a proportion.*

$3 \cdot d = 80 \cdot 10.5$ *Find the cross products.*

$3d = 840$

$\frac{3d}{3} = \frac{840}{3}$ *Divide both sides by 3.*

$d = 280 \text{ mi}$

The distance between the cities is 280 miles.

Think and Discuss

1. **Explain** how you can tell whether a model with a scale factor of $\frac{5}{3}$ is larger or smaller than the original object.

2. **Describe** how to find the scale factor if an antenna is 60 feet long and a scale drawing shows the length as 1 foot long.

5-8 **Exercises**

California Standards Practice
NS1.3

go.hrw.com
Homework Help Online
KEYWORD: MS8CA 5-8
Parent Resources Online
KEYWORD: MS8CA Parent

GUIDED PRACTICE

See Example **1**   Identify the scale factor.

1.

	Grizzly Bear	Model
Height (in.)	84	6

2.

	Moray Eel	Model
Length (ft)	5	$1\frac{1}{2}$

See Example **2**   **3.** In a photograph, a sculpture is 4.2 cm tall and 2.5 cm wide. The scale factor is $\frac{1}{16}$. Find the size of the actual sculpture.

See Example **3**   **4.** Ms. Jackson is driving from South Bend to Indianapolis. She measures a distance of 4.3 cm between the cities on her Indiana road map. What is the actual distance between the cities if the map scale is 1 cm = 30 mi?

INDEPENDENT PRACTICE

See Example **1**   Identify the scale factor.

5.

	Eagle	Model
Wingspan (in.)	90	6

6.

	Dolphin	Model
Length (cm)	260	13

See Example **2**   **7.** On a scale drawing, a tree is $6\frac{3}{4}$ inches tall. The scale factor is $\frac{1}{20}$. Find the height of the actual tree.

See Example **3**   **8.** **Measurement** On a road map of Virginia, the distance from Alexandria to Roanoke is 7.6 cm. What is the actual distance between the cities if the map scale is 2 cm = 50 mi?

PRACTICE AND PROBLEM SOLVING

Extra Practice
See page EP11.

The scale factor of each model is 1:12. Find the missing dimensions.

	Item	Actual Dimensions	Model Dimensions
9.	Lamp	Height: ■	Height: $1\frac{1}{3}$ in.
10.	Couch	Height: 32 in. Length: 69 in.	Height: ■ Length: ■
11.	Chair	Height: $51\frac{1}{2}$ in.	Height: ■

12. A building shaped like a pair of binoculars is a scale model of an actual pair of binoculars. The scale is 9 ft = 1 in. What is the height of the building if the height of the actual binoculars is 5 inches?

13. **Critical Thinking** A countertop is 18 ft long. How long is it on a scale drawing with the scale 1 in. = 3 yd?

14. **Write About It** A scale for a scale drawing is 10 cm = 1 mm. Which will be larger, the actual object or the scale drawing? Explain.

Use the map for Exercises 15–16.

15. In 1863, Confederate troops marched from Chambersburg to Gettysburg in search of badly needed shoes. Use the ruler and the scale of the map to estimate how far the Confederate soldiers, many of whom were barefoot, marched.

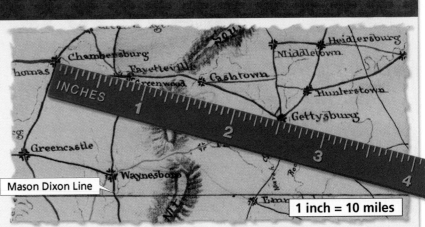

1 inch = 10 miles

16. Before the Civil War, the Mason-Dixon Line was considered the dividing line between the North and the South. If Gettysburg is about 8.1 miles north of the Mason-Dixon Line, how far apart in inches are Gettysburg and the Mason-Dixon Line on the map?

17. **Reasoning** Toby is making a scale model of the battlefield at Fredericksburg. The area he wants to model measures about 11 mi by 7.5 mi. He plans to put the model on a 3.25 ft by 3.25 ft square table. On each side of the model he wants to leave at least 3 in. between the model and the table edges. What is the largest scale he can use?

18. ★ **Challenge** A map of Vicksburg, Mississippi, has a scale of "1 mile to the inch." The map has been reduced so that 5 inches on the original map appears as 1.5 inches on the reduced map. If the distance between two points on the reduced map is 1.75 inches, what is the actual distance in miles?

This painting by H.A. Ogden depicts General Robert E. Lee at Fredericksburg in 1862.

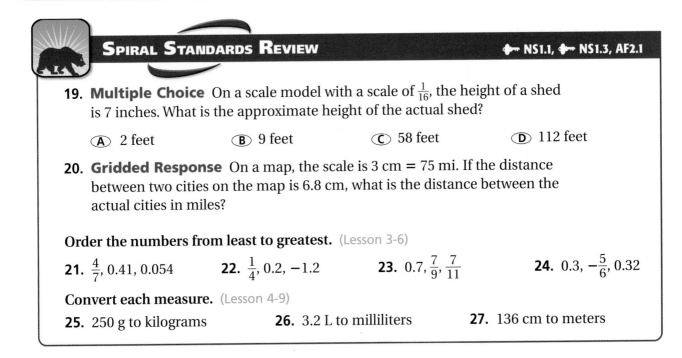

SPIRAL STANDARDS REVIEW   🔑 NS1.1, 🔑 NS1.3, AF2.1

19. **Multiple Choice** On a scale model with a scale of $\frac{1}{16}$, the height of a shed is 7 inches. What is the approximate height of the actual shed?

Ⓐ 2 feet   Ⓑ 9 feet   Ⓒ 58 feet   Ⓓ 112 feet

20. **Gridded Response** On a map, the scale is 3 cm = 75 mi. If the distance between two cities on the map is 6.8 cm, what is the distance between the actual cities in miles?

Order the numbers from least to greatest. (Lesson 3-6)

21. $\frac{4}{7}$, 0.41, 0.054   22. $\frac{1}{4}$, 0.2, −1.2   23. 0.7, $\frac{7}{9}$, $\frac{7}{11}$ 24. 0.3, −$\frac{5}{6}$, 0.32

Convert each measure. (Lesson 4-9)

25. 250 g to kilograms   26. 3.2 L to milliliters   27. 136 cm to meters

READY TO GO ON?

Quiz for Lessons 5-6 Through 5-8

✓ **5-6** **Similar Figures and Proportions**

1. Tell whether the triangles are similar.

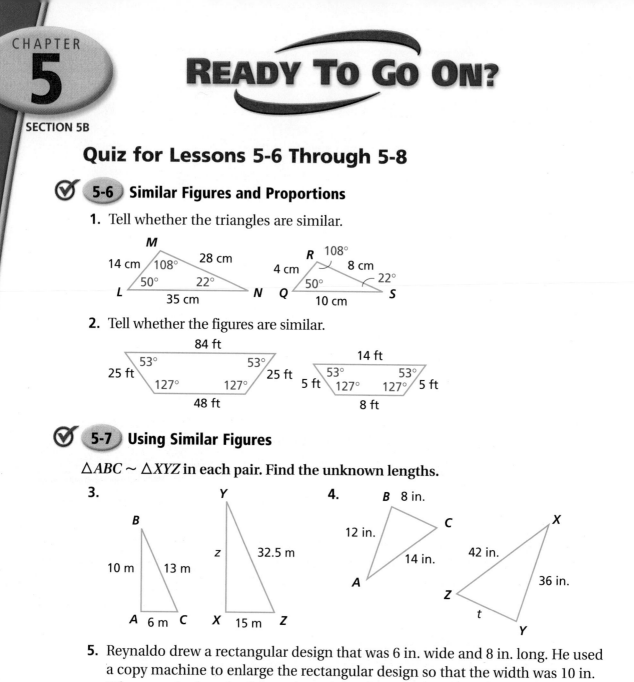

2. Tell whether the figures are similar.

✓ **5-7** **Using Similar Figures**

$\triangle ABC \sim \triangle XYZ$ in each pair. Find the unknown lengths.

3.

4.

5. Reynaldo drew a rectangular design that was 6 in. wide and 8 in. long. He used a copy machine to enlarge the rectangular design so that the width was 10 in. What was the length of the enlarged design?

6. Redon is 6 ft 2 in. tall, and his shadow is 4 ft 1 in. long. At the same time a building casts a shadow that is 19 ft 10 in. long. Estimate the height of the building.

✓ **5-8** **Scale Drawings and Scale Models**

7. An actor is 6 ft tall. On a billboard for a new movie, the actor's picture is enlarged so that his height is 16.8 ft. What is the scale factor?

8. On a scale drawing, a driveway is 6 in. long. The scale factor is $\frac{1}{24}$. Find the length of the actual driveway.

9. A map of Texas has a scale of 1 in. = 65 mi. If the distance from Dallas to San Antonio is 260 mi, what is the distance in inches between two cities on the map?

Bug Juice When campers get thirsty, out comes the well-known camp beverage bug juice! The recipes show how two camps, Camp Big Sky and Camp Wild Flowers, make their bug juice. Each camp has 180 campers. During a typical day, each camper drinks two 8-ounce cups of bug juice.

1. How many ounces of bug juice are consumed at each camp each day?

2. How much does it cost to make two quarts of bug juice at each camp?

3. Each camp has budgeted $30 per day for bug juice. Is $30 a day enough? How do you know? Show your work.

4. Campers begin to complain. They want their bug juice "buggier." How could each camp change its recipe, continue to serve 180 campers two 8-ounce cups of bug juice daily, and not spend more than $40 per day for bug juice? Explain your reasoning.

Camp Big Sky
Bug Juice Recipe

- One 4 oz packet of mix A
- Add tap water to make 2 quarts of bug juice.

Camp Wild Flowers
Bug Juice Recipe

- One 0.14 oz packet of mix B
- 4 oz sugar
- Add tap water to make 2 quarts of bug juice.

Prices

4 oz packet of mix A	$0.78
0.14 oz packet of mix B	$0.20
1 lb of sugar	$0.36

Game Time

Water Works

You have three glasses: a 3-ounce glass, a 5-ounce glass, and an 8-ounce glass. The 8-ounce glass is full of water, and the other two glasses are empty. By pouring water from one glass to another, how can you get exactly 6 ounces of water in one of the glasses? The step-by-step solution is described below.

① Fill the 5 oz glass using water from the 8 oz glass.

② Fill the 3 oz glass using water from the 5 oz glass.

③ Pour the water from the 3 oz glass into the 8 oz glass.

You now have 6 ounces of water in the 8-ounce glass.

Start again, but this time try to get exactly 4 ounces of water in one glass. (*Hint:* Find a way to get 1 ounce of water. Start by pouring water into the 3-ounce glass.)

Next, using 3-ounce, 8-ounce, and 11-ounce glasses, try to get exactly 9 ounces of water in one glass. Start with the 11-ounce glass full of water. (*Hint:* Start by pouring water into the 8-ounce glass.)

Look at the sizes of the glasses in each problem. The volume of the third glass is the sum of the volumes of the first two glasses: $3 + 5 = 8$ and $3 + 8 = 11$. Using any amounts for the two smaller glasses, and starting with the largest glass full, you can get any multiple of the smaller glass's volume. Try it and see.

Concentration

Each card in a deck of cards has a ratio on one side. Place each card face down. Each player or team takes a turn flipping over two cards. If the ratios on the cards are equivalent, the player or team can keep the pair. If not, the next player or team flips two cards. After every card has been turned over, the player or team with the most pairs wins.

go.hrw.com
Game Time Extra
KEYWORD: MS8CA Games

A complete copy of the rules and the game pieces are available online.

Materials
- 2 paper plates
- scissors
- markers

It's in the Bag!

PROJECT **Paper Plate Proportions**

Serve up some proportions on this book made from paper plates.

① Fold one of the paper plates in half. Cut out a narrow rectangle along the folded edge. The rectangle should be as long as the diameter of plate's inner circle. When you open the plate, you will have a narrow window in the center. **Figure A**

② Fold the second paper plate in half and then unfold it. Cut slits on both sides of the crease beginning from the edge of the plate to the inner circle. **Figure B**

③ Roll up the plate with the slits so that the two slits touch each other. Then slide this plate into the narrow window in the other plate. **Figure C**

④ When the rolled-up plate is halfway through the window, unroll it so that the slits fit on the sides of the window. **Figure D**

⑤ Close the book so that all the plates are folded in half.

Taking Note of the Math

Write the number and name of the chapter on the cover of the book. Then review the chapter, using the inside pages to take notes on ratios, rates, proportions, and similar figures.

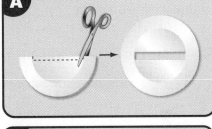

A

B

C

D

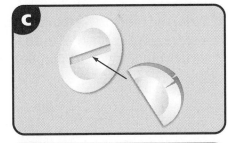

It's in the Bag! **273**

Vocabulary

Complete the sentences below with vocabulary words from the list above.

1. __?__ figures have the same shape but not necessarily the same size.

2. A(n) __?__ is a comparison of two numbers, and a(n) __?__ is a ratio that compares two quantities measured in different units.

3. The ratio used to enlarge or reduce similar figures is a(n) __?__ .

5-1 Ratios (pp. 232–235)

 NS1.2

EXAMPLE

■ Write the ratio of 2 servings of bread to 4 servings of vegetables in all three forms. Write your answers in simplest form.

$\frac{2}{4} = \frac{1}{2}$ *Write the ratio 2 to 4 in simplest form.*

$\frac{1}{2}$, 1 to 2, 1:2

EXERCISES

There are 3 red, 7 blue, and 5 yellow balloons.

4. Write the ratio of blue balloons to total balloons in all three forms. Write your answer in simplest form.

5. Tell whether the ratio of red to blue balloons or the ratio of yellow balloons to total balloons is greater.

5-2 Rates (pp. 236–239)

NS1.2, AF2.2, AF2.3

EXAMPLE

■ Find each unit price. Then decide which has the lowest price per ounce.

$\frac{\$2.70}{5\ oz}$ or $\frac{\$4.32}{12\ oz}$

$\frac{\$2.70}{5\ oz} = \frac{\$0.54}{oz}$ and $\frac{\$4.32}{12\ oz} = \frac{\$0.36}{oz}$

Since $0.36 < 0.54$, $\frac{\$4.32}{12\ oz}$ has the lowest price per ounce.

EXERCISES

Find each average rate of speed.

6. 540 ft in 90 s   7. 436 mi in 4 hr

Find each unit price. Then decide which is the better buy.

8. $\frac{\$56}{25\ gal}$ or $\frac{\$32.05}{15\ gal}$ 9. $\frac{\$160}{5\ g}$ or $\frac{\$315}{9\ g}$

5-3 Identifying and Writing Proportions (pp. 240–243)

NS1.2

EXAMPLES

■ Determine whether $\frac{5}{12}$ and $\frac{3}{9}$ are proportional.

$\frac{5}{12}$ *$\frac{5}{12}$ is already in simplest form.*

$\frac{3}{9} = \frac{1}{3}$ *Simplify $\frac{3}{9}$.*

$\frac{5}{12} \neq \frac{1}{3}$ *The ratios are not proportional.*

■ Find a ratio equivalent to $\frac{5}{12}$. Then use the ratios to write a proportion.

$\frac{5}{12} = \frac{5 \cdot 3}{12 \cdot 3} = \frac{15}{36}$ *Write an equivalent ratio.*

$\frac{5}{12} = \frac{15}{36}$ *Write a proportion.*

EXERCISES

Determine whether the ratios are proportional.

10. $\frac{9}{27} , \frac{6}{20}$ 11. $\frac{15}{25} , \frac{20}{30}$

12. $\frac{21}{14} , \frac{18}{12}$ 13. $\frac{2}{5} , \frac{4}{7}$

14. $\frac{8}{10} , \frac{20}{25}$ 15. $\frac{18}{39} , \frac{24}{52}$

Find a ratio equivalent to each ratio. Then use the ratios to write a proportion.

16. $\frac{10}{12}$ 17. $\frac{45}{50}$

18. $\frac{9}{15}$ 19. $\frac{4}{9}$

5-4 Solving Proportions (pp. 244–248)

NS1.3, AF2.2, AF2.3

EXAMPLE

■ Use cross products to solve $\frac{p}{8} = \frac{10}{12}$.

$\frac{p}{8} = \frac{10}{12}$

$p \cdot 12 = 8 \cdot 10$ *Multiply the cross products.*

$12p = 80$

$\frac{12p}{12} = \frac{80}{12}$ *Divide each side by 12.*

$p = \frac{20}{3}$, or $6\frac{2}{3}$

EXERCISES

Use cross products to solve each proportion.

20. $\frac{4}{6} = \frac{n}{3}$ 21. $\frac{2}{a} = \frac{5}{15}$

22. $\frac{b}{1.5} = \frac{8}{3}$ 23. $\frac{16}{11} = \frac{96}{x}$

24. $\frac{2}{y} = \frac{1}{5}$ 25. $\frac{7}{2} = \frac{70}{w}$

5-5 Customary Measurements (pp. 249–252)

NS1.3, AF2.1

EXAMPLES

■ Choose the most appropriate customary unit for the weight of a mouse. Justify your answer.

Ounces—the weight of a mouse is similar to the weight of a slice of bread.

■ Convert 5 mi to feet.

$\frac{\text{feet} \longrightarrow 5{,}280}{\text{miles} \longrightarrow 1} = \frac{x}{5}$

$x = 5{,}280 \cdot 5 = 26{,}400 \text{ ft}$

EXERCISES

Choose the most appropriate customary unit for each measurement. Justify your answer.

26. the height of a giraffe
27. the capacity of a washing machine
28. the width of a cell phone

Convert each measure.

29. 32 fl oz to pints
30. 1.5 tons to pounds
31. 13,200 ft to miles

5-6 Similar Figures and Proportions (pp. 258–261)

 Prep for NS1.3

EXAMPLE

■ **Tell whether the figures are similar.**

The corresponding angles of the figures have equal measures.

$$\frac{5}{30} \stackrel{?}{=} \frac{3}{18} \stackrel{?}{=} \frac{5}{30} \stackrel{?}{=} \frac{3}{18}$$

$$\frac{1}{6} = \frac{1}{6} = \frac{1}{6} = \frac{1}{6}$$

The ratios of the corresponding sides are equivalent. The figures are similar.

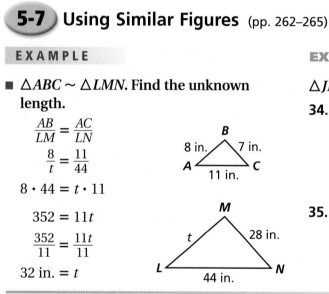

EXERCISES

Tell whether the figures are similar.

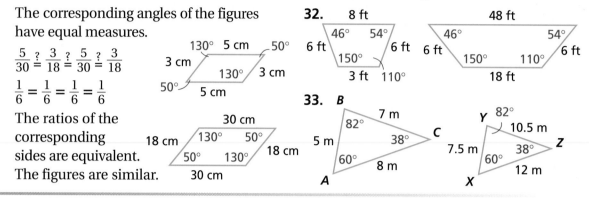

32.

33.

5-7 Using Similar Figures (pp. 262–265)

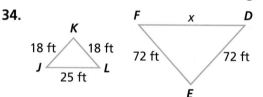 NS1.3

EXAMPLE

■ $\triangle ABC \sim \triangle LMN$. **Find the unknown length.**

$$\frac{AB}{LM} = \frac{AC}{LN}$$

$$\frac{8}{t} = \frac{11}{44}$$

$$8 \cdot 44 = t \cdot 11$$

$$352 = 11t$$

$$\frac{352}{11} = \frac{11t}{11}$$

$$32 \text{ in.} = t$$

EXERCISES

$\triangle JKL \sim \triangle DEF$. **Find the unknown length.**

34.

35. A tree casts a $30\frac{1}{2}$ ft shadow at the time of day when a 2 ft stake casts a $7\frac{2}{3}$ ft shadow. Estimate the height of the tree.

5-8 Scale Drawings and Scale Models (pp. 266–269)

 NS1.3

EXAMPLE

■ A model boat is 4 inches long. The scale factor is $\frac{1}{24}$. How long is the actual boat?

$$\frac{\text{model}}{\text{boat}} = \frac{1}{24}$$

$$\frac{4}{n} = \frac{1}{24} \qquad \textit{Write a proportion.}$$

$$4 \cdot 24 = n \cdot 1 \qquad \textit{Find the cross products.}$$

$$96 = n \qquad \textit{Solve.}$$

The boat is 96 inches long.

EXERCISES

36. The Wright brothers' *Flyer* had a 484-inch wingspan. Carla bought a model of the plane with a scale factor of $\frac{1}{40}$. What is the model's wingspan?

37. The distance from Austin to Houston on a map is 4.3 inches. The map scale is 1 inch = 38 miles. What is the actual distance?

A soccer team has 4 sixth-graders, 5 seventh-graders, and 4 eighth-graders.
Write each ratio in all three forms.

1. seventh-graders to sixth-graders

2. eighth-graders to total team members

3. Stan found 12 pennies, 15 nickels, 7 dimes, and 5 quarters. Tell whether the ratio of pennies to quarters or the ratio of nickels to dimes is greater.

4. Lenny sold 576 tacos in 48 hours. What was Lenny's average rate of taco sales?

5. A store sells a 5 lb box of detergent for $5.25 and a 10 lb box of detergent for $9.75. Which size box has the lowest price per pound?

Find a ratio equivalent to each ratio. Then use the ratios to write a proportion.

6. $\frac{22}{30}$

7. $\frac{7}{9}$

8. $\frac{18}{54}$

9. $\frac{10}{17}$

Use cross products to solve each proportion.

10. $\frac{9}{12} = \frac{m}{6}$

11. $\frac{x}{2} = \frac{18}{6}$

12. $\frac{3}{7} = \frac{21}{t}$

13. $\frac{5}{p} = \frac{10}{2}$

14. A submarine travels 56 miles in 4 hours. At this rate, how many hours will it take the submarine to travel 700 miles?

Convert each measure.

15. 13,200 ft to miles

16. 3.5 lb to ounces

17. 17 qt to gallons

Tell whether the figures are similar.

18.

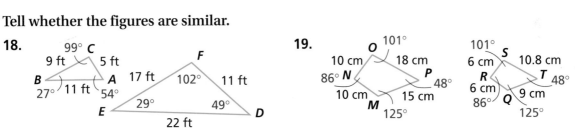

19.

△WYZ ~ △MNO in each pair. Find the unknown lengths.

20.

21.

22. An 8-foot flagpole casts a shadow that is 6 feet long at the same time as a nearby tree casts a shadow that is 21 feet long. How tall is the tree?

23. A scale model of a building is 8 in. by 12 in. If the scale is 1 in. = 15 ft, what are the dimensions of the actual building?

24. The distance from Portland to Seaside is 75 mi. What is the distance in inches between the two towns on a map if the scale is $1\frac{1}{4}$ in. = 25 mi?

STRATEGIES FOR SUCCESS

Gridded Response: Write Gridded Responses

When responding to a test item that requires you to place your answer in a grid, you must fill in the grid on your answer sheet correctly, or the item will be marked as incorrect.

EXAMPLE 1

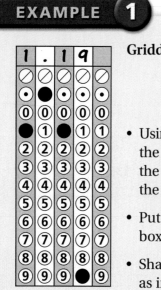

Gridded Response: Solve the equation $0.23 + r = 1.42$.

$$
\begin{array}{r}
0.23 + r = 1.42 \\
-\,0.23 \qquad\quad -\,0.23 \\
\hline
r = 1.19
\end{array}
$$

- Using a pencil, write your answer in the answer boxes at the top of the grid. Put the first digit of your answer in the leftmost box, or put the last digit of your answer in the rightmost box. On some grids, the fraction bar and the decimal point have a designated box.

- Put only one digit or symbol in each box. Do not leave a blank box in the middle of an answer.

- Shade the bubble for each digit or symbol in the same column as in the answer box.

EXAMPLE 2

Gridded Response: Divide. $3 \div 1\frac{4}{5}$

$$3 \div 1\frac{4}{5} = \frac{3}{1} \div \frac{9}{5}$$

$$= \frac{3}{1} \cdot \frac{5}{9}$$

$$= \frac{15}{9} = \frac{5}{3} = 1\frac{2}{3} = 1.\overline{6}$$

The answer simplifies to $\frac{5}{3}$, $1\frac{2}{3}$, or $1.\overline{6}$.

- Mixed numbers and repeating decimals cannot be gridded, so you must grid the answer as $\frac{5}{3}$.

- Write your answer in the answer boxes at the top of the grid.

- Put only one digit or symbol in each box. Do not leave a blank box in the middle of an answer.

- Shade the bubble for each digit or symbol in the same column as in the answer box.

Grid formats may vary from test to test. The grid in this book is used often, but it is not used on every test that has gridded-response questions. Always examine the grid when taking a standardized test to be sure you know how to fill it in correctly.

Read each statement, and then answer the questions that follow.

Sample A
A student correctly solved an equation for *x* and got 42 as a result. Then the student filled in the grid as shown.

1. What error did the student make when filling in the grid?

2. Explain a second method of filling in the answer correctly.

Sample B
A student correctly multiplied 0.16 and 0.07. Then the student filled in the grid as shown.

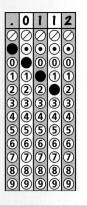

3. What error did the student make when filling in the grid?

4. Explain how to fill in the answer correctly.

Sample C
A student subtracted −12 from 5 and got an answer of −17. Then the student filled in the grid as shown.

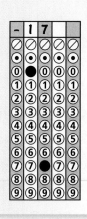

5. What error did the student make when finding the answer?

6. Explain why you cannot fill in a negative number on a grid.

7. Explain how to fill in the answer to 5 − (−12) correctly.

Sample D
A student correctly added $\frac{5}{6} + \frac{11}{12}$ and got $1\frac{9}{12}$ as a result. Then the student filled in the grid as shown.

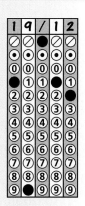

8. What answer is shown in the grid?

9. Explain why you cannot show a mixed number in a grid.

10. Write two equivalent forms of the answer $1\frac{9}{12}$ that could be filled in the grid correctly.

Cumulative Assessment, Chapters 1–5

Multiple Choice

1. What is the unknown length *b* in similar triangles *ABC* and *DEF*?

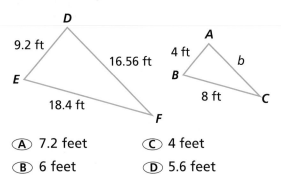

Ⓐ 7.2 feet   Ⓒ 4 feet

Ⓑ 6 feet   Ⓓ 5.6 feet

2. The total length of the Golden Gate Bridge in San Francisco, California, is 8,981 feet. If a car is traveling at a speed of 45 miles per hour, how many minutes would it take the car to cross the bridge?

Ⓐ 0.04 minute   Ⓒ 1.7 minutes

Ⓑ 1.28 minutes   Ⓓ 2.27 minutes

3. For which equation is $x = \frac{2}{5}$ the solution?

Ⓐ $5x = \frac{25}{2}$

Ⓑ $\frac{1}{5}x = \frac{2}{25}$

Ⓒ $\frac{1}{5}x = 2$

Ⓓ $5x = \frac{1}{2}$

4. A hot air balloon descends 38.5 meters in 22 seconds. If the balloon continues to descend at this rate, how long will it take to descend 125 meters?

Ⓐ 25.25 seconds   Ⓒ 71.43 seconds

Ⓑ 86.5 seconds   Ⓓ 218.75 seconds

5. Which value completes the table of equivalent ratios?

Microphones	3	9	15	36
Karaoke Machines	1	3	?	12

Ⓐ 5   Ⓒ 8

Ⓑ 7   Ⓓ 9

6. On a baseball field, the distance from home plate to the pitcher's mound is $60\frac{1}{2}$ feet. The distance from home plate to second base is about $127\frac{7}{24}$ feet. What is the difference between the two distances?

Ⓐ $61\frac{1}{3}$ feet   Ⓒ $66\frac{19}{24}$ feet

Ⓑ $66\frac{5}{6}$ feet   Ⓓ $66\frac{5}{24}$ feet

7. Which word phrase best describes the expression $n - 6$?

Ⓐ 6 more than a number

Ⓑ A number less than 6

Ⓒ 6 minus a number

Ⓓ A number decreased by 6

8. A football weighs about $\frac{3}{20}$ kilogram. If a coach has 15 footballs in a large bag, which estimate best describes the total weight of the footballs?

Ⓐ Not quite 3 kilograms

Ⓑ A little more than 2 kilograms

Ⓒ Almost 1 kilogram

Ⓓ Between 1 and 2 kilograms

9. What is the value of the expression
13 × 4 + 6 ÷ 2?

  Ⓐ 29   Ⓒ 65
  Ⓑ 55   Ⓓ 91

10. On a scale drawing, a cell phone tower
is 1.25 feet tall. The scale factor is $\frac{1}{150}$.
What is the height of the actual cell
phone tower?

  Ⓐ 37.5 ft   Ⓒ 148 ft
  Ⓑ 120 ft   Ⓓ 187.5 ft

11. A box of trail mix includes 4 ounces
of raisins, 8 ounces of granola, and
2 ounces of sunflower seeds. What is
the ratio of the number of ounces of
granola to ounces of trail mix?

  Ⓐ 1:3   Ⓒ 4:3
  Ⓑ 1:8   Ⓓ 4:7

 If a diagram or graph is not provided,
quickly sketch one to clarify the
information provided in the test item.

Gridded Response

12. The Liberty Bell, a symbol of freedom
in the United States, weighs 2,080
pounds. How many tons does the
Liberty Bell weigh?

13. Find the quotient of −104 ÷ (−8).

14. A grasshopper is $1\frac{3}{4}$ inches long, and
a cricket is $\frac{7}{8}$ inch long. How many
inches longer is the grasshopper than
the cricket?

15. A florist is preparing bouquets of
flowers for an exhibit. The florist has
84 tulips and 56 daisies. Each bouquet
will have the same number of tulips
and the same number of daisies. How
many bouquets can the florist make
for this exhibit?

Short Response

16. Small posters cost $6.50 each, medium
posters cost $10.00 each, and large
posters cost $14.50 each. Write an
algebraic expression that can be used
to determine the cost of s small posters,
m medium posters, and ℓ large posters.
Then evaluate the expression to
determine how much Angel will pay
for 3 small posters, 2 medium posters,
and 1 large poster. Show your work.

17. A lamppost casts a shadow that is 18
feet long. At the same time of day,
Alyce casts a shadow that is 4.2 feet
long. Alyce is 5.3 feet tall. Draw a
picture of the situation. Set up and
solve a proportion to find the height of
the lamppost to the nearest foot. Show
your work.

Extended Response

18. Riley is drawing a map of the state
of Virginia. From east to west, the
greatest distance across the state is
about 430 miles. From north to south,
the greatest distance is about
200 miles.

  a. Riley is using a map scale of 1 inch =
  24 miles. Find the length of the map
  from east to west and the length
  from north to south. Round your
  answers to the nearest tenth.

  b. The length between two cities on
  Riley's map is 9 inches. What is the
  distance between the cities in miles?

  c. If an airplane travels at a speed of
  520 miles per hour, about how
  many minutes will it take for the
  plane to fly from east to west across
  the widest part of Virginia? Show
  your work.

CHAPTER 6

Percents

CONCEPT CONNECTION

go.hrw.com
Chapter Project Online
KEYWORD: MS8CA Ch6

Wind turbines are used to produce electricity. You can use a percent to describe the portion of California's electricity that comes from wind power.

Wind turbines
Tehachapi Mountains

ARE YOU READY?

✓ Vocabulary

Choose the best term from the list to complete each sentence.

1. A statement that two ratios are equivalent is called a(n) __?__.

2. To write $\frac{2}{3}$ as a(n) __?__, divide the numerator by the denominator.

3. A(n) __?__, such as 3:4, is a comparison of two quantities.

4. The __?__ of $\frac{9}{24}$ is $\frac{3}{8}$.

decimal

equation

fraction

proportion

ratio

simplest form

Complete these exercises to review skills you will need for this chapter.

✓ Write Fractions as Decimals

Write each fraction as a decimal.

5. $\frac{8}{10}$ 6. $\frac{53}{100}$ 7. $\frac{739}{1,000}$ 8. $\frac{7}{100}$

9. $\frac{2}{5}$ 10. $\frac{5}{8}$ 11. $\frac{7}{12}$ 12. $\frac{13}{20}$

✓ Write Decimals as Fractions

Write each decimal as a fraction in simplest form.

13. 0.05 14. 0.92 15. 0.013 16. 0.8

17. 0.006 18. 0.305 19. 0.0007 20. 1.04

✓ Solve Equations by Dividing

Solve each equation.

21. $100n = 300$ 22. $38 = 0.4x$ 23. $16p = 1,200$

24. $9 = 72y$ 25. $0.07m = 56$ 26. $25 = 100t$

✓ Solve Proportions

Solve each proportion.

27. $\frac{2}{3} = \frac{x}{12}$ 28. $\frac{x}{20} = \frac{3}{4}$ 29. $\frac{8}{15} = \frac{x}{45}$

30. $\frac{16}{28} = \frac{4}{n}$ 31. $\frac{p}{100} = \frac{12}{36}$ 32. $\frac{42}{12} = \frac{14}{n}$

33. $\frac{8}{y} = \frac{10}{5}$ 34. $\frac{6}{9} = \frac{d}{24}$ 35. $\frac{21}{a} = \frac{7}{5}$

Unpacking the Standards

The information below "unpacks" the standards. The Academic Vocabulary is highlighted and defined to help you understand the language of the standards. Refer to the lessons listed after each standard for help with the math terms and phrases. The Chapter Concept shows how the standard is applied in this chapter.

California Standard	Academic Vocabulary	Chapter Concept
NS1.4 Calculate given percentages of quantities and solve problems involving discounts at sales, interest earned, and tips. (Lessons 6-3, 6-4, 6-5, 6-6, 6-7) (Lab 6-4)	**quantity** an amount **discount** a decrease in the usual price of an item *Example:* If a pair of jeans is on sale for $5.00 off, the amount of discount is $5.00. **tip** money paid for a service in addition to the amount of a bill *Example:* Servers in restaurants often receive a tip of 15% of the cost of a meal.	You find a percent of a number to help you solve many types of problems. *Example:* Find 25% of 60. 25% is equal to $\frac{1}{4}$, so find $\frac{1}{4}$ of 60. $\frac{1}{4} \cdot 60 = \frac{60}{4} = 15$ 25% of 60 is 15.
NS1.3 Use proportions to solve problems (e.g., determine the value of N if $\frac{4}{7} = \frac{N}{21}$, find the length of a side of a polygon similar to a known polygon). **Use cross-multiplication as a method for solving such problems,** understanding it as the multiplication of both sides of an equation by a multiplicative inverse. (Lessons 6-4, 6-5)	**determine** find **method** a way of doing something	You write proportions and use them to solve problems involving percents. *Example:* Find 30% of 80. $\frac{30}{100} = \frac{n}{80}$ $30 \cdot 80 = 100 \cdot n$ $2{,}400 = 100n$ $24 = n$ 30% of 80 is 24.
AF1.1 Write and solve one-step linear equations in one variable. (Lessons 6-5, 6-7)	**solve** find the value or values of an unknown quantity that make one side of an equation equal to the other side (that make the equation true) *Example:* $2 \cdot \square = 6$ $2 \cdot 3 = 6$ **one-step** describes an equation that can be solved using one operation *Example:* $x + 2 = 6$ is a one-step equation because it can be solved by using one operation—subtraction.	You write equations and use them to solve problems involving percents.

Standards NS2.1 and NS2.4 are also covered in this chapter. To see these standards unpacked, go to Chapter 3, p. 126 (NS2.4), and Chapter 4, p. 168 (NS2.1).

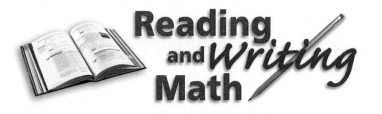

Reading and Writing Math

Study Strategy: Use Multiple Representations

When a new math concept is introduced, the explanation given often presents the topic in more than one way. As you study, pay attention to any models, tables, lists, graphs, diagrams, symbols, and words used to describe a concept.

In this example, the concept of finding equivalent fractions is represented in model, number, and word form.

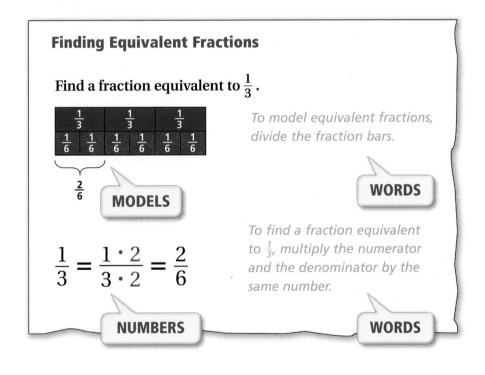

Finding Equivalent Fractions

Find a fraction equivalent to $\frac{1}{3}$.

$\frac{1}{3}$	$\frac{1}{3}$	$\frac{1}{3}$
$\frac{1}{6}$ $\frac{1}{6}$	$\frac{1}{6}$ $\frac{1}{6}$	$\frac{1}{6}$ $\frac{1}{6}$

$\frac{2}{6}$

MODELS

To model equivalent fractions, divide the fraction bars.

WORDS

$$\frac{1}{3} = \frac{1 \cdot 2}{3 \cdot 2} = \frac{2}{6}$$

To find a fraction equivalent to $\frac{1}{3}$, multiply the numerator and the denominator by the same number.

NUMBERS

WORDS

Try This

1. Explain why it could be beneficial to represent a new idea in more than one way when taking notes.

2. Explain how you can use models and numbers to find equivalent fractions. Which method do you prefer? Explain.

Introduction to Percents

California Standards

Preparation for ➤ **NS1.4**
Calculate given percentages of **quantities** and solve problems involving discounts at sales, interest earned, and tips.
Also covered: ➤ **NS2.4**

Vocabulary
percent

Why learn this? You can use percents to describe how much land is covered by rain forests.

Rain forests cover less than 6 out of every 100 square miles of Earth's land. You can write this ratio, 6 to 100, as a *percent*, 6%.

A **percent** is a ratio of a number to 100. The symbol % is used to indicate a percent.

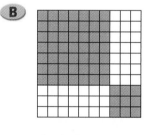

$$\frac{6}{100} = 6\%$$

EXAMPLE 1 **Modeling Percents**

Write the percent modeled by each grid.

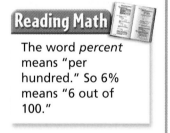

A

$\dfrac{\text{shaded}}{\text{total}} \longrightarrow \dfrac{47}{100} = 47\%$

B

$\dfrac{\text{shaded}}{\text{total}} \longrightarrow \dfrac{49 + 9}{100} = \dfrac{58}{100} = 58\%$

You can write percents as fractions or decimals.

EXAMPLE 2 **Writing Percents as Fractions**

Write 35% as a fraction in simplest form.

$35\% = \dfrac{35}{100}$ *Write the percent as a fraction with a denominator of 100.*

$\quad = \dfrac{7}{20}$ *Simplify.*

So 35% can be written as $\dfrac{7}{20}$.

EXAMPLE 3 **Writing Percents as Decimals**

Write 43% as a decimal.

Method 1: Use pencil and paper.	Method 2: Use mental math.

$43\% = \dfrac{43}{100}$ *Write the percent as a fraction.*

$\underset{\frown}{43.}\% = 0.43$ *Move the decimal point two places to the left.*

$= 0.43$ *Divide 43 by 100.*

Think and Discuss

1. Tell in your own words what *percent* means.

2. Explain how to write 5% as a decimal.

6-1 Exercises

California Standards Practice
Preparation for ← NS1.4;
← NS1.3, ← NS2.4

go.hrw.com
Homework Help Online
KEYWORD: MS8CA 6-1
Parent Resources Online
KEYWORD: MS8CA Parent

GUIDED PRACTICE

See Example 1 Write the percent modeled by each grid.

1. **2.** **3.**

See Example 2 Write each percent as a fraction in simplest form.

4. 65%   **5.** 82%   **6.** 12%   **7.** 38%   **8.** 75%

See Example 3 Write each percent as a decimal.

9. 22%   **10.** 51%   **11.** 8.07%   **12.** 1.6%   **13.** 11%

INDEPENDENT PRACTICE

Write the percent modeled by each grid.

See Example 1   **14.**   **15.**   **16.**

See Example 2 **Write each percent as a fraction in simplest form.**

17. 55% **18.** 34% **19.** 83% **20.** 53% **21.** 81%

See Example 3 **Write each percent as a decimal.**

22. 48% **23.** 9.8% **24.** 30.2% **25.** 66.3% **26.** 8.39%

PRACTICE AND PROBLEM SOLVING

Extra Practice
See page EP12. **Write each percent as a fraction in simplest form and as a decimal.**

27. 2.70% **28.** 7.6% **29.** 44% **30.** 3.148% **31.** 10.5%

Compare. Write <, >, or =.

32. $\frac{18}{100}$ ▨ 22% **33.** $\frac{35}{52}$ ▨ 72% **34.** $\frac{10}{50}$ ▨ 22% **35.** $\frac{11}{20}$ ▨ 56%

36. 41% ▨ $\frac{13}{30}$ **37.** $\frac{17}{20}$ ▨ 85% **38.** $\frac{3}{5}$ ▨ 60% **39.** 15% ▨ $\frac{4}{30}$

40. Multi-Step A nutrition label states that one serving of tortilla chips contains 7 grams of fat and 11% of the recommended daily allowance (RDA) of fat.

   a. Write a ratio that represents the percent RDA of fat in one serving of tortilla chips.

   b. Use the ratio from part **a** to write and solve a proportion to determine how many grams of fat are in the recommended daily allowance.

41. Choose a Strategy During class, Brad finished 63% of his homework, and Liz completed $\frac{5}{7}$ of her homework. Who must finish a greater percent of homework at home?

42. Write About It Compare ratios and percents. How are they alike? How are they different?

43. Challenge Write each of the following as a percent: 0.4 and 0.03.

SPIRAL STANDARDS REVIEW

NS1.3, Prep for NS1.4, NS2.1

44. Multiple Choice Which inequality is a true statement?

  Ⓐ 24% > $\frac{1}{4}$ Ⓑ 0.76 < 76%   Ⓒ 8% < 0.8   Ⓓ $\frac{1}{5}$ < 5%

45. Short Response Nineteen out of the 25 students on Sean's team sold mugs, and 68% of the students on Chi's team sold caps. Which team had a greater percent of students participate in the fundraiser?

Add or subtract. (Lessons 4-2 and 4-3)

46. $\frac{7}{8} - \frac{3}{7}$ **47.** $6\frac{1}{10} + 5\frac{7}{9}$ **48.** $5\frac{2}{3} - \frac{3}{4}$ **49.** $\frac{5}{12} + 2\frac{4}{5}$

Solve each proportion. (Lesson 5-4)

50. $\frac{a}{8} = \frac{27}{12}$ **51.** $\frac{28}{91} = \frac{4}{x}$ **52.** $\frac{360}{n} = \frac{30}{12}$ **53.** $\frac{11}{1} = \frac{m}{9}$

Fractions, Decimals, and Percents

California Standards

Preparation for ◄— NS1.4
Calculate given percentages of quantities and solve problems involving discounts at sales, interest earned, and tips.

Why learn this? You can use a fraction, a decimal, or a percent to describe how much of a goal has been reached.

A group of students plan to collect 2,000 cans of food for a food bank. After 10 days, they have 800 cans of food.

The models show that 800 out of 2,000 can be written as $\frac{800}{2,000}$, $\frac{2}{5}$, 0.4, or 40%. The students have reached 40% of their goal.

EXAMPLE 1 **Writing Decimals as Percents**

Write 0.2 as a percent.

Method 1: Use pencil and paper.	Method 2: Use mental math.
$0.2 = \frac{2}{10} = \frac{20}{100}$ *Write the decimal as a fraction with a denominator of 100.*	$0.20 = 20.0\%$ *Move the decimal point two places to the right and add a percent sign.*
$= 20\%$ *Write the numerator with a percent sign.*	$= 20\%$

EXAMPLE 2 **Writing Fractions as Percents**

Write $\frac{4}{5}$ as a percent.

Remember!

To divide 4 by 5, use long division and place a decimal point followed by a zero after the 4.

$$\begin{array}{r} 0.8 \\ 5\overline{)4.0} \end{array}$$

Method 1: Use pencil and paper.	Method 2: Use mental math.
$\frac{4}{5} = 4 \div 5$ *Use division to write the fraction as a decimal.*	$\frac{4 \cdot 20}{5 \cdot 20} = \frac{80}{100}$ *Write an equivalent fraction with a denominator of 100.*
$= 0.8$	
$= 0.80$ *Write the decimal as a percent.*	$= 80\%$ *Write the numerator with a percent sign.*
$= 80\%$	

EXAMPLE 3 **Data Analysis Application**

Reasoning

In a survey, 55 people were asked whether they prefer cats or dogs. Twenty-nine people said they prefer cats. To the nearest tenth of a percent, what percent of the people surveyed said they prefer cats?

29 out of 55 $= \frac{29}{55}$ *Set up a ratio.*

$= 29 \div 55$ *Use division to write the fraction as a decimal.*

$= 0.5272...$

$= 52.72...\%$ *Write the decimal as a percent.*

$\approx 52.7\%$ *Round to the nearest tenth of a percent.*

About 52.7% of the people surveyed said they prefer cats.

Check Use estimation to check that the answer is reasonable.

$\frac{29}{55} \approx \frac{25}{50} \approx \frac{1}{2}$, or 50%

Because 50% is close to 52.7%, the answer is reasonable.

Think and Discuss

1. **Describe** two methods you could use to write $\frac{3}{4}$ as a percent.

2. **Write** the ratio 25:100 as a fraction, as a decimal, and as a percent.

6-2 Exercises

California Standards Practice
Preparation for ⟵ NS1.4; NS2.1

go.hrw.com
Homework Help Online
KEYWORD: MS8CA 6-2
Parent Resources Online
KEYWORD: MS8CA Parent

GUIDED PRACTICE

See Example 1   Write each decimal as a percent.

1. 0.6   **2.** 0.32   **3.** 0.544   **4.** 0.06   **5.** 0.087

See Example 2   Write each fraction as a percent.

6. $\frac{1}{4}$ **7.** $\frac{3}{25}$ **8.** $\frac{11}{20}$ **9.** $\frac{7}{40}$ **10.** $\frac{5}{8}$

See Example 3   **11.** In a survey, 50 students were asked whether they prefer bananas or apples. Twenty students said they prefer apples. What percent of the students surveyed said they prefer apples?

12. Li correctly answered 34 out of 36 questions on a test. To the nearest percent, what percent of the questions did Li answer correctly?

INDEPENDENT PRACTICE

See Example **1** Write each decimal as a percent.

13. 0.15 **14.** 0.83 **15.** 0.325 **16.** 0.081 **17.** 0.42

See Example **2** Write each fraction as a percent.

18. $\frac{3}{4}$ **19.** $\frac{2}{5}$ **20.** $\frac{3}{8}$ **21.** $\frac{3}{16}$ **22.** $\frac{7}{25}$

See Example **3** **23.** In a theme-park survey, 75 visitors were asked whether they prefer the Ferris wheel or the roller coaster. Thirty visitors prefer the Ferris wheel. What percent of the visitors surveyed said they prefer the Ferris wheel?

24. Jake scored a goal in 5 out of his last 12 soccer games. To the nearest tenth of a percent, in what percent of the games did Jake score a goal?

PRACTICE AND PROBLEM SOLVING

Extra Practice
See page EP12.

Compare. Write <, >, or =.

25. 45% ▨ $\frac{2}{5}$ **26.** 9% ▨ 0.9 **27.** $\frac{7}{12}$ ▨ 60% **28.** 0.037 ▨ 37%

29. **Reasoning** One-half of the 900 students at Jefferson Middle School are boys. One-tenth of the boys are in the band, and one-fifth of those play the trumpet. What percent of the students at Jefferson are boys who play the trumpet in the band?

30. **Science** Rain forests are home to 90,000 of the 250,000 identified plant species in the world. What percent of the world's identified plant species are found in rain forests?

31. **What's the Error?** A student wrote $\frac{2}{5}$ as 0.4%. What was the error?

32. **Write About It** Describe two ways to change a fraction to a percent.

33. **Challenge** A desert area's average rainfall is 12 inches a year. This year the area received 15 inches of rain. What percent of the average rainfall amount is 15 inches?

SPIRAL STANDARDS REVIEW ◆— NS1.3, Prep for ◆— NS1.4, NS2.1, NS2.2, ◆— NS2.4

34. **Multiple Choice** Which value is NOT equivalent to 45%?

Ⓐ $\frac{9}{20}$ Ⓑ 0.45 Ⓒ $\frac{45}{100}$ Ⓓ 0.045

35. **Short Response** Melanie's room measures 10 ft by 12 ft. Her rug covers 90 ft². Explain how to determine the percent of floor covered by the rug.

Multiply or divide. Write each answer in simplest form. (Lessons 4-4 and 4-5)

36. $9\frac{3}{4} \cdot 2\frac{1}{2}$ **37.** $\frac{9}{10} \div \frac{2}{5}$ **38.** $\frac{4}{5} \cdot 5\frac{1}{4}$ **39.** $3\frac{2}{3} \div 33$

40. The actual length of a room is 6 m. The scale factor of a model is 1:15. What is the length of the room in the model? (Lesson 5-8)

6-3 Estimating with Percents

California Standards

NS1.4 Calculate given percentages of quantities and solve problems involving **discounts at sales,** interest earned, and **tips.**

Also covered: **NS2.1**

Why learn this? You can estimate with percents to determine the best deal on a hair dryer.

The table shows common percents and their fraction equivalents. You can estimate a percent of a number by substituting a fraction that is close to a given percent.

Percent	10%	20%	25%	$33\frac{1}{3}$%	50%	$66\frac{2}{3}$%
Fraction	$\frac{1}{10}$	$\frac{1}{5}$	$\frac{1}{4}$	$\frac{1}{3}$	$\frac{1}{2}$	$\frac{2}{3}$

EXAMPLE 1 Using Fractions to Estimate Percents

Use a fraction to estimate 48% of 79.

$48\% \text{ of } 79 \approx \frac{1}{2} \cdot 79$ *Think: 48% is about 50% and 50% is equivalent to $\frac{1}{2}$.*

$\approx \frac{1}{2} \cdot 80$ *Change 79 to a compatible number.*

≈ 40 *Multiply.*

48% of 79 is about 40.

Remember!

Compatible numbers are close to the numbers in a problem and help you use mental math.

See Skills Bank, p. SB10.

You can estimate sale prices by substituting a fraction for a percent of discount.

EXAMPLE 2 *Consumer Math Application*

Carissa's Corner is offering 20% off a hair dryer that costs $19.99. The same hair dryer costs $14.99 at Hair Haven. Which store offers the better deal?

First find the discount on the hair dryer at Carissa's Corner.

$20\% \text{ of } \$19.99 = \frac{1}{5} \cdot \$19.99$ *Think: 20% is equivalent to $\frac{1}{5}$.*

$\approx \frac{1}{5} \cdot \$20$ *Change $19.99 to a compatible number.*

$\approx \$4$ *Multiply.*

The discount is approximately $4. Since $20 − $4 = $16, the $14.99 hair dryer at Hair Haven is the better deal.

Another way to estimate percents is to find 1% or 10% of a number. You can do this by moving the decimal point in the number.

1% of 45 = 45.0

= 0.45

To find 1% of a number, move the decimal point two places to the left.

10% of 45 = 45.0

= 4.5

To find 10% of a number, move the decimal point one place to the left.

EXAMPLE 3 Estimating with Simple Percents

Use 1% or 10% to estimate the percent of each number.

A **3% of 59**

59 is about 60, so find 3% of 60.

1% of 60 = 60.0

3% of 60 = 3 · 0.60 = 1.8   *3% equals 3 · 1%.*

3% of 59 is about 1.8.

B **18% of 45**

18% is about 20%, so find 20% of 45.

10% of 45 = 45.0

20% of 45 = 2 · 4.5 = 9.0   *20% equals 2 · 10%.*

18% of 45 is about 9.

EXAMPLE 4 Consumer Math Application

Reasoning

Eric and Selena spent $25.85 for their meals at a restaurant. About how much money should they leave for a 15% tip?

Since $25.85 is about $26, find 15% of $26.

15% = 10% + 5%   *Think: 15% is 10% plus 5%.*

10% of $26 = $2.60

5% of $26 = $2.60 ÷ 2 = $1.30   *5% is $\frac{1}{2}$ of 10%, so divide $2.60 by 2.*

$2.60 + $1.30 = $3.90   *Add the 10% and 5% estimates.*

Eric and Selena should leave about $3.90 for a 15% tip.

Think and Discuss

1. Describe two ways to estimate 51% of 88.

2. Explain why you might divide by 7 or multiply by $\frac{1}{7}$ to estimate a 15% tip.

3. Give an example of a situation in which an estimate of a percent is sufficient and a situation in which an exact percent is necessary.

6-3 **Exercises**

California Standards Practice
NS1.4, NS2.1

go.hrw.com
Homework Help Online
KEYWORD: MS8CA 6-3
Parent Resources Online
KEYWORD: MS8CA Parent

GUIDED PRACTICE

See Example 1 Use a fraction to estimate the percent of each number.

1. 30% of 86　　**2.** 52% of 83　　**3.** 10% of 48　　**4.** 27% of 63

See Example 2 **5.** Darden has $35 to spend on a backpack. He finds one on sale for 35% off the regular price of $43.99. Does Darden have enough money to buy the backpack? Explain.

See Example 3 Use 1% or 10% to estimate the percent of each number.

6. 5% of 82　　**7.** 39% of 19　　**8.** 21% of 68　　**9.** 7% of 109

See Example 4 **10.** Mrs. Coronado spent $23 on a manicure. About how much money should she leave for a 15% tip?

INDEPENDENT PRACTICE

See Example 1 Use a fraction to estimate the percent of each number.

11. 8% of 261　　**12.** 34% of 93　　**13.** 53% of 142　　**14.** 23% of 98

15. 51% of 432　　**16.** 18% of 42　　**17.** 11% of 132　　**18.** 54% of 39

See Example 2 **19. Consumer Math** A pair of shoes at The Value Store costs $20. Fancy Feet has the same shoes on sale for 25% off the regular price of $23.99. Which store offers the better price on the shoes?

See Example 3 Use 1% or 10% to estimate the percent of each number.

20. 41% of 16　　**21.** 8% of 310　　**22.** 83% of 70　　**23.** 2% of 634

24. 58% of 81　　**25.** 24% of 49　　**26.** 11% of 99　　**27.** 63% of 39

See Example 4 **28.** Marc's lunch cost $8.92. He wants to leave a 15% tip for the service. About how much should his tip be?

PRACTICE AND PROBLEM SOLVING

Extra Practice
See page EP12.

Estimate.

29. 31% of 180　　**30.** 18% of 150　　**31.** 3% of 96　　**32.** 2% of 198

33. 78% of 90　　**34.** 52% of 234　　**35.** 19% of 75　　**36.** 4% of 311

37. The new package of Marti's Snacks contains 20% more snack mix than the old package. There were 22 ounces of snack mix in the old package. About how many ounces are in the new package?

38. Frameworks charges $60.85 for framing. Including the 7% sales tax, about how much will it cost to have a painting framed?

39. Multi-Step Camden's lunch cost $11.67, and he left a $2.00 tip. About how much more than 15% of the bill did Camden leave for the tip?

40. Sports Last season, Ali had a hit 19.3% of the times he came to bat. If Ali batted 82 times last season, about how many hits did he have?

41. Business The table shows the results of a survey about the Internet. The number of people interviewed was 391.

Information People Are Willing to Give Out on the Internet	
Information	**Percent of People**
E-mail address	78
Work phone number	53
Street address	49
Home phone number	35
Credit card number	33
Social Security number	11

   a. Estimate the number of people willing to give out their e-mail address.

   b. Estimate the number of people not willing to give out their credit card number.

42. Multi-Step Sandi earns $43,000 per year. This year, she plans to spend about 27% of her income on rent.

   a. About how much does Sandi plan to spend on rent this year?

   b. About how much does she plan to spend on rent each month?

43. Reasoning Use information from the table in Exercise 41 to write a problem that can be solved by using estimation of a percent.

44. Write About It Explain why it might be important to know whether your estimate of a percent is too high or too low. Give an example.

45. Challenge Use the table from Exercise 41 to estimate how many more people will give out their work phone number than their Social Security number. Show your work using two different methods.

SPIRAL STANDARDS REVIEW ← NS1.3, ← NS1.4, ← NS2.3

46. Multiple Choice About 65% of the people answering a survey said that they have read a "blog," or Web log, online. Sixty-six people were surveyed. Which is the best estimate of the number of people surveyed who have read a blog?

   Ⓐ 30   Ⓑ 35   Ⓒ 45   Ⓓ 50

47. Short Response Ryan's dinner bill is $35.00. He wants to leave a 15% tip. Explain how to use mental math to determine how much he should leave as a tip.

Find each product. (Lesson 2-4)

48. $-6 \cdot 31$ **49.** $14 \cdot (-4)$ **50.** $-9 \cdot (-7)$ **51.** $-5 \cdot 24$

52. Brandi's room was painted in a color that is a blend of 3 parts red paint and 2 parts white paint. How many quarts of white paint does Brandi need to mix with 6 quarts of red paint to match the paint in her room? (Lesson 5-4)

Explore Percents

go.hrw.com
Lab Resources Online
KEYWORD: MS8CA Lab6

California Standards

➤ **NS1.4** Calculate given **percentages of quantities** and solve problems involving discounts at sales, interest earned, and tips.

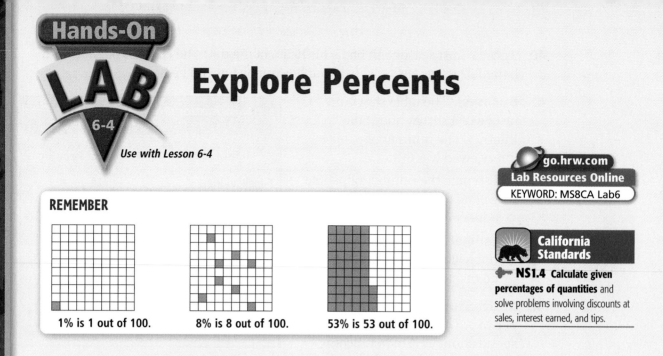

REMEMBER

1% is 1 out of 100.   8% is 8 out of 100.   53% is 53 out of 100.

You can use 10-by-10 grids to model percents, including those less than 1 or greater than 100.

Activity 1

1 Use 10-by-10 grids to model 132%.

Think: 132% means 132 out of 100.

Shade 100 squares plus 32 squares to model 132%.

2 Use a 10-by-10 grid to model 0.5%.

Think: One square equals 1%, so $\frac{1}{2}$ of one square equals 0.5%.

Shade $\frac{1}{2}$ of one square to model 0.5%.

Think and Discuss

1. Explain how to model 36.75% on a 10-by-10 grid.

2. How can you model 0.7%? Explain your answer.

Try This

Use 10-by-10 grids to model each percent.

1. 280%   **2.** $16\frac{1}{2}$%   **3.** 0.25%   **4.** 65%   **5.** 140.75%

You can use a percent bar and a quantity bar to model finding a percent of a number.

Activity 2

1 Find 65% of 60.

Percent bar

| 0 | 10 | 20 | 30 | 40 | 50 | 60 | 70 | 80 | 90 | 100% |

Divide the percent bar into 10 equal parts, and label it as shown.

Quantity bar

0 60

Think: 100% of 60 is 60, the total quantity. Label 60 equal to 100% on the quantity bar.

Quantity bar

0 .... 30 60

Divide the quantity bar in half and label the midpoint.

Quantity bar

0 ...... 15 ...... 30 ...... 45 60

Divide each half in half.

Quantity bar

0 .. 7.5 .. 15 .. 22.5 .. 30 .. 37.5 .. 45 .. 52.5 .. 60

What point on the quantity bar lines up with 65% on the percent bar?
It appears that 65% of 60 is about 39.   *Check by multiplying: 0.65 · 60 = 39.*

2 Find 125% of 60.   *Think: 125% of a whole is greater than the whole.*
   Extend the bars to find 125% of a number.   *Since the whole is 60, line up 60 with 100%.*

Percent bar

| 0 | 10 | 20 | 30 | 40 | 50 | 60 | 70 | 80 | 90 | 100 | 110 | 120 | 130 | 140 | 150% |

Quantity bar

0 .. 7.5 .. 15 .. 22.5 .. 30 .. 37.5 .. 45 .. 52.5 .. 60 .. 67.5 .. 75 .. 82.5 .. 90

What point on the quantity bar lines up with 125% on the percent bar?
It appears that 125% of 60 is about 75.   *Check by multiplying 1.25 · 60 = 75.*

Think and Discuss

1. Explain how to use a percent bar and a quantity bar to find a percent of a number.

2. Explain how using a percent bar and a quantity bar to model finding a percent of a number involves estimation.

Try This

Use a percent bar and a quantity bar to find the percent of each number. Use a calculator to check your answers.

1. 75% of 36   **2.** 60% of 15   **3.** 135% of 40   **4.** 112% of 25   **5.** 25% of 75

California Standards

🐾 **NS1.4** Calculate given percentages of quantities and solve problems involving discounts at sales, interest earned, and tips.

Also covered: 🐾 **NS1.3**

Math Builders

For more on proportions, see the Proportion Builder on page MB2.

Why learn this? You can find a percent of a number to determine how many pounds of water a person's body contains.

The human body is made up mostly of water. In fact, about 67% of a person's total (100%) body weight is water. If Cameron weighs 90 pounds, about how much of his weight is water?

Recall that a percent is a part of 100. Since you want to know the part of Cameron's body that is water, you can set up and solve a proportion to find the answer.

$$\text{Part} \rightarrow \frac{67}{100} = \frac{n}{90} \leftarrow \text{Part}$$
$$\text{Whole} \rightarrow \qquad\qquad \leftarrow \text{Whole}$$

In Lesson 5-4, you learned to solve proportions by setting the cross products equal to each other.

E X A M P L E **1** **Using Proportions to Find Percents of Numbers**

Find the percent of each number.

A 67% of 90

$$\frac{67}{100} = \frac{n}{90}$$ *Write a proportion.*

$$67 \cdot 90 = 100 \cdot n$$ *Set the cross products equal.*

$$6{,}030 = 100n$$ *Multiply.*

$$\frac{6{,}030}{100} = \frac{100n}{100}$$ *Divide each side by 100.*

$$60.3 = n$$

67% of 90 is 60.3.

B 145% of 210

$$\frac{145}{100} = \frac{n}{210}$$ *Write a proportion.*

$$145 \cdot 210 = 100 \cdot n$$ *Set the cross products equal.*

$$30{,}450 = 100n$$ *Multiply.*

$$\frac{30{,}450}{100} = \frac{100n}{100}$$ *Divide each side by 100.*

$$304.5 = n$$

145% of 210 is 304.5.

Helpful Hint

When solving a problem with a percent greater than 100%, the *part* will be greater than the *whole*.

In addition to using proportions, you can find a percent of a number by using decimal equivalents.

EXAMPLE **2** Using Decimal Equivalents to Find Percents of Numbers

Reasoning

Find the percent of each number. Check whether your answer is reasonable.

A **8% of 50**

8% of 50 = 0.08 · 50   *Write the percent as a decimal.*
          = 4   *Multiply.*

Check

Since 10% of 50 is 5, a reasonable answer for 8% of 50 is 4.

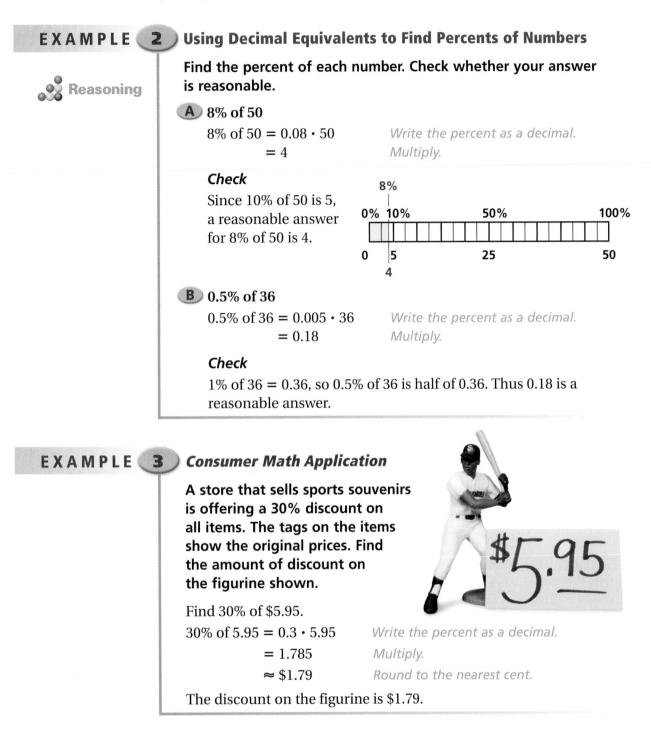

B **0.5% of 36**

0.5% of 36 = 0.005 · 36   *Write the percent as a decimal.*
           = 0.18   *Multiply.*

Check

1% of 36 = 0.36, so 0.5% of 36 is half of 0.36. Thus 0.18 is a reasonable answer.

EXAMPLE **3** *Consumer Math Application*

A store that sells sports souvenirs is offering a 30% discount on all items. The tags on the items show the original prices. Find the amount of discount on the figurine shown.

$5.95

Find 30% of $5.95.

30% of 5.95 = 0.3 · 5.95   *Write the percent as a decimal.*
            = 1.785   *Multiply.*
            ≈ $1.79   *Round to the nearest cent.*

The discount on the figurine is $1.79.

Think and Discuss

1. Explain how to set up a proportion to find 150% of a number.

2. Describe a situation in which you might need to find a percent of a number.

6-4 **Exercises**

California Standards Practice
◆━ NS1.3, ◆━ NS1.4

go.hrw.com
Homework Help Online
KEYWORD: MS8CA 6-4
Parent Resources Online
KEYWORD: MS8CA Parent

GUIDED PRACTICE

See Example ① Find the percent of each number.

1. 30% of 80   **2.** 38% of 400   **3.** 200% of 10   **4.** 180% of 90

See Example ② Find the percent of each number. Check whether your answer is reasonable.

5. 16% of 50   **6.** 7% of 200   **7.** 47% of 900   **8.** 40% of 75

See Example ③ **9.** Ms. Ghosh's meal at a restaurant cost $20.25. She wants to leave a tip that is exactly 16% of the meal's cost. How much of a tip should Ms. Ghosh leave?

INDEPENDENT PRACTICE

See Example ① Find the percent of each number.

10. 80% of 35   **11.** 16% of 70   **12.** 150% of 80   **13.** 118% of 3,000

14. 5% of 58   **15.** 1% of 4   **16.** 103% of 50   **17.** 225% of 8

See Example ② Find the percent of each number. Check whether your answer is reasonable.

18. 9% of 40   **19.** 20% of 65   **20.** 36% of 50   **21.** 2.9% of 60

22. 5% of 12   **23.** 220% of 18   **24.** 0.2% of 160   **25.** 155% of 8

See Example ③ **26.** In 2004, there were 19,396 bulldogs registered by the American Kennel Club. Approximately 86% of this number were registered in 2003. About how many bulldogs were registered in 2003?

PRACTICE AND PROBLEM SOLVING

Extra Practice
See page EP13.

Solve.

27. 60% of 10 is what number?   **28.** What number is 25% of 160?

29. What number is 15% of 30?   **30.** 10% of 84 is what number?

31. 25% of 47 is what number?   **32.** What number is 59% of 20?

33. What number is 125% of 4,100?   **34.** 150% of 150 is what number?

Find the percent of each number. If necessary, round to the nearest tenth.

35. 160% of 50   **36.** 350% of 20   **37.** 480% of 25   **38.** 115% of 200

39. 18% of 3.4   **40.** 0.9% of 43   **41.** 98% of 4.3   **42.** 1.22% of 56

43. Consumer Math Fun Tees is offering a 30% discount on all merchandise. Find the amount of discount on a T-shirt that was originally priced at $15.99.

44. Multi-Step Shoe Style is discounting everything in the store by 25%. What is the sale price of a pair of flip-flops that was originally priced at $10?

45. **Nutrition** The United States Department of Agriculture recommends that women should eat 25 g of fiber each day. A granola bar provides 9% of that amount. How many grams of fiber does it contain?

46. **Metals** The percent of pure gold in 14-karat gold is about 58.3%. A 14-karat gold ring has a mass of 5.6 grams. About how many grams of pure gold are in the ring?

47. **Earth Science** In 2005, wind turbines in the United States could produce 9,149 megawatts of electricity. Wind turbines in California could produce about 23.5% of this amount. About how many megawatts of electricity could the wind turbines in California produce in 2005?

48. **Reasoning** Trahn purchased a pair of slacks for $39.95 and a jacket for $64.00. The sales tax rate on his purchases was 5.5%. Find the total cost of Trahn's purchases, including sales tax.

49. The graph shows the results of a student survey about computers. Use the graph to predict how many students in your class have a computer at home.

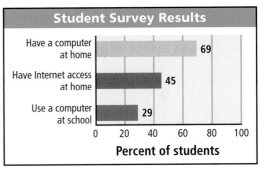

Student Survey Results

Have a computer at home: 69
Have Internet access at home: 45
Use a computer at school: 29

Percent of students

50. **What's the Error?** A student used the proportion $\frac{n}{100} = \frac{5}{26}$ to find 5% of 26. What did the student do wrong?

51. **Write About It** Describe two ways to find 18% of 40.

52. **Challenge** François's starting pay was $6.25 per hour. During his annual review, he received a 5% raise. Find François's pay raise to the nearest cent and the amount he will earn with his raise. Then find 105% of $6.25. What can you conclude?

SPIRAL STANDARDS REVIEW ◆━ NS1.1, ◆━ NS1.3, ◆━ NS1.4

53. **Multiple Choice** Of the 875 students enrolled at Sycamore Valley Middle School, 48% are boys. How many of the students are boys?

(A) 250   (B) 310   (C) 420   (D) 440

54. **Gridded Response** A children's multivitamin has 80% of the recommended daily allowance of zinc. The recommended daily allowance is 15 mg. How many milligrams of zinc does the vitamin provide?

55. Monica buys 3 pounds of peaches for $5.25. What is the cost per pound? (Lesson 5-2)

56. Kevin types 295 words in 5 minutes. At what rate does Kevin type? (Lesson 5-2)

Order the numbers from least to greatest. (Lesson 3-6)

57. $\frac{1}{4}$, 0.2, $-\frac{1}{4}$ 58. -0.8, $-\frac{7}{8}$, -0.9 59. $\frac{7}{8}$, 0.87, $\frac{6}{7}$

6-5 Solving Percent Problems

California Standards

━ **NS1.4** Calculate given percentages of quantities and solve problems involving **discounts at sales,** interest earned, and tips.

Also covered: ━ **NS1.3,** ━ **AF1.1**

Who uses this? Biologists can use proportions or equations to determine what percent of each day an animal sleeps.

Sloths sleep an average of 16.5 hours per day. To find out what percent of a 24-hour day 16.5 hours is, you can use a proportion or an equation.

Proportion method

$$\text{Part} \rightarrow \frac{n}{100} = \frac{16.5}{24} \begin{array}{l} \leftarrow \text{Part} \\ \leftarrow \text{Whole} \end{array}$$

$$\text{Whole} \rightarrow$$

$$n \cdot 24 = 100 \cdot 16.5$$
$$24n = 1{,}650$$
$$n = 68.75$$

Equation method

What percent of 24 is 16.5?

$$\downarrow \quad \downarrow\,\downarrow\,\downarrow\,\downarrow$$

$$n \quad \cdot 24 = 16.5$$
$$n = \frac{16.5}{24}$$
$$n = 0.6875$$

Sloths spend about 69% of the day sleeping!

EXAMPLE **1** **Using Proportions to Solve Problems with Percents**

Solve.

A What percent of 90 is 45?

$$\frac{n}{100} = \frac{45}{90}$$ *Write a proportion.*

$$n \cdot 90 = 100 \cdot 45$$ *Set the cross products equal.*

$$90n = 4{,}500$$ *Multiply.*

$$\frac{90n}{90} = \frac{4{,}500}{90}$$ *Divide each side by 90.*

$$n = 50$$

50% of 90 is 45.

B 12 is 8% of what number?

$$\frac{8}{100} = \frac{12}{n}$$ *Write a proportion.*

$$8 \cdot n = 100 \cdot 12$$ *Set the cross products equal.*

$$8n = 1{,}200$$ *Multiply.*

$$\frac{8n}{8} = \frac{1{,}200}{8}$$ *Divide each side by 8.*

$$n = 150$$

12 is 8% of 150.

EXAMPLE **2** Using Equations to Solve Problems with Percents

Solve.

A What percent of 75 is 105?

$n \cdot 75 = 105$ *Write an equation.*

$\dfrac{n \cdot 75}{75} = \dfrac{105}{75}$ *Divide each side by 75.*

$n = 1.4$

$n = 140\%$ *Write the decimal as a percent.*

140% of 75 is 105.

B 48 is 20% of what number?

$48 = 20\% \cdot n$ *Write an equation.*

$48 = 0.2 \cdot n$ *Write 20% as a decimal.*

$\dfrac{48}{0.2} = \dfrac{0.2 \cdot n}{0.2}$ *Divide each side by 0.2.*

$240 = n$

48 is 20% of 240.

EXAMPLE **3** Finding Sales Tax

Helpful Hint

The *sales tax rate* is the percent used to calculate sales tax.

Ravi bought a T-shirt with a retail sales price of $12 and paid $0.99 sales tax. What is the sales tax rate where Ravi bought the T-shirt?

Restate the question: What percent of $12 is $0.99?

$\dfrac{n}{100} = \dfrac{0.99}{12}$ *Write a proportion.*

$n \cdot 12 = 100 \cdot 0.99$ *Set the cross products equal.*

$12n = 99$ *Multiply.*

$\dfrac{12n}{12} = \dfrac{99}{12}$ *Divide each side by 12.*

$n = 8.25$

8.25% of $12 is $0.99. The sales tax rate where Ravi bought the T-shirt is 8.25%.

Think and Discuss

1. Describe two methods for solving percent problems.

2. Explain whether you prefer to use the proportion method or the equation method when solving percent problems.

3. Tell what the first step is in solving a sales tax problem.

6-5 **Exercises**

California
Standards Practice
🔑 NS1.4

go.hrw.com
Homework Help Online
KEYWORD: MS8CA 6-5
Parent Resources Online
KEYWORD: MS8CA Parent

GUIDED PRACTICE

Solve.

See Example **1**
1. What percent of 100 is 25?
2. What percent of 5 is 4?
3. 6 is 10% of what number?
4. 8 is 20% of what number?

See Example **2**
5. What percent of 50 is 9?
6. What percent of 30 is 27?
7. 7 is 14% of what number?
8. 30 is 15% of what number?

See Example **3**
9. The sales tax on a $120 skateboard at Surf 'n' Skate is $9.60. What is the sales tax rate?

INDEPENDENT PRACTICE

Solve.

See Example **1**
10. What percent of 60 is 40?
11. What percent of 48 is 16?
12. What percent of 45 is 9?
13. What percent of 6 is 18?
14. 56 is 140% of what number?
15. 45 is 20% of what number?

See Example **2**
16. What percent of 80 is 10?
17. What percent of 12.4 is 12.4?
18. 18 is 15% of what number?
19. 9 is 30% of what number?
20. 210% of what number is 147?
21. 8.8 is 40% of what number?

See Example **3**
22. A pack of 12 cinnamon-scented pencils sells for $3.00 at a school booster club sale. What is the sales tax rate if the total cost of the pencils is $3.21?

PRACTICE AND PROBLEM SOLVING

Extra Practice
See page EP13.

Solve. Round to the nearest tenth, if necessary.
23. 5 is what percent of 9?
24. What is 45% of 39?
25. 55 is 80% of what number?
26. 12 is what percent of 19?
27. What is 155% of 50?
28. 5.8 is 0.9% of what number?
29. 36% of what number is 57?
30. What percent of 64 is 40?

31. **Multi-Step** The advertised cost of admission to a water park in a nearby city is $25 per student. A student paid $30 for admission and received $3.75 in change. What is the sales tax rate in that city?

32. **Consumer Math** The table shows the cost of sunscreen purchased in Beach City and Desert City with and without sales tax. Which city has a greater sales tax rate? Give the sales tax rate for each city.

	Cost	Cost + Tax
Beach City	$10	$10.83
Desert City	$5	$5.42

33. Reasoning What number is always used when you set up a proportion to solve a percent problem? Explain.

34. Health The circle graph shows the approximate distribution of blood types among people in the United States.

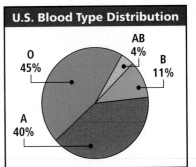

U.S. Blood Type Distribution

a. In a survey, 126 people had type O blood. Predict how many people were surveyed.

b. How many of the people surveyed had type AB blood?

35. Music Beethoven wrote 9 trios for the piano, violin, and cello. These trios make up 20% of the chamber music pieces Beethoven wrote. How many pieces of chamber music did he write?

36. Consumer Math A pair of jeans that regularly cost $25.50 are on sale for $5.10 off the regular price. What is the percent of discount on the jeans?

37. What's the Question? The first lap of an auto race is 2,500 m. This is 10% of the total race distance. The answer is 10. What is the question?

38. Write About It If 35 is 110% of a number, is the number greater than or less than 35? Explain.

39. Challenge Kayleen has been offered two jobs. The first job offers an annual salary of $32,000. The second job offers an annual salary of $10,000 plus 8% commission on all of her sales. How much money per year would Kayleen need to make in sales to earn enough commission to make more money at the second job?

SPIRAL STANDARDS REVIEW   ◆— NS1.4, NS2.1, NS2.2, ◆— AF1.1

40. Multiple Choice Thirty children from an after-school club went to the matinee. This is 20% of the children in the club. How many children are in the club?

Ⓐ 6 　　　　　 Ⓑ 67 　　　　　 Ⓒ 150 　　　　　 Ⓓ 600

41. Gridded Response Jason saves 30% of his monthly paycheck for college. He earned $250 last month. How many dollars did he save for college?

Solve. Write each answer in simplest form. (Lesson 4-6)

42. $\frac{2}{5}x = 2\frac{1}{2}$ 　　　　 **43.** $m - \frac{1}{3} = \frac{5}{8}$ 　　　　 **44.** $\frac{3}{4} = y + \frac{1}{10}$ 　　　　 **45.** $\frac{1}{5}n = \frac{7}{10}$

Find the percent of each number. If necessary, round to the nearest hundredth.
(Lesson 6-4)

46. 45% of 26 　　　 **47.** 22% of 30 　　　 **48.** 15% of 17 　　　 **49.** 68% of 98

READY TO GO ON?

Quiz for Lessons 6-1 Through 6-5

6-1 Introduction to Percents

Write each percent as a fraction in simplest form.

1. 9%   **2.** 43%   **3.** 5%   **4.** 18%

Write each percent as a decimal.

5. 22%   **6.** 90%   **7.** 29%   **8.** 5%

6-2 Fractions, Decimals, and Percents

Write each decimal as a percent.

9. 0.85   **10.** 0.026   **11.** 0.1111   **12.** 0.56

Write each fraction as a percent. Round to the nearest tenth of a percent, if necessary.

13. $\frac{8}{25}$ **14.** $\frac{11}{20}$ **15.** $\frac{55}{78}$ **16.** $\frac{13}{32}$

6-3 Estimating with Percents

Estimate.

17. 49% of 46   **18.** 9% of 25   **19.** 36% of 150   **20.** 5% of 60
21. 18% of 80   **22.** 26% of 115   **23.** 91% of 300   **24.** 42% of 197

25. Carlton spent $21.85 on lunch for himself and a friend. About how much should he leave for a 15% tip?

6-4 Percent of a Number

Find the percent of each number.

26. 25% of 84   **27.** 52% of 300   **28.** 0.5% of 40   **29.** 160% of 450
30. 41% of 122   **31.** 178% of 35   **32.** 29% of 88   **33.** 80% of 176

34. Students get a 15% discount off the original prices at the Everything Fluorescent store during its back-to-school sale. Find the amount of discount on fluorescent notebooks originally priced at $7.99.

6-5 Solving Percent Problems

Solve. Round to the nearest tenth, if necessary.

35. 14 is 44% of what number?   **36.** 22 is what percent of 900?

37. 99 is what percent of 396?   **38.** 75 is 24% of what number?

39. The sales tax on a $105 digital camera is $7.15. What is the sales tax rate?

Focus on Problem Solving

California Standards

MR2.6 Indicate the relative advantages of exact and approximate solutions to problems and give answers to a specified degree of accuracy.
Also covered: ← **NS1.4, MR2.4**

Plan

Make a Plan

- **Estimate or find an exact answer**

Sometimes an estimate is sufficient when you are solving a problem. Other times you need to find an exact answer. Before you try to solve a problem, you should decide whether an estimate will be sufficient. Usually if a problem includes the word *about*, then you can estimate the answer.

Read each problem. Decide whether you need an exact answer or whether you can solve the problem with an estimate. Explain how you know.

1. Barry has $21.50 left from his allowance. He wants to buy a book for $5.85 and a CD for $14.99. Assuming these prices include tax, does Barry have enough money left to buy both the book and the CD?

2. Last weekend Valerie practiced playing the drums for 3 hours. This is 40% of the total time she spent practicing last week. How much time did Valerie spend practicing last week?

3. Amber is shopping for a winter coat. She finds one that costs $157. The coat is on sale and is discounted 25% today only. About how much money will Amber save if she buys the coat today?

4. Marcus is planning a budget. He plans to spend less than 35% of his allowance each week on entertainment. Last week Marcus spent $7.42 on entertainment. If Marcus gets $20.00 each week, did he stay within his budget?

5. An upright piano is on sale for 20% off the original price. The original price is $9,840. What is the sale price?

6. The Mapleton Middle School band has 41 students. Six of the students in the band play percussion instruments. Do more than 15% of the students play percussion instruments?

6-6 Percent of Change

California Standards

🔑 **NS1.4** Calculate given percentages of quantities and solve problems involving **discounts at sales,** interest earned, and tips.

Vocabulary

percent of change
percent of increase
percent of decrease

Who uses this? Safety experts can use percents of change to determine trends in numbers of injuries.

The U.S. Consumer Product Safety Commission has reported that, in 2000, 4,390 injuries related to motorized scooters were treated in hospital emergency rooms. This was a 230% increase from 1999's report of 1,330 injuries.

A percent can be used to describe an amount of change. The **percent of change** is the amount, stated as a percent, that a number increases or decreases. If the amount goes up, it is a **percent of increase**. If the amount goes down, it is a **percent of decrease**.

You can find the percent of change by using the following formula.

$$\textbf{percent of change} = \frac{\textbf{amount of change}}{\textbf{original amount}}$$

EXAMPLE 1 **Finding Percent of Change**

Reasoning

Find each percent of change. Round answers to the nearest tenth of a percent, if necessary.

A **27 is decreased to 20.**

$27 - 20 = 7$	*Find the amount of change.*
percent of change $= \frac{7}{27}$	*Substitute values into formula.*
≈ 0.259259	*Divide.*
$\approx 25.9\%$	*Write as a percent. Round.*

The percent of decrease is about 25.9%.

B **32 is increased to 67.**

$67 - 32 = 35$	*Find the amount of change.*
percent of change $= \frac{35}{32}$	*Substitute values into formula.*
$= 1.09375$	*Divide.*
$\approx 109.4\%$	*Write as a percent. Round.*

The percent of increase is about 109.4%.

EXAMPLE **2** **Using Percent of Change**

Reasoning

The regular price of an MP3 player at TechSource is $79.99. This week the MP3 player is on sale for 25% off. What is the sale price?

Step 1: Find the amount of the discount.

$25\% \cdot 79.99 = d$	*Think: 25% of $79.99 is what number?*
$0.25 \cdot 79.99 = d$	*Write the percent as a decimal.*
$19.9975 = d$	
$\$20.00 \approx d$	*Round to the nearest cent.*

The amount of the discount is $20.00.

Step 2: Find the sale price.

regular price	−	amount of discount	=	sale price
$79.99	−	$20.00	=	$59.99

The sale price is $59.99.

EXAMPLE **3** *Business Application*

Reasoning

Winter Wonders buys snow globes from a manufacturer for $9.20 each and sells them at a 95% increase in price. What is the retail price of the snow globes?

Step 1: Find the amount n of increase.

Think: 95% of $9.20 is what number?

$95\% \cdot 9.20 = n$

$0.95 \cdot 9.20 = n$ *Write the percent as a decimal.*

$8.74 = n$

Step 2: Find the retail price.

wholesale price	+	amount of increase	=	retail price
$9.20	+	$8.74	=	$17.94

The retail price of the snow globes is $17.94 each.

Think and Discuss

1. Explain what is meant by a 100% decrease.

2. Give an example in which the amount of increase is greater than the original amount. What do you know about the percent of increase?

California Standards Practice

🔑 NS1.4

go.hrw.com
Homework Help Online
KEYWORD: MS8CA 6-6
Parent Resources Online
KEYWORD: MS8CA Parent

GUIDED PRACTICE

See Example ① **Find each percent of change. Round answers to the nearest tenth of a percent, if necessary.**

1. 25 is decreased to 18.

2. 36 is increased to 84.

3. 62 is decreased to 52.

4. 28 is increased to 96.

See Example ② **5.** The regular price of a sweater is $42.99. It is on sale for 20% off. Find the sale price.

See Example ③ **6. Business** The retail price of a pair of shoes is a 98% increase from its wholesale price. The wholesale price of the shoes is $12.50. What is the retail price?

INDEPENDENT PRACTICE

See Example ① **Find each percent of change. Round answers to the nearest tenth of a percent, if necessary.**

7. 72 is decreased to 45.

8. 55 is increased to 90.

9. 180 is decreased to 140.

10. 230 is increased to 250.

See Example ② **11.** A skateboard that sells for $65 is on sale for 15% off. Find the sale price.

See Example ③ **12. Business** A jeweler buys a ring from an artisan for $85. He sells the ring in his store at a 135% increase in price. What is the retail price of the ring?

PRACTICE AND PROBLEM SOLVING

Extra Practice
See page EP13.

Find each percent of change, amount of increase, or amount of decrease. Round answers to the nearest tenth, if necessary.

13. $8.80 is increased to $17.60.

14. 6.2 is decreased to 5.9.

15. 39.2 is increased to 56.3.

16. $325 is decreased to $100.

17. 75 is decreased by 40%.

18. 28 is increased by 150%.

19. A water tank holds 45 gallons of water. A new water tank can hold 25% more water. What is the capacity of the new water tank?

20. Business Marla makes stretchy beaded purses and sells them to Bangles 'n' Beads for $7 each. Bangles 'n' Beads makes a profit of 28% on each purse. Find the retail price of the purses.

21. Multi-Step A store is discounting all of its stock. The original price of a pair of sunglasses was $44.95. The sale price is $26.97. At this discount rate, what was the original price of a bathing suit that has a sale price of $28.95?

22. Reasoning Explain why a change in price from $20 to $10 is a 50% decrease, but a change in price from $10 to $20 is a 100% increase.

23. The information at right shows the expenses for the Kramer family for one year.

    a. The Kramers spent $2,905 on auto expenses. What was their income for the year?

    b. How much money was spent on household expenses?

    c. The Kramers pay $14,400 per year on their mortgage. What percent of their household expenses is this? Round your answer to the nearest tenth.

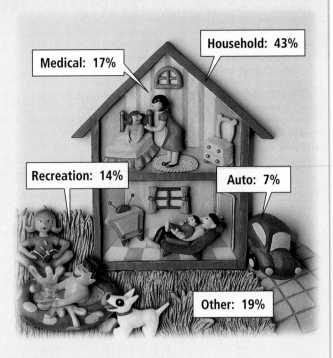

Medical: 17%

Household: 43%

Recreation: 14%

Auto: 7%

Other: 19%

24. United States health expenses were $428.7 billion in 1985 and $991.4 billion in 1995. What was the percent of increase in health expenses during this ten-year period? Round your answer to the nearest tenth of a percent.

25. In 1990, the total amount of energy consumed for transportation in the United States was 22,540 trillion British thermal units (Btu). From 1950 to 1990, there was a 165% increase in energy consumed for transportation. About how many Btu of energy were consumed in 1950?

26. ⭐ **Challenge** In 1960, 21.5% of U.S. households did not have a telephone. This statistic decreased by 75.8% between 1960 and 1990. In 1990, what percent of U.S. households had a telephone?

SPIRAL STANDARDS REVIEW

NS1.4, NS2.4, AF2.1

27. **Multiple Choice** Find the percent of change if the price of a 20-ounce bottle of water increases from $0.85 to $1.25. Round to the nearest tenth.

    Ⓐ 47.1%   Ⓑ 40.0%   Ⓒ 32.0%   Ⓓ 1.7%

28. **Extended Response** A store buys jeans from the manufacturer for $30 each and sells them at a 50% increase in price. At the end of the season, the store puts the jeans on sale for 50% off. Is the sale price $30? Explain your reasoning.

Find the greatest common divisor (GCD). (Lesson 3-2)

29. 24, 80   30. 66, 93   31. 6, 84   32. 30, 75

Convert each measure. (Lesson 5-5)

33. 34 mi to feet   34. 52 oz to pounds   35. 164 lb to tons

6-7 Simple Interest

California Standards

NS1.4 Calculate given percentages of quantities and solve problems involving discounts at sales, **interest earned**, and tips.

Also covered: AF1.1

Vocabulary

interest
simple interest
principal

Why learn this? You can use simple interest to determine how much money a savings account will earn.

When you keep money in a savings account, your money earns *interest*. **Interest** is an amount that is collected or paid for the use of money. For example, the bank pays you interest to use your money to conduct its business. Likewise, when you borrow money from the bank, the bank collects interest on its loan to you.

One type of interest, called **simple interest**, is money paid only on the *principal*. The **principal** is the amount of money deposited or borrowed. To solve problems involving simple interest, you can use the following formula.

Simple interest is money paid only on the principal.

Rate of interest is the percent charged or earned.

$$I = P \cdot r \cdot t$$

Principal is the amount of money borrowed or invested.

Time that the money is borrowed or invested (in years)

Notice that the interest rate is expressed as a decimal and the time is expressed in years.

EXAMPLE 1 Using the Simple Interest Formula

Find each missing value.

A $I = \blacksquare$, $P = \$225$, $r = 3\%$, $t = 2$ years

$I = P \cdot r \cdot t$

$I = 225 \cdot 0.03 \cdot 2$ *Substitute. Use 0.03 for 3%.*

$I = 13.5$ *Multiply.*

The simple interest is $13.50.

B $I = \$300$, $P = \$1,000$, $r = \blacksquare$, $t = 5$ years

$I = P \cdot r \cdot t$

$300 = 1,000 \cdot r \cdot 5$ *Substitute.*

$300 = 5,000r$ *Multiply.*

$\dfrac{300}{5,000} = \dfrac{5,000r}{5,000}$ *Divide each side by 5,000.*

$0.06 = r$

The interest rate is 6%.

EXAMPLE 2 **PROBLEM SOLVING APPLICATION**

Olivia deposits $7,000 in an account that earns 7% simple interest. About how long will it take for her account balance to reach $8,000?

1 **Understand the Problem**

Rewrite the question as a statement:

- Find the number of years it will take for Olivia's account balance to reach $8,000.

List the **important information:**

- The principal is $7,000.

- The interest rate is 7%.

- Her account balance will be $8,000.

2 **Make a Plan**

Olivia's account balance A includes the principal plus the interest: $A = P + I$. Once you solve for I, you can use $I = P \cdot r \cdot t$ to find the time.

3 **Solve**

$$A = P + I$$

$$8{,}000 = \quad 7{,}000 + I \qquad \textit{Substitute.}$$

$$\underline{-7{,}000 \quad -7{,}000} \qquad \textit{Subtract 7,000 from each side.}$$

$$1{,}000 = I$$

$$I = P \cdot r \cdot t$$

$$1{,}000 = 7{,}000 \cdot 0.07 \cdot t \qquad \textit{Substitute. Use 0.07 for 7\%.}$$

$$1{,}000 = 490t \qquad \textit{Multiply.}$$

$$\frac{1{,}000}{490} = \frac{490t}{490} \qquad \textit{Divide each side by 490.}$$

$$2.04 \approx t \qquad \textit{Round to the nearest hundredth.}$$

It will take just over 2 years.

4 **Look Back**

The account earns 7% of $7,000, which is $490, per year. So after 2 years, the interest will be $980, giving a total account balance of $7,980. An answer of just over 2 years for the account to reach $8,000 makes sense.

Think and Discuss

1. Write the value of t for a time period of 6 months.

2. Show how to find r if $I = \$10$, $P = \$100$, and $t = 2$ years.

GUIDED PRACTICE

See Example ① **Find each missing value.**

1. $I = $ ▮, $P = \$300$, $r = 4\%$, $t = 2$ years

2. $I = $ ▮, $P = \$500$, $r = 2\%$, $t = 1$ year

3. $I = \$120$, $P = $ ▮, $r = 6\%$, $t = 5$ years

4. $I = \$240$, $P = \$4,000$, $r = $ ▮, $t = 2$ years

See Example ② 5. Scott deposits \$8,000 in an account that earns 6% simple interest. How long will it be before the total amount is \$10,000?

INDEPENDENT PRACTICE

See Example ① **Find each missing value.**

6. $I = $ ▮, $P = \$600$, $r = 7\%$, $t = 2$ years

7. $I = $ ▮, $P = \$12,000$, $r = 3\%$, $t = 9$ years

8. $I = \$364$, $P = \$1,300$, $r = $ ▮, $t = 7$ years

9. $I = \$440$, $P = $ ▮, $r = 5\%$, $t = 4$ years

10. $I = \$455$, $P = $ ▮, $r = 7\%$, $t = 5$ years

11. $I = \$231$, $P = \$700$, $r = $ ▮, $t = 3$ years

See Example ② 12. Broderick deposits \$6,000 in an account that earns 5.5% simple interest. How long will it be before the total amount is \$9,000?

13. Teresa deposits \$4,000 in an account that earns 7% simple interest. How long will it be before the total amount is \$6,500?

PRACTICE AND PROBLEM SOLVING

Extra Practice
See page EP13.

Complete the table.

	Principal	Interest Rate	Time	Simple Interest
14.	\$2,455	3%	▮	\$441.90
15.	▮	4.25%	3 years	\$663
16.	\$18,500	▮	42 months	\$1,942.50
17.	\$425.50	5%	10 years	▮
18.	▮	6%	3 years	\$2,952

19. **Finance** How many years will it take for \$4,000 to double at a simple interest rate of 5%?

20. **Banking** After 2 years, a savings account earning simple interest held \$585.75. The original deposit was \$550. What was the interest rate?

Reasoning Use the graph for Exercises 21–23.

21. How much more interest was earned on $8,000 deposited for 6 months in a statement savings account than in a passbook savings account?

22. How much money was lost on $5,000 invested in S&P 500 stocks for one year?

23. Compare the returns on $12,000 invested in the high-yield 1-year CD and the Dow Jones industrials for one year.

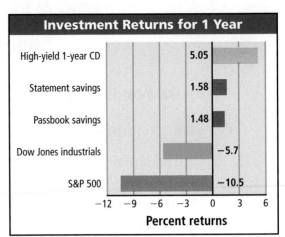

Investment Returns for 1 Year

High-yield 1-year CD	5.05
Statement savings	1.58
Passbook savings	1.48
Dow Jones industrials	−5.7
S&P 500	−10.5

Percent returns

24. **Art** Alexandra can buy a movable artist's-work-and-storage furniture set from her art instructor. She would buy it on credit for $5,000 at a simple interest rate of 4% for 3 years. She can purchase a similar furniture set online for $5,500 plus a $295 shipping and handling fee. Including interest, which set costs less? How much would Alexandra pay for the set?

25. **Write a Problem** Use the graph in Exercises 21–23 to write a problem that can be solved by using the simple interest formula.

26. **Write About It** Explain whether you would pay more simple interest on a loan if you used plan A or plan B.

Plan A: $1,500 for 8 years at 6%   **Plan B:** $1,500 for 6 years at 8%

27. **Challenge** The Jacksons are opening a savings account for their child's college education. In 18 years, they will need about $134,000. If the account earns 6% simple interest, how much money must the Jacksons invest now to cover the cost of the college education?

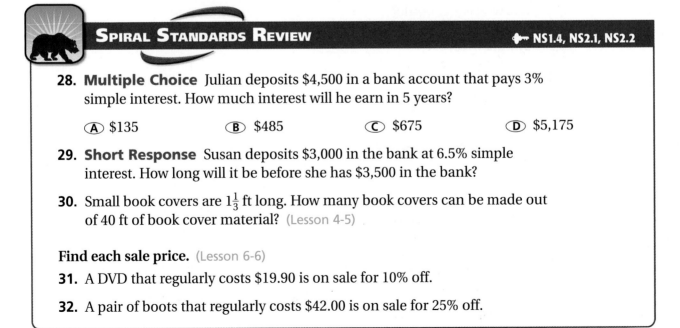

SPIRAL STANDARDS REVIEW   NS1.4, NS2.1, NS2.2

28. **Multiple Choice** Julian deposits $4,500 in a bank account that pays 3% simple interest. How much interest will he earn in 5 years?

    Ⓐ $135   Ⓑ $485   Ⓒ $675   Ⓓ $5,175

29. **Short Response** Susan deposits $3,000 in the bank at 6.5% simple interest. How long will it be before she has $3,500 in the bank?

30. Small book covers are $1\frac{1}{3}$ ft long. How many book covers can be made out of 40 ft of book cover material? (Lesson 4-5)

Find each sale price. (Lesson 6-6)

31. A DVD that regularly costs $19.90 is on sale for 10% off.

32. A pair of boots that regularly costs $42.00 is on sale for 25% off.

Quiz for Lessons 6-6 Through 6-7

☑ 6-6 Percent of Change

Find each percent of change. Round answers to the nearest tenth of a percent, if necessary.

1. 37 is decreased to 17.
2. 121 is increased to 321.
3. 89 is decreased to 84.
4. 45 is increased to 60.
5. 61 is decreased to 33.
6. 86 is increased to 95.

When customers purchase a contract for cell phone service, providers often include the phone at a discounted price. Prices for cell phones from On-the-Go Cellular are listed in the table. Use the table for Exercises 7–9.

On-the-Go Cellular Phones	
Regular Price	Price with 2-year Contract
$49	Free
$99	$39.60
$149	$47.68
$189	$52.92
$229	$57.25

7. Find the percent discount on the $99 phone with a 2-year contract.
8. Find the percent discount on the $149 phone with a 2-year contract.

9. What happens to the percent discount that On-the-Go Cellular gives on its phones as the price of the phone increases?

10. Since Frank is increasing the distance of his daily runs, he needs to carry more water. His current water bottle holds 16 ounces. Frank's new bottle holds 25% more water than his current bottle. What is the capacity of Frank's new water bottle?

☑ 6-7 Simple Interest

Find each missing value.

11. $I = $ ▢ , $P = \$750$, $r = 4\%$, $t = 3$ years
12. $I = \$120$, $P = $ ▢ , $r = 3\%$, $t = 5$ years
13. $I = \$180$, $P = \$1500$, $r = $ ▢ , $t = 2$ years
14. $I = \$220$, $P = \$680$, $r = 8\%$, $t = $ ▢

15. Leslie wants to deposit $10,000 in an account that earns 5% simple interest so that she will have $12,000 when she starts college. How long will it take her account to reach $12,000?

16. Harrison deposits $345 in a savings account that earns 4.2% simple interest. How long will it take for the total amount in the account to reach $410?

Bargain Shopping Shannon and Mary are training for a triathlon. Mary notices that a local sporting goods store is having a weekend sale on bike helmets. Both girls decide to replace their old helmets.

The girls see two signs when they enter the store on Saturday morning. One sign advertises the weekend sale. A second sign notes an early morning special.

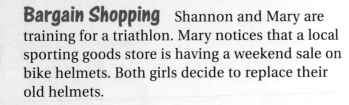

END OF WEEK SALE 40% off the regular price of all bike helmets.

EARLY BIRD SPECIAL! 8:00 A.M. – 11:00 A.M. Take an extra $\frac{1}{3}$ off the END of WEEK SALE price of all bike helmets!

1. The helmet Shannon wants has a regular price of $54. What is the cost of this helmet during the weekend sale?

2. How much money will Shannon save off the weekend sale price if she buys her favorite helmet before 11:00 A.M.?

3. The helmet that Mary prefers regularly costs $48. What is the cost of this helmet during the weekend early shopper special?

4. Shannon thinks that with the combined sales the bike helmets are now 70% off the regular price. Mary disagrees. She thinks the total discount is less than 70%. Who has figured the discount correctly, Shannon or Mary? Explain your answer.

Game Time

Lighten Up

On a digital clock, up to seven segments make up each digit on the display. You can label each segment as shown below.

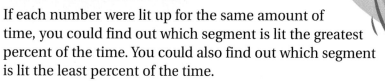

If each number were lit up for the same amount of time, you could find out which segment is lit the greatest percent of the time. You could also find out which segment is lit the least percent of the time.

For each number 0–9, list the letters of the segments that are used when that number is showing. The first few numbers have been done for you.

Once you have determined which segments are lit for each number, count how many times each segment is lit. What percent of the time is each segment lit?

Percent Bingo

Use the bingo cards with numbers and percents provided online. The caller has a collection of percent problems. The caller reads a problem. Then the players solve the problem, and the solution is a number or a percent. If players have the solution on their card, they mark it off. Normal bingo rules apply. You can win with a horizontal, vertical, or diagonal row.

go.hrw.com
Game Time Extra
KEYWORD: MS8CA Games

A complete copy of the rules and game pieces is available online.

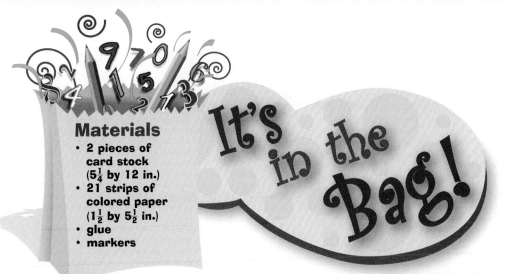

Materials
- 2 pieces of card stock ($5\frac{1}{4}$ by 12 in.)
- 21 strips of colored paper ($1\frac{1}{2}$ by $5\frac{1}{2}$ in.)
- glue
- markers

It's in the Bag!

PROJECT Percent Strips

This colorful booklet holds questions and answers about percents.

Directions

① Fold one piece of card stock in half. Cut along the crease to make two rectangles that are each $5\frac{1}{4}$ inches by 6 inches. You will use these later as covers for your booklet.

② On the other piece of card stock, make accordion folds about $\frac{3}{4}$-inch wide. When you are done, there should be 16 panels. These panels will be the pages of your booklet. **Figure A**

③ Fold up the accordion strip. Glue the covers to the top and bottom panels of the strip. **Figure B**

④ Open the front cover. Glue a strip of colored paper to the top and bottom of the first page. **Figure C**

⑤ Turn the page. Glue a strip of colored paper to the back of the first page between the other two strips. **Figure D**

⑥ Glue strips to the other pages in the same way.

A

B

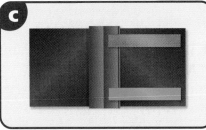

C

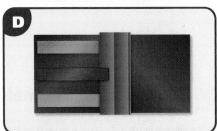

D

Putting the Math into Action

Write a question about percents on the front of each strip. Write the answer on the back. Trade books with another student and put your knowledge of percents to the test.

Study Guide: Review

Vocabulary

Complete the sentences below with vocabulary words from the list above.

1. __?__ is an amount that is collected or paid for the use of money. The equation $I = P \cdot r \cdot t$ is used for calculating __?__. The letter P represents the __?__ and the letter r represents the annual rate.

2. The ratio of an amount of increase to the original amount is the __?__.

3. The ratio of an amount of decrease to the original amount is the __?__.

4. A(n) __?__ is a ratio whose denominator is 100.

6-1 Introduction to Percents (pp. 286–288)

Prep for ◆▬ NS1.4, ◆▬ NS2.4

EXAMPLE

■ Write 12% as a fraction in simplest form and as a decimal.

$$12\% = \frac{12}{100}$$

$$= \frac{12 \div 4}{100 \div 4}$$

$$= \frac{3}{25}$$

$$12\% = \frac{12}{100}$$

$$= 0.12$$

EXERCISES

Write each percent as a fraction in simplest form and as a decimal.

5. 78%   6. 40%

7. 5%   8. 16%

9. 65%   10. 89%

6-2 Fractions, Decimals, and Percents (pp. 289–291)

Prep for ◆▬ NS1.4

EXAMPLE

Write as a percent.

■ $\frac{7}{8}$

$$\frac{7}{8} = 7 \div 8$$

$$= 0.875$$

$$= 87.5\%$$

■ 0.82

$$0.82 = \frac{82}{100}$$

$$= 82\%$$

EXERCISES

Write as a percent. Round to the nearest tenth of a percent, if necessary.

11. $\frac{3}{5}$ 12. $\frac{1}{6}$

13. 0.06   14. 0.8

15. $\frac{2}{3}$ 16. 0.0056

6-3 Estimating with Percents (pp. 292–295)

 NS1.4, NS2.1

EXAMPLE

■ Estimate 26% of 77.

26% of 77 $\approx \frac{1}{4} \cdot 77$ *26% is about 25% and 25% is equivalent to $\frac{1}{4}$.*

     $\approx \frac{1}{4} \cdot 80$ *Change 77 to 80.*

     ≈ 20 *Multiply.*

26% of 77 is about 20.

EXERCISES

Estimate.

17. 22% of 44   **18.** 74% of 120

19. 43% of 64   **20.** 31% of 97

21. 49% of 82   **22.** 6% of 53

23. Byron and Kate's dinner cost $18.23. About how much money should they leave for a 15% tip?

6-4 Percent of a Number (pp. 298–301)

 NS1.3, NS1.4

EXAMPLE

■ Find the percent of the number.

125% of 610

$\frac{125}{100} = \frac{n}{610}$ *Write a proportion.*

$125 \cdot 610 = 100 \cdot n$

$76{,}250 = 100n$

$\frac{76{,}250}{100} = \frac{100n}{100}$

$762.5 = n$

125% of 610 is 762.5.

EXERCISES

Find the percent of each number.

24. 16% of 425   **25.** 48% of 50

26. 7% of 63   **27.** 96% of 125

28. 130% of 21   **29.** 72% of 75

30. Canyon Middle School has 1,247 students. About 38% of the students are in the sixth grade. About how many sixth-graders currently attend Canyon Middle School?

6-5 Solving Percent Problems (pp. 302–305)

NS1.3, NS1.4, AF1.1

EXAMPLE

■ Solve.

80 is 32% of what number?

$80 = 32\% \cdot n$ *Write an equation.*

$80 = 0.32 \cdot n$ *Write 32% as a decimal.*

$\frac{80}{0.32} = \frac{0.32 \cdot n}{0.32}$ *Divide each side by 0.32.*

$250 = n$

80 is 32% of 250.

EXERCISES

Solve.

31. 20% of what number is 25?

32. 4 is what percent of 50?

33. 30 is 250% of what number?

34. What percent of 96 is 36?

35. 6 is 75% of what number?

36. 200 is what percent of 720?

37. The sales tax on a $25 shirt purchased at a store in Oak Park is $1.99. What is the sales tax rate in Oak Park?

6-6 Percent of Change (pp. 308–311)

EXAMPLE

Find each percent of change. Round answers to the nearest tenth, if necessary.

■ **25 is decreased to 16.**

$25 - 16 = 9$

percent of change $= \dfrac{9}{25}$

$\qquad\qquad = 0.36$

$\qquad\qquad = 36\%$

The percent of decrease is 36%.

■ **13.5 is increased to 27.**

$27 - 13.5 = 13.5$

percent of change $= \dfrac{13.5}{13.5}$

$\qquad\qquad = 1$

$\qquad\qquad = 100\%$

The percent of increase is 100%.

EXERCISES

Find each percent of change. Round answers to the nearest tenth, if necessary.

38. 54 is increased to 81.

39. 14 is decreased to 12.

40. 110 is increased to 143.

41. 90 is decreased to 15.2.

42. 26 is increased to 32.

43. 84 is decreased to 21.

44. The regular price of a new pair of skis is $245. This week the skis are on sale for 15% off. Find the sale price.

45. Bianca makes beaded bracelets. Each bracelet costs $3.25 to make. Bianca sells them at a 140% increase in price. What is the price of each bracelet?

6-7 Simple Interest (pp. 312–315)

EXAMPLE

Find each missing value.

■ $I =$ , $P = \$545$, $r = 1.5\%$, $t = 2$ years

$I = P \cdot r \cdot t$

$I = 545 \cdot 0.015 \cdot 2$ *Substitute.*

$I = 16.35$ *Multiply.*

The simple interest is $16.35.

■ $I = \$825$, $P =$ , $r = 6\%$, $t = 11$ years

$I = P \cdot r \cdot t$

$825 = P \cdot 0.06 \cdot 11$ *Substitute.*

$825 = P \cdot 0.66$ *Multiply.*

$\dfrac{825}{0.66} = \dfrac{P \cdot 0.66}{0.66}$ *Divide each side by 0.66.*

$1{,}250 = P$

The principal is $1,250.

EXERCISES

Find each missing value.

46. $I =$ ▢, $P = \$1{,}000$, $r = 3\%$, $t = 6$ months

47. $I = \$452.16$, $P = \$1{,}256$, $r = 12\%$, $t =$ ▢

48. $I =$ ▢, $P = \$675$, $r = 4.5\%$, $t = 8$ years

49. $I = \$555.75$, $P = \$950$, $r =$ ▢, $t = 15$ years

50. $I = \$172.50$, $P =$ ▢, $r = 5\%$, $t = 18$ months

51. Craig deposits $1,000 in a savings account that earns 5% simple interest. How long will it take for the total amount in his account to reach $1,350?

52. Zach deposits $755 in an account that earns 4.2% simple interest. How long will it take for the total amount in the account to reach $1,050?

CHAPTER TEST

Write each percent as a fraction in simplest form and as a decimal.

1. 95% **2.** 37.5% **3.** 4% **4.** 0.01%

Write as a percent. Round to the nearest tenth of a percent, if necessary.

5. 0.75 **6.** 0.06 **7.** 0.8 **8.** 0.0039

9. $\frac{3}{10}$ **10.** $\frac{9}{20}$ **11.** $\frac{5}{16}$ **12.** $\frac{7}{21}$

Estimate.

13. 48% of 8 **14.** 3% of 119 **15.** 26% of 32 **16.** 76% of 280

17. The Pattersons spent $47.89 for a meal at a restaurant. About how much should they leave for a 15% tip?

Find the percent of each number.

18. 90% of 200 **19.** 35% of 210 **20.** 16% of 85

21. 250% of 30 **22.** 38% of 11 **23.** 5% of 145

Solve.

24. 36 is what percent of 150? **25.** What percent of 145 is 29?

26. 51 is what percent of 340? **27.** 36 is 40% of what number?

28. 70 is 14% of what number? **29.** 25 is 20% of what number?

30. Hampton Middle School is expecting 376 sixth-graders next year. This is 40% of the expected school enrollment. How many students are expected to enroll in the school next year?

Find each percent of change. Round answers to the nearest tenth, if necessary.

31. 30 is increased to 45. **32.** 115 is decreased to 46.

33. 116 is increased to 145. **34.** 129 is decreased to 32.

35. A community theater sold 8,500 tickets to performances during its first year. By its tenth year, ticket sales had increased by 34%. How many tickets did the theater sell during its tenth year?

Find each missing value.

36. $I =$ ▓, $P = \$500$, $r = 5\%$, $t = 1$ year **37.** $I = \$702$, $P = \$1,200$, $r = 3.9\%$, $t =$ ▓

38. $I = \$468$, $P = \$900$, $r =$ ▓, $t = 8$ years **39.** $I = \$37.50$, $P =$ ▓, $r = 10\%$, $t = 6$ months

40. Kate invested $3,500 at a 5% simple interest rate. How many years will it take for the original amount to double?

Cumulative Assessment, Chapters 1–6

Multiple Choice

1. The figures shown are similar. What is the value of x?

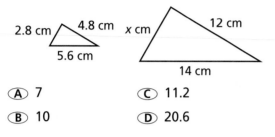

2.8 cm   4.8 cm x cm   12 cm
5.6 cm
14 cm

    Ⓐ 7   Ⓒ 11.2

    Ⓑ 10   Ⓓ 20.6

2. What is 12% of 256?

    Ⓐ 21.33   Ⓒ 30.72

    Ⓑ 24.25   Ⓓ 64.20

3. At Lincoln Middle School, $\frac{3}{4}$ of the students are taking a world language class. Of those students, $\frac{1}{3}$ are taking Spanish. What fraction of the students at Lincoln Middle School are taking Spanish?

    Ⓐ $\frac{1}{4}$ Ⓒ $\frac{4}{9}$

    Ⓑ $\frac{5}{12}$ Ⓓ $\frac{4}{7}$

4. What is the least common multiple of 6, 8, and 12?

    Ⓐ 6   Ⓒ 24

    Ⓑ 12   Ⓓ 48

5. Peaches cost $1.90 per pound. Ty bought a bag of peaches for $4.56. Which equation could be used to find the number of pounds p Ty bought?

    Ⓐ $1.9p = 4.56$

    Ⓑ $4.56p = 1.9$

    Ⓒ $\frac{p}{1.9} = 4.56$

    Ⓓ $\frac{p}{4.56} = 1.9$

6. What value of n makes the following equation true?

$$n - \frac{4}{5} = \frac{7}{10}$$

    Ⓐ $\frac{1}{2}$ Ⓒ $1\frac{1}{2}$

    Ⓑ $\frac{2}{3}$ Ⓓ $2\frac{1}{3}$

7. A basketball goal that usually sells for $825 goes on sale for 20% off. What is the sale price of the basketball goal?

    Ⓐ $580   Ⓒ $680

    Ⓑ $660   Ⓓ $720

8. Which expression is equivalent to $2 + (4 \cdot 8)$?

    Ⓐ $(2 + 4) \cdot (2 + 8)$

    Ⓑ $2 \cdot (4 + 8)$

    Ⓒ $4 + (2 \cdot 8)$

    Ⓓ $(4 \cdot 8) + 2$

9. Amanda wants to leave a 15% tip for a haircut that cost $24.00. Which is closest to the amount of the tip that Amanda should leave?

    Ⓐ $2.50   Ⓒ $3.75

    Ⓑ $3.00   Ⓓ $4.75

10. What is the value of the expression $3(x + 4) + 6x$ for $x = 8$?

    Ⓐ 50   Ⓒ 84

    Ⓑ 76   Ⓓ 104

11. What is the value of $8\frac{2}{5} - 2\frac{3}{4}$?

   Ⓐ $5\frac{9}{20}$ Ⓒ $6\frac{1}{9}$

   Ⓑ $5\frac{13}{20}$ Ⓓ $6\frac{7}{20}$

12. How long will it take Mr. Garza to drive 216 miles at an average speed of 48 miles per hour?

   Ⓐ 3.0 hours   Ⓒ 4.0 hours

   Ⓑ 3.5 hours   Ⓓ 4.5 hours

13. The temperature in San Diego was 73°F warmer than the temperature in Barrow, Alaska. If the temperature in San Diego was 66°F, what was the temperature in Barrow?

   Ⓐ −19°F   Ⓒ 7°F

   Ⓑ −7°F   Ⓓ 19°F

Make sure that your answer makes sense before marking it as your response. Reread the question and determine whether your answer is reasonable.

Gridded Response

14. Jarvis deposits $1,200 in an account that earns 3% simple interest. How many years will it take him to earn $432 in interest?

15. Simplify the expression $93 + 3^2 \cdot 6^2 - 4^3$.

16. To make lemon-lime punch, Sylas needs to use 3 lemons for every 2 limes. If Sylas uses 24 limes, how many lemons will he need?

17. A jumping spider has a length of 1.8 centimeters. What is the spider's length in millimeters?

18. What is the denominator of the value of $\frac{3}{2} + \frac{5}{6}$ when written in simplest form?

Short Response

19. The graph shows the number of boys and the number of girls who participated in a talent show.

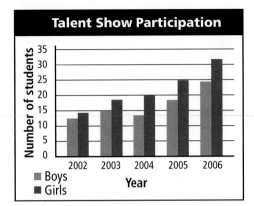

Approximately what percent of students participating in the talent show in 2006 were boys? Explain how you found your answer.

20. A homemaker association has 134 members. If 31 of these members are experts in canning vegetables, are more or less than 25% of the members canning experts? Explain how you know.

Extended Response

21. Riley and Louie each have $5,000 to invest. They both invest at a 2.5% simple interest rate.

   a. Riley keeps her money invested for 7 years. How much interest will she earn? How much will her investment be worth?

   b. What is the value of Louie's investment if he invests for 3 years, then removes and spends $1,000, and then invests what is remaining for 4 more years at a rate of 4%?

   c. Using the information from parts **a** and **b**, who has more money in 7 years, Louie or Riley? Explain your reasoning.

Collecting, Displaying, and Analyzing Data

CONCEPT CONNECTION

go.hrw.com
Chapter Project Online
KEYWORD: MS8CA Ch7

Most California sea lions live along the North American coast of the Pacific Ocean. You can use data to find the mean mass of a sea lion.

California sea lion
off the coast of California

ARE YOU READY?

✓ Vocabulary

Choose the best term from the list to complete each sentence.

circle

frequency

interval

line segment

scale

1. A part of a line consisting of two endpoints and all points between those endpoints is called a(n) __?__.

2. A(n) __?__ is the amount of space between the marked values on the __?__ of a graph.

3. The number of times an item occurs is called its __?__.

Complete these exercises to review skills you will need for this chapter.

✓ Order Whole Numbers

Order the numbers from least to greatest.

4. 45, 23, 65, 15, 42, 18

5. 103, 105, 102, 118, 87, 104

6. 56, 65, 24, 19, 76, 33, 82

7. 8, 3, 6, 2, 5, 9, 3, 4, 2

✓ Whole Number Operations

Add or subtract.

8. $18 + 26$

9. $23 + 17$

10. $75 + 37$

11. $98 + 64$

12. $133 - 35$

13. $54 - 29$

14. $200 - 88$

15. $1,055 - 899$

✓ Locate Points on a Number Line

Copy the number line. Then graph each number.

16. 15

17. 2

18. 18

19. 7

✓ Read a Table

Use the data in the table for Exercises 20 and 21.

20. Which animal is the fastest?

21. Which animal is faster, a rabbit or a zebra?

Top Speeds of Some Animals	
Animal	Speed (mi/h)
Elephant	25
Lion	50
Rabbit	35
Zebra	40

Unpacking the Standards

The information below "unpacks" the standards. The Academic Vocabulary is highlighted and defined to help you understand the language of the standards. Refer to the lessons listed after each standard for help with the math terms and phrases. The Chapter Concept shows how the standard is applied in this chapter.

California Standard	Academic Vocabulary	Chapter Concept
SDAP2.2 Identify different ways of selecting a sample (e.g., convenience sampling, responses to a survey, random sampling) and which method makes a sample more representative for a population. (Lesson 7-7) (Lab 7-7)	**identify** recognize or describe **representative** serving as a typical example ***Example:*** A group of 40 sixth graders selected at random is likely to be representative of all sixth graders at a school.	You learn different ways of choosing samples and determine which types of samples best reflect an entire group.
SDAP2.3 Analyze data displays and explain why the way in which the question was asked might have influenced the results obtained and why the way in which the results were displayed might have influenced the conclusions reached. (Lessons 7-4, 7-5, 7-8)	**analyze** examine closely to look for important facts and patterns **influenced** had an effect on **displayed** shown **conclusions** statements based on reasoning and data	You analyze various types of graphs and determine whether they are misleading.
SDAP2.4 Identify data that represent sampling errors and explain why the sample (and the display) might be biased. (Lesson 7-8)	**biased** in this case, not representative of the entire group being studied	You recognize possible errors in selecting samples and tell how these errors could affect a graph of the results of a survey.
SDAP2.5 Identify claims based on statistical data and, in simple cases, evaluate the validity of the claims. (Lessons 7-4, 7-5, 7-6, 7-8)	**statistical** relating to numerical information **validity** measure of how well a statement is supported by data and reasoning	You analyze statements made about data to decide whether the statements are reasonable.

Standards SDAP1.1, SDAP1.2, SDAP1.3, SDAP1.4, and SDAP2.1 are also covered in this chapter.

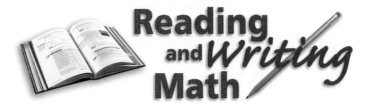

Reading and Writing Math

Reading Strategy: Read a Lesson for Understanding

Before you begin reading a lesson, find out which standard or standards are the main focus of the lesson. These standards are located at the top of the first page of the lesson. Reading with the standards in mind will help guide you through the lesson material. You can use the following tips to help you follow the math as you read.

California Standards

➤ **NS1.4** Calculate given percentages of quantities and solve problems involving **discounts at sales,** interest earned, **and tips.**

Identify the standard or standards of the lesson. Then skim through the lesson to get a sense of how the standards are covered.

"How do I find the percent of a number?"

As you read through the lesson, write down any questions, problems, or trouble spots you may have.

Find the percent of each number.

8% of 50

$8\% \text{ of } 50 = 0.08 \cdot 50$ *Write the percent as a decimal.*

$= 4$ *Multiply.*

Work through each example, as the examples help demonstrate the standards.

Think and Discuss

1. **Explain** how to set up a proportion to find 150% of a number.

Check your understanding of the lesson by answering the Think and Discuss questions.

Try This

Use Lesson 6-7 in your textbook to answer each question.

1. What is the standard of the lesson?

2. What new terms are defined in the lesson?

3. What skills are being taught in Example 1 of the lesson?

4. Which parts of the lesson can you use to answer Think and Discuss question 2?

LAB
7-1

Collect Data to Explore the Mean

Use with Lesson 7-1

California Standards

SDAP1.1 Compute the range, **mean,** median, and mode **of data sets.**

go.hrw.com
Lab Resources Online
KEYWORD: MS8CA Lab7

You can use counters to find a single number that describes an entire set of data. Consider the set of data in the table.

First use counters to make stacks that match the data.

Now move some of the counters so that all of the stacks are the same height.

All of the stacks have 4 counters. The set of data can be described by the number 4. It is the *mean* (average) of the set of data.

| 2 | 5 | 4 | 3 | 6 |

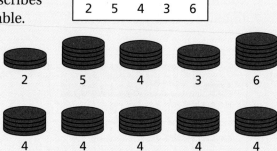

Activity

❶ Ella surveys five people to find out how many brothers and sisters they have.

❷ She collects the data and records the results.

❸ Use counters to show the data.

❹ Move counters so that all of the stacks are the same height. The mean is 2.

Number of Siblings

| 2 | 3 | 1 | 1 | 3 |

Think and Discuss

1. Suppose one of the people surveyed had 8 brothers and sisters instead of 3. How would this change the mean?

2. All of the students in a classroom have 3 textbooks. What is the mean of the set of data? How do you know?

Try This

1. Collect data by surveying four friends to find out how many pets they have. Use counters to find the mean of the set of data.

7-1 Mean, Median, Mode, and Range

California Standards

SDAP1.1 Compute the range, mean, median, and mode of data sets.

Vocabulary

mean
median
mode
range

Why learn this? You can use the mean to determine the average height that the players on a volleyball team can jump.

Players on a volleyball team measured how high they could jump. The results in inches are recorded in the table.

| 13 | 23 | 21 | 20 | 21 | 24 | 18 |

One way to describe this data set is to find the *mean*. The **mean** is the sum of all the items divided by the number of items in the set. Sometimes the mean is also called the *average*.

EXAMPLE 1 Finding the Mean of a Data Set

Find the mean of each data set.

A

Heights of Vertical Jumps (in.)						
13	23	21	20	21	24	18

$13 + 23 + 21 + 20 + 21 + 24 + 18 = 140$ *Add all values.*
$140 \div 7 = 20$ *Divide the sum by the number of items.*

The mean is 20 inches.

B

Numbers of Pets Owned				
2	4	1	1	2

$2 + 4 + 1 + 1 + 2 = 10$ *Add all values.*
$10 \div 5 = 2$ *Divide the sum by the number of items.*

The mean is 2. The average number of pets that these five people own is 2.

Check

Move the counters so that each stack has the same number.

The mean is 2.

Some other descriptions of a set of data are called the *median*, *mode*, and *range*.

- The **median** is the middle value when the data are in numerical order, or the mean of the two middle values if there are an even number of items.

- The **mode** is the value or values that occur most often. There may be more than one mode for a data set. When all values occur an equal number of times, the data set has no mode.

- The **range** is the difference between the least and greatest values in the set.

EXAMPLE **2** Finding the Mean, Median, Mode, and Range of a Data Set

Find the mean, median, mode, and range of each data set.

NFL Career Touchdowns			
Marcus Allen	145	Franco Harris	100
Jim Brown	126	Walter Payton	125

mean: $\dfrac{145 + 126 + 100 + 125}{4}$

$= 124$

Add all values. Divide the sum by the number of items.

median: Write the data in numerical order: 100, 125, 126, 145

100, (125, 126) 145

$\dfrac{125 + 126}{2} = 125.5$

There are an even number of items, so find the mean of the two middle values.

mode: none

No value occurs most often.

range: $145 - 100 = 45$

Subtract the least value from the greatest value.

The mean is 124 touchdowns; the median is 125.5 touchdowns; there is no mode; and the range is 45 touchdowns.

Think and Discuss

1. **Describe** what you can say about the values in a data set if the set has a small range.

2. **Tell** how many modes are in the following data set. Explain your answer. 15, 12, 13, 15, 12, 11

3. **Describe** how adding 20 inches to the data set in Example 1A would affect the mean.

7-1 Exercises

California Standards Practice
SDAP1.1, SDAP1.4

go.hrw.com
Homework Help Online
KEYWORD: MS8CA 7-1
Parent Resources Online
KEYWORD: MS8CA Parent

GUIDED PRACTICE

See Example ① Find the mean of the data set.

1.

Number of Petals	13	24	35	18	15	27

See Example ② Find the mean, median, mode, and range of the data set.

2.

Masses of Sea Lions (kg)	117	141	132	125	118	146	117

INDEPENDENT PRACTICE

See Example ① Find the mean of the data set.

3.

Numbers of Books Read	6	4	10	5	6	8

See Example ② Find the mean, median, mode, and range of each data set.

4.

Ages of Students (yr)	14	16	15	17	16	12

5.

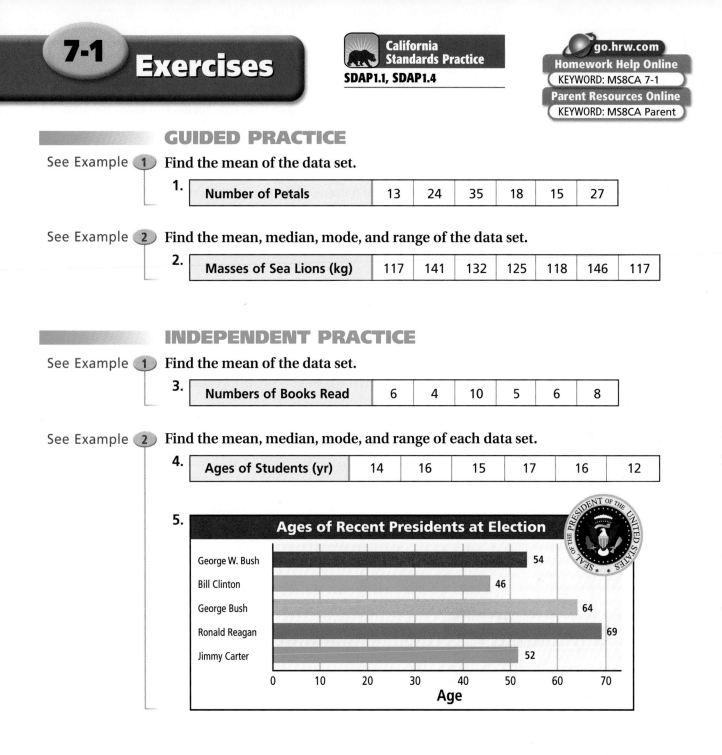

Ages of Recent Presidents at Election

George W. Bush — 54
Bill Clinton — 46
George Bush — 64
Ronald Reagan — 69
Jimmy Carter — 52

Age

PRACTICE AND PROBLEM SOLVING

Extra Practice
See page EP14.

6. Frank has 3 nickels, 5 dimes, and 2 quarters. Find the range, mean, median, and mode of the values of Frank's coins.

7. **Education** For the six New England states, the mean scores on the math section of the SAT one year were as follows: Connecticut, 509; Maine, 500; Massachusetts, 513; New Hampshire, 519; Rhode Island, 500; and Vermont, 508. Create a table using this data. Then find the range, mean, median, and mode.

8. **Critical Thinking** Gina spent $4, $5, $7, $7, and $6 over the past 5 days buying lunch. Is the mean more useful than the median for describing this data set? Explain.

Reasoning Find each missing value.

9. 3, 5, 7, 9, ; mean: 7

10. 15, 17, ▇, 28, 30; mean: 23

11. 10, 9, ▇, 4, 8, 8, 4, 7; mode: 4

12. 7, 2, ▇, 15, 20, 8, 14, 29; median: 13

13. 50, 100, 75, 60, ▇, 25, 105, 40; median: 65

14. 14, 8, 17, 21, ▇, 11, 3, 13; range: 20

15. **Reasoning** Find the set of 5 items of data that has a range of 9, a mean of 11, a median of 12, and a mode of 15.

16. **What's the Error?** Joey says that the mean of the set of data is 23.5. Describe Joey's error.

Numbers of Flowers in Bouquets	25	20	21	22	25	25

17. **What's the Question?** On an exam, three students scored 75, four students scored 82, three students scored 88, four students scored 93, and one student scored 99. If the answer is 88, what is the question?

18. **Challenge** In the Super Bowls from 1997 to 2002, the winning team won by a mean of $12\frac{1}{6}$ points. By how many points did the Green Bay Packers win in 1997?

Year	Super Bowl Champion	Points Won By
2002	New England Patriots	3
2001	Baltimore Ravens	27
2000	St. Louis Rams	7
1999	Denver Broncos	15
1998	Denver Broncos	7
1997	Green Bay Packers	▇

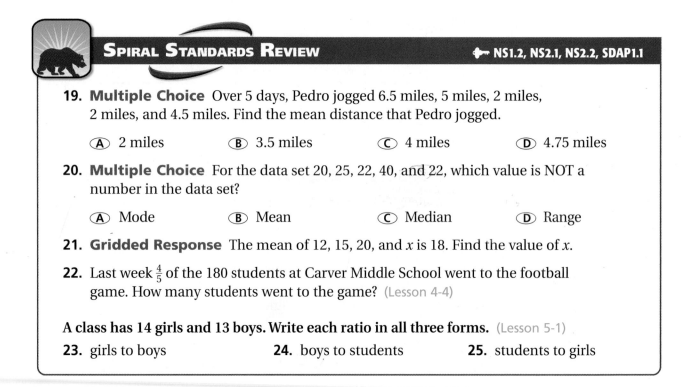

SPIRAL STANDARDS REVIEW 🔑 NS1.2, NS2.1, NS2.2, SDAP1.1

19. **Multiple Choice** Over 5 days, Pedro jogged 6.5 miles, 5 miles, 2 miles, 2 miles, and 4.5 miles. Find the mean distance that Pedro jogged.

ⓐ 2 miles   ⓑ 3.5 miles   ⓒ 4 miles   ⓓ 4.75 miles

20. **Multiple Choice** For the data set 20, 25, 22, 40, and 22, which value is NOT a number in the data set?

ⓐ Mode   ⓑ Mean   ⓒ Median   ⓓ Range

21. **Gridded Response** The mean of 12, 15, 20, and x is 18. Find the value of x.

22. Last week $\frac{4}{5}$ of the 180 students at Carver Middle School went to the football game. How many students went to the game? (Lesson 4-4)

A class has 14 girls and 13 boys. Write each ratio in all three forms. (Lesson 5-1)

23. girls to boys   **24.** boys to students   **25.** students to girls

Additional Data and Outliers

California Standards

SDAP1.2 Understand how additional data added to data sets may affect these computations.
Also covered: **SDAP1.1, SDAP1.3**

Vocabulary
outlier

Why learn this? You can determine how additional data affect the mean, median, mode, and range of the number of Olympic medals won by the U.S.

The mean, median, mode, and range may change when you add data to a data set.

USA's Jim Shea in Men's Skeleton at the 2002 Winter Olympics

EXAMPLE 1 Sports Application

A Find the mean, median, mode, and range of the data in the table.

U.S. Winter Olympic Medals Won							
Year	2002	1998	1994	1992	1988	1984	1980	1976
Medals	34	13	13	11	6	8	12	10

mean: $\dfrac{34 + 13 + 13 + 11 + 6 + 8 + 12 + 10}{8} = 13.375$

median: Write the data in numerical order:
 6, 8, 10, (11, 12,) 13, 13, 34.

$\dfrac{11 + 12}{2} = 11.5$ *Find the mean of the two middle values.*

mode: 13   *The value 13 occurs most often.*

range: $34 - 6 = 28$ *Subtract the least value from the greatest value.*

B The United States also won 8 medals in 1972 and 5 medals in 1968. Add this data to the data in the table and find the mean, median, mode, and range.

mean: 12   *The mean decreased by 1.375.*
median: 10.5   *The median decreased by 1.*
modes: 8, 13   *There is an additional mode.*
range: 29   *The range increased by 1.*

An **outlier** is a value in a set that is very different from the other values. One way to identify an outlier is by making a *line plot*. A line plot uses a number line and x's or other symbols to show the frequencies of values.

EXAMPLE 2
Identifying Outliers

California LINK
Science

San Francisco garter snakes have turquoise bellies and red- and black-striped bodies. These snakes are quite rare and have been on the endangered species list since 1967.

A park ranger is measuring a population of endangered San Francisco garter snakes. Which length represents an outlier?

Length of Garter Snakes (in.)													
18	24	23	30	25	33	36	55	20	21	30	31	32	28

Step 1: Draw a number line.

Step 2: For each snake, use an x on the number line to represent its length in inches.

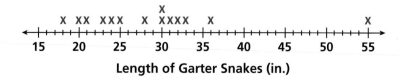

Length of Garter Snakes (in.)

The line plot shows that the value 55 is much greater than the other values in the set. The length of 55 inches represents an outlier.

An outlier can greatly affect the mean and range of a data set.

EXAMPLE 3
Social Studies Application

Helpful Hint

Sherman Bull's age is an outlier because he is much older than the others in the group.

In 2001, 64-year-old Sherman Bull became the oldest person to reach the top of Mount Everest. Other climbers to reach the summit that day were 33, 31, 31, 32, 33, and 28 years old. Find the mean, median, mode, and range without and with Bull's age, and explain the changes.

Data without Bull's age:
mean: ≈ 31.3 median: 31.5
modes: 31, 33   range: 5

Data with Bull's age:
mean: 36   median: 32
modes: 31, 33   range: 36

When you add Bull's age, the mean increases by 4.7, the modes stay the same, the median increases by 0.5, and the range increases by 31. The mean and the range are most affected by the outlier.

Think and Discuss

1. **Explain** how an outlier with a large value will affect the mean of a data set. What is the effect of a small outlier value?

2. **Describe** how a line plot can be used to identify an outlier.

GUIDED PRACTICE

See Example ① **1. Sports** The graph shows how many times some countries have won the Davis Cup in tennis from 1900 to 2000.

    a. Find the mean, median, mode, and range of the data.

    b. The United States won 31 Davis Cups between 1900 and 2000. Add this number to the data and find the mean, median, mode, and range.

Davis Cup Wins 1900 to 2000

France	🎾 🎾 🎾 🎾
Germany	🎾
Sweden	🎾 🎾 🎾 🎾
Spain	🎾

🎾 = 2 wins

See Example ② **2.** The points scored per game by a high-school football team in one season were 20, 17, 20, 19, 14, 23, 7, 17, 16, and 21. Which score represents an outlier?

See Example ③ **3.** In 1998, 77-year-old John Glenn became the oldest person to travel into space. Other astronauts traveling on that same mission were 43, 37, 38, 46, 35, and 42 years old. Find the mean, median, mode, and range of all their ages with and without Glenn's age, and explain the changes.

INDEPENDENT PRACTICE

See Example ① **4. History** The table shows the ages of the 10 youngest signers of the Declaration of Independence.

    a. Find the mean, median, mode, and range of the data.

Ages of 10 Youngest Signers of Declaration of Independence						
Age	26	29	30	31	33	34
Number Of Signers	//	/	/	/	///	//

    b. Benjamin Franklin was 70 years old when he signed the Declaration of Independence. Add his age to the data in the table and find the mean, median, mode, and range.

See Example ② **5.** The data set 6, 9, 5, 5, 5, 6, 4, and 5 represents the number of pups born into eight wolf packs in a national park in one year. Which number of pups represents an outlier?

See Example ③ **6. Geography** The map shows the population densities of several states along the Atlantic coast. Find the mean, median, mode, and range of the data with and without Maine's population density, and explain the changes.

Population Density (people per square mile)

Maine 41

Massachusetts 788

New Jersey 1,098

Rhode Island 948

Connecticut 677

Extra Practice
See page EP14.

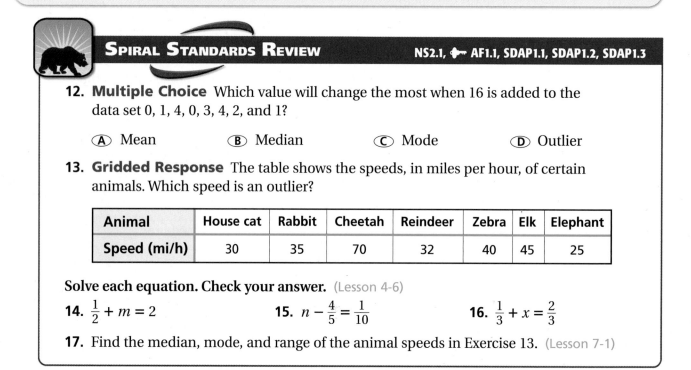

On September 13, 1922, the temperature in El Azizia, Libya, reached 136°F, the record high for the planet. (*Source: The World Almanac and Book of Facts*)

7. What are the mean, median, and mode of the highest recorded temperatures on each continent?

8. **a.** Which temperature is an outlier?

   b. What are the mean, median, and mode of the temperatures if the outlier is not included?

Continent	Highest Temperature (°F)
Africa	136
Antarctica	59
Asia	129
Australia	128
Europe	122
North America	134
South America	120

This satellite map shows the world's surface temperature. The dark blue areas are coldest, and the deep red areas are hottest.

go.hrw.com
Web Extra!
KEYWORD: MS8CA Heat

9. **What's the Error?** A student stated that the median temperature would rise to 120.6°F if a new record high of 75°F were recorded in Antarctica. Explain the error. How would the median temperature actually be affected if a high of 75°F were recorded in Antarctica?

10. **Write About It** Explain why the mean is affected more than the median when an outlier is removed from a data set.

11. **Challenge** Suppose a new high temperature were recorded in Europe, and the new mean temperature became 120°F. What is Europe's new high temperature?

SPIRAL STANDARDS REVIEW NS2.1, ← AF1.1, SDAP1.1, SDAP1.2, SDAP1.3

12. **Multiple Choice** Which value will change the most when 16 is added to the data set 0, 1, 4, 0, 3, 4, 2, and 1?

Ⓐ Mean   Ⓑ Median   Ⓒ Mode   Ⓓ Outlier

13. **Gridded Response** The table shows the speeds, in miles per hour, of certain animals. Which speed is an outlier?

Animal	House cat	Rabbit	Cheetah	Reindeer	Zebra	Elk	Elephant
Speed (mi/h)	30	35	70	32	40	45	25

Solve each equation. Check your answer. (Lesson 4-6)

14. $\frac{1}{2} + m = 2$ 15. $n - \frac{4}{5} = \frac{1}{10}$ 16. $\frac{1}{3} + x = \frac{2}{3}$

17. Find the median, mode, and range of the animal speeds in Exercise 13. (Lesson 7-1)

7-3 Choosing the Most Useful Measure

California Standards

SDAP1.4 Know why a specific measure of central tendency (mean, median) provides the most useful information in a given context.
Also covered: **SDAP1.1, SDAP1.3**

Why learn this? You can decide whether the mean or median gives the most useful information about a set of clarinet prices.

Recall that the mean and median describe the center of a data set. How do you decide which of these measures to use when describing a set of data? You should choose the measure that is most useful for the situation.

The measure you choose may depend on the data itself. As you saw in Lesson 7-2, an outlier can greatly affect the mean. For this reason, the mean may not be the best measure to describe a set of data with an outlier.

EXAMPLE 1 Describing a Data Set

Christi is shopping for a used clarinet. She found 10 clarinets with the prices shown. What are the mean and median of this data set? If Christi wants to know the price of a typical clarinet, is one measure more useful than the other? Explain.

Prices:
$145 $180
$160 $170
$130 $150
$190 $500
$185 $165

Step 1: Find the mean and median.

> **Mean: $197.50**
>
> **Median: $167.50**

Step 2: Choose the more useful measure.

The $500 clarinet is an outlier. Because of this outlier, the mean is higher than all but one of the prices. For this reason, the mean is not a good choice to describe the typical price.

The median is a more useful description of the typical price. Most of the clarinets cost about $167.50.

The measure that you choose to describe a data set may depend on how the information is being used.

For instance, if you wanted to convince someone that clarinets are too expensive, you might choose the mean to describe the data set in Example 1. The mean makes the price of used clarinets seem higher than the median does.

EXAMPLE 2 **Using a Data Set to Persuade**

The list shows the number of minutes Rebecca spent talking on her cell phone during each of the last 8 months.

540, 600, 430, 500, 670, 410, 560, 430

She wants to convince her father that she does not spend too much time on the phone. Should Rebecca use the mean, median, or mode to describe the data set? Explain.

Mean: 517.5 minutes   **Median: 520 minutes**   Mode: 430 minutes

Rebecca should use the measure that makes the number of minutes she talks per month seem lowest. She should use the mode.

Think and Discuss

1. **Explain** whether the mode would be a good measure to describe the typical age of students in your math class.

7-3 Exercises

GUIDED PRACTICE

See Example 1   1. Kate read books that were 240, 190, 180, 160, 195, 170, 240, and 165 pages long. What are the mean and median of this data set? Is one measure more useful than the other for describing the typical length of the books that Kate read? Explain.

See Example 2   2. The line plot shows the number of minutes it took Jamal to download 10 different television programs. Should he use the mean, median, or mode of the data to convince his parents that he needs a faster Internet connection? Explain.

Time to Download (min)

INDEPENDENT PRACTICE

See Example 1   3. The passengers in a van are 14, 14, 14, 14, 15, 14, and 34 years old. What are the mean and median of this data set? Is one measure more useful than the other for describing the typical age of a passenger in the van? Explain.

See Example 2   4. The table shows the low temperatures in a town on 11 days in winter. Should the town's mayor use the mean, median, or mode to convince tourists that the town is not too cold during winter? Explain.

Daily Low Temperatures (°F)					
21	11	12	27	35	30
	40	35	20	14	8

Tell whether the mean, median, or mode would be the best measure for each situation. Explain your choice.

5. Melinda wants to know whether her test score falls in the top half or bottom half of the test scores for her class.

6. Franco wants to know the most common number of pets among students in his class.

7. The circle graph shows the results of a survey.
   a. What is the mode of the data?
   b. Can the mean or median be used to describe the data? Why or why not?

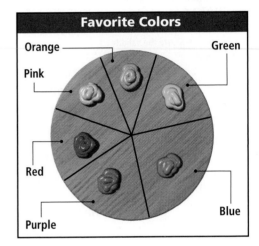

Favorite Colors

Orange — Green
Pink
Red
Purple
Blue

8. **Reasoning** The lengths, in minutes, of the movies at a theater are 98, 103, 96, 88, 93, 98, 108, 100, and 98. Is the median more useful than the mean for describing this data set? Explain.

9. **Write About It** An electronics store sells digital cameras that cost $480, $385, $75, $440, and $370. To convince customers the store has low prices, the manager advertises the mean of these prices. Explain why the advertisement might be misleading.

10. **Challenge** The table shows the number of rainy days per month in a town. Describe a situation in which you would use the mode to describe the data set. Then do the same for the median and the mean.

Number of Rainy Days per Month, 2006					
23	25	11	9	6	8
5	6	6	18	26	25

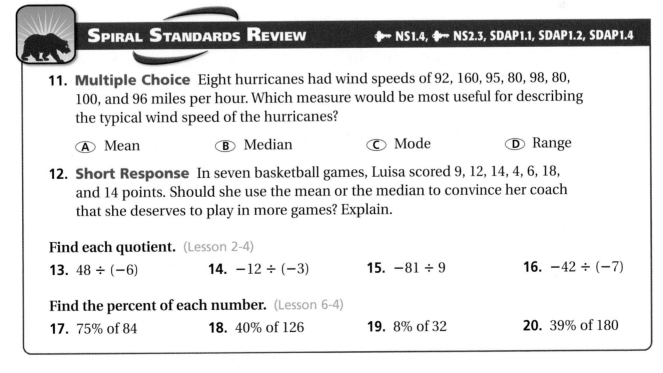

SPIRAL STANDARDS REVIEW
NS1.4, NS2.3, SDAP1.1, SDAP1.2, SDAP1.4

11. **Multiple Choice** Eight hurricanes had wind speeds of 92, 160, 95, 80, 98, 80, 100, and 96 miles per hour. Which measure would be most useful for describing the typical wind speed of the hurricanes?

   (A) Mean   (B) Median   (C) Mode   (D) Range

12. **Short Response** In seven basketball games, Luisa scored 9, 12, 14, 4, 6, 18, and 14 points. Should she use the mean or the median to convince her coach that she deserves to play in more games? Explain.

Find each quotient. (Lesson 2-4)

13. $48 \div (-6)$ 14. $-12 \div (-3)$ 15. $-81 \div 9$ 16. $-42 \div (-7)$

Find the percent of each number. (Lesson 6-4)

17. 75% of 84   18. 40% of 126   19. 8% of 32   20. 39% of 180

California Standards

◆— **SDAP2.5** Identify claims based on statistical data and, in simple cases, evaluate the validity of the claims.

Also covered: ◆— **SDAP2.3**

Vocabulary

bar graph
circle graph
sector
line graph

Why learn this? You can analyze graphs to decide whether a claim based on data from an election is reasonable.

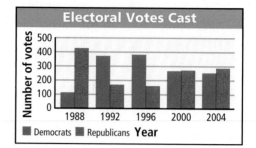

Graphs are often used to display and compare data. They can present a large amount of information in a way that is easy to understand.

A **bar graph** uses vertical or horizontal bars to display data. This graph is a *double-bar graph*. It shows two related sets of data. The blue bars represent the number of electoral votes cast by Democrats, and the red bars represent the number of electoral votes cast by Republicans.

E X A M P L E 1 Analyzing a Bar Graph

Use the bar graph to answer each question.

A In which year shown in the graph did Democrats cast the greatest number of electoral votes?

The blue bar for 1996 is the longest blue bar, so Democrats cast the greatest number of electoral votes in 1996.

B About how many more electoral votes did Republicans cast than Democrats did in 2004?

The bars for 2004 show that Republicans cast about 290 votes and Democrats cast about 250 votes. Republicans cast about 40 more electoral votes than Democrats did in 2004.

C Brendon claims that Republicans cast about 5 times as many electoral votes as Democrats did in 1988. Is his claim valid? Explain.

No. In 1988, Republicans cast about 400 votes and Democrats cast about 100 votes. Republicans cast about 4 times as many electoral votes as Democrats did.

A **circle graph**, also called a pie chart, shows how a set of data is divided into parts. The entire circle displays 100% of the data. Each **sector**, or slice, represents one part of the data set.

The circle graph on the next page shows the results of a survey about pet ownership. The graph makes it easy to see that half of the people surveyed have no pets.

EXAMPLE 2 Analyzing a Circle Graph

Leon surveyed 30 people about pet ownership. The circle graph shows his results. Use the graph to answer each question.

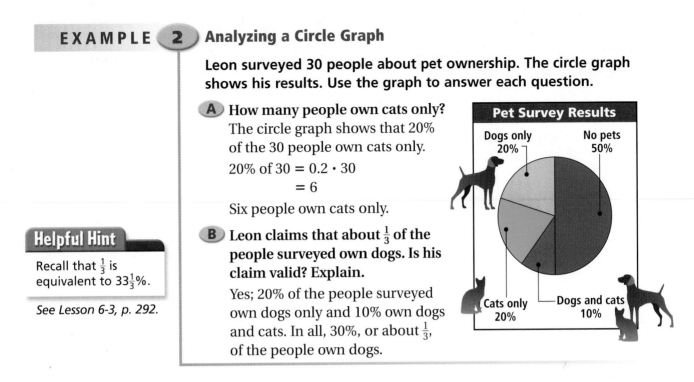

A How many people own cats only?

The circle graph shows that 20% of the 30 people own cats only.

20% of 30 = 0.2 · 30
= 6

Six people own cats only.

Helpful Hint

Recall that $\frac{1}{3}$ is equivalent to $33\frac{1}{3}$%.

See Lesson 6-3, p. 292.

B Leon claims that about $\frac{1}{3}$ of the people surveyed own dogs. Is his claim valid? Explain.

Yes; 20% of the people surveyed own dogs only and 10% own dogs and cats. In all, 30%, or about $\frac{1}{3}$, of the people own dogs.

In a **line graph**, data points on a coordinate grid are connected with line segments. Line graphs are often used to show how numerical data changes over time.

EXAMPLE 3 Analyzing a Line Graph

Use the line graph to answer each question.

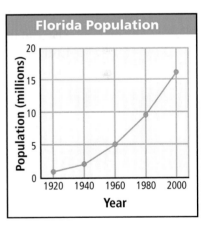

A What was the approximate population of Florida in 1990?

Find the point on the line graph that is halfway between 1980 and 2000. The population at this point is about 13 million.

B Ernesto claims that the population of Florida grew by about 10 million people between 1940 and 2000. Is his claim valid? Explain.

No. The population of Florida in 1940 was about 2 million. The population in 2000 was about 16 million. The population grew by about 14 million people between these two years.

Think and Discuss

1. Compare bar graphs and circle graphs.

California Standards Practice
🔑 SDAP2.3, 🔑 SDAP2.5

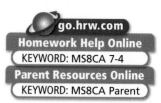

go.hrw.com
Homework Help Online
KEYWORD: MS8CA 7-4
Parent Resources Online
KEYWORD: MS8CA Parent

GUIDED PRACTICE

See Example ① **Use the bar graph for Exercises 1 and 2.**

1. Which state received the most precipitation in 24 hours?

2. Neil claims that the maximum 24-hour precipitation for Virginia is about 20 inches more than it is for Oklahoma. Is his claim valid? Explain.

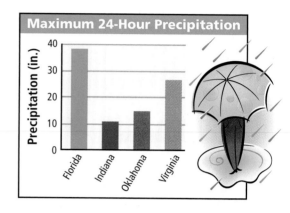

See Example ② **Use the circle graph for Exercises 3 and 4.**

3. What percent of overseas visitors to the United States came from Asia or the Caribbean in 2005?

4. Tricia claims that more than half of the overseas visitors to the United States in 2005 came from Europe. Is her claim valid? Explain.

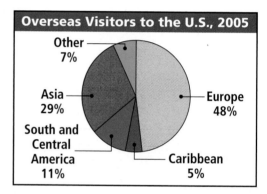

See Example ③ **Use the line graph for Exercises 5 and 6.**

5. What was the approximate average cost of a major league baseball ticket in 2003?

6. Donnell claims that the increase in the average ticket price from 1997 to 2001 was greater than the increase from 1993 to 1997. Is his claim valid? Explain.

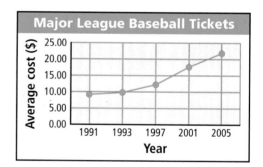

INDEPENDENT PRACTICE

See Example ① **Use the bar graph above for Exercise 7.**

7. Karen claims that the maximum 24-hour precipitation for Florida is more than twice the maximum for Oklahoma. Is her claim valid? Explain.

See Example ② **Use the circle graph above for Exercises 8 and 9.**

8. If about 21,700,000 overseas visitors came to the United States in 2005, about how many came from Asia?

9. Lisa claims that fewer overseas visitors came to the United States from Africa than from South and Central America. Is her claim valid? Explain.

See Example ③ **Use the line graph on page 344 for Exercises 10 and 11.**

10. Estimate the year in which the average cost of a major league baseball ticket first reached $15.

11. Yoshio claims that a family of four would have spent about $70 on tickets to attend a game in 2005. Is his claim valid? Explain.

PRACTICE AND PROBLEM SOLVING

Extra Practice
See page EP14.

12. Earth Science The graph shows the number of acres burned by wildfires in the United States from 1995 to 2000.

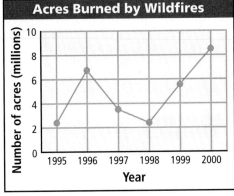

Source: National Interagency Fire Center

   a. During which years did wildfires burn more than 6 million acres?

   b. Explain whether the graph would be useful in predicting future data values.

13. Reasoning A group of students were asked how they like to spend their free time. Of the students surveyed, 47% said they play video games, 59% said they go to the mall, and 41% said they play sports. Can you make a circle graph to display these data? Explain.

14. Write About It What math skills do you use when interpreting information in a circle graph?

15. Challenge A line graph shows that a town's population was 4,500 in 1980, 5,300 in 1990, and 6,100 in 2000. Assuming the population continues to grow at the same rate, what population will the line graph show in 2010?

SPIRAL STANDARDS REVIEW   ← NS1.4, SDAP1.1, SDAP1.4, ← SDAP2.3, ← SDAP2.5

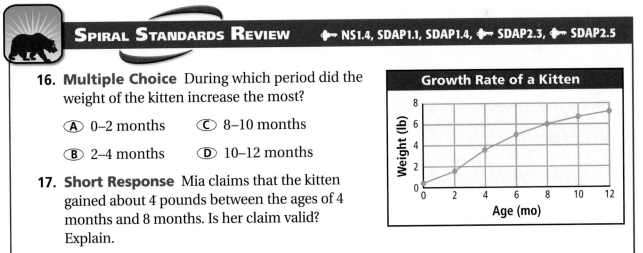

16. Multiple Choice During which period did the weight of the kitten increase the most?

   Ⓐ 0–2 months   Ⓒ 8–10 months

   Ⓑ 2–4 months   Ⓓ 10–12 months

17. Short Response Mia claims that the kitten gained about 4 pounds between the ages of 4 months and 8 months. Is her claim valid? Explain.

18. The regular price of a computer monitor is $499. The monitor is on sale for 15% off. Find the sale price of the monitor. (Lesson 6-6)

19. The number of e-mails Veronica received each day in one week were 12, 15, 14, 38, 11, 16, and 13. What are the mean and median of this data set? Which measure or measures would be most useful for describing the typical number of e-mails Veronica received per day? Explain. (Lesson 7-3)

Technology LAB 7-4

Use Technology to Display Data

Use after Lesson 7-4

go.hrw.com
Lab Resources Online
KEYWORD: MS8CA Lab7

There are several ways to display data, including bar graphs, line graphs, and circle graphs. A spreadsheet provides a quick way to create these graphs.

California Standards

Extension of ◆ **SDAP2.3** Analyze **data displays** and explain why the way in which the question was asked might have influenced the results obtained and why the way in which the results were displayed might have influenced the conclusions reached.

Activity

Use a spreadsheet to display the Kennedy Middle School Student Council budget shown in the table at right.

Student Council Budget	
Activity	**Amount ($)**
Assemblies	275
Dances	587
Spring Festival	412
Awards Banquet	384
Other	250

❶ Open the spreadsheet program, and enter the data as shown below. Enter the activities in column A and the amount budgeted in column B. Include the column titles in row 1.

	A	B	C
1	Activity	Amount ($)	
2	Assemblies	275	
3	Dances	587	
4	Spring Festival	412	
5	Awards Banquet	384	
6	Other	250	
7			

❷ Highlight the data by clicking on cell A1 and dragging the cursor to cell B6. Click the Chart Wizard icon 📊. Then click **FINISH** to choose the first type of column graph.

Chart Wizard – Step 1 of 4 – Chart Type

Standard Types | Custom Types

Chart type:
- Column
- Bar
- Line
- Pie
- XY (Scatter)
- Area
- Doughnut
- Radar
- Surface
- Bubble

Chart sub-type:

Clustered Column. Compares values across categories.

Press and Hold to View Sample

Cancel | < Back | Next > | Finish

3 The bar graph of the data appears as shown. Resize or reposition the graph, if necessary.

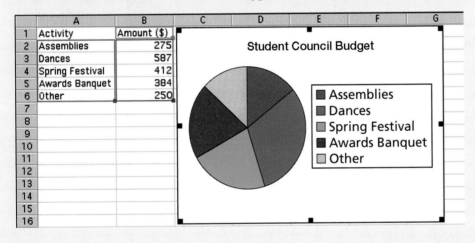

	A	B
1	Activity	Amount ($)
2	Assemblies	275
3	Dances	587
4	Spring Festival	412
5	Awards Banquet	384
6	Other	250

Student Council Budget

To see a circle graph of the data, select the bar graph (as shown above). Click the Chart Wizard icon and choose "Pie," which is the circle graph. Then click **FINISH** to choose the first type of circle graph.

	A	B
1	Activity	Amount ($)
2	Assemblies	275
3	Dances	587
4	Spring Festival	412
5	Awards Banquet	384
6	Other	250

Student Council Budget

- Assemblies
- Dances
- Spring Festival
- Awards Banquet
- Other

Think and Discuss

1. Which graph best displays the Student Council budget? Why?

2. Would a line graph be an appropriate display of the Student Council budget data? Explain.

Try This

1. The table shows the number of points scored by members of a girls' basketball team in one season. Use a spreadsheet to create a bar graph and a circle graph of the data.

Player	Ana	Angel	Mary	Nia	Tina	Zoe
Points Scored	201	145	89	40	21	8

2. Explain how you could use each graph to determine which player scored the most points.

7-5 Misleading Graphs

California Standards

🔑 **SDAP2.3** Analyze data displays and explain why the way in which the question was asked might have influenced the results obtained and **why the way in which the results were displayed might have influenced the conclusions reached.**

Also covered: 🔑 **SDAP2.5**

Why learn this? You can recognize advertisements that use graphs to distort information.

Sometimes data is presented in a way that influences how the data is interpreted. A data display that distorts information in order to persuade can be *misleading*.

An axis in a graph can be "broken" to make the graph easier to read. However, a broken axis can also be misleading. In the graph at right, the cost per minute for service with Company B looks like it is twice as much as the cost for service with Company A. In fact, the difference is only $0.10 per minute.

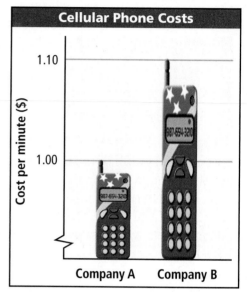

Cellular Phone Costs

Cost per minute ($)

1.10

1.00

Company A   Company B

EXAMPLE 1 *Social Studies Application*

Both bar graphs show the same data. Which graph could be misleading? Why?

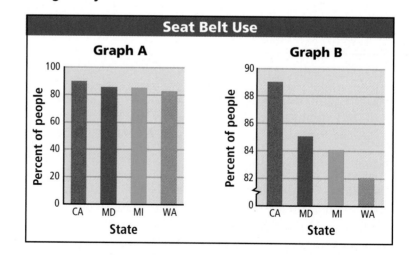

Seat Belt Use

Graph A

Percent of people

CA   MD   MI   WA

State

Graph B

Percent of people

CA   MD   MI   WA

State

Graph B could be misleading. Because the vertical axis on graph B is broken, people might conclude that the percent of people in California who wear seat belts is much greater than the percents in the other states.

348 *Chapter 7 Collecting, Displaying, and Analyzing Data*

There are other ways in which graphs can be misleading. For example, the scales in bar and line graphs might have unequal intervals, or the bars in a bar graph might have unequal widths. Icons in a pictograph can also be misleading because of their size and the number that they represent.

EXAMPLE 2 Analyzing Misleading Graphs

Explain why each graph could be misleading.

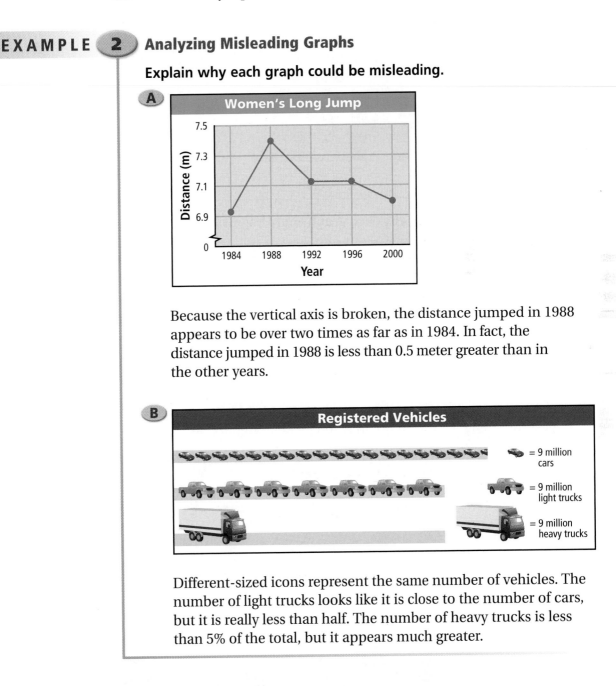

A

Women's Long Jump

Because the vertical axis is broken, the distance jumped in 1988 appears to be over two times as far as in 1984. In fact, the distance jumped in 1988 is less than 0.5 meter greater than in the other years.

B

Registered Vehicles

= 9 million cars

= 9 million light trucks

= 9 million heavy trucks

Different-sized icons represent the same number of vehicles. The number of light trucks looks like it is close to the number of cars, but it is really less than half. The number of heavy trucks is less than 5% of the total, but it appears much greater.

Think and Discuss

1. **Describe** what might indicate that a graph is misleading.

2. **Give an example** of a situation in which a misleading graph might be used to persuade readers.

California
Standards Practice
🔑 SDAP2.3, 🔑 SDAP2.5

go.hrw.com
Homework Help Online
KEYWORD: MS8CA 7-5
Parent Resources Online
KEYWORD: MS8CA Parent

GUIDED PRACTICE

See Example ① **1.** Which graph could be misleading? Why?

See Example ② Explain why each graph could be misleading.

INDEPENDENT PRACTICE

See Example ① **4.** Which graph could be misleading? Why?

See Example ② Explain why each graph could be misleading.

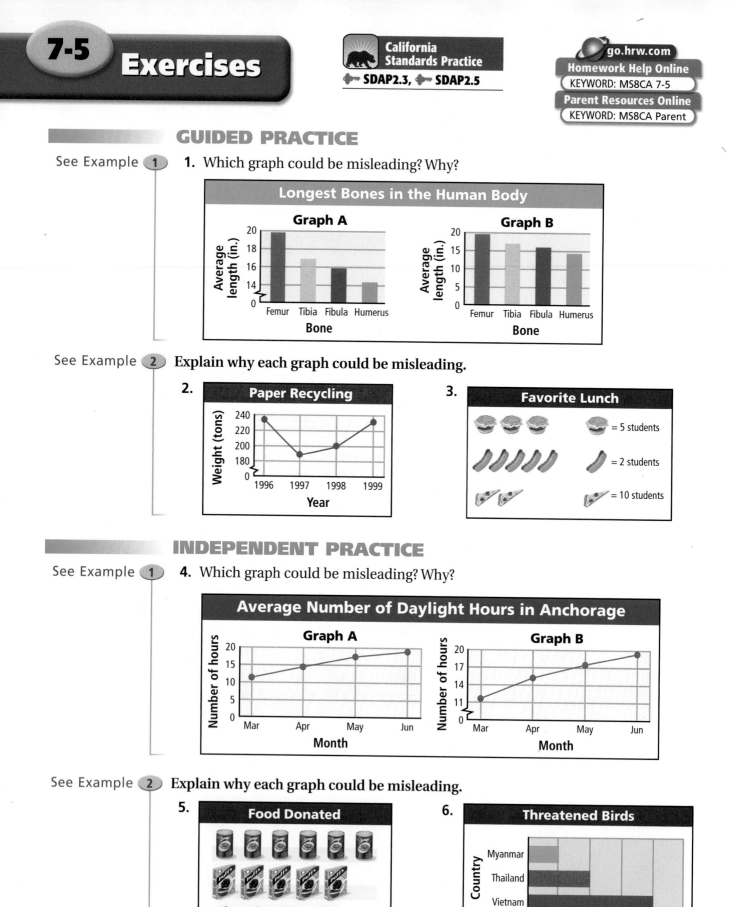

PRACTICE AND PROBLEM SOLVING

Extra Practice
See page EP15.

7. **Reasoning** Explain why the graphs below are misleading. Then tell how you can redraw them so that they are not misleading.

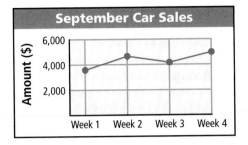

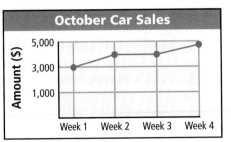

8. **Social Studies** The Appalachian Trail is a 2,160-mile footpath that runs from Maine to Georgia. The bar graph shows the number of miles of trail in three states. Redraw the graph so that it is not misleading. Then compare the two graphs.

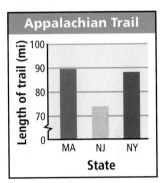

9. **Choose a Strategy** Tanya had $1.19 in coins. None of the coins were dollars or 50-cent pieces. Josie asked Tanya for change for a dollar, but she did not have the correct change. Which coins did Tanya have?

10. **Write About It** Why is it important to closely examine graphs in ads?

11. **Challenge** A company asked 10 people about their favorite brand of toothpaste. Three people chose Sparkle, one chose Smile, and six chose Purely White. An advertisement for Sparkle states, "Three times as many people prefer Sparkle over Smile!" Explain why this statement is misleading.

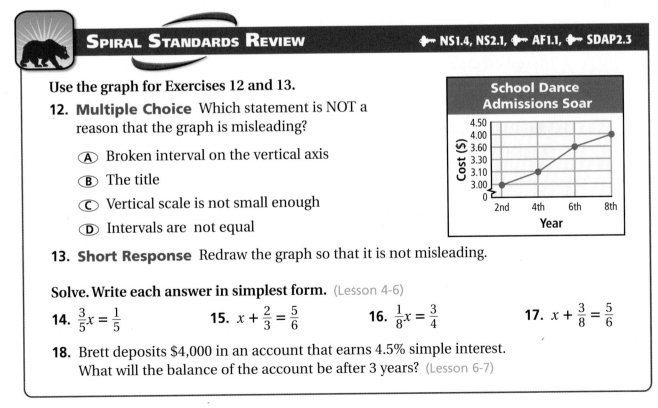

SPIRAL STANDARDS REVIEW ✦ NS1.4, NS2.1, ✦ AF1.1, ✦ SDAP2.3

Use the graph for Exercises 12 and 13.

12. **Multiple Choice** Which statement is NOT a reason that the graph is misleading?

Ⓐ Broken interval on the vertical axis

Ⓑ The title

Ⓒ Vertical scale is not small enough

Ⓓ Intervals are not equal

13. **Short Response** Redraw the graph so that it is not misleading.

Solve. Write each answer in simplest form. (Lesson 4-6)

14. $\frac{3}{5}x = \frac{1}{5}$ 15. $x + \frac{2}{3} = \frac{5}{6}$ 16. $\frac{1}{8}x = \frac{3}{4}$ 17. $x + \frac{3}{8} = \frac{5}{6}$

18. Brett deposits $4,000 in an account that earns 4.5% simple interest. What will the balance of the account be after 3 years? (Lesson 6-7)

READY TO GO ON?

Quiz for Lessons 7-1 Through 7-5

☑ **7-1** **Mean, Median, Mode, and Range**

Find the mean, median, mode, and range of each data set.

1.

Distance (mi)					
5	6	4	7	3	5

2.

Test Scores				
78	80	85	92	90

3.

Ages of Students (yr)							
11	13	12	12	12	13	9	14

4.

Number of Pages in Each Book						
145	119	156	158	125	128	135

☑ **7-2** **Additional Data and Outliers**

5. The four states with the longest coastlines are Alaska, Florida, California, and Hawaii. Alaska's coastline is 6,640 miles. Florida's coastline is 1,350 miles. California's coastline is 840 miles, and Hawaii's coastline is 750 miles. Find the mean, median, mode, and range of the lengths with and without Alaska's, and explain the changes.

☑ **7-3** **Choosing the Most Useful Measure**

6. The list shows the number of mice sold at a pet store over a 10-day period.

5, 6, 4, 5, 5, 4, 24, 5, 6, 6

What are the mean and median of this data set? If the pet store owner wants to know the number of mice sold on a typical day, is one measure more useful than the other? Explain.

☑ **7-4** **Analyzing Data Displays**

Use the circle graph for problems 7 and 8.

7. Approximately what percent of students picked cheese as their favorite topping?

8. Gabriel claims that more students picked pepperoni than green peppers and sausage combined. Is his claim valid? Explain.

Favorite Pizza Toppings

☑ **7-5** **Misleading Graphs**

9. Which graph is misleading? Explain.

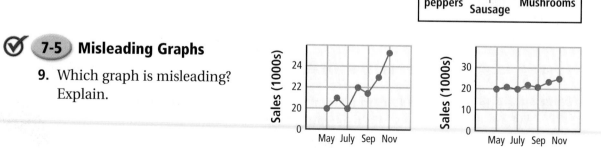

Focus on Problem Solving

California Standards

MR1.1 Analyze problems by identifying relationships, distinguishing relevant from irrelevant information, identifying missing information, sequencing and prioritizing information, and observing patterns.
Also covered: **NS2.0, MR2.4**

Solve

- **Choose an operation: addition or subtraction**

In order to decide whether to add or subtract to solve a problem, you need to determine what action is taking place in the problem. If you are combining or putting together numbers, you need to add. If you are taking away or finding how far apart two numbers are, you need to subtract.

Determine the action in each problem. Then determine which operation could be used to solve the problem. Use the table for problems 5 and 6.

1. Betty, Raymond, and Helen ran a three-person relay race. Their individual times were 48 seconds, 55 seconds, and 51 seconds. What was their total time?

2. The Scots pine and the sessile oak are trees native to Northern Ireland. The height of a mature Scots pine is 111 feet, and the height of a mature sessile oak is 90 feet. How much taller is the Scots pine than the sessile oak?

3. Mr. Hutchins has $35.00 to buy supplies for his social studies class. He wants to buy items that cost $19.75, $8.49, and $7.10. Does Mr. Hutchins have enough money to buy all of the supplies?

4. The running time for the 1998 movie *Antz* is 83 minutes. Jordan has watched 25 minutes of the movie. How many minutes does he have left to watch?

Sizes of Marine Mammals	
Mammal	**Weight (kg)**
Killer whale	3,600
Manatee	400
Sea lion	200
Walrus	750

5. The table gives the approximate weights of four marine mammals. How much more does the killer whale weigh than the sea lion?

6. Find the total weight of the manatee, the sea lion, and the walrus. Do these three mammals together weigh more or less than the killer whale?

7-6 Populations and Samples

Vocabulary
population
sample
random sample

Who uses this? Biologists use samples to study animal populations.

In 2002, there were claims that Chronic Wasting Disease (CWD), or Mad Elk Disease, was spreading westward across North America. In order to evaluate these claims, the elk population had to be tested.

A **population** is an entire group of objects or individuals that is considered for a survey. All of the elk in North America is an example of a population.

Surveying or testing every member of a large group can be difficult or impossible. Instead, researchers often study a sample. A **sample** is a part of a population.

EXAMPLE 1 Deciding When to Use a Sample

For each situation, explain whether it makes sense to use a sample.

A A biologist wants to determine the average wingspan of the six bald eagles at a zoo.

The entire population is small. It does not make sense to use a sample because every member of the population can be measured.

B A biologist wants to determine the average wingspan of bald eagles in the United States.

The entire population is large. It would be difficult to measure the wingspan of every bald eagle in the United States. It makes sense to use a sample.

In a **random sample**, each member of the population has an equal chance of being selected. A random sample is more likely to be representative of a population than samples that are chosen in other ways.

EXAMPLE 2 **Comparing Samples**

About 36% of all households in the United States have a pet dog. Brad surveys a random sample of households from two towns. Compare the samples with the national percent.

Household Dog Ownership		
Sample	Number with Dogs	Number without Dogs
Town A	11	9
Town B	7	13

For each sample, find the percent of the households that have dogs.

Town A: $\dfrac{\text{number of households with dogs}}{\text{total number of households}} = \dfrac{11}{(11+9)} = \dfrac{11}{20} = 0.55 = 55\%$

Town B: $\dfrac{\text{number of households with dogs}}{\text{total number of households}} = \dfrac{7}{(7+13)} = \dfrac{7}{20} = 0.35 = 35\%$

The data suggest that dog ownership in Town B is close to the national percentage, but dog ownership in Town A is greater than the national percentage.

Given data about a random sample, you can make predictions or evaluate claims about the entire population.

EXAMPLE 3 **Evaluating Claims Based on Statistical Data**

Reasoning

A biologist estimates that more than 700 of the 4,500 elk at a wildlife preserve are infected with a parasite. A random sample of 50 elk shows that 8 of them are infected. Determine whether the biologist's estimate is likely to be accurate.

Set up a proportion to predict the total number of infected elk.

$\dfrac{\text{infected elk in sample}}{\text{size of sample}} = \dfrac{\text{infected elk in population}}{\text{size of population}}$

$\dfrac{8}{50} = \dfrac{x}{4{,}500}$ *Let x represent the number of infected elk at the presereve.*

$36{,}000 = 50x$ *The cross products are equal.*

$\dfrac{36{,}000}{50} = \dfrac{50x}{50}$ *Divide each side by 50.*

$720 = x$

Based on the sample, you can predict that there are 720 infected elk at the preserve. The biologist's estimate is likely to be accurate.

> **Remember!**
>
> In the proportion $\frac{a}{b} = \frac{c}{d}$, the cross products $a \cdot d$ and $b \cdot c$ are equal.
>
> *See Lesson 5-4, p. 244.*

Think and Discuss

1. Describe a situation in which you would want to use a sample rather than survey the entire population.

7-6 **Exercises**

California Standards Practice
SDAP2.1, ↞ SDAP2.5

go.hrw.com
Homework Help Online
KEYWORD: MS8CA 7-6
Parent Resources Online
KEYWORD: MS8CA Parent

GUIDED PRACTICE

See Example ① **For each situation, explain whether it makes sense to use a sample.**

1. A reporter wants to know the favorite painters of employees at a local art museum.

2. You want to know the types of calculators used by middle-school students across the country.

See Example ② 3. About 12% of adults in the United States visit a zoo each year. Malika surveys a random sample of adults from two cities in her state. Compare the samples with the national percent.

Zoo Attendance in the Past Year		
Sample	Yes	No
City A	3	22
City B	10	15

See Example ③ 4. A factory produces 150,000 lightbulbs per day. The manager of the factory estimates that fewer than 1,000 defective bulbs are produced each day. In a random sample of 250 lightbulbs, there are 2 defective bulbs. Determine whether the manager's estimate is likely to be accurate. Explain.

INDEPENDENT PRACTICE

See Example ① **For each situation, explain whether it makes sense to use a sample.**

5. You want to know how many hours per week the students in your social studies class spend on their homework.

6. A newspaper publisher wants to know how many of the newspaper's readers own a computer.

See Example ② 7. In 2005, the average American spent 6 hours per week using the Internet. Laura surveys a random sample of 20 people in two towns. Compare the samples with the national average.

Internet Use (hours per week)	
Town A	11, 8, 7, 2, 9, 4, 2, 0, 7, 2, 8, 20, 4, 5, 8, 6, 3, 0, 2, 10
Town B	3, 12, 4, 0, 5, 7, 3, 0, 2, 4, 10, 5, 2, 2, 9, 6, 2, 2, 5, 11

See Example ③ 8. A university has 30,600 students. A school counselor estimates that 2% of the students speak three or more languages. In a random sample of 240 students, 20 speak three or more languages. Determine whether the counselor's estimate is likely to be accurate.

PRACTICE AND PROBLEM SOLVING

Extra Practice
See page EP15.

9. **Estimation** A brand of mixed nuts contains cashews. Tyler counts 51 nuts in one package, 13 of which are cashews. He counts 52 nuts in another package, 10 of which are cashews. Based on these samples, estimate the percent of nuts in a package that are cashews.

10. **Science** A biologist chooses a random sample of 50 out of 750 fruit flies and finds that two of them have deformed wings. She claims that about 30 of the 750 fruit flies have deformed wings. Do you agree? Explain.

11. A field of poppies has an area of 400 square meters. A random sample within the field has an area of 16 square meters and contains 23 California poppies. Predict the number of California poppies in the entire field.

12. **Consumer Math** On June 12, 2006, the average price of regular gasoline in the United States was $2.91 per gallon. The table shows the price of regular gas at a sample of 10 gas stations in Los Angeles on this date. Compare the sample to the national average.

Price per Gallon of Regular Gas in Los Angeles
$3.05, $3.10, $3.49, $3.18, $3.24, $3.20, $3.05, $3.39, $3.18, $3.12

The California poppy is the California state flower. It was originally called the golden poppy for its golden yellow color.

13. **Write a Problem** Use results from a newspaper poll or survey to write a problem about using a sample to make a prediction.

14. **Write About It** The graph shows the results of a 2005 survey of 651 visitors to Yosemite National Park. Identify the population being studied. Then explain whether the data was collected from a sample or from the entire population.

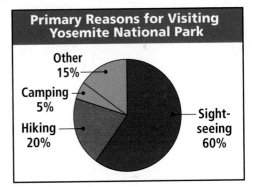

Primary Reasons for Visiting Yosemite National Park

Other 15%
Camping 5%
Hiking 20%
Sight-seeing 60%

15. **Challenge** There are 80 students in a soccer club. Cara chooses a random sample of 2 students and finds that one of them is also a member of the chess club. Cara concludes that 40 students in the soccer club also belong to the chess club. Do you agree? Why or why not?

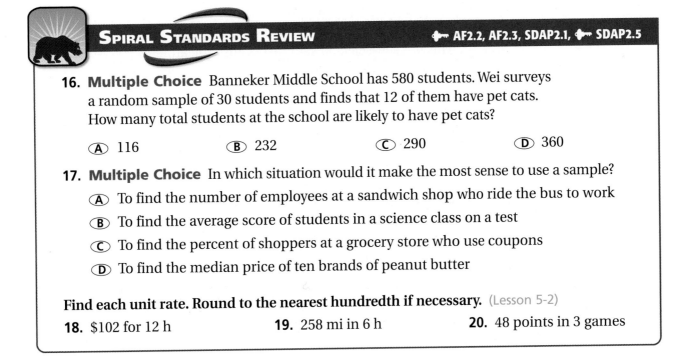

SPIRAL STANDARDS REVIEW   **AF2.2, AF2.3, SDAP2.1, SDAP2.5**

16. **Multiple Choice** Banneker Middle School has 580 students. Wei surveys a random sample of 30 students and finds that 12 of them have pet cats. How many total students at the school are likely to have pet cats?

   Ⓐ 116   Ⓑ 232   Ⓒ 290   Ⓓ 360

17. **Multiple Choice** In which situation would it make the most sense to use a sample?

   Ⓐ To find the number of employees at a sandwich shop who ride the bus to work

   Ⓑ To find the average score of students in a science class on a test

   Ⓒ To find the percent of shoppers at a grocery store who use coupons

   Ⓓ To find the median price of ten brands of peanut butter

Find each unit rate. Round to the nearest hundredth if necessary. (Lesson 5-2)

18. $102 for 12 h   19. 258 mi in 6 h   20. 48 points in 3 games

7-7 Selecting Samples

California Standards

SDAP2.2 **Identify different ways of selecting a sample (e.g., convenience sampling, responses to a survey, random sampling) and which method makes a sample more representative for a population.**

Why learn this? You can use sampling to learn about the athletes in a race.

Recall that in a *random sample* each member of the population has an equal chance of being selected. Some other types of sampling methods are described below.

Athletes in the Long Beach Marathon

Vocabulary
systematic sample
convenience sample
self-selected sample

Sampling Methods	
Method	**Description**
systematic sample	A member of the population is selected at random, and then others are selected by using a pattern.
convenience sample	The most-available members of the population are chosen.
self-selected sample	Members of the population volunteer to respond to a survey.

EXAMPLE 1 Identifying Sampling Methods

Reasoning

Race organizers want to know how often participants train for a race. Identify each type of sampling method.

A The organizers provide written surveys at the finish line for athletes who wish to fill them out.

This is a self-selected sample because the athletes choose whether to complete the surveys.

B The organizers randomly choose one of the first ten names on an alphabetical list of the athletes' names. Then they select every tenth name after that.

This is a systematic sample. The first name is chosen at random, and then the other names are chosen by using a pattern.

C The organizers interview a group of 50 athletes as the athletes arrive at the race.

This is a convenience sample because the group of athletes is easy for the organizers to reach.

Random samples and systematic samples are more likely to be representative of a population than either convenience samples or self-selected samples.

EXAMPLE 2 Analyzing Sampling Methods

Reasoning

Determine which sampling method will better represent the entire population. Justify your answer.

Student Attendance at Football Games	
Sampling Method	**Results of Survey**
Arnie surveys 80 students by randomly choosing names from the school directory.	62% attend football games.
Vic surveys 28 students that were sitting near him during lunch.	81% attend football games.

Arnie's method produces results that better represent the entire student population because he uses a random sample.

Vic's method produces results that are not as representative of the entire student population because he uses a convenience sample.

Think and Discuss

1. Explain why it might be difficult to obtain a truly random sample of a very large population.

 **7-7 Exercises**

California Standards Practice
SDAP2.2

go.hrw.com
Homework Help Online
KEYWORD: MS8CA 7-7
Parent Resources Online
KEYWORD: MS8CA Parent

GUIDED PRACTICE

See Example 1 — A state senator wants to know whether voters in her district support a new tax law. Identify each type of sampling method.

1. A staff member randomly chooses 500 names from a list of the district's registered voters.

2. A staff member posts a survey on the senator's Web site.

See Example 2 — **3.** Determine which sampling method will better represent the entire population. Justify your answer.

Lone Star Cars: Customer Satisfaction	
Sampling Method	**Results of Survey**
Nadia surveys 200 customers on the car lot one Saturday morning.	92% are satisfied.
Daria surveys every 25th customer listed in the company's computer records.	68% are satisfied.

INDEPENDENT PRACTICE

See Example 1   A school librarian wants to know how often students at the school use text messaging. Identify each type of sampling method.

4. The librarian randomly selects a name from the first 20 names on a list of all students at the school and then chooses every 20th name after that.

5. The librarian surveys 40 students who are in the library during lunch period.

See Example 2   **6.** Determine which sampling method will better represent the entire population. Justify your answer.

Midville Morning News: Subscription Renewals	
Sampling Method	**Results of Survey**
Suzanne puts a mail-in survey in one issue of the newspaper.	61% intend to renew subscription.
Vonetta telephones 150 randomly selected subscribers.	82% intend to renew subscription.

PRACTICE AND PROBLEM SOLVING

Extra Practice
See page EP15.

Jasmine wants to survey a sample of the students taking art at her school. Describe how Jasmine could select each type of sample.

7. random sample   **8.** convenience sample   **9.** self-selected sample

10. Reasoning Explain why surveying 100 people who are listed in the phone book may not be a random sample.

11. Write About It Suppose you want to know whether the sixth-grade students at your school spend more time watching TV or using a computer. How might you choose a random sample from the population?

12. Challenge A manager surveyed 200 company employees and determined that 40 walk to work. If 300 of the company's 9,200 employees walk to work, do you think the manager chose a random sample? Explain.

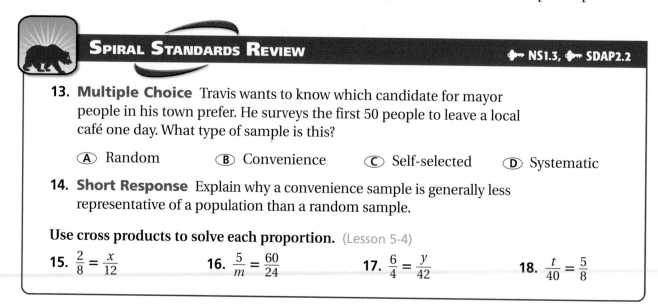

SPIRAL STANDARDS REVIEW
➤ NS1.3, ➤ SDAP2.2

13. Multiple Choice Travis wants to know which candidate for mayor people in his town prefer. He surveys the first 50 people to leave a local café one day. What type of sample is this?

Ⓐ Random   Ⓑ Convenience   Ⓒ Self-selected   Ⓓ Systematic

14. Short Response Explain why a convenience sample is generally less representative of a population than a random sample.

Use cross products to solve each proportion. (Lesson 5-4)

15. $\frac{2}{8} = \frac{x}{12}$ **16.** $\frac{5}{m} = \frac{60}{24}$ **17.** $\frac{6}{4} = \frac{y}{42}$ **18.** $\frac{t}{40} = \frac{5}{8}$

Explore Samples

Use with Lesson 7-7

go.hrw.com
Lab Resources Online
KEYWORD: MS8CA Lab7

California Standards

🔑 **SDAP2.2** Identify different ways of selecting a sample (e.g., convenience sampling, responses to a survey, random sampling) and which method makes a sample more representative for a population.

You can predict data about a population by collecting data from a representative sample.

Activity

Your school district has been discussing the possibility of school uniforms. Each school will get to choose its uniform and colors. Your class has been chosen to make the selection for your school. To be fair, you want the other students in the school to have some input. You conduct a survey to see what the majority of students in your school want.

1 Model the survey by following the steps below.

  a. Choose your population. For example:

  - every student in the school
  - only your class
  - all 6th grade students
  - all girls
  - all boys
  - teachers

  b. Choose two different sampling methods. Discuss the pros and cons of each method listed.

  - random
  - systematic
  - convenience
  - self-selected response

  c. Decide what colors and what uniform choices to present to your sample. For example:

  - pants
  - sweaters
  - school colors
  - shorts
  - jackets
  - navy blue
  - skirts
  - vests
  - forest green

Think and Discuss

1. Explain why choosing the teachers as your population might not be the best choice.

2. How did you decide which colors to present to your sample?

Try This

1. Create forms for your survey listing the different options. Then survey your sample. Make a table of your results. Explain what your table tells you about the population.

California Standards

SDAP2.4 Identify data that represent sampling errors and explain why the sample (and the display) might be biased.

Also covered: **SDAP2.3, SDAP2.5**

Vocabulary
biased sample
biased question

Why learn this? Identifying possible bias in surveys can help you decide whether claims made by reporters are valid.

Do We Need a New Downtown Station?

Yes 85%

No 15%

A reporter wants to know whether city residents support the building of a new downtown subway station. The reporter surveys 80 subway riders and graphs the results.

A **biased sample** is a sample that does not fairly represent the population. The reporter's sample could be biased because subway riders may be more likely to support a new station than city residents who do not ride the subway would be.

EXAMPLE 1 Identifying Potentially Biased Samples

Determine whether each sample may be biased. Explain.

A The first 50 people exiting a movie are surveyed to find out what type of movie people in the town like to see.

The sample is biased. It is likely that not everyone in the town likes to see the same type of movie that these 50 people just saw.

B A librarian randomly chooses 100 books from the library's database to calculate the average length of a library book.

The sample is not biased. It is a random sample.

The results of a survey may also be affected by *biased questions*. A **biased question** is one that leads people to give a certain answer.

EXAMPLE 2 Identifying Potentially Biased Questions

Determine whether each survey question may be biased. Explain.

A Do you prefer the sleek and stylish cell phone or this plainer one?

The question is biased. People may be more likely to choose a cell phone that is described as sleek and stylish than one that is described as plain.

B In the next election, do you intend to vote for Martinez or Chen?

The question is not biased. It does not lead people to choose one candidate over the other.

To decide whether a claim based on a survey is valid, check whether the sample or the survey question is biased. In addition, make sure that the sample was taken from the correct population.

EXAMPLE **3** **Evaluating Survey Claims**

Determine whether each claim is valid. Explain.

A Ashton conducts a survey to find out how teenagers in his town spend their free time.

Sample: 40 teenagers at a local soccer game

Question: What is your favorite hobby?

Claim: Playing sports is the most popular hobby among teenagers in Ashton's town.

The claim may not be valid. The sample is biased because teenagers at a soccer game may be more likely to play sports than other teenagers would.

Results:

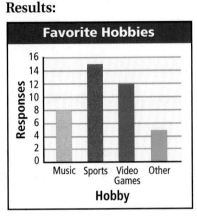

B The manager of a bookstore conducts a survey to find out whether customers like the store's new Web site.

Sample: 100 customers selected at random from the store's database

Question: What is your opinion of our new, more user-friendly Web site?

Claim: A majority of the bookstore's customers like the new Web site.

The claim may not be valid. The question is biased because customers may be more likely to have a favorable opinion of a Web site that is described as new and user friendly.

Results:

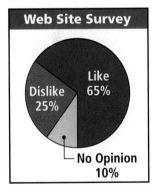

Think and Discuss

1. Explain why biased questions can lead to survey results that are not valid.

2. Give an example of a biased question and of a fair question that you could ask the students in your class about their favorite books.

3. Explain why a claim based on a self-selected sample may not be valid.

California Standards Practice

← SDAP2.3, ← SDAP2.4, ← SDAP2.5

go.hrw.com
Homework Help Online
KEYWORD: MS8CA 7-8
Parent Resources Online
KEYWORD: MS8CA Parent

GUIDED PRACTICE

See Example 1 **Determine whether the sample may be biased. Explain.**

1. A company selects every fifth customer from its computer database and then surveys those customers to find out how they like their service.

See Example 2 **Determine whether each survey question may be biased. Explain.**

2. Do you approve or disapprove of the governor's tax proposal?

3. Do you agree that putting computers in every classroom is the best way to improve education?

See Example 3 4. Ellen conducts a survey to find out what is important to people in her city when they buy a car. Determine whether Ellen's claim is valid. Explain.
Sample: 50 people at a car show
Question: What is the most important factor when you buy a car?
Claim: Having the latest features is the most important factor for car buyers in Ellen's city.

Results:

Most Important Factor When Buying a Car

Looks 30%
Safety 12%
Cost 14%
Latest Features 44%

INDEPENDENT PRACTICE

See Example 1 **Determine whether the sample may be biased. Explain.**

5. A disc jockey asks the first 10 listeners who call in whether they liked the last song that was played.

See Example 2 **Determine whether each survey question may be biased. Explain.**

6. Should the historic Main Street Theater be replaced by an unneeded shopping center?

7. What is your favorite brand of jeans?

See Example 3 8. Manuel conducts a survey to find out the preferred news source of students at his school. Determine whether Manuel's claim is valid. Explain.
Sample: 30 students chosen at random from the school directory
Question: What is your preferred source of news?
Claim: Most students at Manuel's school prefer to get their news from the Internet.

Results:

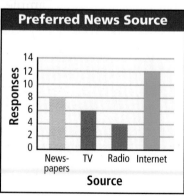

Preferred News Source

Extra Practice
See page EP15.

For each situation, describe a survey sample and a survey question that would be likely to lead to valid results.

9. A teacher wants to know whether his students prefer to have a class party at an ice-skating rink or at an amusement park.

10. The mayor of a city wants to know whether registered voters approve of adding a bike lane on First Street.

11. **Reasoning** A local news show asks viewers to call in their answers to the question "Does the city need a new airport?" Two-thirds of the 240 callers say no. The same question is asked of 240 people who are contacted by phone from a random selection of local telephone numbers. Only 28% of these people answer no. Which result is probably more valid? Explain.

12. **What's the Error?** The students in Jacy's science class put their names in a hat. Of the 28 names in the hat, Jacy draws 15 names. She finds that 6 of these 15 students say that their favorite subject is science. Jacy predicts that 254 of the 635 students at her school would say that their favorite subject is science. What is the error in Jacy's prediction?

13. **Write About It** Explain why the question "How much time do you waste each week watching television?" is biased and describe how you could reword it to make it more fair.

14. **Challenge** A newspaper conducts a survey to find out whether residents of a town think a new playground should be built. Write a biased question that might give the results shown in the table.

Playground Survey Results	
Approve	20%
Disapprove	75%
No opinion	5%

SPIRAL STANDARDS REVIEW NS2.3, AF1.1, AF1.4, SDAP2.4, SDAP2.5

15. **Multiple Choice** A researcher wants to know about the driving habits of people in her state. She chooses 200 people at random from the state's database of licensed drivers. She asks the question "In the past month, how many times have you put other people at risk by talking on your cell phone while driving?" Which of the following best explains why the survey results may not be valid?

Ⓐ The sample is biased.   Ⓒ The sample is from the wrong population.

Ⓑ The question is biased.   Ⓓ The question is not related to the topic.

16. **Short Response** Give an example of a biased sample. Explain why it is biased.

Simplify each expression. (Lesson 1-3)

17. $24 \div 2^2 + 4$ 18. $(3^2 - 1) \div 4$ 19. $10 \cdot (2 + 1) - 9 \cdot 2$ 20. $4^3 - (5^2 + 1)$

Solve each equation. Check your answer. (Lesson 2-5)

21. $m - 4 = -9$ 22. $-6 + x = 18$ 23. $3p = -27$ 24. $\frac{y}{4} = -20$

READY TO GO ON?

Quiz for Lessons 7-6 Through 7-8

7-6 Populations and Samples

For each situation, explain whether it makes sense to use a sample.

1. The manager of a radio station wants to know how many hours per week listeners tune in to the station.

2. Enrique wants to know the average length of the songs on his favorite CD.

3. A biologist estimates that there are 1,800 fish in a quarry. To test this estimate, a student caught 150 fish from the quarry, tagged them, and released them. A few days later, the student caught 50 fish and noted that 4 were tagged. Determine whether the biologist's estimate is likely to be accurate.

7-7 Selecting Samples

A park ranger would like to know how often visitors to the park go camping each year. Identify each type of sampling method.

4. The ranger places survey forms in the park's gift shop.

5. The ranger surveys the first 50 visitors who pass through the park's information booth.

6. Determine which sampling method will better represent the entire population. Justify your answer.

Skateboard Ownership: Riverdale Students	
Sampling Method	**Survey Results**
Jamison surveys 20 students at a local skate park.	90% own a skateboard.
Sheila surveys every 20th student entering the Riverdale cafeteria one day at lunch.	16% own a skateboard.

7-8 Identifying Sampling Errors and Bias

Determine whether each sample may be biased. Explain.

7. Rickie surveys people at an amusement park to find out the average size of people's immediate family.

8. Theo surveys every fourth person entering a grocery store to find out the average number of pets in people's homes.

Determine whether the survey question may be biased. Explain.

9. Do you agree with many experts that global warming is the most important problem we face?

CONCEPT CONNECTION

CHAPTER
7

Big Money Prizes A radio station is planning a contest. Each winner will select a money envelope. The station is planning on having 150 winners and giving away $6,000. The table shows the plan for filling the envelopes.

1. The station wants to describe the typical amount of money a winner will receive. What are the mean, median, mode, and range of the amounts won?

2. The sponsors decide to double the amount of money they give away. The station manager wants to do this by doubling the amount of money in each envelope. Make a table showing how much money would be in each envelope.

3. How does the station manager's plan affect the mean, median, mode, and range of the amounts won?

Number of Envelopes	Amount of Money
1	$5,000
2	$250
4	$50
12	$10
6	$5
25	$2
100	$1

4. The DJs think it would be better to double the number of winners rather than doubling the amount of money in each envelope. They want to double the number of envelopes containing each amount of money. Make a new table that shows their plan.

5. How does the DJs' plan affect the mean, median, mode, and range of the amounts won?

Game Time

Code Breaker

A *cryptogram* is a message written in code. One of the most common types of codes is a substitution code, in which each letter of a text is replaced with a different letter. The table shows one way to replace the letters in a text to make a coded message.

Original Letter	A	B	C	D	E	F	G	H	I	J	K	L	M
Code Letter	J	E	O	H	K	A	U	B	L	Y	V	G	P
Original Letter	N	O	P	Q	R	S	T	U	V	W	X	Y	Z
Code Letter	X	N	S	D	Z	Q	M	W	C	R	F	T	I

With this code, the word MATH is written PJMB. You can also use the table as a key to decode messages. Try decoding the following message.

J EJZ UZJSB OJX EK WQKH MN HLQSGJT HJMJ.

Suppose you want to crack a substitution code but are not given the key. You can use letter frequencies to help you. The bar graph below shows the number of times each letter of the English language is likely to appear in a text of 100 letters.

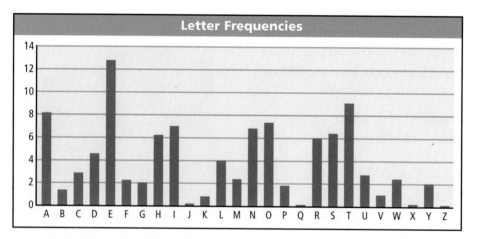

From the graph, you can see that E is the mode. In a coded text, the letter that appears most frequently is likely to represent the letter E. The letter that appears the second most frequently is likely to represent the letter T. Count the number of times each letter appears in the following message. Then use the letter frequencies and a bit of guesswork to decode the message. (*Hint:* In this code, P represents the letter M.)

KSQ PQUR, KSQ PQHGUR, URH KSQ PXHQ KQWW VXE DXPQKSGRT UCXEK U DQK XZ HUKU.

Materials
- 2 pieces of card stock
- 6 sandwich-size zipper bags
- clear packaging tape
- graph paper
- scissors

It's in the Bag!

PROJECT **Graphing According to Me**

Create different types of graphs and make a zippered accordion book to hold them all.

Directions

❶ Place one piece of card stock that is $6\frac{1}{2}$ inches by 7 inches next to one of the bags. The opening of the bag should be at the top, and there should be a small space between the card stock and the bag. Tape the card stock and bag together on the front and back sides. **Figure A**

❷ Lay another bag down next to the first, keeping a small space between them. Tape them together, front and back. **Figure B**

❸ Continue with the rest of the bags. At the end of the chain, tape a second piece of card stock that is $6\frac{1}{2}$ inches by 7 inches to the last bag. **Figure C**

❹ Fold the bags accordion-style, back and forth, with the two card stock covers on the front and back.

❺ Cut out squares of graph paper so they will fit in the bags.

Taking Note of the Math

Write the number and title of the chapter on the cover. On each piece of graph paper, draw and label an example of one type of graph from the chapter. Store the graphs in the bags.

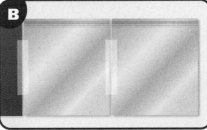

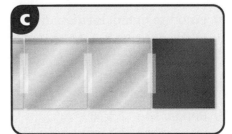

Study Guide: Review

Vocabulary

Complete the sentences below with vocabulary words from the list above.

1. When gathering information about a(n) ___?___, researchers often study part of the group, called a(n) ___?___.

2. The sum of the data values divided by the number of data items is called the ___?___ of the data.

7-1 Mean, Median, Mode, and Range (pp. 331–334)

 SDAP1.1

EXAMPLE

■ Find the mean, median, mode, and range of the data set 3, 7, 10, 2, and 3.

Mean: $3 + 7 + 10 + 2 + 3 = 25$ $\frac{25}{5} = 5$

Median: 2, 3, 3, 7, 10

Mode: 3

Range: $10 - 2 = 8$

EXERCISES

Find the mean, median, mode, and range of each data set.

3. 324, 233, 324, 399, 233, 299

4. 48, 39, 27, 52, 45, 47, 49, 37

5. 27, 25, 20, 32, 35, 35, 29

6. 115, 104, 110, 108, 118

7-2 Additional Data and Outliers (pp. 335–338)

 SDAP1.1, SDAP1.2, SDAP1.3

EXAMPLE

■ Find the mean, median, mode, and range with and without the outlier.

10, 4, 7, 8, 34, 7, 7, 12, 5, 8   *The outlier is 34.*

With: **mean** = 10.2, **mode** = 7, **median** = 7.5, **range** = 30

Without: **mean** ≈ 7.555, **mode** = 7, **median** = 7, **range** = 7

EXERCISES

Find the mean, median, mode, and range of each data set with and without the outlier.

7. 12, 11, 9, 38, 10, 8, 12

8. 34, 12, 32, 45, 32

9. 16, 12, 15, 52, 10, 13

7-3 Choosing the Most Useful Measure (pp. 339–341)

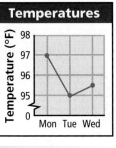SDAP1.1, SDAP1.3, SDAP1.4

EXAMPLE

■ The list shows Jared's scores in 8 rounds of golf.

84, 88, 92, 86, 128, 90, 85, 91

What are the mean and median of this data set? Is one measure more useful than the other for describing Jared's typical golf score? Explain.

Mean: 93
Median: 89
The mean is greater than all but one of the scores because of the outlier (the score of 128). Therefore, the median best describes the typical score.

EXERCISES

10. Grant scored 26, 25, 28, 24, and 27 points in his last 5 basketball games. What are the mean and median of this data set? Is one measure more useful than the other for describing Grant's typical score? Explain.

11. The table shows the amount in dollars a salesperson sold during one week.

Day	Mon	Tue	Wed	Thu	Fri
Sales ($)	495	501	490	520	375

Should she use the mean, median, or mode of the data to convince her boss that she deserves a raise? Explain.

7-4 Analyzing Data Displays (pp. 342–345)

SDAP2.3, SDAP2.5

EXAMPLE

■ The bar graph shows the number of students in each grade of a middle school.

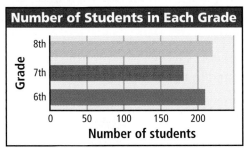

Which grades have more than 200 students?

The sixth and eighth grades

EXERCISES

Use the bar graph at left for Exercises 12–14.

12. About how many more students are in the sixth grade than in the seventh grade?

13. Victor claims that there are fewer than 500 students at the middle school. Is Victor's claim valid? Explain.

14. Carlie claims that there are about 40 more eighth-grade students than seventh-grade students. Is Carlie's claim valid? Explain.

7-5 Misleading Graphs (pp. 348–351)

SDAP2.3, SDAP2.5

EXAMPLE

■ Explain why the graph could be misleading.

The vertical axis is broken, so it appears that A's sales are more than twice B's.

Shoe Sales

EXERCISES

15. Explain why the graph could be misleading.

Temperatures

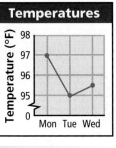

7-6 Populations and Samples (pp. 354–357)

 NS1.3, SDAP2.1, SDAP2.5

EXAMPLE

■ A school's yearbook includes 1,350 photos. Steve estimates that 35 of the photos are black and white. In a random sample of 150 yearbook photos, four of them are black and white. Determine whether Steve's estimate is likely to be accurate. Explain.

$$\frac{4}{150} = \frac{x}{1,350}$$
$$5,400 = 150x$$
$$36 = x$$

Let x represent the number of black and white photos in the yearbook.

Based on the sample, about 36 of the photos are black and white. Steve's estimate is likely to be accurate.

EXERCISES

For each situation, explain whether it makes sense to use a sample.

16. A researcher wants to know the average number of items bought by customers at a grocery store.

17. A researcher wants to know how many brands of oatmeal a grocery store sells.

18. A press prints 200,000 posters each day. The manager of the press estimates that fewer than 50 posters with defects are printed each day. In a random sample of 2,000 posters, there are two with defects. Determine whether the manager's estimate is likely to be accurate. Explain.

7-7 Selecting Samples (pp. 358–360)

SDAP2.2

EXAMPLE

The owner of a sporting goods store wants to know what percentage of his customers play soccer. The owner places printed surveys at the checkout counter. Identify the type of sampling method.

This is a self-selected sample because customers choose whether to fill out the surveys.

EXERCISES

Kristen wants to know what fraction of the students at her school ride their bikes to school. Identify each type of sampling method.

19. Kristen surveys every tenth student listed in the school directory.

20. Kristen suveys 30 students in the school cafeteria.

21. Kristen surveys 25 students chosen at random using a computer program.

7-8 Identifying Sampling Errors and Bias (pp. 362–365)

SDAP2.3, SDAP2.4, SDAP2.5

EXAMPLE

■ Members of a hiking club are surveyed to determine what type of shoes people prefer. Determine whether the sample may be biased. Explain.

The sample is biased. People in a hiking club may be more likely than other people to choose hiking boots as their favorite type of shoes.

EXERCISES

22. A park employee surveys 20 joggers in a park to determine whether more bike trails should be added to the park. Determine whether the sample may be biased. Explain.

23. Determine whether the survey question "How many hours do you exercise each week?" may be biased. Explain.

Use the data set 12, 18, 12, 22, 28, 23, 32, 10, 29, and 36 for problems 1 and 2.

1. Find the mean, median, mode, and range of the data set.

2. How would the outlier 57 affect the mean, median, and mode?

3. The list shows the number of miles Marcus ran during the last 8 track practices.

    1.5, 3, 4.5, 5, 2.5, 4, 1.5, 6

    What are the mean and median of this data set? Which measure or measures would be most useful for describing the typical distance Marcus runs during practice? Explain.

Use the circle graph for problems 4 and 5.

4. Approximately what percent of the students are seventh graders?

5. The school population is 1,200 students. Anaya claims that more than 500 students are in the eighth grade. Is Anaya's claim valid? Explain.

6. A small business produces 5,000 hand-made tiles per week. The owner estimates that fewer than 120 of the tiles made each week are defective. In a random sample of 250 tiles, 5 have defects. Determine whether the owner's estimate is likely to be accurate. Explain.

7. Explain why the bar graph at right could be misleading.

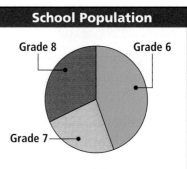

School Population

Grade 8   Grade 6

Grade 7

The manager of a skating rink wants to know what type of music skaters prefer. Identify each type of sampling method.

8. The manager surveys 30 people seated at the snack bar.

9. The manager surveys every 50th person who rents skates during one week.

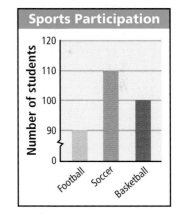

Sports Participation

Number of students

120
110
100
90
0

Football   Soccer   Basketball

Determine whether each sample may be biased. Explain.

10. A reporter determines the average number of words in the articles of a magazine by randomly selecting 50 articles from the magazine database.

11. To learn about people's favorite musical instruments, a reporter surveys the first 50 people leaving a rock concert.

Determine whether each survey question may be biased. Explain.

12. Do you prefer the fresh, clean scent of Brand A soap or the strong odor of Brand B soap?

13. Do you plan to vote for Scott or Vanessa in the student council election?

STRATEGIES FOR SUCCESS

Extended Response: Understand the Scores

Extended-response test items usually involve multiple steps and require a detailed explanation. The items are often scored using a 4-point rubric. A complete and correct response is worth 4 points, a partial response is worth 2 to 3 points, an incorrect response with no work shown is worth 1 point, and no response at all is worth 0 points.

EXAMPLE

Extended Response A 10-pound bag of apples costs $4. Write and solve a proportion to find how much a 15-pound bag of apples would cost at the same rate. Explain how the increase in weight is related to the increase in cost.

Here are examples of how different responses were scored using the scoring rubric shown.

4-point response:

Let c = the cost of the 15 lb bag.
$$\frac{10 \text{ pounds}}{\$4} = \frac{15 \text{ pounds}}{c}$$
$$10 \cdot c = 4 \cdot 15$$
$$\frac{10c}{10} = \frac{60}{10}$$
$$c = 6$$

The 15 lb bag costs $6.

For every additional 5 pounds, the cost increases by 2 dollars.

3-point response:

Let c = the cost of the 15 lb bag.
$$\frac{10 \text{ pounds}}{\$4} = \frac{15 \text{ pounds}}{c}$$
$$10 \cdot c = 4 \cdot 15$$
$$\frac{10c}{10} = \frac{60}{10}$$
$$c = 6$$

The 15 lb bag costs $6.

For every additional 5 pounds, the cost increases by 6 dollars.

The proportion is set up and solved correctly, and all work is shown, but the explanation is incorrect.

2-point response:

Let c = the cost of the apples.
$$\frac{10 \text{ pounds}}{\$4} = \frac{c}{15 \text{ pounds}}$$
$$10 \cdot 15 = 4 \cdot c$$
$$\frac{150}{4} = \frac{4c}{4}$$
$$37.5 = c$$

1-point response:

$$37.5 = c$$

The answer is incorrect, no work is shown, and no explanation is given.

The proportion is set up incorrectly, and no explanation is given.

After you complete an extended-response test item, double-check that you have answered all parts.

Read each test item and answer the questions that follow using the scoring rubric below.

Scoring Rubric

4 Points: The student correctly answers all parts of the question, shows all work, and provides a complete and correct explanation.

3 Points: The student answers all parts of the question, shows all work, and provides a complete explanation that demonstrates understanding, but the student makes minor errors in computation.

2 Points: The student does not answer all parts of the question but shows all work and provides a complete and correct explanation for the parts answered, or the student correctly answers all parts of the question but does not show all work or does not provide an explanation.

1 Point: The student gives incorrect answers and shows little or no work or explanation, or the student does not follow directions.

0 Points: The student gives no response.

Item A
Extended Response Alex drew a model of a birdhouse using a scale of 1 inch to 3 inches. On the drawing, the house is 6 inches tall. Define a variable, and then write and solve a proportion to find how many inches tall the actual birdhouse is.

1. Should the response shown receive a score of 4 points? Why or why not?

$$\frac{1 \ inch}{6 \ inches} = \frac{3 \ inches}{h}$$
$$1 \cdot h = 3 \cdot 6$$
$$h = 18$$
The actual birdhouse is 18 inches tall.

Item B
Extended Response The list below shows the ages of the employees at a discount store. What are the mean and median of the data? Is one measure more useful than the other for describing the typical age of an employee at the store? Explain.

68, 22, 16, 23, 21, 17, 25, 20

2. What should you add to the response shown, if anything, so that it receives full credit?

The mean is 26.5. The median is 21.5. The measure that best describes the typical age is the median.

Item C
Extended Response The figures are similar. Find the value of x and the sum of the side lengths of one of the figures.

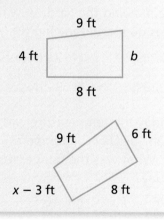

3. What needs to be included in a response that would receive 4 points?

4. Write a response that would receive full credit.

MASTERING THE STANDARDS

go.hrw.com
Standards Practice Online
KEYWORD: MS8CA Practice

Cumulative Assessment, Chapters 1–7

Multiple Choice

1. Which expression is true for the data set? 15, 18, 13, 15, 16, 14

   Ⓐ Mean < mode

   Ⓑ Median > mean

   Ⓒ Median = mean

   Ⓓ Median = mode

2. What is the first step to complete in simplifying this expression?

   $\frac{2}{5} + [3 - 5(2)] \div 6$

   Ⓐ Multiply 5 and 2.

   Ⓑ Divide by 6.

   Ⓒ Subtract 5 from 3.

   Ⓓ Divide 2 by 5.

3. Harrison spends $3\frac{1}{2}$ hours a week working in his yard. He spends $1\frac{1}{3}$ hours pulling weeds. He spends the rest of the time mowing the yard. How much time does he spend mowing the yard?

   Ⓐ $1\frac{1}{6}$ hours   Ⓒ $2\frac{1}{3}$ hours

   Ⓑ $2\frac{1}{6}$ hours   Ⓓ $3\frac{1}{3}$ hours

4. On Monday the temperature was −13°F. On Tuesday the temperature rose 7°F. What was the temperature on Tuesday?

   Ⓐ −20°F   Ⓒ −6°F

   Ⓑ −8°F   Ⓓ 7°F

5. What is the value of the expression $b(c - 4)$ when $b = 8$ and $c = 10$?

   Ⓐ 40   Ⓒ 76

   Ⓑ 48   Ⓓ 86

6. Gina is conducting a survey about her school's cafeteria. Which survey question would be the least biased?

   Ⓐ What is your favorite meal served by the cafeteria?

   Ⓑ Don't you agree that the cafeteria's chili is much too spicy?

   Ⓒ Should the cafeteria serve healthy pasta or greasy hamburgers?

   Ⓓ Do you think students should waste money on the cafeteria's vending machines?

7. Ron eats $\frac{1}{4}$ cup of cereal every day as part of his breakfast. He has had a total of 16 cups of cereal this year. How many days has he eaten cereal?

   Ⓐ 4 days   Ⓒ 32 days

   Ⓑ 16 days   Ⓓ 64 days

8. A store is offering lip gloss at 25% off its original price. The original price of lip gloss is $7.59. What is the sale price?

   Ⓐ $5.69   Ⓒ $3.80

   Ⓑ $4.93   Ⓓ $1.90

9. Jamie is making a fruit salad. She needs $2\frac{1}{4}$ cups of crushed pineapple, $3\frac{3}{4}$ cups of sliced apples, $1\frac{1}{3}$ cups of mandarin oranges, and $2\frac{2}{3}$ cups of red grapes. How many cups total of fruit does she need for the fruit salad?

   Ⓐ 6 cups   Ⓒ 10 cups

   Ⓑ 8 cups   Ⓓ 12 cups

10. Which equation has a solution of 8?

   Ⓐ $2x = 18$ Ⓒ $x + 6 = 24$

   Ⓑ $x - 4 = 12$ Ⓓ $\frac{x}{4} = 2$

11. Which statement is best supported by the data?

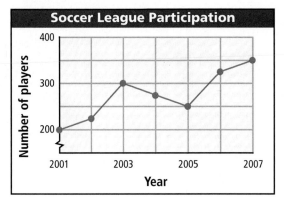

   Ⓐ More students played soccer in 2005 than in 2002.

   Ⓑ From 2001–2007, soccer participation increased by 100%.

   Ⓒ From 2002–2006, soccer participation decreased by 144%.

   Ⓓ Participation increased between 2004 and 2005.

 Read a graph or diagram as closely as you read the actual test question. These visual aids contain important information.

Gridded Response

12. To the nearest hundredth, what is the difference between the median and the mean of the data set?

14, 11, 14, 11, 13, 12, 9, 15, 16

13. Greg is separating his marbles into sets. He has 16 green marbles and 20 red marbles. Each set must have the same number of green marbles and the same number of red marbles. What is the greatest number of marble sets that Greg can make if he wants to use every marble?

Short Response

14. The graph shows the results of a survey. Aaron read the graph and determined that more than $\frac{1}{5}$ of the students chose drama as their favorite type of movie. Do you agree with Aaron? Why or why not?

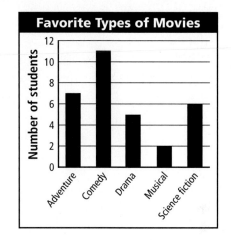

15. A land developer purchases 120 acres of land and plans to divide one part into five 5-acre lots, another part into two 10-acre lots, and the rest into $\frac{1}{2}$-acre lots. Each lot will be sold for a future home site. How many total lots can the developer plan to sell?

Extended Response

16. Mr. Parker wants to identify the types of activities in which high school students participate after school, so he surveys the twelfth-graders in his science classes. The table shows the results of the survey.

Activity	Boys	Girls
Play sports	36	24
Talk to friends	6	30
Do homework	15	18
Work	5	4

   a. Use the data in the table to construct a double-bar graph.

   b. What is the mean number of girls per activity? Show your work.

   c. What type of sample is used? Is this sample representative of the population? Explain.

Probability

CONCEPT CONNECTION

go.hrw.com
Chapter Project Online
KEYWORD: MS8CA Ch8

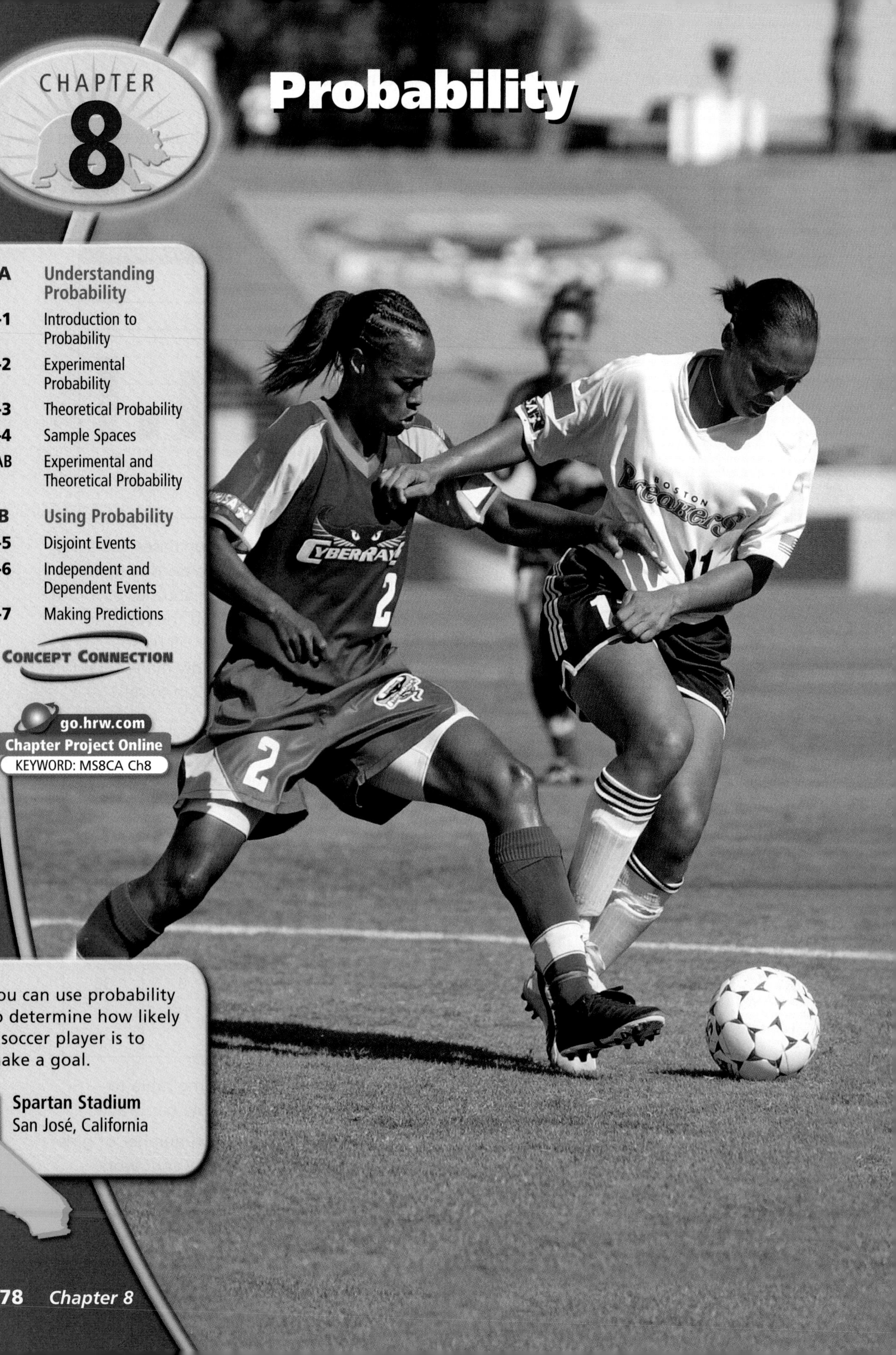

You can use probability to determine how likely a soccer player is to make a goal.

Spartan Stadium
San José, California

ARE YOU READY?

✓ Vocabulary

Choose the best term from the list to complete each sentence.

composite number

even number

odd number

percent

prime number

ratio

1. A(n) __?__ is a comparison of two quantities, often written as a fraction.

2. A(n) __?__ is an integer that is divisible by 2.

3. A(n) __?__ is a ratio that compares a number to 100.

4. A(n) __?__ is a number greater than 1 that has more than two whole number factors.

5. A(n) __?__ is an integer that is not divisible by 2.

Complete these exercises to review skills you will need for this chapter.

✓ Simplify Fractions

Write each fraction in simplest form.

6. $\frac{6}{9}$ 7. $\frac{12}{15}$ 8. $\frac{8}{10}$ 9. $\frac{20}{24}$

10. $\frac{2}{4}$ 11. $\frac{7}{35}$ 12. $\frac{12}{22}$ 13. $\frac{72}{81}$

✓ Write Fractions as Decimals

Write each fraction as a decimal.

14. $\frac{3}{5}$ 15. $\frac{9}{20}$ 16. $\frac{57}{100}$ 17. $\frac{12}{25}$

18. $\frac{3}{25}$ 19. $\frac{1}{2}$ 20. $\frac{7}{10}$ 21. $\frac{9}{5}$

✓ Percents and Decimals

Write each decimal as a percent.

22. 0.14   23. 0.08   24. 0.75   25. 0.38

26. 0.27   27. 1.89   28. 0.234   29. 0.0025

✓ Multiply Fractions

Multiply. Write each answer in simplest form.

30. $\frac{1}{2} \cdot \frac{1}{4}$ 31. $\frac{2}{3} \cdot \frac{3}{5}$ 32. $\frac{3}{10} \cdot \frac{1}{2}$ 33. $\frac{5}{6} \cdot \frac{3}{4}$

Unpacking the Standards

The information below "unpacks" the standards. The Academic Vocabulary is highlighted and defined to help you understand the language of the standards. Refer to the lessons listed after each standard for help with the math terms and phrases. The Chapter Concept shows how the standard is applied in this chapter.

California Standard	Academic Vocabulary	Chapter Concept
SDAP3.1 Represent all possible outcomes for compound events in an organized way (e.g., tables, grids, tree diagrams) and express the theoretical probability of each outcome. (Lessons 8-4, 8-5; Lab 8-4)	**represent** show or describe **organized** arranged in an orderly way **grid** a type of display in which information is shown in rows and columns	You list the outcomes of compound events. You find the theoretical probability of each outcome.
SDAP3.3 Represent probabilities as ratios, proportions, decimals between 0 and 1, and percentages between 0 and 100 and verify that the probabilities computed are reasonable; know that if *P* is the probability of an event, $1 - P$ is the probability of an event not occurring. (Lessons 8-1, 8-2, 8-3, 8-4, 8-6, 8-7; Lab 8-4)	**verify** check **occurring** happening	You write probabilities in different forms. **Example:** The theoretical probability that a coin will land on heads can be written as $\frac{1}{2}$, **0.5**, or **50%**. You find the probability of an event not occurring.
SDAP3.4 Understand that the probability of either of two disjoint events occurring is the sum of the two individual probabilities and that the probability of one event following another, in independent trials, is the product of the two probabilities. (Lessons 8-5, 8-6)	**individual** separate	You find the probability of disjoint events and independent events. **Example:** The probability of choosing an *F* or an *R* from the letters in the word *firefly* is $\frac{2}{7} + \frac{1}{7} = \frac{3}{7}$.
SDAP3.5 Understand the difference between independent and dependent events. (Lesson 8-6)	**difference** way in which two or more things are not alike	You determine whether a set of events is independent or dependent.

Standards NS1.3 and SDAP3.2 are also covered in this chapter. To see standard NS1.3 unpacked, go to Chapter 5, p. 230.

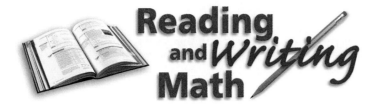

Reading and Writing Math

Reading Strategy: Read Problems for Understanding

To best understand a word problem, read it once to note what concept is being reviewed. Then read the problem again, slowly and carefully, to identify what the problem is asking. As you read, highlight the key information. When dealing with a multi-step problem, break the problem into parts and then make a plan to solve it.

---

20. Banking After 2 years, a savings account earning simple interest held $585.75. The original deposit was $550. What was the interest rate?

Step	Question	Answer
Step 1	What concept is being reviewed?	• using the simple interest formula
Step 2	What are you being asked to do?	• Find the interest rate of the savings account.
Step 3	What is the key information needed to solve the problem?	• The principal is $550. • The principal earns interest for 2 years. • The account balance is $585.75.
Step 4	What is my plan to solve this multi-part problem?	• Subtract the principal from the account balance to find the amount of interest. • Substitute the values for the interest, principal, and time into the formula $I = prt$. • Solve for r.

Try This

For each problem, complete each step in the four-step method described above.

1. Shawna wants to make violet paint by mixing 1 part purple paint and 5 parts white paint. If Shawna needs 3 ounces of violet paint, how many ounces of white paint will she need?

2. At a party, each child receives the same number and type of party favors. There are 16 kazoos, 24 snappers, 8 hats, and 32 pieces of gum. What is the greatest number of children that may be at the party?

8-1 Introduction to Probability

California Standards

SDAP3.3 Represent probabilities as ratios, proportions, decimals between 0 and 1, and percentages between 0 and 100 and verify that the probabilities computed are reasonable; know that if *P* is the probability of an event, 1 − *P* is the probability of an event not occurring.

Vocabulary
experiment
trial
outcome
event
probability
complement

Why learn this? You can use probability to determine how likely you are to roll a certain number on a number cube.

An activity involving chance, such as rolling a number cube, is called an **experiment** . Each repetition or observation of an experiment is a **trial** , and each result is an **outcome** . A set of one or more outcomes is an **event** . For example, rolling a 5 (one outcome) can be an event, or rolling an even number (more than one outcome) can be an event.

The **probability** of an event, written *P*(event), is the measure of how likely the event is to occur. Probability is a measure between 0 and 1. You can write probability as a ratio, a decimal, or a percent.

Impossible	Unlikely	As likely as not	Likely	Certain
0	$\frac{1}{4}$	$\frac{1}{2}$	$\frac{3}{4}$	1
0	0.25	0.5	0.75	1.0
0%	25%	50%	75%	100%

EXAMPLE 1 **Determining the Likelihood of an Event**

Determine whether each event is impossible, unlikely, as likely as not, likely, or certain.

A rolling an even number on a number cube

There are 6 possible outcomes:

Even	*Not* Even
2, 4, 6	1, 3, 5

Half of the outcomes are even.

Rolling an even number is as likely as not.

B rolling a 5 on a number cube

There are 6 possible outcomes:

5	*Not* 5
5	1, 2, 3, 4, 6

Only one outcome is a five.

Rolling a 5 is unlikely.

When a number cube is rolled, either a 5 will be rolled or it will not. Rolling a 5 and not rolling a 5 are examples of *complementary events*. The **complement** of an event is the set of all outcomes that are *not* the event.

Because it is certain that either an event or its complement will occur when an activity is performed, the sum of the probabilities is 1.

$$P(\text{event}) + P(\text{complement}) = 1$$

EXAMPLE 2 **Using Complements**

A bag contains 6 blue marbles, 6 red marbles, 3 green marbles, and 1 yellow marble. The probability of randomly drawing a red marble is $\frac{6}{16}$, or $\frac{3}{8}$. What is the probability of not drawing a red marble?

$$P(\text{event}) + P(\text{complement}) = 1$$
$$P(\text{red}) + P(\text{not red}) = 1$$

$$\frac{3}{8} + P(\text{not red}) = 1 \qquad \textit{Substitute } \tfrac{3}{8} \textit{ for P(red).}$$

$$-\frac{3}{8} \qquad\qquad\qquad = -\frac{3}{8} \qquad \textit{Subtract } \tfrac{3}{8} \textit{ from both sides.}$$

$$P(\text{not red}) = \frac{5}{8} \qquad \textit{Simplify.}$$

The probability of not drawing a red marble is $\frac{5}{8}$.

Check Find the sum of the probabilities of drawing a red marble and not drawing a red marble.

$$P(\text{red}) + P(\text{not red}) = \frac{3}{8} + \frac{5}{8} = \frac{8}{8} = 1$$

The sum of the probabilities is 1, so the answer is reasonable.

EXAMPLE 3 *School Application*

Eric's math teacher almost always gives a pop quiz if the class did not ask many questions during the lesson on the previous class day. If it is Monday and no one asked questions during class on Friday, should Eric expect a pop quiz? Explain.

Since Eric's teacher often gives quizzes on days after few questions were asked, a quiz on Monday is likely.

Think and Discuss

1. **Describe** an event that has a probability of 0% and an event that has a probability of 100%.

2. **Give an example** of a real-world event and its complement.

California
Standards Practice

🔑 SDAP3.3

go.hrw.com
Homework Help Online
KEYWORD: MS8CA 8-1
Parent Resources Online
KEYWORD: MS8CA Parent

GUIDED PRACTICE

See Example ① **Determine whether each event is impossible, unlikely, as likely as not, likely, or certain.**

1. rolling a number greater than 5 with a number cube

2. drawing a blue marble from a bag of black and white marbles

See Example ② **3.** A bag contains 8 purple beads, 2 blue beads, and 2 pink beads. The probability of randomly drawing a pink bead is $\frac{1}{6}$. What is the probability of not drawing a pink bead?

See Example ③ **4.** Natalie almost always sleeps in on Saturday mornings when she does not have to work. If it is Saturday morning and Natalie does not have to work, would you expect Natalie to sleep in? Explain.

INDEPENDENT PRACTICE

See Example ① **Determine whether each event is impossible, unlikely, as likely as not, likely, or certain.**

5. randomly drawing a red or pink card from a deck of red and pink cards

6. flipping a coin and getting tails

7. rolling a 6 on a number cube five times in a row

See Example ② **8.** The probability of rolling a 5 or 6 with a number cube is $\frac{1}{3}$. What is the probability of not rolling a 5 or 6?

9. The probability of randomly drawing a green marble from a bag of green, red, and blue marbles is $\frac{3}{5}$. What is the probability of randomly drawing a red or blue marble?

See Example ③ **10.** Tim rarely spends more than 30 minutes watching TV in the afternoon. If Tim began watching TV at 4:00 P.M., would you expect that he is still watching TV at 5:00 P.M? Explain.

PRACTICE AND PROBLEM SOLVING

Extra Practice
See page EP16.

A bag contains 24 checkers; 12 are red and 12 are black. Determine whether each event is impossible, unlikely, as likely as not, likely, or certain.

11. randomly drawing a red checker

12. randomly drawing a white checker

13. randomly drawing a red or black checker

14. randomly drawing a black checker

15. Exercise Luka almost always jogs in the afternoon when the weather is not cold or rainy. The sky is cloudy and the temperature is 41°F. How likely is it that Luka will jog this afternoon?

16. Science A researcher's garden contains 900 sweet pea plants. More than 700 of the plants have purple flowers and about 200 have white flowers. Would you expect that one plant randomly selected from the garden will have purple or white flowers? Explain.

17. Science Sharks belong to a class of fishes that have skeletons made of cartilage. Bony fishes, which account for 95% of all species of fish, have skeletons made of bone.

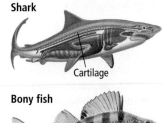

Shark

Cartilage

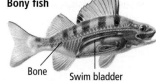

Bony fish

Bone   Swim bladder

a. How likely is it that a fish you cannot identify at a pet store is a bony fish? Explain.

b. Only bony fishes have swim bladders, which keep them from sinking. How likely is it that a shark has a swim bladder? Explain.

18. Earth Science The graph shows the carbon dioxide levels in the atmosphere from 1958 to 1994. How likely is it that the level of carbon dioxide fell from 1994 to 2000? Explain.

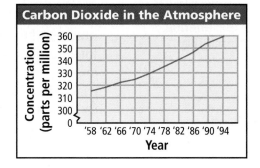

Carbon Dioxide in the Atmosphere

Concentration (parts per million): 360, 350, 340, 330, 320, 310, 300, 0

Year: '58 '62 '66 '70 '74 '78 '82 '86 '90 '94

19. Write a Problem Describe an event that involves rolling a number cube. Determine the likelihood that the event will occur.

20. Write About It Explain how to tell whether an event is as likely as not.

21. Challenge A bag contains 10 red marbles and 8 blue marbles, all the same size and weight. Keiko randomly draws 2 red marbles from the bag and does not replace them. Will Keiko be more likely to draw a red marble than a blue marble on her next draw? Explain.

SPIRAL STANDARDS REVIEW   ✦ NS1.4, ✦ AF2.2, ✦ SDAP3.3

22. Multiple Choice Which percent best shows the probability that Kito will randomly draw an even number from five cards numbered 2, 4, 6, 8, and 10?

Ⓐ 75%   Ⓑ 25%   Ⓒ 50%   Ⓓ 100%

23. Short Response Based on past games, the probability that a basketball player will make his next free throw is $\frac{5}{12}$. What is the probability that the player will not make his next free throw? Explain how you determined your answer.

24. The sales tax on a $45 DVD player is $3.38. What is the sales tax rate to the nearest tenth of a percent? (Lesson 6-5)

Find each unit rate. Round to the nearest hundredth, if necessary. (Lesson 5-2)

25. $1.00 for 6 lemons   **26.** 84 pages in 3 hours   **27.** $2.20 for 4 pairs

8-2 Experimental Probability

California Standards

SDAP3.2 Use data to estimate the probability of future events (e.g., batting averages or number of accidents per mile driven).

Also covered: 🔑 **SDAP3.3**

Vocabulary

experimental probability

Why learn this? You can use experimental probability to find the likelihood that a hockey player will make a save.

Experimental probability is one way of estimating the probability of an event. The **experimental probability** of an event is found by comparing the number of times the event occurs to the total number of trials when repeating an experiment many times. The more trials you have, the more accurate the estimate is likely to be.

EXPERIMENTAL PROBABILITY

$$\text{probability} \approx \frac{\text{number of times the event occurs}}{\text{total number of trials}}$$

EXAMPLE **1** *Sports Application*

 Reasoning

Tanya made saves on 15 out of 25 shots. What is the experimental probability that she will make a save on the next shot? Write your answer as a ratio, as a decimal, and as a percent. Then explain why your answer is reasonable.

$$P(\text{event}) \approx \frac{\text{number of times the event occurs}}{\text{total number of trials}}$$

$$P(\text{save}) \approx \frac{\text{number of saves made}}{\text{total number of shots attempted}}$$

$$= \frac{15}{25} \qquad \textit{Substitute data from the experiment.}$$

$$= \frac{3}{5} \qquad \textit{Write in simplest form.}$$

$$= 0.6 = 60\% \qquad \textit{Write as a decimal and as a percent.}$$

Writing Math

"*P*(event)" represents the probability that an event will occur. For example, the probability of a flipped coin landing heads up could be written as "*P*(heads)."

The experimental probability that Tanya will make a save on the next shot is $\frac{3}{5}$, or 0.6, or 60%.

Tanya made saves on more than half of the 25 shots, so the experimental probability that she will make a save on the next shot should be greater than $\frac{1}{2}$, or 50%. An answer of 60% is reasonable.

EXAMPLE 2 *Weather Application*

For the past three weeks, Karl has been recording the daily high temperatures for a science project. His results are shown below.

Week 1	Temp (°F)	Week 2	Temp (°F)	Week 3	Temp (°F)
Sun	76	Sun	72	Sun	78
Mon	74	Mon	79	Mon	76
Tue	79	Tue	78	Tue	77
Wed	80	Wed	79	Wed	75
Thu	77	Thu	77	Thu	79
Fri	76	Fri	74	Fri	77
Sat	75	Sat	73	Sat	75

A What is the experimental probability that the temperature will be above 75°F on the next day?

The number of days the temperature was above 75°F is 14.

$$P(\text{above } 75°F) \approx \frac{\text{number of days above } 75°F}{\text{total number of days}}$$

$$= \frac{14}{21} \qquad \textit{Substitute data.}$$

$$= \frac{2}{3} \qquad \textit{Write in simplest form.}$$

The experimental probability that the temperature will be above 75°F on the next day is $\frac{2}{3}$.

B What is the experimental probability that the temperature will not be above 75°F on the next day?

$$P(\text{above } 75°F) + P(\text{not above } 75°F) = 1 \qquad \textit{Use the complement.}$$

$$\frac{2}{3} + P(\text{not above } 75°F) = 1 \qquad \textit{Substitute.}$$

$$-\frac{2}{3} \qquad\qquad\qquad\qquad = -\frac{2}{3} \qquad \textit{Subtract } \frac{2}{3} \textit{ from both sides.}$$

$$P(\text{not above } 75°F) = \frac{1}{3} \qquad \textit{Simplify.}$$

The experimental probability that the temperature will not be above 75°F on the next day is $\frac{1}{3}$.

Think and Discuss

1. Describe a real-world situation in which you could estimate probability using experimental probability.

2. Explain how experimental probability could be used for making predictions.

California Standards Practice
SDAP3.2, ⟜ SDAP3.3

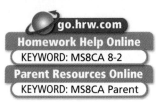

go.hrw.com
Homework Help Online
KEYWORD: MS8CA 8-2
Parent Resources Online
KEYWORD: MS8CA Parent

GUIDED PRACTICE

See Example ① 1. During soccer practice, Teri scored a goal on 6 out of 31 tries. What is the experimental probability that she will score a goal on her next try? Write your answer as a ratio, as a decimal, and as a percent. Then explain why your answer is reasonable.

See Example ② 2. **Government** A reporter surveys 75 people to determine whether they plan to vote for or against a proposed amendment. Of these people, 65 plan to vote for the amendment.

    a. What is the experimental probability that the next person surveyed would say he or she plans to vote for the amendment?

    b. What is the experimental probability that the next person surveyed would say he or she plans to vote against the amendment?

INDEPENDENT PRACTICE

See Example ① 3. **Sports** Jack hit a baseball on 13 out of 30 tries during practice. What is the experimental probability that he will hit the ball on his next try? Write your answer as a ratio, as a decimal, and as a percent. Then explain why your answer is reasonable.

4. Cam hit the bull's-eye in darts 8 times out of 15 throws. What is the experimental probability that Cam's next throw will hit the bull's-eye? Explain why your answer is reasonable.

See Example ② 5. For the past two weeks, Benita has been recording the number of people at Eastside Park at lunchtime. During that time, there were 50 or more people at the park 9 out of 14 days.

    a. What is the experimental probability that there will be 50 or more people at the park during lunchtime on the fifteenth day?

    b. What is the experimental probability that there will not be 50 or more people at the park during lunchtime on the fifteenth day?

PRACTICE AND PROBLEM SOLVING

Extra Practice
See page EP16.

6. **Recreation** While bowling with friends, Alexis rolls a strike in 4 out of the 10 frames. What is the experimental probability that Alexis will roll a strike in the first frame of the next game?

7. Jeremiah is greeting customers at a music store. Of the first 25 people he sees enter the store, 16 are wearing jackets and 9 are not. What is the experimental probability that the next person to enter the store will be wearing a jacket?

8. **Reasoning** Claudia finds that the experimental probability of her cat waking her between 5:00 A.M. and 6:00 A.M. is $\frac{8}{11}$. About what percent of the time does Claudia's cat not wake her between 5:00 A.M. and 6:00 A.M.?

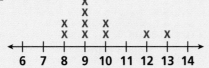

9. **Multi-Step** The line plot shows the depth of snow in inches recorded in Buffalo, New York, over a 10-day period.

```
                    X
                    X
            X   X   X
            X   X   X       X   X
    +---+---+---+---+---+---+---+---+---+
    6   7   8   9  10  11  12  13  14
```

a. What is the median depth of snow for the 10-day period?

b. What is the experimental probability that the snow will be less than 6 in. deep on the eleventh day?

c. What is the experimental probability that the snow will be more than 10 in. deep on the eleventh day?

10. The table shows the high temperatures recorded on July 4 in Orlando, Florida, over an eight-year period.

a. What is the experimental probability that the high temperature on the next July 4 will be below 90°F?

b. What is the experimental probability that the high temperature on the next July 4 will be above 100°F?

Year	Temp (°F)	Year	Temp (°F)
1994	86.0	1998	96.8
1995	95.0	1999	89.1
1996	78.8	2000	90.0
1997	98.6	2001	91.0

Source: Old Farmers' Almanac

11. ⭐ **Challenge** A toy company finds that the experimental probability of manufacturing a defective balance ball is $\frac{3}{50}$. About how many defective balls are likely to be in a batch of 1,800 balls?

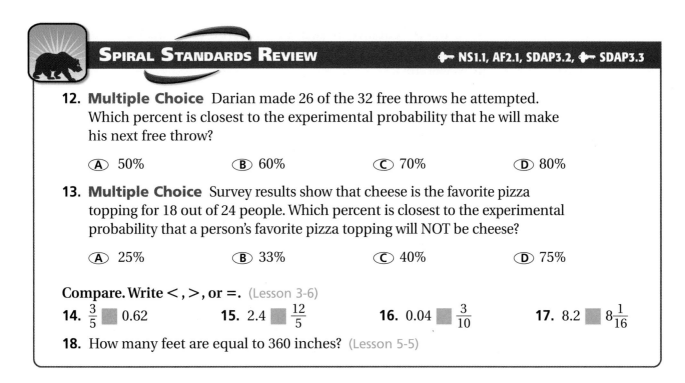

SPIRAL STANDARDS REVIEW   🔑 NS1.1, AF2.1, SDAP3.2, 🔑 SDAP3.3

12. **Multiple Choice** Darian made 26 of the 32 free throws he attempted. Which percent is closest to the experimental probability that he will make his next free throw?

Ⓐ 50%   Ⓑ 60%   Ⓒ 70%   Ⓓ 80%

13. **Multiple Choice** Survey results show that cheese is the favorite pizza topping for 18 out of 24 people. Which percent is closest to the experimental probability that a person's favorite pizza topping will NOT be cheese?

Ⓐ 25%   Ⓑ 33%   Ⓒ 40%   Ⓓ 75%

Compare. Write < , > , or =. (Lesson 3-6)

14. $\frac{3}{5}$ ▨ 0.62   15. 2.4 ▨ $\frac{12}{5}$ 16. 0.04 ▨ $\frac{3}{10}$ 17. 8.2 ▨ $8\frac{1}{16}$

18. How many feet are equal to 360 inches? (Lesson 5-5)

8-3) Theoretical Probability

California Standards

◆━ **SDAP3.3** Represent probabilities as ratios, proportions, decimals between 0 and 1, and percentages between 0 and 100 and verify that the probabilities computed are reasonable; know that if *P* is the probability of an event, 1– *P* is the probability of an event not occurring.

Vocabulary
theoretical probability

Why learn this? Knowing how to determine theoretical probability can help you play board games.

In a board game, players use tiles with the letters of the alphabet to form words. Of the 125 tiles used in the game, 15 have the letter *E* on them.

To determine the probability of drawing an *E*, you can draw tiles from a bag and record your results to find the experimental probability, or you can calculate the *theoretical probability*. **Theoretical probability** is used to find the probability of an event when all outcomes are equally likely.

> ### THEORETICAL PROBABILITY
> $$\text{probability} = \frac{\text{number of ways the event can occur}}{\text{total number of equally likely outcomes}}$$

If each possible outcome of an experiment is equally likely, then the experiment is said to be fair. Experiments involving number cubes and coins are usually assumed to be fair.

EXAMPLE 1) Finding Theoretical Probability

Reasoning

Find the probability of each event. Write your answer as a ratio, as a decimal, and as a percent. Then explain why your answer is reasonable.

Ⓐ drawing one of the 15 *E*'s from a bag of 125 tiles

$$P = \frac{\text{number of ways the event can occur}}{\text{total number of equally likely outcomes}}$$

$P(E) = \dfrac{\text{number of }E\text{'s}}{\text{total number of tiles}}$ *Write the ratio.*

$= \dfrac{15}{125}$ *Substitute.*

$= \dfrac{3}{25}$ *Write in simplest form.*

$= 0.12 = 12\%$ *Write as a decimal and as a percent.*

The theoretical probability of drawing an *E* is $\frac{3}{25}$, 0.12, or 12%.

Fewer than $\frac{1}{5}$ of the 125 tiles are *E*'s, so the theoretical probability of drawing an *E* should be less than $\frac{1}{5}$, or 20%. An answer of 12% is reasonable.

390 *Chapter 8 Probability*

Find the probability of each event. Write your answer as a ratio, as a decimal, and as a percent.

B rolling a number greater than 2 on a fair number cube

There are four outcomes greater than 2: 3, 4, 5, and 6.

There are six possible outcomes: 1, 2, 3, 4, 5, and 6.

$$P(\text{greater than 2}) = \frac{\text{number of ways the event can occur}}{\text{total number of equally likely outcomes}}$$

$$= \frac{4}{6} \qquad \textit{Write the ratio.}$$

$$= \frac{2}{3} \qquad \textit{Write in simplest form.}$$

$$\approx 0.667 \approx 66.7\% \qquad \textit{Write as a decimal and a percent.}$$

The theoretical probability of rolling a number greater than 2 is $\frac{2}{3}$, or approximately 0.667, or approximately 66.7%.

EXAMPLE 2 *School Application*

There are 11 boys and 16 girls in Mr. Ashley's class. Mr. Ashley has written the name of each student on a craft stick. He randomly draws one of these sticks to choose a student to answer a question.

A Find the theoretical probability of drawing a boy's name.

$$P(\text{boy}) = \frac{\text{number of boys in class}}{\text{total number of students in class}}$$

$$P(\text{boy}) = \frac{11}{27}$$

B Find the theoretical probability of drawing a girl's name.

Remember!

The sum of the probabilities of an event and its complement is 1.

$$P(\text{boy}) + P(\text{girl}) = 1 \qquad \textit{Substitute } \tfrac{11}{27} \textit{ for P(boy).}$$

$$\frac{11}{27} + P(\text{girl}) = 1$$

$$-\frac{11}{27} \qquad\qquad = -\frac{11}{27} \qquad \textit{Subtract } \tfrac{11}{27} \textit{ from both sides.}$$

$$P(\text{girl}) = \frac{16}{27} \qquad \textit{Simplify.}$$

Think and Discuss

1. Give an example of an experiment in which all of the outcomes are not equally likely. Explain.

2. Describe how the probability in Example 2 would be affected if each girl's name were listed on two sticks instead of just one.

California
Standards Practice
🔑 SDAP3.3, SDAP3.4

go.hrw.com
Homework Help Online
KEYWORD: MS8CA 8-3
Parent Resources Online
KEYWORD: MS8CA Parent

GUIDED PRACTICE

See Example ① Find the probability of each event. Write your answer as a ratio, as a decimal, and as a percent. Then explain why your answer is reasonable.

1. randomly choosing a red marble from a bag of 15 red, 15 blue, 15 green, 15 yellow, 15 black, and 15 white marbles

2. randomly choosing an orange straw from a box of 12 orange straws, 12 yellow straws, and 15 purple straws

See Example ② A set of cards includes 15 yellow cards, 10 green cards, and 10 blue cards. Find the probability of each event when a card is chosen at random.

3. yellow   4. green   5. not yellow

INDEPENDENT PRACTICE

See Example ① Find the probability of each event. Write your answer as a ratio, as a decimal, and as a percent. Then explain why your answer is reasonable.

6. randomly drawing a heart from a shuffled deck of 52 cards with 13-card suits: diamonds, hearts, clubs, and spades

7. randomly drawing a purple disk from a game with 10 red, 10 purple, 13 orange, and 13 white disks of the same size and shape

8. randomly drawing one of the two blank game tiles from a complete set of 100 tiles

See Example ② Sifu has 6 girls and 8 boys in his karate class. He randomly selects one student to demonstrate a self-defense technique. Find the probability of each event.

9. selecting a girl   10. selecting a boy

PRACTICE AND PROBLEM SOLVING

Extra Practice
See page EP16.

Reasoning A spinner is divided equally into 10 sectors. The numbers 1 through 5 are each placed in two different sectors. Find the probability of each event.

11. $P(3)$ 12. $P(\text{greater than } 3)$

13. $P(\text{less than } 3)$ 14. $P(5)$

15. $P(8)$ 16. $P(\text{less than } 6)$

17. **Games** Mahjong is a traditional Chinese game played with 144 decorated tiles—36 bamboo tiles, 36 circle tiles, 36 character tiles, 16 wind tiles, 12 dragon tiles, and 8 bonus tiles. Suppose the tiles are all placed facedown and you choose one at random. What is the probability that you will NOT choose a dragon tile?

Recreation The table shows the approximate number of visitors to five different amusement parks in the United States in one year. Find the probability that a randomly selected visitor to one of the amusement parks visited the parks listed in Exercises 18 and 19. Write each answer as a decimal and as a percent.

Amusement Parks	Number of Visitors
Disney World, FL	15,640,000
Disneyland, CA	13,680,000
SeaWorld, FL	4,900,000
Busch Gardens, FL	4,200,000
SeaWorld, CA	3,700,000

18. a park in Florida

19. a park in California

20. Gardening A package of mixed lettuce seeds contains 150 green lettuce seeds and 50 red lettuce seeds. What is the probability that a randomly selected seed will be a red lettuce seed? Write your answer as a percent.

21. Choose a Strategy Francis, Amanda, Raymond, and Albert wore different-colored T-shirts. The colors were tan, orange, purple, and aqua. Neither Raymond nor Amanda ever wears orange, and neither Francis nor Raymond ever wears aqua. Albert wore purple. What color was each person's T-shirt?

22. Write About It Suppose the theoretical probability of an event happening is $\frac{3}{8}$. Explain what each number in the ratio represents.

23. Challenge A spinner is divided into three sectors. Half of the spinner is red, $\frac{1}{3}$ is blue, and $\frac{1}{6}$ is green. What is the probability that the spinner will land on either red or green?

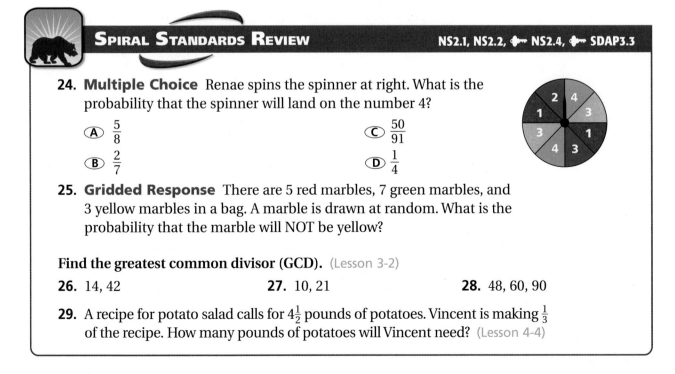

24. Multiple Choice Renae spins the spinner at right. What is the probability that the spinner will land on the number 4?

Ⓐ $\frac{5}{8}$

Ⓒ $\frac{50}{91}$

Ⓑ $\frac{2}{7}$

Ⓓ $\frac{1}{4}$

25. Gridded Response There are 5 red marbles, 7 green marbles, and 3 yellow marbles in a bag. A marble is drawn at random. What is the probability that the marble will NOT be yellow?

Find the greatest common divisor (GCD). (Lesson 3-2)

26. 14, 42

27. 10, 21

28. 48, 60, 90

29. A recipe for potato salad calls for $4\frac{1}{2}$ pounds of potatoes. Vincent is making $\frac{1}{3}$ of the recipe. How many pounds of potatoes will Vincent need? (Lesson 4-4)

8-4 Sample Spaces

California Standards

SDAP3.1 Represent all possible outcomes for compound events in an organized way (e.g., tables, grids, tree diagrams) and express the theoretical probability of each outcome.

Also covered: **SDAP3.3**

Vocabulary
sample space
compound event
Fundamental
  Counting Principle

> **Why learn this?** You can find a sample space to determine the probability of winning a game of Rock, Paper, Scissors. (See Example 2).

Together, all the possible outcomes of an experiment make up the **sample space**. For example, when you toss a coin, the sample space is landing on heads or tails.

A **compound event** includes two or more simple events. Tossing one coin is a simple event; tossing two coins is a compound event. You can make a table to show all possible outcomes of an experiment involving a compound event.

EXAMPLE 1 **Using a Table to Find a Sample Space**

Reasoning

Lucia flips two quarters at the same time. Use a table to find all the possible outcomes. What is the theoretical probability of each outcome?

Each quarter can land heads up or tails up. Let H = heads and T = tails.

Quarter 1	Quarter 2
H	H
H	T
T	H
T	T

Record each possible outcome.

HH: 2 heads

HT: 1 head, 1 tail

TH: 1 head, 1 tail

TT: 2 tails

Find the probability of each outcome.

$$P(\text{2 heads}) = \frac{1}{4} \qquad P(\text{2 tails}) = \frac{1}{4}$$
$$P(\text{1 head, 1 tail}) = \frac{2}{4} = \frac{1}{2}$$

When the number of possible outcomes of an experiment increases, it may be easier to track all the possible outcomes on a *tree diagram*.

In the game of Rock, Paper, Scissors, two players move their hands into one of three positions at the same time: Rock (a fist), Paper (all fingers extended), or Scissors (first two fingers extended in a V). According to the rules, Rock beats Scissors, Scissors beats Paper, and Paper beats Rock.

EXAMPLE 2 Using a Tree Diagram to Find a Sample Space

Reasoning

Ren and Marisa play a round of Rock, Paper, Scissors. Use a tree diagram to find all the possible outcomes. What is the probability that Ren will win the round?

To make a tree diagram, first list each hand position for Ren. Then for each of Ren's hand positions, list each hand position for Marisa.

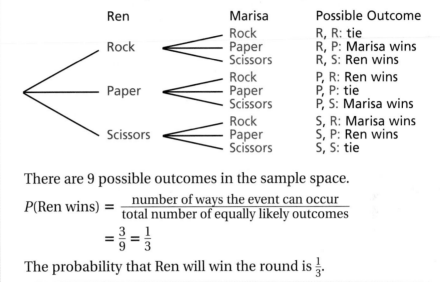

Ren	Marisa	Possible Outcome
Rock	Rock	R, R: tie
	Paper	R, P: Marisa wins
	Scissors	R, S: Ren wins
Paper	Rock	P, R: Ren wins
	Paper	P, P: tie
	Scissors	P, S: Marisa wins
Scissors	Rock	S, R: Marisa wins
	Paper	S, P: Ren wins
	Scissors	S, S: tie

There are 9 possible outcomes in the sample space.

$$P(\text{Ren wins}) = \frac{\text{number of ways the event can occur}}{\text{total number of equally likely outcomes}}$$

$$= \frac{3}{9} = \frac{1}{3}$$

The probability that Ren will win the round is $\frac{1}{3}$.

The **Fundamental Counting Principle** states that you can find the total number of outcomes for a compound event by multiplying the number of outcomes for each simple event.

EXAMPLE 3 *Recreation Application*

In a game, each player rolls a number cube and spins a spinner. The spinner is divided into thirds, numbered 1, 2, and 3. How many outcomes are possible during one player's turn?

The number cube has 6 outcomes.   *List the number of outcomes*
The spinner has 3 outcomes.   *for each simple event.*

$6 \cdot 3 = 18$ *Use the Fundamental Counting Principle.*

There are 18 possible outcomes during one player's turn.

Think and Discuss

1. Compare using a tree diagram and using the Fundamental Counting Principle to find a sample space.

2. Find the size of the sample space for flipping 5 coins.

California
Standards Practice
SDAP3.1, SDAP3.3

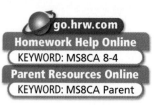

go.hrw.com
Homework Help Online
KEYWORD: MS8CA 8-4
Parent Resources Online
KEYWORD: MS8CA Parent

GUIDED PRACTICE

See Example **1** 1. Enrique tosses a coin and spins the spinner at right. Use a table to find all the possible outcomes. What is the theoretical probability of each outcome?

See Example **2** 2. At a picnic, people can choose tacos from 2 types of tortilla (corn or flour) and 3 types of filling (chicken, beef, or beans).

a. Use a tree diagram to find all the possible taco types.

b. Angela picks a taco at random from a basket that contains one taco of each type. What is the probability that she will choose a corn tortilla with chicken filling?

See Example **3** 3. A game includes a number cube and a spinner divided into 4 equal sectors. A player rolls the number cube and spins the spinner. How many outcomes are possible?

INDEPENDENT PRACTICE

See Example **1** 4. A spinner is divided into fourths and numbered 1 through 4. Jory spins the spinner and tosses a coin. Use a table to find all the possible outcomes. What is the theoretical probability of each outcome?

See Example **2** 5. Berto tosses a coin and spins the spinner at right.

a. Use a tree diagram to find all the possible outcomes.

b. What is the probability that the coin will land on heads and the spinner will stop on 3?

6. A bookstore is giving out bookmarks to its customers. Customers can choose from 4 colors (green, red, orange, or blue) and 2 styles (cloth or paper).

a. Use a tree diagram to find all the possible bookmark types.

b. Spencer picks a bookmark at random from a box that contains one bookmark of each type. What is the probability that he will choose an orange cloth bookmark?

See Example **3** 7. A pizza shop offers thick crust, thin crust, or stuffed crust. The choices of toppings are pepperoni, cheese, hamburger, Italian sausage, Canadian bacon, onions, bell peppers, mushrooms, and pineapple. How many different one-topping pizzas could you order?

PRACTICE AND PROBLEM SOLVING

Extra Practice
See page EP16.

8. Andie has a blue sweater, a red sweater, and a purple sweater. She has a white shirt and a tan shirt. How many different ways can she wear a sweater and a shirt together?

9. **Health** For each pair of food groups, give the number of possible outcomes if one item is chosen from each group.

a. group A and group B

b. group B and group D

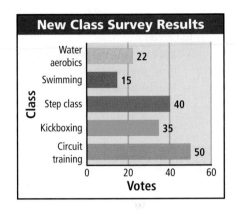

Group A	Group B	Group C	Group D
milk	beef	bread	vegetables
cheese	fish	cereal	fruit
yogurt	poultry	pasta	
		rice	

10. **Health** The graph shows the kinds of classes that health club members would like to see offered.

a. If the health club offers the four most popular classes at different times on the same day, how many ways could they be arranged?

b. If the health club offers each of the five classes on a different weekday, how many ways could they be arranged?

New Class Survey Results

Class / Votes:
- Water aerobics: 22
- Swimming: 15
- Step class: 40
- Kickboxing: 35
- Circuit training: 50

(x-axis: Votes, 0 to 60)

11. **Recreation** There are 3 trails from the South Canyon trailhead to Lake Solitude. There are 4 trails from Lake Solitude to Hidden Lake. How many possible routes could you take to hike from the South Canyon trailhead to Hidden Lake that go by Lake Solitude?

12. **What's the Question?** Dan has 4 face cards and 5 number cards. He shuffles the cards separately and places each set in a separate pile. The answer is 20 possible outcomes. What is the question?

13. **Write About It** Explain how to determine the size of the sample space when you toss three number cubes at the same time.

14. **Challenge** Suppose you flip a penny, a nickel, and a dime at the same time. What are all the possible outcomes?

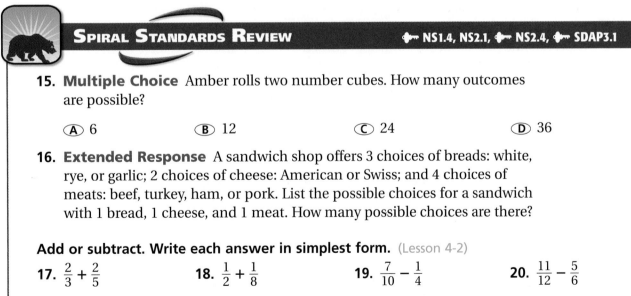

SPIRAL STANDARDS REVIEW ⟵ NS1.4, NS2.1, ⟵ NS2.4, ⟵ SDAP3.1

15. **Multiple Choice** Amber rolls two number cubes. How many outcomes are possible?

Ⓐ 6 Ⓑ 12 Ⓒ 24 Ⓓ 36

16. **Extended Response** A sandwich shop offers 3 choices of breads: white, rye, or garlic; 2 choices of cheese: American or Swiss; and 4 choices of meats: beef, turkey, ham, or pork. List the possible choices for a sandwich with 1 bread, 1 cheese, and 1 meat. How many possible choices are there?

Add or subtract. Write each answer in simplest form. (Lesson 4-2)

17. $\frac{2}{3} + \frac{2}{5}$ 18. $\frac{1}{2} + \frac{1}{8}$ 19. $\frac{7}{10} - \frac{1}{4}$ 20. $\frac{11}{12} - \frac{5}{6}$

21. Belinda deposits $450 into a savings account that earns simple interest at a rate of 2.5%. How much interest will the account earn in 6 years? (Lesson 6-7)

Experimental and Theoretical Probability

Use with Lesson 8-4

go.hrw.com
Lab Resources Online
KEYWORD: MS8CA Lab8

California Standards

SDAP3.2 Use data to estimate the probability of future events (e.g., batting averages or number of accidents per mile driven).
Also covered: ☞ **SDAP3.1,** ☞ **SDAP3.3**

REMEMBER

- The experimental probability of an event is the ratio of the number of times the event occurs to the total number of trials.
- The theoretical probability of an event is the ratio of the number of ways the event can occur to the total number of equally likely outcomes.

Activity 1

1 Write the letters *A, B, C,* and *D* on four slips of paper. Fold the slips in half and place them in a bag or other small container.

2 You will be choosing these slips of paper without looking. Predict the number of times you expect to choose *A* when you repeat the experiment 12 times.

3 Choose a slip of paper, note the result, and replace the slip. Repeat this 12 times, mixing the slips between trials. Record your results in a table like the one shown.

4 How many times did you choose *A*? How does this number compare to your prediction?

5 What is the experimental probability of choosing *A*? What is the theoretical probability of choosing *A*?

6 Combine your results with those of your classmates. Find the experimental probability of choosing *A* based on the combined results.

Outcome	Number of Times Chosen
A	//
B	////
C	ﬓ
D	/

Think and Discuss

1. How is the experimental probability of choosing *A* based on the combined results different from the experimental probability of choosing *A* based on the results of your own experiment?

2. How many times would you expect to choose *A* if you repeat the experiment 500 times?

Try This

1. What is the theoretical probability of choosing *A* from five slips of paper with the letters *A, B, C, D,* and *E*?

2. Predict the number of times you would expect to choose *A* from the five slips in problem 1 if you repeat the experiment 500 times.

Activity 2

1 Write the letters *A*, *B*, *C*, and *D* and the numbers 1, 2, and 3 on slips of paper. Fold the slips in half. Place the slips with the letters in one bag and the slips with the numbers in a different bag.

2 In this activity, you will be choosing one slip of paper from each bag without looking. What is the sample space for this experiment? Predict the number of times you expect to choose *A* and 1 (*A*-1) when you repeat the experiment 24 times.

3 Choose a slip of paper from each bag, note the results, and replace the slips. Repeat this 24 times, mixing the slips between trials. Record your results in a table like the one shown.

4 How many times did you choose *A*-1? How does this number compare to your prediction?

Outcome	Number of Times Chosen
A-1	/
A-2	~~llll~~
A-3	//
B-1	/

5 Combine your results with those of your classmates. Find the experimental probability of choosing *A*-1 based on the combined results.

Think and Discuss

1. What do you think is the theoretical probability of choosing *A*-1? Why?

2. How many times would you expect to choose *A*-1 if you repeat the experiment 600 times?

3. Explain the difference between the experimental probability of an event and the theoretical probability of the event.

Try This

1. Suppose you toss a penny and a nickel at the same time.

   a. What is the sample space for this experiment?

   b. Predict the number of times you would expect both coins to land heads up if you repeat the experiment 100 times.

   c. Predict the number of times you would expect one coin to land heads up and one coin to land tails up if you repeat the experiment 1,000 times.

2. You spin the spinner at right and roll a number cube at the same time.

   a. What is the sample space for this experiment?

   b. Describe an experiment you could conduct to find the experimental probability of spinning green and rolling a 4 at the same time.

READY TO GO ON?

Quiz for Lessons 8-1 Through 8-4

☑ **8-1** **Introduction to Probability**

Determine whether each event is impossible, unlikely, as likely as not, likely, or certain.

1. rolling 2 number cubes and getting a sum of 2

2. guessing the answer to a true/false question correctly

3. drawing a black marble from a bag containing 2 blue, 3 yellow, and 4 white marbles

4. The probability of Ashur's soccer team winning its next game is $\frac{7}{10}$. What is the probability of Ashur's team not winning the next game?

☑ **8-2** **Experimental Probability**

5. Carl is conducting a survey for the school paper. He finds that 7 students have no pets, 15 have one pet, and 9 have at least two pets. What is the experimental probability that the next student Carl asks will not have a pet?

6. During her ride home from school, Dana sees 15 cars driven by men and 34 cars driven by women. What is the experimental probability that the next car Dana sees will be driven by a man?

☑ **8-3** **Theoretical Probability**

A spinner with 10 equal sectors numbered 1 through 10 is spun. Find the probability of each event. Write your answer as a ratio, as a decimal, and as a percent.

7. $P(5)$

8. $P(\text{prime number})$

9. $P(\text{even number})$

10. $P(20)$

11. Sabina has a list of 8 CDs and 5 DVDs that she would like to buy. Her friends randomly select one of the items from the list to give her as a gift. What is the probability Sabina's friends will select a CD? a DVD?

☑ **8-4** **Sample Spaces**

12. Shelly and Anthony are playing a game using a number cube and a nickel. Each player rolls the number cube and flips the coin. Use a tree diagram to show all the possible outcomes during one turn. What is the probability of rolling a 5 and getting tails?

13. A yogurt shop offers 4 different flavors of yogurt and 3 different fruit toppings. How many different desserts are possible if you can choose one flavor of yogurt and one topping?

Focus on Problem Solving

California Standards

MR1.1 Analyze problems by identifying relationships, distinguishing relevant from irrelevant information, identifying missing information, sequencing **and prioritizing information,** and observing patterns.
Also covered: **SDAP3.2,**
SDAP3.3

Understand

Understand the Problem

• **Identify important details**

When you are solving word problems, you need to identify information that is important to the problem. Read the problem several times to find all the important details. Sometimes it is helpful to read the problem aloud so that you can hear the words. Highlight the facts that are needed to solve the problem. Then list any other information that is necessary.

Highlight the important information in each problem, and then list any other important details.

1 A bag of bubble gum has 25 pink pieces, 20 blue pieces, and 15 green pieces. Lauren selects 1 piece of bubble gum without looking. What is the probability that it is not blue?

2 Regina has a bag of marbles that contains 6 red marbles, 3 green marbles, and 4 blue marbles. Regina pulls 1 marble from the bag without looking. What is the probability that the marble is red?

3 Marco is counting the cars he sees on his ride home from school. Of 20 cars, 10 are white, 6 are red, 2 are blue, and 2 are green. What is the experimental probability that the next car Marco sees will be red?

4 Frederica has 28 socks in a drawer; 8 are red, 6 are blue, 10 are white, and 4 are yellow. What is the probability that she will randomly pull a brown sock from the drawer?

5 During the first 20 minutes of lunch, 5 male students, 7 female students, and 3 teachers went through the lunch line. What is the experimental probability that the next person through the line will be a teacher?

 **8-5** **Disjoint Events**

YOU'VE WON!
HOLLYWOOD

 **California Standards**

SDAP3.4 Understand that the probability of either of two disjoint events occurring is the sum of the two individual probabilities and that the probability of one event following another, in independent trials, is the product of the two probabilities.

Also covered: 🔑 **SDAP3.1**

Why learn this? Understanding disjoint events can help you to find the probability of winning a prize.

On a game show, the letters in the word *Hollywood* are printed on cards and shuffled. A contestant will win a trip to Hollywood if the first card she chooses is printed with an *O* or an *L*.

Choosing an *O* or an *L* on the first card is a set of *disjoint events*. **Disjoint events** are events that cannot all occur in the same trial of an experiment.

EXAMPLE **1** **Identifying Disjoint Events**

Vocabulary
disjoint events

Determine whether each set of events is disjoint. Explain.

A choosing a red apple or a green apple from a basket containing red apples, green apples, bananas, and oranges

The events are disjoint. You cannot choose a piece of fruit that is both a green apple and a red apple.

B rolling a 6 or rolling an even number on a number cube

The events are not disjoint. Because 6 is an even number, you can roll a 6 and an even number at the same time.

Reading Math

Disjoint events are sometimes called mutually exclusive events.

Probability of Two Disjoint Events

$$P(A \text{ or } B) = P(A) + P(B)$$

Probability of either event · Probability of one event · Probability of other event

---

EXAMPLE **2** **Finding the Probability of Disjoint Events**

Find the probability of each set of disjoint events.

A choosing an *O* or an *L* from the letters in the word *Hollywood*

$P(O) = \frac{3}{9}$ $P(L) = \frac{2}{9}$

$P(O \text{ or } L) = P(O) + P(L)$ *Add the probabilities of*
$= \frac{3}{9} + \frac{2}{9} = \frac{5}{9}$ *the individual events.*

The probability of choosing an *O* or an *L* is $\frac{5}{9}$.

Find the probability of each set of disjoint events.

B choosing a green bead or a purple bead from a box that holds only 10 green beads, 18 purple beads, and 14 blue beads

$$P(\text{green}) = \frac{10}{42} \qquad P(\text{purple}) = \frac{18}{42}$$

$$P(\text{green or purple}) = P(\text{green}) + P(\text{purple})$$

$$= \frac{10}{42} + \frac{18}{42}$$

$$= \frac{28}{42} = \frac{2}{3}$$

The probability of choosing a green bead or a purple bead is $\frac{2}{3}$.

EXAMPLE 3 *Recreation Application*

Maya is playing a board game. She rolls two number cubes. If the sum of the numbers rolled is 11 or 12, she will get another turn. Use a grid to find the sample space. Then find the probability that Maya will get another turn.

Step 1 Use a grid to find the sample space.

First Roll

	1	2	3	4	5	6
1	2	3	4	5	6	7
2	3	4	5	6	7	8
3	4	5	6	7	8	9
4	5	6	7	8	9	10
5	6	7	8	9	10	(11)
6	7	8	9	10	(11)	(12)

(Second Roll — vertical axis label)

The grid shows all possible sums.

There are 36 equally likely outcomes in the sample space.

Step 2 Find the probability of the set of disjoint events.

$$P(\text{sum of 11}) = \frac{2}{36} \qquad P(\text{sum of 12}) = \frac{1}{36}$$

$$P(\text{sum of 11 or sum of 12}) = P(\text{sum of 11}) + P(\text{sum of 12})$$

$$= \frac{2}{36} + \frac{1}{36}$$

$$= \frac{3}{36} = \frac{1}{12}$$

The probability that Maya will get another turn is $\frac{1}{12}$.

Think and Discuss

1. Explain why choosing an *A* or a vowel from the letters of the alphabet would not represent an example of disjoint events.

California Standards Practice
→ **SDAP3.1, SDAP3.2,**
→ **SDAP3.3, SDAP3.4**

go.hrw.com
Homework Help Online
KEYWORD: MS8CA 8-5
Parent Resources Online
KEYWORD: MS8CA Parent

GUIDED PRACTICE

See Example ① **Determine whether each set of events is disjoint. Explain.**

1. rolling a number cube and getting a 5 or a number less than 3

2. choosing an 11-year-old or choosing a sixth-grader from among the students at a middle school

See Example ② **Find the probability of each set of disjoint events.**

3. tossing a coin and its landing on heads or tails

4. spinning red or green on a spinner that has four equal sectors colored red, green, blue, and yellow

5. drawing a black marble or a red marble from a bag that contains only 4 white marbles, 3 black marbles, and 2 red marbles

See Example ③ 6. Adam tosses two coins at the same time. Use a grid to find the sample space. Then find the probability that both coins land on heads or both coins land on tails.

INDEPENDENT PRACTICE

See Example ① **Determine whether each set of events is disjoint. Explain.**

7. choosing a multiple of 4 or a multiple of 5 from among the numbers 1–100

8. drawing a red bead or a pink bead from a bag that contains only 10 red beads and 10 pink beads

See Example ② **Find the probability of each set of disjoint events.**

9. choosing a boy or a girl from among a class of 13 boys and 17 girls

10. choosing an *A* or an *E* from a list of the five vowels

11. choosing a number less than 3 or a number greater than 12 from a set of 20 cards numbered 1–20

See Example ③ 12. Sumi spins the two spinners shown. She wins a prize if the sum of the numbers she spins is 6 or 7. Use a grid to find the sample space. Then find the probability that Sumi will win a prize.

PRACTICE AND PROBLEM SOLVING

Extra Practice
See page EP17.

Find the probability of each set of disjoint events when two number cubes are rolled.

13. The sum is 3 or 4.

14. The sum is 5 or 9.

15. The sum is 8 or 10.

16. The sum is 6, 7, or 8.

Sports The graph shows the experimental probabilities of different outcomes when Rob bats in a baseball game. Find the probability of each set of disjoint events.

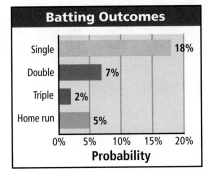

Batting Outcomes

Single 18%
Double 7%
Triple 2%
Home run 5%

0%   5%   10%   15%   20%
Probability

17. Rob hits a single or a double.

18. Rob hits a triple or a home run.

19. Consumer Math A cereal company is putting prize cards in some of its boxes. For every 10,000 boxes, there is 1 card for a video game system, 25 cards for a DVD, and 100 cards for a movie ticket. What is the probability, written as a percent, that Diego will win a video game system or a DVD if he buys a box of the cereal?

20. In every 60-second period, a traffic light is green for 30 seconds, yellow for 6 seconds, and red for 24 seconds. What is the probability that the light is green or yellow when a driver arrives at the light?

21. Reasoning A weather report states that there is a 60% chance of rain on Saturday and a 60% chance of rain on Sunday. Explain why the chance of rain on Saturday or Sunday is not equal to 120%.

22. Write About It The spinner is divided into 3 equal sectors. Explain why the probability that the spinner does not land on red is the same as the probability that the spinner lands on green or blue.

23. Challenge Nadia rolls a number cube. What is the probability that she rolls an odd number or a prime number?

SPIRAL STANDARDS REVIEW

AF2.1, ⟵ SDAP3.3, SDAP3.4

24. Multiple Choice A set of cards are numbered 1 through 12. You choose one card at random. What is the probability that you choose an even number or a 5?

(A) $\frac{1}{6}$ (B) $\frac{1}{2}$ (C) $\frac{7}{12}$ (D) $\frac{5}{6}$

25. Multiple Choice A tray contains 5 cheese tamales, 5 pork tamales, and 10 chicken tamales. Andy chooses a tamale at random. What is the probability that he chooses a pork tamale or a chicken tamale?

(A) $\frac{1}{4}$ (B) $\frac{1}{2}$ (C) $\frac{2}{3}$ (D) $\frac{3}{4}$

Convert each measure. (Lesson 4-9)

26. 3 kilograms to grams   **27.** 560 centimeters to meters   **28.** 0.8 liter to milliliters

29. A drawer holds 10 metal spoons and 15 plastic spoons. If Merina chooses a spoon from the drawer at random, what is the probability that she will choose a plastic spoon? (Lesson 8-3)

8-6 Independent and Dependent Events

California Standards

SDAP3.5 Understand the difference between independent and dependent events.
Also covered: SDAP3.3, SDAP3.4

Vocabulary
independent events
dependent events

Why learn this? You can determine whether one event affects the probability of a second event.

Raji and Kara must each choose a topic from a list of topics to research for their class. If Raji can choose the same topic as Kara and vice versa, the events are *independent*. For **independent events**, the occurrence of one event has no effect on the probability that a second event will occur.

If once Raji chooses a topic, Kara must choose from the remaining topics, then the events are *dependent*. Kara has fewer topics to choose from after Raji chooses. For **dependent events**, the occurrence of one event *does* have an effect on the probability that a second event will occur.

EXAMPLE 1 Determining Whether Events Are Independent or Dependent

Decide whether each set of events is independent or dependent. Explain your answer.

A Erika rolls a 3 on one number cube and a 2 on another number cube.

The outcome of rolling one number cube does not affect the outcome of rolling the second number cube.

The events are independent.

B Tomoko chooses a seventh-grader for her team from a group of seventh- and eighth-graders, and then Juan chooses a different seventh-grader from the remaining students.

Juan cannot pick the same student that Tomoko picked, and there are fewer students for Juan to choose from after Tomoko chooses.

The events are dependent.

C Mica has three $10 bills and two $20 bills in her wallet. She takes out a bill at random, replaces it, and then takes out a second bill at random. Both are $20 bills.

Since Mica replaces the first bill, the outcome of picking the first bill does not affect the outcome of picking the second bill.

The events are independent.

---

406 *Chapter 8 Probability*

To find the probability that two independent events will happen, multiply the probabilities of the two events.

Probability of Two Independent Events

$$P(A \text{ and } B) = P(A) \cdot P(B)$$

Probability of both events *Probability of first event* *Probability of second event*

EXAMPLE 2 **Finding the Probability of Independent Events**

Find the probability of flipping a coin and getting heads and then rolling a 6 on a number cube.

The outcome of flipping the coin does not affect the outcome of rolling the number cube, so the events are independent.

$P(\text{heads and } 6) = P(\text{heads}) \cdot P(6)$

$\qquad = \frac{1}{2} \cdot \frac{1}{6}$ *There are 2 ways a coin can land and 6 ways a number cube can land.*

$\qquad = \frac{1}{12}$ *Multiply.*

The probability of getting heads and a 6 is $\frac{1}{12}$.

EXAMPLE 3 *Earth Science Application*

A weather report states that there is a 20% chance of rain on Saturday and an 80% chance of rain on Sunday. If the chance of rain on Sunday is independent of the chance of rain on Saturday, what is the probability that it will rain on both days?

$P(\text{rain Sat. and rain Sun.}) = P(\text{rain Sat.}) \cdot P(\text{rain Sun.})$

$\qquad = 20\% \cdot 80\%$ *Substitute 20% for P(rain Sat.) and 80% for P(rain Sun.)*

$\qquad = 0.20 \cdot 0.80$ *Write the percents as decimals.*

$\qquad = 0.16$ *Multiply.*

$\qquad = 16\%$ *Write the decimal as a percent.*

Helpful Hint

To multiply two percents, first rewrite them as decimals or as fractions.

The probability that it will rain on both Saturday and Sunday is 16%.

Think and Discuss

1. **Compare** probabilities of independent and disjoint events.

2. **Explain** whether the probability of two independent events is greater than or less than the probability of each individual event.

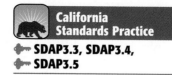

GUIDED PRACTICE

See Example **1** Decide whether each set of events is independent or dependent. Explain your answer.

1. A student flips heads on one coin and tails on a second coin.

2. A student chooses a red marble from a bag of marbles and then chooses another red marble without replacing the first.

3. A teacher randomly chooses two students from a class of 15 boys and 10 girls. Both of the students are girls.

See Example **2** Find the probability of each set of independent events.

4. a flipped coin landing heads up and rolling a 5 or a 6 on a number cube

5. drawing a 5 from 10 cards numbered 1 through 10 and rolling a 2 on a number cube

See Example **3** **6.** Based on past seasons, a basketball player has a 90% chance of making a free throw and a 50% chance of making a field goal. The player attempts both a free throw and a field goal in the last minute of a game. If the shots are independent of each other, what is the probability that the player will make both of them?

INDEPENDENT PRACTICE

See Example **1** Decide whether each set of events is independent or dependent. Explain your answer.

7. A student chooses a fiction book at random from a list of books and then chooses a second fiction book from those remaining.

8. A woman chooses a lily from one bunch of flowers and then chooses a tulip from a different bunch.

9. A student spins twice using a spinner divided into red, yellow, and blue sectors. Both times, the spinner stops on a red sector.

See Example **2** Find the probability of each set of independent events.

10. drawing a red marble from a bag of 6 red and 4 blue marbles, replacing it, and then drawing a blue marble

11. rolling an even number on a number cube and rolling an odd number on a second roll of the same cube

See Example **3** **12.** Each morning, Mr. Samms passes two traffic lights. There is a 30% chance that the first light will be green, and a 30% chance that the second light will be green. If the timing of the lights is independent of each other, what is the probability that both lights will be green when Mr. Samms reaches them?

13. A card is chosen randomly from a set of cards labeled with the numbers 1 through 8. A second card is chosen after the first card is replaced. Are these independent or dependent events? What is the probability that both cards will be labeled with even numbers?

14. On a multiple-choice test, each question has five possible answers. A student does not know the answers to two questions, so he guesses. What is the probability that the student will get both answers wrong?

Find the probability of each event for the spinners shown.

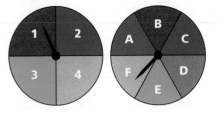

15. The spinners land on 1 and *F*.

16. The spinners land on an even number and *A*.

17. Science If a cat has 5 kittens, what is the probability that all of the kittens are female? (Assume that having a male and having a female are equally likely events.)

18. Write a Problem Describe two events that are independent, and make up a probability problem about them.

19. Write About It At the beginning of a board game, players take turns drawing 7 tiles. Are drawing *A*'s on the first two tiles dependent or independent events? Explain.

20. Challenge Weather forecasters have accurately predicted rain in one community $\frac{4}{5}$ of the time. If their prediction on one day is independent of their prediction on the next day, what is the probability that they will accurately predict rain two days in a row?

SPIRAL STANDARDS REVIEW

NS2.1, ← SDAP3.3, SDAP3.4, ← SDAP3.5

21. Multiple Choice A bag contains 5 red marbles and 5 purple marbles. What is the probability of drawing a red marble and then a purple marble, if the first marble is replaced before drawing the second marble?

   Ⓐ $\frac{1}{4}$ Ⓑ $\frac{1}{3}$ Ⓒ $\frac{2}{5}$ Ⓓ $\frac{1}{2}$

22. Short Response José has 3 brown socks, 5 blue socks, and 6 black socks in his sock drawer. He picked one sock and then another sock out of the drawer. Are the events independent or dependent? Explain your answer.

23. Fritz jogged $1\frac{3}{4}$ mi on Monday, $2\frac{1}{2}$ mi on Wednesday, and 3 mi on Friday. How many miles did he jog altogether on these days? (Lesson 4-3)

24. Find the probability of choosing a sixth-grader or a seventh-grader from a team that includes 5 sixth-graders, 9 seventh-graders, and 4 eighth-graders. (Lesson 8-5)

8-7 Making Predictions

California Standards

SDAP3.2 Use data to estimate the probability of future events (e.g., batting averages or number of accidents per mile driven).

Also covered: ☞ **NS1.3,** ☞ **SDAP3.3**

Vocabulary
prediction

Why learn this? You can use probability to predict how many of an airline's flights are likely to be on time.

A **prediction** is a guess about something in the future. Suppose you know the experimental probability that an airline's flight will be on time. You can use the probability to predict how many flights out of 1,000 will be on time.

E X A M P L E 1 Using Experimental Probability to Make Predictions

Based on a sample survey, an airline claims that its flights have a 92% probability of being on time. Out of 1,000 flights, how many would you predict will be on time?

You can write a proportion. Remember that *percent* means "per hundred."

$$\frac{92}{100} = \frac{x}{1,000}$$ *Think: 92 out of 100 is how many out of 1,000?*

$$100 \cdot x = 92 \cdot 1,000$$ *The cross products are equal.*

$$100x = 92,000$$

$$\frac{100x}{100} = \frac{92,000}{100}$$ *Divide both sides by 100.*

$$x = 920$$

You can predict that about 920 of 1,000 flights will be on time.

Math Builders

For more on proportions, see the Proportion Builder on page MB2.

E X A M P L E 2 Using Theoretical Probability to Make Predictions

If you roll a number cube 24 times, how many times do you expect to roll a 5?

$$P(\text{rolling a } 5) = \frac{1}{6}$$

$$\frac{1}{6} = \frac{x}{24}$$ *Think: 1 out of 6 is how many out of 24?*

$$6 \cdot x = 1 \cdot 24$$ *The cross products are equal.*

$$6x = 24$$

$$\frac{6x}{6} = \frac{24}{6}$$ *Divide both sides by 6.*

$$x = 4$$

You can expect to roll a 5 about 4 times.

EXAMPLE 3

PROBLEM
SOLVING

Reasoning

PROBLEM SOLVING APPLICATION

A stadium sells yearly parking passes. If you have a parking pass, you can park at the stadium for any event during that year.

Based on a sample group of fans, the managers of the stadium estimate that the probability that a person with a pass will attend any one event is 80%. The parking lot has 300 spaces for people with parking passes. If the managers want the lot to be full at every event, how many passes should they sell?

1 Understand the Problem

The **answer** will be the number of parking passes they should sell.

List the **important information:**

- P(person with pass attends event) $= 80\%$
- There are 300 parking spaces.

2 Make a Plan

The managers want to fill all 300 spaces. But, on average, only 80% of parking pass holders will attend. So 80% of pass holders must equal 300. You can write an equation to find this number.

3 Solve

$$\frac{80}{100} = \frac{300}{x}$$ *Think: 80 out of 100 is 300 out of how many?*

$$100 \cdot 300 = 80 \cdot x$$ *The cross products are equal.*

$$30{,}000 = 80x$$

$$\frac{30{,}000}{80} = \frac{80x}{80}$$ *Divide both sides by 80.*

$$375 = x$$

The managers should sell 375 parking passes.

4 Look Back

If the managers sold only 300 passes, the parking lot would not usually be full because only about 80% of the people with passes will attend any one event. The managers should sell more than 300 passes, so 375 is a reasonable answer.

Think and Discuss

1. Tell whether you expect to be exactly right if you make a prediction based on a sample. Explain your answer.

8-7

Exercises

California
Standards Practice

⬥— NS1.3, ⬥— SDAP2.4,
SDAP3.2, ⬥— SDAP3.3

go.hrw.com
Homework Help Online
KEYWORD: MR8CA 8-7
Parent Resources Online
KEYWORD: MR8CA Parent

GUIDED PRACTICE

See Example ① **1.** Based on a sample survey, a local newspaper states that 12% of the city's residents have volunteered at an animal shelter. Out of 5,000 residents, how many would you predict have volunteered at the animal shelter?

See Example ② **2.** If you roll a fair number cube 30 times, how many times would you expect to roll a number that is a multiple of 3?

See Example ③ **3.** **Recreation** Airlines routinely overbook flights, which means that they sell more tickets than there are seats on the planes. Suppose an airline estimates that 93% of customers will show up for a particular flight. If the plane seats 186 people, how many tickets should the airline sell?

INDEPENDENT PRACTICE

See Example ① **4.** Based on a sample survey, a local newspaper claims that 64% of the town's households receive their paper. Out of 15,000 households, how many would you predict receive the paper?

See Example ② **5.** If you flip a coin 64 times, how many times do you expect the coin to show tails?

6. A bag contains 2 black chips, 5 red chips, and 4 white chips. You pick a chip from the bag, record its color, and put the chip back in the bag. If you repeat this process 99 times, how many times do you expect to remove a red chip from the bag?

See Example ③ **7.** **Science** The director of a blood bank is eager to increase his supply of O negative blood, because O negative blood can be given to people with any blood type. The probability that a person has O negative blood is 7%. The director would like to have 9 O negative donors each day. How many total donors does the director need to find each day to reach his goal of O negative donors?

PRACTICE AND PROBLEM SOLVING

Extra Practice
See page EP17.

8. A sample survey of 50 people in Harrisburg indicates that 10 of them know the name of the mayor of their neighboring city.

   a. Out of 5,500 Harrisburg residents, how many would you expect to know the name of the mayor of the neighboring city?

   b. Multi-Step Out of 600 Harrisburg residents, how many would you predict do not know the name of the mayor of the neighboring city?

9. Reasoning A survey is being conducted as people exit a frozen yogurt store. They are being asked if they prefer frozen yogurt or ice cream. Should predictions be made about the population of the town based on the survey? Explain.

The Native Canadians lived in Canada before the Europeans arrived. The French were the first Europeans to settle successfully in Canada.

The graph shows the results of a survey of 400 Canadian citizens.

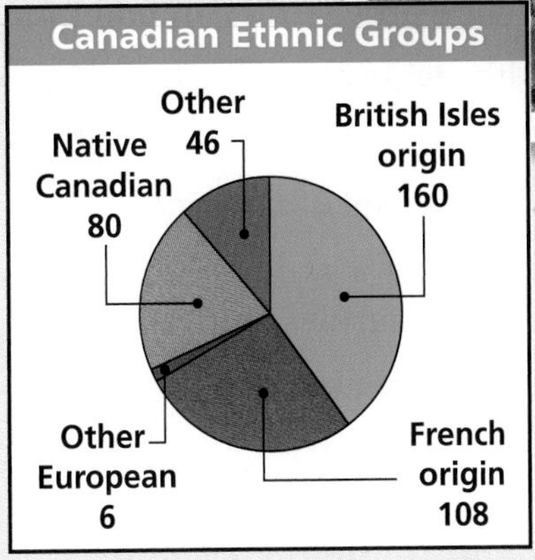

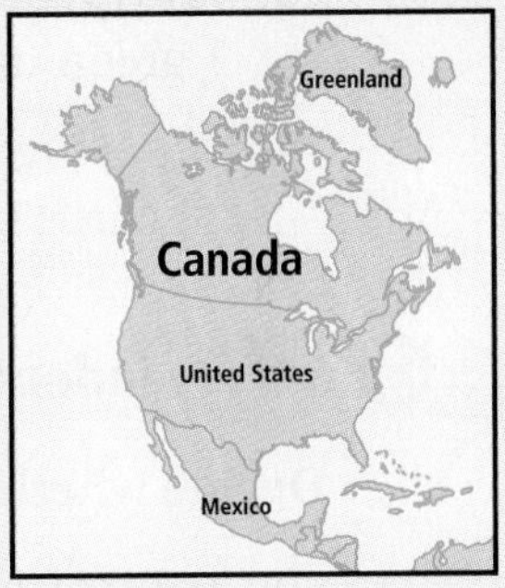

10. Out of 75 Canadians, how many would you predict are of French origin?

11. A random group of Canadians includes 18 Native Canadians. How many total Canadians would you predict are in the group?

12. **? What's the Error?** A student said that in any group of Canadians, 20 of them will be Native Canadians. What mistake did this student make?

Canadian Ethnic Groups

Other 46
Native Canadian 80
British Isles origin 160
Other European 6
French origin 108

13. **✐ Write About It** How could you predict the number of people of French *or* Native Canadian origin in a group of 150 Canadians?

14. **★ Challenge** In a group of Canadians, 15 are in the Other European origin category. Predict how many Canadians in the same group are NOT in that category.

SPIRAL STANDARDS REVIEW   ← NS2.3, ← AF1.1, SDAP3.2, ← SDAP3.3

15. Multiple Choice Jay played a game and won 24 out of 100 times. Which is the best prediction of the number of times Jay will win if he plays 75 games?

(A) 6   (B) 12   (C) 15   (D) 18

16. Multiple Choice You roll a fair number cube 36 times. How many times do you expect to roll a 4?

(A) 36   (B) 9   (C) 6   (D) $\frac{1}{6}$

Solve each equation. Check your answers. (Lesson 2-5)

17. $x + 10 = -2$ **18.** $x - 20 = -5$ **19.** $-9x = 45$ **20.** $x \div (-2) = -5$

A fair number cube is rolled. Find each probability. (Lesson 8-3)

21. $P(5)$ **22.** $P(\text{not } 2)$ **23.** $P(\text{not } 0)$ **24.** $P(\text{number divisible by 3})$

READY TO GO ON?

Quiz for Lessons 8-5 Through 8-7

✓ 8-5 Disjoint Events

Determine whether each set of events is disjoint. Explain.

1. rolling a number cube and getting an odd number or an even number

2. choosing a flag with stripes or choosing a flag with stars from the flags of the world's nations

Find the probability of each set of disjoint events.

3. drawing a blue marble or a white marble from a bag that contains only 1 green marble, 5 blue marbles, and 3 white marbles

4. choosing a number less than 5 or a number greater than 16 from a set of 20 cards numbered 1–20

✓ 8-6 Independent and Dependent Events

Decide whether each set of events is independent or dependent. Explain.

5. Winny rolls two number cubes and gets a 5 on one and a 3 on the other.

6. A card with hearts is drawn from a full deck of cards and not replaced. Then a card with clubs is drawn from the same deck.

A bag contains only 8 blue and 7 yellow marbles. Use this information for Exercises 7 and 8.

7. Find the probability of randomly drawing a blue marble and then randomly drawing a yellow marble after replacing the first marble.

8. Find the probability of randomly drawing a blue marble and then randomly drawing another blue marble after replacing the first marble.

9. The experimental probability that a kicker will make a field goal is 90%. What is the probability that the kicker will make his next 2 attempted field goals?

✓ 8-7 Making Predictions

10. Based on a sample survey, 26% of the local people have a pet dog. Out of 600 local people, how many people do you predict will have a pet dog?

11. If you roll a number cube 54 times, how many times do you expect to roll a number less than 3?

12. Based on previous attendance, the managers for a summer concert series estimate the probability that a person will attend any one event to be 90%. The chairs set up around the stage seat 450 people. If the managers want to be at full capacity every concert, how many tickets should they sell?

Spin to Win Jasper Middle School is having a spring carnival for students and their families. Every guest may spin either the Big Wheel or the Lucky Circle. Guests win a door prize if the Big Wheel's spinner lands on *A* or if the Lucky Circle's spinner lands on an even number.

1. Is a guest more likely to win a door prize by spinning the Big Wheel or by spinning the Lucky Circle? Explain.

2. Miguel chooses to spin the Big Wheel. His sister, Anna, chooses to spin the Lucky Circle. How many different outcomes of their spins are possible?

3. What is the probability that Miguel and Anna both win a door prize?

4. Find the probability that two guests in a row win a prize spinning the Big Wheel.

5. During the carnival, 160 guests spin the Big Wheel and 125 guests spin the Lucky Circle. Which spinner do you predict will have the greater number of winners? Explain.

Game Time

Probability Brain Teasers

Can you solve these riddles that involve probability? Watch out—some of them are tricky!

1 In Wade City, 5% of the residents have unlisted phone numbers. If you selected 100 people at random from the town's phone directory, how many of them would you predict have unlisted numbers?

2 Amanda has a drawer that contains 24 black socks and 18 white socks. If she reaches into the drawer without looking, how many socks does she have to pull out in order to be *certain* that she will have two socks of the same color?

3 Dale, Melvin, Carter, and Ken went out to eat. Each person ordered something different. When the food came, the waiter could not remember who had ordered what, so he set the plates down at random in front of the four friends. What is the probability that exactly three of the boys got what they ordered?

Round and Round and Round

This is a game for two players.

The object of this game is to determine which of the three spinners is the winning spinner (lands on the greater number most often).

Both players choose a spinner and spin at the same time. Record which spinner lands on the greater number. Repeat this 19 more times, keeping track of which spinner wins each time. Repeat this process until you have played spinner A against spinner B, spinner B against spinner C, and spinner A against spinner C. Spin each pair of spinners 20 times and record the results.

Which spinner wins more often, A or B?
Which spinner wins more often, B or C?
Which spinner wins more often, A or C?
Is there anything surprising about your results?

go.hrw.com
Game Time Extra
KEYWORD: MS8CA Games

A complete copy of the rules and game pieces are available online.

Materials
- CD with case
- white paper
- scissors
- markers
- glue
- brass fastener
- large paper clip
- stapler

It's in the Bag!

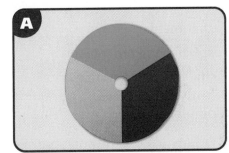
A

PROJECT — CD Spinner

Use a CD to make a spinner. Then take notes on probability in a booklet that you store in the CD case.

Directions

❶ Trace around the CD to make a circle on white paper. Divide the circle into thirds, color each third a different color, and cut out the circle. Glue the circle onto the CD. **Figure A**

B

❷ Carefully remove the plastic CD holder from the back of the CD case. Place the CD in the holder and insert a brass fastener into the center of the CD. Bend the ends of the fastener so it stays in place, and put the holder back into the CD case. **Figure B**

❸ Attach a large paper clip to the brass fastener to make a spinner. **Figure C**

C

❹ Cut several sheets of white paper so they are $4\frac{3}{4}$ inches by $4\frac{3}{4}$ inches. Staple them together to form a booklet that fits in the cover of the CD case.

Taking Note of the Math

Use the booklet to record notes on probability. Be sure to include probabilities related to the spinner that you made.

CHAPTER 8 PROBABILITY

Vocabulary

Complete the sentences below with vocabulary words from the list above.

1. For ___?___, the outcome of one event has no effect on the outcome of a second event.

2. A(n) ___?___ is a result of an experiment.

8-1 Introduction to Probability (pp. 382–385)

 SDAP3.3

EXAMPLE

■ A spinner is divided equally into 8 sectors numbered 1 through 8. The likelihood of each event is described.

landing on:

0	impossible
5	unlikely
an even number	as likely as not

EXERCISES

Determine whether each event is impossible, unlikely, as likely as not, likely, or certain.

3. rolling a sum of 12 with two number cubes

4. rolling a sum of 24 with two number cubes

8-2 Experimental Probability (pp. 386–389)

 SDAP3.2, SDAP3.3

EXAMPLE

■ Of 50 people surveyed, 21 said they liked mysteries better than comedies. What is the probability that the next person surveyed will prefer mysteries?

$P(\text{mysteries}) = \frac{21}{50}$

EXERCISES

Of Sami's first 15 grades, 10 have been above 82.

5. What is the probability that her next grade will be above 82?

6. What is the probability that her next grade will not be above 82?

8-3 Theoretical Probability (pp. 390–393)

SDAP3.3

EXAMPLE

■ Find the probability of drawing a 4 from a standard deck of 52 playing cards. Write your answer as a ratio, as a decimal, and as a percent.

$$P(4) = \frac{\text{number of 4's in deck}}{\text{number of cards in deck}}$$

$$= \frac{4}{52}$$

$$= \frac{1}{13}$$

$$\approx 0.077 \approx 7.7\%$$

EXERCISES

Find each probability. Write your answer as a ratio, as a decimal, and as a percent.

7. There are 9 girls and 12 boys on the student council. What is the probability that a girl will be chosen as president?

8. Anita rolls a number cube. What is the probability that she will roll a number less than 4?

9. Jefferson chooses a marble from a bag containing only 6 blue, 9 white, 3 orange, and 11 green marbles. What is the probability that he will select a green marble?

8-4 Sample Spaces (pp. 394–397)

SDAP3.1, SDAP3.3

EXAMPLE

■ Anita tosses a coin and rolls a number cube. How many outcomes are possible?

The coin has 2 outcomes. *List the number*
The number cube has 6 *of outcomes.*
outcomes.

$2 \cdot 6 = 12$ *Use the Fundamental Counting Principle.*

There are 12 possible outcomes.

EXERCISES

Chen spins each of the spinners once.

10. What are all the possible outcomes?

11. What is the theoretical probability of each outcome?

8-5 Disjoint Events (pp. 402–405)

SDAP3.1, SDAP3.4

EXAMPLE

■ Tina has 24 U.S. stamps, 10 Canadian stamps, and 6 Mexican stamps. If she chooses a stamp at random, what is the probability that she will choose a Canadian or a Mexican stamp?

$$P(\text{Can.}) = \frac{10}{40} \qquad P(\text{Mex.}) = \frac{6}{40}$$

$$P(\text{Can. or Mex.}) = \frac{10}{40} + \frac{6}{40}$$

$$= \frac{16}{40} = \frac{2}{5}$$

EXERCISES

Find the probability of each set of disjoint events.

12. choosing either an *E* or a *Y* from the letters in the word *freeway*

13. drawing a blue marble or a green marble from a bag that contains only 3 red marbles, 5 green marbles, and 6 blue marbles

14. rolling a number less than 2 or greater than 5 on a number cube

8-6 Independent and Dependent Events (pp. 406–409)

SDAP3.3, SDAP3.4, SDAP3.5

EXAMPLE

■ There are 4 red marbles, 3 green marbles, 6 blue marbles, and 2 black marbles in a bag. What is the probability that Angie will pick a green marble and then a black marble after replacing the first marble?

$P(\text{green}) = \frac{3}{15} = \frac{1}{5}$

$P(\text{black}) = \frac{2}{15}$

$P(\text{green, then black}) = \frac{1}{5} \cdot \frac{2}{15} = \frac{2}{75}$

The probability of picking a green marble and then a black marble is $\frac{2}{75}$.

EXERCISES

Decide whether each set of events is independent or dependent. Explain your answer.

15. Michelle tosses a quarter and a penny and gets heads on both coins.

16. Kevin takes a book at random from a shelf, puts it aside, and then takes a second book. Both books were written before 1950.

17. Each letter of the word *probability* is written on a card and put in a bag. What is the probability of picking a vowel (*a, e, i, o,* or *u*) on the first try and again on the second try if the first card is replaced?

18. Based on past games, a golfer has a 4% chance of making a hole-in-one on each hole in miniature golf. What is the probability that the golfer will make a hole-in-one on each of her next 2 holes?

8-7 Making Predictions (pp. 410–413)

NS1.3, SDAP3.2, SDAP3.3

EXAMPLE

■ If you spin the spinner 30 times, how many times do you expect it to land on red?

$P(\text{red}) = \frac{1}{3}$

$\frac{1}{3} = \frac{x}{30}$

$3 \cdot x = 1 \cdot 30$ *The cross products are equal.*

$3x = 30$

$\frac{3x}{3} = \frac{30}{3}$ *Divide both sides by 3.*

$x = 10$

You can expect it to land on red about 10 times.

EXERCISES

19. Based on a sample survey, about 2% of the items produced by a company are defective. Out of 5,000 items, how many can you predict will be defective?

20. If you roll a fair number cube 50 times, how many times can you expect to roll an even number?

21. In a sample survey, 500 teenagers indicated that 175 of them use their computers regularly. Out of 4,500 teenagers, predict how many use their computers regularly.

22. In a sample survey, 100 sixth-grade students indicated that 20 of them take music lessons. Out of 500 sixth-grade students, predict how many take music lessons.

CHAPTER TEST

A box contains 3 orange cubes, 2 white cubes, 3 black cubes, and 4 blue cubes. Determine whether each event is impossible, unlikely, as likely as not, likely, or certain.

1. randomly choosing an orange or black cube

2. randomly choosing a white cube

3. randomly choosing a purple cube

4. The baseball game has a 64% chance of being rained out. What is the probability that it will NOT be rained out?

5. Josh threw darts at a dartboard 10 times. Assume that he threw the darts randomly and did not aim. Based on his results, what is the experimental probability that Josh's next dart will land in the center circle?

Rachel spins a spinner that is divided into 10 equal sectors numbered 1 through 10. Find each probability. Write your answer as a ratio, as a decimal, and as a percent.

6. P(odd number)   7. P(composite number)   8. P(number greater than 10)

9. Emilio randomly guesses at the answers to 2 true–false questions on a quiz. Use a tree diagram to show all the possible outcomes. What is the probability that the correct answer to both questions is "true"?

10. A brand of jeans comes in 8 different waist sizes: 28, 30, 32, 34, 36, 38, 40, and 42. The jeans also come in three different colors: blue, black, and tan. How many different types of jeans are possible?

Find the probability of each event.

11. randomly choosing a silver tack or a white tack from a box that contains only 15 blue tacks, 5 red tacks, 20 white tacks, and 8 silver tacks

12. spinning red on a spinner with equally sized red, blue, yellow, and green sectors, and flipping a coin that lands tails up

13. choosing a card labeled *vanilla* from a group of cards labeled *vanilla, chocolate, strawberry,* and *swirl,* and then choosing a card labeled *chocolate* after replacing the first card

14. The experimental probability that Ryan will have math homework on a given school day is 80%. On how many of the next 30 school days can Ryan expect to have math homework?

15. If you roll a number cube 36 times, how many times should you expect to roll an even number?

Cumulative Assessment, Chapters 1–8

Multiple Choice

1. In a box containing 115 marbles, 25 are blue, 22 are brown, and 68 are red. What is the probability of randomly selecting a blue marble?

Ⓐ $\frac{115}{25}$ Ⓒ $\frac{5}{23}$

Ⓑ $\frac{22}{115}$ Ⓓ Not here

2. Convert 805 centimeters to meters.

Ⓐ 80.5 m   Ⓒ 0.0805 m

Ⓑ 8.05 m   Ⓓ 0.00805 m

3. What is the value of $(-8 - 4)^2 + 4^1$?

Ⓐ −143   Ⓒ 145

Ⓑ 0   Ⓓ 148

4. The graph shows a town's high temperatures over a 5-day period. What was the mean high temperature over these 5 days?

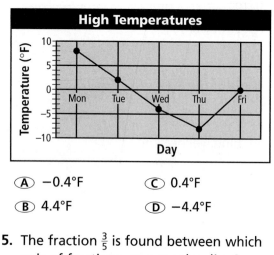

Ⓐ −0.4°F   Ⓒ 0.4°F

Ⓑ 4.4°F   Ⓓ −4.4°F

5. The fraction $\frac{3}{5}$ is found between which pair of fractions on a number line?

Ⓐ $\frac{7}{10}$ and $\frac{3}{4}$ Ⓒ $\frac{2}{5}$ and $\frac{1}{2}$

Ⓑ $\frac{2}{7}$ and $\frac{8}{11}$ Ⓓ $\frac{1}{3}$ and $\frac{5}{13}$

6. Stu wants to leave a 15% tip for his dinner that cost $13.40. About how much tip should Stu leave?

Ⓐ $1.50   Ⓒ $2.00

Ⓑ $1.75   Ⓓ $2.50

7. What is $2\frac{5}{12} \times \frac{12}{7}$?

Ⓐ $\frac{5}{7}$ Ⓒ $2\frac{17}{19}$

Ⓑ $2\frac{5}{7}$ Ⓓ $4\frac{1}{7}$

8. Jason delivers newspapers. He earns $0.22 for every newspaper he delivers. He wants to buy a new printer for his computer that costs $264. If n equals the number of newspapers he delivers, which equation can be used to find the number of newspapers Jason needs to deliver in order to have enough money to buy the printer?

Ⓐ $n - 0.22 = 264$ Ⓒ $\frac{n}{0.22} = 264$

Ⓑ $0.22 + n = 264$ Ⓓ $0.22n = 264$

9. The weights of four puppies are listed below. Which puppy is the heaviest?

Puppy	Weight (lb)
Toby	$5\frac{1}{4}$
Rusty	$5\frac{2}{5}$
Alex	$5\frac{5}{8}$
Jax	$5\frac{2}{3}$

Ⓐ Toby   Ⓒ Alex

Ⓑ Rusty   Ⓓ Jax

10. A fair number cube is rolled. What is the probability that the cube will NOT land on 4?

   (A) $\frac{1}{6}$ (C) $\frac{2}{3}$

   (B) $\frac{1}{3}$ (D) $\frac{5}{6}$

 A probability can be written as a decimal, ratio, or percent. Probabilities are always between 0 and 1 (or 0% and 100%). The greater the probability, the more likely the event is to occur.

11. There were 18 teachers and 45 students registered to participate in a 5K walk-a-thon. Which ratio accurately compares the number of students to the number of teachers?

   (A) 1:5   (C) 3:15

   (B) 5:2   (D) 18:45

12. What is 70% of 30?

   (A) 0.21   (C) 21

   (B) 2.1   (D) 210

Gridded Response

13. Nancy is stenciling 5-inch-wide stars, end-to-end, around her rectangular bedroom. Her bedroom is $12\frac{3}{4}$ feet wide and $15\frac{1}{4}$ feet long. How many whole stars will Nancy stencil?

14. Anji bought 4 shirts for $56.80. She later bought a shirt for $19.20. What was the mean cost of all the shirts in dollars?

15. Rosa has a coupon for 60% off the before-tax total of two pairs of shoes. The first pair of shoes is marked $45, and the second pair is marked $32. What is Rosa's total cost, in dollars, after a 5.5% sales tax is added?

16. What is the value of x? $12 = x - \frac{3}{4}$

Short Response

17. John asked a group of teenagers how many hours of television they watch per day during the summer. He put his results in a table.

Hours	2	3	4	5
Teenagers	II	JHT II	JHT I	JHT

  a. Based on this survey, what is the probability that a teenager will spend 4 hours a day watching television in the summer?

  b. John plans to ask 500 teenagers the same survey question. How many of those teenagers can he predict watch 2 hours of television per day during the summer? Explain.

18. Rhonda has 3 different-color T-shirts—red, blue, and green—and a pair of blue jeans and a pair of white jeans. She randomly chooses a T-shirt and a pair of jeans. What is the probability that she will pair the red T-shirt with the white jeans? Show how you found your answer.

Extended Response

19. A bag contains only 5 blue blocks, 3 red blocks, and 2 yellow blocks.

  a. What is the probability that Tip will draw a red block or a blue block if he draws one block from the bag at random? Show your work.

  b. What is the probability that Tip will draw a red block and then a blue block at random if the first block is replaced before the second is drawn? Show the steps necessary to find your answer.

  c. Explain how you know whether the events in part **b** are independent or dependent.

Geometric Figures

CONCEPT CONNECTION

go.hrw.com
Chapter Project Online
KEYWORD: MS8CA Ch9

Polygons such as triangles and rectangles appear in the structures of many bridges.

Golden Gate Bridge
San Francisco

ARE YOU READY?

✓ Vocabulary

Choose the best term from the list to complete each sentence.

clockwise

counterclockwise

horizontal

protractor

quadrilateral

ruler

triangle

vertical

1. A closed figure with three sides is a __?__, and a closed figure with four sides is a __?__.

2. A __?__ is used to measure and draw angles.

3.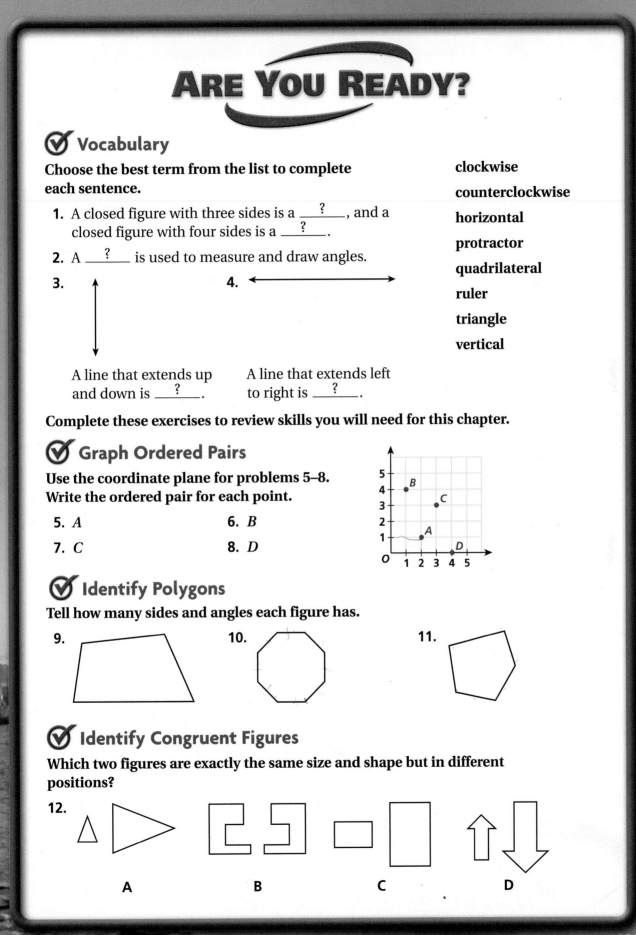

   A line that extends up and down is __?__.

4. A line that extends left to right is __?__.

Complete these exercises to review skills you will need for this chapter.

✓ Graph Ordered Pairs

Use the coordinate plane for problems 5–8. Write the ordered pair for each point.

5. *A*

6. *B*

7. *C*

8. *D*

✓ Identify Polygons

Tell how many sides and angles each figure has.

9.

10.

11.

✓ Identify Congruent Figures

Which two figures are exactly the same size and shape but in different positions?

12.

A   B   C   D

Unpacking the Standards

The information below "unpacks" the standards. The Academic Vocabulary is highlighted and defined to help you understand the language of the standards. Refer to the lessons listed after each standard for help with the math terms and phrases. The Chapter Concept shows how the standard is applied in this chapter.

California Standard	Academic Vocabulary	Chapter Concept
MG2.1 Identify angles as vertical, adjacent, complementary, or supplementary and provide descriptions of these terms. (Lessons 9-3, 9-4, 9-7)	**identify** recognize and describe **terms** words or phrases	You determine the relationship between angles and describe these relationships. *Example:* The angles below are complementary because the sum of their measures is 90°. 30° 60°
MG2.2 Use the properties of complementary and supplementary angles and the sum of the angles of a triangle to solve problems involving an unknown angle. (Lessons 9-4, 9-7) (Lab 9-7)	**properties** in this case, characteristics or features of geometric figures **unknown angle** an angle whose measure is not known	You use facts about angles and triangles to find unknown angle measures. *Example:* The angles below are supplementary, so the sum of their measures is 180°. 150° a The value of *a* is 30° because 150° + 30° = 180°.
MG2.3 Draw quadrilaterals and triangles from given information about them (e.g., a quadrilateral having equal sides but no right angles, a right isosceles triangle). (Lesson 9-8) (Lab 9-6)	**given information** information that is provided in a problem **e.g.** an abbreviation that stands for the Latin phrase *exempli gratia*, which means "for example" **equal sides** sides that have the same length	You draw triangles and quadrilaterals that fit a given description. *Example:* The triangle below is equilateral because it has three equal sides.

Standard AF1.1 is also covered in this chapter. To see this standard unpacked, go to Chapter 1, p. 4.

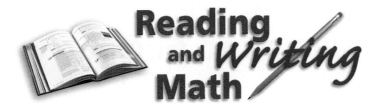

Reading and Writing Math

California Standards

English–Language Arts
Reading 6.2.4

Writing Strategy: Keep a Math Journal

Keeping a math journal can help you improve your writing and reasoning skills and help you make sense of math topics that might be confusing.

You can use your journal to reflect on what you have learned in class or to summarize important concepts and vocabulary. Most important, though, your math journal can help you see your progress throughout the year.

Journal Entry:
Read the entry Lydia wrote in her math journal about similar figures.

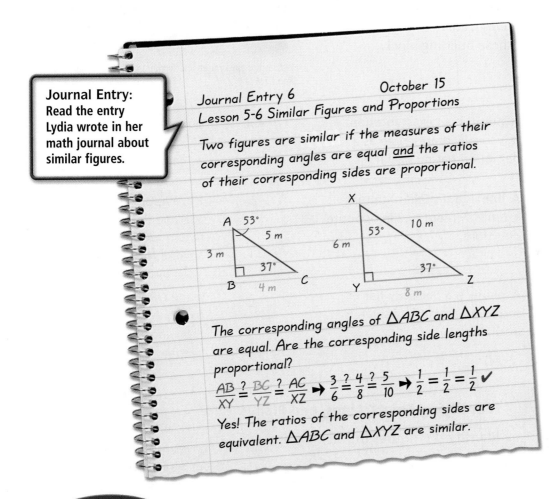

Journal Entry 6   October 15
Lesson 5-6 Similar Figures and Proportions

Two figures are similar if the measures of their corresponding angles are equal <u>and</u> the ratios of their corresponding sides are proportional.

The corresponding angles of $\triangle ABC$ and $\triangle XYZ$ are equal. Are the corresponding side lengths proportional?

$$\frac{AB}{XY} \overset{?}{=} \frac{BC}{YZ} \overset{?}{=} \frac{AC}{XZ} \rightarrow \frac{3}{6} \overset{?}{=} \frac{4}{8} \overset{?}{=} \frac{5}{10} \rightarrow \frac{1}{2} = \frac{1}{2} = \frac{1}{2} \checkmark$$

Yes! The ratios of the corresponding sides are equivalent. $\triangle ABC$ and $\triangle XYZ$ are similar.

Try This

In your math journal, make an entry each day this week. Use the following ideas to begin your entries. Be sure to date each entry.

- What I already know about this lesson is . . .

- The skills I need to be successful in this lesson are . . .

- What challenges did I have? How did I handle these challenges?

Introduction to Geometry

California Standards

Preparation for MG2.1
Identify angles as vertical, adjacent, complementary, or supplementary and provide descriptions of these terms.

Vocabulary
point
line
plane
ray
line segment
congruent

Helpful Hint

A number line is an example of a line, and a coordinate plane is an example of a plane.

Who uses this? Artists often use basic geometric figures when creating their works. (See Exercises 16 and 20.)

Points, *lines*, and *planes* are the most basic figures of geometry. Other geometric figures, such as *line segments* and *rays*, are defined in terms of these building blocks.

Wassily Kandinsky used line segments in his painting *Red Circle*.

A **point** is an exact location. It is usually represented as a dot, but it has no size at all.	• *A*	point *A* *Use a capital letter to name a point.*
A **line** is a straight path that extends without end in opposite directions.		$\overleftrightarrow{XY}$, $\overleftrightarrow{YX}$, or ℓ *Use two points on the line or a lowercase letter to name a line.*
A **plane** is a perfectly flat surface that extends infinitely in all directions.		plane *QRS* *Use three points in any order, not on the same line, to name a plane.*

EXAMPLE **1** **Identifying Points, Lines, and Planes**

Identify the figures in the diagram.

A three points
    A, *E*, and *D*   *Choose any three points.*

B two lines
    $\overleftrightarrow{BD}$, $\overleftrightarrow{CE}$ *Choose any two points on a line to name a line.*

C a plane
    plane *ABC*   *Choose any three points not on the same line to name a plane.*

| A **ray** is a part of a line. It has one endpoint and extends without end in one direction. | 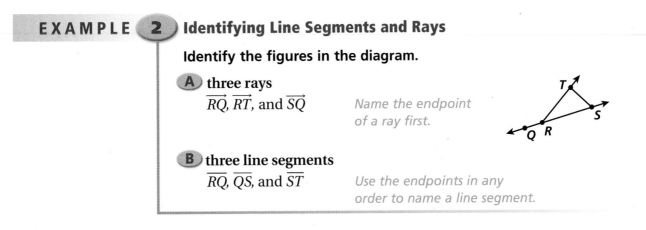 $\overrightarrow{GH}$
Name the endpoint first when naming a ray. |
| A **line segment** is a part of a line or a ray that extends from one endpoint to another. | $\overline{LM}$ or $\overline{ML}$
Use the endpoints to name a line segment. |

EXAMPLE 2 **Identifying Line Segments and Rays**

Identify the figures in the diagram.

A three rays
$\overrightarrow{RQ}$, $\overrightarrow{RT}$, and $\overrightarrow{SQ}$ *Name the endpoint of a ray first.*

B three line segments
$\overline{RQ}$, $\overline{QS}$, and $\overline{ST}$ *Use the endpoints in any order to name a line segment.*

Figures are **congruent** if they have the same shape and size. Line segments are congruent if they have the same length.

You can use **tick marks** to indicate congruent line segments. In the triangle at right, line segments AB and BC are congruent.

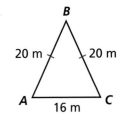

EXAMPLE 3 **Identifying Congruent Line Segments**

Identify the line segments that are congruent in the figure.

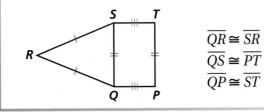

$\overline{QR} \cong \overline{SR}$ *One tick mark*
$\overline{QS} \cong \overline{PT}$ *Two tick marks*
$\overline{QP} \cong \overline{ST}$ *Three tick marks*

Think and Discuss

1. **Explain** why a line and a plane can be named in more than two ways. How many ways can a line segment be named?

2. **Explain** why it is important to choose three points that are not on the same line when naming a plane.

California Standards Practice
Preparation for MG2.1 and MG2.3

go.hrw.com
Homework Help Online
KEYWORD: MS8CA 9-1
Parent Resources Online
KEYWORD: MS8CA Parent

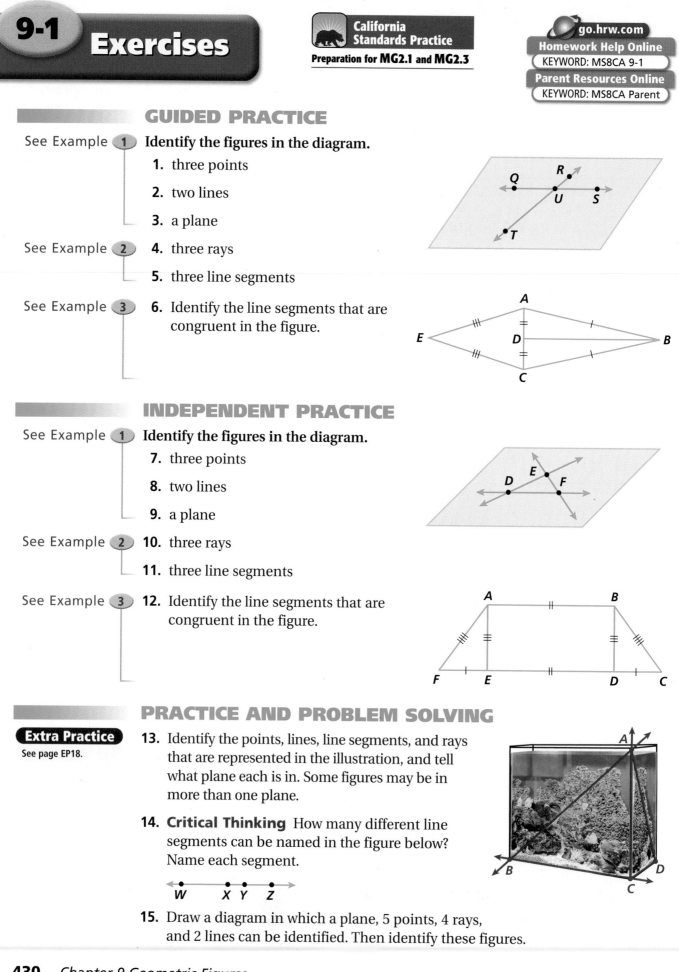

GUIDED PRACTICE

See Example ① **Identify the figures in the diagram.**

1. three points

2. two lines

3. a plane

See Example ② **4.** three rays

5. three line segments

See Example ③ **6.** Identify the line segments that are congruent in the figure.

INDEPENDENT PRACTICE

See Example ① **Identify the figures in the diagram.**

7. three points

8. two lines

9. a plane

See Example ② **10.** three rays

11. three line segments

See Example ③ **12.** Identify the line segments that are congruent in the figure.

PRACTICE AND PROBLEM SOLVING

Extra Practice
See page EP18.

13. Identify the points, lines, line segments, and rays that are represented in the illustration, and tell what plane each is in. Some figures may be in more than one plane.

14. Critical Thinking How many different line segments can be named in the figure below? Name each segment.

15. Draw a diagram in which a plane, 5 points, 4 rays, and 2 lines can be identified. Then identify these figures.

16. The artwork at right, by Diana Ong, is called *Blocs*.

   a. Copy the line segments in the artwork. Add tick marks to show line segments that appear to be congruent.

   b. Label the endpoints of the segments, including the points of intersection. Then name four pairs of line segments that appear to be congruent.

17. Draw a figure that includes at least three sets of congruent line segments. Label the endpoints and use notation to tell which line segments are congruent.

18. **Reasoning** Can two endpoints be shared by two different line segments? Make a drawing to illustrate your answer.

19. ✏️ **Write About It** Explain the difference between a line, a line segment, and a ray. Is it possible to estimate the length of any of these figures? If so, tell which ones and why.

20. ⭐ **Challenge** The sandstone sculpture at right, by Georges Vantongerloo, is called *Interrelation of Volumes*. Explain whether two separate faces on the front of the sculpture could be in the same plane.

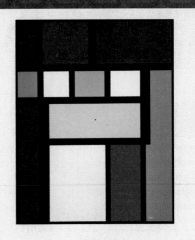

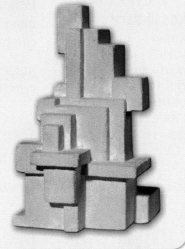

---

21. **Multiple Choice** Identify the line segments that are congruent in the figure.

   I $\overline{AB}, \overline{BC}$ **II** $\overline{AB}, \overline{CD}$

   III $\overline{BC}, \overline{CD}$ **IV** $\overline{BC}, \overline{AD}$

   Ⓐ I only   Ⓑ I and III   Ⓒ II and IV   Ⓓ II only

22. **Short Response** Draw a plane that contains each of the following: points *A*, *B*, and *C*; line segment *AB*; ray *BC*; and line *AC*.

Find each product or quotient. (Lesson 2-4)

23. $-48 \div (-3)$ **24.** $-2 \cdot (-6)$ **25.** $-56 \div 8$ **26.** $5 \cdot (-13)$

Find each sale price. (Lesson 6-6)

27. A tennis racket that regularly costs $79.00 is on sale for 15% off.

28. Ribbon that regularly costs $1.60 per yard is on sale for 20% off.

Measuring and Classifying Angles

California Standards

Preparation for MG2.1
Identify angles as vertical, adjacent, complementary, or supplementary and provide descriptions of these terms.
Also covered: **Prep for MG2.3**

Vocabulary
angle
vertex
acute angle
right angle
obtuse angle
straight angle

Who uses this? Runners can adjust the angle that a treadmill makes with the ground in order to have an easier or more intense workout.

An **angle** is formed by two rays with a common endpoint, called the **vertex**. An angle can be named by its vertex or by its vertex and a point from each ray. The middle point in the name must be the vertex. The angle of the treadmill can be called ∠F, ∠EFG, or ∠GFE.

Angles are measured in degrees. Use the symbol ° to show degrees.

E X A M P L E **1** **Measuring an Angle with a Protractor**

Use a protractor to measure the angle.

- Place the center point of the protractor on the vertex of the angle.
- Place the protractor so $\overrightarrow{YZ}$ passes through the 0° mark.
- Using the scale that starts with 0° along $\overrightarrow{YZ}$, read the measure where $\overrightarrow{YX}$ crosses.
- The measure of ∠XYZ is 75°. Write this as m∠XYZ = 75°.

Reading Math

m∠XYZ is read "the measure of angle XYZ."

E X A M P L E **2** **Drawing an Angle with a Protractor**

Use a protractor to draw an angle that measures 150°.

- Draw a ray on a sheet of paper.
- Place the center point of the protractor on the endpoint of the ray. Make sure the ray passes through the 0° mark.
- Make a mark at 150° above the scale on the protractor.
- Draw a ray from the endpoint of the first ray through the mark at 150°.

You can classify an angle by its measure.

An **acute angle** measures less than 90°.

A **right angle** measures exactly 90°.

An **obtuse angle** measures more than 90° and less than 180°.

A **straight angle** measures exactly 180°.

EXAMPLE 3 Classifying Angles

Classify each angle as acute, right, obtuse, or straight.

A

The angle measures more than 90° and less than 180°, so it is an obtuse angle.

B

The angle measures less than 90°, so it is an acute angle.

EXAMPLE 4 *Architectural Application*

An architect designed this floor plan for a five-sided room of a house. Classify ∠A, ∠B, and ∠D in the floor plan.

∠A   right angle   *The angle is marked as a right angle.*

∠B   obtuse angle   *The angle measures more than 90° and less than 180°.*

∠D   acute angle   *The angle measures less than 90°.*

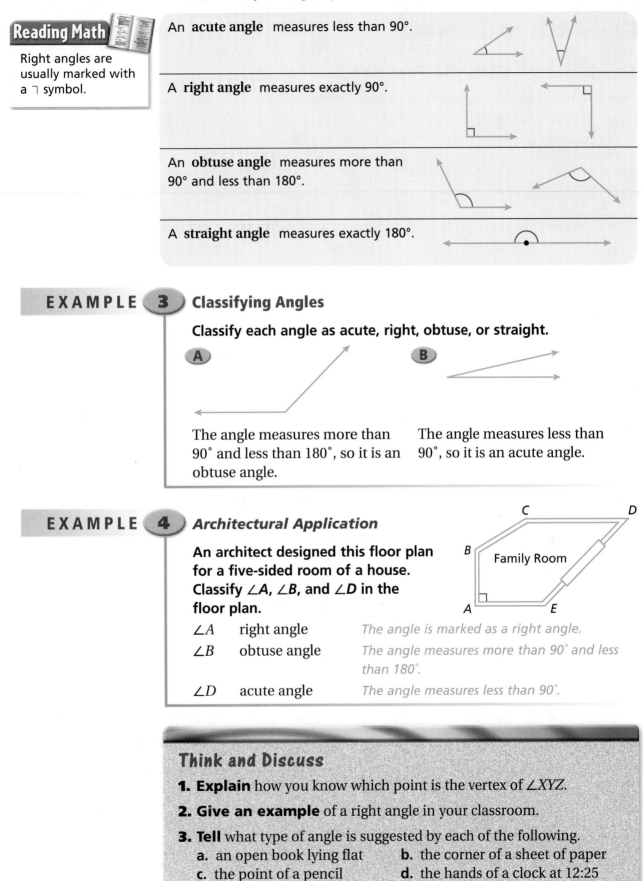

Think and Discuss

1. Explain how you know which point is the vertex of ∠XYZ.

2. Give an example of a right angle in your classroom.

3. Tell what type of angle is suggested by each of the following.
   a. an open book lying flat   **b.** the corner of a sheet of paper
   c. the point of a pencil   **d.** the hands of a clock at 12:25

California Standards Practice
Preparation for MG2.1 and MG2.3

go.hrw.com
Homework Help Online
KEYWORD: MS8CA 9-2
Parent Resources Online
KEYWORD: MS8CA Parent

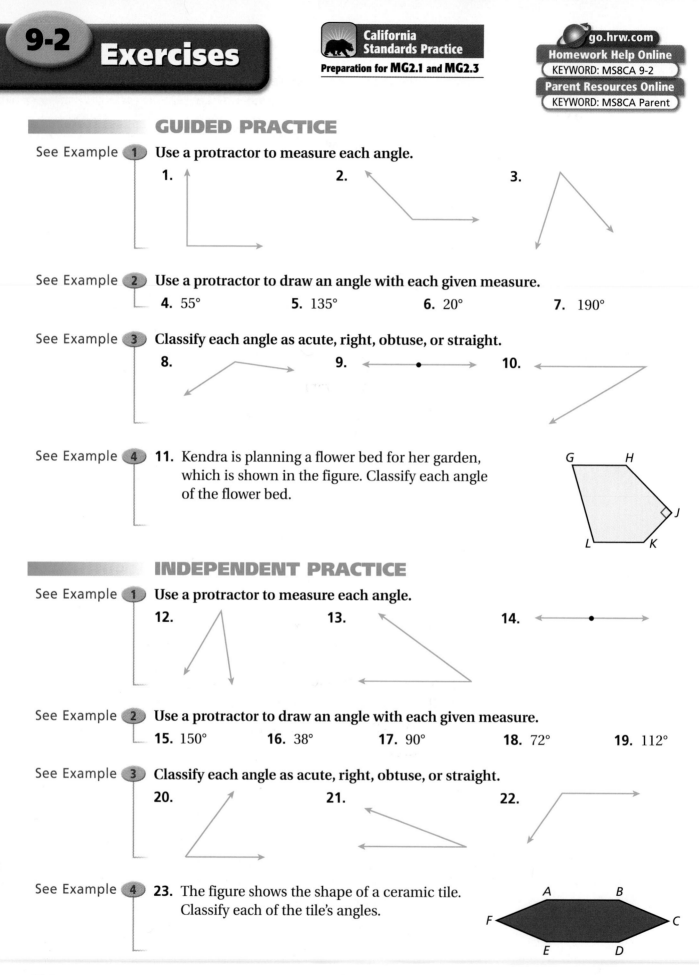

GUIDED PRACTICE

See Example 1 Use a protractor to measure each angle.

1.   **2.**   **3.**

See Example 2 Use a protractor to draw an angle with each given measure.

4. 55°   **5.** 135°   **6.** 20°   **7.** 190°

See Example 3 Classify each angle as acute, right, obtuse, or straight.

8.   **9.**   **10.**

See Example 4 **11.** Kendra is planning a flower bed for her garden, which is shown in the figure. Classify each angle of the flower bed.

INDEPENDENT PRACTICE

See Example 1 Use a protractor to measure each angle.

12.   **13.**   **14.**

See Example 2 Use a protractor to draw an angle with each given measure.

15. 150°   **16.** 38°   **17.** 90°   **18.** 72°   **19.** 112°

See Example 3 Classify each angle as acute, right, obtuse, or straight.

20.   **21.**   **22.**

See Example 4 **23.** The figure shows the shape of a ceramic tile. Classify each of the tile's angles.

PRACTICE AND PROBLEM SOLVING

Extra Practice
See page EP18.

Use a protractor to draw each angle.

24. an acute angle whose measure is less than 45°

25. an obtuse angle whose measure is between 100° and 160°

26. a right angle

Classify the smallest angle formed by the hands on each clock.

27.   **28.**   **29.**

30. Reasoning Can two acute angles that share a vertex form a right angle? Justify your answer with a diagram.

31. What's the Error? A student wrote that the measure of this angle is 156°. Explain the error the student may have made, and give the correct measure of the angle. How can the student avoid making the same mistake again?

32. Write About It Describe how an acute angle and an obtuse angle are different.

33. Challenge How many times during the day do the hands of a clock form a straight angle?

SPIRAL STANDARDS REVIEW   ← NS1.4, ← SDAP3.3

34. Multiple Choice The figure shows a plan for a skateboard ramp. What type of angle is ∠B?

    Ⓐ Acute   Ⓑ Right   Ⓒ Obtuse   Ⓓ Straight

35. Multiple Choice Which of the following is another name for ∠PQR?

    Ⓐ ∠P   Ⓑ ∠RQP   Ⓒ ∠PRQ   Ⓓ ∠QPR

Find the percent of each number. (Lesson 6-4)

36. 12% of 30   **37.** 30% of 60   **38.** 65% of 110   **39.** 82% of 360

Determine whether each survey question may be biased. Explain. (Lesson 7-8)

40. What do you plan to do during summer vacation?

41. How many hours do you waste each month at the mall?

9-3 Angle Relationships

California Standards

MG2.1 Identify angles as vertical, adjacent, complementary, or supplementary and provide descriptions of these terms.

Vocabulary
vertical angles
adjacent angles
complementary angles
supplementary angles

Why learn this? Angle relationships play an important role in many sports and games, such as miniature golf and tennis.

In miniature golf a player who understands angles has a better knowledge of where to aim the ball. In the miniature-golf hole shown, m∠1 = m∠2, m∠3 = m∠4, and m∠5 = m∠6.

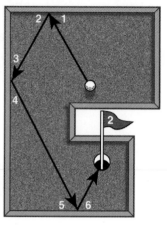

Angles are *congruent* if they have the same measure.

Adjacent angles are two angles that are side by side and have a common vertex and ray. Adjacent angles may or may not be congruent.

∠MRN and ∠NRP are adjacent angles. They share vertex R and $\overrightarrow{RN}$.

∠NRP and ∠PRQ are adjacent angles. They share vertex R and $\overrightarrow{RP}$.

Vertical angles are two angles that are formed by two intersecting lines and are not adjacent. Vertical angles have the same measure, so they are always congruent.

∠MRQ and ∠NRP are vertical angles.

∠MRN and ∠PRQ are vertical angles.

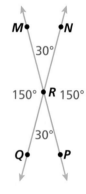

EXAMPLE **1** **Identifying Adjacent and Vertical Angles**

Tell whether the numbered angles are adjacent or vertical.

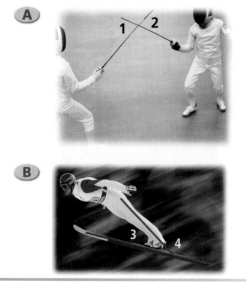

A

∠1 and ∠2 are formed by two intersecting lines and are not adjacent.

They are vertical angles.

B

∠3 and ∠4 are side by side and have a common vertex and ray.

They are adjacent angles.

Complementary angles are two angles whose measures have a sum of 90°.

65° + 25° = 90°

∠LMN and ∠NMP are complementary.

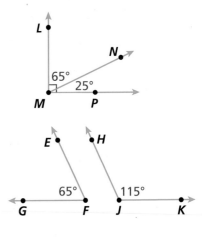

Supplementary angles are two angles whose measures have a sum of 180°.

65° + 115° = 180°

∠GFE and ∠HJK are supplementary.

E X A M P L E 2 **Identifying Complementary and Supplementary Angles**

Remember!

If the angle you are measuring is obtuse, then its measure is greater than 90°. If the angle you are measuring is acute, then its measure is less than 90°.

See Lesson 9-2, p. 433.

Use the protractor diagram to tell whether the angles are complementary, supplementary, or neither.

A ∠DXE and ∠AXB

m∠DXE = 55° and m∠AXB = 35°
Since 55° + 35° = 90°, ∠DXE and ∠AXB are complementary.

B ∠DXE and ∠BXC

m∠DXE = 55°
To find m∠BXC, start with the measure of ∠AXC, which is 75°, and subtract the measure of ∠AXB, which is 35°.
m∠BXC = 75° − 35° = 40°.
Since 55° + 40° = 95°, ∠DXE and ∠BXC are neither complementary nor supplementary.

C ∠AXC and ∠CXE

m∠AXC = 75° and m∠CXE = 105°
Since 75° + 105° = 180°, ∠AXC and ∠CXE are supplementary.

Think and Discuss

1. **Tell** whether the angles in Example 1B are supplementary, complementary, or neither.

2. **List** three different terms that may apply to a pair of angles, and explain what these terms mean.

3. **Discuss** whether two angles can be both vertical and adjacent.

9-3 Exercises

California Standards Practice
MG2.1

go.hrw.com
Homework Help Online
KEYWORD: MS8CA 9-3
Parent Resources Online
KEYWORD: MS8CA Parent

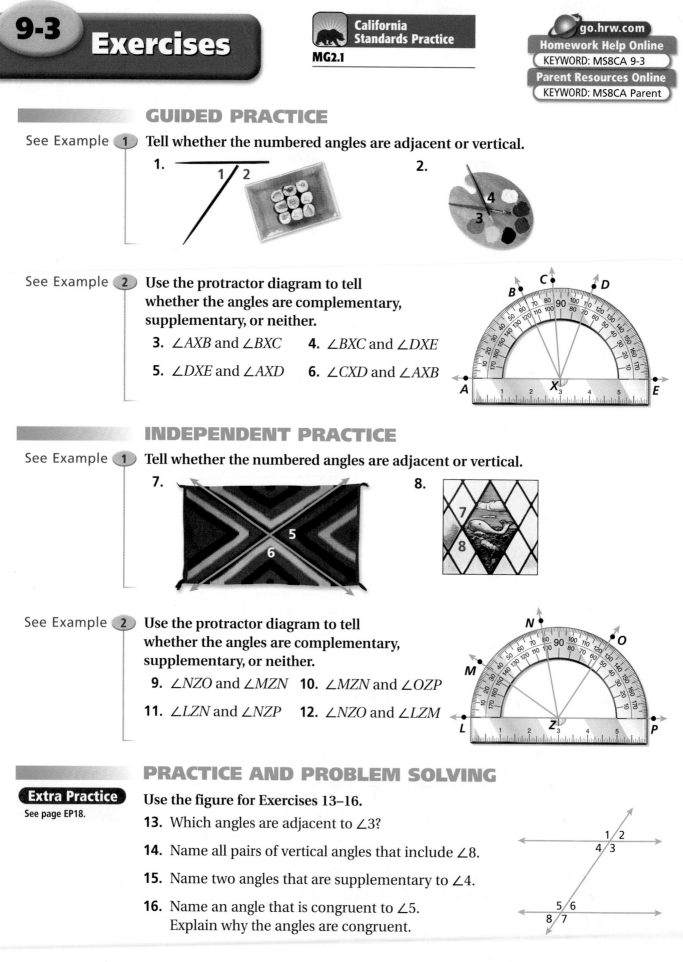

GUIDED PRACTICE

See Example 1 Tell whether the numbered angles are adjacent or vertical.

1.

2.

See Example 2 Use the protractor diagram to tell whether the angles are complementary, supplementary, or neither.

3. $\angle AXB$ and $\angle BXC$ **4.** $\angle BXC$ and $\angle DXE$

5. $\angle DXE$ and $\angle AXD$ **6.** $\angle CXD$ and $\angle AXB$

INDEPENDENT PRACTICE

See Example 1 Tell whether the numbered angles are adjacent or vertical.

7.

8.

See Example 2 Use the protractor diagram to tell whether the angles are complementary, supplementary, or neither.

9. $\angle NZO$ and $\angle MZN$ **10.** $\angle MZN$ and $\angle OZP$

11. $\angle LZN$ and $\angle NZP$ **12.** $\angle NZO$ and $\angle LZM$

PRACTICE AND PROBLEM SOLVING

Extra Practice
See page EP18.

Use the figure for Exercises 13–16.

13. Which angles are adjacent to $\angle 3$?

14. Name all pairs of vertical angles that include $\angle 8$.

15. Name two angles that are supplementary to $\angle 4$.

16. Name an angle that is congruent to $\angle 5$. Explain why the angles are congruent.

Tell whether each statement is sometimes, always, or never true. Explain.

17. Vertical angles are congruent.

18. Complementary angles are congruent.

19. Complementary angles are supplementary.

Engineering The photo shows part of the San Francisco–Oakland Bay Bridge. Determine whether each statement is true or false. Explain.

20. ∠1 and ∠3 are congruent.

21. ∠3 and ∠4 are supplementary.

22. ∠2 and ∠4 are adjacent.

An average of 280,000 vehicles cross the Bay Bridge each day, making it the nation's busiest toll bridge.

23. Use a protractor to draw an angle that measures 50°. Then draw an angle that is adjacent and complementary to this angle. Explain how you know that the angles are adjacent and complementary.

24. **Reasoning** Explain whether two obtuse angles can be supplementary.

25. **Critical Thinking** Draw and name a pair of angles that are *not* adjacent but share a vertex and a ray.

26. **Write About It** Angles *C* and *D* are each complementary to angle *F*. Describe the relationship between angle *C* and angle *D*.

27. **Challenge** Two vertical angles are supplementary. What is the measure of each angle?

SPIRAL STANDARDS REVIEW AF2.2, AF2.3, MG2.1, SDAP3.3

28. Multiple Choice Which type of angles are always congruent?

Ⓐ Adjacent   Ⓑ Complementary   Ⓒ Supplementary   Ⓓ Vertical

29. Multiple Choice Which statement is NOT true?

Ⓐ ∠*EAF* and ∠*BAC* are vertical angles.

Ⓑ ∠*DAE* and ∠*DAC* are adjacent angles.

Ⓒ ∠*FAE* and ∠*EAD* are complementary angles.

Ⓓ ∠*FAD* and ∠*DAC* are supplementary angles.

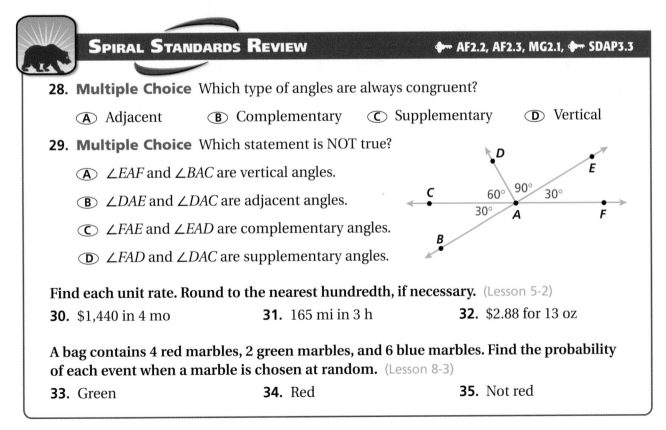

Find each unit rate. Round to the nearest hundredth, if necessary. (Lesson 5-2)

30. $1,440 in 4 mo   **31.** 165 mi in 3 h   **32.** $2.88 for 13 oz

A bag contains 4 red marbles, 2 green marbles, and 6 blue marbles. Find the probability of each event when a marble is chosen at random. (Lesson 8-3)

33. Green   **34.** Red   **35.** Not red

Finding Angle Measures

California Standards

MG2.2 Use the properties of complementary and supplementary angles and the sum of the angles of a triangle **to solve problems involving an unknown angle.**

Also covered: **AF1.1, MG2.1**

Who uses this? Model-ship builders can use angle measures to correctly position a ship's rigging. (See Example 2.)

You can use what you know about the properties of vertical, complementary, and supplementary angles to solve problems that involve angle measures.

EXAMPLE 1 **Finding an Unknown Angle Measure**

Find each unknown angle measure.

A **The angles are complementary.**

Since the angles are complementary, the sum of the angle measures is 90°.

$$55° + a = 90°$$
$$\underline{-55° \qquad -55°}$$ *Subtract 55° from both sides.*
$$a = 35°$$

B **The angles are supplementary.**

Since the angles are supplementary, the sum of the angle measures is 180°.

$$75° + b = 180°$$
$$\underline{-75° \qquad -75°}$$ *Subtract 75° from both sides.*
$$b = 105°$$

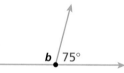

C **The angles are vertical angles.**

Since the angles are vertical angles, the angles are congruent.

$$c = 51°$$ *Congruent angles have the same measure.*

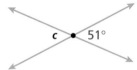

D $\angle JGF \cong \angle KGH;$ m$\angle FGH = 180°$

Since $\angle JGF$ and $\angle KGH$ are congruent, m$\angle KGH = 22°$.

m$\angle JGF +$ m$\angle JGK +$ m$\angle KGH = 180°$ *The sum of the measures is 180°.*

$$22° \quad + \quad d \quad + \quad 22° = 180°$$ *Substitute.*
$$44° + d = 180°$$ *Add.*
$$\underline{-44° \qquad -44°}$$ *Subtract 44° from both sides.*
$$d = 136°$$

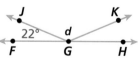

A ship's rigging includes its sails and the masts, beams, and ropes that support and control the sails. To put the rigging on a model of a ship, you must first find the measures of the angles formed by the ropes and the masts.

EXAMPLE 2 Recreation Application

The diagram shows some of the rigging for a model of a ship. Use the information in the diagram to find the unknown angle measures *a, b,* and *c.* Show your work.

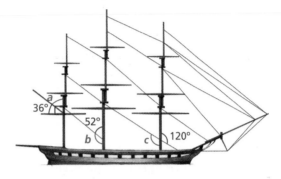

Helpful Hint

Adjacent angles that form a right angle are complementary.

Step 1: The angles labeled *a* and 36° are complementary. To find *a,* use properties of complementary angles.

$36° + a =\ \ 90°$ *The sum of the measures is 90°.*
$\underline{-36°\qquad\quad -36°}$ *Subtract 36° from both sides.*
$a =\ \ 54°$

Step 2: The angles labeled *b* and 52° are supplementary. To find *b,* use properties of supplementary angles.

$52° + b =\ \ 180°$ *The sum of the measures is 180°.*
$\underline{-52°\qquad\quad -52°}$ *Subtract 52° from both sides.*
$b =\ \ 128°$

Step 3: The angles labeled *c* and 120° are vertical angles. To find *c,* use properties of vertical angles.

$c = 120°$ *Vertical angles are congruent.*

Think and Discuss

1. **Explain** how to find the measure of ∠1 if ∠1 and ∠2 are supplementary and m∠2 = 120°.

2. **Explain** how to find the measure of ∠P if ∠P and ∠Q are complementary and m∠Q = 25°.

3. **Explain** how you can determine that the acute angles in Example 1A are complementary just by looking at the diagram.

California
Standards Practice
MG2.1, ⚷ **MG2.2**

go.hrw.com
Homework Help Online
KEYWORD: MS8CA 9-4
Parent Resources Online
KEYWORD: MS8CA Parent

GUIDED PRACTICE

See Example ① **Find each unknown angle measure.**

1. The angles are complementary.

81°
a

2. The angles are supplementary.

150° b

3. The angles are complementary.

34°
c

4. $\angle JKM \cong \angle LKN$; m$\angle JKL = 180°$

J   K   L
30° d
M   N

See Example ② 5. **Architecture** The X-shaped bracing on this building helps the structure withstand powerful winds. Use the information in the diagram to find the unknown angle measures a, b, and c. Show your work.

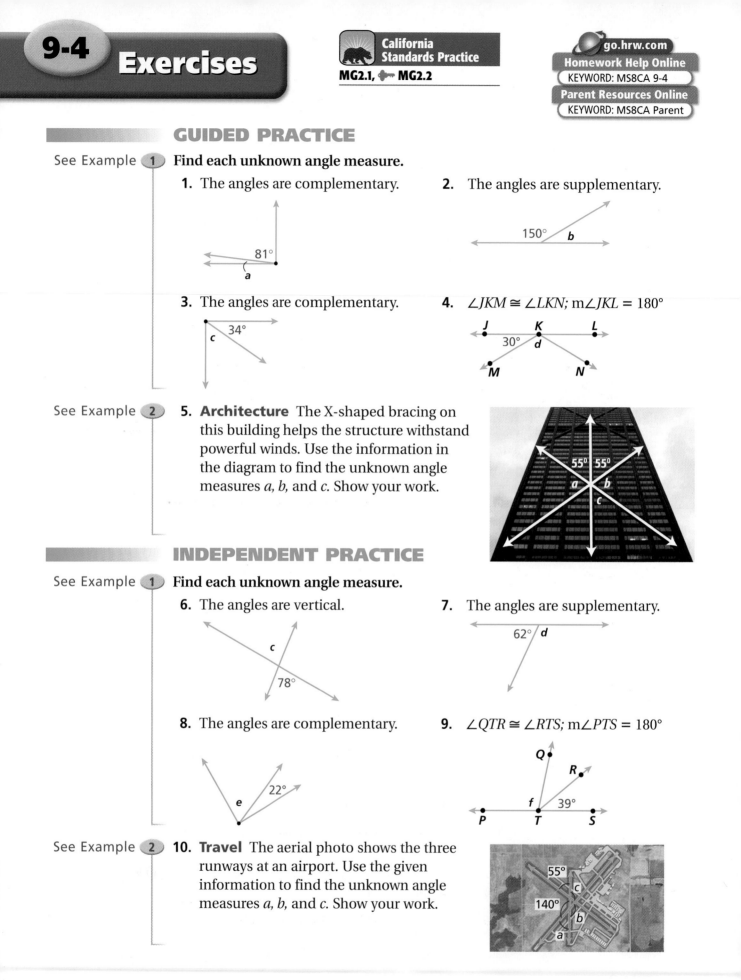

55° 55°
a   b
c

INDEPENDENT PRACTICE

See Example ① **Find each unknown angle measure.**

6. The angles are vertical.

c
78°

7. The angles are supplementary.

62° d

8. The angles are complementary.

22°
e

9. $\angle QTR \cong \angle RTS$; m$\angle PTS = 180°$

Q
R
f   39°
P   T   S

See Example ② 10. **Travel** The aerial photo shows the three runways at an airport. Use the given information to find the unknown angle measures a, b, and c. Show your work.

55°
c
140°
b
a

PRACTICE AND PROBLEM SOLVING

Extra Practice

See page EP18.

Find the measure of the angle that is complementary to each given angle.

11. 47° **12.** 62° **13.** 55° **14.** 31°

Find the measure of the angle that is supplementary to each given angle.

15. 75° **16.** 102° **17.** 136° **18.** 81°

Use the figure for Exercises 19 and 20.

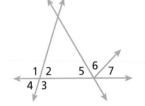

19. If m∠2 = 72°, what are the measures of ∠1, ∠3, and ∠4?

20. If m∠5 = 59° and m∠7 = 45°, what is the measure of ∠6?

21. Reasoning Angles A and B are complementary. The measure of angle A equals the measure of angle B. What is the measure of each angle?

22. What's the Error? A student states that one angle in a pair of complementary angles measures 94°. Explain why the student must have made an error.

23. Write About It Angles X and Y are supplementary. Explain how to find the measure of ∠X, given the measure of ∠Y.

24. Challenge The measure of angle A is 38°. Angle B is complementary to angle A. Angle C is supplementary to angle B. What is the measure of angle C?

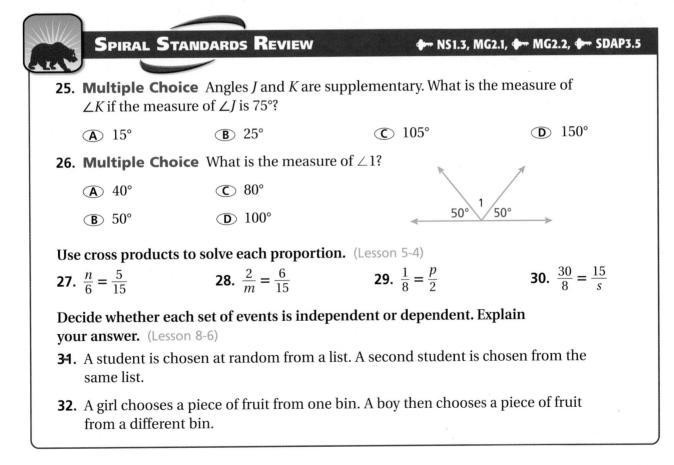

SPIRAL STANDARDS REVIEW   ← NS1.3, MG2.1, ← MG2.2, ← SDAP3.5

25. Multiple Choice Angles J and K are supplementary. What is the measure of ∠K if the measure of ∠J is 75°?

Ⓐ 15° Ⓑ 25° Ⓒ 105° Ⓓ 150°

26. Multiple Choice What is the measure of ∠1?

Ⓐ 40° Ⓒ 80°

Ⓑ 50° Ⓓ 100°

50° 1 50°

Use cross products to solve each proportion. (Lesson 5-4)

27. $\frac{n}{6} = \frac{5}{15}$ **28.** $\frac{2}{m} = \frac{6}{15}$ **29.** $\frac{1}{8} = \frac{p}{2}$ **30.** $\frac{30}{8} = \frac{15}{s}$

Decide whether each set of events is independent or dependent. Explain your answer. (Lesson 8-6)

31. A student is chosen at random from a list. A second student is chosen from the same list.

32. A girl chooses a piece of fruit from one bin. A boy then chooses a piece of fruit from a different bin.

Explore Parallel Lines and Transversals

Use with Lesson 9-4

go.hrw.com
Lab Resources Online
KEYWORD: MS8CA Lab9

California Standards

Extension of MG2.1 Identify angles as vertical, adjacent, complementary, or supplementary and provide descriptions of these terms.
Also covered: **Extension of**
MG2.2

REMEMBER
- Two angles are supplementary if the sum of their measures is 180°.
- Angles with measures less than 90° are acute.
- Angles with measures greater than 90° but less than 180° are obtuse.

Parallel lines are lines in the same plane that never cross. When two parallel lines are intersected by a third line, the angles formed have special relationships. This third line is called a *transversal*.

In San Francisco, California, many streets are parallel such as Lombard St. and Broadway.

Lombard St.

Broadway

Columbus Ave. is a transversal that runs diagonally across them. The eight angles that are formed are labeled on the diagram below.

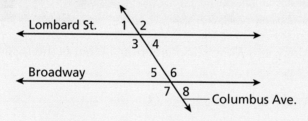

Activity

1 Copy the table below. Then measure angles 1–8 in the diagram below. Write these measures in your table.

Angle Number	Angle Measure
1	
2	
3	
4	
5	
6	
7	
8	

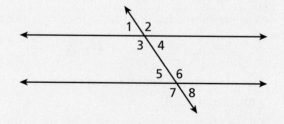

2 Use the table you completed and the corresponding diagram for the following problems.

   a. Angles inside the parallel lines are *interior angles*. Name them.

   b. Angles outside the parallel lines are *exterior angles*. Name them.

   c. Angles 3 and 6 and angles 4 and 5 are *alternate interior angles*. What do you notice about angles 3 and 6? What do you notice about angles 4 and 5?

   d. Angles 2 and 7 and angles 1 and 8 are *alternate exterior angles*. How do the measures of each pair of alternate exterior angles compare?

   e. Angles 1 and 5 are *corresponding angles* because they are in the same position on each of the parallel lines. How do the measures of angles 1 and 5 compare? Name another set of corresponding angles.

   f. Add the measures of angles 1 and 2. Now add the measures of angles 3 and 8. What can you say about the relationship of the angles in each of these sets? Name two other angles that have the same relationship.

Think and Discuss

1. $\overleftrightarrow{FG}$ and $\overleftrightarrow{LO}$ are parallel. Tell what you know about the angles that are labeled 1 through 8.

2. If angle 2 measures 125°, what are the measures of angles 1, 3, 4, 5, 6, 7, and 8?

3. If a transversal intersects two parallel lines and one of the angles formed measures 90°, discuss the relationship between all the angles.

Try This

Use a protractor to measure one angle in each diagram. Then find the measures of all the other angles without using a protractor. Tell how to find each angle measure.

1.

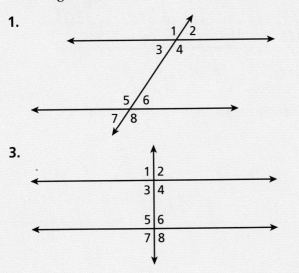

2.

3.

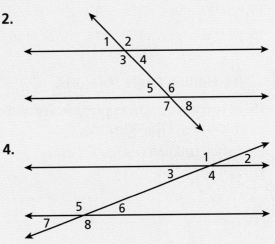

4.

Quiz for Lessons 9-1 Through 9-4

9-1 Introduction to Geometry

Identify the figures in the diagram.

1. three points
2. two lines
3. a plane
4. two line segments
5. two rays

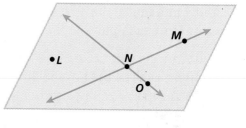

9-2 Measuring and Classifying Angles

Use a protractor to measure each angle. Then classify each angle as acute, right, obtuse, or straight.

6.

7.

8.

9.

10. The quarterback of a football team throws a long pass, and the angle the path of the ball makes with the ground is 30°. Draw an angle with this measurement.

9-3 Angle Relationships

Use the protractor diagram to tell whether the angles are complementary, supplementary, or neither.

11. ∠DXE and ∠AXD
12. ∠AXB and ∠CXD
13. ∠DXE and ∠AXB
14. ∠BXC and ∠DXE

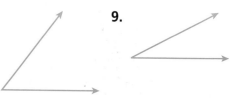

9-4 Finding Angle Measures

15. If two angles are supplementary and one angle measures 97°, what is the measure of the other angle?

Find each unknown angle measure.

16.

17.

18.

19.

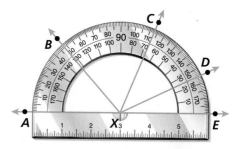

Focus on Problem Solving

California Standards

MR2.4 Use a variety of methods, **such as** words, numbers, symbols, charts, graphs, tables, **diagrams,** and models, **to explain mathematical reasoning.**
Also covered: **NS2.1, NS2.2, ◆ MG2.2**

Make a Plan

Plan

• **Draw a diagram**

Sometimes a problem seems difficult because it is described in words only. You can draw a diagram to help you picture the problem.

Try to label all the information you are given on your diagram. Then use the diagram to solve the problem.

Read each problem. Draw a diagram to help you solve the problem. Then solve.

1. Bob used a ruler to draw a triangle. First he drew a line segment 3 in. long and labeled it $\overline{AB}$. From B, he drew a line segment $2\frac{1}{2}$ in. long and labeled the endpoint C. What is the length of $\overline{AC}$ if the perimeter of Bob's triangle is $10\frac{1}{2}$ in?

2. Karen has a vegetable garden that is 12 feet long and 10 feet wide. She plans to plant tomatoes in one-half of the garden. She will divide the other half of the garden equally into three beds, where she'll grow cabbage, pumpkins, and radishes.
   a. What are the possible whole number dimensions of the tomato bed?
   b. What fraction of the garden will Karen use to grow cabbage?

3. Pam draws three parallel lines that are an equal distance apart. The two outside lines are 8 cm apart. How far apart is the middle line from the outside lines?

4. Jan connected the following points on a coordinate grid: (2, 4), (4, 6), (6, 6), (6, 2), (3, 2), and (2, 4).
   a. How many sides and angles does Jan's figure have?
   b. How many right angles does the figure have?

5. Triangle *ABC* is isoceles. The measure of angle *B* is equal to the measure of angle *C*. The measure of angle *B* equals 50°. What is the measure of angle *A*?

9-5 Classifying Polygons

California Standards

Preparation for MG2.3 Draw quadrilaterals and triangles from given information about them (e.g., a quadrilateral having equal sides but no right angles, a right isosceles triangle).

Vocabulary
polygon
vertex
regular polygon

Reading Math

Vertices is the plural form of *vertex*.

Who uses this? In many cultures weavers use geometric shapes such as triangles and rectangles in their work.

Triangles and rectangles are examples of *polygons*. A **polygon** is a closed plane figure formed by three or more line segments. Each line segment forms a side of the polygon. Each side meets exactly two other sides, one on each end, in a common endpoint. Each endpoint is a **vertex** of the polygon.

The Paracas were an ancient native culture of Peru. Among the items that have been excavated from their lands are color tapestries, such as this one.

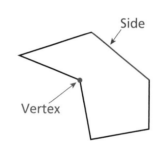

Side

Vertex

The polygon at left has six sides and six vertices.

EXAMPLE **1** **Identifying Polygons**

Determine whether each figure is a polygon. Explain your answer.

A

The figure is a polygon. It is a closed figure with 5 sides.

B

The figure is not a polygon. It is not a closed figure.

C

The figure is not a polygon. Not all of the sides of the figure are line segments.

D

The figure is not a polygon. There are sides that meet more than two other sides.

Polygons are classified by the number of sides and angles they have.

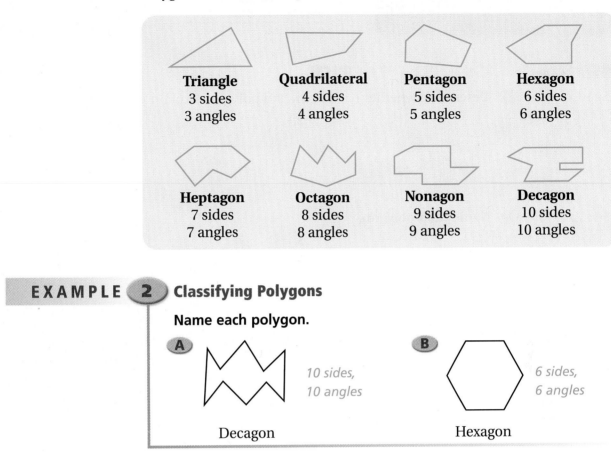

Triangle
3 sides
3 angles

Quadrilateral
4 sides
4 angles

Pentagon
5 sides
5 angles

Hexagon
6 sides
6 angles

Heptagon
7 sides
7 angles

Octagon
8 sides
8 angles

Nonagon
9 sides
9 angles

Decagon
10 sides
10 angles

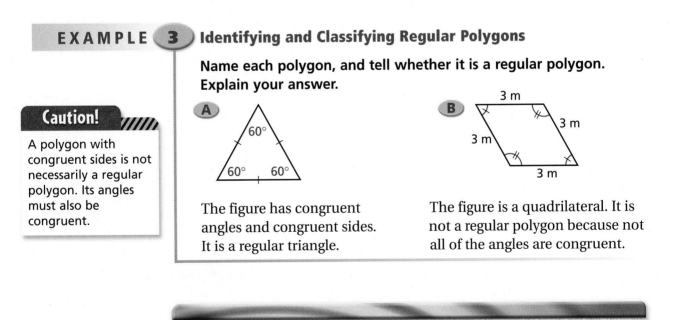

EXAMPLE **2** **Classifying Polygons**

Name each polygon.

A
10 sides,
10 angles

Decagon

B
6 sides,
6 angles

Hexagon

A **regular polygon** is a polygon in which all sides are congruent and all angles are congruent.

EXAMPLE **3** **Identifying and Classifying Regular Polygons**

Name each polygon, and tell whether it is a regular polygon. Explain your answer.

Caution!

A polygon with congruent sides is not necessarily a regular polygon. Its angles must also be congruent.

A

60°

60°   60°

The figure has congruent angles and congruent sides. It is a regular triangle.

B

3 m

3 m

3 m

3 m

The figure is a quadrilateral. It is not a regular polygon because not all of the angles are congruent.

Think and Discuss

1. Name three reasons why a given figure might not be a polygon.

California Standards Practice

Preparation for MG2.3

go.hrw.com
Homework Help Online
KEYWORD: MS8CA 9-5
Parent Resources Online
KEYWORD: MS8CA Parent

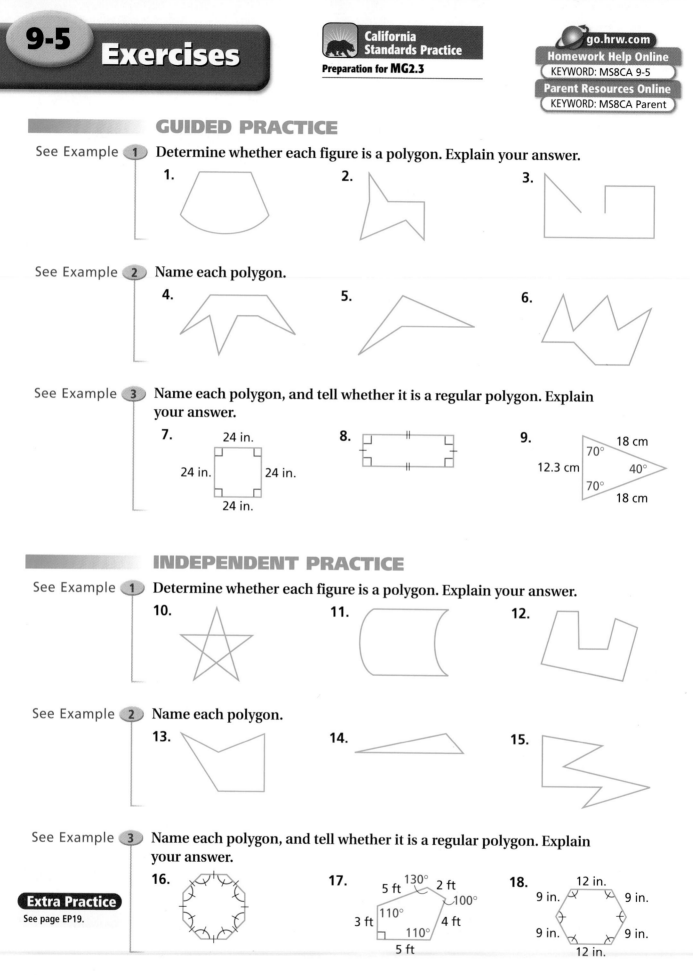

GUIDED PRACTICE

See Example **1** Determine whether each figure is a polygon. Explain your answer.

1.

2.

3.

See Example **2** Name each polygon.

4.

5.

6.

See Example **3** Name each polygon, and tell whether it is a regular polygon. Explain your answer.

7.
24 in.
24 in. 24 in.
24 in.

8.

9.
18 cm
70° 40°
12.3 cm
70°
18 cm

INDEPENDENT PRACTICE

See Example **1** Determine whether each figure is a polygon. Explain your answer.

10.

11.

12.

See Example **2** Name each polygon.

13.

14.

15.

See Example **3** Name each polygon, and tell whether it is a regular polygon. Explain your answer.

Extra Practice
See page EP19.

16.

17.
5 ft 130° 2 ft
110° 100°
3 ft 4 ft
110°
5 ft

18.
12 in.
9 in. 9 in.
9 in. 9 in.
12 in.

Quilting is an art form that has existed in many countries for hundreds of years. Some cultures record their histories and traditions through the colors and patterns in quilts.

19. The design of the quilt at right is made of triangles.

  a. Name two other polygons in the pattern.

  b. Which of the polygons in the pattern appear to be regular?

Use the photograph of the star quilt for Exercises 20 and 21.

20. The large star in the quilt pattern is made of smaller shapes stitched together. These smaller shapes are all the same type of polygon. What type of polygon are the smaller shapes?

21. A polygon can be named by the number of its sides followed by *-gon*. For example, a polygon with 14 sides is called a 14-gon. What is the name of the large star-shaped polygon on the quilt?

22. ⭐ **Challenge** The quilt at right has a modern design. Find and copy one of each type of polygon, from a triangle up to a decagon, onto your paper from the design. Write the name of each polygon next to its drawing.

go.hrw.com
Web Extra!
KEYWORD: MS8CA Quilt

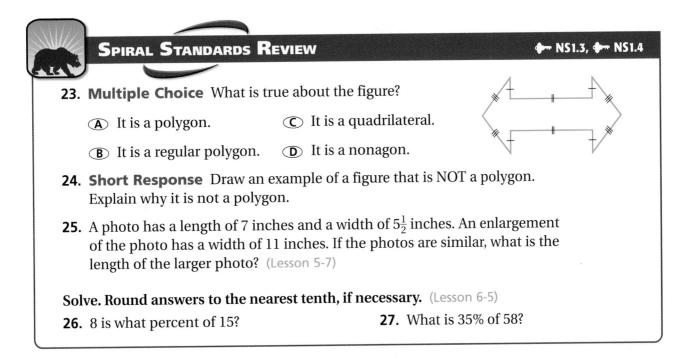

SPIRAL STANDARDS REVIEW   ➔ NS1.3, ➔ NS1.4

23. **Multiple Choice** What is true about the figure?

  Ⓐ It is a polygon.   Ⓒ It is a quadrilateral.

  Ⓑ It is a regular polygon.   Ⓓ It is a nonagon.

24. **Short Response** Draw an example of a figure that is NOT a polygon. Explain why it is not a polygon.

25. A photo has a length of 7 inches and a width of $5\frac{1}{2}$ inches. An enlargement of the photo has a width of 11 inches. If the photos are similar, what is the length of the larger photo? (Lesson 5-7)

Solve. Round answers to the nearest tenth, if necessary. (Lesson 6-5)

26. 8 is what percent of 15?   27. What is 35% of 58?

Classifying Triangles

California Standards

Preparation for **MG2.3** Draw quadrilaterals and **triangles from given information about them (e.g.,** a quadrilateral having equal sides but no right angles, **a right isosceles triangle).**

Why learn this? You can use special types of triangles to describe the shapes of the faces of crystals. (See Exercise 20.)

One way to classify triangles is by the lengths of their sides. Another way is by the measures of their angles.

Vocabulary
scalene triangle
isosceles triangle
equilateral triangle
acute triangle
obtuse triangle
right triangle

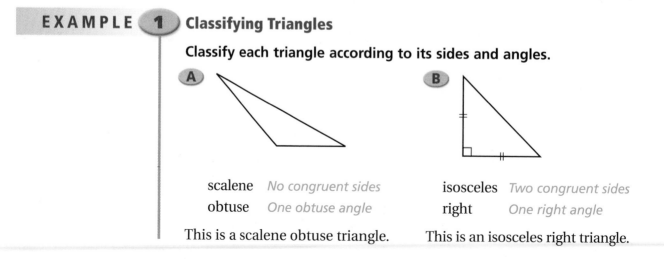

Triangles classified by sides

A **scalene triangle** has no congruent sides.

An **isosceles triangle** has at least 2 congruent sides.

In an **equilateral triangle**, all of the sides are congruent.

Triangles classified by angles

In an **acute triangle**, all of the angles are acute.

An **obtuse triangle** has exactly one obtuse angle.

A **right triangle** has exactly one right angle.

EXAMPLE  **Classifying Triangles**

Classify each triangle according to its sides and angles.

Ⓐ

Ⓑ

scalene   *No congruent sides*
obtuse   *One obtuse angle*

isosceles   *Two congruent sides*
right   *One right angle*

This is a scalene obtuse triangle.

This is an isosceles right triangle.

Classify each triangle according to its sides and angles.

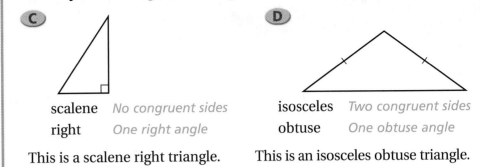

C		D	
scalene	No congruent sides	isosceles	Two congruent sides
right	One right angle	obtuse	One obtuse angle
This is a scalene right triangle.		This is an isosceles obtuse triangle.	

EXAMPLE 2 Identifying Triangles

Identify the different types of triangles in the figure, and determine how many of each there are.

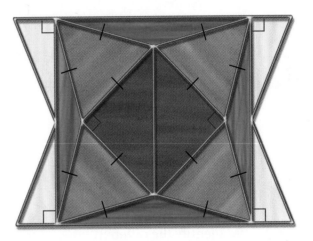

Type	How Many	Colors	Type	How Many	Colors
Scalene	4	Yellow	Right	6	Purple, yellow
Isosceles	10	Green, pink, purple	Obtuse	4	Green
Equilateral	4	Pink	Acute	4	Pink

Think and Discuss

1. Draw an isosceles acute triangle and an isosceles obtuse triangle.

2. Draw a triangle that is right and scalene.

3. Explain why any equilateral triangle is also an isosceles triangle, but not all isosceles triangles are equilateral triangles.

9-6

Exercises

California Standards Practice
Preparation for MG2.3

go.hrw.com
Homework Help Online
KEYWORD: MS8CA 9-6
Parent Resources Online
KEYWORD: MS8CA Parent

GUIDED PRACTICE

See Example **1** Classify each triangle according to its sides and angles.

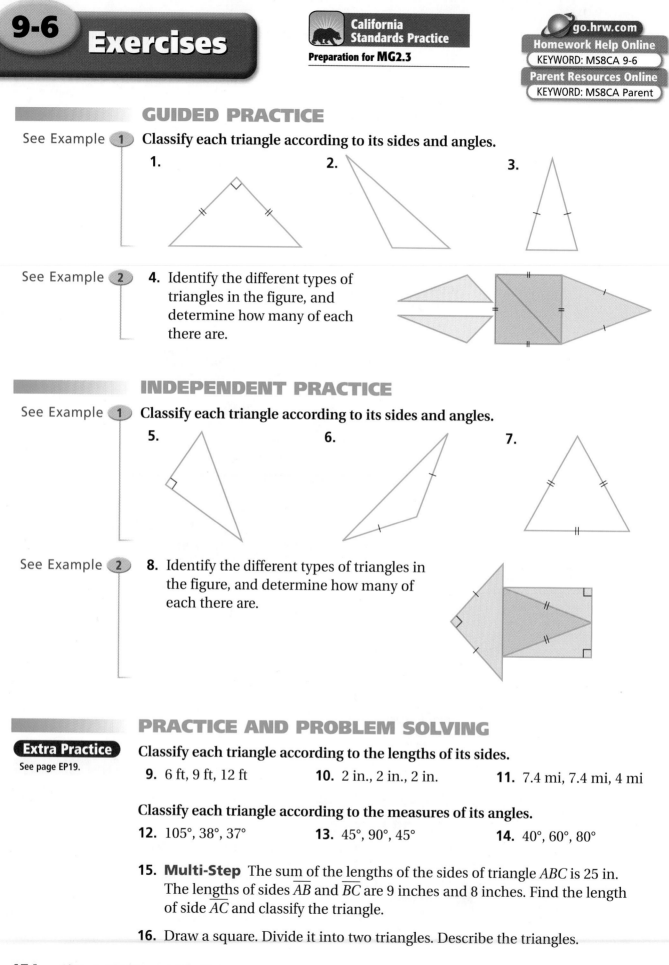

1.

2.

3.

See Example **2** 4. Identify the different types of triangles in the figure, and determine how many of each there are.

INDEPENDENT PRACTICE

See Example **1** Classify each triangle according to its sides and angles.

5.

6.

7.

See Example **2** 8. Identify the different types of triangles in the figure, and determine how many of each there are.

PRACTICE AND PROBLEM SOLVING

Extra Practice
See page EP19.

Classify each triangle according to the lengths of its sides.

9. 6 ft, 9 ft, 12 ft   **10.** 2 in., 2 in., 2 in.   **11.** 7.4 mi, 7.4 mi, 4 mi

Classify each triangle according to the measures of its angles.

12. 105°, 38°, 37°   **13.** 45°, 90°, 45°   **14.** 40°, 60°, 80°

15. Multi-Step The sum of the lengths of the sides of triangle ABC is 25 in. The lengths of sides $\overline{AB}$ and $\overline{BC}$ are 9 inches and 8 inches. Find the length of side $\overline{AC}$ and classify the triangle.

16. Draw a square. Divide it into two triangles. Describe the triangles.

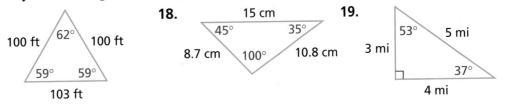

Classify each triangle according to its sides and angles.

17.
100 ft, 100 ft, 62°, 59°, 59°, 103 ft

18.
15 cm, 45°, 35°, 8.7 cm, 100°, 10.8 cm

19.
53°, 5 mi, 3 mi, 37°, 4 mi

Architecture

The Washington Monument opened in 1888—105 years after Congress proposed a memorial to honor the first president of the United States.

20. Earth Science Each flat surface of a crystal is a triangle whose sides are all different lengths. What kind of triangle is each surface of the crystal?

21. Architecture The Washington Monument is an obelisk, the top of which is a pyramid. The pyramid has four triangular faces. The bottom edge of each face measures 10.5 m. The other edges measure 17.0 m. What kind of triangle is each face of the pyramid?

22. Critical Thinking A line segment connects each vertex of a regular octagon to the vertex opposite it. How many triangles are within the octagon? What type of triangles are they?

23. Choose a Strategy How many triangles are in the figure?

Ⓐ 6   Ⓑ 9   Ⓒ 10   Ⓓ 13

24. Write About It Is it possible for an equilateral triangle to be obtuse? Explain your answer.

25. Challenge The centers of circles *A*, *B*, *C*, *D*, and *E* are connected by line segments. Classify each triangle in the figure, given that the diameter of circle *D* is 4 and *DE* = 5, *BD* = 6, *CB* = 8, and *AC* = 8.

SPIRAL STANDARDS REVIEW   🔑 NS1.1, 🔑 MG2.2

26. Multiple Choice Based on the angle measures given, which triangle is NOT acute?

Ⓐ 60°, 60°, 60°   Ⓑ 90°, 45°, 45°   Ⓒ 54°, 54°, 72°   Ⓓ 75°, 45°, 60°

27. Multiple Choice Which of the following best describes the triangle?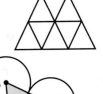

Ⓐ Scalene, right triangle   Ⓒ Isosceles, obtuse triangle

Ⓑ Isosceles, acute triangle   Ⓓ Equilateral, acute triangle

28. Order the numbers $\frac{3}{7}$, -0.4, 2.3, and $1\frac{3}{10}$ from least to greatest. (Lesson 3-6)

Find each unknown angle measure. (Lesson 9-4)

29.
32°, *a*

30.
b, 54°

31.
45°, *c*

Hands-On LAB 9-6

Construct Triangles

Use with Lesson 9-6

go.hrw.com
Lab Resources Online
KEYWORD: MS8CA Lab9

California Standards

🔑 **MG2.3 Draw** quadrilaterals and **triangles from given information about them** (e.g., a quadrilateral having equal sides but no right angles, **a right isosceles triangle**).

REMEMBER
- A scalene triangle has no congruent sides.
- An isosceles triangle has at least two congruent sides.
- In an acute triangle, all of the angles are acute.
- An obtuse triangle has exactly one obtuse angle.
- A right triangle has exactly one right angle.

You can use a compass, straightedge, and protractor to construct triangles from given information.

Activity 1

Construct an acute isosceles triangle.

❶ Use a straightedge to draw line segment $\overline{AB}$.

❷ Use the straightedge to draw a line through point A that forms an acute angle with the segment.

❸ Open a compass to the same length as $\overline{AB}$.

❹ Holding the point of the compass on A, draw an arc that passes through the line. Label the intersection of the arc and the line as point C.

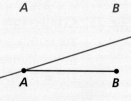

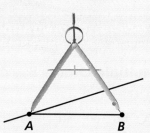

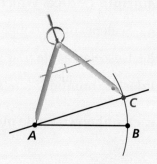

❺ Use the straightedge to draw $\overline{BC}$. This is the third side of the triangle.

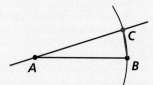

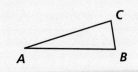

1. Which sides of the triangle are congruent? How do you know that they are congruent?

2. Explain how to check whether the triangle is acute.

Try This

1. Construct an obtuse isosceles triangle.

Activity 2

Construct a right scalene triangle.

❶ Use a straightedge to draw a line segment $\overline{AB}$.

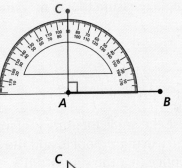

❷ Use a protractor and the straightedge to draw a line segment $\overline{AC}$ that forms a 90° angle with $\overline{AB}$. Draw $\overline{AC}$ so that its length is different from the length of $\overline{AB}$.

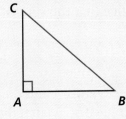

❸ Use the straightedge to draw the third side of the triangle, $\overline{BC}$.

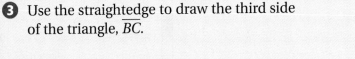

Think and Discuss

1. How do you know that the triangle is a right triangle?

2. Explain how to check whether the triangle is scalene.

Try This

1. Construct an acute scalene triangle.

2. Construct an obtuse scalene triangle.

3. Construct a right isosceles triangle.

4. Martina wants to draw an equilateral triangle. She first draws $\overline{DE}$. Then she opens her compass to the same length as $\overline{DE}$, and draws an arc while holding the point of the compass on D. Tell how Martina can use her compass and straightedge to finish the triangle.

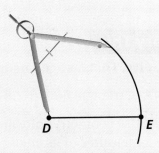

Angles in Triangles

Use with Lesson 9-7

go.hrw.com
Lab Resources Online
KEYWORD: MS8CA Lab9

California Standards

◆ **MG2.2 Use** the properties of complementary and supplementary angles and **the sum of the angles of a triangle to solve problems involving an unknown angle.**

The sum of the angle measures is the same for any triangle. You can use geometry software to find this sum and to check that the sum is the same for many different triangles.

Activity

① Use the geometry software to make triangle *ABC*. Then use the angle measure tool to measure ∠*B*.

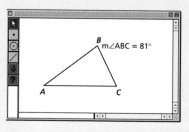

② Use the angle measure tool to measure ∠*C* and ∠*A*. Then use the calculator tool to add the measures of the three angles. Notice that the sum is 180°.

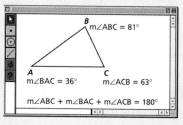

③ Select vertex *A* and drag it around to change the shape of triangle *ABC*. Watch the angle sum. Change the shape of the triangle again and then again. Be sure to make acute and obtuse triangles.

Notice that the sum of the angle measures is always 180°, regardless of the triangle's shape.

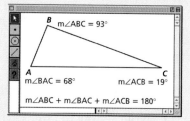

Think and Discuss

1. Can you use geometry software to draw a triangle with two obtuse angles? Explain.

Try This

Solve. Then use geometry software to check each answer.

1. In triangle *ABC*, m∠*B* = 49.15° and m∠*A* = 113.75°. Find m∠*C*.

2. Use geometry software to construct an acute triangle *XYZ*. Give the measures of its angles, and check that their sum is 180°.

Angle Measures in Triangles

Why learn this? You can correctly fold paper airplanes by finding angle measures in triangles. (See Exercise 4.)

If you tear off the corners of a triangle and put all three of them together, you will find that they form a straight angle. This illustrates that the sum of the measures of the angles in a triangle is 180°.

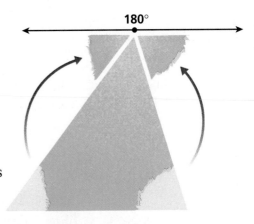

ANGLES OF A TRIANGLE	
The sum of the measures of the angles in a triangle is 180°.	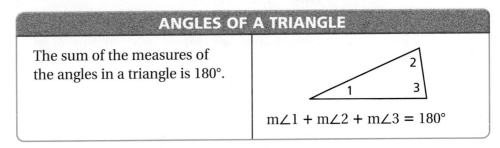 $m\angle 1 + m\angle 2 + m\angle 3 = 180°$

EXAMPLE 1 Finding an Angle Measure in a Triangle

Find the unknown angle measure in each triangle.

A

25°   *x*   37°

$$25° + 37° + x = 180°$$ *The sum of the angle measures in a triangle is 180°.*

$$62° + x = 180°$$ *Add 25° and 37°.*

$$\underline{-62° \qquad\quad -62°}$$ *Subtract 62° from both sides.*

$$x = 118°$$

The measure of the unknown angle is 118°.

B

59°   *y*

$$59° + 90° + y = 180°$$ *The sum of the angle measures in a triangle is 180°.*

$$149° + y = 180°$$ *Add 59° and 90°.*

$$\underline{-149° \qquad\quad -149°}$$ *Subtract 149° from both sides.*

$$y = 31°$$

The measure of the unknown angle is 31°.

9-7 Angle Measures in Triangles   **459**

The figure shows one of the steps in folding an origami swan. Find the unknown angle measure *x*. Show your work.

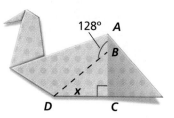

Step 1: Find the measure of ∠DBC.

$$m\angle DBA + m\angle DBC = 180°$$
$$128° + m\angle DBC = 180°$$ *Substitue 128° for m∠DBA.*
$$m\angle DBC = 52°$$ *Subtract 128° from both sides.*

Step 2: Find the angle measure *x*.

$$52° + 90° + x = 180°$$ *Sum of angle measures is 180°.*
$$142° + x = 180°$$ *Add 52° and 90°.*
$$x = 38°$$ *Subtract 142° from both sides.*

> **Helpful Hint**
>
> Adjacent angles that form a straight angle are supplementary.

Think and Discuss

1. Explain how to find the measure of an angle in a triangle when you know the measures of the two other angles.

9-7 Exercises

go.hrw.com
Homework Help Online
KEYWORD: MS8CA 9-7
Parent Resources Online
KEYWORD: MS8CA Parent

GUIDED PRACTICE

See Example ① **Find the unknown angle measure in each triangle.**

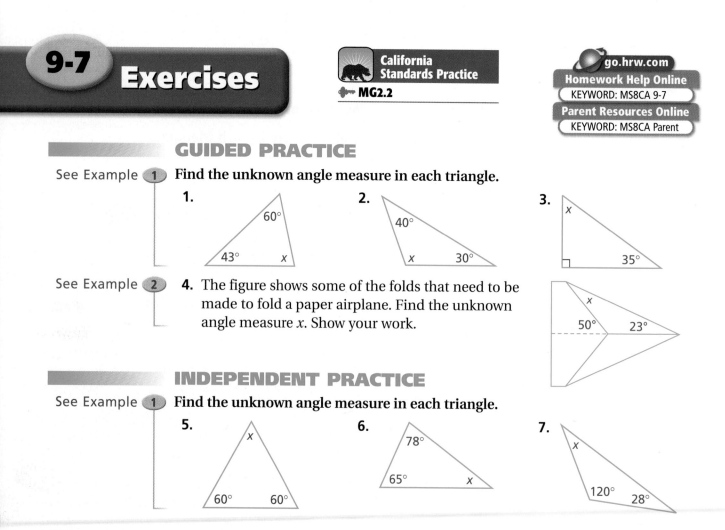

See Example ② **4.** The figure shows some of the folds that need to be made to fold a paper airplane. Find the unknown angle measure *x*. Show your work.

INDEPENDENT PRACTICE

See Example ① **Find the unknown angle measure in each triangle.**

8. The diagram shows a section of roller-coaster track. Find the unknown angle measure x. Show your work.

PRACTICE AND PROBLEM SOLVING

Extra Practice
See page EP19.

Find the measure of the third angle in each triangle, given two angle measures. Then classify the triangle.

9. 56°, 101°   **10.** 18°, 63°   **11.** 62°, 58°   **12.** 41°, 49°

Use the diagram to find the measure of each indicated angle.

13. ∠KNJ   **14.** ∠LKM

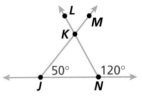

15. Earth Science A sundial consists of a circular base and a right triangle mounted upright on the base. One acute angle in the right triangle measures 52°. What is the measure of the other acute angle?

16. Reasoning What is the measure of each angle in an isosceles right triangle? (*Hint:* Two of the angles in the triangle are congruent.)

17. Write About It Explain why a triangle cannot have two right angles.

18. Challenge The diagram shows a triangle formed by the lines of sight between a lighthouse, a tugboat, and a cargo ship. What are the unknown angle measures of the triangle?

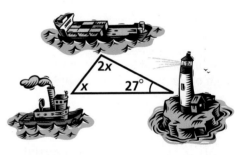

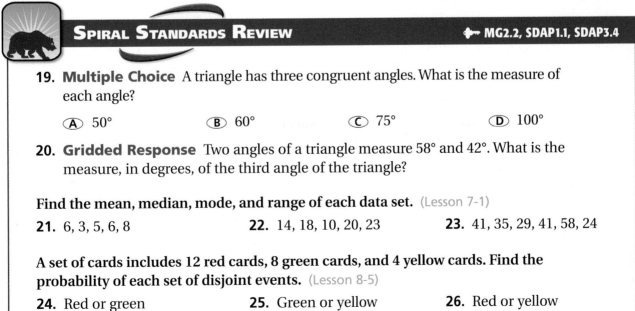

SPIRAL STANDARDS REVIEW   🔑 MG2.2, SDAP1.1, SDAP3.4

19. Multiple Choice A triangle has three congruent angles. What is the measure of each angle?

Ⓐ 50°   Ⓑ 60°   Ⓒ 75°   Ⓓ 100°

20. Gridded Response Two angles of a triangle measure 58° and 42°. What is the measure, in degrees, of the third angle of the triangle?

Find the mean, median, mode, and range of each data set. (Lesson 7-1)

21. 6, 3, 5, 6, 8   **22.** 14, 18, 10, 20, 23   **23.** 41, 35, 29, 41, 58, 24

A set of cards includes 12 red cards, 8 green cards, and 4 yellow cards. Find the probability of each set of disjoint events. (Lesson 8-5)

24. Red or green   **25.** Green or yellow   **26.** Red or yellow

9-8 Classifying Quadrilaterals

California Standards

MG2.3 Draw quadrilaterals and triangles from given information about them (e.g., a quadrilateral having equal sides but no right angles, a right isosceles triangle).

Why learn this? You can use quadrilaterals to describe national flags. (See Exercise 25.)

Some quadrilaterals have properties that classify them as *special quadrilaterals*.

Vocabulary
parallelogram
rectangle
rhombus
square
trapezoid

Helpful Hint

Arrowheads are used to show sides that are parallel to each other.

Parallelogram		Both pairs of opposite sides are parallel. You can also classify a quadrilateral as a parallelogram if both pairs of opposite sides or both pairs of opposite angles are congruent.
Rectangle		Parallelogram with four right angles.
Rhombus		Parallelogram with four congruent sides.
Square		Parallelogram with four congruent sides and four right angles.
Trapezoid		Exactly one pair of opposite sides is parallel.

Quadrilaterals can have more than one name because the special quadrilaterals sometimes share properties. For example, squares are both a type of rectangle and a type of rhombus.

EXAMPLE 1 Classifying Quadrilaterals

Give all of the names that apply to each quadrilateral. Then give the name that best describes it.

A

The figure has opposite sides that are congruent, so it is a parallelogram. It has four right angles, so it is also a rectangle.

Rectangle best describes this quadrilateral.

Give all of the names that apply to each quadrilateral. Then give the name that best describes it.

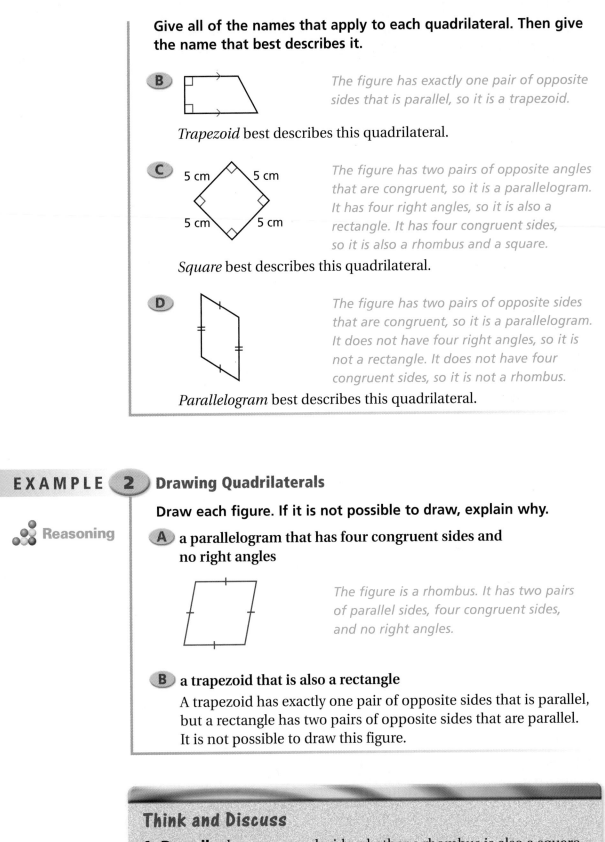

B *The figure has exactly one pair of opposite sides that is parallel, so it is a trapezoid.*

Trapezoid best describes this quadrilateral.

C 5 cm 5 cm 5 cm 5 cm

The figure has two pairs of opposite angles that are congruent, so it is a parallelogram. It has four right angles, so it is also a rectangle. It has four congruent sides, so it is also a rhombus and a square.

Square best describes this quadrilateral.

D *The figure has two pairs of opposite sides that are congruent, so it is a parallelogram. It does not have four right angles, so it is not a rectangle. It does not have four congruent sides, so it is not a rhombus.*

Parallelogram best describes this quadrilateral.

EXAMPLE 2   Drawing Quadrilaterals

Reasoning

Draw each figure. If it is not possible to draw, explain why.

A a parallelogram that has four congruent sides and no right angles

The figure is a rhombus. It has two pairs of parallel sides, four congruent sides, and no right angles.

B a trapezoid that is also a rectangle

A trapezoid has exactly one pair of opposite sides that is parallel, but a rectangle has two pairs of opposite sides that are parallel. It is not possible to draw this figure.

Think and Discuss

1. **Describe** how you can decide whether a rhombus is also a square. Use drawings to justify your answer.

2. **Draw** a Venn diagram to show how the properties of the five quadrilaterals relate.

California Standards Practice
Preparation for MG2.3; MG2.3

go.hrw.com
Homework Help Online
KEYWORD: MS8CA 9-8
Parent Resources Online
KEYWORD: MS8CA Parent

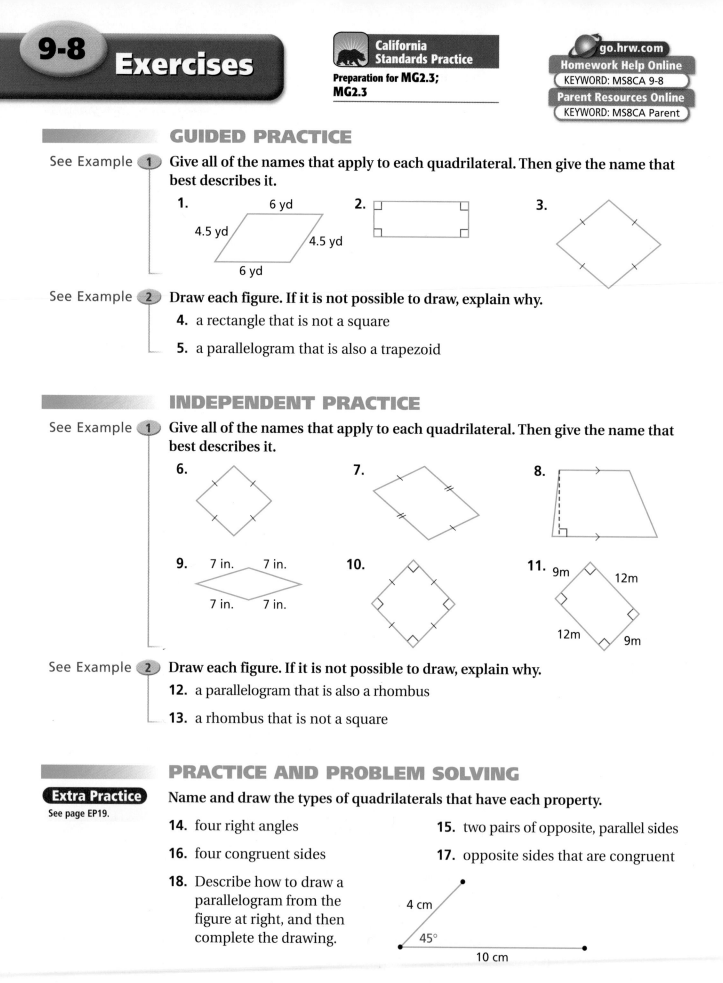

GUIDED PRACTICE

See Example **1**   Give all of the names that apply to each quadrilateral. Then give the name that best describes it.

1. 6 yd / 4.5 yd / 4.5 yd / 6 yd

2.

3.

See Example **2**   Draw each figure. If it is not possible to draw, explain why.

4. a rectangle that is not a square

5. a parallelogram that is also a trapezoid

INDEPENDENT PRACTICE

See Example **1**   Give all of the names that apply to each quadrilateral. Then give the name that best describes it.

6.

7.

8.

9. 7 in. 7 in. / 7 in. 7 in.

10.

11. 9m 12m / 12m 9m

See Example **2**   Draw each figure. If it is not possible to draw, explain why.

12. a parallelogram that is also a rhombus

13. a rhombus that is not a square

PRACTICE AND PROBLEM SOLVING

Extra Practice
See page EP19.

Name and draw the types of quadrilaterals that have each property.

14. four right angles

15. two pairs of opposite, parallel sides

16. four congruent sides

17. opposite sides that are congruent

18. Describe how to draw a parallelogram from the figure at right, and then complete the drawing.

4 cm / 45° / 10 cm

Tell whether each statement is true or false. Explain your answer.

19. All squares are rhombuses.

20. All rectangles are parallelograms.

21. All squares are rectangles.

22. All rhombuses are rectangles.

23. Some trapezoids are squares.

24. Some rectangles are squares.

25. Social Studies Name the polygons made by each color in the flag of the Bahamas. Give the specific names of any quadrilaterals you find.

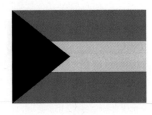

26. Graph the points $A(-2, -2)$, $B(4, 1)$, $C(3, 4)$, and $D(-1, 2)$, and draw line segments to connect the points. What kind of quadrilateral did you draw?

27. Bandon Highway is being built perpendicular to Avenue A and Avenue B, which are parallel. What kinds of polygons could be made by adding a fourth road?

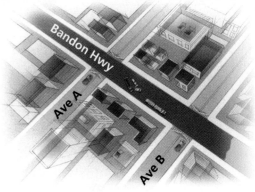

28. Write a Problem Draw a design, or find one in a book, and then write a problem about the design that involves identifying quadrilaterals.

29. Write About It Quadrilaterals can be found on many college campuses. Describe two special quadrilaterals that you commonly find in the world around you.

30. Challenge The coordinates of three vertices of a parallelogram are $(-1, 1)$, $(2, 1)$, and $(0, -4)$. What are the coordinates of the fourth vertex?

31. Short Response Draw a trapezoid with two right angles. Explain how you know that the figure is a trapezoid.

32. Extended Response Graph the points $A(-1, 5)$, $B(4, 3)$, $C(2, -2)$, and $D(-3, 0)$. Draw segments AB, BC, CD, and AD, and give all of the names that apply to the quadrilateral. Then give the name that best describes it.

Use the data set 43, 28, 33, 49, 18, 44, 57, 34, 40, and 57 for Exercises 33 and 34. (Lesson 7-2)

33. Find the mean, median, mode, and range of the data.

34. Add the values 65 and 18 to the data, and find the mean, median, mode, and range.

35. The probability that it will rain tomorrow is 20%. What is the probability that it will not rain tomorrow? Write your answer as a fraction, as a decimal, and as a percent. (Lesson 8-1)

Congruent Figures

California Standards

Extension of 🔑 **MG2.2** Use the properties of complementary and supplementary angles and the sum of the angles of a triangle to **solve problems involving an unknown angle.**

Who uses this? Surveyors can use congruent figures to find the distance across a stream. (See Exercise 19.)

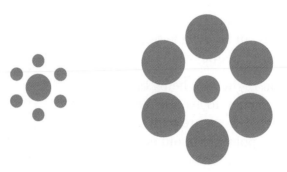

Vocabulary
Side-Side-Side Rule

Look at the two patterns. Which center circle do you think is bigger? In spite of appearances, the two center circles are congruent. Their apparent differences are optical illusions. One way to determine whether figures are congruent is to see whether one figure will fit exactly over the other one.

E X A M P L E   1   Identifying Congruent Figures in the Real World

Identify any figures that appear to be congruent.

> **Remember!**
>
> Two figures are congruent if they have the same shape and size.
>
> *See Lesson 9-1, p. 429.*

Ⓐ

The squares on a checkerboard are congruent. The checkers are also congruent.

Ⓑ

The rings on a target are not congruent. Each ring is larger than the one inside of it.

If all of the corresponding sides and angles of two polygons are congruent, then the polygons are congruent. For triangles, if the corresponding sides are congruent, then the corresponding angles will always be congruent. This is called the **Side-Side-Side Rule** . Because of this rule, when determining whether triangles are congruent, you only need to determine whether the sides are congruent.

EXAMPLE **2** Identifying Congruent Triangles

Determine whether the triangles
are congruent.

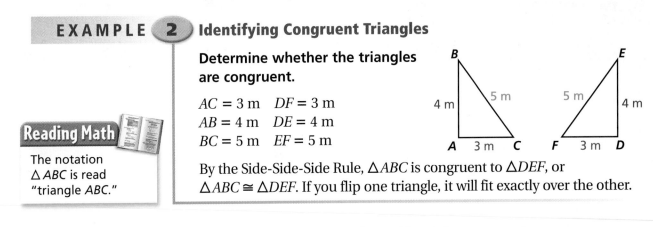

$AC = 3 \text{ m}$ $DF = 3 \text{ m}$
$AB = 4 \text{ m}$ $DE = 4 \text{ m}$
$BC = 5 \text{ m}$ $EF = 5 \text{ m}$

By the Side-Side-Side Rule, △*ABC* is congruent to △*DEF*, or
△*ABC* ≅ △*DEF*. If you flip one triangle, it will fit exactly over the other.

For polygons with more than three sides, it is not enough to compare
the measures of their sides. For example, the corresponding sides of
the figures below are congruent, but the figures are not congruent.

If you know that two figures are congruent, you can find missing
measures in the figures.

EXAMPLE **3** Using Congruence to Find Missing Measures

Determine the missing measure in each set of congruent
polygons.

A

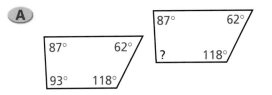

The corresponding angles
of congruent polygons
are congruent.

The missing angle measure is 93°.

B

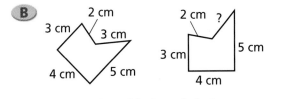

The corresponding sides
of congruent polygons
are congruent.

The missing side length is 3 cm.

Think and Discuss

1. **Draw** an illustration to explain whether an isosceles triangle can
   be congruent to a right triangle.

2. **Explain** why congruent figures are always similar figures.

California Standards Practice
Extension of ◆━◆ MG2.2

go.hrw.com
Homework Help Online
KEYWORD: MS8CA 9-9
Parent Resources Online
KEYWORD: MS8CA Parent

GUIDED PRACTICE

See Example ① **Identify any figures that appear to be congruent.**

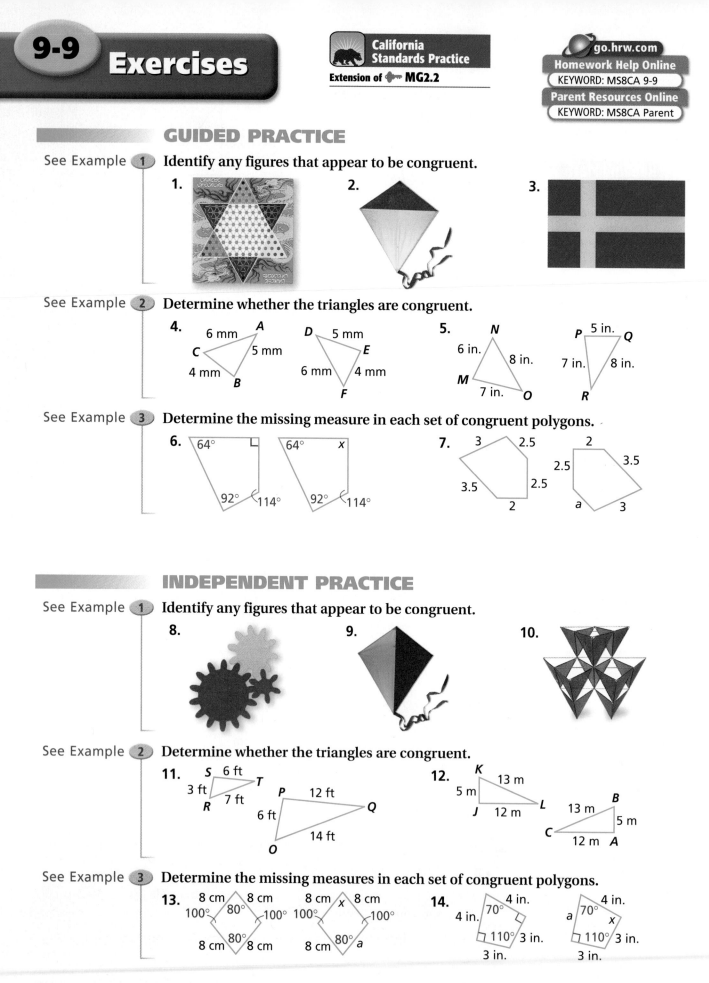

1.

2.

3.

See Example ② **Determine whether the triangles are congruent.**

4.
6 mm   A
C   5 mm
4 mm   B
D   5 mm   E
6 mm   4 mm   F

5.
N
6 in.   8 in.
M
7 in.   O
P   5 in.   Q
7 in.   8 in.
R

See Example ③ **Determine the missing measure in each set of congruent polygons.**

6.
64°   □
92°   114°
64°   x
92°   114°

7.
3   2.5
3.5   2.5
2
2
2.5   3.5
a   3

INDEPENDENT PRACTICE

See Example ① **Identify any figures that appear to be congruent.**

8.

9.

10.

See Example ② **Determine whether the triangles are congruent.**

11.
S   6 ft   T
3 ft
R   7 ft
P   12 ft   Q
6 ft
14 ft
O

12.
K   13 m
5 m
J   12 m   L
B
13 m   5 m
C   12 m   A

See Example ③ **Determine the missing measures in each set of congruent polygons.**

13.
8 cm   8 cm
100°   80°   100°
8 cm   80°   8 cm
8 cm   x   8 cm
100°   100°
8 cm   80°   a

14.
4 in.   4 in.
4 in.   70°
110°   3 in.
3 in.
a   70°   x
110°   3 in.
3 in.

PRACTICE AND PROBLEM SOLVING

Extra Practice
See page EP19.

Tell the minimum amount of information needed to determine whether the figures are congruent.

15. two triangles   **16.** two squares   **17.** two rectangles   **18.** two pentagons

19. Surveying In the figure, trees *A* and *B* are on opposite sides of the stream. Jamil wants to string a rope from one tree to the other. Triangles *ABC* and *DEC* are congruent. What is the distance between the trees?

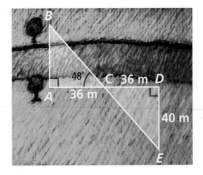

20. Hobbies In the quilt block, which figures appear congruent?

21. Choose a Strategy Anji and her brother Art walked to school along the routes in the figure. They started at 7:40 A.M. and walked at the same rate. Who arrived first?
  (A) Anji   (B) Art   (C) They arrived at the same time.

22. Write About It Explain how you can determine whether two triangles are congruent.

23. Challenge If all of the angles in two triangles have the same measure, are the triangles necessarily congruent?

24. Multiple Choice Which figures appear to be congruent?

  (A)   (B)   (C)   (D)

25. Multiple Choice Determine the missing measure in the congruent triangles.

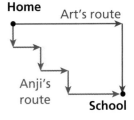

  (A) 4 mm   (C) 6 mm

  (B) 5 mm   (D) Cannot be determined

Multiply or divide. Write each answer in simplest form. (Lessons 4-4 and 4-5)

26. $1\frac{1}{3} \cdot 6$ **27.** $4\frac{7}{8} \div 13$ **28.** $\frac{2}{5} \cdot \frac{5}{6}$ **29.** $\frac{1}{9} \div \frac{2}{3}$

Find the measure of the third angle in each triangle, given two angle measures. Then classify the triangle. (Lesson 9-7)

30. $25°, 48°$ **31.** $125°, 30°$ **32.** $60°, 60°$ **33.** $72°, 18°$

READY TO GO ON?

Quiz for Lessons 9-5 Through 9-9

9-5 **Classifying Polygons**

Name each polygon, and tell whether it is a regular polygon.
Explain your answer.

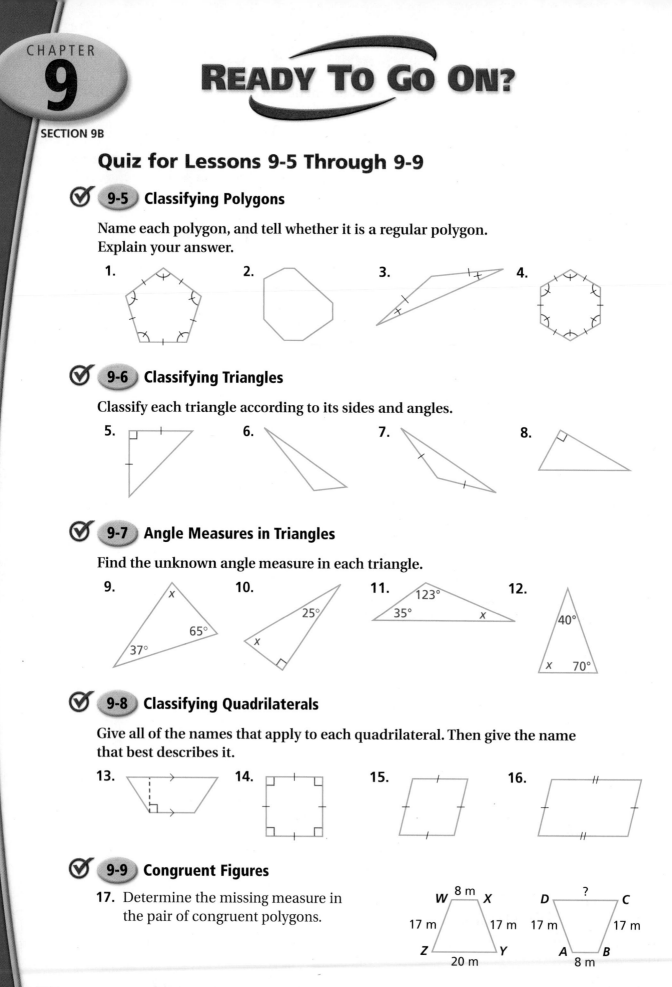

1.

2.

3.

4.

9-6 **Classifying Triangles**

Classify each triangle according to its sides and angles.

5.

6.

7.

8.

9-7 **Angle Measures in Triangles**

Find the unknown angle measure in each triangle.

9.
x
65°
37°

10.
25°
x

11.
123°
35°
x

12.
40°
x   70°

9-8 **Classifying Quadrilaterals**

Give all of the names that apply to each quadrilateral. Then give the name
that best describes it.

13.

14.

15.

16.

9-9 **Congruent Figures**

17. Determine the missing measure in
the pair of congruent polygons.

W 8 m X
17 m   17 m
Z   Y
   20 m

D   ?   C
17 m   17 m
A   B
   8 m

CONCEPT CONNECTION

Start Your Engines Several friends are racing remote-controlled cars. They use chalk to lay out the race course shown in the figure. Kendall examines the course beforehand to prepare for the race.

1. Kendall knows that figure *ABCD* is a trapezoid. What can he conclude about $\overline{AB}$ and $\overline{DC}$?

2. Using a protractor, Kendall measures ∠*ADF* as 81° and ∠*DFA* as 66°. He wants to know the angle at which he should turn his car as he goes from *C* to *A* to *D*. Explain how he can find the measure of ∠*CAD* without using a protractor. Then find the angle measure.

3. Triangle *DEC* is equilateral. How long is the section of the course from *E* to *D*?

4. $\overline{AC}$ is congruent to $\overline{DB}$, and $\overline{AC}$ is 33 feet long. What is the total length of the course?

5. Kendall's car moves at about 10 feet per second. Estimate the time it will take his car to complete the course.

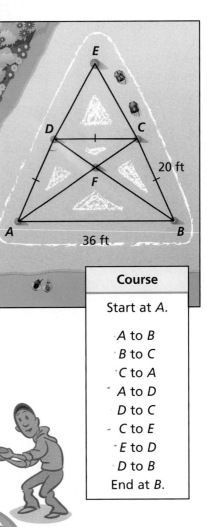

Course
Start at *A*.
A to *B*
B to *C*
C to *A*
A to *D*
D to *C*
C to *E*
E to *D*
D to *B*
End at *B*.

Tangrams

A tangram is an ancient Chinese puzzle. The seven shapes that make this square can be arranged to make many other figures. Copy the shapes that make this square, and then cut them apart. See if you can arrange the pieces to make the figures below.

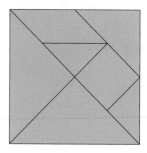

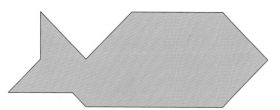

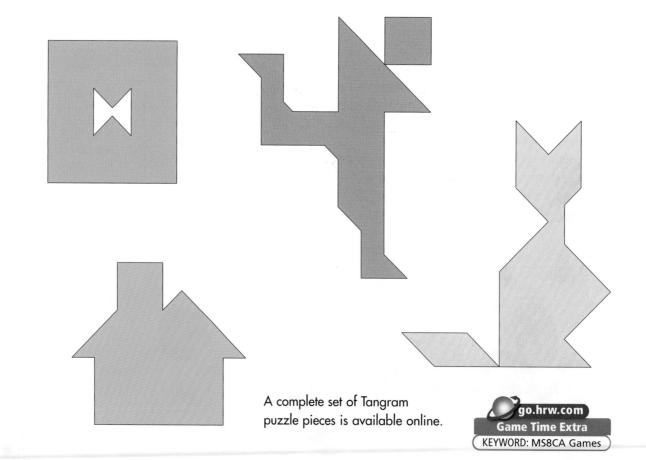

A complete set of Tangram puzzle pieces is available online.

go.hrw.com
Game Time Extra
KEYWORD: MS8CA Games

Materials
- 6 sheets of construction paper
- card stock
- scissors
- hole punch
- 4 electrical ties
- white paper
- markers

It's in the Bag!

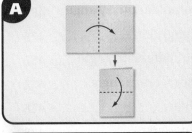

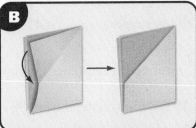

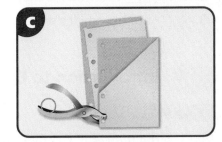

PROJECT Brochure Book of Geometric Figures

Make an organizer to hold brochures that summarize each lesson of the chapter.

Directions

1 Start with sheets of construction paper that are 12 inches by 18 inches. Fold one sheet in half to make it 12 inches by 9 inches and then in half again to make it 6 inches by 9 inches. **Figure A**

2 Hold the paper with the folds at the bottom and on the right-hand side. Turn the top left-hand corner back and under to form a pocket. **Figure B**

3 Turn the whole thing over and fold the top right-hand corner back and under to form a pocket. Repeat steps 1–3 with the other sheets of construction paper.

4 Cut out two pieces of card stock that are 6 inches by 9 inches. Punch four equally spaced holes down the length of each piece. Similarly, punch four equally spaced holes on each pocket as shown. **Figure C**

5 Stack the six pockets and put the card stock covers on the front and back of the stack. Insert electrical ties into the holes to hold everything together.

Taking Note of the Math

Fold sheets of plain white paper into thirds like a brochure. Use the brochures to take notes on the lessons of the chapter. Store the brochures in the pockets of your organizer.

Vocabulary

Complete the sentences below with vocabulary words from the list above.

1. Every equilateral triangle is also a(n) __?__ triangle.

2. A(n) __?__ is a triangle that has exactly one angle that is greater than 90°.

3. __?__ are two angles whose measures have a sum of 90°.

9-1 Introduction to Geometry (pp. 428–431)

 Prep for MG2.1

EXAMPLES

Identify the figures in the diagram.

- points: A, B, C
- lines: $\overleftrightarrow{AB}$
- planes: ABC
- rays: $\overrightarrow{BA}$; $\overrightarrow{AB}$
- line segments: $\overline{AB}$; $\overline{BC}$

EXERCISES

Identify the figures in the diagram.

4. points
5. lines
6. planes
7. rays
8. line segments

9-2 Measuring and Classifying Angles (pp. 432–435)

 Prep for MG2.1

EXAMPLE

- Classify each angle as acute, right, obtuse, or straight.

m∠A = 80°
80° < 90°, so ∠A is acute.

EXERCISES

Classify each angle as acute, right, obtuse, or straight.

9. m∠x = 60°   10. m∠x = 100°

11. m∠x = 45°   12. m∠x = 180°

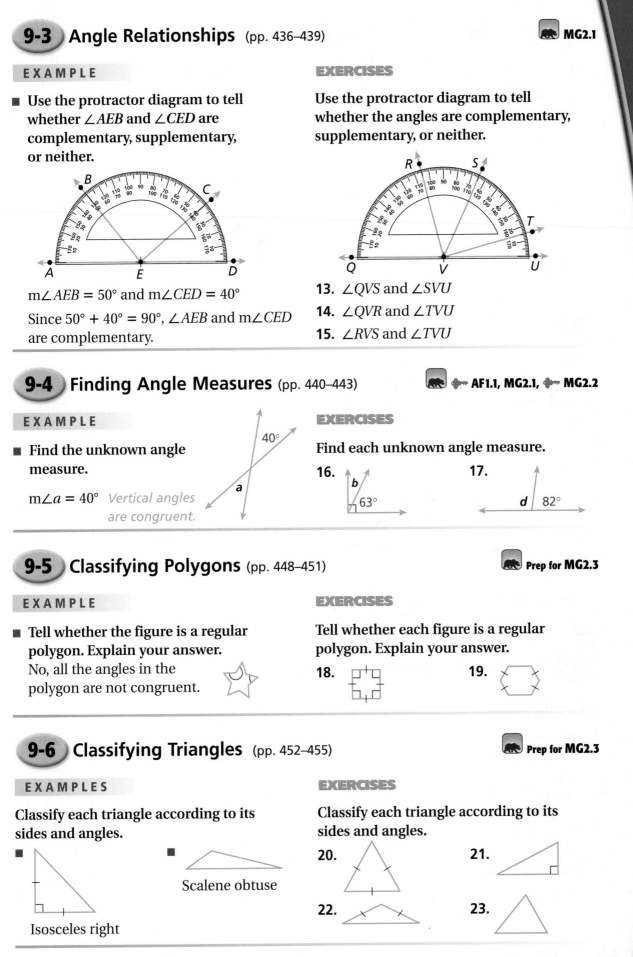

9-3 Angle Relationships (pp. 436–439)

MG2.1

EXAMPLE

■ Use the protractor diagram to tell whether ∠AEB and ∠CED are complementary, supplementary, or neither.

m∠AEB = 50° and m∠CED = 40°

Since 50° + 40° = 90°, ∠AEB and m∠CED are complementary.

EXERCISES

Use the protractor diagram to tell whether the angles are complementary, supplementary, or neither.

13. ∠QVS and ∠SVU
14. ∠QVR and ∠TVU
15. ∠RVS and ∠TVU

9-4 Finding Angle Measures (pp. 440–443)

AF1.1, MG2.1, MG2.2

EXAMPLE

■ Find the unknown angle measure.

m∠a = 40° *Vertical angles are congruent.*

EXERCISES

Find each unknown angle measure.

16. b / 63°

17. d / 82°

9-5 Classifying Polygons (pp. 448–451)

Prep for MG2.3

EXAMPLE

■ Tell whether the figure is a regular polygon. Explain your answer.
No, all the angles in the polygon are not congruent.

EXERCISES

Tell whether each figure is a regular polygon. Explain your answer.

18.

19.

9-6 Classifying Triangles (pp. 452–455)

Prep for MG2.3

EXAMPLES

Classify each triangle according to its sides and angles.

■

■ Scalene obtuse

Isosceles right

EXERCISES

Classify each triangle according to its sides and angles.

20.

21.

22.

23.

9-7 Angle Measures in Triangles (pp. 459–461)

AF1.1, MG2.1, MG2.2

EXAMPLE

■ Find the unknown angle measure in the triangle.

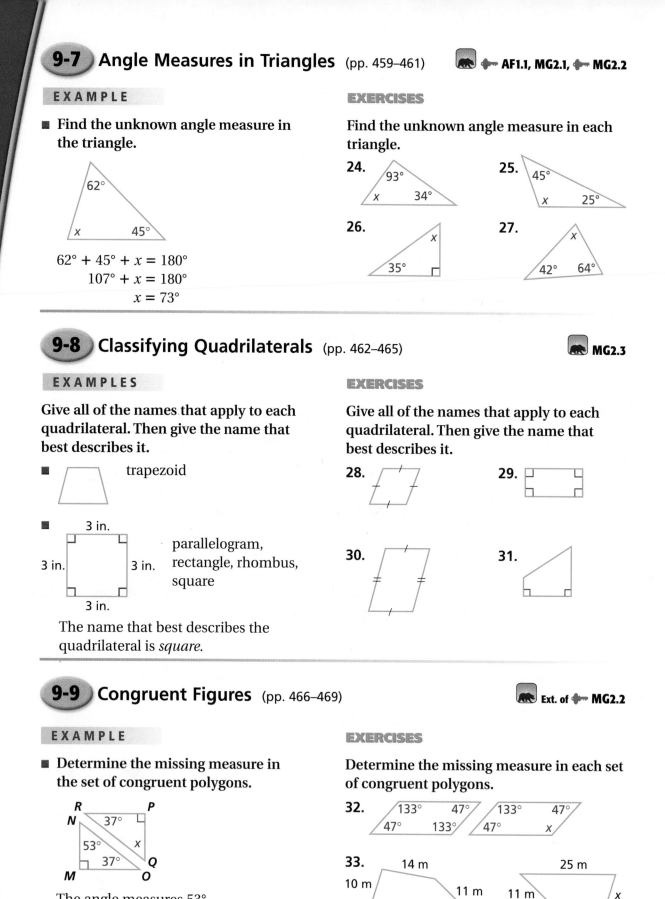

$62° + 45° + x = 180°$
$107° + x = 180°$
$x = 73°$

EXERCISES

Find the unknown angle measure in each triangle.

24.

93°
x   34°

25.

45°
x   25°

26.

x
35°

27.

x
42° 64°

9-8 Classifying Quadrilaterals (pp. 462–465)

MG2.3

EXAMPLES

Give all of the names that apply to each quadrilateral. Then give the name that best describes it.

■ trapezoid

■ 3 in.
3 in.   3 in.
3 in.

parallelogram, rectangle, rhombus, square

The name that best describes the quadrilateral is *square*.

EXERCISES

Give all of the names that apply to each quadrilateral. Then give the name that best describes it.

28.

29.

30.

31.

9-9 Congruent Figures (pp. 466–469)

Ext. of MG2.2

EXAMPLE

■ Determine the missing measure in the set of congruent polygons.

R   P
N   37°
53°   x
37°   Q
M   O

The angle measures 53°.

EXERCISES

Determine the missing measure in each set of congruent polygons.

32.
133°   47°   133°   47°
47°   133°   47°   x

33.
14 m   25 m
10 m   11 m
11 m   x
25 m   14 m

CHAPTER TEST

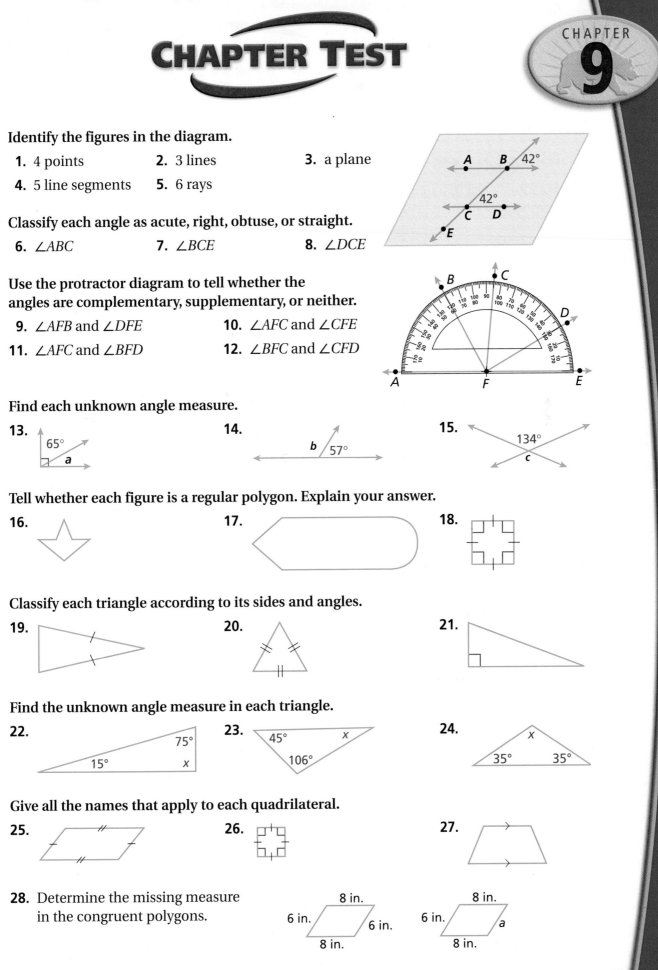

Identify the figures in the diagram.

1. 4 points
2. 3 lines
3. a plane
4. 5 line segments
5. 6 rays

Classify each angle as acute, right, obtuse, or straight.

6. $\angle ABC$
7. $\angle BCE$
8. $\angle DCE$

Use the protractor diagram to tell whether the angles are complementary, supplementary, or neither.

9. $\angle AFB$ and $\angle DFE$
10. $\angle AFC$ and $\angle CFE$
11. $\angle AFC$ and $\angle BFD$
12. $\angle BFC$ and $\angle CFD$

Find each unknown angle measure.

13.
14.
15.

Tell whether each figure is a regular polygon. Explain your answer.

16.
17.
18.

Classify each triangle according to its sides and angles.

19.
20.
21.

Find the unknown angle measure in each triangle.

22.
23.
24.

Give all the names that apply to each quadrilateral.

25.
26.
27.

28. Determine the missing measure in the congruent polygons.

Chapter Test **477**

STRATEGIES FOR SUCCESS

Multiple Choice: Identifying Keywords and Context Clues

When reading a test item, pay attention to key words and context clues given in the problem statement. These clues will guide you in providing a correct response.

EXAMPLE 1

Which angle is obtuse?

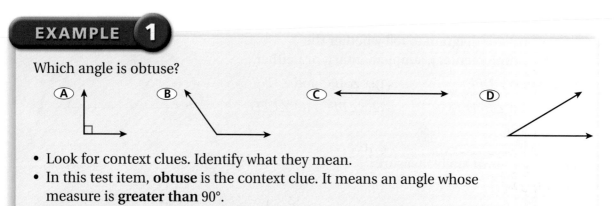

- Look for context clues. Identify what they mean.
- In this test item, **obtuse** is the context clue. It means an angle whose measure is **greater than** 90°.

Find the choice that shows an **obtuse** angle.
A: This angle's measure is 90° because it has a right angle symbol.
B: This angle's measure is greater than 90°. It is an obtuse angle.
C: This angle's measure is 180° because it is a straight angle.
D: This angle's measure is less than 90°. It is an acute angle.

The correct answer is B.

EXAMPLE 2

Kenneth makes flower deliveries along Oak Street. He starts at the flower shop on Oak Street. His first delivery is 8 blocks directly west of the shop. His second delivery takes him 4 blocks directly east of his first delivery. His third delivery takes him 5 blocks east of his second delivery. Write an expression using integers to model this situation.

(A) $-4 - 5 + 8$ (B) $8 + 4 - 5$ (C) $-8 - 4 - 5$ (D) $-8 + 4 + 5$

- Look for key words.
- In this test item, the key words are **expression** and **integers.**

Find the choice that shows the correct **integer expression** to model the situation.
A: The first delivery is 8 blocks west. This expression does not begin with –8.
B: The first delivery is 8 blocks west. This expression does not begin with –8.
C: The expression begins with –8, but 4 blocks east would be + 4.
D: This expression's integers correctly correspond to the deliveries.

The correct answer is D.

If you do not understand what a word means, reread the sentences that surround the word and make a logical guess.

Read each test item and answer the questions that follow.

Item A
Multiple Choice Jenny had $3\frac{1}{2}$ gallons of indigo paint. She used $\frac{3}{4}$ gallon to paint a bathroom. How much paint does Jenny have left?

Ⓐ $2\frac{3}{4}$ gallons   Ⓒ $4\frac{1}{4}$ gallons

Ⓑ $3\frac{1}{4}$ gallons   Ⓓ $4\frac{2}{3}$ gallons

---

1. If you did not know that *indigo* is a color, which other word or words in the problem could help you guess its meaning? Explain.

2. Which words in the problem tell you which operation you need to use to solve this problem?

3. Which answer choices can you eliminate immediately? Explain.

Item B
Multiple Choice Tavon climbed from an elevation of –45 feet to an elevation of 218 feet. What was Tavon's change in elevation?

Ⓐ 153 feet   Ⓒ 233 feet

Ⓑ 173 feet   Ⓓ 263 feet

---

4. What other words in the problem can help you guess the meaning of *elevation*?

5. Which operation should you use to solve this problem? How do you know?

Item C
Multiple Choice Madeline has 28 daisies and 42 violets. Find the GCD to find the greatest number of wrist corsages that can be made if each corsage has the same number of daisies and the same number of violets.

Ⓐ 4   Ⓒ 14

Ⓑ 7   Ⓓ 21

---

6. What is the math term that describes what is being tested?

7. Identify the keywords in this problem statement.

Item D
Multiple Choice An office supply store states that 4 out of 5 customers would recommend the store to another person. Given this information, what percent of customers would NOT recommend the office supply store to someone else?

Ⓐ 10%   Ⓒ 40%

Ⓑ 20%   Ⓓ 80%

---

8. What information is needed to solve this problem?

9. Which choice can be eliminated immediately? Why?

10. Write a proportion to find the percent of customers who would recommend the office store to someone else.

11. Describe two different ways to solve this problem.

Cumulative Assessment, Chapters 1–9

Multiple Choice

1. Each student in a school is assigned a 2-letter password. Each letter can be from A to Z. What is the probability that a student will get the password DD?

Ⓐ $\frac{1}{676}$ Ⓒ $\frac{1}{52}$

Ⓑ $\frac{1}{338}$ Ⓓ $\frac{1}{26}$

2. Terri is $60\frac{1}{2}$ inches tall. Steve is $65\frac{1}{4}$ inches tall. What is the difference, in inches, in their heights?

Ⓐ $4\frac{1}{4}$ Ⓒ $4\frac{3}{4}$

Ⓑ $4\frac{1}{2}$ Ⓓ $5\frac{1}{4}$

3. In the figure below, which of the following angle pairs are NOT adjacent?

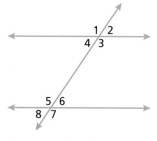

Ⓐ ∠1 and ∠2   Ⓒ ∠1 and ∠3

Ⓑ ∠5 and ∠8   Ⓓ ∠6 and ∠7

4. Nolan spent $\frac{1}{2}$ hour traveling to his orthodontist appointment, $\frac{3}{5}$ hour at his appointment, and $\frac{3}{4}$ hour traveling home. What is the total amount of time Nolan spent for this appointment?

Ⓐ $\frac{7}{11}$ hour   Ⓒ $1\frac{17}{20}$ hours

Ⓑ $\frac{37}{60}$ hour   Ⓓ $\frac{13}{5}$ hours

5. A store sells two dozen rolls of toilet paper for $4.84. What is the unit rate for one roll of toilet paper?

Ⓐ $0.13/roll of toilet paper

Ⓑ $0.20/roll of toilet paper

Ⓒ $0.40/roll of toilet paper

Ⓓ $1.21/roll of toilet paper

6. Which of the following best describes the triangle below?

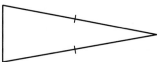

Ⓐ Acute isosceles triangle

Ⓑ Equilateral triangle

Ⓒ Obtuse right triangle

Ⓓ Obtuse scalene triangle

7. Which expression represents "twice the difference of a number and 8"?

Ⓐ $2(x + 8)$ Ⓒ $2(x - 8)$

Ⓑ $2x - 8$ Ⓓ $2x + 8$

8. For which equation is $x = 1$ NOT the solution?

Ⓐ $3x = 3$ Ⓒ $-x + 6 = 5$

Ⓑ $8 - x = 9$ Ⓓ $8 + x = 9$

9. Which of the following decimals is closest to 0?

Ⓐ 0.08   Ⓒ 0.2

Ⓑ −0.07   Ⓓ −0.1

10. The graph shows how Amy spends her earnings each month. Amy earned $200 in May. How much did she spend on transportation and clothing combined?

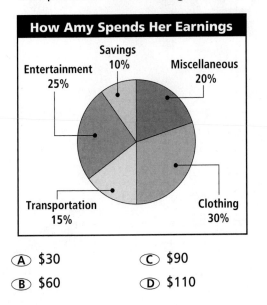

How Amy Spends Her Earnings

Savings 10%
Entertainment 25%
Miscellaneous 20%
Transportation 15%
Clothing 30%

Ⓐ $30   Ⓒ $90

Ⓑ $60   Ⓓ $110

Once you have answered a short- or extended-response question, check to make sure you have answered all parts of the question.

Gridded Response

11. What is the unknown angle measure in degrees?

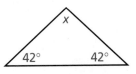

42°   42° x

12. Two angles are complementary. If the measure of one angle is 36°, what is the measure of the second angle in degrees?

13. An antiques dealer bought a chair for $85. The dealer sold the chair at her shop for 45% more than what she paid. To the nearest whole dollar, what was the price of the chair?

14. What is the value of the expression $4x^2$ for $x = 2$?

Short Response

15. Find the unknown angle measure x. Explain how you determined your answer.

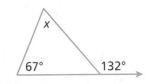

67°   132° x

16. Taylor's goal is to spend less than 35% of her allowance each month on cell phone bills. Last month, Taylor spent $45 on cell phone bills. If she gets $120 each month as her allowance, did she achieve her goal? Explain your answer.

17. The table shows ten distances hit by a baseball player.

Distances (ft)				
334	360	350	343	330
320	265	327	335	270

Is the mean distance of this player's hits more than or less than the median distance? Explain how you found your answer.

Extended Response

18. A bird lays 2 eggs. For each egg, there is a 50% chance that the chick will be male and a 50% chance that the chick will be female.

a. Make a tree diagram showing the possible outcomes for two chicks.

b. Find the probability of each of the following outcomes.

- Both chicks are male.
- Both chicks are female.
- One chick is male and one chick is female.

c. What is the probability that neither chick is female? Explain how you determined your answer.

CHAPTER 10

Measurement and Geometry

CONCEPT CONNECTION

go.hrw.com
Chapter Project Online
KEYWORD: MS8CA Ch10

The diameter of the trunk of a giant sequoia tree can be determined by measuring the distance around the trunk and then using a formula.

Mariposa Grove
Yosemite National Park

ARE YOU READY?

☑ Vocabulary

Choose the best term from the list to complete each sentence.

1. A(n) __?__ is a quadrilateral with exactly one pair of parallel sides.

2. A(n) __?__ is a four-sided figure with opposite sides that are congruent and parallel.

3. The __?__ of a circle is one-half the __?__ of the circle.

diameter

parallelogram

radius

right triangle

trapezoid

Complete these exercises to review skills you will need for this chapter.

☑ Round Whole Numbers

Round each number to the nearest ten and nearest hundred.

4. 1,535   **5.** 294   **6.** 30,758   **7.** 497

☑ Round Decimals

Round each number to the nearest whole number and nearest tenth.

8. 6.18   **9.** 10.50   **10.** 513.93   **11.** 29.06

☑ Multiply with Decimals

Multiply.

12. $5.63 \cdot 8$ **13.** $9.67 \cdot 4.3$ **14.** $8.34 \cdot 16$ **15.** $6.08 \cdot 0.56$

16. $0.82 \cdot 21$ **17.** $2.74 \cdot 6.6$ **18.** $40 \cdot 9.54$ **19.** $0.33 \cdot 0.08$

☑ Order of Operations

Simplify each expression.

20. $2 \cdot 9 + 2 \cdot 6$ **21.** $2(15 + 8)$ **22.** $4 \cdot 6.8 + 7 \cdot 9.3$

23. $14(25.9 + 13.6)$ **24.** $(27.3 + 0.7) \div 2^2$ **25.** $5 \cdot 3^3 - 8.02$

26. $(63 \div 7) \cdot 4^2$ **27.** $1.1 + 3 \cdot 4.3$ **28.** $66 \cdot [5 + (3 + 3)^2]$

☑ Identify Polygons

Name each figure.

29.   **30.** 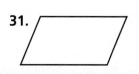   **31.**

Unpacking the Standards

The information below "unpacks" the standards. The Academic Vocabulary is highlighted and defined to help you understand the language of the standards. Refer to the lessons listed after each standard for help with the math terms and phrases. The Chapter Concept shows how the standard is applied in this chapter.

California Standard	Academic Vocabulary	Chapter Concept
AF3.1 Use variables in expressions describing geometric quantities (e.g., $P = 2w + 2\ell$, $A = \frac{1}{2}bh$, $C = \pi d$—the formula for the perimeter of a rectangle, the area of a triangle, and the circumference of a circle, respectively). (Lessons 10-1 to 10-5, 10-8 to 10-10) (Labs 10-3, 10-4, 10-8)	**formula** rule showing relationships among quantities ***Example:*** A formula for the perimeter of a rectangle is $P = 2w + 2\ell$. **respectively** in the order given	You use formulas for perimeter, area, circumference, and other geometric measurements. ***Example:*** Find the perimeter P of a rectangle with a width of 4 m and a length of 6 m. $P = 2w + 2\ell$ $P = 2(4) + 2(6)$ $P = 8 + 12$ $P = 20$ The perimeter is 20 m.
AF3.2 Express in symbolic form simple relationships arising from geometry. (Lessons 10-1 to 10-6, 10-8 to 10-10) (Labs 10-3, 10-4, 10-8)	**express** communicate **symbolic** written using symbols or signs; standing for something else	You use variables to write expressions and equations for measurements such as area, volume, and circumference.
MG1.1 Understand the concept of a constant such as π; know the formulas for the circumference and area of a circle. (Lessons 10-2, 10-5, 10-6) (Lab 10-2)	**concept** idea **constant** a value that does not change	You know what the constant π represents. You understand the formulas for the circumference and area of circles.
MG1.3 Know and use the formulas for the volume of triangular prisms and cylinders (area of base × height); compare these formulas and explain the similarity between them and the formula for the volume of a rectangular solid. (Lessons 10-8, 10-9) (Lab 10-8)	**similarity** quality or feature that two or more things have in common	You find the volume of prisms and cylinders. ***Example:*** Find the volume of a triangular prism with a base of 14 m² and a height of 6 m. $V = Bh$ $V = 14 \cdot 6$ $V = 84$ The volume is 84 m³.

Standards NS2.1, AF1.1, AF1.2, and MG1.2 are also covered in this chapter. To see standards NS2.1, AF1.1, and AF1.2 unpacked, go to Chapter 1, p. 4 (AF1.1 and AF1.2) and Chapter 4, p. 168 (NS2.1).

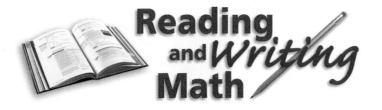

Reading Strategy: Read and Interpret Graphics

Figures, diagrams, tables, and graphs provide important data. Knowing how to read these graphics will help you understand and solve related problems.

Similar Figures
$\triangle ABC$ and $\triangle JKL$ are similar. 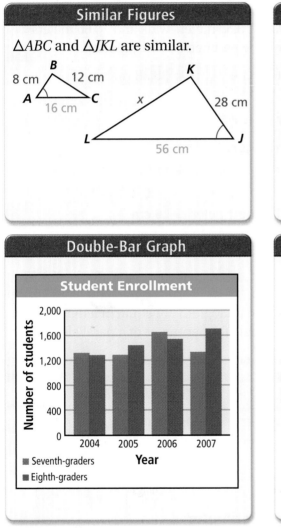

How to Read
Read all labels. $AB = 8$ cm; $AC = 16$ cm; $BC = 12$ cm; $JK = 28$ cm; $JL = 56$ cm; $KL = x$ cm; $\angle A$ corresponds to $\angle J$.
Be careful about what you assume. You may think $\overline{AB}$ corresponds to $\overline{LK}$, but this is not so. Since $\angle A$ corresponds to $\angle J$, you know $\overline{AB}$ corresponds to $\overline{JK}$.

Double-Bar Graph

How to Read
Read the title of the graph and any special notes. Blue indicates seventh-graders. Purple indicates eighth-graders.
Read each axis label and note the intervals of each scale. **x-axis**—year increases by 1. **y-axis**—enrollment increases by 400 students.
Determine what information is presented. student enrollment for seventh- and eighth-graders per year

Try This

Look up each graphic in your textbook and answer the following questions.

1. Lesson 5-6 Exercise 1: Which side of the smaller triangle corresponds to $\overline{BC}$? Which angle corresponds to $\angle EDF$?

2. Lesson 7-4 Example 1: By what interval does the *x*-axis scale increase? About how many electoral votes were cast by Republicans in 2000?

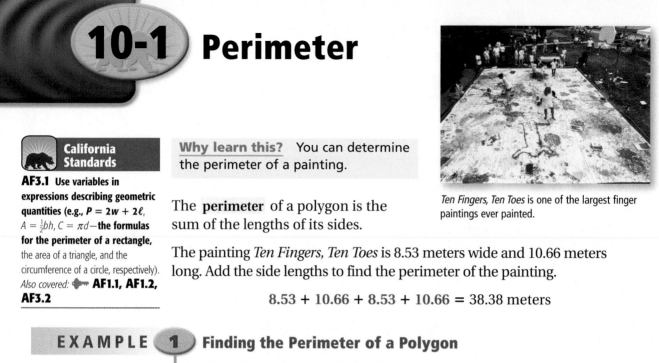

Ten Fingers, Ten Toes is one of the largest finger paintings ever painted.

California Standards

AF3.1 Use variables in expressions describing geometric quantities (e.g., $P = 2w + 2\ell$, $A = \frac{1}{2}bh$, $C = \pi d$—the formulas for the perimeter of a rectangle, the area of a triangle, and the circumference of a circle, respectively). *Also covered:* 🔑 **AF1.1, AF1.2, AF3.2**

Why learn this? You can determine the perimeter of a painting.

The **perimeter** of a polygon is the sum of the lengths of its sides.

The painting *Ten Fingers, Ten Toes* is 8.53 meters wide and 10.66 meters long. Add the side lengths to find the perimeter of the painting.

$$8.53 + 10.66 + 8.53 + 10.66 = 38.38 \text{ meters}$$

EXAMPLE ① **Finding the Perimeter of a Polygon**

Vocabulary
perimeter

Find the perimeter of the figure.

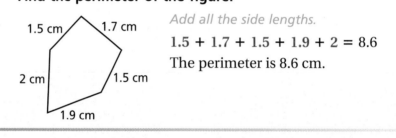

Add all the side lengths.

$1.5 + 1.7 + 1.5 + 1.9 + 2 = 8.6$

The perimeter is 8.6 cm.

Recall that the opposite sides of a parallogram are equal in length. You can use this relationship to find a formula for perimeter of a parallelogram.

PERIMETER OF A PARALLELOGRAM

The perimeter *P* of a parallelogram is the sum of twice its width *w* and twice its length *ℓ*.

$P = w + w + \ell + \ell$
$P = 2w + 2\ell$

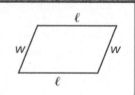

EXAMPLE ② **Using a Formula to Find Perimeter**

Find the perimeter *P* of the parallelogram.

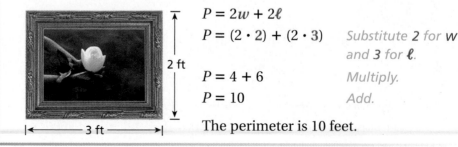

2 ft

3 ft

$P = 2w + 2\ell$
$P = (2 \cdot 2) + (2 \cdot 3)$ *Substitute 2 for w and 3 for ℓ.*
$P = 4 + 6$ *Multiply.*
$P = 10$ *Add.*

The perimeter is 10 feet.

EXAMPLE 3 **Finding Unknown Side Lengths and the Perimeter of a Polygon**

Find each unknown measure.

:∴: **Reasoning**

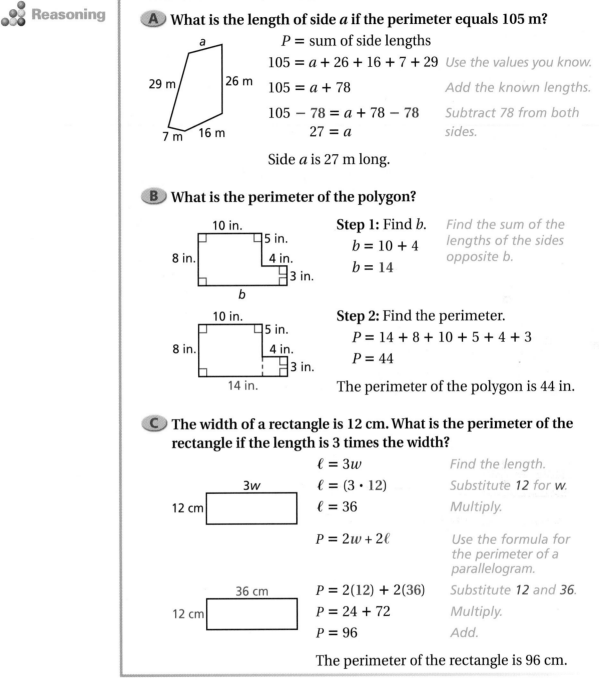

A What is the length of side *a* if the perimeter equals 105 m?

P = sum of side lengths

105 = *a* + 26 + 16 + 7 + 29   *Use the values you know.*

105 = *a* + 78   *Add the known lengths.*

105 − 78 = *a* + 78 − 78   *Subtract 78 from both*
27 = *a*   *sides.*

Side *a* is 27 m long.

B What is the perimeter of the polygon?

Step 1: Find *b*.   *Find the sum of the*
b = 10 + 4   *lengths of the sides*
b = 14   *opposite b.*

Step 2: Find the perimeter.

P = 14 + 8 + 10 + 5 + 4 + 3
P = 44

The perimeter of the polygon is 44 in.

C The width of a rectangle is 12 cm. What is the perimeter of the rectangle if the length is 3 times the width?

ℓ = 3*w*   *Find the length.*

ℓ = (3 · 12)   *Substitute 12 for w.*

ℓ = 36   *Multiply.*

P = 2*w* + 2ℓ   *Use the formula for*
the perimeter of a
parallelogram.

P = 2(12) + 2(36)   *Substitute 12 and 36.*

P = 24 + 72   *Multiply.*

P = 96   *Add.*

The perimeter of the rectangle is 96 cm.

Think and Discuss

1. Explain how to find the perimeter of a regular pentagon if you know the length of one side.

2. Tell what formula you can use to find the perimeter of a square.

California
Standards Practice
NS2.1, AF3.1, AF3.2

go.hrw.com
Homework Help Online
KEYWORD: MS8CA 10-1
Parent Resources Online
KEYWORD: MS8CA Parent

GUIDED PRACTICE

See Example 1 **Find the perimeter of each figure.**

1. 0.5 in. 0.5 in. 0.5 in. 0.5 in.

2. 7 cm 9 cm 12 cm

See Example 2 **Find the perimeter *P* of each parallelogram.**

3. 12 m 8 m

4. 28.5 cm. 25.4 cm.

See Example 3 **Find the unknown measure.**

5. What is the length of side *b* if the perimeter equals 21 yd?

b 3 yd 4 yd 4 yd 3 yd

INDEPENDENT PRACTICE

See Example 1 **Find the perimeter of each figure.**

6. 3 ft $1\frac{1}{4}$ ft $2\frac{3}{4}$ ft

7. regular octagon 12 in.

See Example 2 **Find the perimeter *P* of each parallelogram.**

8. 11 in. 5 in.

9. 1.75 cm

10. $2\frac{1}{2}$ m 7 m

See Example 3 **Find each unknown measure.**

11. What is the perimeter of the polygon?

6 m 5 m 4 m *b* 11 m

12. The width of a rectangle is 15 ft. What is the perimeter of the rectangle if the length is 5 ft longer than the width?

PRACTICE AND PROBLEM SOLVING

Extra Practice
See page EP20.

Reasoning Use the figure *ACDEFG* for Exercises 13–15.

13. What is the length of side *FE*?

14. If the perimeter of rectangle *BCDE* is 34 in., what is the length of side *BC*?

15. Use your answer from Exercise 14 to find the perimeter of figure *ACDEFG*.

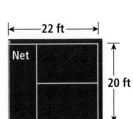

Find the perimeter of each figure.

16. a triangle with side lengths 6 in., 8 in., and 10 in.

17. a regular dodecagon (12-sided figure) with side length 3 m

18. Sports The diagram shows one-half of a badminton court.

   a. What are the dimensions of the whole court?

   b. What is the perimeter of the whole court?

   c. Is the perimeter of the half court $\frac{1}{2}$ of the perimeter of the whole court? Explain.

19. What's the Error? A student found the perimeter of a 10-inch-by-13-inch rectangle to be 23 inches. Explain the student's error. Then find the correct perimeter.

20. Write About It Explain how to find the unknown length of a side of a triangle that has a perimeter of 24 yd and two sides that measure 6 yd and 8 yd.

21. Challenge The perimeter of a regular octagon is 20 m. What is the length of one side of the octagon?

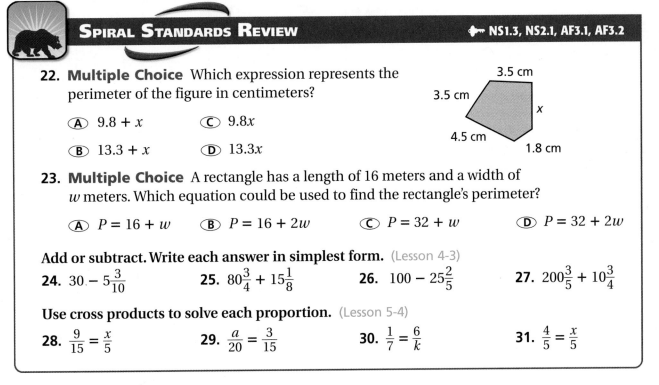

SPIRAL STANDARDS REVIEW

NS1.3, NS2.1, AF3.1, AF3.2

22. Multiple Choice Which expression represents the perimeter of the figure in centimeters?

   (A) $9.8 + x$ (C) $9.8x$

   (B) $13.3 + x$ (D) $13.3x$

23. Multiple Choice A rectangle has a length of 16 meters and a width of *w* meters. Which equation could be used to find the rectangle's perimeter?

   (A) $P = 16 + w$ (B) $P = 16 + 2w$ (C) $P = 32 + w$ (D) $P = 32 + 2w$

Add or subtract. Write each answer in simplest form. (Lesson 4-3)

24. $30 - 5\frac{3}{10}$ **25.** $80\frac{3}{4} + 15\frac{1}{8}$ **26.** $100 - 25\frac{2}{5}$ **27.** $200\frac{3}{5} + 10\frac{3}{4}$

Use cross products to solve each proportion. (Lesson 5-4)

28. $\frac{9}{15} = \frac{x}{5}$ **29.** $\frac{a}{20} = \frac{3}{15}$ **30.** $\frac{1}{7} = \frac{6}{k}$ **31.** $\frac{4}{5} = \frac{x}{5}$

 **Hands-On**

LAB
10-2

Explore Circumference

Use with Lesson 10-2

 **go.hrw.com**
Lab Resources Online
KEYWORD: MS8CA Lab10

In this lab, you will measure objects to investigate the distance around a circle. The distance around a circle is called the *circumference*.

California Standards

MG1.2 Know common estimates of π (3.14; $\frac{22}{7}$) and use these values to estimate and calculate the circumference and the area **of circles; compare with actual measurements.**
Also covered: ⟶ **MG1.1**

Activity 1

1 Choose a cylindrical object, such as a can or a mug. Tightly wrap a piece of string around the object, and mark the string where it meets itself. Measure this length on the string, and record it in a table like the one below as the circumference.

2 Using a ruler, measure the distance across the object through its center. Record this as the *diameter*.

3 Use a calculator to find the ratio of the circumference C to the diameter d. Round this value to the nearest hundredth, and record it in the table.

4 Repeat the process with three more cylindrical objects.

	Object 1	Object 2	Object 3	Object 4
Circumference *C*				
Diameter *d*				
$\frac{C}{d}$				

Think and Discuss

1. Describe what you notice about the ratio $\frac{C}{d}$ in your table.

Try This

Find the ratio $\frac{C}{d}$ for each circle. Round to the nearest hundredth.

1. 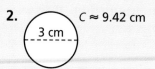 4 in. $C \approx 12.57$ in.

2. 3 cm $C \approx 9.42$ cm

3. 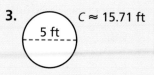 5 ft $C \approx 15.71$ ft

The ratio of the circumference of a circle to its diameter is always the same. This ratio is called *pi*, which is represented by the Greek letter π. As you saw in Activity 1, the value of π is close to 3. You can approximate π as 3.14 or $\frac{22}{7}$.

For any circle, $\frac{C}{d} = \pi$. You can solve this equation for C to give an equation for the circumference of a circle in terms of the diameter. The equation is $C = \pi d$.

Activity 2

① Open your compass to a width of 4 cm. Use the compass to draw a circle with a radius of 4 cm. What is the diameter of the circle?

4 cm

② Use the equation $C = \pi d$ and the approximation $\pi \approx 3.14$ to predict the circumference of the circle.

③ Carefully lay a piece of string on top of the circle. Make sure the string matches the circle as closely as possible.

④ Mark the string where it meets itself, and measure this length.

⑤ Repeat the process, this time starting with a circle whose radius is 3.5 cm. Use the equation $C = \pi d$ to predict the circle's circumference, and then check the prediction by using a string to measure the circumference.

Think and Discuss

1. In each case, how did the length of the string compare with the circumference that you predicted?

2. If you know the diameter of a circle, what should you do to find the circle's circumference?

3. If you know the circumference of a circle, what should you do to find the circle's diameter?

Try This

Find the circumference of each circle. Use 3.14 as an estimate for π.

1.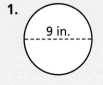
9 in.

2.
5 ft

3.
10 cm

Circles and Circumference

California Standards

MG1.1 Understand the concept of a constant such as π; know the formulas for the circumference and area of a circle.

Also covered: **AF1.1, AF3.1, AF3.2, MG1.2**

Who uses this? You can determine the circumference of a circular floor. (See Example 2.)

A **circle** is the set of all points in a plane that are the same distance from a given point, called the **center** .

Vocabulary
circle
center
radius (radii)
diameter
circumference
pi

Diameter
A line segment that passes through the center of the circle and has both endpoints on the circle.

Circumference
The distance around a circle.

Center A circle is named by its center.

Radius (plural radii) A line segment with one endpoint at the center of the circle and the other endpoint on the circle.

Notice that the length of the diameter is twice the length of the radius, $d = 2r$.

EXAMPLE 1 **Naming Parts of a Circle**

Name the circle, a diameter, and three radii.

The center is point O, so this is circle O.
$\overline{AB}$ is a diameter.
$\overline{OA}$, $\overline{OB}$, and $\overline{OC}$ are radii.

The ratio of the circumference to the diameter, $\frac{C}{d}$, is the same for any circle. This ratio is represented by the Greek letter π, which is read "**pi** ." The decimal representation of *pi* starts with 3.14159265 . . . and goes on forever without repeating. Most people approximate π using either 3.14 or $\frac{22}{7}$.

Because $\frac{C}{d} = \pi$, you can multiply both sides of the equation by d to get a formula for circumference. You can also substitute $2r$ for d because $d = 2r$.

$$\frac{C}{d} = \pi$$
$$\frac{C}{d} \cdot d = \pi \cdot d$$
$$C = \pi d$$
$$C = \pi(2r) = 2\pi r$$

Circumference of a Circle	
Words	Formula
The circumference of any circle is equal to π times the diameter, or 2π times the radius.	$C = \pi d$ or $C = 2\pi r$

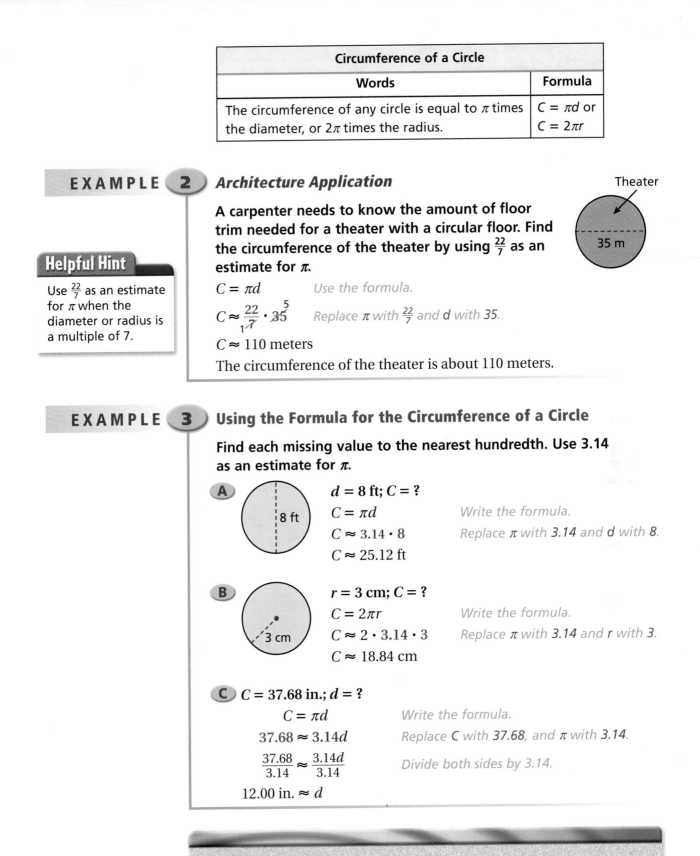

EXAMPLE 2 Architecture Application

A carpenter needs to know the amount of floor trim needed for a theater with a circular floor. Find the circumference of the theater by using $\frac{22}{7}$ as an estimate for π.

$C = \pi d$ *Use the formula.*

$C \approx \dfrac{22}{\underset{1}{7}} \cdot \overset{5}{\cancel{35}}$ *Replace π with $\frac{22}{7}$ and d with 35.*

$C \approx 110$ meters

The circumference of the theater is about 110 meters.

Theater

35 m

Helpful Hint

Use $\frac{22}{7}$ as an estimate for π when the diameter or radius is a multiple of 7.

EXAMPLE 3 Using the Formula for the Circumference of a Circle

Find each missing value to the nearest hundredth. Use 3.14 as an estimate for π.

A

8 ft

$d = 8$ ft; $C = ?$

$C = \pi d$ *Write the formula.*

$C \approx 3.14 \cdot 8$ *Replace π with 3.14 and d with 8.*

$C \approx 25.12$ ft

B

3 cm

$r = 3$ cm; $C = ?$

$C = 2\pi r$ *Write the formula.*

$C \approx 2 \cdot 3.14 \cdot 3$ *Replace π with 3.14 and r with 3.*

$C \approx 18.84$ cm

C $C = 37.68$ in.; $d = ?$

$C = \pi d$ *Write the formula.*

$37.68 \approx 3.14d$ *Replace C with 37.68, and π with 3.14.*

$\dfrac{37.68}{3.14} \approx \dfrac{3.14d}{3.14}$ *Divide both sides by 3.14.*

12.00 in. $\approx d$

Think and Discuss

1. **Explain** how to find the radius in Example 3C.

2. **Tell** whether rounding *pi* to 3 will result in an overestimation or an underestimation of the circumference of a circle.

California Standards Practice

AF3.1, MG1.1, MG1.2

go.hrw.com
Homework Help Online
KEYWORD: MS8CA 10-2
Parent Resources Online
KEYWORD: MS8CA Parent

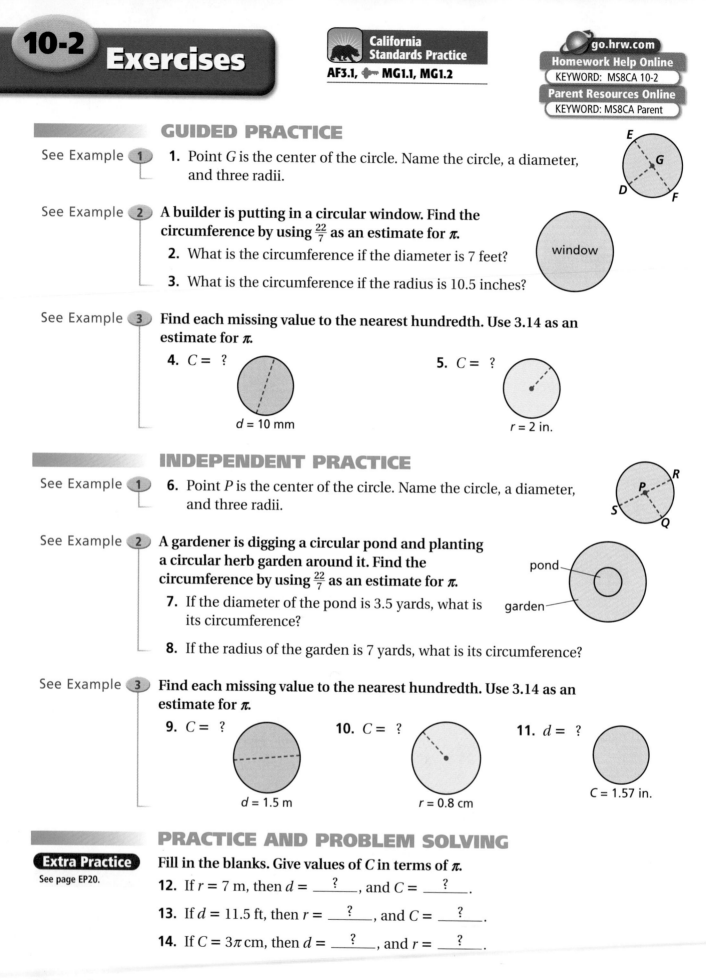

GUIDED PRACTICE

See Example **1**

1. Point G is the center of the circle. Name the circle, a diameter, and three radii.

See Example **2**

A builder is putting in a circular window. Find the circumference by using $\frac{22}{7}$ as an estimate for π.

2. What is the circumference if the diameter is 7 feet?

3. What is the circumference if the radius is 10.5 inches?

See Example **3**

Find each missing value to the nearest hundredth. Use 3.14 as an estimate for π.

4. $C =$?

$d = 10$ mm

5. $C =$?

$r = 2$ in.

INDEPENDENT PRACTICE

See Example **1**

6. Point P is the center of the circle. Name the circle, a diameter, and three radii.

See Example **2**

A gardener is digging a circular pond and planting a circular herb garden around it. Find the circumference by using $\frac{22}{7}$ as an estimate for π.

7. If the diameter of the pond is 3.5 yards, what is its circumference?

8. If the radius of the garden is 7 yards, what is its circumference?

See Example **3**

Find each missing value to the nearest hundredth. Use 3.14 as an estimate for π.

9. $C =$?

$d = 1.5$ m

10. $C =$?

$r = 0.8$ cm

11. $d =$?

$C = 1.57$ in.

PRACTICE AND PROBLEM SOLVING

Extra Practice
See page EP20.

Fill in the blanks. Give values of C in terms of π.

12. If $r = 7$ m, then $d =$ ___?___, and $C =$ ___?___.

13. If $d = 11.5$ ft, then $r =$ ___?___, and $C =$ ___?___.

14. If $C = 3\pi$ cm, then $d =$ ___?___, and $r =$ ___?___.

15. Measurement Draw a circle. Name the center *P* and make the radius 2 in. long.

    a. Draw the diameter $\overline{AB}$ and give its length.

    b. Find the circumference. Use 3.14 as an estimate for π. Round your answer to the nearest hundredth.

16. Recreation What is the circumference of a circular hoop with a 3 ft diameter? Use 3.14 as an estimate for π.

17. Forestry The circumference of the base of a giant sequoia tree is 91 feet. To the nearest foot, what is the diameter of the base of the tree?

18. How many times greater is the circumference of the top of the purple cylinder than the top of the blue cylinder?

radius = 6 cm   diameter = 4 cm

19. Reasoning If the circumference of a circle is 22.5 centimeters, which method can you use to find the radius?

   Ⓐ Divide 22.5 by π.

   Ⓑ Multiply 22.5 by π.

   Ⓒ Divide 22.5 by π and then divide the quotient by 2.

   Ⓓ Multiply 22.5 by π and then multiply the product by 2.

20. Write About It The circumference of a circle is 3.14 m. Explain how you can find the diameter and radius of the circle.

21. Challenge An Olympic outdoor archery target is made up of 10 equally spaced concentric circles. *Concentric* means that the center of each of the circles is the same. If the diameter of the largest circle on the target is 122 cm and the diameter of the smallest circle is 12.2 centimeters, what is the diameter of the fourth largest circle?

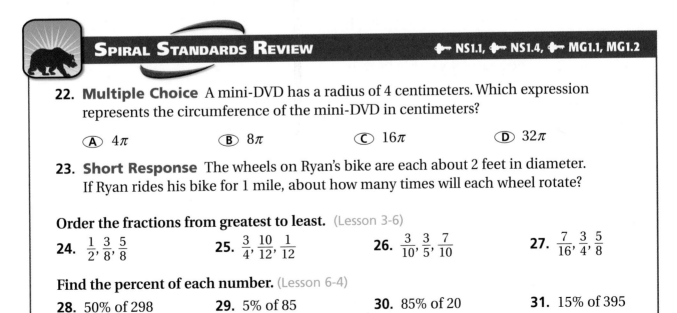

SPIRAL STANDARDS REVIEW   ✦ NS1.1, ✦ NS1.4, ✦ MG1.1, MG1.2

22. Multiple Choice A mini-DVD has a radius of 4 centimeters. Which expression represents the circumference of the mini-DVD in centimeters?

   Ⓐ 4π Ⓑ 8π Ⓒ 16π Ⓓ 32π

23. Short Response The wheels on Ryan's bike are each about 2 feet in diameter. If Ryan rides his bike for 1 mile, about how many times will each wheel rotate?

Order the fractions from greatest to least. (Lesson 3-6)

24. $\frac{1}{2}, \frac{3}{8}, \frac{5}{8}$ **25.** $\frac{3}{4}, \frac{10}{12}, \frac{1}{12}$ **26.** $\frac{3}{10}, \frac{3}{5}, \frac{7}{10}$ **27.** $\frac{7}{16}, \frac{3}{4}, \frac{5}{8}$

Find the percent of each number. (Lesson 6-4)

28. 50% of 298   **29.** 5% of 85   **30.** 85% of 20   **31.** 15% of 395

Hands-On

LAB
10-3

Explore Area of Parallelograms

Use with Lesson 10-3

The area of a rectangle can be found by multiplying its length ℓ by its width w. You can use a rectangle to find the area of other types of parallelograms.

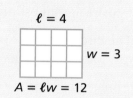

$\ell = 4$
$w = 3$
$A = \ell w = 12$

California Standards

AF3.2 Express in symbolic form simple relationships arising from geometry. *Also covered:* **AF3.1**

Activity

❶ On a sheet of graph paper, draw a parallelogram like the one shown.

❷ Cut out the parallelogram. Then cut a right triangle off the end of the parallelogram by cutting along the altitude.

❸ Move the triangle to the other side of the figure to make a rectangle.

❹ What are the length and width of the rectangle? What is the area of the rectangle?

❺ Find the area of the parallelogram.

❻ How is the area of the parallelogram related to the area of the rectangle?

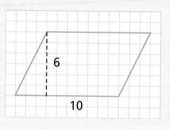

6
10

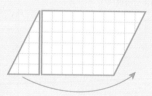

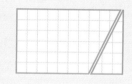

Think and Discuss

1. How are the length and width of the rectangle related to the base b and height h of the parallelogram?

2. Suppose a parallelogram has base b and height h. Write a formula for the area of the parallelogram.

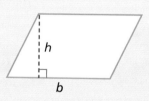

h
b

Try This

1. Show how to use your formula to find the area of the parallelogram at right.

2. Explain what must be true about the areas of the parallelograms below.

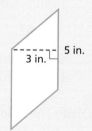

5 in.
3 in.

10-3 Area of Parallelograms

California Standards

AF3.1 Use variables in expressions describing geometric quantities (e.g., $P = 2w + 2\ell$, $A = \frac{1}{2}bh$, $C = \pi d$—the formulas for the perimeter of a rectangle, the area of a triangle, and the circumference of a circle, respectively).
Also covered: **NS2.1, ← AF1.1, AF2.1, AF3.2**

Vocabulary
area
base
height

Reading Math

Two lines or segments are *perpendicular* if they intersect to form right angles.

Why learn this? You can determine the number of square tiles needed to make a patio. (See Example 4.)

The **area** of a figure is the number of non-overlapping unit squares needed to cover the figure. Area is measured in square units.

The **base** of a parallelogram is the length of one side. Its **height** is the perpendicular distance from the base to the opposite side.

For a rectangle, the base is the same as the length, and the height is the same as the width.

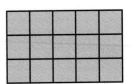

Area = 15 square units

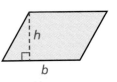

AREA OF PARALLELOGRAMS AND RECTANGLES		
Parallelograms The area A of a parallelogram is the product of its base b and height h.	5 3 $5 \cdot 3 = 15$ units²	$A = bh$
Rectangles The area A of a rectangle is the product of its length ℓ and width w.	5 3 $5 \cdot 3 = 15$ units²	$A = \ell w$

EXAMPLE 1 **Finding the Area of a Parallelogram**

Find the area of the parallelogram.

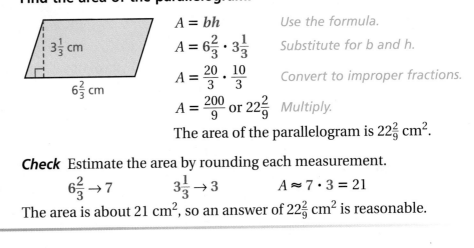

$3\frac{1}{3}$ cm

$6\frac{2}{3}$ cm

$A = bh$ *Use the formula.*

$A = 6\frac{2}{3} \cdot 3\frac{1}{3}$ *Substitute for b and h.*

$A = \frac{20}{3} \cdot \frac{10}{3}$ *Convert to improper fractions.*

$A = \frac{200}{9}$ or $22\frac{2}{9}$ *Multiply.*

The area of the parallelogram is $22\frac{2}{9}$ cm².

Check Estimate the area by rounding each measurement.

$6\frac{2}{3} \rightarrow 7$ $3\frac{1}{3} \rightarrow 3$ $A \approx 7 \cdot 3 = 21$

The area is about 21 cm², so an answer of $22\frac{2}{9}$ cm² is reasonable.

EXAMPLE **2** **Finding the Area of a Rectangle**

Find the area of the rectangle.

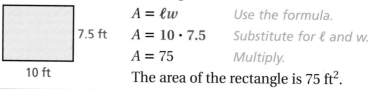

$A = \ell w$	*Use the formula.*
$A = 10 \cdot 7.5$	*Substitute for ℓ and w.*
$A = 75$	*Multiply.*

The area of the rectangle is 75 ft².

EXAMPLE **3** **Finding Length or Width of a Rectangle**

Bethany and her dad are planting a rectangular garden. The area of the garden is 1,080 ft², and the width is 24 ft. What is the length of the garden?

$A = \ell w$ *Use the formula for the area of a rectangle.*

$1{,}080 = \ell \cdot 24$ *Substitute 1,080 for A and 24 for w.*

$\dfrac{1{,}080}{24} = \dfrac{\ell \cdot 24}{24}$ *Divide both sides by 24 to isolate ℓ.*

$45 = \ell$

The length of the garden is 45 ft.

EXAMPLE **4** **Landscaping Application**

🔵 **Reasoning**

Birgit and Mark are building a rectangular patio measuring 9 yd by 7 yd. How many square feet of tile will they need?

Step 1: Draw and label a diagram.

Step 2: Convert the units.

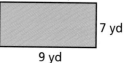

The patio is measured in yards, but the answer should be in square feet.

$9 \ \text{yd} \cdot \dfrac{3 \ \text{ft}}{1 \ \text{yd}} = 27 \ \text{ft}$ *Convert yards to feet by multiplying by a ratio equal to 1.*

$7 \ \text{yd} \cdot \dfrac{3 \ \text{ft}}{1 \ \text{yd}} = 21 \ \text{ft}$

Step 3: Find the area of the patio in square feet.

$A = \ell w$ *Use the formula for the area of a rectangle.*

$A = 27 \cdot 21$ *Substitute 27 for ℓ and 21 for w.*

$A = 567$ *Multiply.*

Birgit and Mark need 567 ft² of tile.

Think and Discuss

1. Write a formula for the area of a square, using an exponent.

2. Explain why the area of a nonrectangular parallelogram with side lengths 5 in. and 3 in. is not 15 in².

10-3 **Exercises**

California Standards Practice
NS2.1, AF2.1, AF3.1, AF3.2

go.hrw.com
Homework Help Online
KEYWORD: MS8CA 10-3
Parent Resources Online
KEYWORD: MS8CA Parent

GUIDED PRACTICE

See Example 1 Find the area of each parallelogram.

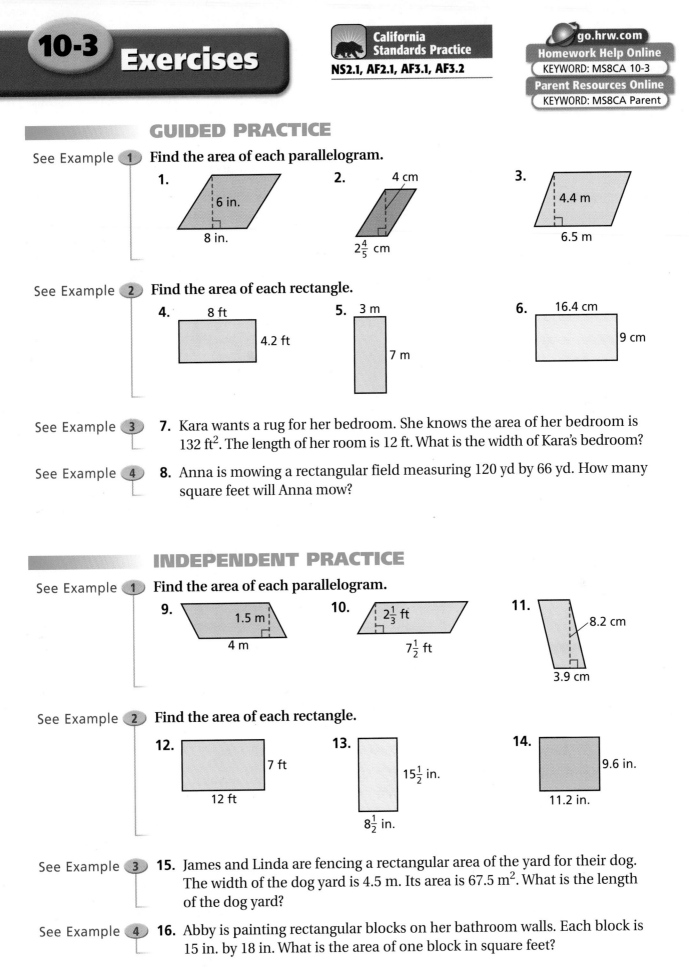

1.

6 in.

8 in.

2.

4 cm

$2\frac{4}{5}$ cm

3.

4.4 m

6.5 m

See Example 2 Find the area of each rectangle.

4.

8 ft

4.2 ft

5.

3 m

7 m

6.

16.4 cm

9 cm

See Example 3 **7.** Kara wants a rug for her bedroom. She knows the area of her bedroom is 132 ft². The length of her room is 12 ft. What is the width of Kara's bedroom?

See Example 4 **8.** Anna is mowing a rectangular field measuring 120 yd by 66 yd. How many square feet will Anna mow?

INDEPENDENT PRACTICE

See Example 1 Find the area of each parallelogram.

9.

1.5 m

4 m

10.

$2\frac{1}{3}$ ft

$7\frac{1}{2}$ ft

11.

8.2 cm

3.9 cm

See Example 2 Find the area of each rectangle.

12.

7 ft

12 ft

13.

$15\frac{1}{2}$ in.

$8\frac{1}{2}$ in.

14.

9.6 in.

11.2 in.

See Example 3 **15.** James and Linda are fencing a rectangular area of the yard for their dog. The width of the dog yard is 4.5 m. Its area is 67.5 m². What is the length of the dog yard?

See Example 4 **16.** Abby is painting rectangular blocks on her bathroom walls. Each block is 15 in. by 18 in. What is the area of one block in square feet?

PRACTICE AND PROBLEM SOLVING

Extra Practice
See page EP20.

Fill in the blanks.

17. rectangle: $\ell = 9$ yd; $w =$ ___?___ ; $A = 72$ yd^2

18. parallelogram: $b =$ ___?___ ; $h = 4.2$ m; $A = 29.4$ m^2

Graph the polygon with the given vertices. Then find the area of the polygon.

19. $(2, 0), (2, -2), (9, 0), (9, -2)$

20. $(4, 1), (4, 7), (8, 4), (8, 10)$

21. Art Without the frame, the painting *Havana Player* by Christian Pierre measures about 16 in. by 20 in. The width of the frame is $3\frac{1}{2}$ in.

   a. What is the area of the painting?

   b. What is the perimeter of the painting?

   c. What is the total area covered by the painting and the frame?

22. What is the height of a parallelogram with an area of 66 in^2 and a base of 11 in.?

23. Choose a Strategy The area of a parallelogram is 84 cm^2. If the base is 5 cm longer than the height, what is the length of the base?

   Ⓐ 5 cm Ⓑ 7 cm Ⓒ 12 cm Ⓓ 14 cm

24. Write About It A rectangle and a parallelogram have sides that measure 3 m, 4 m, 3 m, and 4 m. Do the figures necessarily have the same area? Explain.

25. Challenge Two parallelograms have the same base length, but the height of the first is half that of the second. What is the ratio of the area of the first parallelogram to that of the second? What would the ratio be if both the height and the base of the first parallelogram were half those of the second?

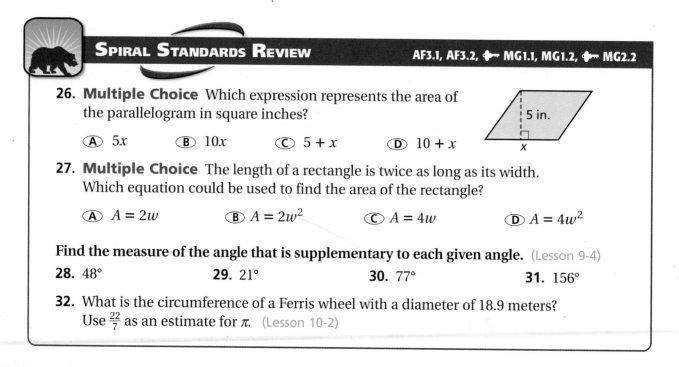

SPIRAL STANDARDS REVIEW

AF3.1, AF3.2, ✦ MG1.1, MG1.2, ✦ MG2.2

26. Multiple Choice Which expression represents the area of the parallelogram in square inches?

   Ⓐ $5x$ Ⓑ $10x$ Ⓒ $5 + x$ Ⓓ $10 + x$

5 in.

x

27. Multiple Choice The length of a rectangle is twice as long as its width. Which equation could be used to find the area of the rectangle?

   Ⓐ $A = 2w$ Ⓑ $A = 2w^2$ Ⓒ $A = 4w$ Ⓓ $A = 4w^2$

Find the measure of the angle that is supplementary to each given angle. (Lesson 9-4)

28. 48°   **29.** 21°   **30.** 77°   **31.** 156°

32. What is the circumference of a Ferris wheel with a diameter of 18.9 meters? Use $\frac{22}{7}$ as an estimate for π. (Lesson 10-2)

Explore Area of Triangles and Trapezoids

Use with Lesson 10-4

California Standards

AF3.2 Express in symbolic form simple relationships arising from geometry.
Also covered: **AF3.1**

You can use a parallelogram to find the area of a triangle or trapezoid.

Activity 1

1. On a sheet of graph paper, draw a triangle with a base of 7 units and a height of 4 units.

2. Cut out the triangle. Then use the triangle to trace and cut out a second triangle that is congruent to it. Arrange the two triangles to form a parallelogram.

3. Compare the areas of the triangle and the parallelogram.

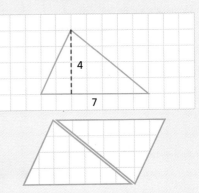

Think and Discuss

1. How are the base and height of the triangle related to the base and height of the parallelogram? Write a formula for the area of the triangle at right.

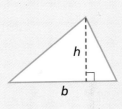

Try This

1. Find the area of a triangle with a base of 10 and a height of 5.

Activity 2

1. On a sheet of graph paper, draw a trapezoid with bases 4 units and 8 units long and a height of 3 units.

2. Cut out the trapezoid. Then use the trapezoid to trace and cut out a second trapezoid that is congruent to it. Arrange the two trapezoids to form a parallelogram.

3. Compare the areas of the trapezoid and the parallelogram.

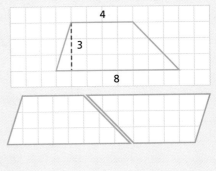

Think and Discuss

1. What is the length of the base of the parallelogram at right? What is the parallelogram's area? What is the area of one of the trapezoids?

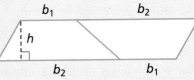

Try This

1. Find the area of a trapezoid with bases 4 and 6 and a height of 8.

10-4 Area of Triangles and Trapezoids

California Standards

AF3.1 Use variables in expressions describing geometric quantities (e.g., $P = 2w + 2\ell$, $A = \frac{1}{2}bh$, $C = \pi d$—the formulas for the perimeter of a rectangle, **the area of a triangle**, and the circumference of a circle, respectively). *Also covered:* **AF1.2, AF3.2**

Why learn this? You can use the area of triangles and trapezoids to approximate the area of some states. (See Example 3.)

The base of a triangle can be any side. The height of a triangle is the perpendicular distance from the line containing the base to the opposite vertex.

You can divide any parallelogram into two congruent triangles. The area of each triangle is half the area of the parallelogram.

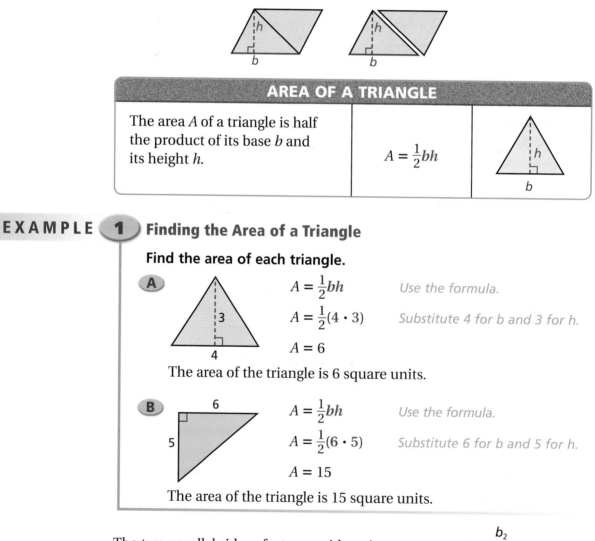

AREA OF A TRIANGLE		
The area A of a triangle is half the product of its base b and its height h.	$A = \frac{1}{2}bh$	

EXAMPLE 1 Finding the Area of a Triangle

Find the area of each triangle.

A

$A = \frac{1}{2}bh$ *Use the formula.*

$A = \frac{1}{2}(4 \cdot 3)$ *Substitute 4 for b and 3 for h.*

$A = 6$

The area of the triangle is 6 square units.

B

$A = \frac{1}{2}bh$ *Use the formula.*

$A = \frac{1}{2}(6 \cdot 5)$ *Substitute 6 for b and 5 for h.*

$A = 15$

The area of the triangle is 15 square units.

The two parallel sides of a trapezoid are its bases, b_1 and b_2. The height of a trapezoid is the perpendicular distance between the bases.

You can form a parallelogram from any two congruent trapezoids. The parallelogram has a base of $b_1 + b_2$ and a height of h. The area of each trapezoid is half the area of the parallelogram.

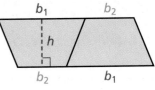

AREA OF A TRAPEZOID		
The area of a trapezoid is half its height multiplied by the sum of the lengths of its two bases.	$A = \frac{1}{2}h(b_1 + b_2)$	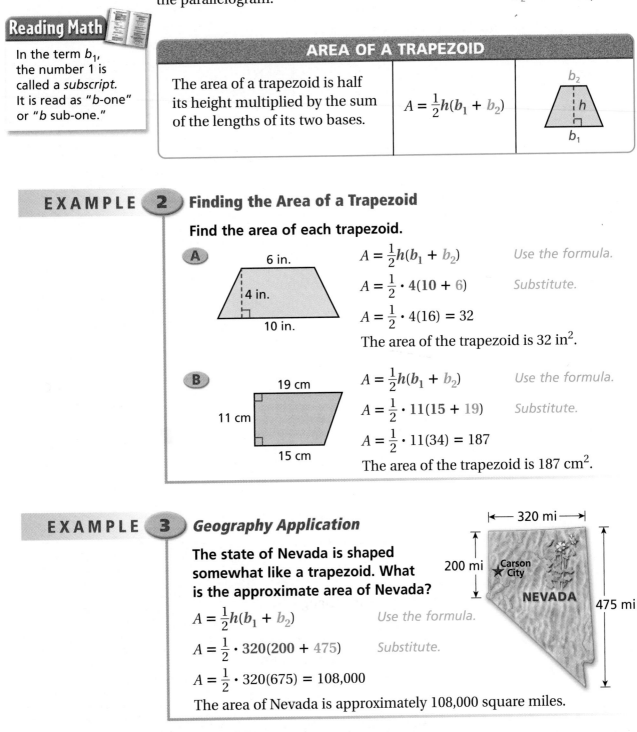

EXAMPLE 2 **Finding the Area of a Trapezoid**

Find the area of each trapezoid.

A

6 in.
4 in.
10 in.

$A = \frac{1}{2}h(b_1 + b_2)$ *Use the formula.*

$A = \frac{1}{2} \cdot 4(10 + 6)$ *Substitute.*

$A = \frac{1}{2} \cdot 4(16) = 32$

The area of the trapezoid is 32 in^2.

B

19 cm
11 cm
15 cm

$A = \frac{1}{2}h(b_1 + b_2)$ *Use the formula.*

$A = \frac{1}{2} \cdot 11(15 + 19)$ *Substitute.*

$A = \frac{1}{2} \cdot 11(34) = 187$

The area of the trapezoid is 187 cm^2.

EXAMPLE 3 *Geography Application*

The state of Nevada is shaped somewhat like a trapezoid. What is the approximate area of Nevada?

320 mi
200 mi
Carson City
NEVADA
475 mi

$A = \frac{1}{2}h(b_1 + b_2)$ *Use the formula.*

$A = \frac{1}{2} \cdot 320(200 + 475)$ *Substitute.*

$A = \frac{1}{2} \cdot 320(675) = 108,000$

The area of Nevada is approximately 108,000 square miles.

Think and Discuss

1. Explain how to find the area of a trapezoid.

10-4
Exercises

California
Standards Practice
AF3.1, AF3.2

go.hrw.com
Homework Help Online
KEYWORD: MS8CA 10-4
Parent Resources Online
KEYWORD: MS8CA Parent

GUIDED PRACTICE

See Example ① **Find the area of each triangle.**

1.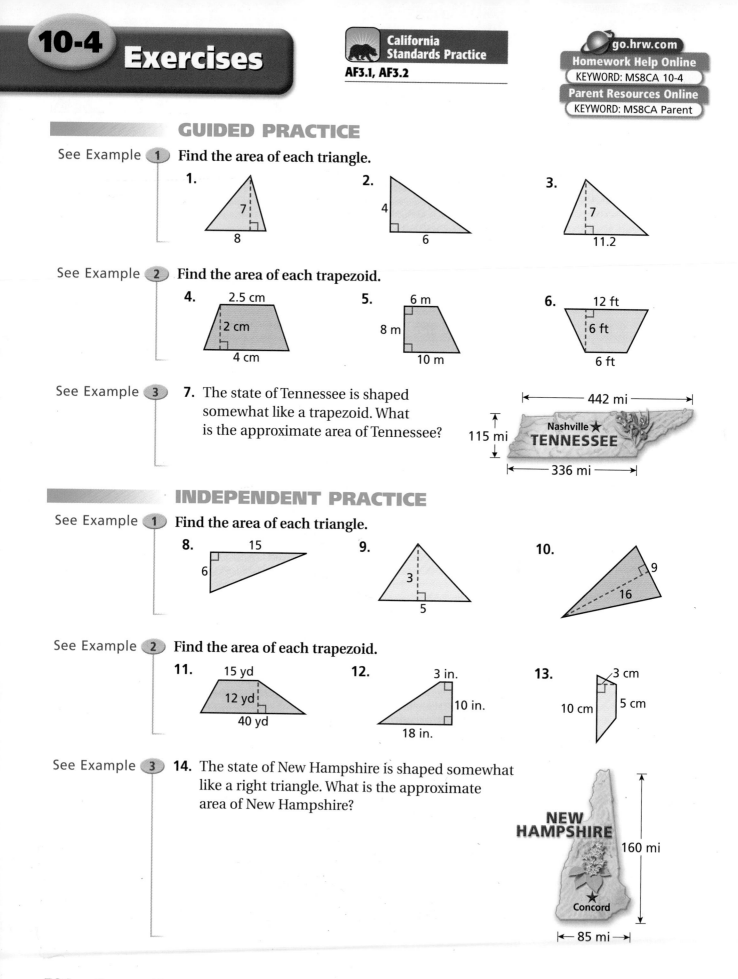
7
8

2.
4
6

3.
7
11.2

See Example ② **Find the area of each trapezoid.**

4.
2.5 cm
2 cm
4 cm

5.
6 m
8 m
10 m

6.
12 ft
6 ft
6 ft

See Example ③ **7.** The state of Tennessee is shaped somewhat like a trapezoid. What is the approximate area of Tennessee?

442 mi
Nashville ★
TENNESSEE
115 mi
336 mi

INDEPENDENT PRACTICE

See Example ① **Find the area of each triangle.**

8.
15
6

9.
3
5

10.
9
16

See Example ② **Find the area of each trapezoid.**

11.
15 yd
12 yd
40 yd

12.
3 in.
10 in.
18 in.

13.
3 cm
10 cm
5 cm

See Example ③ **14.** The state of New Hampshire is shaped somewhat like a right triangle. What is the approximate area of New Hampshire?

NEW HAMPSHIRE
160 mi
Concord
85 mi

PRACTICE AND PROBLEM SOLVING

Extra Practice
See page EP20.

Find the missing measurement of each triangle.

15. $b = 8$ cm
$h = $ ▨
$A = 18$ cm^2

16. $b = 16$ ft
$h = 0.7$ ft
$A = $ ▨

17. $b = $ ▨
$h = 95$ in.
$A = 1,045$ in^2

Graph the polygon with the given vertices. Then find the area of the polygon.

18. (1, 2), (4, 5), (8, 2), (8, 5)

19. (1, −6), (5, −1), (7, −6)

20. (2, 3), (2, 10), (7, 6), (7, 8)

21. (3, 0), (3, 4), (−3, 0)

22. What is the height of a trapezoid with an area of 9 m^2 and bases that measure 2.4 m and 3.6 m?

23. Multi-Step The state of Colorado is somewhat rectangular in shape. Estimate the perimeter and area of Colorado.

24. What's the Error? A student says the area of the triangle shown at right is 33 cm^2. Explain why the student is incorrect.

25. Write About It Explain how to use the formulas for the area of a rectangle and the area of a triangle to estimate the area of Nevada. (See Example 3.)

26. Challenge The state of North Dakota is trapezoidal in shape and has an area of 70,704 mi^2. If the southern border is 359 mi and the distance between the northern border and the southern border is 210 mi, what is the approximate length of the northern border?

SPIRAL STANDARDS REVIEW

AF3.1, AF3.2, ◆ MG2.2

27. Multiple Choice Which expression represents the area of the trapezoid in square centimeters?

Ⓐ $4x$ Ⓒ $15x$

Ⓑ $8x$ Ⓓ $16x$

28. Short Response Find the height of a triangle with an area of 54 in^2 and a base of 12 in. Show how you used a formula to determine your answer.

Find the measure of the third angle in each triangle, given two angle measures. (Lesson 9-7)

29. 45°, 45°

30. 71°, 57°

31. 103°, 28°

32. 62°, 19°

33. Write an expression for the perimeter of a rectangle with a length of ℓ cm and a width of 18 cm. (Lesson 10-1)

California Standards

MG1.2 Know common estimates of π (3.14; $\frac{22}{7}$) and use these values to estimate and calculate the circumference and the area of circles; compare with actual measurements.
Also covered: **AF3.1, AF3.2,** **MG1.1**

Why learn this? You can determine the area of a circular rug. (See Example 3.)

A circle can be cut into equal-sized sections and arranged to resemble a parallelogram. The smaller the sections, the more closely the resulting figure resembles a parallelogram. The height h of the parallelogram is equal to the radius r of the circle, and the base b of the parallelogram is equal to one-half the circumference C of the circle. So the area of the parallelogram can be written as follows:

$$A = bh, \text{ or } A = \frac{1}{2}Cr$$

$$A = \frac{1}{2}(2\pi r)r \qquad \textit{Because } C = 2\pi r, \textit{ substitute } 2\pi r \textit{ for } C.$$

$$A = \pi r^2$$

AREA OF A CIRCLE		
The area A of a circle is the product of π and the square of the circle's radius r.	$A = \pi r^2$	

EXAMPLE 1 *Estimation Application*

Reasoning

Remember!

The order of operations calls for evaluating the exponents before multiplying.

Find the area of the circle by using a formula. Then use an estimate to check whether your answer is reasonable.

$A = \pi r^2$ *Use the formula.*

$A \approx 3.14 \cdot 4^2$ *Use 3.14 as an estimate for π, and use 4 for r.*

$A \approx 3.14 \cdot 16$ *Evaluate the power.*

$A \approx 50.24$ square units   *Multiply.*

Check Use the grid to estimate the area.
$32 + 20 = 52$ square units   **32** *squares are completely inside the circle.*
                                     20 *squares are mostly inside the circle.*
Because 52 is close to 50.24, an answer of 50.24 square units is reasonable.

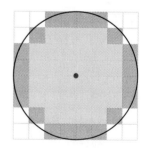

EXAMPLE 2 Finding the Area of a Circle

Find the area of each circle to the nearest tenth. Use 3.14 as an estimate for π.

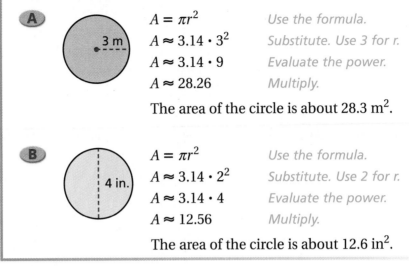

A

3 m

$A = \pi r^2$ *Use the formula.*

$A \approx 3.14 \cdot 3^2$ *Substitute. Use 3 for r.*

$A \approx 3.14 \cdot 9$ *Evaluate the power.*

$A \approx 28.26$ *Multiply.*

The area of the circle is about 28.3 m^2.

B

4 in.

$A = \pi r^2$ *Use the formula.*

$A \approx 3.14 \cdot 2^2$ *Substitute. Use 2 for r.*

$A \approx 3.14 \cdot 4$ *Evaluate the power.*

$A \approx 12.56$ *Multiply.*

The area of the circle is about 12.6 in^2.

EXAMPLE 3 *Social Studies Application*

Social Studies

Nomads in Mongolia carried their homes wherever they roamed. These homes, called *yurts*, were made of wood and felt.

A group of historians are building a yurt to display at a local multicultural fair. The yurt has a height of 8 feet 9 inches at its center, and it has a circular floor of radius 7 feet. What is the area of a circular rug that will completely cover the floor of the yurt? Use $\frac{22}{7}$ as an estimate for π.

$A = \pi r^2$ *Use the formula for the area of a circle.*

$A \approx \frac{22}{7} \cdot 7^2$ *Substitute. Use 7 for r.*

$A \approx \frac{22}{\cancel{7}_1} \cdot \cancel{49}^7$ *Evaluate the power. Then simplify.*

$A \approx 22 \cdot 7$

$A \approx 154$ *Multiply.*

The area of a rug that will cover the floor of the yurt is about 154 ft^2.

Check Estimate the area by using compatible numbers.

$\pi \to 3$ $7^2 \to 50$ $A = \pi \cdot 7^2 \approx 3 \cdot 50 = 150$

The area is about 150 ft^2, so an answer of 154 ft^2 is reasonable.

Think and Discuss

1. Compare finding the area of a circle when given the radius with finding the area when given the diameter.

2. Give an example of a circular object in your classroom. Tell how you could estimate the area of the object, and then estimate.

10-5 Exercises

California
Standards Practice
AF3.1, ⟵ MG1.1, MG1.2

go.hrw.com
Homework Help Online
KEYWORD: MS8CA 10-5
Parent Resources Online
KEYWORD: MS8CA Parent

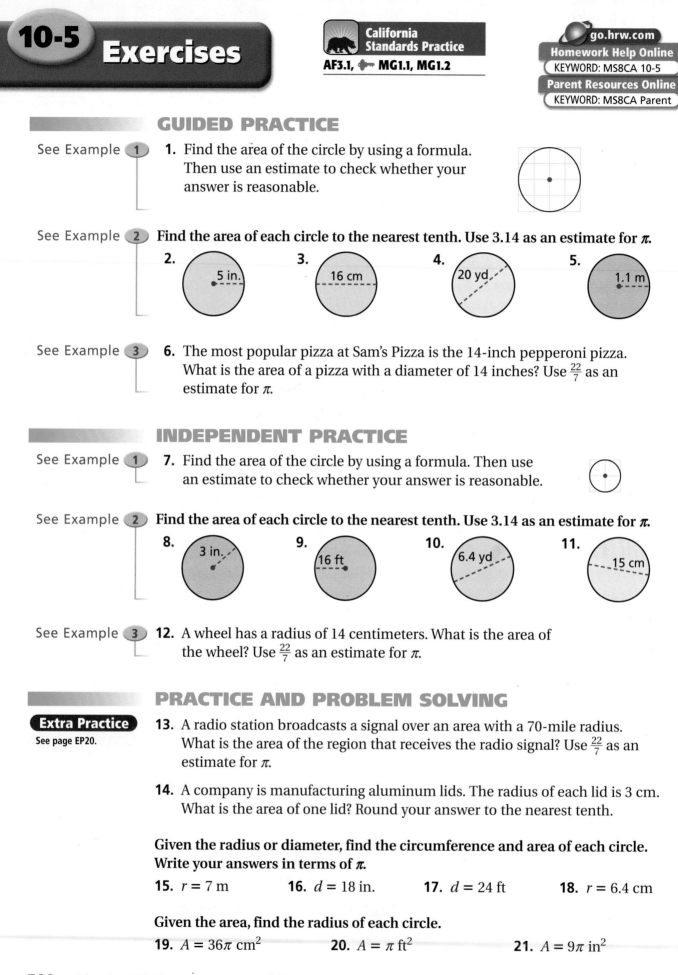

GUIDED PRACTICE

See Example ① 1. Find the area of the circle by using a formula. Then use an estimate to check whether your answer is reasonable.

See Example ② Find the area of each circle to the nearest tenth. Use 3.14 as an estimate for π.

2. 5 in.   3. 16 cm   4. 20 yd   5. 1.1 m

See Example ③ 6. The most popular pizza at Sam's Pizza is the 14-inch pepperoni pizza. What is the area of a pizza with a diameter of 14 inches? Use $\frac{22}{7}$ as an estimate for π.

INDEPENDENT PRACTICE

See Example ① 7. Find the area of the circle by using a formula. Then use an estimate to check whether your answer is reasonable.

See Example ② Find the area of each circle to the nearest tenth. Use 3.14 as an estimate for π.

8. 3 in.   9. 16 ft   10. 6.4 yd   11. 15 cm

See Example ③ 12. A wheel has a radius of 14 centimeters. What is the area of the wheel? Use $\frac{22}{7}$ as an estimate for π.

PRACTICE AND PROBLEM SOLVING

Extra Practice
See page EP20.

13. A radio station broadcasts a signal over an area with a 70-mile radius. What is the area of the region that receives the radio signal? Use $\frac{22}{7}$ as an estimate for π.

14. A company is manufacturing aluminum lids. The radius of each lid is 3 cm. What is the area of one lid? Round your answer to the nearest tenth.

Given the radius or diameter, find the circumference and area of each circle. Write your answers in terms of π.

15. $r = 7$ m   16. $d = 18$ in.   17. $d = 24$ ft   18. $r = 6.4$ cm

Given the area, find the radius of each circle.

19. $A = 36\pi$ cm^2 20. $A = \pi$ ft^2 21. $A = 9\pi$ in^2

22. A hiker was last seen near a fire tower in the Catalina Mountains. Searchers are sent to the surrounding area to find the missing hiker.

   a. Assume the hiker could walk in any direction at a rate of 3 miles per hour. How large an area would searchers have to cover if the hiker was last seen 2 hours ago? Use 3.14 as an estimate for π. Round your answer to the nearest square mile.

   b. How much additional area would the searchers have to cover if the hiker was last seen 3 hours ago?

23. Science The tower of a wind turbine is about the height of a 20-story building. Each turbine can produce 24 megawatt-hours of electricity in one day. Find the area covered by the blades of the turbine when they are rotating. Use 3.14 as an estimate for π. Round your answer to the nearest tenth.

187 ft

24. Reasoning Two circles have the same radius. Is the combined area of the two circles the same as the area of a circle with twice the radius?

25. What's the Question? Chang painted half of a free-throw circle that has a diameter of 12 ft. The answer is 56.52 ft². What is the question?

26. Write About It Describe how to find the area of a circle when given only the circumference of the circle.

27. Challenge How does the area of a circle change if you multiply the radius by a factor of *n*, where *n* is a whole number?

SPIRAL STANDARDS REVIEW   AF3.1, AF3.2, ➔ MG1.1, MG1.2, MG2.1

28. Multiple Choice A circle has a circumference of 10π feet. Which expression represents the area of the circle in square feet?

   (A) 20π (B) 25π (C) 100π (D) 400π

29. Short Response A pizza parlor offers a large pizza with a 12-inch diameter. It also offers a "mega" pizza with a 24-inch diameter. The slogan used to advertise the mega pizza is "Twice the pizza of a large, and twice the fun." Is the mega pizza twice as big as the large? If not, how much bigger is it? Explain.

Use the diagram to give an example of each type of angle pair. (Lesson 9-3)

30. vertical

31. adjacent

32. supplementary

33. Write an expression for the area of a triangle with a base of *b* inches and a height of 12 inches. (Lesson 10-4)

10-6 Area of Irregular and Composite Figures

California Standards

Extension of AF3.1 Use variables in expressions describing geometric quantities (e.g., $P = 2w + 2\ell$, $A = \frac{1}{2}bh$, $C = \pi d$—**the formulas for** the perimeter of a rectangle, **the area of a triangle**, and the circumference of a circle, respectively).
Also covered: **AF3.2, MG1.1, MG1.2**

Why learn this? You can determine how much carpet is needed to cover the floor of an unusually shaped closet. (See Example 3.)

A **composite figure** is made up of simple geometric shapes, such as triangles and rectangles. You can find the area of composite and other irregular figures by separating them into non-overlapping familiar figures. The sum of the areas of these figures is the area of the entire figure. You can also estimate the area of irregular figures by using graph paper.

EXAMPLE 1 Estimating the Area of an Irregular Figure

Vocabulary
composite figure

Estimate the area of the figure. Each square represents 1 ft².

Count the number of filled or almost-filled squares: 35 yellow squares.

Count the number of squares that are about half-filled: 6 blue squares.

Add the number of filled squares plus $\frac{1}{2}$ the number of half-filled squares: $35 + \left(\frac{1}{2} \cdot 6\right) = 35 + 3 = 38$.

The area of the figure is about 38 ft².

EXAMPLE 2 Finding the Area of a Composite Figure

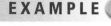

Find the area of the composite figure. Use 3.14 as an estimate for π.

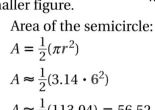

Step 1: Separate the figure into smaller, familiar figures.

Step 2: Find the area of each smaller figure.

Area of the square:	Area of the semicircle:
$A = s^2$	$A = \frac{1}{2}(\pi r^2)$
$A = 12^2 = 144$	$A \approx \frac{1}{2}(3.14 \cdot 6^2)$
	$A \approx \frac{1}{2}(113.04) = 56.52$

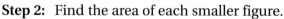

Helpful Hint

The area of a semicircle is $\frac{1}{2}$ the area of a circle.
$A = \frac{1}{2}(\pi r^2)$

Step 3: Add the areas to find the total area.
$$A \approx 144 + 56.52 = 200.52$$
The area of the composite figure is about 200.52 m².

EXAMPLE 3 **PROBLEM SOLVING APPLICATION**

Chandra wants to carpet the floor of her closet. A floor plan of the closet is shown at right. How much carpet does she need?

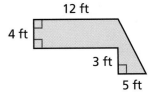

1 Understand the Problem

Rewrite the question as a statement:

- Find the amount of carpet needed to cover the floor of the closet.

List the **important information:**

- The floor of the closet is a composite figure.
- The amount of carpet needed is equal to the area of the floor.

Helpful Hint

There are often several different ways to separate a composite figure into familiar figures.

2 Make a Plan

Find the area of the floor by separating the figure into familiar figures: a rectangle and a triangle. Then add the areas of the rectangle and triangle to find the total area.

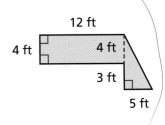

3 Solve

Find the area of each smaller figure.

Area of the rectangle:

$A = \ell w$

$A = 12 \cdot 4$

$A = 48 \text{ ft}^2$

Area of the triangle:

$A = \frac{1}{2}bh$

$A = \frac{1}{2}(5)(3 + 4)$

$A = \frac{1}{2}(35) = 17.5 \text{ ft}^2$

Add the areas to find the total area.

$A = 48 + 17.5 = 65.5$

Chandra needs 65.5 ft^2 of carpet.

4 Look Back

The area of the closet floor must be greater than the area of the rectangle (48 ft^2), so the answer is reasonable.

Think and Discuss

1. Describe two different ways to find the area of the composite figure at right.

2. Explain why the area of the figure at right must be less than 32 in^2.

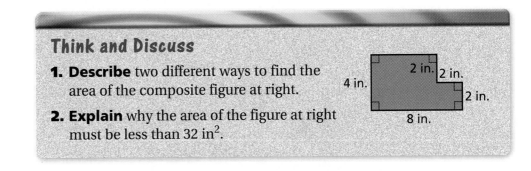

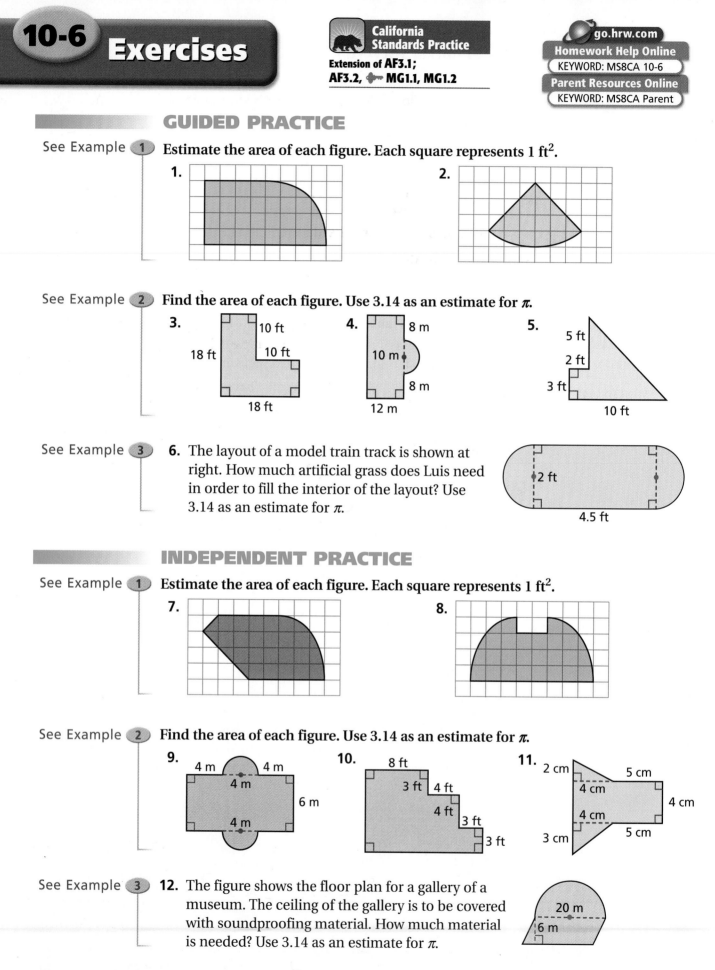

California
Standards Practice
Extension of AF3.1;
AF3.2, ━ MG1.1, MG1.2

go.hrw.com
Homework Help Online
KEYWORD: MS8CA 10-6
Parent Resources Online
KEYWORD: MS8CA Parent

GUIDED PRACTICE

See Example 1 Estimate the area of each figure. Each square represents 1 ft².

1.

2.

See Example 2 Find the area of each figure. Use 3.14 as an estimate for π.

3.
10 ft
18 ft   10 ft
18 ft

4.
8 m
10 m
8 m
12 m

5.
5 ft
2 ft
3 ft
10 ft

See Example 3 **6.** The layout of a model train track is shown at right. How much artificial grass does Luis need in order to fill the interior of the layout? Use 3.14 as an estimate for π.

2 ft
4.5 ft

INDEPENDENT PRACTICE

See Example 1 Estimate the area of each figure. Each square represents 1 ft².

7.

8.

See Example 2 Find the area of each figure. Use 3.14 as an estimate for π.

9.
4 m   4 m
4 m
6 m
4 m

10.
8 ft
3 ft 4 ft
4 ft
3 ft
3 ft

11.
2 cm   5 cm
4 cm
4 cm
4 cm
3 cm   5 cm

See Example 3 **12.** The figure shows the floor plan for a gallery of a museum. The ceiling of the gallery is to be covered with soundproofing material. How much material is needed? Use 3.14 as an estimate for π.

20 m
6 m

Find the area and perimeter of each figure. Use 3.14 as an estimate for π.

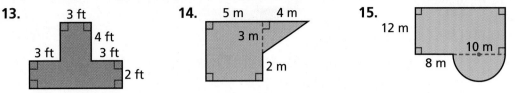

13. 3 ft, 4 ft, 3 ft, 3 ft, 2 ft

14. 5 m, 4 m, 3 m, 2 m

15. 12 m, 10 m, 8 m

16. **Multi-Step** A figure has vertices $A(-8, 5)$, $B(-4, 5)$, $C(-4, 2)$, $D(3, 2)$, $E(3, -2)$, $F(6, -2)$, $G(6, -4)$, and $H(-8, -4)$. Graph the figure on a coordinate plane. Then find the area and perimeter of the figure.

17. **Reasoning** The figure at right is made up of an isosceles triangle and a square. The perimeter of the figure is 44 feet. What is the value of x?

x ft, 7 ft, 7 ft

18. **Choose a Strategy** A figure is formed by combining a square and a triangle. Its total area is 32.5 m². The area of the triangle is 7.5 m². What is the length of each side of the square?

Ⓐ 5 m   Ⓑ 15 m   Ⓒ 16.25 m   Ⓓ 25 m

19. **Write About It** Describe how to find the area of the composite figure at right.

12 in., 5 in., 6 in., 4 in.

20. **Challenge** Find the area and perimeter of the figure at right. Use 3.14 as an estimate for π.

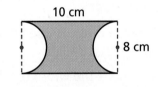

10 cm, 8 cm

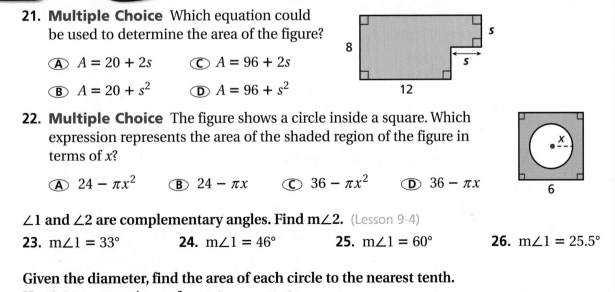

21. **Multiple Choice** Which equation could be used to determine the area of the figure?

Ⓐ $A = 20 + 2s$ Ⓒ $A = 96 + 2s$

Ⓑ $A = 20 + s^2$ Ⓓ $A = 96 + s^2$

8, s, s, 12

22. **Multiple Choice** The figure shows a circle inside a square. Which expression represents the area of the shaded region of the figure in terms of x?

Ⓐ $24 - \pi x^2$ Ⓑ $24 - \pi x$ Ⓒ $36 - \pi x^2$ Ⓓ $36 - \pi x$

x, 6

$\angle 1$ and $\angle 2$ are complementary angles. Find m$\angle 2$. (Lesson 9-4)

23. m$\angle 1 = 33°$ **24.** m$\angle 1 = 46°$ **25.** m$\angle 1 = 60°$ **26.** m$\angle 1 = 25.5°$

Given the diameter, find the area of each circle to the nearest tenth. Use 3.14 as an estimate for π. (Lesson 10-5)

27. $d = 30$ m   **28.** $d = 5.5$ cm   **29.** $d = 18$ in.   **30.** $d = 11$ ft

Quiz for Lessons 10-1 Through 10-6

10-1 **Perimeter**

Find the perimeter of each figure.

1.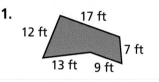

2.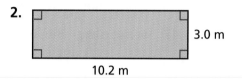

10-2 **Circles and Circumference**

3. What is the circumference of the circle? Use 3.14 as an estimate for π.

4. If the circumference of a wheel is 94 cm, what is its approximate diameter?

10-3 **Area of Parallelograms**

5. Find the area of the parallelogram.

6. The area of a rectangular courtyard is 1,508 m², and the length is 52 m. What is the width of the courtyard?

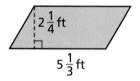

10-4 **Area of Triangles and Trapezoids**

7. Find the area of the trapezoid at right.

8. A triangle has an area of 45 cm² and a base of 12.5 cm. What is the height of the triangle?

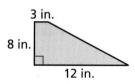

10-5 **Area of Circles**

9. Find the area of the circle to the nearest tenth. Use $\frac{22}{7}$ as an estimate for π.

10-6 **Area of Irregular and Composite Figures**

Find the area of each figure to the nearest tenth. Use 3.14 as an estimate for π.

10.

11.

12.

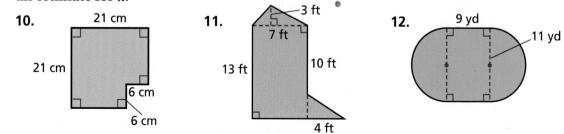

Focus on
Problem Solving

California Standards

MR3.2 Note the method of deriving the solution and demonstrate a conceptual understanding of the derivation by solving similar problems. *Also covered:* 🔑 **NS2.0, MR1.1**

Solve
• Choose the operation

Read the whole problem before you try to solve it. Determine what action is taking place in the problem. Then decide whether you need to add, subtract, multiply, or divide in order to solve the problem.

Action	Operation
Combining or putting together	Add
Removing or taking away Comparing or finding the difference	Subtract
Combining equal groups	Multiply
Sharing equally or separating into equal groups	Divide

Read each problem and determine the action taking place. Choose an operation, and then solve the problem.

1 There are 3 lily ponds in the botanical gardens. They are identical in size and shape. The total area of the ponds is 165 ft^2. What is the area of each lily pond?

2 The greenhouse is made up of 6 rectangular rooms with an area of $4,800 \text{ ft}^2$ each. What is the total area of the greenhouse?

3 A shady area with 17 different varieties of magnolia trees, which bloom from March to June, surrounds the plaza in Magnolia Park. In the center of the plaza, there is a circular bed of shrubs as shown in the diagram. If the total area of the park is 625 ft^2, what is the area of the plaza?

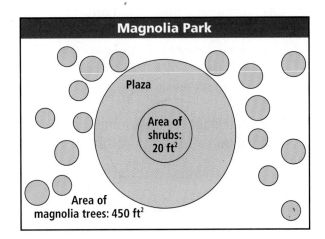

Magnolia Park

Plaza

Area of shrubs: 20 ft^2

Area of magnolia trees: 450 ft^2

Hands-On LAB 10-7

Explore Three-Dimensional Figures

Use with Lesson 10-7

go.hrw.com
Lab Resources Online
KEYWORD: MS8CA Lab10

REMEMBER
- Congruent figures have the same shape and size.
- A polygon is a closed plane figure formed by three or more sides. Each side meets exactly two other sides in a vertex.
- The radius of a circle is a line segment with one endpoint at the center of the circle and the other endpoint on the circle.

California Standards

Preparation for MG1.3 Know and use the formulas for the volume of triangular prisms and cylinders (area of base × height); compare these formulas and explain the similarity between them and the formula for the volume of a rectangular solid.

A *prism* is a three-dimensional figure with two parallel and congruent polygons called bases. The remaining edges join corresponding vertices of the bases so that the remaining surfaces are rectangles. You can use this definition to make models of prisms.

Activity 1

1 Use a straightedge and protractor to draw two equilateral triangles with side lengths of 4 centimeters on cardboard. Then cut them out. (*Hint:* Each angle of an equilateral triangle measures 60°.)

2 Cut out a rectangle from heavy paper that measures 12 centimeters by 6 centimeters. Fold the paper into thirds as shown.

3 Tape the edges of the triangles to the edges of the folded paper to form a prism.

4 Cut out two squares with side lengths of 3 centimeters from cardboard.

5 Cut out a rectangle from heavy paper that measures 12 centimeters by 6 centimeters. Fold the paper into fourths as shown.

6 Tape the edges of the squares to the edges of the folded paper to form a prism.

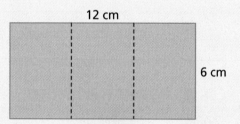

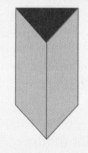

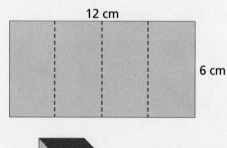

Think and Discuss

1. What shape are the bases of each prism that you modeled?

2. What shape are the other surfaces of each prism?

3. A prism is named for the shape of its bases. For example, a prism with rectangular bases is called a rectangular prism. Give the name of each prism you modeled.

4. How is the second prism you modeled different from the first prism? How are they alike?

Try This

Tell whether each figure below is a prism. Explain your answer.

1.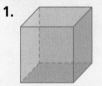

2.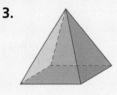

3.

A *cylinder* is a three-dimensional figure with two parallel congruent circular bases. The third surface of a cylinder consists of all parallel circles of the same radius whose centers lie on the line segment joining the centers of the bases. You can use this definition to model a cylinder.

Activity 2

1 Use a compass to draw at least 10 circles with a radius of 3 centimeters each on cardboard, and then cut them out.

2 Poke a hole through the center of each circle.

3 Straighten part of a paper clip and push it through the centers of the cardboard circles to make them model a cylinder. Use the paper clip to keep the stack of cardboard circles aligned.

Think and Discuss

1. Describe the bases of the cylinder.

2. How is your model of a cylinder different from your models of prisms? How are they the same?

Try This

Tell whether each figure below is a cylinder. Explain your answer.

1.

2.

3.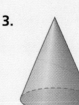

California Standards

Preparation for **MG1.3** Know and use the formulas for the volume of triangular prisms and cylinders (area of base × height); compare these formulas and explain the similarity between them and the formula for the volume of a rectangular solid.

Vocabulary
polyhedron
face
edge
vertex
cube
base

Why learn this? You can name and describe the surfaces of three-dimensional objects, such as sculptures.

A **polyhedron** is a three-dimensional object with flat surfaces, called **faces**, that are polygons.

When two faces of a three-dimensional figure share a side, they form an **edge**. A point at which three or more edges meet is a **vertex** (plural: *vertices*).

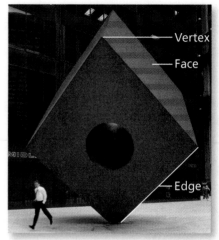

This sculpture, *Red Cube*, in front of a bank in New York City, was created by Isamu Noguchi.

A **cube** is formed by 6 congruent square faces. It has 8 vertices and 12 edges. The sculpture in front of this building is based on a cube. The artist's work is not a polyhedron because of the hole cut through the middle.

EXAMPLE 1 Identifying Faces, Edges, and Vertices

Identify the number of faces, edges, and vertices on each three-dimensional figure.

A
5 faces
9 edges
6 vertices

B
6 faces
12 edges
8 vertices

Two types of polyhedrons are *prisms* and *pyramids*. Prisms and pyramids are named for the shape of their bases. A **base** of a three-dimensional figure is a face by which the figure is measured or classified.

Helpful Hint

The bottom face of a prism is not always one of its bases. For example, the bottom face of the triangular prism in Example 1A is not one of its triangular bases.

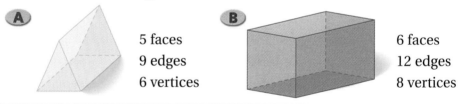

PRISMS	PYRAMIDS
• Two parallel congruent bases that are polygons • Remaining faces are rectangles	• One base that is a polygon • Remaining faces are triangles

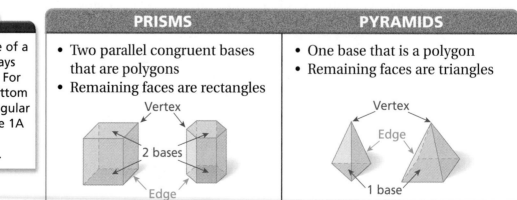

Other three-dimensional figures include *cylinders* and *cones*. These figures are not polyhedrons because their surfaces are not polygons.

CYLINDERS	CONES
• Two parallel congruent bases that are circles • Bases connected by a curved surface 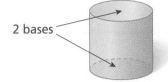2 bases	• One base that is a circle • Curved surface that comes to a point 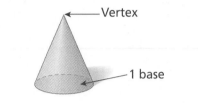Vertex 1 base

EXAMPLE 2 Naming Three-Dimensional Figures

Name each three-dimensional figure represented by each object.

A

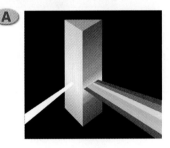

All the faces are flat and are polygons.

The figure is a polyhedron.

There are two congruent, parallel bases, so the figure is a prism.

The bases are triangles.

The figure is a triangular prism.

B

There is a curved surface.

The figure is not a polyhedron.

There is a flat, circular base.

The curved surface comes to a point.

The figure represents a cone.

C

All the faces are flat and are polygons.

The figure is a polyhedron.

It has one base and the other faces are triangles that meet at a point, so the figure is a pyramid.

The base is a square.

The figure is a square pyramid.

Think and Discuss

1. **Explain** how a pyramid and a prism are alike and how they are different.

2. **Explain** how a cone and a pyramid are alike and how they are different.

10-7 Exercises

California
Standards Practice
Preparation for MG1.3

go.hrw.com
Homework Help Online
KEYWORD: MS8CA 10-7
Parent Resources Online
KEYWORD: MS8CA Parent

GUIDED PRACTICE

See Example 1 Identify the number of faces, edges, and vertices on each three-dimensional figure.

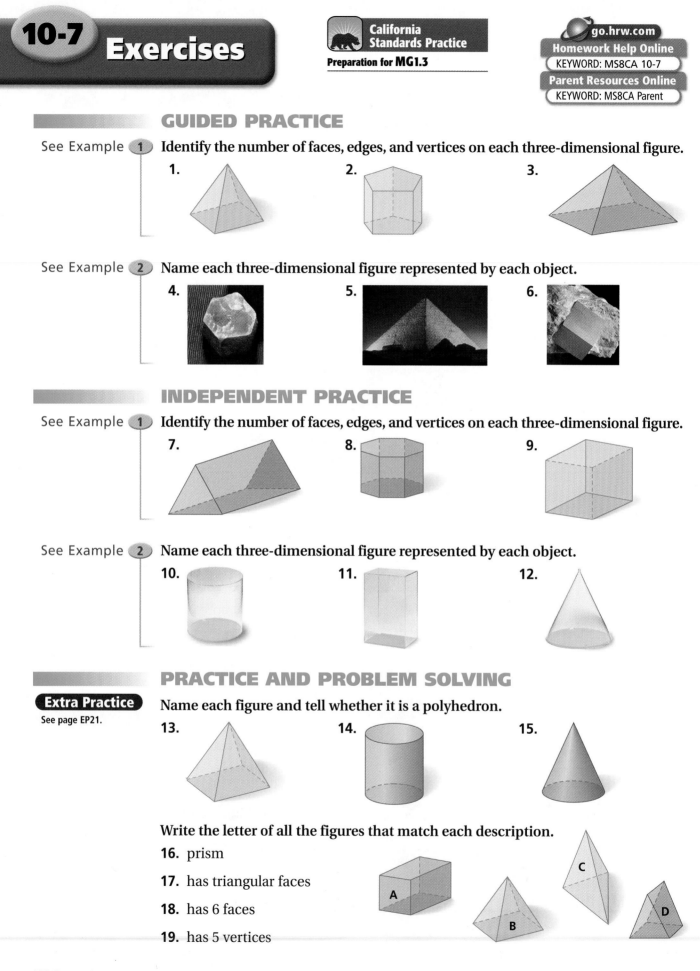

1.

2.

3.

See Example 2 Name each three-dimensional figure represented by each object.

4.

5.

6.

INDEPENDENT PRACTICE

See Example 1 Identify the number of faces, edges, and vertices on each three-dimensional figure.

7.

8.

9.

See Example 2 Name each three-dimensional figure represented by each object.

10.

11.

12.

PRACTICE AND PROBLEM SOLVING

Extra Practice
See page EP21.

Name each figure and tell whether it is a polyhedron.

13.

14.

15.

Write the letter of all the figures that match each description.

16. prism

17. has triangular faces

18. has 6 faces

19. has 5 vertices

Write *true* or *false* for each statement.

20. A cone does not have a flat surface.

21. The bases of a cylinder are congruent.

22. All pyramids have five or more vertices.

23. All of the edges of a cube are congruent.

24. Architecture Name the three-dimensional figure represented by each building.

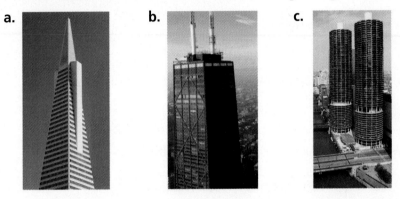

a. b. c.

25. Critical Thinking Li makes candles with her mother. She made a candle in the shape of a pyramid that had 9 faces. How many sides did the base of the candle have? Name the polyhedron formed by the candle.

26. What's the Error? A student says that any polyhedron can be named if the number of faces it has is known. What is the student's error?

27. Write About It How are a cone and cylinder alike? How are they different?

28. Challenge A square pyramid is cut in half, and the cut is made parallel to the base of the pyramid. What are the shapes of the faces of the bottom half of the pyramid?

SPIRAL STANDARDS REVIEW   NS1.1, MG2.3

29. Multiple Choice Which figure has the greatest number of faces?

Ⓐ Cone   Ⓑ Cube   Ⓒ Octagonal prism   Ⓓ Triangular prism

30. Multiple Choice Which figure has a circular base?

Ⓐ Cube   Ⓑ Cylinder   Ⓒ Square pyramid   Ⓓ Triangular prism

Compare. Write <, >, or =. (Lesson 3-6)

31. 9.04 ▒ 9.404   **32.** 12.7 ▒ 12.70   **33.** 0.03 ▒ 0.003   **34.** 5.12 ▒ 5.125

Draw each figure. If it is not possible to draw, explain why. (Lesson 9-8)

35. a quadrilateral with 4 right angles, but not all sides congruent

36. a parallelogram with 4 congruent sides, but no right angles

37. a trapezoid with 4 right angles

Explore Volume of Prisms and Cylinders

Use with Lessons 10-8 and 10-9

go.hrw.com
Lab Resources Online
KEYWORD: MS8CA Lab10

> **REMEMBER**
> • Volume is the number of cubic units needed to fill a space.

California Standards

MG1.3 Know and use the formulas for the volume of triangular prisms and cylinders (area of base × height); compare these formulas and explain the similarity between them and the formula for the volume of a rectangular solid. *Also covered:* **AF3.1, AF3.2**

You can use centimeter cubes to help you find the volume of a *prism*.

Activity 1

Use the steps and diagrams below to fill in the table.

	Length (ℓ)	Width (w)	Height (h)	Total Number of Cubes (V)
Figure A	▪	▪	▪	▪
Figure B	▪	▪	▪	▪
Figure C	▪	▪	▪	▪

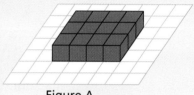

Figure A

1. Draw a 4 × 3 rectangle on centimeter graph paper. Place centimeter cubes on the rectangle. *(Figure A)* How many cubes did you use? What is the height of this prism?

2. Make a prism that is 2 units tall. *(Figure B)* How many cubes did you use?

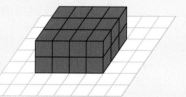

Figure B

3. Make a prism that is 5 units tall. *(Figure C)* How many cubes did you use?

Think and Discuss

1. How can you use the length, width, and height of a prism to find the total number of cubes without counting them?

2. Use your answer from Problem **1** to write a formula for the volume of a prism.

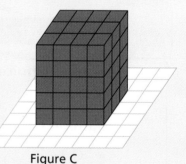

Figure C

3. When the height of the prism is doubled, what happens to the volume?

Try This

Build each rectangular prism and find its volume.

1. ℓ = 4; w = 2; h = 3   **2.** ℓ = 1; w = 4; h = 5   **3.** ℓ = 3; w = 3; h = 3   **4.** ℓ = 5; w = 10; h = 2

5. Estimate the volume of a shoe box. Fill it with centimeter cubes. How close was your estimate?

You can use graph paper and centimeter cubes to estimate the volume of a *cylinder*.

Activity 2

Use the steps below to fill in the table to estimate the volume of a can.

	Estimated Area of Base (A)	Height (h)	Volume (V)
Can	■	■	■

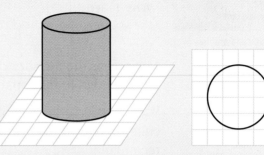

1. Trace around the bottom of a can on graph paper. Count the squares inside the circle to estimate the area *A* of the bottom of the can.

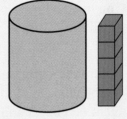

2. Use centimeter cubes to find the height of the can.

3. Use centimeter cubes to build a prism that covers the area of the circle and is the height of the can. Find the volume of the can by counting the cubes used to build the prism or by using $V = A \times h$.

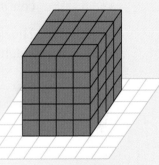

Think and Discuss

1. If you measure the radius of the base, what expression can you use to find the exact area of the circle?

2. Use the expression you found in Problem **1** to write a formula for the volume of a cylinder.

3. When the height of the cylinder is doubled, how does the volume change?

Try This

Estimate the volume of different-sized cans.

		Estimated Area of Base (A)	Height (h)	Volume (V)
1.	Tuna Can	■	■	■
2.		■	■	■
3.		■	■	■

10-8 Volume of Prisms

California Standards

MG1.3 Know and use the formulas for the volume of **triangular prisms** and cylinders **(area of base × height);** compare these formulas and **explain the similarity between them and the formula for the volume of a rectangular solid.**

Also covered: **AF3.1, AF3.2**

Vocabulary
volume

Why learn this? You can determine the volume of a tent. (See Example 3.)

Volume is the number of cubic units needed to fill a space.

You need 10, or 5 · 2, centimeter cubes to cover the bottom of this rectangular prism.

You need 3 layers of 10 cubes each to fill the prism. It takes 30, or 5 · 2 · 3, cubes.

Volume is expressed in cubic units, so the volume of the prism is 5 cm · 2 cm · 3 cm = 30 cubic centimeters, or 30 cm^3.

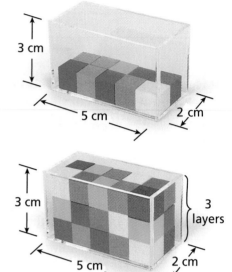

The volume of a rectangular prism is the area of its base times its height. This formula can be used to find the volume of any prism.

VOLUME OF A PRISM

The volume V of a prism is the area of its base B times its height h.

$$V = Bh$$

EXAMPLE 1 Finding the Volume of a Rectangular Prism

Math Builders

For more on volume of prisms, see the Volume Builder on page MB4.

Find the volume of the rectangular prism.
Step 1: Find the area of the base.

$B = 80 \cdot 36$	*The base is a rectangle.*
$B = 2{,}880$	*Multiply.*

Step 2: Find the volume.

$V = Bh$	*Write the formula.*
$V = 2{,}880 \cdot 20$	*Substitute for B and h.*
$V = 57{,}600$	*Multiply.*

The volume of the prism is 57,600 in^3.

You can also use the formula $V = Bh$ to find the volume of a triangular prism. For triangular prisms, B represents the area of a triangle, rather than a rectangle.

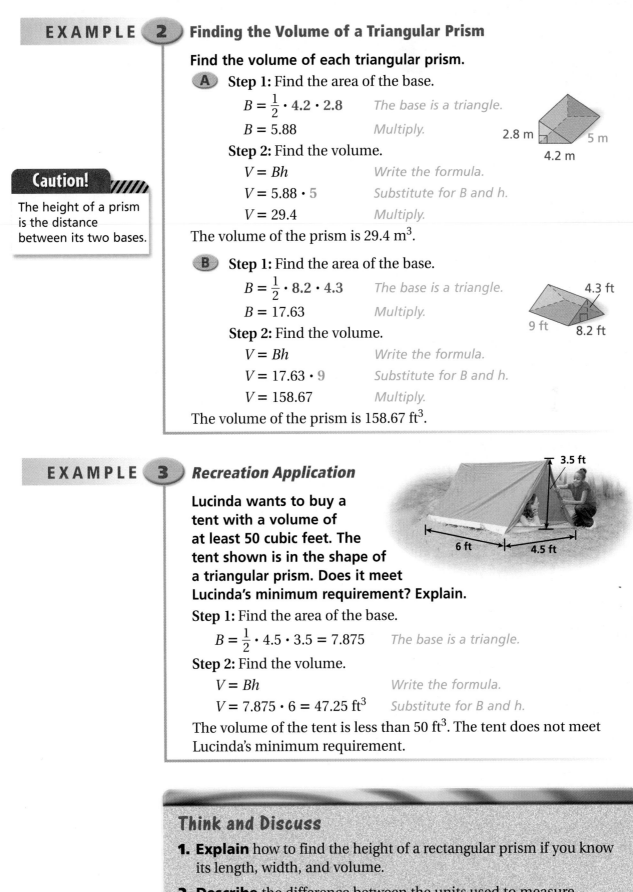

EXAMPLE 2   **Finding the Volume of a Triangular Prism**

Find the volume of each triangular prism.

A   **Step 1:** Find the area of the base.

$$B = \frac{1}{2} \cdot 4.2 \cdot 2.8 \qquad \textit{The base is a triangle.}$$

$$B = 5.88 \qquad \textit{Multiply.}$$

Step 2: Find the volume.

$$V = Bh \qquad \textit{Write the formula.}$$

$$V = 5.88 \cdot 5 \qquad \textit{Substitute for B and h.}$$

$$V = 29.4 \qquad \textit{Multiply.}$$

The volume of the prism is 29.4 m³.

2.8 m   5 m

4.2 m

Caution!

The height of a prism is the distance between its two bases.

B   **Step 1:** Find the area of the base.

$$B = \frac{1}{2} \cdot 8.2 \cdot 4.3 \qquad \textit{The base is a triangle.}$$

$$B = 17.63 \qquad \textit{Multiply.}$$

Step 2: Find the volume.

$$V = Bh \qquad \textit{Write the formula.}$$

$$V = 17.63 \cdot 9 \qquad \textit{Substitute for B and h.}$$

$$V = 158.67 \qquad \textit{Multiply.}$$

The volume of the prism is 158.67 ft³.

4.3 ft

9 ft   8.2 ft

EXAMPLE 3   *Recreation Application*

Lucinda wants to buy a tent with a volume of at least 50 cubic feet. The tent shown is in the shape of a triangular prism. Does it meet Lucinda's minimum requirement? Explain.

3.5 ft

6 ft   4.5 ft

Step 1: Find the area of the base.

$$B = \frac{1}{2} \cdot 4.5 \cdot 3.5 = 7.875 \qquad \textit{The base is a triangle.}$$

Step 2: Find the volume.

$$V = Bh \qquad \textit{Write the formula.}$$

$$V = 7.875 \cdot 6 = 47.25 \text{ ft}^3 \qquad \textit{Substitute for B and h.}$$

The volume of the tent is less than 50 ft³. The tent does not meet Lucinda's minimum requirement.

Think and Discuss

1. Explain how to find the height of a rectangular prism if you know its length, width, and volume.

2. Describe the difference between the units used to measure perimeter, area, and volume.

California Standards Practice
AF3.1, MG1.3

GUIDED PRACTICE

See Example ① Find the volume of each rectangular prism.

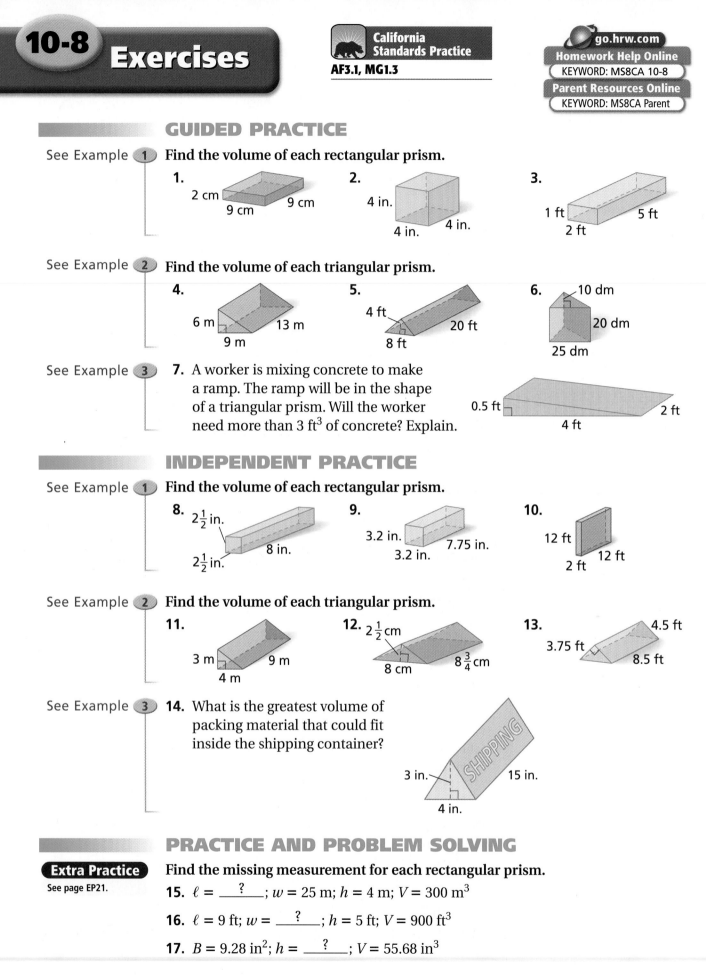

1. 2 cm, 9 cm, 9 cm

2. 4 in., 4 in., 4 in.

3. 1 ft, 2 ft, 5 ft

See Example ② Find the volume of each triangular prism.

4. 6 m, 9 m, 13 m

5. 4 ft, 8 ft, 20 ft

6. 10 dm, 20 dm, 25 dm

See Example ③ **7.** A worker is mixing concrete to make a ramp. The ramp will be in the shape of a triangular prism. Will the worker need more than 3 ft³ of concrete? Explain.

0.5 ft, 4 ft, 2 ft

INDEPENDENT PRACTICE

See Example ① Find the volume of each rectangular prism.

8. $2\frac{1}{2}$ in., 8 in., $2\frac{1}{2}$ in.

9. 3.2 in., 3.2 in., 7.75 in.

10. 12 ft, 2 ft, 12 ft

See Example ② Find the volume of each triangular prism.

11. 3 m, 4 m, 9 m

12. $2\frac{1}{2}$ cm, 8 cm, $8\frac{3}{4}$ cm

13. 4.5 ft, 3.75 ft, 8.5 ft

See Example ③ **14.** What is the greatest volume of packing material that could fit inside the shipping container?

3 in., 4 in., 15 in. SHIPPING

PRACTICE AND PROBLEM SOLVING

Extra Practice
See page EP21.

Find the missing measurement for each rectangular prism.

15. $\ell =$ ___?___ ; $w = 25$ m; $h = 4$ m; $V = 300$ m³

16. $\ell = 9$ ft; $w =$ ___?___ ; $h = 5$ ft; $V = 900$ ft³

17. $B = 9.28$ in²; $h =$ ___?___ ; $V = 55.68$ in³

The density of a substance is a measure of its mass per unit of volume. The density of a particular substance is always the same. The formula for density D is the mass m of a substance divided by its volume V, or $D = \frac{m}{V}$.

18. Find the volume of each substance in the table.

19. Calculate the density of each substance.

20. Water has a density of 1 g/cm³. A substance whose density is less than that of water will float. Which of the substances in the table will float in water?

21. A fresh egg has a density of approximately 1.2 g/cm³. A spoiled egg has a density of about 0.9 g/cm³. How can you tell whether an egg is fresh without cracking it open?

22. **Multi-Step** Alicia has a solid rectangular prism of a substance she believes is gold. The dimensions of the prism are 2 cm by 1 cm by 2 cm, and the mass is 20.08 g. Is the substance that Alicia has gold? Explain.

23. **Write About It** How is finding the volume of a triangular prism similar to finding the volume of a rectangular prism? How is it different?

24. ⭐ **Challenge** A solid rectangular prism of silver has a mass of 84 g. What are some possible dimensions of the prism?

Iron filings are attracted by a magnet.

Copper is used in color-coded telephone wires.

Rectangular Prisms				
Substance	Length (cm)	Width (cm)	Height (cm)	Mass (g)
Copper	2	1	5	89.6
Gold	$\frac{2}{3}$	$\frac{3}{4}$	2	19.32
Iron pyrite	0.25	2	7	17.57
Pine	10	10	3	120
Silver	2.5	4	2	210

Gold is used to make many pieces of jewelry.

25. **Multiple Choice** A triangular prism has a volume of 1,080 ft³. The area of the prism's base is 72 ft². What is the height of the prism?

    Ⓐ 15 ft   Ⓑ 120 ft   Ⓒ 135 ft   Ⓓ 77,760 ft

26. **Gridded Response** What is the volume, in cubic inches, of the prism shown?

3 in.   16 in.   3 in.

Find the GCD of each set of numbers. (Lesson 3-2)

27. 12, 18, 24   **28.** 15, 18, 30   **29.** 16, 24, 42   **30.** 18, 54, 63

California Standards

MG1.3 Know and use the formulas for the volume of triangular prisms and **cylinders** (area of base × height); compare these formulas and explain the similarity between them and the formula for the volume of a rectangular solid.
Also covered: **AF3.1, AF3.2**

Why learn this? You can determine the volume of a phonograph cylinder.

A phonograph is a machine used for playing recorded music. Thomas Edison invented the first phonograph in 1877. The main part of this phonograph was a cylinder.

To find the volume of a cylinder, you can use the same method as you did for prisms: Multiply the area of the base by the height. The area of the circular base is πr^2.

$$V = Bh$$
$$= \pi r^2 h$$

E X A M P L E **1** **Finding the Volume of a Cylinder**

Math Builders

For more on volume, see the Volume Builder on page MB4.

Find the volume V of each cylinder to the nearest cubic unit.

A 4 in. / 15 in.

$V = \pi r^2 h$	*Write the formula.*
$V \approx 3.14 \times 4^2 \times 15$	*Replace π with 3.14, r with 4, and h with 15.*
$V \approx 753.6$	*Multiply.*

The volume is about 754 in³.

B 6 ft / 18 ft

6 ft ÷ 2 = 3 ft	*Find the radius.*
$V = \pi r^2 h$	*Write the formula.*
$V \approx 3.14 \times 3^2 \times 18$	*Replace π with 3.14, r with 3, and h with 18.*
$V \approx 508.68$	*Multiply.*

The volume is about 509 ft³.

C $r = 5$ / $h = 24$ cm

$V = \pi r^2 h$	*Write the formula.*
$V \approx 3.14 \times 5^2 \times 24$	*Replace π with 3.14, r with 5, and h with 24.*
$V \approx 1,884$	*Multiply.*

The volume is about 1,884 cm³.

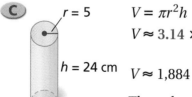

EXAMPLE **2** *Music Application*

The cylinder in Edison's first phonograph had a 4 in. diameter and a height of 3.375 in. The standard phonograph manufactured 21 years later had a 2 in. diameter and a height of 4 in. Estimate the volume of each cylinder to the nearest cubic inch.

Remember!

The value of *pi* can be approximated as 3.14 or $\frac{22}{7}$.

A Edison's first phonograph

4 in. ÷ 2 = 2 in.	*Find the radius.*
$V = \pi r^2 h$	*Write the formula.*
$V \approx 3.14 \times 2^2 \times 3.375$	*Replace π with 3.14, r with 2, and h with 3.375.*
$V \approx 42.39$	*Multiply.*

The volume of Edison's first phonograph was about 42 in³.

B Edison's standard phonograph

2 in. ÷ 2 = 1 in.	*Find the radius.*
$V = \pi r^2 h$	*Write the formula.*
$V \approx 3.14 \times 1^2 \times 4$	*Replace π with 3.14, r with 1, and h with 4.*
$V \approx 12.56$	*Multiply.*

The volume of the standard phonograph was about 13 in³.

EXAMPLE **3** **Comparing Volumes of Cylinders**

Find which cylinder has the greater volume.

Cylinder 1: $V = \pi r^2 h$
$V \approx 3.14 \times 6^2 \times 12$
$V \approx 1,356.48$ cm³

Cylinder 2: $V = \pi r^2 h$
$V \approx 3.14 \times 4^2 \times 16$
$V \approx 803.84$ cm³

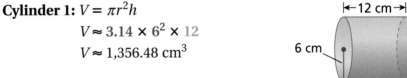

Cylinder 1 has the greater volume because 1,356.48 cm³ > 803.84 cm³.

Think and Discuss

1. Explain how the formula for the volume of a cylinder is similar to the formula for the volume of a rectangular prism.

2. Explain which parts of a cylinder are represented by πr^2 and h in the formula $V = \pi r^2 h$.

California
Standards Practice
AF3.1, MG1.3

go.hrw.com
Homework Help Online
KEYWORD: MS8CA 10-9
Parent Resources Online
KEYWORD: MS8CA Parent

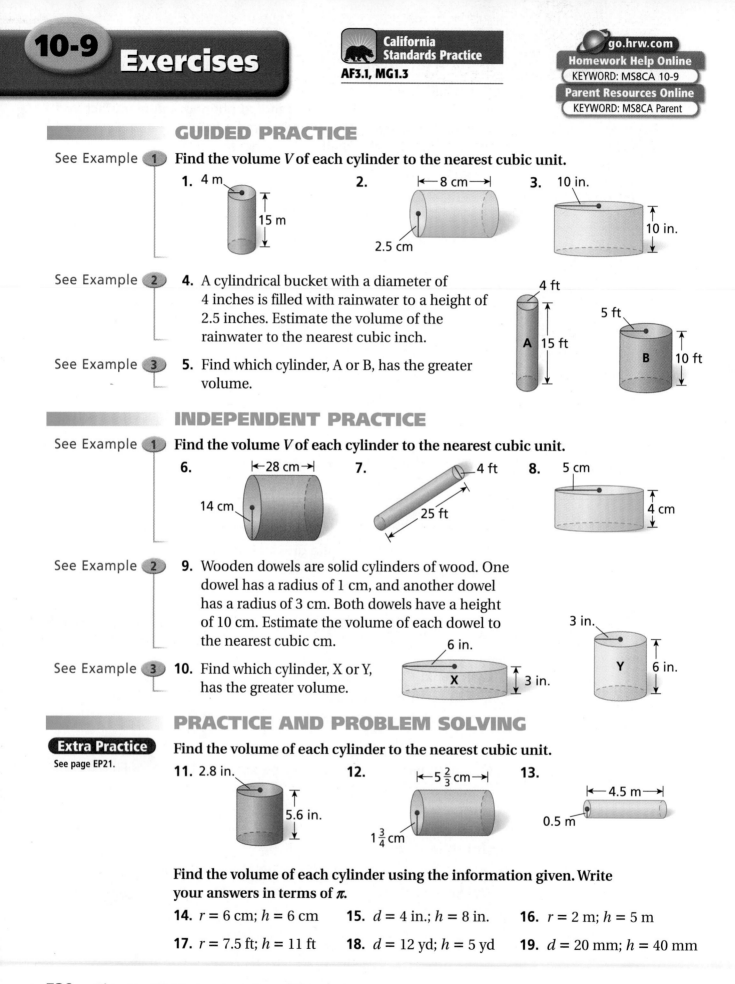

GUIDED PRACTICE

See Example **1** Find the volume V of each cylinder to the nearest cubic unit.

1. 4 m   15 m

2. 8 cm   2.5 cm

3. 10 in.   10 in.

See Example **2** **4.** A cylindrical bucket with a diameter of 4 inches is filled with rainwater to a height of 2.5 inches. Estimate the volume of the rainwater to the nearest cubic inch.

4 ft
A 15 ft

5 ft
B 10 ft

See Example **3** **5.** Find which cylinder, A or B, has the greater volume.

INDEPENDENT PRACTICE

See Example **1** Find the volume V of each cylinder to the nearest cubic unit.

6. 28 cm   14 cm

7. 4 ft   25 ft

8. 5 cm   4 cm

See Example **2** **9.** Wooden dowels are solid cylinders of wood. One dowel has a radius of 1 cm, and another dowel has a radius of 3 cm. Both dowels have a height of 10 cm. Estimate the volume of each dowel to the nearest cubic cm.

See Example **3** **10.** Find which cylinder, X or Y, has the greater volume.

6 in.
X 3 in.

3 in.
Y 6 in.

PRACTICE AND PROBLEM SOLVING

Extra Practice
See page EP21.

Find the volume of each cylinder to the nearest cubic unit.

11. 2.8 in.   5.6 in.

12. $5\frac{2}{3}$ cm $1\frac{3}{4}$ cm

13. 4.5 m   0.5 m

Find the volume of each cylinder using the information given. Write your answers in terms of π.

14. $r = 6$ cm; $h = 6$ cm

15. $d = 4$ in.; $h = 8$ in.

16. $r = 2$ m; $h = 5$ m

17. $r = 7.5$ ft; $h = 11$ ft

18. $d = 12$ yd; $h = 5$ yd

19. $d = 20$ mm; $h = 40$ mm

Multi-Step Find the volume of the shaded portion of each figure to the nearest cubic unit.

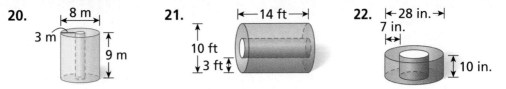

20. 8 m, 3 m, 9 m

21. ←14 ft→, 10 ft, 3 ft

22. ←28 in.→, 7 in., 10 in.

23. Measurement Could this blue can hold 200 cm³ of juice? How do you know?

5 cm, 10 cm

24. Science A scientist filled a cylindrical beaker with 942 mm³ of a chemical solution. The area of the base of the cylinder is 78.5 mm². What is the height of the solution?

25. Reasoning Fran, Gene, Helen, and Ira have cylinders with different volumes. Gene's cylinder holds more than Fran's. Ira's cylinder holds more than Helen's, but less than Fran's. Whose cylinder has the largest volume? What color cylinder does each person have?

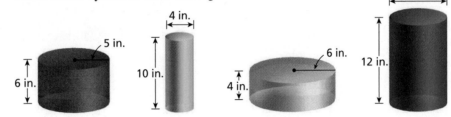

5 in., 6 in.

4 in., 10 in.

6 in., 4 in.

8 in., 12 in.

26. Write About It How is finding the volume of a cylinder similar to finding the volume of a triangular prism? How is it different?

27. Challenge Find the volume of the shaded portion.

$1\frac{1}{2}$ cm, 4 cm, 4 cm, 4 cm

28. Multiple Choice Find the volume of a cylinder with a height of $2\frac{1}{3}$ feet and a radius of $1\frac{1}{2}$ feet. Use $\frac{22}{7}$ as an estimate for π.

Ⓐ $19\frac{3}{4}$ ft³   Ⓑ $16\frac{1}{2}$ ft³   Ⓒ 11 ft³   Ⓓ $5\frac{1}{2}$ ft³

29. Short Response Chicken noodle soup is sold in a can that is 11 cm tall and has a radius of 2.5 cm. Tomato soup is sold in a can that is 7.5 cm tall and has a radius of 4 cm. Find the volume of both cans. Which can holds more soup?

Find each sum. (Lesson 2-2)

30. $-26 + 14$ **31.** $-7 + (-18)$ **32.** $37 + (-25)$

33. Find the volume of the triangular prism. (Lesson 10-8)

4 ft, 12 ft, 8 ft

Model Three-Dimensional Figures

Use with Lesson 10-10

go.hrw.com
Lab Resources Online
KEYWORD: MS8CA Lab10

California Standards

Preparation for AF3.2 Express in symbolic form simple relationships arising from geometry.

You can build a solid figure by cutting its faces from paper, taping them together, and then folding them to form the solid. A pattern of shapes that can be folded to form a solid figure is called a *net*.

Activity

1 To make a pattern for a rectangular prism follow the steps below.

a. Draw the following rectangles and cut them out:

Two 2 in. × 3 in. rectangles

Two 1 in. × 3 in. rectangles

Two 1 in. × 2 in. rectangles

b. Tape the pieces together to form the prism.

c. Remove the tape from some of the edges so that the pattern lies flat.

2 Create a net for a cylinder.

Think: What shapes can make a cylinder?

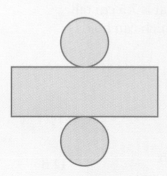

If a cylinder is "unfolded," the bases of the cylinder are circles, and the curved surface is a rectangle.

The net is made up of two circles and a rectangle.

3 Create a net for a square pyramid.

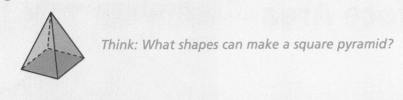

Think: What shapes can make a square pyramid?

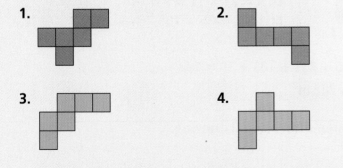

If the square pyramid is "unfolded," the base is a square, and the sides are triangles.

The net is made up of a square and four triangles.

Think and Discuss

1. Compare the nets for a rectangular prism and a cube.

2. Tell what shapes will always appear in a net for a triangular pyramid.

3. Tell what shapes will always appear in a net for a hexagonal prism.

Try This

Tell whether each net can be folded to form a cube. If not, explain.

1.
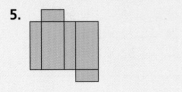

2.

3.

4.

Name a three-dimensional figure that can be formed from each net.

5.

6.

10-10 Surface Area

California Standards

AF3.1 Use variables in expressions describing geometric quantities (e.g., $P = 2w + 2\ell$, $A = \frac{1}{2}bh$, $C = \pi d$—the formulas for the perimeter of a rectangle, the area of a triangle, and the circumference of a circle, respectively).
Also covered: **AF3.2**

Vocabulary
surface area
net

Who uses this? Architects can determine how much aluminum sheeting is needed to cover a sports arena by calculating the arena's surface area. (See Exercise 20.)

The Walter Pyramid is a sports arena at California State University Long Beach.

The **surface area** of a three-dimensional figure is the sum of the areas of its surfaces. To help you see all the surfaces of a three-dimensional figure, you can use a *net*. A **net** is an arrangement of two-dimensional figures that can be folded to form a three-dimensional figure.

EXAMPLE 1 Finding the Surface Area of a Prism

Find the surface area S of each prism.

Reasoning

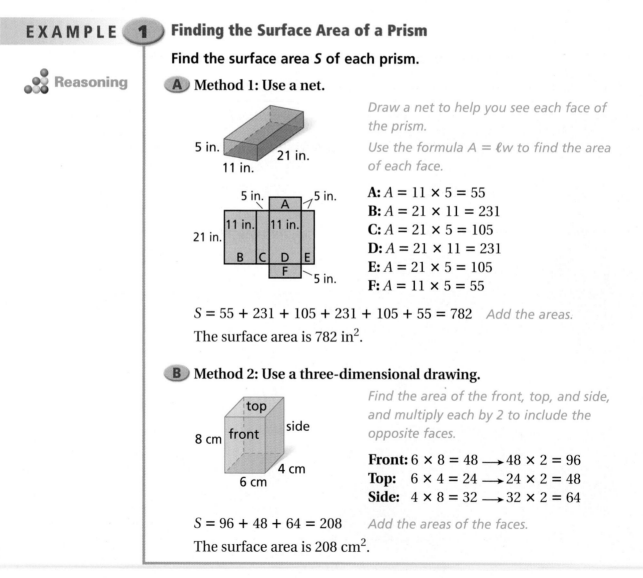

A Method 1: Use a net.

Draw a net to help you see each face of the prism.

Use the formula $A = \ell w$ to find the area of each face.

A: $A = 11 \times 5 = 55$
B: $A = 21 \times 11 = 231$
C: $A = 21 \times 5 = 105$
D: $A = 21 \times 11 = 231$
E: $A = 21 \times 5 = 105$
F: $A = 11 \times 5 = 55$

$S = 55 + 231 + 105 + 231 + 105 + 55 = 782$ *Add the areas.*

The surface area is 782 in².

B Method 2: Use a three-dimensional drawing.

Find the area of the front, top, and side, and multiply each by 2 to include the opposite faces.

Front: $6 \times 8 = 48 \longrightarrow 48 \times 2 = 96$
Top: $6 \times 4 = 24 \longrightarrow 24 \times 2 = 48$
Side: $4 \times 8 = 32 \longrightarrow 32 \times 2 = 64$

$S = 96 + 48 + 64 = 208$ *Add the areas of the faces.*

The surface area is 208 cm².

The surface area of a pyramid equals the sum of the area of the base and the areas of the triangular faces. To find the surface area of a pyramid, think of its net.

EXAMPLE 2 **Finding the Surface Area of a Pyramid**

Find the surface area S of the pyramid.

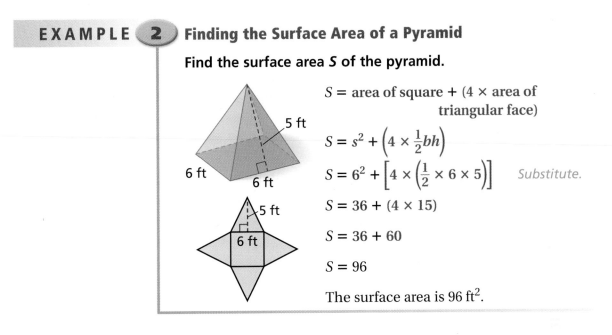

S = area of square + (4 × area of triangular face)

$S = s^2 + \left(4 \times \frac{1}{2}bh\right)$

$S = 6^2 + \left[4 \times \left(\frac{1}{2} \times 6 \times 5\right)\right]$ *Substitute.*

$S = 36 + (4 \times 15)$

$S = 36 + 60$

$S = 96$

The surface area is 96 ft^2.

The surface area of a cylinder equals the sum of the area of its bases and the area of its curved surface.

EXAMPLE 3 **Finding the Surface Area of a Cylinder**

Find the surface area S of the cylinder. Write your answer in terms of π.

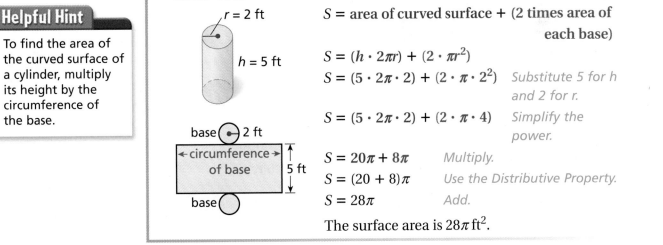

Helpful Hint

To find the area of the curved surface of a cylinder, multiply its height by the circumference of the base.

S = area of curved surface + (2 times area of each base)

$S = (h \cdot 2\pi r) + (2 \cdot \pi r^2)$

$S = (5 \cdot 2\pi \cdot 2) + (2 \cdot \pi \cdot 2^2)$ *Substitute 5 for h and 2 for r.*

$S = (5 \cdot 2\pi \cdot 2) + (2 \cdot \pi \cdot 4)$ *Simplify the power.*

$S = 20\pi + 8\pi$ *Multiply.*

$S = (20 + 8)\pi$ *Use the Distributive Property.*

$S = 28\pi$ *Add.*

The surface area is 28π ft^2.

Think and Discuss

1. Describe how to find the surface area of a pentagonal prism.

2. Tell how to find the surface area of a cube if you know the area of one face.

10-10
Exercises

California Standards Practice
AF3.1, AF3.2

go.hrw.com
Homework Help Online
KEYWORD: MS8CA 10-10
Parent Resources Online
KEYWORD: MS8CA Parent

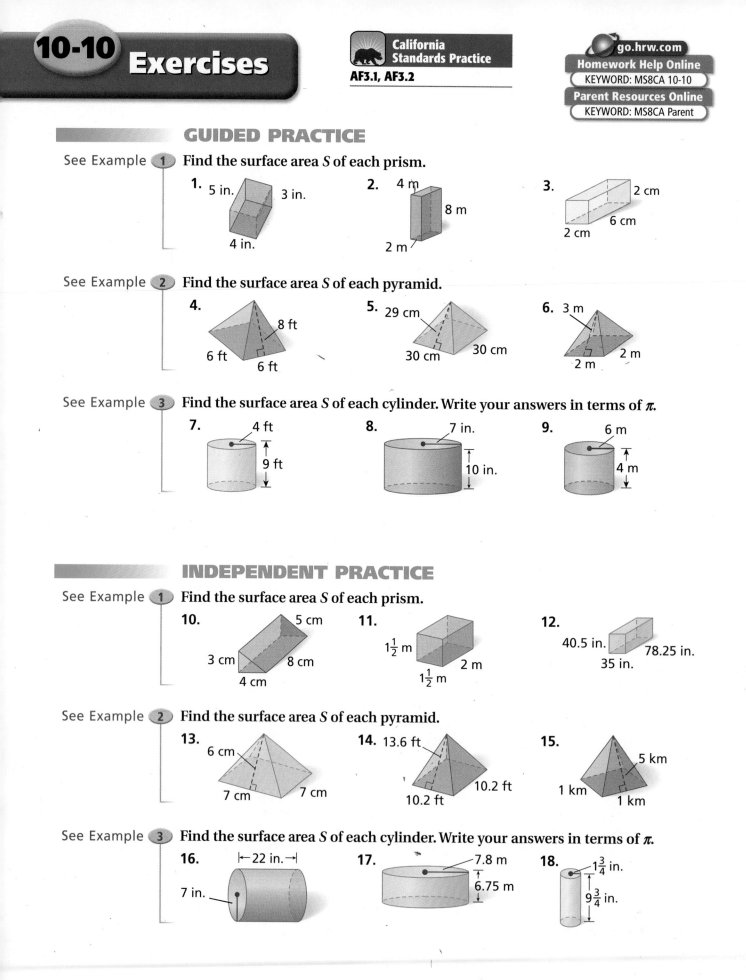

GUIDED PRACTICE

See Example ① Find the surface area S of each prism.

1. 5 in. 3 in. 4 in.

2. 4 m 8 m 2 m

3. 2 cm 6 cm 2 cm

See Example ② Find the surface area S of each pyramid.

4. 8 ft 6 ft 6 ft

5. 29 cm 30 cm 30 cm

6. 3 m 2 m 2 m

See Example ③ Find the surface area S of each cylinder. Write your answers in terms of π.

7. 4 ft 9 ft

8. 7 in. 10 in.

9. 6 m 4 m

INDEPENDENT PRACTICE

See Example ① Find the surface area S of each prism.

10. 5 cm 3 cm 8 cm 4 cm

11. $1\frac{1}{2}$ m 2 m $1\frac{1}{2}$ m

12. 40.5 in. 78.25 in. 35 in.

See Example ② Find the surface area S of each pyramid.

13. 6 cm 7 cm 7 cm

14. 13.6 ft 10.2 ft 10.2 ft

15. 5 km 1 km 1 km

See Example ③ Find the surface area S of each cylinder. Write your answers in terms of π.

16. ⟵ 22 in. ⟶ 7 in.

17. 7.8 m 6.75 m

18. $1\frac{3}{4}$ in. $9\frac{3}{4}$ in.

PRACTICE AND PROBLEM SOLVING

Extra Practice
See page EP21.

19. You are designing a container for oatmeal. Your first design is a rectangular prism with a height of 12 in., a width of 8 in., and a depth of 3 in.

  a. What is the surface area of the package?

  b. You redesign the package as a cylinder with the same surface area as the prism from part **a.** If the radius of the cylinder is 2 in., what is the height of the cylinder? Round to the nearest tenth of an inch.

20. Architecture A sports arena is shaped like a square pyramid. The side length of the base is 345 ft, and the height of the triangular faces is about 257 ft. What is the surface area of the aluminum sheeting that covers the triangular faces of the pyramid?

Estimation Estimate the surface area of each figure.

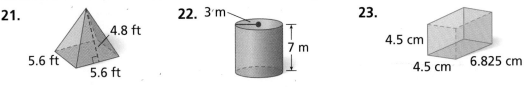

21.   4.8 ft   5.6 ft   5.6 ft

22. 3 m   7 m

23. 4.5 cm   4.5 cm   6.825 cm

24. Critical Thinking If each of the dimensions of a rectangular prism is halved, how does this affect the surface area?

25. What's the Question? The surface area of a cube is 150 cm². The answer is 5 cm. What is the question?

26. Write About It How is finding the surface area of a rectangular pyramid different from finding the surface area of a triangular prism?

27. Challenge This cube is made of 27 smaller cubes whose sides measure 1 in. Remove one small cube from each of the eight corners of the larger cube. What is the surface area of the solid formed?

---

28. Multiple Choice A cylinder has a radius of r meters and a height of 6 meters. Which expression could be used to determine the surface area of the cylinder?

  Ⓐ $\pi r^2 + 6\pi r$ Ⓑ $\pi r^2 + 12\pi r$ Ⓒ $2\pi r^2 + 6\pi r$ Ⓓ $2\pi r^2 + 12\pi r$

29. Short Response Write an expression in terms of x that could be used to determine the surface area of a cube with a side length of x inches.

Solve each equation. (Lesson 1-8)

30. $12 + y = 23$ **31.** $38 + y = 80$ **32.** $y + 76 = 230$

Find each sum or difference. Write the answer in simplest form. (Lesson 4-3)

33. $5\frac{2}{3} - 1\frac{1}{9}$ **34.** $1\frac{1}{4} + 2\frac{3}{8}$ **35.** $2\frac{5}{6} - 2\frac{3}{4}$ **36.** $4\frac{2}{5} + 3\frac{3}{10}$

READY TO GO ON?

Quiz for Lessons 10-7 Through 10-10

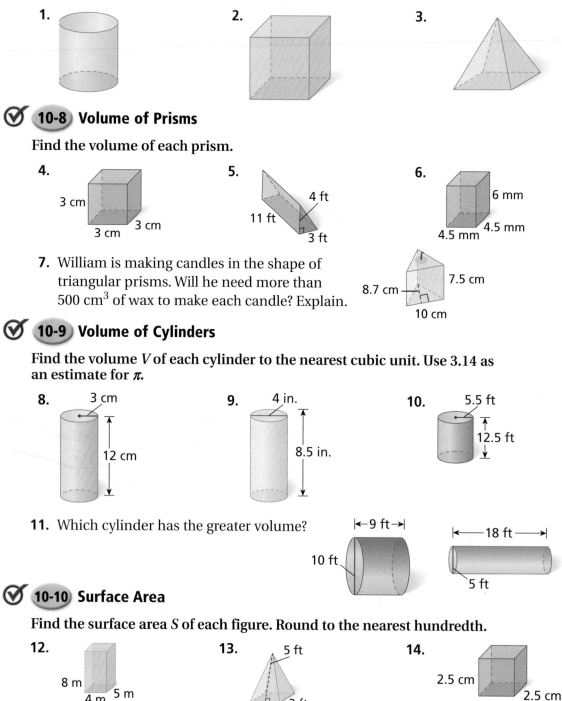

✓ **10-7** **Three-Dimensional Figures**

Identify the number of faces, edges, and vertices on each figure. Then name the figure and tell whether it is a polyhedron.

1.

2.

3.

✓ **10-8** **Volume of Prisms**

Find the volume of each prism.

4.
3 cm
3 cm
3 cm

5.
4 ft
11 ft
3 ft

6.
6 mm
4.5 mm
4.5 mm

7. William is making candles in the shape of triangular prisms. Will he need more than 500 cm³ of wax to make each candle? Explain.

8.7 cm
7.5 cm
10 cm

✓ **10-9** **Volume of Cylinders**

Find the volume *V* of each cylinder to the nearest cubic unit. Use 3.14 as an estimate for π.

8.
3 cm
12 cm

9.
4 in.
8.5 in.

10.
5.5 ft
12.5 ft

11. Which cylinder has the greater volume?

|←9 ft→|
10 ft

|← 18 ft →|
5 ft

✓ **10-10** **Surface Area**

Find the surface area *S* of each figure. Round to the nearest hundredth.

12.
8 m
4 m
5 m

13.
5 ft
3 ft   3 ft

14.
2.5 cm
2.5 cm
2.5 cm

CONCEPT CONNECTION

At Home in Space The International Space Station is a state-of-the-art laboratory in space. It is where we can learn to live and work "off planet." The space station is large enough to accommodate more than 30 experiments and provide living space for 6 astronauts. It is in the shape of a rectangular prism.

1. The table below shows the volumes of rectangular prisms that each have an 18-square-foot area for their bases but have different heights. Describe any patterns or proportional relationships in the table.

2. Write a rule to show how the volumes in the table are related to the heights.

3. According to NASA, the average floor space in U.S. houses is about 1,800 ft². Ceilings are 8 ft high on average. How many cubic feet are in a house with these average measurements?

4. The space station has 43,000 ft³ of pressurized volume. About how many houses with the measurements from Problem 3 would fit in the space station? Explain.

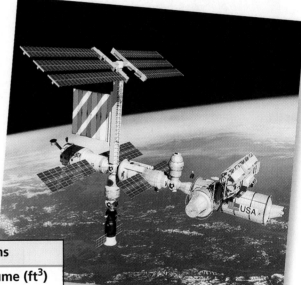

Volume of Rectangular Prisms		
Area (ft²)	Height (ft)	Volume (ft³)
18	1	18
18	2	36
18	3	54
18	4	72
18	5	90
18	6	108
18	7	126
18	8	144

Game Time

Polygon Hide-and-Seek

Use the figure to name each polygon described.

1. an obtuse scalene triangle
2. a right isosceles triangle
3. a parallelogram with no right angles
4. a trapezoid with two congruent sides
5. a pentagon with three congruent sides

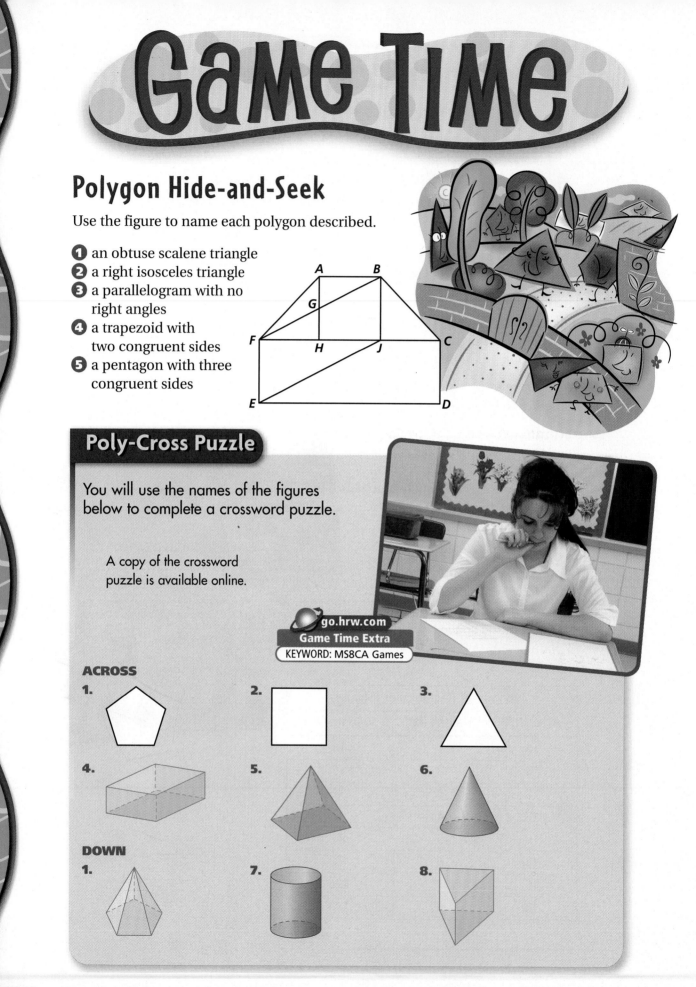

Poly-Cross Puzzle

You will use the names of the figures below to complete a crossword puzzle.

A copy of the crossword puzzle is available online.

go.hrw.com
Game Time Extra
KEYWORD: MS8CA Games

ACROSS

1.

2.

3.

4.

5.

6.

DOWN

1.

7.

8.

Materials
- colored file folder
- scissors
- 8 library pockets
- glue stick
- index cards
- black construction paper
- markers
- tag
- string

It's in the Bag!

PROJECT ## Area and Volume Suitcase

Carry your notes from Chapter 10 in this handy suitcase.

Directions

❶ Cut the tabs off a colored file folder to form a rectangular folder with straight sides.
Figure A

❷ Open the folder. Glue library pockets inside the folder so that there are four on each side. Place an index card in each pocket.
Figure B

❸ Cut out "handles" from the construction paper. Glue these to the folder as shown.
Figure C

❹ Use a piece of string to attach a tag to one of the handles. Write your name and the name of your class on the tag. Write the name and number of the chapter on the front of the folder.

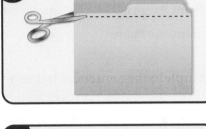

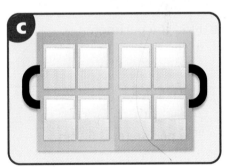

Taking Note of the Math

Write the names of the chapter's lessons on the library pockets. Then take notes on each lesson on the appropriate index card.

Vocabulary

area 497	cube 518	*pi* 492
base (parallelogram) 497	diameter 492	polyhedron 518
base (prism or cylinder) . . 518	edge 518	radius (radii) 492
center 492	face 518	surface area 534
circle 492	height 497	vertex 518
circumference 492	net 534	volume 524
composite figure 510	perimeter 486	

Complete the sentences below with vocabulary words from the list above.

1. A ___?___ is a three-dimensional object with flat faces that are polygons.

2. The number of cubic units needed to fill a space is called ___?___.

10-1 Perimeter (pp. 486–489)

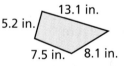 AF1.1, AF1.2, AF3.1, AF3.2

EXAMPLE

■ **Find the perimeter of the figure.**

Add all the side lengths.

9 cm, 12 cm, 10 cm, 5 cm, 16 cm

$P = 9 + 10 + 5 + 16 + 12 = 52$
The perimeter is 52 cm.

EXERCISES

3. Find the perimeter of the figure.

13.1 in. 5.2 in. 7.5 in. 8.1 in.

4. What is the length of side *n* if the perimeter is 20 ft?

4 ft, 1 ft, 1 ft, 3 ft, 1 ft, 3 ft, *n*

10-2 Circles and Circumference (pp. 492–495)

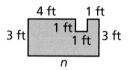 AF1.1, AF3.1, AF3.2, MG1.1, MG1.2

EXAMPLE

■ **Find the circumference of the circle. Use 3.14 as an estimate for π.**

$C = \pi d$
$C \approx 3.14 \cdot 6 \approx 18.84$ cm

d = 6 cm

EXERCISES

Find each missing value to the nearest hundredth. Use 3.14 as an estimate for π.

5. *d* = 10 ft; C = ___?___
6. C = 28.26 m; *d* = ___?___
7. *r* = 8 cm; C = ___?___
8. C = 69.08 ft; *r* = ___?___

10-3 Area of Parallelograms (pp. 497–500)

NS2.1, AF1.1, AF2.1, AF3.1, AF3.2

EXAMPLE

■ Find the area.

14 in.

8.6 in.

$A = \ell w$
$A = 14 \cdot 8.6 = 120.4$
The area of the rectangle is 120.4 in².

EXERCISES

Find the area of each polygon.

9.   8.6 cm

5.9 cm

10.

24.3 yd

34 yd

10-4 Area of Triangles and Trapezoids (pp. 502–505)

AF1.2, AF3.1, AF3.2

EXAMPLE

■ Find the area.

2.9 m

4.8 m

$A = \frac{1}{2}bh$
$A = \frac{1}{2}(4.8 \cdot 2.9) = 6.96$

The area of the triangle is 6.96 m².

EXERCISES

Find the area of each polygon.

11.

28 in.

19 in.

12.   7.6 cm

12.5 cm

9.8 cm

10-5 Area of Circles (pp. 506–509)

AF3.1, AF3.2, MG1.1, MG1.2

EXAMPLE

■ Find the area to the nearest tenth. Use 3.14 as an estimate for π.

5 in.

$A = \pi r^2$
$A \approx 3.14 \cdot 5^2 \approx 78.5$
The area of the circle is about 78.5 in².

EXERCISES

Find the area of each circle to the nearest tenth. Use 3.14 as an estimate for π.

13.

3.4 m

14.

17 ft

10-6 Area of Irregular and Composite Figures (pp. 510–513)

Ext. of AF3.1, AF3.2, MG1.1, MG1.2

EXAMPLE

■ Find the area of the irregular figure.

Separate the figure into a rectangle and a triangle.

$A = \ell w$
$\quad = 4 \cdot 8 = 32 \text{ m}^2$

$A = \frac{1}{2}bh$
$\quad = \frac{1}{2}(3 \cdot 4) = 6 \text{ m}^2$

$A = 32 + 6 = 38 \text{ m}^2$

3 m
4 m
4 m
8 m

EXERCISES

Find the area of each figure. Use 3.14 as an estimate for π.

15.

2 ft
3.5 ft   3.5 ft
7 ft

16.   2 m

3 m   2 m

5 m

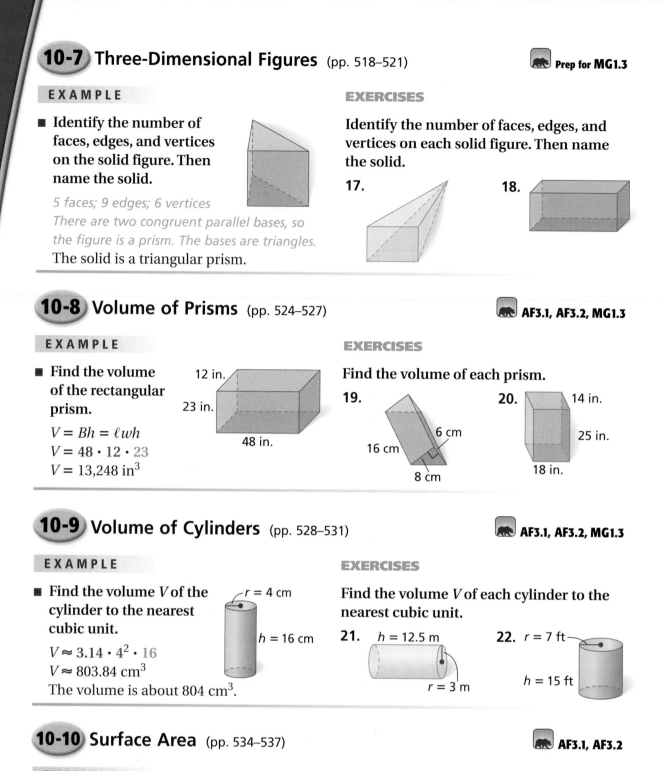

10-7 Three-Dimensional Figures (pp. 518–521)

Prep for MG1.3

EXAMPLE

■ Identify the number of faces, edges, and vertices on the solid figure. Then name the solid.

5 faces; 9 edges; 6 vertices
There are two congruent parallel bases, so the figure is a prism. The bases are triangles.
The solid is a triangular prism.

EXERCISES

Identify the number of faces, edges, and vertices on each solid figure. Then name the solid.

17.

18.

10-8 Volume of Prisms (pp. 524–527)

AF3.1, AF3.2, MG1.3

EXAMPLE

■ Find the volume of the rectangular prism.

12 in.
23 in.
48 in.

$V = Bh = \ell wh$
$V = 48 \cdot 12 \cdot 23$
$V = 13{,}248 \text{ in}^3$

EXERCISES

Find the volume of each prism.

19.
6 cm
16 cm
8 cm

20.
14 in.
25 in.
18 in.

10-9 Volume of Cylinders (pp. 528–531)

AF3.1, AF3.2, MG1.3

EXAMPLE

■ Find the volume V of the cylinder to the nearest cubic unit.

$r = 4$ cm
$h = 16$ cm

$V \approx 3.14 \cdot 4^2 \cdot 16$
$V \approx 803.84 \text{ cm}^3$
The volume is about 804 cm³.

EXERCISES

Find the volume V of each cylinder to the nearest cubic unit.

21. $h = 12.5$ m
$r = 3$ m

22. $r = 7$ ft
$h = 15$ ft

10-10 Surface Area (pp. 534–537)

AF3.1, AF3.2

EXAMPLE

■ Find the surface area S of the cylinder.

2 in.
6 in.

$S = h \cdot (2\pi r) + 2 \cdot (\pi r^2)$
$S \approx 6 \cdot (2 \cdot 3.14 \cdot 2) + 2 \cdot (3.14 \cdot 2^2)$
$S \approx 100.48 \text{ in}^2$

EXERCISES

Find the surface area S of each solid.

23.
$h = 10$ m
5 m   5 m

24.
2 cm
3 cm
9 cm

CHAPTER TEST

1. Find the perimeter of the trapezoid.

10.5 in.
9.1 in.
6.3 in.
17.2 in.

Find the area of each figure.

2.
12 m
8 m

3.
8.7 ft
13.6 ft

4.
11 ft
3 ft
10 ft
5 ft
4 ft

5. A patio is in the shape of a trapezoid.
   What is the area of the patio?

   A   24 ft   B
   6 ft
   D   C
   32 ft

Find the circumference and area of each circle. Use 3.14 as an estimate for π. Round to the nearest hundredth.

6.
A   V
$2\frac{1}{2}$ m
P

7.
J
O
10 in.
D

8.
9 cm
H
F
S

Name each figure and tell whether it is a polyhedron. If it is a polyhedron, identify the number of faces, edges, and vertices.

9.

10.

11.

Find the volume of each three-dimensional figure. Use 3.14 as an estimate for π.

12.
8 m
6 m   4 m

13.
3 in.
4 in.

14.
12 cm
10 cm   18 cm

15. Patricia has two cylinder-shaped jars. Jar A has a radius of 6 cm
    and a height of 9 cm. Jar B has a diameter of 8 cm and a height
    of 17 cm. Which jar has the greater volume? How much greater?

Find the surface area S of each three-dimensional figure.

16.
3 in.
6 in.
3 in.

17.
4 ft
2 ft   2 ft

18.
5.2 cm
7.2 cm
5.4 cm

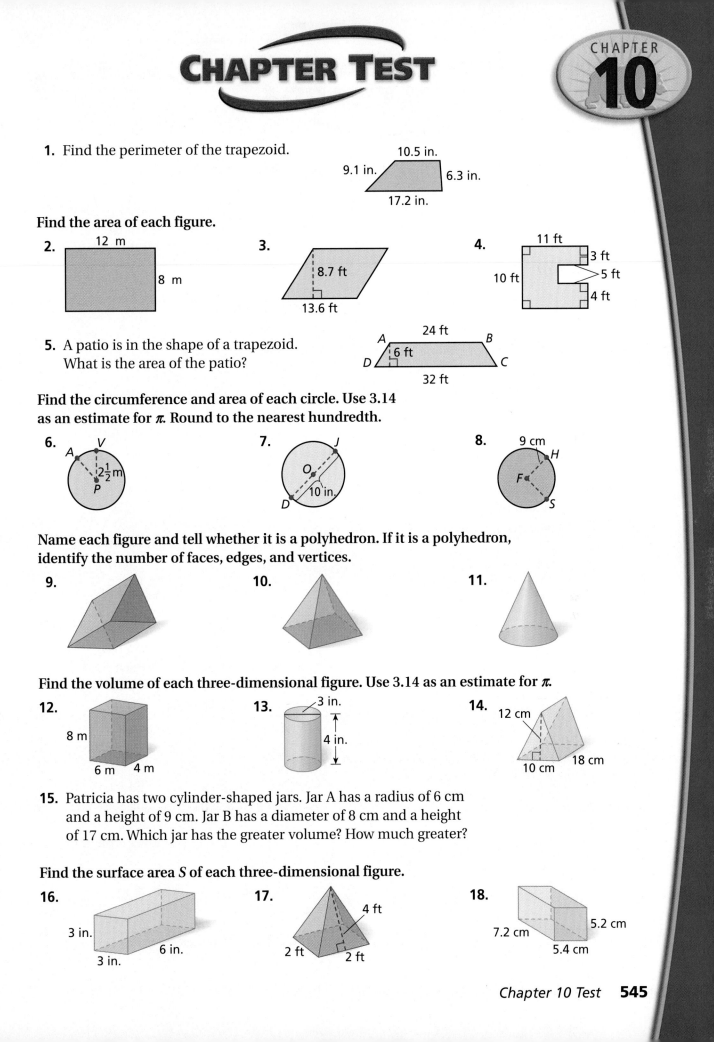

MASTERING THE STANDARDS

Cumulative Assessment, Chapters 1–10

Multiple Choice

1. Which of the following numbers is greatest?

  Ⓐ -0.07 Ⓒ $-\frac{7}{10}$

  Ⓑ $-\frac{1}{7}$ Ⓓ -0.7

2. A recipe for punch calls for 6 cups of lemonade, 2 cups of orange juice, and 2 cups of cranberry juice. What is the ratio of cups of lemonade to cups of punch?

  Ⓐ 1:3   Ⓒ 3:5

  Ⓑ 3:2   Ⓓ 6:1

3. Frozen dinners are on sale for 2 for $5.00. Which proportion could be used to solve for x, the cost of 3 frozen dinners?

  Ⓐ $\frac{2}{x} = \frac{5}{3}$ Ⓒ $\frac{2}{5} = \frac{x}{3}$

  Ⓑ $\frac{2}{3} = \frac{x}{5}$ Ⓓ $\frac{2}{5} = \frac{3}{x}$

4. What is the greatest common divisor of 24, 36, and 51?

  Ⓐ 3   Ⓒ 8

  Ⓑ 6   Ⓓ 9

5. Justin has 3 cups of flour in a canister. He uses $\frac{1}{3}$ cup of flour in a sauce recipe. He uses $\frac{3}{4}$ of what is remaining in the canister to make pasta. How much flour is left?

  Ⓐ $\frac{2}{3}$ cup   Ⓒ $1\frac{11}{12}$ cups

  Ⓑ 1 cup   Ⓓ 2 cups

6. Which expression represents the area of the trapezoid in terms of h?

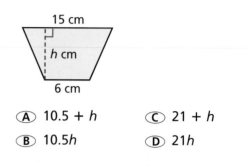

  Ⓐ $10.5 + h$ Ⓒ $21 + h$

  Ⓑ $10.5h$ Ⓓ $21h$

7. What is the volume of the prism?

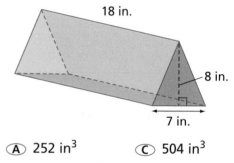

  Ⓐ 252 in^3 Ⓒ 504 in^3

  Ⓑ 434 in^3 Ⓓ 1,008 in^3

8. A round antique tabletop has a diameter of 3 feet. Which measurement is closest to the area of the tabletop?

  Ⓐ 7.1 ft^2 Ⓒ 18.8 ft^2

  Ⓑ 9.4 ft^2 Ⓓ 28.3 ft^2

9. The scale on a map is 1 in:50 mi. If Cincinnati, Ohio, is about 300 miles from Chicago, Illinois, about how far apart are the two cities on the map?

  Ⓐ 5 in.   Ⓒ 7 in.

  Ⓑ 6 in.   Ⓓ 8 in.

10. In March of 2005, Steve Fossett became the first man to complete the first solo, nonstop flight around the world. He did not even stop to refuel. The 36,818-kilometer voyage took 67 hours and 2 minutes. How many kilometers did he travel per minute? Round to the nearest kilometer.

(A) 5 km/min   (C) 23 km/min

(B) 9 km/min   (D) 26 km/min

Pay attention to the units in problems. If the units in a problem do not match the units in the answer choices, you will need to convert from one unit to another.

Gridded Response

The table shows the number of people who attended the Super Bowl from 1967 to 1971. Use the table for items 11 and 12.

11. What was the mean attendance? Round to the nearest whole number.

Superbowl Attendance					
Year	1967	1968	1969	1970	1971
Number of People	61,946	75,546	75,389	80,562	79,204

12. In 1972, Super Bowl attendance was 81,023. If this value is added to the data set, by how much does the mean attendance increase? Round to the nearest whole number.

13. The probability that it will rain on Tuesday is 0.2. What is the probability that it will NOT rain on Tuesday?

14. Solve the equation $\frac{2}{7}k = \frac{1}{6}$ for k.

15. A watermelon has a mass of 2.89 kg. What is the mass of the watermelon in grams?

Short Response

16. Triangle *WXY* is isosceles. The two short sides have a length of 18 mm. The other side has as length of 30 mm.

    a. Draw a triangle that is similar to triangle *WXY*.

    b. Write a proportion to prove that the two triangles are similar.

17. Determine the measures of angles 1, 2, and 3 in the figure below. Explain how you determined each angle measure.

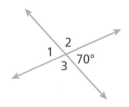

18. Carole has a piece of fabric that is 2 yards long. She wants to cut the fabric into 2.4-inch strips. Let *s* equal one of the fabric strips. Write and solve an equation to find how many 2.4-inch strips Carole can cut from the piece of fabric.

Extended Response

19. There are 3 pools in Marcie's neighborhood where she can go swimming. Two of the pools are cylindrical. Pool 1 has a radius of 9 feet and a depth of 6 feet. Pool 2 has a diameter of 20 feet and a depth of 5 feet.

    a. Find the volume of each cylindrical pool. Which pool has the greater volume?

    b. What is the circumference of pool 1?

    c. The third pool is shaped like a rectangular prism. It has a depth of 5 feet, a width of 8 feet, and approximately the same volume as pool 2. Write an equation that could be used to find the length ℓ of pool 3. Then solve your equation.

Preview of Grade 7

Multi-Step Equations and Inequalities

CONCEPT CONNECTION

go.hrw.com
Chapter Project Online
KEYWORD: MS8CA Ch11

The best length for a surfboard depends on a surfer's body type and skill level. An algebraic inequality can be used to represent possible surfboard lengths.

Surfer
California coast

ARE YOU READY?

✓ Vocabulary

Choose the best term from the list to complete each sentence.

1. __?__ are mathematical operations that undo each other.

2. To solve an equation you need to __?__.

3. A(n) __?__ is a mathematical statement that two expressions are equivalent.

4. A(n) __?__ is a mathematical statement that two ratios are equivalent.

isolate the variable

equation

proportion

inverse operations

expression

Complete these exercises to review skills you will need for this chapter.

✓ Add Whole Numbers, Decimals, Fractions, and Integers

Add.

5. $24 + 16$

6. $-34 + (-47)$

7. $35 + (-61)$

8. $-12 + (-29) + 53$

9. $2.7 + 3.5$

10. $\frac{2}{3} + \frac{1}{2}$

11. $5.87 + 10.6$

12. $\frac{8}{9} + \frac{9}{11}$

✓ Evaluate Expressions

Evaluate each expression for $a = 7$ and $b = -2$.

13. $a - b$

14. $b - a$

15. $\frac{b}{a}$

16. $2a + 3b$

17. $\frac{-4a}{b}$

18. $3a - \frac{8}{b}$

19. $1.2a + 2.3b$

20. $-5a - (-6b)$

✓ Solve Equations by Dividing

Solve.

21. $8x = -72$

22. $-12a = -60$

23. $\frac{2}{3}y = 16$

24. $-12b = 9$

25. $12 = -4x$

26. $13 = \frac{1}{2}c$

27. $-2.4 = -0.8p$

28. $\frac{3}{4} = 6x$

✓ Solve Proportions

Solve.

29. $\frac{3}{4} = \frac{x}{24}$

30. $\frac{8}{9} = \frac{4}{a}$

31. $\frac{12}{5} = \frac{15}{c}$

32. $\frac{y}{50} = \frac{35}{20}$

33. $\frac{2}{3} = \frac{18}{w}$

34. $\frac{35}{21} = \frac{d}{3}$

35. $\frac{7}{13} = \frac{h}{195}$

36. $\frac{9}{15} = \frac{27}{p}$

Unpacking the Standards

The information below "unpacks" the standards. The Academic Vocabulary is highlighted and defined to help you understand the language of the standards. Refer to the lessons listed after each standard for help with the math terms and phrases. The Chapter Concept shows how the standard is applied in this chapter.

California Standard	Academic Vocabulary	Chapter Concept
Preview of Grade 7 ⟜ AF1.3 **Simplify** numerical expressions by **applying** properties of rational numbers (e.g., identity, inverse, **distributive, associative, and commutative**) and **justify** the process used. (Lessons 11-2, 11-3)	**simplify** rewrite in a simpler form **applying** using **justify** give a reason for	You use mathematical properties to write expressions in a simpler form. You give reasons for each step when you simplify expressions.
Preview of Grade 7 ⟜ AF4.0 **Students solve** simple linear equations and **inequalities over the rational numbers.** (Lessons 11-6, 11-7)	**solve** find the value or values of a variable that make an equation or inequality true **over** for the set of	You find the set of values that make an inequality true. ***Example:*** $x + 4 < 10$ $x + 4 - 4 < 10 - 4$ $x < 6$ Any number less than 6 is a solution of the inequality.
Preview of Grade 7 ⟜ AF4.1 **Solve two-step linear equations and inequalities in one variable over the rational numbers,** interpret the solution or solutions in the context from which they arose, and verify the reasonableness of the results. (Lessons 11-1, 11-8) (Lab 11-1)	**two-step** refers to an equation or inequality that can be solved by using two operations	You solve two-step linear equations and inequalities. ***Example:*** $2x + 5 = 13$ $2x + 5 - 5 = 13 - 5$ $2x = 8$ $\dfrac{2x}{2} = \dfrac{8}{2}$ $x = 4$
Preview of Algebra I ⟜ 5.0 **Students solve multistep** problems, including word problems, **involving** linear equations and linear inequalities **in one variable** and provide justification for each step. (Lessons 11-3, 11-4)	**multistep** needing more than one step **involving** needing the use of	You solve equations when finding the solution involves two or more steps.

Standards 6AF1.2, 6AF3.1, 6AF3.2, and 7AF1.1 are also covered in this chapter. To see standards 6AF1.2, 6AF3.1, and 6AF3.2 unpacked, go to Chapter 1, p. 4 (6AF1.2), and Chapter 10, p. 484 (6AF3.1 and 6AF3.2).

Study Strategy: Prepare for Your Final Exam

Math is a cumulative subject, so your exam will cover all of the material you have learned from the beginning of the course. Being prepared is the key for you to be successful on your exam.

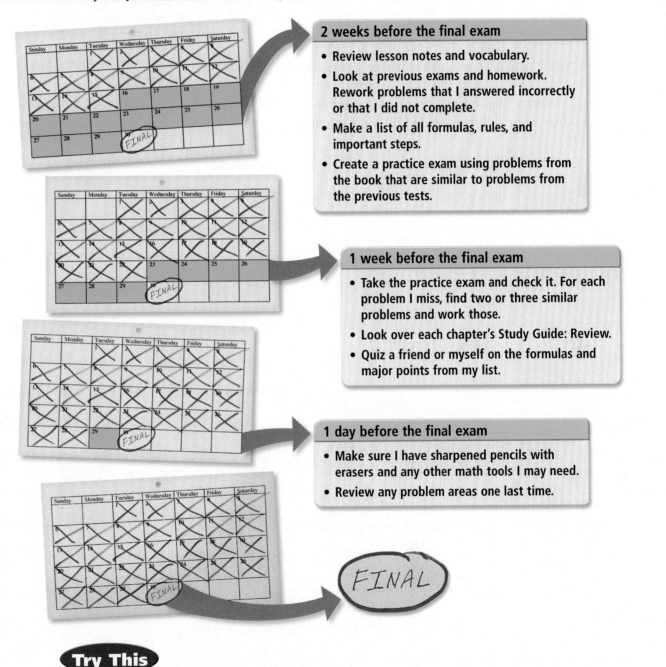

2 weeks before the final exam

- Review lesson notes and vocabulary.
- Look at previous exams and homework. Rework problems that I answered incorrectly or that I did not complete.
- Make a list of all formulas, rules, and important steps.
- Create a practice exam using problems from the book that are similar to problems from the previous tests.

1 week before the final exam

- Take the practice exam and check it. For each problem I miss, find two or three similar problems and work those.
- Look over each chapter's Study Guide: Review.
- Quiz a friend or myself on the formulas and major points from my list.

1 day before the final exam

- Make sure I have sharpened pencils with erasers and any other math tools I may need.
- Review any problem areas one last time.

Try This

1. Create a timeline that you will use to study for your final exam.

Model Two-Step Equations

go.hrw.com
Lab Resources Online
KEYWORD: MS8CA Lab11

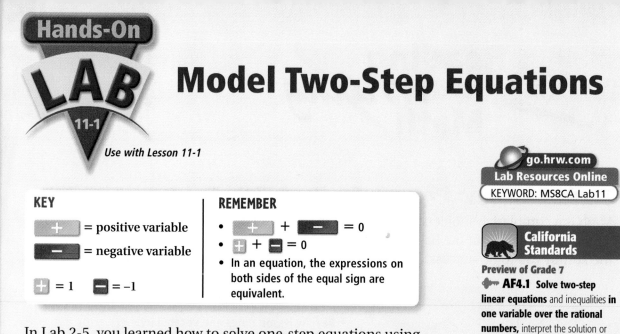

KEY

 = positive variable

 = negative variable

 = 1   = −1

REMEMBER

- + = 0
- + = 0
- In an equation, the expressions on both sides of the equal sign are equivalent.

California Standards

Preview of Grade 7
☞ **AF4.1** Solve two-step **linear equations** and inequalities **in one variable over the rational numbers,** interpret the solution or solutions in the context from which they arose, and verify the resonableness of the results.

In Lab 2-5, you learned how to solve one-step equations using algebra tiles. You can also use algebra tiles to solve two-step equations. When solving a two-step equation, it is easiest to perform addition and subtraction before multiplication and division.

Activity

1 Use algebra tiles to model and solve $2p + 2 = 10$.

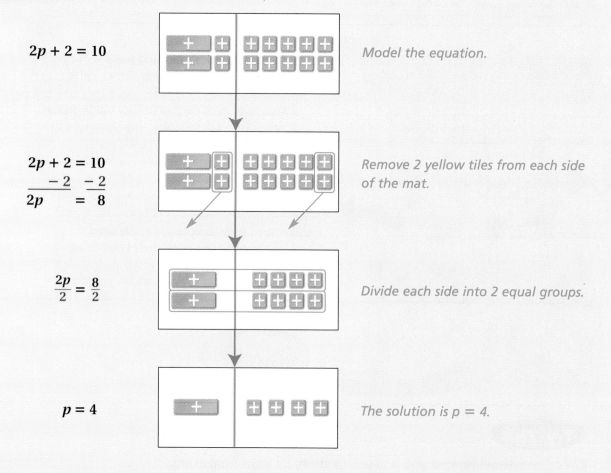

$2p + 2 = 10$ Model the equation.

$$\begin{array}{r} 2p + 2 = 10 \\ \underline{-2 \quad -2} \\ 2p \quad = 8 \end{array}$$ Remove 2 yellow tiles from each side of the mat.

$\dfrac{2p}{2} = \dfrac{8}{2}$ Divide each side into 2 equal groups.

$p = 4$ The solution is p = 4.

❷ Use algebra tiles to model and solve $3n + 6 = -15$.

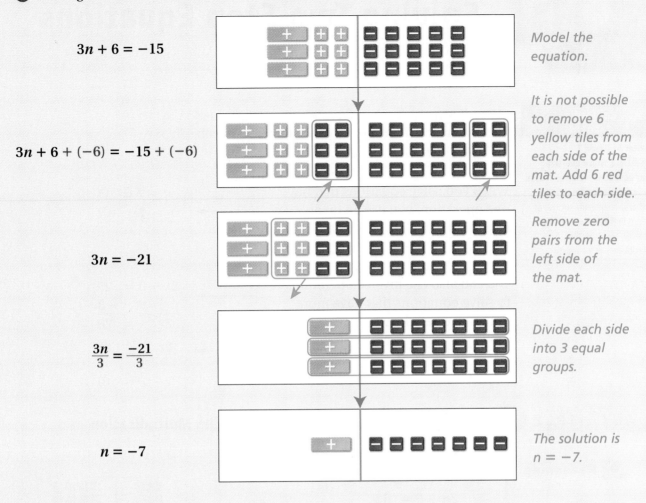

$3n + 6 = -15$ *Model the equation.*

$3n + 6 + (-6) = -15 + (-6)$ *It is not possible to remove 6 yellow tiles from each side of the mat. Add 6 red tiles to each side.*

$3n = -21$ *Remove zero pairs from the left side of the mat.*

$\dfrac{3n}{3} = \dfrac{-21}{3}$ *Divide each side into 3 equal groups.*

$n = -7$ *The solution is $n = -7$.*

Think and Discuss

1. When you add a value to one side of an equation, why do you also have to add the same value to the other side?

2. When you solved $3n + 6 = -15$ in the activity, why were you able to remove six yellow unit tiles and six red unit tiles from the left side of the equation?

3. Model and solve $3x - 5 = 10$. Explain each step.

4. How would you check the solution to $3n + 6 = -15$ using algebra tiles?

Try This

Use algebra tiles to model and solve each equation.

1. $4 + 2x = 20$ 2. $3r + 7 = -8$ 3. $-4m + 3 = -25$

4. $-2n - 5 = 17$ 5. $10 = 2j - 4$ 6. $5 + r = 7$

7. $4h + 2h + 3 = 15$ 8. $-3g = 9$ 9. $5k + (-7) = 13$

11-1 Solving Two-Step Equations

California Standards

Preview of Grade 7

🔑 **AF4.1 Solve two-step linear equations** and inequalities **in one variable over the rational numbers,** interpret the solution or solutions in the context from which they arose, and verify the reasonableness of the results.

Why learn this? You can solve a two-step equation to determine the monthly cost of a tennis-club membership. (See Example 3.)

When you solve equations that have one operation, you use an inverse operation to isolate the variable.

$$\begin{array}{rr} n + 7 = & 15 \\ -7 & -7 \\ \hline n \ = & 8 \end{array}$$

You can also use inverse operations to solve equations that have more than one operation.

$$\begin{array}{rr} 2x + 3 = & 23 \\ -3 & -3 \\ \hline 2x \ = & 20 \end{array}$$

Use the inverse of multiplying by 2 to isolate x.

$$\frac{2x}{2} = \frac{20}{2}$$

$$x \ = \ 10$$

EXAMPLE 1 Solving Two-Step Equations Containing Multiplication

Reasoning

Solve.

A $2n + 5 = 13$

$$\begin{array}{rr} 2n + 5 = & 13 \\ -5 & -5 \\ \hline 2n \ = & 8 \end{array}$$ *Subtract 5 from both sides.*

$$\frac{2n}{2} = \frac{8}{2}$$ *Divide both sides by 2.*

$$n = 4$$

Helpful Hint

Reverse the order of operations when solving equations that have more than one operation.

B $19 = -3p - 8$

$$19 = -3p - 8$$

$$\begin{array}{rr} +8 & +8 \\ \hline 27 = & -3p \end{array}$$ *Add 8 to both sides.*

$$\frac{27}{-3} = \frac{-3p}{-3}$$ *Divide both sides by −3.*

$$-9 = p$$

Check

$$19 = -3p - 8$$

$$19 \overset{?}{=} -3(-9) - 8$$ *Substitute −9 for p.*

$$19 \overset{?}{=} 27 - 8$$

$$19 \overset{?}{=} 19 ✔$$ *−9 is a solution.*

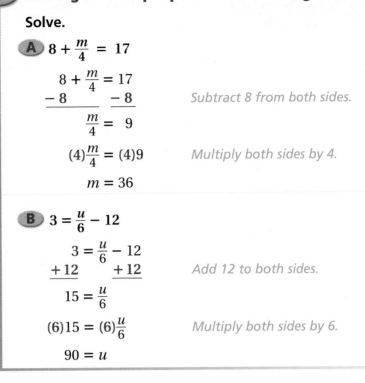

EXAMPLE 2 **Solving Two-Step Equations Containing Division**

Solve.

A $8 + \frac{m}{4} = 17$

$$8 + \frac{m}{4} = 17$$
$$\underline{-8 \qquad\quad -8} \qquad \text{\textit{Subtract 8 from both sides.}}$$
$$\frac{m}{4} = 9$$
$$(4)\frac{m}{4} = (4)9 \qquad \text{\textit{Multiply both sides by 4.}}$$
$$m = 36$$

B $3 = \frac{u}{6} - 12$

$$3 = \frac{u}{6} - 12$$
$$\underline{+12 \qquad\quad +12} \qquad \text{\textit{Add 12 to both sides.}}$$
$$15 = \frac{u}{6}$$
$$(6)15 = (6)\frac{u}{6} \qquad \text{\textit{Multiply both sides by 6.}}$$
$$90 = u$$

EXAMPLE 3 *Fitness Application*

A new one-year membership at Vista Tennis Center costs $160. A registration fee of $28 is paid up front, and the rest is paid monthly. How much do new members pay each month?

| registration fee | plus | 12 • monthly cost | is | $160 |

Let m represent the monthly cost.

$\boxed{\$28}$ + $\boxed{12m}$ = $\boxed{\$160}$

$$28 + 12m = 160$$
$$\underline{-28 \qquad\qquad -28} \qquad \text{\textit{Subtract 28 from both sides.}}$$
$$12m = 132$$
$$\frac{12m}{12} = \frac{132}{12} \qquad \text{\textit{Divide both sides by 12.}}$$
$$m = 11$$

New members pay $11 per month for a one-year membership.

Think and Discuss

1. **Explain** how you decide which inverse operation to use first when solving a two-step equation.

2. **Tell** the steps you would follow to solve $-1 + 2x = 7$.

California
Standards Practice
Preview of Grade 7 ✦ **AF4.1**

go.hrw.com
Homework Help Online
KEYWORD: MS8CA 11-1
Parent Resources Online
KEYWORD: MS8CA Parent

GUIDED PRACTICE

See Example **1** Solve.

1. $3n + 8 = 29$ **2.** $-4m - 7 = 17$ **3.** $2 = -6x + 4$

See Example **2** Solve.

4. $12 + \dfrac{b}{6} = 16$ **5.** $\dfrac{y}{8} - 15 = 2$ **6.** $10 = -8 + \dfrac{n}{4}$

See Example **3** **7.** A coffee shop sells a ceramic refill mug for $8.95. Each refill costs $1.50. Last month Rose spent $26.95 on a mug and refills. How many refills did she buy?

INDEPENDENT PRACTICE

See Example **1** Solve. Check each answer.

8. $5x + 6 = 41$ **9.** $-9p - 15 = 93$ **10.** $-2m + 14 = 10$

11. $-7 = 7d - 8$ **12.** $-7 = -3c + 14$ **13.** $12y - 11 = 49$

See Example **2** Solve.

14. $24 + \dfrac{h}{4} = 10$ **15.** $\dfrac{k}{5} - 13 = 4$ **16.** $-17 + \dfrac{q}{8} = 13$

17. $24 = \dfrac{m}{10} + 32$ **18.** $-9 = 15 + \dfrac{v}{3}$ **19.** $\dfrac{m}{-7} - 14 = 2$

See Example **3** **20.** Each Saturday, a gym holds a 45-minute yoga class. The weekday yoga classes last 30 minutes. The number of weekday classes varies. Last week, the yoga classes totaled 165 minutes. How many weekday yoga classes were held?

PRACTICE AND PROBLEM SOLVING

Extra Practice
See page EP22.

Translate each equation into words, and then solve the equation.

21. $6 + \dfrac{m}{3} = 18$ **22.** $3x + 15 = 27$ **23.** $2 = \dfrac{n}{5} - 4$

Solve.

24. $18 + \dfrac{y}{4} = 12$ **25.** $5x + 30 = 40$ **26.** $\dfrac{s}{12} - 7 = 8$

27. $-10 + 6g = 110$ **28.** $-8 = \dfrac{z}{7} + 2$ **29.** $46 = -6w - 8$

30. $15 = -7 + \dfrac{r}{3}$ **31.** $-20 = -4p - 12$ **32.** $7 + 2r = 5$

33. **Consumer Math** A long-distance phone company charges $1.01 for the first 25 minutes of a call, and then $0.09 for each additional minute. A call cost $9.56. How long did it last?

34. The school purchased baseball equipment and uniforms for a total cost of $1,836. The equipment cost $612, and the uniforms were $25.50 each. How many uniforms did the school purchase?

YOUR TOTAL COMES TO $76.41 AND 17,843 CALORIES.

As a service to health-conscious customers, many grocery stores have installed scanners that calculate the total number of calories purchased.

35. If you double the number of calories per day that the U.S. Department of Agriculture recommends for children who are 1 to 3 years old and then subtract 100, you get the number of calories per day recommended for teenage boys. Given that 2,500 calories are recommended for teenage boys, how many calories per day are recommended for children?

36. According to the U.S. Department of Agriculture, children who are 4 to 6 years old need about 1,800 calories per day. This is 700 calories more than half the recommended calories for teenage girls. How many calories per day does a teenage girl need?

37. Hector consumed 2,130 calories from food in one day. Of these, he consumed 350 calories at breakfast and 400 calories having a snack. He also ate 2 portions of one of the items shown in the table for lunch and the same for dinner. What did Hector eat for lunch and dinner?

38. ⭐ **Challenge** There are 30 mg of cholesterol in a box of macaroni and cheese. This is 77 mg minus $\frac{1}{10}$ the number of milligrams of sodium it contains. How many milligrams of sodium are in a box of macaroni and cheese?

Calorie Counter		
Food	**Portion**	**Calories**
Stir-fry	1 cup	250
Enchilada	1 whole	310
Chicken sandwich	1 whole	345
Tomato soup	1 cup	160

🪐 **go.hrw.com**
Web Extra!
KEYWORD: MS8CA Health

SPIRAL STANDARDS REVIEW

MG1.3, ⚷ MG2.2

39. Multiple Choice For which equation is $x = -2$ a solution?

Ⓐ $2x + 5 = 9$　　Ⓑ $8 = 10 - x$　　Ⓒ $\frac{x}{2} + 3 = 2$　　Ⓓ $-16 = -4x - 8$

40. Short Response A taxi cab costs $1.25 for the first mile and $0.25 for each additional mile. Write an equation for the total cost of a taxi ride, where x is the number of miles. How many miles can be traveled in the taxi for $8.00?

Find the measure of the third angle in each triangle, given two angle measures.
(Lesson 9-7)

41. 49°, 74°　　　　**42.** 115°, 37°　　　　**43.** 17°, 21°

44. A triangular prism has a base with an area of 18 in² and a height of 9 in. What is the volume of the prism? (Lesson 10-8)

11-2 Simplifying Algebraic Expressions

California Standards

Preview of Grade 7

➤ **AF1.3** Simplify numerical expressions by applying properties of rational numbers (e.g., identity, inverse, **distributive, associative,** and **commutative**) and justify the process used.

Also covered: **6AF1.2, 6AF3.1, 6AF3.2**

Why learn this? You can use an expression with more than one term to describe the length of a talent show.

Individual skits at the talent show can last up to x minutes each, and group skits can last up to y minutes each. The expression $7x + 9y$ represents the maximum length of the talent show if 7 individuals and 9 groups perform.

Vocabulary

term
coefficient

In the expression $7x + 9y$, $7x$ and $9y$ are *terms*. A **term** can be a number, a variable, or a product of numbers and variables. Terms in an expression are separated by plus or minus signs.

Caution!

A variable by itself, such as y, has a coefficient of 1. So $y = 1y$.

In the term $7x$, 7 is called the *coefficient*. A **coefficient** is a number that is multiplied by a variable in an algebraic expression.

Coefficient  Variable

Like terms are terms with the same variables raised to the same powers. The coefficients do not have to be the same. Constants, like 5, $\frac{1}{2}$, and 3.2, are also like terms.

Like Terms	$3x$ and $2x$	w and $\frac{w}{7}$	5 and 1.8
Unlike Terms	$5x^2$ and $2x$ *The exponents are different.*	$6a$ and $6b$ *The variables are different.*	3.2 and n *Only one term contains a variable.*

EXAMPLE 1 Identifying Like Terms

Identify like terms in the list.

$$5a \quad \frac{t}{2} \quad 3y^2 \quad 7t \quad x^2 \quad 4z \quad k \quad 4.5y^2 \quad 2t \quad \frac{2}{3}a$$

Look for like variables with like powers.

Helpful Hint

Use different shapes or colors to indicate sets of like terms.

$$\boxed{5a} \quad \boxed{\frac{t}{2}} \quad \boxed{3y^2} \quad \boxed{7t} \quad x^2 \quad 4z \quad k \quad \boxed{4.5y^2} \quad \boxed{2t} \quad \boxed{\frac{2}{3}a}$$

Like terms: $5a$ and $\frac{2}{3}a$ $\frac{t}{2}$, $7t$, and $2t$ $3y^2$ and $4.5y^2$

To simplify an algebraic expression that contains like terms, combine the terms. Combining like terms is like grouping similar objects.

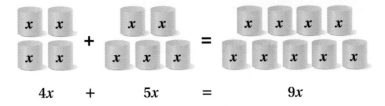

$$4x \quad + \quad 5x \quad = \quad 9x$$

To combine like terms that have variables, use the Distributive Property.
$$4x + 5x = (4 + 5)x = 9x$$

EXAMPLE **2** **Simplifying Algebraic Expressions**

Reasoning

Simplify. Justify your steps using the Commutative, Associative, and Distributive Properties when necessary.

A $7x + 2x$

$7x + 2x$ *7x and 2x are like terms.*

$(7 + 2)x = 9x$ *Distributive Property*

B $5x^3 + 3y + 7x^3 - 2y - 4x^2$

$5x^3 + 3y + 7x^3 - 2y - 4x^2$ *Identify like terms.*

$5x^3 + 7x^3 + 3y - 2y - 4x^2$ *Commutative Property*

$(5 + 7)x^3 + (3 - 2)y - 4x^2$ *Distributive Property*

$\qquad 12x^3 + y - 4x^2$

C $2(a + 2a^2) + 2b$

$2(a + 2a^2) + 2b$

$2a + 4a^2 + 2b$ *Distributive Property*

There are no like terms to combine.

EXAMPLE **3** *Geometry Application*

Remember!

To find the perimeter of a figure, add the lengths of the sides.

See Lesson 10-1, p. 486.

Write an expression for the perimeter of the quadrilateral. Then simplify the expression.

$c + d + d + c$ *Write an expression using the side lengths.*

$c + c + d + d$ *Identify and group like terms.*

$(1 + 1)c + (1 + 1)d$ *Distributive Property*

$\qquad 2c + 2d$

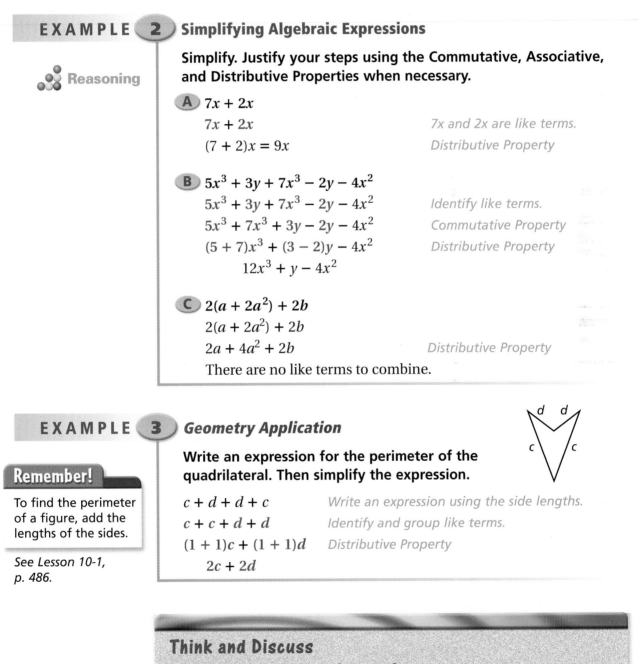

Think and Discuss

1. Explain whether $5x$, $5x^2$, and $5x^3$ are like terms.

2. Explain how you know when an expression cannot be simplified.

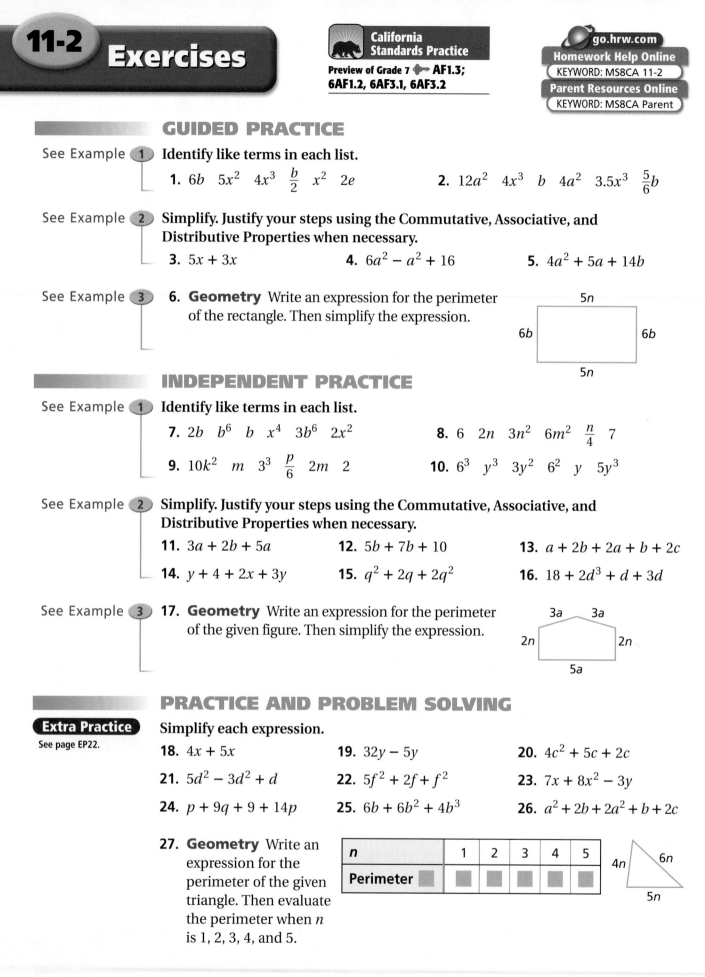

California
Standards Practice
Preview of Grade 7 ➞ **AF1.3;**
6AF1.2, 6AF3.1, 6AF3.2

go.hrw.com
Homework Help Online
KEYWORD: MS8CA 11-2
Parent Resources Online
KEYWORD: MS8CA Parent

GUIDED PRACTICE

See Example ① **Identify like terms in each list.**

1. $6b$ $5x^2$ $4x^3$ $\frac{b}{2}$ x^2 $2e$

2. $12a^2$ $4x^3$ b $4a^2$ $3.5x^3$ $\frac{5}{6}b$

See Example ② **Simplify. Justify your steps using the Commutative, Associative, and Distributive Properties when necessary.**

3. $5x + 3x$

4. $6a^2 - a^2 + 16$

5. $4a^2 + 5a + 14b$

See Example ③ **6. Geometry** Write an expression for the perimeter of the rectangle. Then simplify the expression.

INDEPENDENT PRACTICE

See Example ① **Identify like terms in each list.**

7. $2b$ b^6 b x^4 $3b^6$ $2x^2$

8. 6 $2n$ $3n^2$ $6m^2$ $\frac{n}{4}$ 7

9. $10k^2$ m 3^3 $\frac{p}{6}$ $2m$ 2

10. 6^3 y^3 $3y^2$ 6^2 y $5y^3$

See Example ② **Simplify. Justify your steps using the Commutative, Associative, and Distributive Properties when necessary.**

11. $3a + 2b + 5a$

12. $5b + 7b + 10$

13. $a + 2b + 2a + b + 2c$

14. $y + 4 + 2x + 3y$

15. $q^2 + 2q + 2q^2$

16. $18 + 2d^3 + d + 3d$

See Example ③ **17. Geometry** Write an expression for the perimeter of the given figure. Then simplify the expression.

PRACTICE AND PROBLEM SOLVING

Extra Practice
See page EP22.

Simplify each expression.

18. $4x + 5x$

19. $32y - 5y$

20. $4c^2 + 5c + 2c$

21. $5d^2 - 3d^2 + d$

22. $5f^2 + 2f + f^2$

23. $7x + 8x^2 - 3y$

24. $p + 9q + 9 + 14p$

25. $6b + 6b^2 + 4b^3$

26. $a^2 + 2b + 2a^2 + b + 2c$

27. Geometry Write an expression for the perimeter of the given triangle. Then evaluate the perimeter when n is 1, 2, 3, 4, and 5.

n	1	2	3	4	5
Perimeter					

28. Critical Thinking Determine whether the expression $9m^2 + k$ is equal to $7m^2 + 2(2k - m^2) + 5k$. Use properties to justify your answer.

29. Multi-Step Brad makes d dollars per hour as a cook at a deli. The table shows the number of hours he worked each week in June.

Hours Brad Worked	
Week	**Hours**
1	21.5
2	23
3	15.5
4	19

  a. Write and simplify an expression for the amount of money Brad earned in June.

  b. Evaluate your expression from part **a** for $d = \$9.50$.

  c. What does your answer to part **b** represent?

30. Business Ashley earns $8 per hour working at a grocery store. Last week she worked h hours bagging groceries and twice as many hours stocking shelves. Write and simplify an expression for the amount Ashley earned.

31. Reasoning The terms $3x$, $23x^2$, $6y^2$, $2x$, y^2 and one other term can be written in an expression which, when simplified, equals $5x + 7y^2$. Identify the term missing from the list and write the expression.

32. What's the Question? At one store, a pair of jeans costs $29 and a shirt costs $25. At another store, the same kind of jeans costs $26 and the same kind of shirt costs $20. The answer is $29j - 26j + 25s - 20s = 3j + 5s$. What is the question?

33. Write About It Describe the steps for simplifying the expression $2x + 3 + 5x - 15$.

34. Challenge A rectangle has a width of $x + 2$ and a length of $3x + 1$. Write and simplify an expression for the perimeter of the rectangle.

SPIRAL STANDARDS REVIEW   AF1.2, AF2.1, AF3.1, AF3.2

35. Multiple Choice Translate "six times the sum of x and y" and "five less than y." Which algebraic expression represents the sum of these two verbal expressions?

  Ⓐ $6x + 5$ Ⓑ $6x + 2y - 5$ Ⓒ $6x + 5y + 5$ Ⓓ $6x + 7y - 5$

36. Multiple Choice The side length of a square is $2x + 3$. Which expression represents the perimeter of the square?

  Ⓐ $2x + 12$ Ⓑ $4x + 6$ Ⓒ $6x + 7$ Ⓓ $8x + 12$

Evaluate the expression $9y - 3$ for each given value of the variable. (Lesson 1-5)

37. $y = 2$ **38.** $y = 6$ **39.** $y = 10$ **40.** $y = 18$

Convert each measure. (Lesson 4-9)

41. 23 cm to millimeters   **42.** 600 m to kilometers   **43.** 0.5 g to milligrams

11-3 Solving Multi-Step Equations

California Standards

Preview of Grade 7

🔑 **AF1.3 Simplify** numerical expressions by applying properties of rational numbers (e.g., identity, inverse, **distributive**, **associative**, and **commutative**) and justify the process used.

Also covered: **Preview of Algebra I** 🔑 **5.0**

Why learn this? You can solve a multi-step equation to determine the number of comic books in a collection. (See Example 3.)

Some types of equations require more than two steps to solve. These equations are known as multi-step equations. The first step in solving some multi-step equations is to combine like terms.

E X A M P L E **1** **Combining Like Terms to Solve Equations**

Solve $7n - 1 - 2n = 14$.

$$7n - 1 - 2n = 14$$
$$5n - 1 = 14 \qquad \text{Combine like terms.}$$
$$\underline{+1 \qquad +1} \qquad \text{Add 1 to both sides.}$$
$$5n = 15$$

$$\frac{5n}{5} = \frac{15}{5} \qquad \text{Divide both sides by 5.}$$
$$n = 3$$

You may need to use the Distributive Property to solve an equation that has parentheses. Multiply each term inside the parentheses by the factor that is outside the parentheses. Then combine like terms.

E X A M P L E **2** **Using the Distributive Property to Solve Equations**

Remember!

The Distributive Property states that $a(b + c) = ab + ac$. For instance, $2(3 + 5) = 2(3) + 2(5)$.

See Lesson 1-4, p. 21.

Solve $3(z - 1) + 8 = 14$.

$$3(z - 1) + 8 = 14$$
$$3(z) - 3(1) + 8 = 14 \qquad \text{Distribute 3 on the left side.}$$
$$3z - 3 + 8 = 14 \qquad \text{Simplify.}$$
$$3z + 5 = 14 \qquad \text{Combine like terms.}$$
$$\underline{-5 \qquad -5} \qquad \text{Subtract 5 from both sides.}$$
$$3z = 9$$
$$\frac{3z}{3} = \frac{9}{3} \qquad \text{Divide both sides by 3.}$$
$$z = 3$$

EXAMPLE 3 **PROBLEM SOLVING APPLICATION**

PROBLEM
SOLVING

Reasoning

Jamal owns twice as many comic books as Levi owns. Brooke owns 6 more than the number of comic books Jamal and Levi own combined. Brooke owns 30 comic books. How many does Levi own?

1 Understand the Problem

Rewrite the question as a statement.

• Find the number of comic books that Levi owns.

List the **important information:**

• Jamal owns 2 times as many comic books as Levi owns.

• The number of comic books Jamal owns plus the number Levi owns added to 6 equals the number Brooke owns.

• Brooke owns 30 comic books.

2 Make a Plan

Let c represent the number of comic books Levi owns. Then $2c$ represents the number Jamal owns.

Jamal's books	+	Levi's books	+	6	=	Brooke's books
$2c$	+	c	+	6	=	30

Solve the equation $2c + c + 6 = 30$ for c.

3 Solve

$$2c + c + 6 = 30$$

$$3c + 6 = 30 \qquad \textit{Combine like terms.}$$

$$\underline{-6 \qquad -6} \qquad \textit{Subtract 6 from both sides.}$$

$$3c = 24$$

$$\frac{3c}{3} = \frac{24}{3} \qquad \textit{Divide both sides by 3.}$$

$$c = 8$$

Levi owns 8 comic books.

4 Look Back

Make sure that your answer makes sense in the original problem. Levi has 8 comic books. Jamal has $2(8) = 16$. Brooke has $8 + 16 + 6 = 30$.

Think and Discuss

1. **List** the steps required to solve $-n + 5n + 3 = 27$.

2. **Describe** how to solve the equations $4x + 2 = 10$ and $4(x + 2) = 10$. Are the solutions the same or different? Explain.

11-3 Exercises

California
Standards Practice
Preview of Grade 7 ➡ AF1.3 and
Algebra I ➡ 5.0

go.hrw.com
Homework Help Online
KEYWORD: MS8CA 11-3
Parent Resources Online
KEYWORD: MS8CA Parent

GUIDED PRACTICE

See Example 1   Solve.

1. $14n + 2 - 7n = 37$ **2.** $10x - 11 - 4x = 43$ **3.** $1 = -3 + 4p - 2p$

See Example 2   **4.** $12 - (x + 3) = 10$ **5.** $15 = 2(q + 4) + 3$ **6.** $5(m - 2) + 36 = -4$

See Example 3   **7.** Keisha read twice as many books this year as Ben read. Subtracting 5 from the number of books Keisha and Ben read combined gives the number of books Sheldon read. Sheldon read 10 books. How many books did Ben read?

INDEPENDENT PRACTICE

See Example 1   Solve.

8. $b + 18 + 3b = 74$ **9.** $10x - 3 - 2x = 4$

10. $18w - 10 - 6w = 50$ **11.** $19 = 5n + 7 - 3n$

12. $-27 = -3p + 15 - 3p$ **13.** $-x - 8 + 14x = -34$

See Example 2   **14.** $2(x + 4) + 6 = 22$ **15.** $1 - 3(n + 5) = -8$

16. $43 - 14(p + 7) = -97$ **17.** $18 + 60n - 32 = 76$

18. $0 = 9\left(k - \frac{2}{3}\right) + 33$ **19.** $6(t - 2) - 76 = -142$

See Example 3   **20.** Abby ran 3 times as many laps as Karen. Adding 4 to the number of laps Abby and Karen ran combined gives the number of laps Jill ran. Jill ran 8 laps. How many laps did Karen run?

PRACTICE AND PROBLEM SOLVING

Extra Practice
See page EP22.

Solve.

21. $0.5x + 7 + 1.5x = 5$ **22.** $4(t - 8) + 20 = 5$ **23.** $63 = 8w + 26 - 27$

24. $17 = -5(3 + w) + 7$ **25.** $\frac{1}{4}a - 12 + \frac{7}{4}a = 4$ **26.** $9 = -(r - 5) + 11$

27. $2(b - 3) = -30$ **28.** $8.44 = 0.4h + 6.92 + 0.4h$ **29.** $57 = -25x + 180 - 16x$

30. Consumer Math Three friends ate dinner at a restaurant. The friends decided to add a 15% tip and then split the bill evenly. Each friend paid $10.35. What was the total bill for dinner before tip?

31. Ann earns 1.5 times her normal hourly pay for each hour that she works over 40 hours in a week. Last week she worked 51 hours and earned $378.55. What is her normal hourly pay?

32. Geometry The base angles of an isosceles triangle are congruent. The measure of each of the base angles is twice the measure of the third angle. Find the measures of all three angles.

33. Consumer Math Patrice used a $15 gift certificate when she purchased a pair of sandals. After 8% sales tax was applied to the price of the sandals, the $15 was deducted. Patrice had to pay a total of $12 for the sandals. How much did the sandals cost before tax?

34. Science To convert temperatures between degrees Celsius and degrees Fahrenheit, you can use the formula $F = \frac{9}{5}C + 32$. The table shows the melting points of various elements.

a. What is the melting point in degrees Celsius of gold?

b. What is the melting point in degrees Celsius of hydrogen?

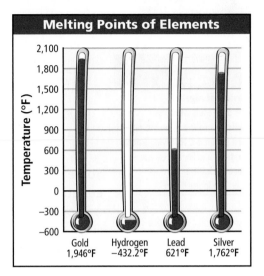

Melting Points of Elements

Gold	Hydrogen	Lead	Silver
1,946°F	−432.2°F	621°F	1,762°F

35. On his first two social studies tests, Billy made an 86 and a 93. What grade must Billy make on the third test to have an average of 90 for all three tests?

36. What's the Question? Three friends shared a taxi ride from the airport to their hotel. After adding a $7.00 tip, the friends divided the cost of the ride evenly. If solving the equation $\frac{1}{3}(c + \$7.00) = \$11.25$ gives the answer, what is the question?

37. Write About It Describe two different ways you could solve the equation $3(x + 4) = 15$.

38. Challenge Are the solutions to the following equations the same? Explain.
$$\frac{3y}{4} + 2 = 4 \text{ and } 3y + 8 = 16$$

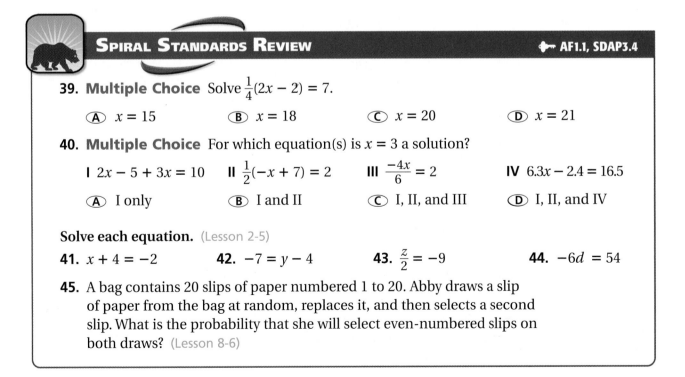

Solving Equations with Variables on Both Sides

California Standards

Preview of Algebra I

← **5.0** Students solve multistep problems, including word problems, involving linear equations and linear inequalities in one variable and provide justification for each step.

Why learn this? You can determine how many weeks you would have to rent a video game console to make buying the console worth the price. (See Example 3.)

Some problems require you to solve equations that have the same variable on both sides of the equal sign. To solve this kind of problem, you need to get the terms with variables on one side of the equal sign.

EXAMPLE 1 **Using Inverse Operations to Group Terms with Variables**

Group the terms with variables on one side of the equal sign, and simplify.

A $6m = 4m + 12$

$$
\begin{array}{ll}
6m = \quad 4m + 12 & \\
\underline{-\,4m \quad -\,4m} & \text{Subtract 4m from both sides.} \\
2m = 12 & \text{Simplify.}
\end{array}
$$

B $-7x - 198 = 5x$

$$
\begin{array}{ll}
-7x - 198 = \quad 5x & \\
\underline{+\,7x \qquad\quad +\,7x} & \text{Add 7x to both sides.} \\
-198 = \quad 12x & \text{Simplify.}
\end{array}
$$

EXAMPLE 2 **Solving Equations with Variables on Both Sides**

Reasoning

Solve.

A $5n = 3n + 26$

$$
\begin{array}{ll}
5n = \quad 3n + 26 & \\
\underline{-\,3n \quad -\,3n} & \text{Subtract 3n from both sides.} \\
2n = \qquad\quad 26 & \text{Simplify.} \\
\dfrac{2n}{2} = \dfrac{26}{2} & \text{Divide both sides by 2.} \\
n = 13 &
\end{array}
$$

Check $\quad 5n = 3n + 26$

$\qquad 5(13) \overset{?}{=} 3(13) + 26 \qquad$ *Substitute 13 for n.*

$\qquad\qquad 65 = 65\ ✔ \qquad$ *65 is a solution.*

Solve.

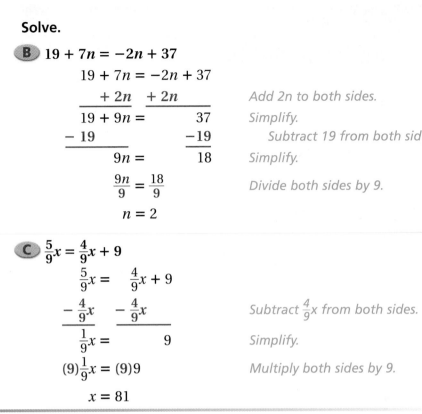

B $19 + 7n = -2n + 37$

$$19 + 7n = -2n + 37$$

$\underline{+\ 2n \qquad +\ 2n}$	Add 2n to both sides.
$19 + 9n = \qquad 37$	Simplify.
$\underline{-\ 19 \qquad\qquad -19}$	Subtract 19 from both sides.
$9n = \qquad 18$	Simplify.
$\dfrac{9n}{9} = \dfrac{18}{9}$	Divide both sides by 9.
$n = 2$	

C $\frac{5}{9}x = \frac{4}{9}x + 9$

$\frac{5}{9}x = \quad \frac{4}{9}x + 9$	
$\underline{-\frac{4}{9}x \qquad -\frac{4}{9}x}$	Subtract $\frac{4}{9}x$ from both sides.
$\frac{1}{9}x = \qquad 9$	Simplify.
$(9)\frac{1}{9}x = (9)9$	Multiply both sides by 9.
$x = 81$	

EXAMPLE 3 *Consumer Math Application*

Mari can buy a video game console for $72.45 and rent a game for $7.95 per week, or she can rent a console and the same game for a total of $22.44 per week. How many weeks would Mari need to rent both the video game and the console to pay as much as she would if she had bought the console and rented the game instead?

Let w represent the number of weeks.

$22.44w = 72.45 + 7.95w$	
$\underline{-\ 7.95w \qquad\qquad -\ 7.95w}$	Subtract 7.95w from both sides.
$14.49w = 72.45$	Simplify.
$\dfrac{14.49w}{14.49} = \dfrac{72.45}{14.49}$	Divide both sides by 14.49.
$w = 5$	

Mari would need to rent the video game and the console for 5 weeks to pay as much as she would have if she had bought the console.

Think and Discuss

1. **Explain** how you would solve $\frac{1}{2}x + 7 = \frac{2}{3}x - 2$.

2. **Describe** how you would decide which variable term to add or subtract on both sides of the equation $-3x + 7 = 4x - 9$.

11-4 **Exercises**

California Standards Practice
Preview of Algebra I ✦ 5.0

go.hrw.com
Homework Help Online
KEYWORD: MS8CA 11-4
Parent Resources Online
KEYWORD: MS8CA Parent

GUIDED PRACTICE

See Example **1** Group the terms with variables on one side of the equal sign, and simplify.

1. $5n = 4n + 32$ **2.** $-6x - 28 = 4x$ **3.** $8w = 32 - 4w$

See Example **2** Solve.

4. $4y = 2y + 40$ **5.** $8 + 6a = -2a + 24$ **6.** $\frac{3}{4}d + 4 = \frac{1}{4}d + 18$

See Example **3** **7. Consumer Math** Members at the Star Theater pay $30.00 per month plus $1.95 for each movie. Nonmembers pay the regular $7.95 admission fee. How many movies would both a member and a nonmember have to see in a month to pay the same amount?

INDEPENDENT PRACTICE

See Example **1** Group the terms with variables on one side of the equal sign, and simplify.

8. $12h = 9h + 84$ **9.** $-10p - 8 = 2p$ **10.** $6q = 18 - 2q$

11. $-4c - 6 = -2c$ **12.** $-7s + 12 = -9s$ **13.** $6 + \frac{4}{5}a = \frac{9}{10}a$

See Example **2** Solve.

14. $9t = 4t + 120$ **15.** $42 + 3b = -4b - 14$ **16.** $\frac{6}{11}x + 4 = \frac{2}{11}x + 16$

17. $1.5a + 6 = 9a + 12$ **18.** $32 - \frac{3}{8}y = \frac{3}{4}y + 5$ **19.** $-6 - 8c = 3c + 16$

See Example **3** **20. Consumer Math** Members at a swim club pay $5 per lesson plus a one-time fee of $60. Nonmembers pay $11 per lesson. How many lessons would both a member and a nonmember have to take to pay the same amount?

PRACTICE AND PROBLEM SOLVING

Extra Practice
See page EP22.

Solve. Check each answer.

21. $3y + 7 = -6y - 56$ **22.** $\frac{7}{8}x + 6 = \frac{3}{8}x + 14$

23. $5r + 6 - 2r = 7r - 10$ **24.** $-10p + 8 = 7p + 12$

25. $9 + 5r = -17 - 8r$ **26.** $8k + 70 = -7k + 10$

27. Reasoning A choir is singing at a festival. On the first night, 12 choir members were absent, so the choir stood in 5 equal rows. On the second night, only 1 member was absent, so the choir stood in 6 equal rows. The same number of people stood in each row each night. How many members are in the choir?

28. Consumer Math Jaline can purchase tile at a store for $0.99 per tile and rent a tile saw for $24. At another store, she can borrow the tile saw for free if she buys tile there for $1.49 per tile. How many tiles must she buy for the cost to be the same at both stores?

The figures in each pair have the same perimeter. Find the value of each variable.

29.

x $x + 4$ x $x + 9$ $x + 5$

30.

$s + 7$ $3s$ $2s + 12$ $2s + 12$ $2s + 12$

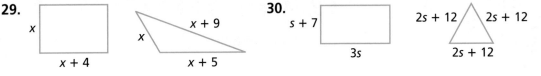

31. Recreation A rock-climbing gym charges nonmembers $18 per day to use the wall plus $7 per day for equipment rental. Members pay an annual fee of $400 plus $5 per day for equipment rental. How many days must both a member and a nonmember use the wall in one year so that both pay the same amount?

32. Multi-Step Two families drove from Denver to Cincinnati. After driving 582 miles the first day, the Smiths spread the rest of the trip equally over the next 3 days. The Chows spread their trip equally over 6 days. The distance the Chows drove each day was equal to the distance the Smiths drove each of the three days.

   a. How many miles did the Chows drive each day?

   b. How far is it from Denver to Cincinnati?

33. What's the Error? To combine terms in the equation $-8a - 4 = 2a + 34$, a student wrote $-6a = 38$. What is the error?

34. Write About It If the same variable is on both sides of an equation, must it have the same value on each side? Explain your answer.

35. Challenge Combine terms before solving the equation $12x - 4 - 12 = 4x + 8 + 8x - 24$. Do you think there is just one solution to the equation? Why or why not?

SPIRAL STANDARDS REVIEW   ← MG1.1, MG1.2, ← MG2.2

36. Multiple Choice For which equation is $x = 0$ NOT a solution?

   (A) $3x + 2 = 2 - x$ (B) $2.5x + 3 = x$ (C) $-x + 4 = 3x + 4$ (D) $6x + 2 = x + 2$

37. Extended Response One calling plan offers long-distance calls for $0.03 per minute. Another plan costs $2.00 per month but offers long-distance service for $0.01 per minute. Write and solve an equation to find the number of long-distance minutes for which the two plans would cost the same. Write your answer in a complete sentence.

Find the measure of the angle that is complementary to each given angle. (Lesson 9-4)

38. $32°$ **39.** $89°$ **40.** $13°$ **41.** $45°$

Given the radius or diameter, find the area of each circle. Use $\frac{22}{7}$ as an estimate for π. (Lesson 10-5)

42. $r = 35$ in.   **43.** $d = 14$ m   **44.** $r = 28$ cm   **45.** $d = 21$ yd

READY TO GO ON?

Quiz for Lessons 11-1 Through 11-4

 11-1 Solving Two-Step Equations

Solve.

1. $-4x + 6 = 54$ **2.** $15 + \frac{y}{3} = 6$ **3.** $\frac{z}{8} - 5 = -3$

4. $-33 = -7a - 5$ **5.** $-27 = \frac{r}{12} - 19$ **6.** $-13 = 11 - 2n$

7. A taxi service charges an initial fee of $1.50 plus $1.50 for every mile traveled. A taxi ride costs $21.00. How many miles did the taxi travel?

 11-2 Simplifying Algebraic Expressions

Simplify each expression.

8. $2y - 2y^2 + 5y^2$ **9.** $x - 4 + 7x - 9$ **10.** $10 + b - 6a - 9b$

11. Write an expression for the perimeter of the given figure. Then simplify the expression.

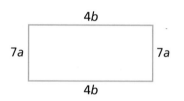

 11-3 Solving Multi-Step Equations

Solve.

12. $3(3b + 2) = -30$ **13.** $13 = 2c + 3 + 5c$ **14.** $\frac{1}{2}(8w - 6) = 17$

15. $6(x - 4) + 10 = 28$ **16.** $6m - 4m + 8 = 34$ **17.** $15 = 5 + 9p - 4p$

18. Peter used a $5.00 gift certificate to help pay for his lunch. After adding a 15% tip to the cost of his meal, Peter still had to pay $2.36 in cash. How much did Peter's meal cost?

 11-4 Solving Equations with Variables on Both Sides

Solve.

19. $12m = 3m + 108$ **20.** $\frac{7}{8}n - 3 = \frac{5}{8}n + 12$

21. $1.2x + 3.7 = 2.2x - 4.5$ **22.** $-7 - 7p = 3p + 23$

23. $2.3q - 16 = 5q + 38$ **24.** $\frac{3}{5}k + \frac{7}{10} = \frac{11}{15}k - \frac{2}{5}$

25. One shuttle service charges $10 for pickup and $0.10 per mile. Another shuttle service has no pickup fee but charges $0.35 per mile. Find the number of miles for which the cost of the two shuttle services is the same.

Focus on Problem Solving

California Standards

6MR1.3 Determine when and how to break a problem into simpler parts.

Also covered: **Preview of Grade 7**

👉 **AF4.1 and Algebra I**

👉 **5.0**

Solve

• Write an equation

When you are asked to solve a problem, be sure to read the entire problem before you begin solving it. Sometimes you will need to perform several steps to solve the problem, and you will need to know all of the information in the problem before you decide which steps to take.

Read each problem and determine what steps are needed to solve it. Then write an equation that can be used to solve the problem.

1 Martin can buy a pair of inline skates and safety equipment for $49.50. At a roller rink, Martin can rent a pair of inline skates for $2.50 per day, but he still needs to buy safety equipment for $19.50. How many days would Martin have to skate in order to pay as much to rent skates and buy safety equipment as he would have to pay to buy both?

2 Christopher draws caricatures at the local mall. He charges $5 for a simple sketch and $15 for a larger drawing. In one day, Christopher earned $175. He drew 20 simple sketches that day. How many larger drawings did he make?

3 Book-club members are required to buy a minimum number of books each year. Leslee bought 3 times the minimum. Denise bought 7 more than the minimum. Together, they bought 23 books. What is the minimum number of books?

4 Coach Willis has won 150 games during his career. This is 10 more than $\frac{1}{2}$ as many games as Coach Gentry has won. How many games has Coach Gentry won?

5 The perimeter of an isosceles triangle is 4 times the length of the shortest side. The longer sides are 4.5 ft longer than the shortest side. What is the length of each side of the triangle?

6 Miss Rankin's class has raised $100.00 for a class trip. The class needs to collect a total of $225.00. How many $0.50 carnations must the class sell to reach its goal?

California Standards

Preview of Grade 7

AF1.1 Use variables and appropriate operations **to write** an expression, an equation, **an inequality,** or a system of equations or inequalities **that represents a verbal description** (e.g., three less than a number, half as large as area *A*).

Vocabulary
inequality
algebraic inequality
solution set
compound inequality

Why learn this? You can use an inequality to describe the number of students in an auditorium. (See Example 1.)

An **inequality** is a statement that compares two expressions by using one of the following symbols: $<$, $>$, $\leq$, $\geq$, or $\neq$.

Symbol	Meaning	Word Phrases
$<$	Is less than	Fewer than, below
$>$	Is greater than	More than, above
$\leq$	Is less than or equal to	At most, no more than
$\geq$	Is greater than or equal to	At least, no less than

EXAMPLE 1 Writing Inequalities

Write an inequality for each situation.

A There are at least 25 students in the auditorium.

number of students $\geq$ 25   *"At least" means greater than or equal to.*

B No more than 150 people can occupy the room.

room capacity $\leq$ 150   *"No more than" means less than or equal to.*

An inequality that contains a variable is an **algebraic inequality**. A value of the variable that makes the inequality true is a solution of the inequality. An inequality may have more than one solution. Together, all of the solutions are called the **solution set**.

You can graph the solutions of an inequality on a number line. If the variable is "greater than" or "less than" a number, then that number is indicated with an open circle.

This open circle shows that 5 is not a solution.

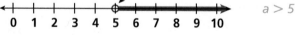

$a > 5$

If the variable is "greater than or equal to" or "less than or equal to" a number, that number is indicated with a closed circle.

This closed circle shows that 3 is a solution.

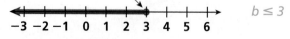

$b \leq 3$

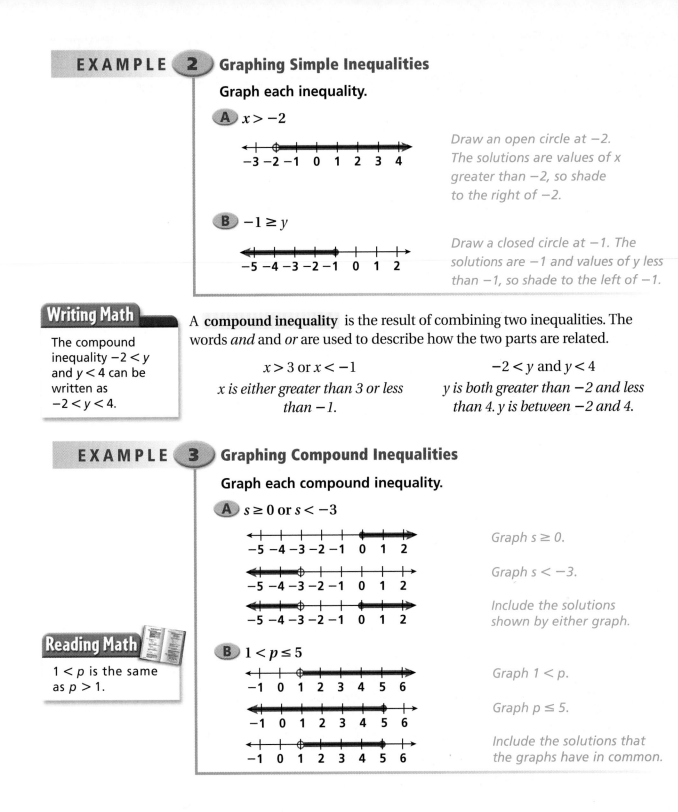

EXAMPLE **2** **Graphing Simple Inequalities**

Graph each inequality.

A $x > -2$

Draw an open circle at −2. The solutions are values of x greater than −2, so shade to the right of −2.

B $-1 \geq y$

Draw a closed circle at −1. The solutions are −1 and values of y less than −1, so shade to the left of −1.

Writing Math

The compound inequality $-2 < y$ and $y < 4$ can be written as $-2 < y < 4$.

A **compound inequality** is the result of combining two inequalities. The words *and* and *or* are used to describe how the two parts are related.

$x > 3$ or $x < -1$

x is either greater than 3 or less than −1.

$-2 < y$ and $y < 4$

y is both greater than −2 and less than 4. y is between −2 and 4.

EXAMPLE **3** **Graphing Compound Inequalities**

Graph each compound inequality.

A $s \geq 0$ or $s < -3$

Graph $s \geq 0$.

Graph $s < -3$.

Include the solutions shown by either graph.

Reading Math

$1 < p$ is the same as $p > 1$.

B $1 < p \leq 5$

Graph $1 < p$.

Graph $p \leq 5$.

Include the solutions that the graphs have in common.

Think and Discuss

1. Compare the graphs of the inequalities $y > 2$ and $y \geq 2$.

2. Explain how to graph each type of compound inequality.

11-5 **Exercises**

California
Standards Practice
Preview of Grade 7 **AF1.1**

go.hrw.com
Homework Help Online
KEYWORD: MS8CA 11-5
Parent Resources Online
KEYWORD: MS8CA Parent

GUIDED PRACTICE

See Example ① **Write an inequality for each situation.**

1. No more than 18 people are allowed in the gallery at one time.

2. There are fewer than 8 fish in the aquarium.

3. The water level is above 45 inches.

See Example ② **Graph each inequality.**

4. $x < 3$ **5.** $\frac{1}{2} \geq r$ **6.** $2.8 < w$ **7.** $y \geq -4$

See Example ③ **Graph each compound inequality.**

8. $a > 2$ or $a \leq -1$ **9.** $-4 < p \leq 6$ **10.** $-2 \leq n < 0$

INDEPENDENT PRACTICE

See Example ① **Write an inequality for each situation.**

11. The temperature is below 40°F.

12. There are at least 24 pictures on the roll of film.

13. No more than 35 tables are in the cafeteria.

14. Fewer than 250 people attended the rally.

See Example ② **Graph each inequality.**

15. $s \geq -1$ **16.** $y < 0$ **17.** $n \leq -3$

18. $2 < x$ **19.** $-6 \leq b$ **20.** $m < -4$

See Example ③ **Graph each compound inequality.**

21. $p > 3$ or $p < 0$ **22.** $1 \leq x \leq 4$ **23.** $-3 < y < -1$

24. $k > 0$ or $k \leq -2$ **25.** $n \geq 1$ or $n \leq -1$ **26.** $-2 < w \leq 2$

PRACTICE AND PROBLEM SOLVING

Extra Practice
See page EP23.

Graph each inequality or compound inequality.

27. $z \leq -5$ **28.** $3 > f$ **29.** $m \geq -2$

30. $3 > y$ or $y \geq 6$ **31.** $-9 < p \leq -3$ **32.** $q > 2$ or $-1 > q$

Write each statement using inequality symbols.

33. The number c is between -2 and 3. **34.** The number y is greater than -10.

Write an inequality shown by each graph.

35.

36.

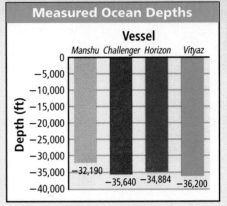

Continental shelf ▬
Continental slope ▬
Continental rise ▬

Abyssal plain

The portion of the earth's surface that lies beneath the ocean and consists of continental crust is the continental margin. The continental margin is divided into the continental shelf, the continental slope, and the continental rise.

37. The continental shelf begins at the shoreline and slopes toward the open ocean. The depth of the continental shelf can reach 200 meters. Write a compound inequality for the depth of the continental shelf.

38. The continental slope begins at the edge of the continental shelf and continues down to the flattest part of the ocean floor. The depth of the continental slope ranges from about 200 meters to about 4,000 meters. Write a compound inequality for the depth of the continental slope.

39. The bar graph shows the depth of the ocean in various locations as measured by different research vessels. For each vessel, write a compound inequality that shows the ranges of depth that it measured.

40. ⭐ **Challenge** Water freezes at 32°F and boils at 212°F. Write three inequalities to show the ranges of temperatures for which water is a solid, a liquid, and a gas.

Deep Flight is designed to explore the ocean in underwater flights.

Measured Ocean Depths

Vessel

Manshu Challenger Horizon Vityaz

Depth (ft)

0
−5,000
−10,000
−15,000
−20,000
−25,000
−30,000
−35,000 — −32,190
−40,000

−35,640 −34,884 −36,200

SPIRAL STANDARDS REVIEW ⬩ NS1.3, ⬩ AF2.2, AF2.3

41. Multiple Choice Which inequality represents *a number that is greater than −4 and less than 3?*

Ⓐ $-4 \geq n \geq 3$　　Ⓑ $-4 < n < 3$　　Ⓒ $-4 > n > 3$　　Ⓓ $-4 \leq n \leq 3$

42. Multiple Choice Which inequality is shown by the graph?

$$\leftarrow\!\!+\!\!+\!\!+\!\!+\!\!+\!\!|\!\!+\!\!|\!\!+\!\!+\!\!\rightarrow$$
−5 −4 −3 −2 −1　0　1　2　3　4　5

Ⓐ $x < -1$ or $x \leq 2$　Ⓑ $x < -1$ or $x \geq 2$　Ⓒ $x \leq -1$ or $x < 2$　Ⓓ $x \leq -1$ or $x > 2$

43. Mateo drove 472 miles in 8 hours. What was his average rate of speed? (Lesson 5-2)

Use cross products to solve each proportion. (Lesson 5-4)

44. $\dfrac{x}{5} = \dfrac{9}{30}$　　　　**45.** $\dfrac{12}{14} = \dfrac{36}{n}$　　　　**46.** $\dfrac{16}{y} = \dfrac{12}{75}$　　　　**47.** $\dfrac{w}{24} = \dfrac{34}{60}$

11-6 Solving Inequalities by Adding or Subtracting

California Standards

Preview of Grade 7

AF4.0 Students solve simple linear equations and inequalities over the rational numbers.

Why learn this? You can solve an inequality to determine the high temperature on a day when the temperature is different than the day before. (See Example 3.)

In Joshua Tree National Park, a day of snow can be followed by a day of sun.

When you add or subtract the same number on both sides of an inequality, the resulting statement will still be true.

$$
\begin{array}{rr}
-2 < & 5 \\
\underline{+7} & \underline{+7} \\
5 < & 12
\end{array}
$$

You can find solution sets of inequalities the same way you find solutions of equations, by isolating the variable.

EXAMPLE **1** **Solving Inequalities by Adding**

Solve. Then graph each solution set on a number line.

A $x - 12 > 32$

$$
\begin{array}{rr}
x - 12 > & 32 \\
\underline{+ 12} & \underline{+ 12} \\
x \quad\quad > & 44
\end{array}
$$

Add 12 to both sides.

Draw an open circle at 44. Solutions are values of x greater than 44, so shade to the right of 44.

Check According to the graph, 55 should be a solution.

$$
\begin{array}{c}
x - 12 > 32 \\
55 - 12 \overset{?}{>} 32 \\
43 > 32 ✔
\end{array}
$$

Substitute 55 for x.

55 is a solution.

B $-14 \geq y - 8$

$$
\begin{array}{rr}
-14 \geq & y - 8 \\
\underline{+ 8} & \underline{+ 8} \\
-6 \geq & y
\end{array}
$$

Add 8 to both sides.

Draw a closed circle at −6. Solutions are −6 and values of y less than −6, so shade to the left of −6.

As shown in Example 1A, you can check the solution to an inequality by choosing any number in the solution set and substituting it into the original inequality.

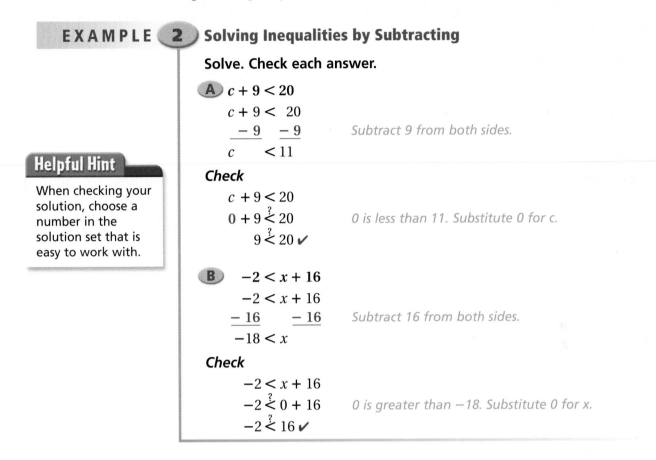

EXAMPLE 2 Solving Inequalities by Subtracting

Solve. Check each answer.

A $c + 9 < 20$

$$c + 9 < 20$$
$$\underline{-9 \phantom{<}-9} \qquad \text{Subtract 9 from both sides.}$$
$$c < 11$$

Check

$$c + 9 < 20$$
$$0 + 9 \overset{?}{<} 20 \qquad \text{0 is less than 11. Substitute 0 for c.}$$
$$9 \overset{?}{<} 20 \checkmark$$

> **Helpful Hint**
>
> When checking your solution, choose a number in the solution set that is easy to work with.

B $-2 < x + 16$

$$-2 < x + 16$$
$$\underline{-16 \phantom{<x}-16} \qquad \text{Subtract 16 from both sides.}$$
$$-18 < x$$

Check

$$-2 < x + 16$$
$$-2 \overset{?}{<} 0 + 16 \qquad \text{0 is greater than } -18. \text{ Substitute 0 for x.}$$
$$-2 \overset{?}{<} 16 \checkmark$$

EXAMPLE 3 *Weather Application*

Sunday's high temperature of 52°F was at least 20°F higher than Monday's high temperature. What was Monday's high temperature?

Sunday's high	was at least	20°F higher than	Monday's high.
52	≥	20	+ t

$$52 \geq 20 + t$$
$$\underline{-20 -20} \qquad \text{Subtract 20 from both sides.}$$
$$32 \geq t \qquad \text{Rewrite the inequality.}$$
$$t \leq 32$$

Monday's high temperature was at most 32°F.

> **Think and Discuss**
>
> **1. Compare** solving addition and subtraction equations with solving addition and subtraction inequalities.
>
> **2. Describe** how to check whether -36 is a solution of $s - 5 > 1$.

California Standards Practice
Preview of Grade 7 ➤ **AF4.0**

go.hrw.com
Homework Help Online
KEYWORD: MS8CA 11-6
Parent Resources Online
KEYWORD: MS8CA Parent

GUIDED PRACTICE

See Example **1** Solve. Then graph each solution set on a number line.

1. $x - 9 < 18$ **2.** $y - 11 \geq -7$ **3.** $4 \geq p - 3$

See Example **2** Solve. Check each answer.

4. $n + 5 > 26$ **5.** $b + 21 \leq -3$ **6.** $9 \leq 12 + k$

See Example **3** **7. Weather** Yesterday's high temperature was 30°F. Tomorrow's weather forecast includes a high temperature that is no more than 12°F warmer than yesterday's. What high temperatures are forecast for tomorrow?

INDEPENDENT PRACTICE

See Example **1** Solve. Then graph each solution set on a number line.

8. $s - 2 > 14$ **9.** $m - 14 < -3$ **10.** $b - 25 > -30$

11. $c - 17 \leq -6$ **12.** $-25 > y - 53$ **13.** $71 \leq x - 9$

See Example **2** Solve. Check each answer.

14. $w + 16 < 4$ **15.** $z + 9 > -3$ **16.** $p + 21 \leq -4$

17. $26 < f + 32$ **18.** $65 > k + 54$ **19.** $n + 29 \geq 25$

See Example **3** **20.** Clark scored at least 12 points more than Josh scored. Josh scored 15 points. How many points did Clark score?

21. Science Adriana is helping track bird populations. She counted 8 fewer birds on Tuesday than on Thursday. She counted at most 32 birds on Thursday. How many birds did Adriana count on Tuesday?

PRACTICE AND PROBLEM SOLVING

Extra Practice
See page EP23.

Solve.

22. $k + 3.2 \geq 8$ **23.** $a - 13 > -10$ **24.** $c - 1\frac{1}{4} < 6\frac{1}{2}$

25. $-20 \geq 18 + m$ **26.** $7.02 < x + 4$ **27.** $g + 3\frac{2}{3} < 10$

28. $-109 > r - 58$ **29.** $5.9 + w \leq 21.6$ **30.** $n - 21.6 > 26$

31. $-150 \leq t + 92$ **32.** $y + 1\frac{1}{8} \geq 4\frac{3}{4}$ **33.** $v + 0.9 \leq 1.5$

34. Consumer Math To get a group discount for baseball tickets, Marco's group must have at least 20 people. The group needs at least 7 more people to sign up. How many have signed up so far?

35. Recreation Mila is 62 inches tall. She needs a surfboard of length ℓ that is at least 12 inches longer than her height. Write and solve an inequality to find the values of ℓ that are suitable lengths for Mila's surfboard.

36. **Transportation** The *shinkansen*, or bullet train, of Japan travels at an average speed of 162.3 miles per hour. It has a top speed of 186 miles per hour. At most, how many more miles per hour can the train travel beyond its average speed before it reaches its maximum speed?

37. **Science** The giant spider crab, the world's largest crab, lives off the southeastern coast of Japan. Giant spider crabs can grow as much as 3.6 meters across. A scientist finds one that could still grow another 0.5 m across. How wide is the giant spider crab that he found?

38. The line graph shows the number of miles Amelia rode her bike in each of the last four months. She wants to ride at least 5 miles more in May than she did in April. At least how many miles does Amelia want to ride in May?

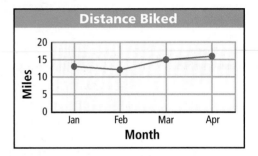

39. **Science** The average human ear can detect sounds that have frequencies between 20 hertz and 20,000 hertz. The average dog ear can detect sounds with frequencies of up to 30,000 hertz greater than those a human ear can detect. Up to how many hertz can a dog hear?

40. **Choose a Strategy** If five days ago was the day after Saturday, what was the day before yesterday?

41. **Write About It** Explain how to solve and check the inequality $n - 9 < -15$.

42. **Challenge** Solve the inequality $x + (4^2 - 2^3)^2 > -1$.

SPIRAL STANDARDS REVIEW   SDAP1.1, SDAP3.4

43. **Multiple Choice** Which inequality has the following graphed solution?

   Ⓐ $x - 2 \geq -2$ Ⓑ $x + 3 \geq 7$ Ⓒ $x - 3 \leq 1$ Ⓓ $x + 5 < 9$

44. **Short Response** The highest-paid employee at the movie theater is the manager, who earns $10.25 per hour. The lowest-paid employees earn $3.90 less per hour than the manager. Write and graph a compound inequality to show all the other hourly wages earned at the movie theater.

Find the mean, median, mode, and range of each data set. (Lesson 7-1)

45. 20, 18, 16, 20, 15, 13, 17   46. 0.4, 0.9, 1.2, 0.6, 0.3, 1.4

47. Find the probability of rolling an even number on a number cube 2 times in a row. (Lesson 8-6)

11-7 Solving Inequalities by Multiplying or Dividing

California Standards

Preview of Grade 7

AF4.0 Students solve simple linear equations and inequalities over the rational numbers.

Who uses this? Melon farmers can solve inequalities to determine how many watermelons they must sell to make a profit. (See Example 3.)

When you multiply or divide both sides of an inequality by the same positive number, the statement will still be true. However, when you multiply or divide both sides by the same *negative* number, you need to reverse the direction of the inequality symbol for the statement to be true.

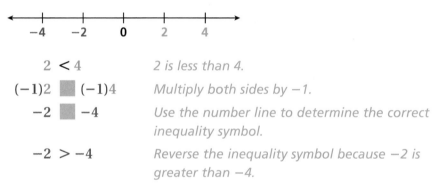

$2 < 4$	*2 is less than 4.*
$(-1)2 \; \blacksquare \; (-1)4$	*Multiply both sides by −1.*
$-2 \; \blacksquare \; -4$	*Use the number line to determine the correct inequality symbol.*
$-2 > -4$	*Reverse the inequality symbol because −2 is greater than −4.*

EXAMPLE 1 Solving Inequalities by Multiplying

Solve.

A $\dfrac{x}{11} < 3$

$$\dfrac{x}{11} < 3$$

$$(11)\dfrac{x}{11} < (11)3 \qquad \text{\textit{Multiply both sides by 11.}}$$

$$x < 33$$

B $4.8 \le \dfrac{r}{-6}$

$$4.8 \le \dfrac{r}{-6}$$

$$(-6)4.8 \ge (-6)\dfrac{r}{-6} \qquad \text{\textit{Multiply both sides by −6, and reverse the inequality symbol.}}$$

$$-28.8 \ge r$$

Check $4.8 \le \dfrac{r}{-6}$

$$4.8 \stackrel{?}{\le} \dfrac{-30}{-6} \qquad \text{\textit{−30 is less than −28.8. Substitute −30 for r.}}$$

$$4.8 \le 5 ✔$$

EXAMPLE 2 Solving Inequalities by Dividing

Solve. Check each answer.

A $4x > 9$

$4x > 9$

$\dfrac{4x}{4} > \dfrac{9}{4}$ *Divide both sides by 4.*

$x > \dfrac{9}{4}$, or $2\dfrac{1}{4}$

Check

$4x > 9$

$4(3) \overset{?}{>} 9$ *3 is greater than $2\frac{1}{4}$. Substitute 3 for x.*

$12 \overset{?}{>} 9$ ✔

B $-60 \geq -12y$

$-60 \geq -12y$

$\dfrac{-60}{-12} \leq \dfrac{-12y}{-12}$ *Divide both sides by -12, and reverse the inequality symbol.*

$5 \leq y$

Check

$-60 \geq -12y$

$-60 \overset{?}{\geq} -12(10)$ *10 is greater than 5. Substitute 10 for y.*

$-60 \overset{?}{\geq} -120$ ✔

EXAMPLE 3 *Agriculture Application*

Reasoning

It cost the Schmidts $517 to raise watermelons. How many watermelons must they sell at $5 apiece to make a profit?

To make a profit, the Schmidts need to earn more than $517. Let w represent the number of watermelons they must sell.

$5w > 517$ *Write an inequality.*

$\dfrac{5w}{5} > \dfrac{517}{5}$ *Divide both sides by 5.*

$w > 103.4$

The Schmidts cannot sell 0.4 watermelon, so they need to sell at least 104 watermelons to earn a profit.

Think and Discuss

1. **Compare** solving multiplication and division equations with solving multiplication and division inequalities.

2. **Explain** how you would solve the inequality $0.5y > 4.5$.

California Standards Practice
Preview of Grade 7 ← AF4.0

go.hrw.com
Homework Help Online
KEYWORD: MS8CA 11-7
Parent Resources Online
KEYWORD: MS8CA Parent

GUIDED PRACTICE

See Example **1** Solve.

1. $\frac{w}{8} < -4$

2. $\frac{z}{-6} \geq 7$

3. $-4 < \frac{p}{-12}$

See Example **2** Solve. Check each answer.

4. $3m > -15$

5. $16 > -8y$

6. $25c \leq 200$

See Example **3** 7. It cost Deirdre $212 to make candles. How many candles must she sell at $8 apiece to make a profit?

INDEPENDENT PRACTICE

See Example **1** Solve.

8. $\frac{s}{5} > 1.4$

9. $\frac{m}{-4} < -13$

10. $\frac{b}{6} > -30$

11. $\frac{c}{-10} \leq 12$

12. $\frac{y}{9} < 2.5$

13. $\frac{x}{1.1} \geq -1$

See Example **2** Solve. Check each answer.

14. $6w < 4$

15. $-5z > -3$

16. $15p \leq -45$

17. $-9f > 27$

18. $20k < 30$

19. $-18n \geq 180$

See Example **3** 20. Attendance at a museum more than tripled from Monday to Saturday. On Monday, 186 people went to the museum. How many people went to the museum on Saturday?

21. It cost George $678 to make wreaths. How many wreaths must he sell at $15 apiece to make a profit?

PRACTICE AND PROBLEM SOLVING

Extra Practice
See page EP23.

Solve.

22. $\frac{a}{65} \leq -10$

23. $0.4p > 1.6$

24. $-\frac{m}{5} < -20$

25. $\frac{2}{3}y \geq 12$

26. $\frac{x}{-9} \leq 3$

27. $\frac{g}{2.1} > 0.3$

28. $\frac{r}{6} \geq \frac{2}{3}$

29. $4w \leq 1\frac{1}{2}$

30. $-10n < 10^2$

31. $-t > -4$

32. $-\frac{y}{12} < 4$

33. $5.6v \geq -14$

34. A community theater group produced 8 plays over the last two years. The group's goal for the next two years is to produce at least $1\frac{1}{2}$ times as many plays as they did in the two previous years. How many plays does the group want to produce in the next two years?

35. Tammy is going to a family reunion 350 miles away. She plans to travel no faster than 70 miles per hour. What is the least amount of time it will take her to get there?

36. **Social Studies** Of the total U.S. population, about 874,000 people are Pacific Islanders. The graph shows where most of these Americans live.

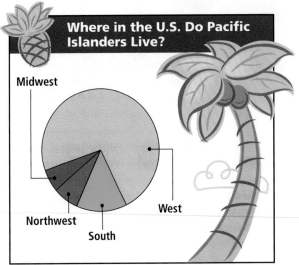

Source: USA Today

a. According to the graph, less than 10% of Pacific Islanders live in the Midwest. How many Pacific Islanders live in the Midwest?

b. According to the graph, between 10% and 20% of Pacific Islanders live in the South. How many Pacific Islanders live in the South?

37. Seventh-graders at Mountain Middle School have sold 360 subscriptions to magazines. This is $\frac{3}{4}$ of the number of subscriptions that they need to sell to reach their goal. How many total subscriptions must they sell to beat their goal?

38. **Recreation** Malcolm has saved $362 to spend on his vacation. He wants to have at least $35 a day available to spend. How many days of vacation does Malcolm have enough money for?

39. **Write a Problem** Write a word problem that can be solved using the inequality $\frac{x}{2} \geq 7$. Solve the inequality.

40. **Write About It** Explain how to solve the inequality $\frac{n}{-8} < -40$.

41. **Challenge** Use what you have learned about solving multi-step equations to solve the inequality $4x - 5 \leq 7x + 4$.

---

42. **Multiple Choice** Solve $\frac{x}{4} > -2$.

   (A) $x > -8$ (B) $x < -8$ (C) $x < 8$ (D) $x > 8$

43. **Gridded Response** It cost John and Jamie $150 to grow tomatoes. They sell each tomato for $0.50. How many tomatoes must they sell to make a profit?

Find the percent of each number. (Lesson 6-4)

44. 45% of 200   45. 112% of 50   46. 14% of 150   47. 1% of 350

48. In 16 tries, Sondra made 9 baskets. What is the experimental probability that Sondra will make a basket the next time she tries? (Lesson 8-2)

Solving Two-Step Inequalities

California Standards

Preview of Grade 7

🔑 **AF4.1** Solve two-step **linear** equations and **inequalities in one variable over the rational numbers,** interpret the solution or solutions in the context from which they arose, and verify the reasonableness of the results.

Why learn this? You can solve a two-step inequality to determine how much money band members need to raise at a car wash. (See Example 2.)

When you solve two-step equations, you can use the order of operations in reverse to isolate the variable. You can use the same process when solving two-step inequalities.

E X A M P L E **1** **Solving Two-Step Inequalities**

Solve. Then graph each solution set on a number line.

A $\frac{x}{5} - 15 < 10$

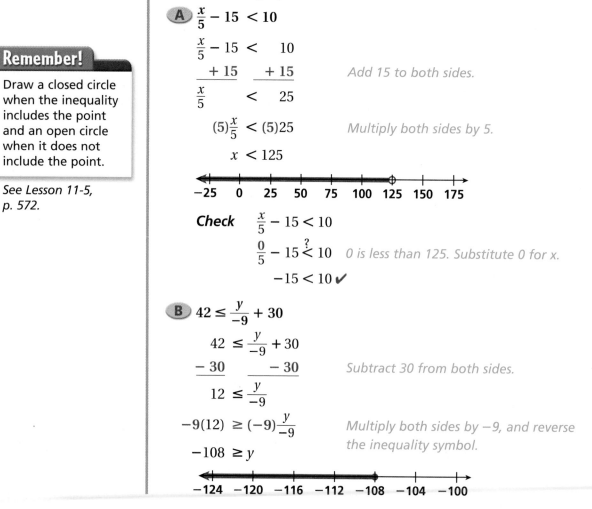

$$\frac{x}{5} - 15 < 10$$
$$\underline{+ 15 \qquad + 15} \qquad \text{\textit{Add 15 to both sides.}}$$
$$\frac{x}{5} \quad < \quad 25$$

$$(5)\frac{x}{5} < (5)25 \qquad \text{\textit{Multiply both sides by 5.}}$$

$$x < 125$$

> **Remember!**
>
> Draw a closed circle when the inequality includes the point and an open circle when it does not include the point.
>
> *See Lesson 11-5, p. 572.*

Check $\quad \frac{x}{5} - 15 < 10$

$$\frac{0}{5} - 15 \overset{?}{<} 10 \qquad \text{\textit{0 is less than 125. Substitute 0 for x.}}$$

$$-15 < 10 \text{ ✔}$$

B $42 \le \frac{y}{-9} + 30$

$$42 \le \frac{y}{-9} + 30$$
$$\underline{-30 \qquad\qquad -30} \qquad \text{\textit{Subtract 30 from both sides.}}$$
$$12 \le \frac{y}{-9}$$

$$-9(12) \ge (-9)\frac{y}{-9} \qquad \text{\textit{Multiply both sides by −9, and reverse}}$$
$$-108 \ge y \qquad\qquad \text{\textit{the inequality symbol.}}$$

Solve. Then graph each solution set on a number line.

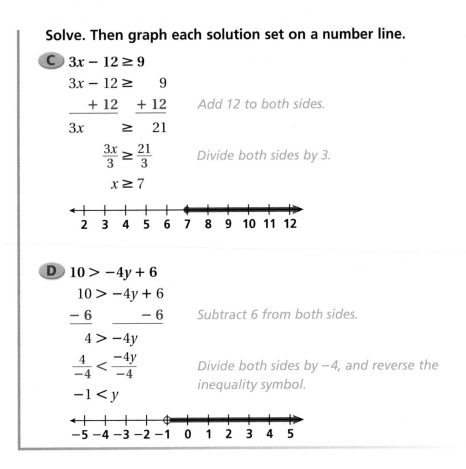

C $3x - 12 \geq 9$

$$3x - 12 \geq \quad 9$$
$$\underline{+ 12 \quad + 12} \qquad \textit{Add 12 to both sides.}$$
$$3x \qquad \geq \quad 21$$

$$\frac{3x}{3} \geq \frac{21}{3} \qquad \textit{Divide both sides by 3.}$$

$$x \geq 7$$

```
 ←—+——+——+——+——+——●━━━━━━━━━━→
   2   3   4   5   6   7   8   9  10  11  12
```

D $10 > -4y + 6$

$$10 > -4y + 6$$
$$\underline{-6 \qquad - 6} \qquad \textit{Subtract 6 from both sides.}$$
$$4 > -4y$$

$$\frac{4}{-4} < \frac{-4y}{-4} \qquad \textit{Divide both sides by } -4, \textit{ and reverse the inequality symbol.}$$

$$-1 < y$$

```
 ←—+——+——+——+——○━━━━━━━━━━━━→
  -5  -4  -3  -2  -1   0   1   2   3   4   5
```

EXAMPLE 2 **School Application**

The 83 members of the Newman Middle School Band are trying to raise at least $5,000 to buy new percussion instruments. They have already raised $850. How much should each student still raise, on average, to meet the goal?

Let d represent the average amount each student should still raise.

$$83d + 850 \geq 5,000 \qquad \textit{Write an inequality.}$$
$$\underline{- 850 \quad - 850} \qquad \textit{Subtract 850 from both sides.}$$
$$83d \qquad \geq 4,150$$

$$\frac{83d}{83} \geq \frac{4,150}{83} \qquad \textit{Divide both sides by 83.}$$

$$d \geq 50$$

On average, each band member should raise at least $50.

Think and Discuss

1. Tell how you would solve the inequality $8x + 5 < 20$.

2. Explain why the *greater than or equal to* symbol was used in the inequality in Example 2.

California Standards Practice
Preview of Grade 7 ➔ AF4.1

go.hrw.com
Homework Help Online
KEYWORD: MS8CA 11-8
Parent Resources Online
KEYWORD: MS8CA Parent

GUIDED PRACTICE

See Example 1 · Solve. Then graph each solution set on a number line.

1. $5x + 3 < 18$

2. $-19 \geq \frac{z}{7} + 23$

3. $3y - 4 \geq 14$

4. $\frac{m}{4} - 2 > -3$

5. $42 \leq -11p - 13$

6. $\frac{n}{-3} - 4 > 4$

See Example 2 · **7.** Three students collected more than $93 washing cars. They used $15 to reimburse their parents for cleaning supplies. Then they divided the remaining money equally. How much did each student earn?

INDEPENDENT PRACTICE

See Example 1 · Solve. Then graph each solution set on a number line.

8. $5s - 7 > -42$

9. $\frac{b}{2} + 3 < 9$

10. $19 \leq -2q + 5$

11. $-8c - 11 \leq 13$

12. $\frac{y}{-4} + 6 > 10$

13. $\frac{x}{9} - 5 \leq -8$

14. $\frac{r}{-2} - 9 > -14$

15. $44 \geq 13j + 18$

16. $\frac{d}{13} - 12 > 27$

See Example 2 · **17.** Rico has $5.00. Bagels cost $0.65 each, and a small container of cream cheese costs $1.00. What is the greatest number of bagels Rico can buy if he also buys one small container of cream cheese?

18. The 35 members of a drill team are trying to raise at least $1,200 to cover travel costs to a training camp. They have already raised $500. How much should each member still raise, on average, to meet the goal?

PRACTICE AND PROBLEM SOLVING

Extra Practice
See page EP23.

Solve.

19. $32 \geq -4x + 8$

20. $0.5 + \frac{n}{5} > -0.5$

21. $1.4 + \frac{c}{3} < 2$

22. $1 < \frac{3}{4}b - 2$

23. $12 + 2w - 8 \leq 20$

24. $5k + 6 - k \geq -14$

25. $\frac{s}{2} + 9 > 12 - 15$

26. $4t - 3 - 10t < 15$

27. $\frac{d}{2} + 1 + \frac{d}{2} \leq 5$

28. Mr. Monroe keeps a bag of small prizes to distribute to his students. He likes to keep at least twice as many prizes in the bag as he has students. The bag currently has 79 prizes in it. Mr. Monroe has 117 students. How many more prizes does he need to buy?

29. Manny needs to buy 5 work shirts that are each the same price. After he uses a $20 gift certificate, he can spend no more than $50. What is the maximum amount that each shirt can cost?

30. Business Darcy earns a salary of $1,400 per month, plus a commission of 4% of her sales. She wants to earn a total of at least $1,600 this month. What is the least amount of sales she needs?

31. Multi-Step The bar graph shows how many students from Warren Middle School participated in a reading challenge each of the past four years. This year, the goal is for at least 10 more students to participate than the average number of participants from the past four years. What is the goal for this year?

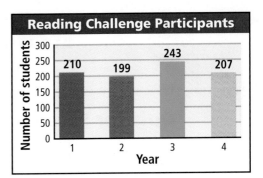

Reading Challenge Participants

32. Consumer Math Michael wants to buy a belt that costs $18. He also wants to buy some shirts that are on sale for $14 each. He has $70. At most, how many shirts can Michael buy together with the belt?

33. Earth Science A granite rock contains the minerals feldspar, quartz, and biotite mica. The rock has $\frac{1}{3}$ as much biotite mica as quartz. The rock is at least 30% quartz. What percent of the rock is feldspar?

Feldspar

Quartz

Biotite mica

Granite

34. What's the Error? A student's solution to the inequality $\frac{x}{-9} - 5 > 2$ was $x > 63$. What error did the student make in the solution?

35. Write About It Explain how to solve the inequality $4y + 6 < -2$.

36. Challenge A student scored 92, 87, and 85 on three tests. She wants her average score for five tests to be at least 90. What is the lowest score the student can get, on average, on her fourth and fifth tests?

SPIRAL STANDARDS REVIEW   NS2.1, NS2.2, SDAP3.1

37. Multiple Choice Which inequality has the following graphed solution?

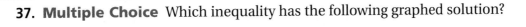

Ⓐ $2x - 5 > 1$ Ⓑ $-x + 3 < 6$ Ⓒ $3x - 12 < -3$ Ⓓ $-5x - 2 > -13$

38. Gridded Response Gretta earns $450 per week plus a 10% commission on book sales. How many dollars of books must she sell to earn at least $650 per week?

Multiply or divide. Write each answer in simplest form. (Lessons 4-4 and 4-5)

39. $\frac{3}{5} \cdot \frac{10}{21}$ **40.** $1\frac{1}{6} \cdot 5\frac{1}{4}$ **41.** $\frac{7}{8} \div \frac{7}{12}$ **42.** $5\frac{7}{10} \div 3$

43. Jamie flips a coin and rolls a number cube. Use a tree diagram to find all of the possible outcomes. What is the probability of getting heads on the coin and 3 on the number cube? (Lesson 8-4)

READY TO GO ON?

Quiz for Lessons 11-5 Through 11-8

✓ 11-5 Introduction to Inequalities

Write an inequality for each situation.

1. Gary has at least 25 blue T-shirts.

2. The room can hold no more than 50 people.

Graph each inequality.

3. $b > -1$ **4.** $5 \le t$ **5.** $-3 \ge x$

Graph each compound inequality.

6. $5 \ge p$ and $p > -1$ **7.** $-8 > g$ or $g \ge -1$ **8.** $-4 \le x < 0$

✓ 11-6 Solving Inequalities by Adding or Subtracting

Solve. Then graph each solution set on a number line.

9. $28 > m - 4$ **10.** $8 + c \ge -13$ **11.** $-1 + v < 1$

12. $5 \le p - 3$ **13.** $-8 > f + 1$ **14.** $-7 - w < 10$

15. A group of climbers are at an altitude of at most 17,500 feet. They are on their way to the top of Mount Everest, which is at an altitude of 29,035 feet. How many more feet do they have left to climb?

✓ 11-7 Solving Inequalities by Multiplying or Dividing

Solve. Check each answer.

16. $-8s > 16$ **17.** $\frac{x}{-2} \le 9$ **18.** $-7 \le \frac{b}{3}$

19. $\frac{c}{-3} \ge -4$ **20.** $28 > 7h$ **21.** $6y < -2$

✓ 11-8 Solving Two-Step Inequalities

Solve. Then graph each solution set on a number line.

22. $2x - 3 > 5$ **23.** $3 \ge -2d + 4$ **24.** $3g - 2 - 10g > 5$

25. $14 < -4a + 6$ **26.** $3.6 + 7.2k < 25.2$ **27.** $3z - 2 \le 13$

28. A concert is being held in a gymnasium that can hold no more than 450 people. The bleachers seat 60 people. There will also be 26 rows of chairs set up. At most, how many people can sit in each row?

29. The 23 members of the Westview Journalism Club are trying to raise at least $2,100 to buy new publishing design software. The members have already raised $1,180. How much should each student still raise, on average, to meet the goal?

CONCEPT CONNECTION

Classy Music Ricky is learning to play the guitar and is thinking about taking classes at one of the schools listed in the table.

1. Last year, Ricky spent $590 on guitar lessons. If he takes classes at Main Street Music and spends the same amount this year, how many classes can he take?

2. How many classes would Ricky have to take in order for the cost at Main Street Music to be the same as the cost at SoundWorks?

School	Cost of Lessons
Main Street Music	Annual registration fee: $50 $12 per class
SoundWorks	Annual registration fee: $14 $16.50 per class
Town Hall	No annual registration fee $18 per class

3. Ricky plans to buy a new guitar this year. He expects to pay $139 for it. His total budget for the guitar and the classes is $600. Write and solve an inequality to find the maximum number of classes Ricky will be able to take if he goes to Main Street Music and stays within his budget.

4. Write and solve inequalities to find the maximum number of classes Ricky will be able to take with a $600 budget if he goes to the other schools. Assuming the three schools are equal in other respects, which of the schools should he choose? Why?

Game Time

Flapjacks

Five pancakes of different sizes are stacked in a random order. How can you get the pancakes in order from largest to smallest by flipping portions of the stack?

To find the answer, stack five disks of different sizes in no particular order. Arrange the disks from largest to smallest in the fewest number of moves possible. Move disks by choosing a disk and flipping over the whole stack from that disk up.

Start with a stack of five.

Flip the stack from the second disk up.

Now flip the stack from the third disk up.

Finally, flip the stack from the second disk up.

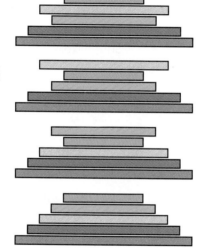

At most, it should take $3n - 2$ turns, where n is the number of disks, to arrange the disks from largest to smallest. The five disks above were arranged in three turns, which is less than $3(5) - 2 = 13$. Try it on your own.

Leaping Counters

Remove all but one of the counters from the board by jumping over each counter with another and removing the jumped counter. The game is over when you can no longer jump a counter. A perfect game would result in one counter being left in the center of the board.

A complete copy of the rules and a game board are available online.

go.hrw.com
Game Time Extra
KEYWORD: MS8CA Games

Materials
- 8 tongue depressors
- 2 pieces of electrical wire
- scissors
- markers

It's in the Bag!

PROJECT Wired for Multi-Step Equations

These "study sticks" will help you sort out the steps in solving equations.

Directions

❶ Twist a piece of electrical wire around each end of a tongue depressor. Twist the wire tightly so that it holds the tongue depressor securely. **Figure A**

❷ Slide another tongue depressor between the ends of the wires. Slide it down as far as possible and then twist the wires together to hold this tongue depressor securely. **Figure B**

❸ Continue in the same way with the remaining tongue depressors.

❹ Twist the wires together at the top to make a handle. Trim the wires as needed.

Taking Note of the Math

Write the title of the chapter on the top tongue depressor. On each of the remaining tongue depressors, write the steps for solving a sample multi-step equation.

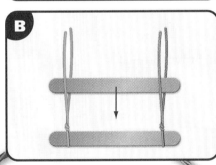

SOLVING MULTISTEP EQUATIONS

$$\frac{4x-3}{7} = 3$$

$$(7)\frac{4x-3}{7} = (7)3$$

$$4x - 3 = 21$$

$$4x - 3 + 3 = 21 + 3$$

$$4x = 24$$

$$\frac{4x}{4} = \frac{24}{4}$$

591

Study Guide: Review

Vocabulary

algebraic inequality	 572	inequality	 572
coefficient	 558	solution set	 572
compound inequality	 573	term	 558

Complete the sentences below with vocabulary words from the list above.

1. A(n) __?__ states that two quantities either are not equal or may not be equal.

2. A(n) __?__ is a combination of more than one inequality.

3. Together, the solutions of an inequality are called the __?__.

11-1 Solving Two-Step Equations (pp. 554–557)

 Preview of 7AF4.1

EXAMPLE

■ Solve $6a - 3 = 15$.

$6a - 3 = 15$

$6a - 3 + 3 = 15 + 3$ *Add 3 to both sides.*

$6a = 18$

$\dfrac{6a}{6} = \dfrac{18}{6}$ *Divide both sides by 6.*

$a = 3$

EXERCISES

Solve.

4. $-5y + 6 = -34$

5. $9 + \dfrac{z}{6} = 14$

6. $-8 = \dfrac{w}{-7} + 13$

7. $4x + 5 = 21$

8. $7b - 4 = 10$

9. $\dfrac{k}{9} + 10 = 12$

10. $\dfrac{a}{5} - 7 = -4$

11. $-5p + 6 = 26$

11-2 Simplifying Algebraic Expressions (pp. 558–561)

Preview of 7AF1.3; 6AF1.2, 6AF3.1, 6AF3.2

EXAMPLES

Simplify each expression.

■ $6a + 4a$

$(6 + 4)a$

$10a$

■ $4x^3 + 5y + 8x^3 - 4y - 5x^2$

$4x^3 + 5y + 8x^3 - 4y - 5x^2$

$12x^3 + y - 5x^2$

EXERCISES

Simplify each expression.

12. $7b^2 + 8 + 3b^2$

13. $12a^2 + 4 + 3a^2 - 2$

14. $x^2 + x^3 + x^4 + 5x^2$

15. $x^2 + 7x - 9 + 5x^2$

16. $10p + 4p - 7p + 5$

11-3 Solving Multi-Step Equations (pp. 562–565)

Preview of 7AF1.3 and 1A5.0

EXAMPLE

■ Solve $\frac{1}{7}(4x - 3) = 3$.

$$\frac{1}{7}(4x - 3) = 3$$

$(7)\frac{1}{7}(4x - 3) = (7)3$ *Multiply.*

$$4x - 3 = 21$$

$4x - 3 + 3 = 21 + 3$ *Add 3 to both sides.*

$$4x = 24$$

$\dfrac{4x}{4} = \dfrac{24}{4}$ *Divide both sides by 4.*

$$x = 6$$

EXERCISES

Solve.

17. $7a + 4 - a = 6$ **18.** $9 = \frac{1}{4}(6j - 18)$

19. $\frac{1}{3}(8b - 5) = 9$ **20.** $52 = -9 + 16y - 19$

21. $4(x + 1) - 3 = 29$ **22.** $9k + k - 4 = 6$

23. Noelle biked twice as many miles as Leila. Adding 2 to the number of miles Noelle and Leila biked combined gives the number of miles Dani biked. Dani biked 17 miles. How many miles did Leila bike?

11-4 Solving Equations with Variables on Both Sides (pp. 566–569)

EXAMPLE

Preview of 1A5.0

■ Solve $8a = 3a + 25$.

$$8a = 3a + 25$$

$8a - 3a = 3a - 3a + 25$ *Subtract.*

$$5a = 25$$

$\dfrac{5a}{5} = \dfrac{25}{5}$ *Divide.*

$$a = 5$$

EXERCISES

Solve.

24. $-6b + 9 = 12b$

25. $5 - 7c = -3c - 19$

26. $18m - 14 = 12m + 2$

27. $20 - 2x = x - 40$

28. $10x + 6 = 54 + 9x$

29. $18 - \frac{1}{2}y = 3 + \frac{1}{3}y$

11-5 Introduction to Inequalities (pp. 572–575)

Preview of 7AF1.1

EXAMPLES

Write an inequality for each situation.

■ You have to be at least 17 years old to drive a car in New Jersey.
age of driver ≥ 17

■ There can be at most 60 people on the bus.
number of people ≤ 60

■ Graph $x < -1$.

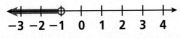

EXERCISES

Write an inequality for each situation.

30. A bridge's load limit is at most 9 tons.

31. The large tree in the park is more than 200 years old.

32. The moving truck holds at least 2 tons of furniture.

33. The hole is not yet 49 feet deep.

Graph each inequality.

34. $y \geq 3$

35. $-2 \leq k < -1$

11-6 Solving Inequalities by Adding or Subtracting (pp. 576–579)

 **Preview of 7AF4.0**

EXAMPLE

Solve. Graph the solution set.

- $b + 6 > -10$

$$b + 6 > -10$$
$$b + 6 - 6 > -10 - 6$$
$$b > -16$$

<-+---○---+---+---+---+---+---+---+->
-20 -16 -12 -8 -4 0 4 8

EXERCISES

Solve. Graph each solution set.

36. $r - 16 > 9$ **37.** $-14 \geq 12 + x$

38. $\frac{3}{4} + g < 8\frac{3}{4}$ **39.** $\frac{5}{6} > \frac{2}{3} + t$

40. $7.46 > r - 1.54$ **41.** $u - 58 \geq -124$

42. The Wildcats scored at least 13 more points than the Stingrays scored. The Stingrays scored 25 points. How many points did the Wildcats score?

11-7 Solving Inequalities by Multiplying or Dividing (pp. 580–583)

Preview of 7AF4.0

EXAMPLE

Solve.

- $\frac{m}{-4} \geq 3.8$

$$\frac{m}{-4} \geq 3.8$$
$$(-4)\frac{m}{-4} \leq (-4)3.8 \quad \textit{Multiply and reverse the inequality symbol.}$$
$$m \leq -15.2$$

EXERCISES

Solve.

43. $\frac{n}{-8} > 6.9$ **44.** $-18 \leq -3p$

45. $\frac{k}{13} < -10$ **46.** $-5p > -25$

47. $2.3 \leq \frac{v}{1.2}$ **48.** $\frac{c}{-11} < -3$

49. $6g < -42$ **50.** $12x \geq 6$

51. It cost Carlita $204 to make beaded purses. How many purses must Carlita sell at $13 apiece to make a profit?

11-8 Solving Two-Step Inequalities (pp. 584–587)

Preview of 7AF4.1

EXAMPLE

Solve. Graph the solution set.

- $\frac{k}{3} - 18 > 24$

$$\frac{k}{3} - 18 > 24$$
$$\frac{k}{3} - 18 + 18 > 24 + 18$$
$$\frac{k}{3} > 42$$
$$(3)\frac{k}{3} > (3)42$$
$$k > 126$$

<-+---+---+---○---+---+---+---+->
114 120 126 132 138 144

EXERCISES

Solve. Graph each solution set.

52. $-7b - 16 > -2$ **53.** $38 + \frac{d}{6} < 37$

54. $15 - 4n + 9 \leq 40$ **55.** $\frac{y}{-3} + 18 \geq 12$

56. $\frac{c}{3} + 7 > -11$ **57.** $32 \geq 4x - 8$

58. $18 + \frac{h}{6} \geq -8$ **59.** $14 > -2t - 6$

60. $-3 < \frac{w}{-4} + 10$ **61.** $\frac{y}{7} + 3.9 \leq 8.9$

62. Luis has $53.55. T-shirts cost $8.95 each, and a belt costs $16.75. How many T-shirts can Luis buy if he also buys a new belt?

CHAPTER TEST

CHAPTER
11

Simplify. Justify your steps using the Commutative, Associative, and Distributive Properties when necessary.

1. $12x + 5x - x + 7$

2. $6 + 3n + 8 - 2n$

3. $x^3 + 2x^3 - x + 12x$

Solve.

4. $3y - 8 = 16$

5. $\frac{x}{3} + 12 = -4$

6. $\frac{a}{6} - 7 = -4$

7. $-7b + 5 = -51$

8. $\frac{1}{3}(5y - 4) = 7$

9. $8r + 7 - 13 = 58$

10. $6 = \frac{1}{5}(12s - 6)$

11. $3(4t - 10) = -54$

12. $-14q = 4q - 126$

13. $5p + 24 = p - 96$

14. $9 - 6k = 3k - 54$

15. $-36d = -70d + 340$

16. The bill for the repair of a computer was $179. The cost of the parts was $44, and the labor charge was $45 per hour. How many hours did it take to repair the computer?

Write an inequality for each situation.

17. You must be more than 4 ft tall to go on the ride.

18. You cannot go more than 65 miles per hour on Route 18.

Graph each inequality.

19. $a < -2$

20. $-5 < d$ and $d \le 2$

21. $c > -1$ or $c < -5$

22. $b \ge 3$

Solve. Then graph each solution set on a number line.

23. $n + 8 < -9$

24. $n - 124 > -59$

25. $-40 > \frac{x}{32}$

26. $-3y \le -48$

27. Rosa wants to save at least $125 to buy a new skateboard. She has already saved $46. How much more does Rosa need to save?

28. Gasoline costs $2.75 a gallon. At most, how many gallons can be bought for $22.00?

Solve. Then graph each solution set on a number line.

29. $m - 7.8 \le 23.7$

30. $18z > -8$

31. $\frac{w}{-4.9} \le 3.4$

32. $-15 < 4a + 9$

33. $2.8 - \frac{c}{4} \ge 7.4$

34. $\frac{d}{5} - 8 > -4$

35. The seventh-grade students at Fulmore Middle School are trying to raise at least $7,500 for the local public library. So far, each of the 198 students has raised an average of $20. How much more money must each seventh-grader collect, on average, to reach the goal?

Chapter Test **595**

STRATEGIES FOR SUCCESS

Any Question Type: Use a Diagram

Diagrams are a helpful tool. If a diagram is included in a test item, study it closely as it may contain useful information. Sometimes it is helpful to draw your own diagram.

EXAMPLE 1

Multiple Choice A small circle is inside a large circle. The diameter of the small circle is 10 feet. If the circumference of the large circle is 4 times the circumference of the small circle, what is the radius of the large circle?

  Ⓐ 20 ft   Ⓑ 30 ft   Ⓒ 40 ft   Ⓓ 120 ft

Draw a diagram to help you visualize the problem.
Draw two circles and label them with all the information given in the problem.

Diameter = 10 ft

The circumference of the large circle is 4 times the circumference of the small circle, so the diameter of the large circle is 4 times the diameter of the small circle. The diameter of the large circle is $4 \cdot 10 = 40$ feet, so its radius is 20 feet.

Choice A is correct.

EXAMPLE 2

Short Response $\triangle ABC$ is similar to $\triangle FDE$. Find the missing length.

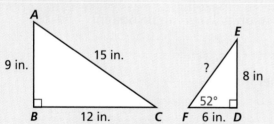

These triangles do not look similar and are not drawn to scale, but the information in the problem says that they are.

Set up a proportion to find the missing length and solve for x. $\dfrac{x}{6} = \dfrac{15}{9}$

The unknown side length is 10 in.

If you have trouble understanding what a test item is asking, draw a diagram to help you visualize the question.

Read each test item and answer the questions that follow.

Item A
Multiple Choice The temperature at the ski lodge was 21°F at 9:00 P.M. At sunrise, the temperature was 34°F. How many degrees did the temperature rise overnight?

- (A) 54°F
- (C) 13°F
- (B) 25°F
- (D) 4°F

1. What information will help you solve the problem?

2. Sketch a diagram to help you solve this problem. Be sure to label the diagram with all of the information you know.

Item B
Short Answer Prove that the two rectangles below are similar. Explain your reasoning.

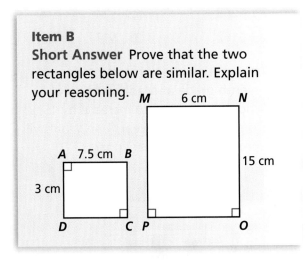

3. What information can you get from the diagram to help you prove that the figures are similar?

4. Do you think the drawings accurately illustrate the given information? If not, why?

5. What is the length of $\overline{DC}$?

Item C
Gridded Response The longest side of a triangle is 14.4 centimeters. Its shortest side is 5.9 centimeters shorter than the longest side. If the perimeter of the triangle is 35.2 centimeters, what is the length of the third side?

6. How do you determine the perimeter of a triangle?

7. Sketch a diagram of the triangle. Explain how sketching the diagram can help you answer the problem.

8. Tell how you would fill in your response to this test item on a grid.

Item D
Multiple Choice Which angle pairs are vertical angles?

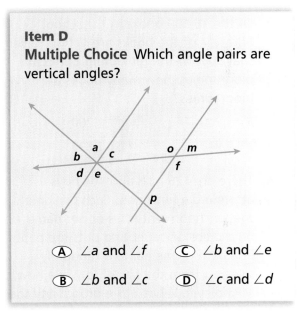

- (A) ∠a and ∠f
- (C) ∠b and ∠e
- (B) ∠b and ∠c
- (D) ∠c and ∠d

9. Which answer choice can you immediately eliminate? Why?

10. How can you use the diagram to help you eliminate the other choices?

11. Explain which answer choice is correct.

MASTERING THE STANDARDS

Cumulative Assessment, Chapters 1–11

Multiple Choice

1. Nolan has 7 red socks, 3 black socks, 10 white socks, and 5 blue socks in a drawer. If Nolan chooses one sock, replaces it, and then chooses a second sock, what is the probability that he will choose 2 white socks?

Ⓐ $\frac{3}{20}$　　Ⓒ $\frac{2}{5}$

Ⓑ $\frac{4}{25}$　　Ⓓ $\frac{19}{25}$

2. Of the 10,500 books in the school library, $\frac{2}{5}$ of the books are fiction. Given that 30% of the remaining books are biographies, how many books are biographies?

Ⓐ 4,200　　Ⓒ 1,260

Ⓑ 2,940　　Ⓓ 1,890

3. There are 126 girls and 104 boys attending a luncheon. Each person at the luncheon writes his or her name on a piece of paper and puts the paper in a barrel. One name is randomly selected from the barrel to win a new MP3 player. What is the probability the person selected is male?

Ⓐ 45.2%　　Ⓒ 82.5%

Ⓑ 54.8%　　Ⓓ Not here

4. A trapezoid has two bases, b_1 and b_2, and height h. For which values of b_1, b_2, and h is the area of the trapezoid equal to 16 in^2?

Ⓐ $b_1 = 8$ in., $b_2 = 4$ in., $h = 2$ in.

Ⓑ $b_1 = 5$ in., $b_2 = 3$ in., $h = 4$ in.

Ⓒ $b_1 = 2$ in., $b_2 = 8$ in., $h = 6$ in.

Ⓓ $b_1 = 2$ in., $b_2 = 4$ in., $h = 4$ in.

5. There were 18 teachers and 45 students registered to participate in a 5K walk-a-thon. Which ratio accurately compares the number of students to the number of teachers?

Ⓐ 1:5　　Ⓒ 3:15

Ⓑ 5:2　　Ⓓ 18:45

6. What is $7 + (-6)$?

Ⓐ -13　　Ⓒ 1

Ⓑ -1　　Ⓓ 13

7. Martha buys a surfboard that costs $405 for 40% off. How much money does she save?

Ⓐ $243　　Ⓒ $24

Ⓑ $162　　Ⓓ $17

8. The total number of students in seventh grade at Madison Middle School is expected to increase by 15% from year three to year four. What will enrollment be in year four?

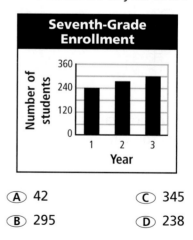

Ⓐ 42　　Ⓒ 345

Ⓑ 295　　Ⓓ 238

9. The two figures are similar. Which proportion can be used to find the missing side length?

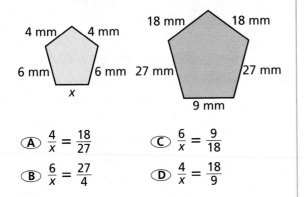

Ⓐ $\frac{4}{x} = \frac{18}{27}$ Ⓒ $\frac{6}{x} = \frac{9}{18}$

Ⓑ $\frac{6}{x} = \frac{27}{4}$ Ⓓ $\frac{4}{x} = \frac{18}{9}$

Create and use a number line to help you order rational numbers quickly.

10. Which rational number is greater than $-3\frac{1}{3}$ but less than $-\frac{4}{5}$?

Ⓐ -0.4 Ⓒ -0.19

Ⓑ $-\frac{22}{5}$ Ⓓ $-\frac{9}{7}$

11. Which equation could be used to find the circumference in inches of a circle with a radius of 5 inches?

Ⓐ $C = 5 \cdot \pi$ Ⓒ $C = 5^2 \cdot \pi$

Ⓑ $C = 10 \cdot \pi$ Ⓓ $C = 10^2 \cdot \pi$

Gridded Response

12. What is the least common multiple of 6, 8, and 10?

13. Freddy counted the number of bats he saw each night for one week. What is the median of the data set?

Number of Bats Spotted
42, 21, 36, 28, 40, 21, 31

14. What is the probability of flipping a coin and getting tails and then rolling a number greater than or equal to 4 on a 6-sided number cube? Write your answer as a decimal.

Short Response

15. Nancy is stenciling 5-inch-wide stars, end-to-end, around her rectangular bedroom. Her bedroom is $12\frac{3}{4}$ feet wide and $15\frac{1}{4}$ feet long. How many whole stars will Nancy stencil?

16. A restaurant offers a choice of 3 main dishes (roast beef, chicken, or fish), 3 vegetables (broccoli, carrots, and corn), and 2 sides (soup or salad). Use a tree diagram to find all the possible outcomes when choosing one main dish, one vegetable, and one side.

17. Hallie is baking 5 batches of bran muffins for the bake sale. Each batch requires $1\frac{2}{3}$ cups of flour. Hallie has $8\frac{1}{4}$ cups of flour. Does she have enough flour to make five batches? Explain your answer.

Extended Response

18. There are 5 blue tiles, 7 red tiles, and 8 yellow tiles in a jar.

    a. If you pick a tile without looking, what is the probability of picking a blue tile? Express this probability as a percent, a fraction, and a decimal.

    b. If you pick a tile without looking, what is the probability of NOT picking a yellow tile? Write your answer in simplest form.

    c. You conduct an experiment in which you pick a tile out of the jar 50 different times. Each time you record the color of tile and then replace the tile before you pick another. How many times would you expect to pick a blue tile? Explain.

÷ # Student +
Handbook

✕

─

⬡ **Extra Practice**. **EP2**

✚ **Skills Bank**

Extra Practice ⋅ Chapter 1

LESSON 1-1

Identify a possible pattern. Use your pattern to write the next three numbers.

1. 13, 21, 29, 37, ▪, ▪, ▪, …

2. 7, 8, 10, 13, ▪, ▪, ▪, …

3. 165, 156, 147, 138, ▪, ▪, ▪, …

4. 19, 33, 47, 61, ▪, ▪, ▪, …

Identify a possible pattern. Use your pattern to draw the next three figures.

5.

6.

LESSON 1-2

Find each value.

7. 5^3

8. 7^3

9. 5^5

10. 6^5

11. 4^1

12. 8^2

13. 12^2

14. 100^3

Write each number using an exponent and the given base.

15. 121, base 11

16. 4,096, base 4

17. 216, base 6

18. Maria decided to donate $1.00 to her favorite charity the first week of the month and to double the amount she donates each week. How much will she donate the sixth week?

LESSON 1-3

Simplify each expression.

19. $9 \div 3 + 6 \cdot 5$

20. $16 + (20 \div 5) - 3^2$

21. $(6 - 3)^3 \div 9 + 7$

22. $(4 \cdot 9) - (9 - 3)^2$

23. $5 + 9 \cdot 2^2 \div 6$

24. $6{,}842 - (5^3 \cdot 5 \cdot 10)$

25. Charlotte bought 4 shirts for $32 each and 3 pairs of pants for $25 each. Simplify the expression $4 \cdot 32 + 3 \cdot 25$ to find out how much she paid for the clothes.

LESSON 1-4

Tell which property is represented.

26. $1 \cdot (2 \cdot 3) = (1 \cdot 2) \cdot 3$

27. $xy = yx$

28. $(x + y) + z = x + (y + z)$

Simplify each expression. Justify each step.

29. $5 + 6 + 19$

30. $5 \cdot 10 \cdot 2$

31. $3 \cdot (5 \cdot 9)$

32. $(25 \cdot 8) \cdot 4$

33. $30 + (121 + 39)$

34. $125 \cdot (2 \cdot 3)$

Use the Distributive Property to find each product.

35. $8 \cdot (2 + 10)$

36. $3 \cdot (19 + 4)$

37. $(10 - 2) \cdot 7$

38. $15 \cdot (13 - 8)$

39. $(47 + 88) \cdot 4$

40. $5 \cdot (157 - 45)$

LESSON 1-5

Evaluate each expression for the given value of the variable.

41. $v \div 5 + v$ for $v = 20$ **42.** $3r - 20 \div r$ for $r = 5$ **43.** $5x^2 + 3x$ for $x = 3$

Evaluate each expression for the given values of the variables.

44. $8m - 6n$ for $m = 4$ and $n = 2$ **45.** $\frac{x}{y} - z$ for $x = 28$, $y = 7$, and $z = 4$

LESSON 1-6

Write each phrase as an algebraic expression.

46. add 7 to 8 times a number   **47.** 6 times the sum of 13 and a number

48. A music store sells packages of guitar strings. David bought s strings for $24. Write an algebraic expression for the cost of one string.

LESSON 1-7

Determine whether the given value of each variable is a solution.

49. $a + 15 = 34$, when $a = 17$ **50.** $t - 9 = 14$, when $t = 23$

LESSON 1-8

Solve each equation. Check your answers.

51. $r + 13 = 36$ **52.** $52 = 24 + n$ **53.** $6 + s = 10$

54. Towns A, B, and C are located along a road that runs east and west. Town A is 34 miles west of town C. Town B is 12 miles west of town C. Find the distance d between town A and town B.

LESSON 1-9

Solve each equation. Check your answers.

55. $z - 9 = 5$ **56.** $v - 17 = 14$ **57.** $24 = w - 6$

58. Reggie withdrew $175 from his bank account to go shopping. After his withdrawal, there was $234 left in Reggie's account. How much money m did Reggie have in his account before his withdrawal?

LESSON 1-10

Solve each equation. Check your answers.

59. $4y = 20$ **60.** $21 = 3t$ **61.** $72 = 9g$

62. The area of a rectangle is 54 in². Its width is 6 in. What is its length ℓ?

LESSON 1-11

Solve each equation. Check your answers.

63. $\frac{n}{4} = 6$ **64.** $7 = \frac{t}{5}$ **65.** $\frac{a}{8} = 12$

66. Sydney likes to run and ride a bike for exercise. Each day, she runs for one-third the time that she rides her bike. Yesterday, Sydney ran for 15 minutes. How many minutes m did she ride her bike?

Extra Practice · Chapter 2

LESSON 2-1

Use a number line to order the integers from least to greatest.

1. $5, -3, -1, 2, 0$ **2.** $-4, -1, 3, 1, 4$ **3.** $-5, 0, -3, 2, 4$

Use a number line to find each absolute value.

4. $|-22|$ **5.** $|9|$ **6.** $|-13|$ **7.** $|21|$

LESSON 2-2

Find each sum.

8. $8 + (-4)$ **9.** $-3 + (-6)$ **10.** $-5 + 9$ **11.** $-7 + (-2)$

Evaluate $c + d$ for the given values.

12. $c = 5, d = -9$ **13.** $c = 12, d = 9$ **14.** $c = -7, d = -2$ **15.** $c = -16, d = 8$

16. The temperature in Pierre at 8:00 A.M. was $-33°F$. It rose $20°F$ in 9 hours. What was the temperature at 5:00 P.M.?

17. A pet-sitting business's income for the month of July was $3,680. Expenses were $3,290. Use integer addition to find the business's total profit or loss.

LESSON 2-3

Find each difference.

18. $6 - (-3)$ **19.** $-4 - (-8)$ **20.** $2 - 7$ **21.** $3 - (-4)$

Evaluate $a - b$ for each set of values.

22. $a = 5, b = -8$ **23.** $a = -12, b = -6$ **24.** $a = 6, b = 13$ **25.** $a = 9, b = -17$

26. The highest mountain in the United States is Mount McKinley at about 20,320 feet. Death Valley, California, is the lowest point at about 282 feet below sea level. What is the difference between the highest and lowest points in the United States?

LESSON 2-4

Find each product or quotient.

27. $-9 \div 3$ **28.** $8 \cdot (-3)$ **29.** $16 \div 4$ **30.** $-7 \cdot 3$

31. $-2 \cdot 9$ **32.** $15 \div (-5)$ **33.** $6 \cdot 7$ **34.** $-72 \div (-12)$

35. A submarine descends below the ocean's surface at a rate of 75 feet per minute. How many feet below the ocean's surface will the submarine be in 12 minutes?

36. While playing a board game, Rosalyn loses 2 points for each incorrect answer and gains 5 points for each correct answer. What is Rosalyn's total score if she gives 4 incorrect answers and 3 correct answers?

LESSON 2-5

Solve each equation. Check your answer.

37. $n - 25 = -18$ **38.** $y + (-13) = 61$ **39.** $21 = \frac{s}{4}$ **40.** $15y = -45$

41. $\frac{k}{-18} = 2$ **42.** $h - (-7) = -42$ **43.** $6 = \frac{z}{9}$ **44.** $68 = 4 + p$

45. Martin deposited $76 and withdrew $100 from his bank account. He now has $202 in his account. How much money did he start with?

LESSON 2-6

Name the quadrant where each point is located.

46. A **47.** R **48.** C **49.** T

Give the coordinates of each point.

50. B **51.** S **52.** D **53.** U

Graph each point on a coordinate plane.

54. $M(2, -1)$ **55.** $W(-4, -2)$ **56.** $A(2, 3)$

LESSON 2-7

Write an equation in two variables that gives the values in each table. Use your equation to find the value of y for the indicated value of x.

57.

x	1	2	3	4	5	10
y	6	7	8	9	10	▉

58.

x	3	5	7	9	11	13
y	9	15	21	27	33	▉

Write an equation for the relationship. Tell what each variable you use represents.

59. The length of a rectangle is 4 cm less than 3 times its width.

60. Darren's age is 5 more than 2 times Nicole's age.

61. Renting a canoe costs $10 plus $5 per hour.

LESSON 2-8

Use the given x-values to write solutions of each equation as ordered pairs.

62. $y = 6x + 2$ for $x = 1, 2, 3, 4$ **63.** $y = 5x - 9$ for $x = 2, 3, 4, 5$

Determine whether the ordered pair is a solution to the given equation.

64. $(2, 3)$; $y = x + 1$ **65.** $(9, 7)$; $y = 3x - 12$

66. $(-1, 4)$; $y = -2x + 6$ **67.** $(0, 8)$; $y = 8x + 8$

Graph each equation.

68. $y = 4x - 3$ **69.** $y = x + 1$

Extra Practice ⋅ Chapter 3

LESSON 3-1

Tell whether each number is prime or composite.

1. 11	**2.** 24	**3.** 61	**4.** 45
5. 39	**6.** 83	**7.** 53	**8.** 77

Write the prime factorization of each number.

9. 78	**10.** 144	**11.** 96	**12.** 95
13. 176	**14.** 156	**15.** 336	**16.** 675
17. 888	**18.** 2,800	**19.** 780	**20.** 682

LESSON 3-2

Find the greatest common divisor (GCD).

21. 6, 15	**22.** 18, 27	**23.** 26, 65	**24.** 60, 25
25. 84, 48	**26.** 90, 34	**27.** 49, 56	**28.** 36, 120
29. 30, 75	**30.** 32, 68	**31.** 81, 75	**32.** 30, 70, 65, 100
33. 21, 77	**34.** 64, 84, 120	**35.** 20, 40, 80, 140	**36.** 49, 98

37. José is making identical gift bags that will be given away as door prizes at his concert. He has 51 posters and 34 T-shirts. What is the greatest number of gift bags José can make using all of the posters and all of the T-shirts?

38. Kieve is arranging chairs for a concert. There are 80 metal chairs and 24 cushioned chairs. Each row will have the same number of metal chairs and the same number of cushioned chairs. What is the greatest number of rows Kieve can make by using all of the chairs?

LESSON 3-3

Find the least common multiple (LCM).

39. 12, 15	**40.** 30, 12	**41.** 16, 32	**42.** 25, 40
43. 30, 75	**44.** 12, 64	**45.** 15, 50	**46.** 15, 30, 50, 100
47. 21, 28	**48.** 15, 22, 30	**49.** 20, 40, 80, 120	**50.** 42, 90

51. Kanisha shoots a basket every 7 seconds. Thomas shoots a basket every 12 seconds. They begin at the same time. How many seconds will have passed when they next shoot a basket at the same time?

52. Ron cleans the glass of his fish tank every 30 days and changes the water every 20 days. If Ron does both today, how many days will pass before he does them both on the same day again?

LESSON 3-4

Find two fractions equivalent to the given fraction.

53. $\frac{1}{5}$ **54.** $\frac{8}{12}$ **55.** $\frac{4}{10}$ **56.** $\frac{14}{50}$

Determine whether the fractions in each pair are equivalent.

57. $\frac{2}{7}$ and $\frac{3}{4}$ **58.** $\frac{4}{6}$ and $\frac{12}{18}$ **59.** $\frac{7}{8}$ and $\frac{20}{24}$ **60.** $\frac{5}{12}$ and $\frac{15}{36}$

Write each as a mixed number.

61. $\frac{19}{5}$ **62.** $\frac{23}{8}$ **63.** $\frac{41}{6}$ **64.** $\frac{98}{15}$

Write each as an improper fraction.

65. $2\frac{1}{5}$ **66.** $2\frac{13}{15}$ **67.** $6\frac{7}{8}$ **68.** $72\frac{1}{3}$

LESSON 3-5

Write each fraction as a decimal. Round to the nearest hundredth, if necessary.

69. $\frac{4}{5}$ **70.** $\frac{6}{8}$ **71.** $\frac{57}{15}$ **72.** $-\frac{75}{10}$

Write each decimal as a fraction in simplest form.

73. 0.85   **74.** -0.04 **75.** 0.875   **76.** 2.6

77. Brianna sold 84 of the 96 CDs that she brought to sell at her concert. What portion of the CDs did she sell? Write your answer as a decimal.

78. Jacob used 44 of the 60 pages in his journal. What portion of the pages did he use? Write your answer as a decimal rounded to the nearest hundredth.

LESSON 3-6

Compare the fractions. Write < or >.

79. $\frac{8}{13}$ ▧ $\frac{5}{13}$ **80.** $\frac{1}{4}$ ▧ $\frac{1}{3}$ **81.** $-\frac{8}{9}$ ▧ $-\frac{11}{12}$ **82.** $\frac{3}{5}$ ▧ $\frac{5}{8}$

Compare the decimals. Write < or >.

83. 0.88 ▧ 0.82   **84.** -1.24 ▧ 1.07   **85.** 4.02 ▧ 4.12   **86.** -1.4 ▧ -1.9

Order the numbers from least to greatest. Graph the numbers on a number line.

87. 0.5, 0.58, $\frac{6}{13}$ **88.** 2.7, 2.59, $2\frac{7}{12}$ **89.** $-0.61, -0.55, -\frac{9}{15}$

90. $\frac{3}{10}, -0.2, \frac{2}{5}$ **91.** $-0.4, -\frac{9}{20}, -0.42$ **92.** 1.7, $1\frac{2}{3}, \frac{8}{5}$

Extra Practice ▪ Chapter 4

LESSON 4-1

1. A stock's price in July was $19\frac{3}{8}$ and its price in October rose to $27\frac{1}{8}$. Estimate the difference between the price in July and the price in October.

Estimate each sum, difference, product or quotient.

2. $\frac{3}{8} + \frac{5}{6}$

3. $\frac{7}{8} - \frac{1}{6}$

4. $5\frac{3}{4} \cdot 2\frac{1}{8}$

5. $7\frac{11}{12} \div 1\frac{7}{10}$

LESSON 4-2

Add or subtract. Write each answer in simplest form.

6. $\frac{3}{7} + \frac{5}{9}$

7. $\frac{7}{8} - \frac{2}{3}$

8. $\frac{7}{12} + \frac{5}{6}$

9. $\frac{9}{10} - \frac{4}{5}$

10. Jacob and Julius spent $\frac{1}{4}$ hour swimming, $\frac{1}{10}$ hour eating a snack, and then $\frac{1}{2}$ hour hiking. How long did these activities take Jacob and Julius?

LESSON 4-3

Add or subtract. Write each answer in simplest form.

11. $9\frac{7}{8} - 4\frac{1}{4}$

12. $3\frac{1}{2} + 2\frac{3}{4}$

13. $9\frac{5}{6} - 6\frac{1}{3}$

14. $5\frac{7}{12} + 2\frac{5}{8}$

15. The average male giraffe is about $17\frac{1}{2}$ feet tall. One of the giraffes at the zoo is $18\frac{1}{8}$ feet tall. How much taller is the giraffe at the zoo than the average male giraffe?

LESSON 4-4

Multiply. Write each answer in simplest form.

16. $\frac{2}{3} \cdot 12\frac{3}{4}$

17. $3\frac{2}{9} \cdot \frac{1}{2}$

18. $\frac{5}{7} \cdot 4\frac{3}{8}$

19. $5\frac{2}{3} \cdot \frac{7}{12}$

20. Mary is $2\frac{1}{2}$ times as old as Victor. If Victor is $7\frac{1}{2}$ years old, how old is Mary?

LESSON 4-5

Divide. Write each answer in simplest form.

21. $\frac{7}{8} \div \frac{5}{6}$

22. $\frac{7}{12} \div \frac{7}{8}$

23. $\frac{2}{3} \div \frac{2}{5}$

24. $2\frac{1}{4} \div \frac{1}{2}$

25. Each serving of chicken weighs $\frac{1}{3}$ pound. Melanie bought 12 pounds of chicken for a party. How many servings does she have?

LESSON 4-6

Solve. Write each answer in simplest form.

26. $\frac{1}{3} + s = \frac{2}{5}$

27. $t - \frac{3}{8} = \frac{1}{6}$

28. $\frac{5}{6} = \frac{1}{3}x$

29. $\frac{2}{3}w = 240$

30. $n - \frac{5}{8} = \frac{5}{6}$

31. $x - \frac{5}{8} = \frac{5}{8}$

32. $\frac{2}{3}y = \frac{3}{4}$

33. $\frac{r}{6} = \frac{1}{8}$

LESSON 4-7

Add or subtract. Estimate to check whether each answer is reasonable.

34. $8.79 + 45.63$ **35.** $34.7 - 7.85$ **36.** $43.67 - 14.81$ **37.** $18 + 7.32$

38. $34.43 + 62.57$ **39.** $8.26 + 7.4$ **40.** $8.75 - 5.43$ **41.** $35.4 - 24.08$

42. Zoe gets to work in 25.5 minutes and gets home from work in 37.5 minutes. How much time does she spend commuting each day?

Multiply. Estimate to check whether each answer is reasonable.

43. $4.3 \cdot 2.8$ **44.** $-3.38 \cdot 0.8$ **45.** $-8 \cdot (-0.07)$ **46.** $7.59 \cdot (-36)$

47. $67.4 \cdot 8.7$ **48.** $5.66 \cdot 16.34$ **49.** $43.9 \cdot 4.7$ **50.** $73.3 \cdot 6.85$

51. Griffin works after school and on weekends. He worked 18.5 hours last week and gets paid $7.90 per hour. How much did he earn last week?

LESSON 4-8

Divide. Estimate to check whether each answer is reasonable.

52. $63.5 \div 2$ **53.** $36.6 \div 6$ **54.** $62.8 \div 8$ **55.** $56.05 \div 2$

56. $16.9 \div (-1.3)$ **57.** $74.25 \div 6.6$ **58.** $-4.8 \div 0.12$ **59.** $-0.63 \div (-0.7)$

60. The diameter of a northern red oak tree grows an average of 0.4 inches per year. At this rate, how long will it take the tree's diameter to grow to 24.8 inches?

LESSON 4-9

Convert each measure.

61. 8.9 m to millimeters   **62.** 56 mg to grams   **63.** 900 mL to liters

64. 2 L to milliliters   **65.** 150 m to kilometers   **66.** 0.002 kg to milligrams

67. Anthony and Melinda are drinking apple juice. Anthony has 300 mL left and Melinda has 0.09L. Who has the greater amount of juice? Use estimation to explain why your answer makes sense.

LESSON 4-10

Solve.

68. $4.7 + s = 9$ **69.** $t - 1.35 = 22$ **70.** $4.8 = 6x$ **71.** $9.6 = \frac{v}{8}$

72. $6.5 + n = 15.9$ **73.** $x - 1.07 = 8.5$ **74.** $6.2y = 21.08$ **75.** $\frac{r}{13} = 3.25$

76. Billy worked 7.5 hours and earned $56.70. What is Billy's hourly wage?

LESSON 5-1

One day, a veterinarian saw 20 cats and 30 dogs. Write each ratio in all three forms. Make sure each ratio is in simplest form.

1. cats to dogs   **2.** dogs to cats   **3.** cats to animals

4. A compact car gets 135 miles per 5 gallons of gas. A midsize car gets 210 miles per 10 gallons of gas. Which car gets more miles per gallon?

LESSON 5-2

5. Danielle skipped a rope 248 times in 4 minutes. On average, how many times did Danielle skip the rope per minute?

6. A serving of 8 crackers contains 128 Calories. What is the number of Calories per cracker?

7. Jamie's family drives 350 miles to her grandparents' house in 7 hours. What is their average speed in miles per hour?

8. A store sells milk in 3 sizes. The 128 fl oz container costs $4.59, the 64 fl oz container costs $3.29, and the 32 fl oz container costs $1.99. Which size milk has the lowest price per fluid ounce?

LESSON 5-3

Determine whether the ratios are proportional.

9. $\frac{25}{40}, \frac{30}{48}$ **10.** $\frac{32}{36}, \frac{24}{28}$ **11.** $\frac{5}{6}, \frac{15}{18}$ **12.** $\frac{21}{49}, \frac{18}{42}$

Find a ratio equivalent to each ratio. Then use the ratios to write a proportion.

13. $\frac{72}{81}$ **14.** $\frac{15}{40}$ **15.** $\frac{24}{32}$ **16.** $\frac{5}{13}$

LESSON 5-4

Use cross products to solve each proportion.

17. $\frac{8}{n} = \frac{12}{18}$ **18.** $\frac{4}{7} = \frac{p}{28}$ **19.** $\frac{u}{14} = \frac{21}{28}$ **20.** $\frac{3}{21} = \frac{t}{49}$

21. $\frac{y}{35} = \frac{63}{45}$ **22.** $\frac{6}{n} = \frac{48}{12}$ **23.** $\frac{32}{x} = \frac{52}{117}$ **24.** $\frac{56}{80} = \frac{105}{m}$

25. The ratio of a person's weight on Earth to his weight on the Moon is 6 to 1. Rafael weighs 90 pounds on Earth. How much would he weigh on the Moon?

26. In 2 weeks, a taxi traveled 2,460 miles. At this rate, how many miles will the taxi travel in one year (52 weeks)?

27. Yvette's phone plan charges $1.00 for every 20 text messages sent. How much will Yvette be charged if she sends 65 text messages?

LESSON 5-5

Choose the most appropriate customary unit for each measurement. Justify your answer.

28. the weight of 6 crackers

29. the capacity of a pond

30. the capacity of a baby's bottle

31. the length of a marathon

Convert each measure.

32. 8 pt to cups

33. 5 ft to inches

34. 6.5 lb to ounces

35. A mass of 1 kilogram weighs about 2.2 pounds. African elephants can have a mass of up to 6,800 kilograms. What is the maximum weight of African elephants, rounded to the nearest thousand pounds?

LESSON 5-6

Tell whether the figures are similar.

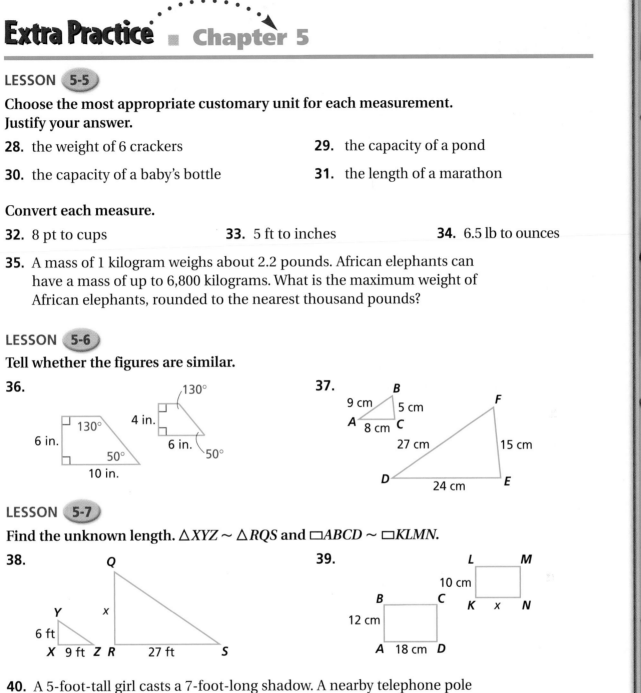

36.

37.

LESSON 5-7

Find the unknown length. $\triangle XYZ \sim \triangle RQS$ and $\square ABCD \sim \square KLMN$.

38.

39.

40. A 5-foot-tall girl casts a 7-foot-long shadow. A nearby telephone pole casts a 35-foot-long shadow. What is the height of the telephone pole?

LESSON 5-8

41. An amoeba is 0.8 millimeter in length. A scale model of the amoeba is 160 millimeters in length. What is the scale factor of the model?

42. A scale model of the Empire State Building is 3.125 feet tall with a scale factor of $\frac{1}{400}$. Find the height of the actual Empire State Building.

43. Kira is drawing a map with a scale of 1 inch = 30 miles. The actual distance from Park City to Gatesville is 80 miles. How far from the dot for Gatesville should Kira draw the dot for Park City?

Extra Practice ▪ Chapter 6

LESSON 6-1

Write the percent modeled by each grid.

1.

2.

3.

Write each percent as a fraction in simplest form.

4. 14%   **5.** 110%   **6.** 20%   **7.** 9%

Write each percent as a decimal.

8. 27%   **9.** 7%   **10.** 125%   **11.** 0.53%

LESSON 6-2

Write each decimal as a percent.

12. 0.06   **13.** 0.54   **14.** 1.69   **15.** 42.0   **16.** 0.898

Write each fraction as a percent.

17. $\frac{15}{40}$ **18.** $\frac{8}{25}$ **19.** $\frac{33}{44}$ **20.** $\frac{17}{20}$ **21.** $1\frac{2}{5}$

22. Yesterday 18 of Ms. Hansen's 24 students finished their science assignment in class. What percent of the students finished the science assignment in class?

23. During football practice, Anton made 13 out of 20 attempted field goals. What percent of the attempted field goals did Anton make?

LESSON 6-3

Use a fraction to estimate the percent of each number.

24. 48% of 200   **25.** 27% of 76   **26.** 65% of 300   **27.** 15% of 15

28. Kel has $25 to spend on a pair of jeans. One pair is on sale for 30% off the regular price of $29.99. Does she have enough money to buy the jeans? Explain.

Use 1% or 10% to estimate the percent of each number.

29. 21% of 88   **30.** 19% of 109   **31.** 2% of 56   **32.** 48% of 200

33. Last year, Maria's retirement fund lost 19%. If the fund was worth $18,000 at the beginning of the year, about how much money did she lose?

34. Every year, about 300 movies are made. Only 13% are considered to be hits. About how many movies are considered hits in a year?

LESSON 6-4

Find the percent of each number. Check whether your answer is reasonable.

35. 35% of 80

36. 55% of 256

37. 75% of 60

38. 2% of 68

39. 17% of 51

40. 0.5% of 80

41. 1% of 8.5

42. 1.25% of 48

43. A cell phone is on sale for a 20% discount. The regular price of the phone is $75.00. What is the amount of discount on the phone?

44. Donna left an 18% tip for a meal that cost $12.50. What is the amount of the tip that Donna left?

LESSON 6-5

Solve.

45. What percent of 150 is 60?

46. What percent of 140 is 28?

47. What percent of 120 is 24?

48. What percent of 90 is 117?

49. 24 is 60% of what number?

50. 9 is 15% of what number?

51. Thomas bought a desk with a retail sales price of $129 and paid $10.32 sales tax. What is the sales tax rate where Thomas bought the desk?

52. The sales tax on a $68 hotel room is $7.48. What is the sales tax rate?

LESSON 6-6

Find each percent of change. Round answers to the nearest tenth of a percent, if necessary.

53. 54 is increased to 68.

54. 90 is decreased to 82.

55. 60 is increased to 80.

56. 76 is decreased to 55.

57. 75 is increased to 120.

58. 50 is decreased to 33.

59. Abby's Appliances sells DVD players at 7% above the wholesale cost of $89. How much does the store charge for a DVD player?

60. A market's old parking lot held 48 cars. The new lot holds 37.5% more cars. How many parking spaces are on the new lot?

61. A regular bag of banana chips contains 12 ounces. A jumbo bag contains $166\frac{2}{3}\%$ more chips. How many ounces does the jumbo bag contain?

LESSON 6-7

Find each missing value.

62. $I = $ ▨ $, P = \$500, r = 5\%, t = 1$ year

63. $I = \$30, P = $ ▨ $, r = 6\%, t = 2$ years

64. $I = \$168, P = \$800, r = $ ▨ $, t = 3$ years

65. $I = \$48, P = \$300, r = 8\%, t = $ ▨

66. Shane deposits $600 in an account that earns 5.5% simple interest. How long will it be before the total amount is $699?

Extra Practice ▪ Chapter 7

LESSON 7-1

Find the mean, median, mode, and range of each data set.

1.

Points Scored				
16	18	23	13	15

2.

Hours Worked							
37	42	43	38	39	40	45	40

LESSON 7-2

3. a. The table shows a student's test scores. Find the mean, median, mode, and range of the test scores.

Test Scores			
78	82	87	95

   b. On the next test the student scored a 92. Find the mean, median, mode, and range with the new test score.

4. The scores Anna received for her balance beam routine in a gymnastics competition were 8.80, 9.90, 8.75, 8.95, 8.95, 8.95, and 9.00. What score represents an outlier?

5. The daily high temperatures for the first seven days of April were 52°F, 63°F, 61°F, 54°F, 52°F, 55°F, and 68°F. On April 8, the high temperature was 88°F. Find the mean, median, mode, and range of the data with and without the high temperature on April 8, and explain the changes.

LESSON 7-3

6. The list shows the number of miles Trey ran per day during training.

   5, 6, 5, 5, 6, 5, 4, 6, 14

   What are the mean and median of this data set? Is one measure more useful than the other for describing the typical distance run per day? Explain.

7. The list shows the prices of used cars at a car dealership.

   $9,200; $3,700; $8,600; $9,400; $8,800;
   $12,400; $8,800; $4,600, $7,500; $10,200

   The manager wants to convince customers that the dealership has low prices on used cars. Should the manager use the mean, median, or mode to describe the data set? Explain.

LESSON 7-4

The circle graph shows the results of a survey of 100 people from Iran who were asked about their ethnic backgrounds. Use the graph for Exercises 8–10.

8. Which ethnic group is the second largest?

9. According to the survey, 3% of the people are Arab. How many of the people surveyed are Arab?

10. Greg claims that about 50% of the people surveyed are Persian. Is his claim valid? Explain.

LESSON 7-5

Explain why each graph could be misleading.

11.
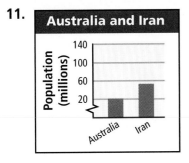

12.
Hungary and Ireland

LESSON 7-6

13. About 22% of adults in the United States visited a beach in 2004. Kiki surveyed a random sample of adults from two towns. Compare the samples with the national percent.

Visited Beach in 2004		
Sample	**Yes**	**No**
Town A	63	87
Town B	38	112

14. A principal estimates that about 100 of the 842 students at a high school have part-time jobs. A random sample of 50 of the students show that 11 of them have part-time jobs. Determine whether the principal's estimate is likely to be accurate.

LESSON 7-7

15. Determine which sampling method will better represent the entire population. Justify your answer.

Election for Mayor	
Sampling Method	**Results of Survey**
Erik surveys 100 voters by randomly choosing names from a voter registration list.	54% plan to vote for Zoe Stott.
Laura surveys 100 voters by visiting a local library one Saturday.	38% plan to vote for Zoe Stott.

LESSON 7-8

Determine whether each sample may be biased. Explain.

16. A bank asks the first 10 customers that enter in the morning if they are satisfied with the bank's late afternoon lobby hours.

17. Members of a polling organization survey 1,000 residents by randomly choosing names from a list of all residents.

Determine whether each survey question may be biased. Explain.

18. What is your favorite type of vegetable?

19. Don't you agree that our school needs a longer lunch period?

Extra Practice ▪ Chapter 8

LESSON 8-1

Determine whether each event is impossible, unlikely, as likely as not, likely, or certain.

1. flipping a coin and getting heads twelve times in a row

2. drawing a green bead from a bag of white and red beads

3. The probability of rolling a 2 on a number cube is $\frac{1}{6}$. What is the probability of not rolling a 2?

LESSON 8-2

4. Bess bowls a strike on 6 out of 15 tries. What is the experimental probability that she will bowl a strike on her next try? Write your answer as a ratio, as a decimal, and as a percent.

5. For the past 10 days, a city planner has counted the number of northbound cars that pass through a particular intersection. During that time, 200 or more cars were counted 9 out of 10 days.

   a. What is the experimental probability that there will be 200 or more northbound cars passing through the intersection on the eleventh day?

   b. What is the experimental probability that there will be fewer than 200 northbound cars passing through the intersection on the eleventh day?

LESSON 8-3

Find the probability of each event. Write your answer as a ratio, as a decimal, and as a percent.

6. rolling a number less than 5 on a fair number cube

7. randomly drawing a pink sock out of a drawer of 6 pink, 4 black, 8 white, and 2 blue socks all of the same size

LESSON 8-4

8. Ronald flips a coin and rolls a number cube at the same time. Use a table to find all the possible outcomes. What is the theoretical probability of each outcome?

9. For lunch, Amy can choose from a salad, a taco, a hamburger, or a fish fillet. She can drink lemonade, milk, juice, or water. Use a tree diagram to find all of the possible outcomes of choosing one food item and one drink. If Amy chooses at random, what is the probability that she will choose a fish fillet and juice?

10. A café makes 23 types of soup. You can get each type in a bowl, a dish, or a cup. How many outcomes are possible?

LESSON 8-5

Determine whether each set of events is disjoint. Explain.

11. rolling a number cube and getting a number less than 3 or a number greater than 3

12. choosing a multiple of 10 or a multiple of 5 from a set of 30 cards numbered 1 to 30

Find the probability of each set of disjoint events.

13. selecting a red marble or a blue marble from a bag that contains 6 green marbles, 3 blue marbles, 4 white marbles, and 7 red marbles

14. rolling either a 5 or an even number on a number cube

15. choosing either an *S* or a *T* from the word ESTABLISHMENT

LESSON 8-6

Decide whether each set of events is independent or dependent. Explain your answer.

16. Mr. Fernandez's class contains 14 boys and 16 girls. Mr. Fernandez randomly picks a boy and a girl to represent the class at the school spelling bee.

17. Mrs. Rogers's class received new math books. Mrs. Rogers selects a student to hand out the new books. She also picks a second student to collect the old books.

18. There are 52 playing cards in a standard card deck. Alex draws a card and holds onto it while Suzi draws a card.

Find the probability of each set of independent events.

19. flipping 2 coins at the same time and getting heads on both coins

20. drawing a 3 from 5 cards numbered 1 through 5 and rolling an even number on a number cube

LESSON 8-7

21. Based on a sample survey, a local newspaper stated that 26% of the population has a pet dog. Out of 600 people, how many people can you predict will have a pet dog?

22. If you roll a number cube 54 times, how many times do you expect to roll a number less than 3?

23. A promotion team is selling tickets for unreserved seats to a concert. The promotion team estimates that 75% of the people who purchase a ticket will attend the concert. If the stadium seats 15,000 people and the promotion team wants to have all of the seats full at the concert, how many concert tickets should they sell?

Extra Practice ▪ Chapter 9

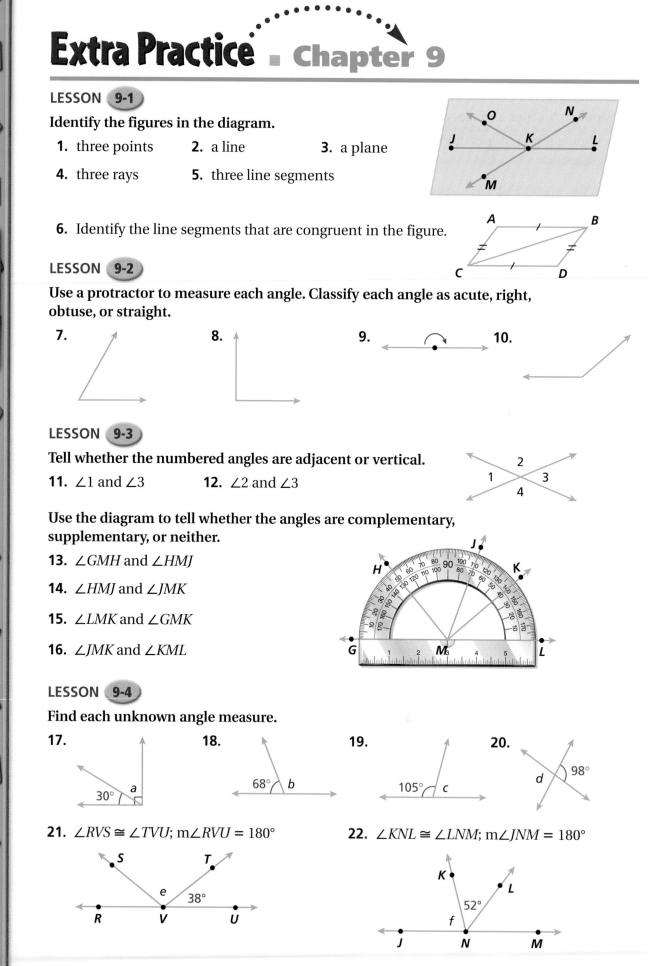

LESSON 9-1

Identify the figures in the diagram.

1. three points

2. a line

3. a plane

4. three rays

5. three line segments

6. Identify the line segments that are congruent in the figure.

LESSON 9-2

Use a protractor to measure each angle. Classify each angle as acute, right, obtuse, or straight.

7.

8.

9.

10.

LESSON 9-3

Tell whether the numbered angles are adjacent or vertical.

11. ∠1 and ∠3

12. ∠2 and ∠3

Use the diagram to tell whether the angles are complementary, supplementary, or neither.

13. ∠GMH and ∠HMJ

14. ∠HMJ and ∠JMK

15. ∠LMK and ∠GMK

16. ∠JMK and ∠KML

LESSON 9-4

Find each unknown angle measure.

17. 30° a

18. 68° b

19. 105° c

20. d 98°

21. ∠RVS ≅ ∠TVU; m∠RVU = 180°

22. ∠KNL ≅ ∠LNM; m∠JNM = 180°

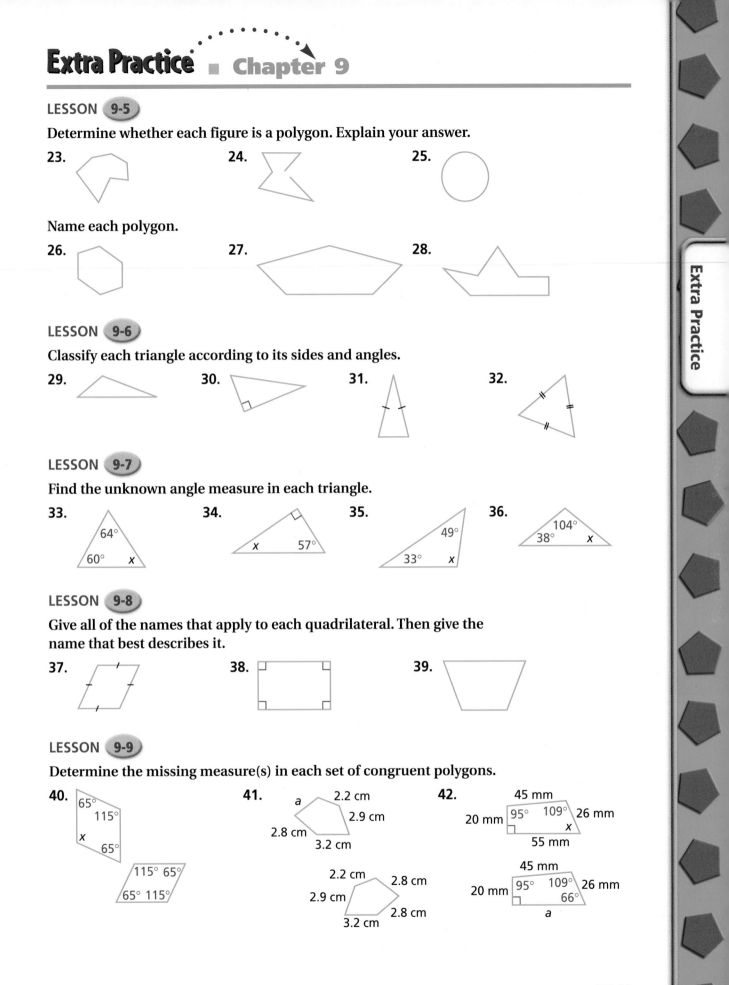

LESSON 9-5

Determine whether each figure is a polygon. Explain your answer.

23.

24.

25.

Name each polygon.

26.

27.

28.

LESSON 9-6

Classify each triangle according to its sides and angles.

29.

30.

31.

32.

LESSON 9-7

Find the unknown angle measure in each triangle.

33.
64°
60° x

34.
x 57°

35.
49°
33° x

36.
104°
38° x

LESSON 9-8

Give all of the names that apply to each quadrilateral. Then give the name that best describes it.

37.

38.

39.

LESSON 9-9

Determine the missing measure(s) in each set of congruent polygons.

40.
65°
115°
x
65°

115° 65°
65° 115°

41.
a   2.2 cm
2.9 cm
2.8 cm
3.2 cm

2.2 cm   2.8 cm
2.9 cm
2.8 cm
3.2 cm

42.
45 mm
20 mm 95° 109° 26 mm
x
55 mm

45 mm
20 mm 95° 109° 26 mm
66°
a

LESSON 10-1

Find the perimeter of each figure.

1.
4.5 cm
4 cm   3 cm
7 cm

2.
11.2 km   11.2 km
11.2 km

3.
$18\frac{1}{2}$ m
$5\frac{1}{2}$ m

4. The length of a rectangle is 18 inches. What is the perimeter of the rectangle if the length is 7 inches longer than the width?

LESSON 10-2

Find the circumference of each circle to the nearest tenth. Use 3.14 or $\frac{22}{7}$ as an estimate for π.

  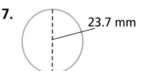

5. 7 yd

6. 16.5 in.

7. 23.7 mm

LESSON 10-3

Find the area of each rectangle or parallelogram.

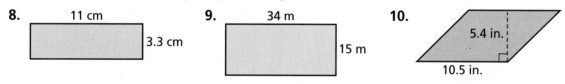

8. 11 cm
3.3 cm

9. 34 m
15 m

10. 5.4 in.
10.5 in.

11. Harry is using 16 Japanese tatami mats to cover a floor. Each mat measures 3 feet by 2 feet. What is the total area that will be covered by the mats?

LESSON 10-4

Find the area of each triangle or trapezoid.

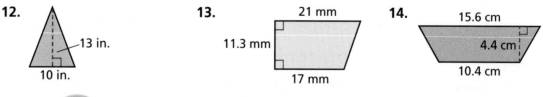

12. 13 in.
10 in.

13. 21 mm
11.3 mm
17 mm

14. 15.6 cm
4.4 cm
10.4 cm

LESSON 10-5

Find the area of each circle to the nearest tenth. Use 3.14 as an estimate for π.

15. 17 in.

16. 29.8 m

17. 104 mm

18. An approximately circular crater on the moon has a radius of about 0.21 mile. To the nearest hundredth of a square mile, what is the approximate area of the crater? Use $\frac{22}{7}$ as an estimate for π.

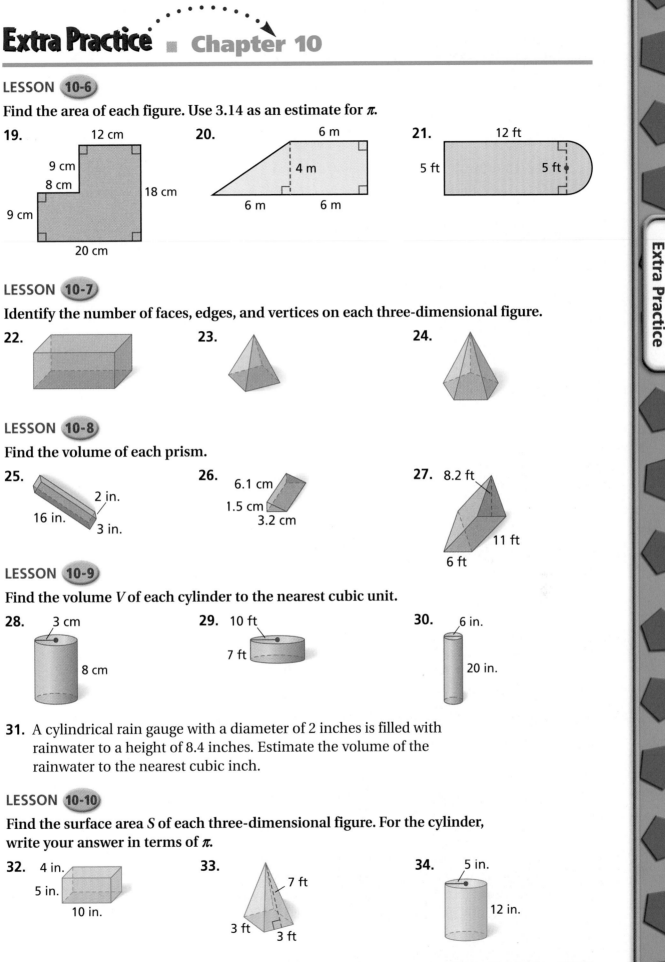

LESSON 10-6

Find the area of each figure. Use 3.14 as an estimate for π.

19.
12 cm
9 cm
8 cm
18 cm
9 cm
20 cm

20.
6 m
4 m
6 m   6 m

21.
12 ft
5 ft   5 ft

LESSON 10-7

Identify the number of faces, edges, and vertices on each three-dimensional figure.

22.

23.

24.

LESSON 10-8

Find the volume of each prism.

25.
2 in.
16 in.
3 in.

26.
6.1 cm
1.5 cm
3.2 cm

27. 8.2 ft
11 ft
6 ft

LESSON 10-9

Find the volume V of each cylinder to the nearest cubic unit.

28. 3 cm
8 cm

29. 10 ft
7 ft

30. 6 in.
20 in.

31. A cylindrical rain gauge with a diameter of 2 inches is filled with rainwater to a height of 8.4 inches. Estimate the volume of the rainwater to the nearest cubic inch.

LESSON 10-10

Find the surface area S of each three-dimensional figure. For the cylinder, write your answer in terms of π.

32. 4 in.
5 in.
10 in.

33.
7 ft
3 ft   3 ft

34. 5 in.
12 in.

LESSON 11-1

Solve.

1. $4c - 13 = 15$

2. $3h + 14 = 23$

3. $-5j - 13 = 22$

4. $\frac{e}{7} + 2 = 5$

5. $\frac{m}{6} - 3 = 1$

6. $\frac{x}{3} + 5 = -13$

LESSON 11-2

Simplify. Justify your steps using the Commutative, Associative, and Distributive Properties when necessary.

7. $5b + 3t + b$

8. $t + 3b + 3t + 3b + x$

9. $8g + 3g + 12$

10. $3u + 6 + 5k + u$

11. $11 + 5t^2 + t + 6t$

12. $y^3 + 3y + 6y^3$

13. Write an expression for the perimeter of the given figure. Then simplify the expression.

LESSON 11-3

Solve.

14. $2w - 11 + 4w = 7$

15. $7v + 5 - v = 11$

16. $-7z + 4 - z = -12$

17. $3(5x - 7) = -36$

18. $2t - 7 - 5t = 11$

19. $6(t + 8) = 66$

20. $12a - 3 - 8a = -1$

21. $2(h - 1) + 3 = 12$

22. $\frac{1}{4}(3s - 14) = 4$

23. $4(t + 5) - 20 = 0$

LESSON 11-4

Group the terms with variables on one side of the equal sign, and simplify.

24. $6a = 4a - 8$

25. $3d - 5 = 7d - 9$

26. $-2j + 6 = j - 3$

27. $2 + 5m = 7 - m$

Solve.

28. $7y - 9 = -2y$

29. $2c - 13 = 5c + 11$

30. $4g + 90 = -60 - 6g$

31. $7d + 4 = 8 - d$

32. $-3p + 8 = -7p - 12$

33. $12k + 23 = -5k + 74$

34. Roberta and Stanley are collecting signatures for a petition. So far, Roberta has twice as many signatures as Stanley. If she collects 30 more signatures, she will have 4 times as many signatures as Stanley currently has. How many signatures has Stanley collected?

LESSON 11-5

Write an inequality for each situation.

35. The cafeteria could hold no more than 50 people.

36. There were fewer than 20 boats in the marina.

Graph each inequality.

37. $y < -2$

38. $f \geq 3$

39. $n \leq -1.5$

40. $x > 4$

Graph each compound inequality.

41. $1 < s < 4$

42. $-1 \leq v < 2$

43. $w < 0$ or $w \geq 5$

44. $-3.5 \leq y < -2$

LESSON 11-6

Solve. Then graph each solution set on a number line.

45. $c - 6 > -5$

46. $v - 3 \geq 1$

47. $w - 6 \leq -7$

48. $a - 2 \leq 5$

Solve. Check each answer.

49. $q + 3 \leq 5$

50. $m + 1 > 0$

51. $p + 7 \leq 4$

52. $z + 2 \geq -3$

53. By Saturday night, 3 inches of rain had fallen in Happy Valley. The weekend forecast predicted at least 8 inches of rain. How much more rain must fall on Sunday for this forecast to be correct?

LESSON 11-7

Solve. Check each answer.

54. $\frac{a}{5} \leq 4.5$

55. $-\frac{v}{2} > 2$

56. $\frac{x}{3.9} \geq -2$

57. $-\frac{c}{4} < 2.3$

58. $13y < 39$

59. $2t \leq 5$

60. $-7r > 56$

61. $3s \geq -4.5$

62. The local candy store buys candy in bulk and then sells it by the pound. If the store owner spends \$135 on peppermints and then sells them for \$3.50 per pound, how many pounds must he sell to make a profit?

LESSON 11-8

Solve. Then graph each solution set on a number line.

63. $\frac{m}{3} - 1 \leq 2$

64. $7.2x - 4.8 > 24$

65. $-5.5h + 2 < 13$

66. $-1 - \frac{s}{3.5} \geq 1$

67. $-\frac{w}{1.5} - 8 \leq -10$

68. $4j - 6 > 16$

69. $5 - 2u < 15$

70. $\frac{r}{7} - 1 \geq 0$

71. $5 - \frac{m}{9} \leq 17$

72. Jill, Serena, and Erin are trying to earn enough money to rent a beach house for a week. They estimate that it will cost at least \$1,650. If Jill has already earned \$600, how much must each of the others earn?

Skills Bank

Read and Write Whole Numbers

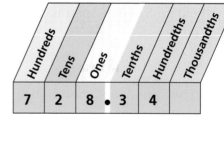 4NS1.1

You can use a place-value chart to read and write whole numbers. Starting from the right, each group of three digits forms a period. Use commas to separate the periods.

Place Value

Hundred-millions	Ten-millions	Millions	Hundred-thousands	Ten-thousands	Thousands	Hundreds	Tens	Ones
1	2	6	3	0	0	5	6	7

EXAMPLE 1

Write 126,300,567 in words.

Use the place-value chart. The word form of the number is one hundred twenty-six million, three hundred thousand, five hundred sixty-seven.

EXAMPLE 2

Write two million, sixty thousand, seven hundred eighty-five in standard form.

The standard form of the number is 2,060,785.

PRACTICE

Write each number in words.

1. 543,201   **2.** 11,239,487   **3.** 2,730,432   **4.** 904,382,121

5. Write one hundred three thousand, five hundred twenty-six in standard form.

Read and Write Decimals

4NS1.6

When reading and writing a decimal, you need to know the place value of the digit in the last decimal place. Also, when writing a decimal in word form remember that "and" goes in place of the decimal for numbers greater than one.

Place Value

Hundreds	Tens	Ones	Tenths	Hundredths	Thousandths
7	2	8 .	3	4	

EXAMPLE

Write 728.34 in words.

Use the place-value chart. The 4 is in the hundredths place, so 728.34 is written as "seven hundred twenty-eight and thirty-four hundredths."

PRACTICE

Write each decimal in words.

1. 17.238   **2.** 9.23   **3.** 534.019   **4.** 33.084   **5.** 4,356.6

Compare and Order Whole Numbers

You can use place values from left to right to compare and order numbers.

EXAMPLE

Compare and order from least to greatest: 42,810; 142,997; 42,729; 42,638.

Start at the leftmost place value.

There is one number with a digit in the greatest place.
It is the greatest of the four numbers.

Compare the remaining three numbers. All values in the next
two places, the ten thousands and thousands, are the same.

In the hundreds place, the values are different.
Use this digit to order the remaining numbers.

42,638; 42,729; 42,810; 142,997

42,810
142,997
42,729
42,638

PRACTICE

Compare and order the numbers in each set from least to greatest.

1. 2,564; 2,546; 2,465; 2,654

2. 6,237; 6,372; 6,273; 6,327

3. 132,957; 232,795; 32,975; 31,999

4. 9,614; 29,461; 129,164; 129,146

Round Whole Numbers

You can use rounding rules to round whole numbers to the nearest 10, 100,
1,000, 10,000, or 100,000.

- If the digit to the right of the rounding place is 5 or greater, increase the digit in
  the rounding place by 1.
- If the digit to the right of the rounding place is less than 5, keep the digit in the
  rounding place the same.

EXAMPLE

Round 12,573 to the nearest 1,000.

12,573   *Find the digit in the thousands place.*

The digit to the right of the thousands place is 5 or greater.
Add 1 to the digit in the thousands place.

12,573 rounded to the nearest 1,000 is 13,000.

PRACTICE

Round each number to the given place value.

1. 15,638; nearest 100

2. 2,737,519; nearest 100,000

3. 9,298; nearest 10

4. 69,504; nearest 10,000

5. 852; nearest 1,000

6. 33,449; nearest 100

Round Decimals

You can use rounding rules to round decimals to the nearest whole number, tenth, hundredth, or thousandth.

EXAMPLE

Round each decimal to the given place value.

A **5.16; tenth**

$6 \geq 5$ So 5.16 rounds to 5.2.

B **13.4563; thousandth**

$3 < 5$ So 13.4563 rounds to 13.456.

PRACTICE

Round each decimal to the given place value.

1. 3.982; tenth

2. 6.3174; hundredth

3. 1.4714; thousandth

4. 48.1526; hundredth

5. 5.0365; thousandth

6. 0.083; tenth

Add Whole Numbers

Addition is used to find the total of two or more quantities. The answer to an addition problem is called the *sum*.

EXAMPLE

4,617 + 5,682

Step 1: Add the ones.	**Step 2:** Add the tens.	**Step 3:** Add the hundreds. Regroup.	**Step 4:** Add the thousands.
$\begin{array}{r} 4,617 \\ + 5,682 \\ \hline 9 \end{array}$	$\begin{array}{r} 4,617 \\ + 5,682 \\ \hline 99 \end{array}$	$\begin{array}{r} {}^{1} \\ 4,617 \\ + 5,682 \\ \hline 299 \end{array}$	$\begin{array}{r} {}^{1} \\ 4,617 \\ + 5,682 \\ \hline 10,299 \end{array}$

The sum is 10,299.

PRACTICE

Find each sum.

1. 711 + 591

2. 2,580 + 2,345

3. 21,470 + 13,329

4. $165 + $304

5. 6,905 + 872

6. 47,231 + 3,254

7. 26,074 + 941

8. 77,350 + 29,475

9. 23 + 47 + 66

Subtract Whole Numbers

4NS2.1, 4NS3.1

Subtraction is used to take away one quantity from another quantity or to compare two quantities. The answer to a subtraction problem is called the *difference*. The difference tells how much greater or smaller one number is than the other.

EXAMPLE

780 − 468

Step 1: Regroup. Subtract the ones.	Step 2: Subtract the tens.	Step 3: Subtract the hundreds.
$\begin{array}{r} 7\,^{7}8\!\!\!/\,^{10}0\!\!\!/ \\ -\;4\,6\,8 \\ \hline 2 \end{array}$	$\begin{array}{r} 7\,^{7}8\!\!\!/\,^{10}0\!\!\!/ \\ -\;4\,6\,8 \\ \hline 1\,2 \end{array}$	$\begin{array}{r} 7\,^{7}8\!\!\!/\,^{10}0\!\!\!/ \\ -\;4\,6\,8 \\ \hline 3\,1\,2 \end{array}$

The difference is 312.

PRACTICE

Find each difference.

1. 6,785 − 2,426

2. 3,000 − 1,930

3. 932 − 868

4. 41,003 − 22,500

5. $1,075 − $918

6. 12,035 − 640

7. 704 − 86

8. 4,875 − 796

9. 8,007 − 228

Multiply and Divide by Powers of Ten

4NS3.2, 5NS2.2

When you *multiply* by powers of ten, move the decimal point one place to the right for each zero in the power of ten. When you *divide* by powers of ten, move the decimal point one place to the left for each zero in the power of ten.

EXAMPLE

Find each product or quotient.

A 0.37 · 100
$$0.37 \cdot 100 = 0.37$$
$$= 37$$

B 43 · 1,000
$$43 \cdot 1,000 = 43.000$$
$$= 43,000$$

C 0.24 ÷ 10
$$0.24 \div 10 = 0.24$$
$$= 0.024$$

D 1,467 ÷ 100
$$1,467 \div 100 = 14\,67.$$
$$= 14.67$$

PRACTICE

Find each product or quotient.

1. 10 × 8.53

2. 0.55 × 100

3. 48.6 × 1,000

4. 2.487 ÷ 1,000

5. 6.03 ÷ 100

6. 3.7 ÷ 10

Multiply Whole Numbers

When you multiply two whole numbers, think of the second number's expanded form, and multiply by each value. The answer to a multiplication problem is called the *product*.

EXAMPLE

621 × 85

Step 1: Think of 85 as 8 tens and 5 ones. Multiply 621 by 5 ones.	Step 2: Multiply 621 by 8 tens.	Step 3: Add the partial products.
621 × 85 3,105 ⟵ 5 × 621	621 × 85 3,105 49,680 ⟵ 80 × 621	621 × 85 3,105 + 49,680 52,785

The product is 52,785.

PRACTICE

Find each product.

1. 493 × 37   **2.** 539 × 82   **3.** 134 × 145   **4.** 857 × 662

Divide Whole Numbers

Division is used to separate a quantity into equal groups. The answer to a division problem is known as the *quotient*.

EXAMPLE

672 ÷ 16

Step 1: Write 672 inside the long division symbol and 16 to the left. Place the first digit of the quotient above the 7 in 672.	Step 2: Multiply 4 by 16, and place the product under 67.	Step 3: Bring down the next digit of the dividend.
$\frac{4}{16\overline{)672}}$ *16 cannot go into 6, so try 67.*	$16\overline{)672}$ *Subtract 64 from 67.* − 64 3	$16\overline{)672}$ *Divide 32 by 16.* − 64 32 −32 0 (quotient 42)

The quotient is 42.

PRACTICE

Find each quotient.

1. 578 ÷ 34   **2.** 736 ÷ 8   **3.** 826 ÷ 118   **4.** 5,989 ÷ 53

Divide with Zeros in the Quotient

4NS3.2, 5NS2.2

Sometimes when dividing, you need to use zeros in the quotient as placeholders.

EXAMPLE

$3,648 \div 12$

Step 1: Divide 36 by 12 because $12 > 3$. $$\begin{array}{r} 3 \\ 12\overline{)3,648} \end{array}$$	**Step 2:** Place a zero in the quotient because $12 > 4$. $$\begin{array}{r} 30 \\ 12\overline{)3,648} \\ -36\downarrow \\ \hline 04 \end{array}$$	**Step 3:** Bring down the 8. $$\begin{array}{r} 304 \\ 12\overline{)3,648} \\ -36\downarrow \\ \hline 048 \\ -48 \\ \hline 0 \end{array}$$

The quotient is 304.

PRACTICE

Find each quotient.

1. $424 \div 4$ **2.** $5,796 \div 28$ **3.** $540 \div 18$ **4.** $7,380 \div 123$

Fractional Part of a Whole

4NS1.5, 4NS1.7

You can use fractions to name parts of a whole. The denominator tells how many equal parts are in the whole. The numerator tells how many of those parts are being considered.

EXAMPLE

Tell what fraction of each whole is shaded.

A $\dfrac{1}{2}$ B $\dfrac{1}{3}$ C $\dfrac{3}{4}$

PRACTICE

Tell what fraction of each whole is shaded.

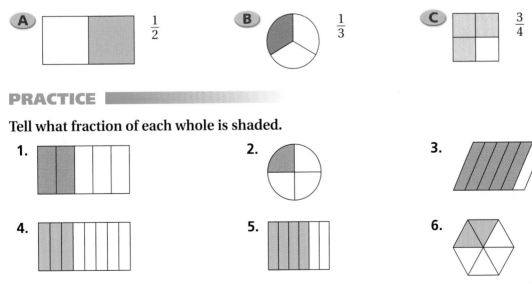

1.   2.   3.

4.   5.   6.

Fractional Part of a Set

You can use fractions to name part of a set. The denominator tells how many items are in the set. The numerator tells how many of those items are being used.

EXAMPLE

Tell what fraction of each set are stars.

A □☆□☆●☆●□□□

3 out of 10 shapes are stars.

$\frac{3}{10}$ of the shapes are stars.

B ☆●☆☆●☆☆

5 out of 7 shapes are stars.

$\frac{5}{7}$ of the shapes are stars.

PRACTICE

Tell what fraction of each set is shaded.

1. ☆☆☆☆☆☆

2. ■■■■□

3. ●☆○○☆○

4. ■■■□□

5. ●○□□

6. ☆⬡■○▯△♡

Divisibility Rules

A number is divisible by another number if the quotient is a whole number with no remainder.

A number is divisible by . . .	Divisible	Not Divisible
2 if the last digit is an even number.	13,776	4,221
3 if the sum of the digits is divisible by 3.	327	97
4 if the last two digits form a number divisible by 4.	3,128	526
5 if the last digit is 0 or 5.	9,415	50,501
6 if the number is divisible by 2 and 3.	762	62
9 if the sum of the digits is divisible by 9.	21,222	96
10 if the last digit is 0.	1,680	8,255

PRACTICE

Determine whether each number is divisible by 2, 3, 4, 5, 6, 9, or 10.

1. 324
2. 501
3. 200
4. 812
5. 60
6. 784
7. 351
8. 3,009
9. 2,345
10. 555,555
11. 1,084
12. 26,000

Factors

A **factor** of a number is any number that divides into the number without leaving a remainder.

EXAMPLE

List all the positive factors of 28.

The possible factors are whole numbers from 1 to 28.

$1 \cdot 28 = 28$ *1 and 28 are factors of 28.*

$2 \cdot 14 = 28$ *2 and 14 are factors of 28.*

$3 \cdot ? = 28$ *No whole number multiplied by 3 equals 28, so 3 is not a factor of 28.*

$4 \cdot 7 = 28$ *4 and 7 are factors of 28.*

$5 \cdot ? = 28$ *No whole number multiplied by 5 equals 28, so 5 is not a factor of 28.*

$6 \cdot ? = 28$ *No whole number multiplied by 6 equals 28, so 6 is not a factor of 28.*

The positive factors of 28 are 1, 2, 4, 7, 14, and 28.

PRACTICE

List all the positive factors of each number.

1. 10   **2.** 8   **3.** 18   **4.** 54   **5.** 27   **6.** 36

Multiples

Multiples of a number can be found by multiplying the number by 1, 2, 3, and so on. *Common multiples* of a set of numbers are multiples of all numbers in the set.

EXAMPLE

Find the first five multiples of 3.

$3 \cdot 1 = 3$ *Multiply 3 times 1.*
$3 \cdot 2 = 6$ *Multiply 3 times 2.*
$3 \cdot 3 = 9$ *Multiply 3 times 3.*

$3 \cdot 4 = 12$ *Multiply 3 times 4.*
$3 \cdot 5 = 15$ *Multiply 3 times 5.*

The first five multiples of 3 are 3, 6, 9, 12, and 15.

PRACTICE

Find the first five multiples of each number.

1. 9   **2.** 10   **3.** 20   **4.** 15   **5.** 7   **6.** 18

7. Find the first five common multiples of 3, 4, and 6.

8. Find the first five common multiples of 2, 5, and 8.

9. Find the first five common multiples of 3, 5, and 10.

Estimate with Whole Numbers

Sometimes in math you do not need an exact answer. Instead, you can use an estimate. An **estimate** is close to the exact answer but is usually easier and faster to find.

To estimate a sum or difference, find the least number and round it to its greatest place value. Round all the other numbers to this place value. Then add or subtract the rounded numbers.

EXAMPLE 1

Estimate each sum or difference.

A 5,439 + 7,516

$$\begin{array}{r} 5{,}000 \\ +\ 8{,}000 \\ \hline 13{,}000 \end{array}$$

The least number is 5,439, so round each number to the thousands place.

The sum is about 13,000

B 2,511 − 167

$$\begin{array}{r} 2{,}500 \\ -\ 200 \\ \hline 2{,}300 \end{array}$$

The least number is 167, so round each number to the hundreds place.

The difference is about 2,300.

You can use *compatible numbers* to estimate products and quotients. **Compatible numbers** are close to the numbers in the problem and can help you do math mentally.

EXAMPLE 2

Estimate each product or quotient.

A 327 · 28

Compatible numbers

$327 \cdot 28 \approx 300 \cdot 30$

$\approx 9{,}000 \longleftarrow$ *Estimate*

The product is about 9,000.

B 637 ÷ 8

Compatible numbers

$637 \div 8 \approx 640 \div 8$

$\approx 80 \longleftarrow$ *Estimate*

The quotient is about 80.

PRACTICE

Use rounding to estimate each sum or difference.

1. 244 + 565 **2.** 7,562 + 1,422 **3.** 643 − 104 **4.** 2,416 − 435

5. 6,570 + 3,409 **6.** 3,912 + 269 **7.** 49,821 − 11,567 **8.** 37,097 − 20,364

Use compatible numbers to estimate each product or quotient.

9. 42 · 7 **10.** 3,957 ÷ 23 **11.** 5,169 · 21 **12.** 813 ÷ 8

13. 78 · 42 **14.** 1,443 ÷ 7 **15.** 98 · 48 **16.** 3,372 ÷ 415

17. 58 · 9 **18.** 27,657 ÷ 67 **19.** 83 · 27 **20.** 468 ÷ 9

Skills Bank

Estimate with Decimals

You can estimate sums and differences of decimals by rounding to the nearest whole number before adding and subtracting.

EXAMPLE 1

Estimate each sum or difference.

A $3.92 + 6.48$
$4 + 6 = 10$ *Round to the nearest whole number.*

B $10.63 - 5.1$
$11 - 5 = 6$ *Round to the nearest whole number.*

When you are estimating a sum, sometimes all of the numbers are close to the same number. When this happens, you can estimate by clustering. **Clustering** means rounding the numbers to the same value.

EXAMPLE 2

Estimate $198.45 + 210.6 + 194.4$.

$$
\begin{array}{rcl}
198.45 & \longrightarrow & 200 \\
210.6 & \longrightarrow & 200 \\
+194.4 & \longrightarrow & +200 \\
\hline
& & 600
\end{array}
$$

Each number is close to 200, so round each number to 200.

You can use compatible numbers to estimate products and quotients of decimals.

EXAMPLE 3

Estimate each product or quotient.

A $26.76 \cdot 2.93$
Compatible numbers
$26.76 \cdot 2.93 \approx 25 \cdot 3$
$\approx 75 \longleftarrow Estimate$

B $42.64 \div 16.51$
Compatible numbers
$42.64 \div 16.51 \approx 45 \div 15$
$\approx 3 \longleftarrow Estimate$

PRACTICE

Use rounding to estimate each sum or difference.

1. $2.74 - 0.86$
2. $26.7 + 4.95$
3. $10.8 + 5.3$
4. $45.98 - 20.5$

Use clustering to estimate each sum.

5. $19.86 + 22.3 + 20.18 + 21.4$
6. $7.48 + 6.95 + 7.35 + 6.84$

Use compatible numbers to estimate each product or quotient.

7. $38.92 \div 4.06$
8. $14.51 \cdot 7.89$
9. $22.47 \div 3.22$
10. $9.64 \cdot 1.769$

Use Formulas

You can use formulas to answer questions about quantities and their relationships. Substitute numerical values for the variables in the formula and then simplify.

EXAMPLE

Sandy drove 50 mi/h for 6 hours. How far did she drive? Use the formula $d = rt$ to find the distance.

$d = rt$

$d = 50 \cdot 6$ *Substitute 50 for the rate, r, and 6 for the time, t.*

$d = 300$ *Multiply.*

The distance d is 300 miles.

PRACTICE

1. Paul ran at an average of 25 feet per second for 10 seconds. How far did Paul run? Use the formula $d = rt$ to find the distance.

2. A triangle has a base of 10 centimeters and a height of 8 centimeters. What is the area of the triangle? Use the formula $A = \frac{1}{2}bh$ to find the area.

3. A rectangular prism has a length of 6 feet, a width of 4 feet, and a height of 2 feet. What is the volume of the prism? Use the formula $V = \ell wh$ to find the volume.

Angle Measures in Quadrilaterals

The sum of the measures of the angles in a quadrilateral is 360°. You can use this fact to find unknown angle measures.

$m\angle 1 + m\angle 2 + m\angle 3 + m\angle 4 = 360°$

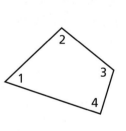

EXAMPLE

Find the unknown angle measure in the quadrilateral.

$98° + 137° + 52° + x = \quad 360°$

$\qquad\qquad 287° + x = \quad 360°$ *Add the measures.*

$\underline{\qquad -287° \qquad -287°}$ *Subtract 287° from both sides.*

$\qquad\qquad\qquad x = \quad 73°$

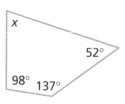

PRACTICE

Find the unknown angle measure in each quadrilateral.

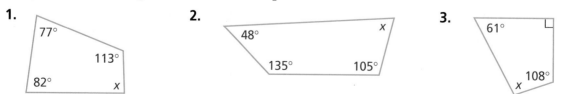

1. 77°, 113°, 82°, x

2. 48°, 135°, 105°, x

3. 61°, 108°, x

Line Segments on the Coordinate Plane

You can find the length of a horizontal or vertical line segment by using the coordinates of its endpoints.

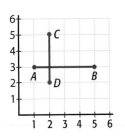

4MG2.2, 4MG2.3

The coordinates of the endpoints of horizontal line segment *AB* are (1, 3) and (5, 3). One way to find the length of a horizontal line segment is to find the difference of the *x*-coordinates of the segment's endpoints.

Endpoints: (**1**, 3) (**5**, 3)

$$5 - 1 = 4$$ *Subtract the x-coordinates.*

$\overline{AB}$ is 4 units long.

The coordinates of the endpoints of vertical line segment *CD* are (2, 2) and (2, 5). One way to find the length of a vertical line segment is to find the difference of the *y*-coordinates of its endpoints.

Endpoints: (2, **2**) (2, **5**)

$$5 - 2 = 3$$ *Subtract the y-coordinates.*

$\overline{CD}$ is 3 units long.

EXAMPLE

Find the length of each line segment with the given endpoints.

A **(7, 12) and (7, 4)**

(7, 12) and (7, 4)   *The segment is vertical because the x-coordinates of the endpoints are the same. Subtract the y-coordinates.*

$$12 - 4 = 8$$

The line segment is 8 units long.

B **(5, −1) and (16, −1)**

(5, −1) and (16, −1)   *The segment is horizontal because the y-coordinates of the endpoints are the same. Subtract the x-coordinates.*

$$16 - 5 = 11$$

The line segment is 11 units long.

PRACTICE

Find the length of each line segment with the given endpoints.

1. (21, 3) and (9, 3)

2. (−6, 11) and (−6, 44)

3. (4, 4) and (4, 12)

4. (−8, 1) and (−8, 15)

5. (7, 10) and (7, 3)

6. (0, 26) and (18, 26)

7. (4, 5) and (4, −5)

8. (6, 2) and (−2, 2)

Identify Parallel and Perpendicular Lines

Parallel lines are lines in the same plane that never intersect. The symbol ∥ means "is parallel to." **Perpendicular lines** intersect to form 90° angles, or right angles. The symbol ⊥ means "is perpendicular to."

EXAMPLE

Tell whether the lines in the figure appear parallel, perpendicular, or neither.

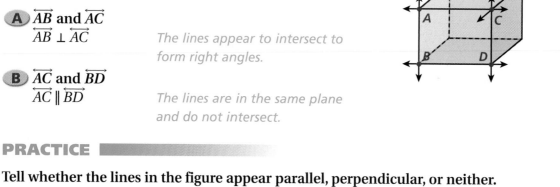

A $\overleftrightarrow{AB}$ and $\overleftrightarrow{AC}$

$\overleftrightarrow{AB} \perp \overleftrightarrow{AC}$ *The lines appear to intersect to form right angles.*

B $\overleftrightarrow{AC}$ and $\overleftrightarrow{BD}$

$\overleftrightarrow{AC} \parallel \overleftrightarrow{BD}$ *The lines are in the same plane and do not intersect.*

PRACTICE

Tell whether the lines in the figure appear parallel, perpendicular, or neither.

1. $\overleftrightarrow{CD}$ and $\overleftrightarrow{BD}$ 2. $\overleftrightarrow{AB}$ and $\overleftrightarrow{CD}$ 3. $\overleftrightarrow{BD}$ and $\overleftrightarrow{CE}$ 4. $\overleftrightarrow{AB}$ and $\overleftrightarrow{BD}$

Display Data in a Bar Graph

A **bar graph** displays data with vertical or horizontal bars. A bar graph can be used to compare data in different categories.

EXAMPLE

Use the given data to make a bar graph.

Step 1: Find an appropriate scale and interval. The scale must include all of the data values. The interval separates the scale into equal parts.

Step 2: Use the data to determine the lengths of the bars. Draw bars of equal width. The bars cannot touch.

Step 3: Title the graph and label the axes.

Coal Reserves (billion metric tons)		
Asia	Europe	Africa
695	404	66

Coal Reserves

800		
600		
400		
200		
	Asia Europe Africa	

Billion metric tons

Continent

PRACTICE

1. Use the given data to make a bar graph.

Students in Mr. Jones's History Classes			
Period 1	28	Period 6	22
Period 2	27	Period 7	7

Display Data in a Line Graph

5SDAP1.2

Data that show change over time are best displayed in a *line graph*. A
line graph displays a set of data using line segments.

EXAMPLE

The population of the American colonies was 50,400
in 1650; 111,900 in 1670; 210,400 in 1690; and
250,800 in 1700. Use the data to make a line graph.

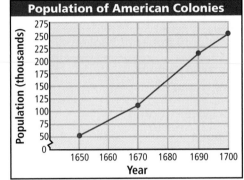

Step 1:   Determine an appropriate scale
          and interval for each axis.

Step 2:   Mark a point for each data value.
          Connect the points with straight lines.

Step 3:   Title the graph and label the axes.

PRACTICE

1.   Enrollment in a school was 2,000 students in 2000; 2,500 students in
     2001; 2,750 students in 2002; and 3,500 students in 2003. Use the data
     to make a line graph.

Display Data in a Histogram

5SDAP1.2

A **histogram** is a bar graph that shows the number of data items that occur
within each interval.

EXAMPLE

Use the frequency table to make a histogram.

Goals Scored per Game			
Goals	0–2	3–5	6–8
Frequency	7	11	3

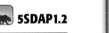

Goals Scored per Game

Step 1:   Choose an appropriate scale and interval.

Step 2:   Draw a bar for the number of goals in each
          interval. The bars should touch but not
          overlap.

Step 3:   Title the graph and label the axes.

PRACTICE

1.   Use the frequency table to make a
     histogram.

Length of U.S. Presidencies				
Years	0–3	4–7	8–11	12–15
Frequency	7	22	12	1

Display Data in a Circle Graph

A **circle graph** uses sections of a circle to compare data that are parts of a whole. Each section of a circle graph is called a *sector*.

EXAMPLE

Use the given data to make a circle graph.

Favorite Books at Booker Middle School	
Type of Book	**Percent**
Mysteries	35%
Science Fiction	25%
Sports	20%
Biographies	15%
Humor	5%

Percent	Angle of Sector
35%	$\frac{35}{100} \cdot 360° = 126°$
25%	$\frac{25}{100} \cdot 360° = 90°$
20%	$\frac{20}{100} \cdot 360° = 72°$
15%	$\frac{15}{100} \cdot 360° = 54°$
5%	$\frac{5}{100} \cdot 360° = 18°$

Step 1: Find the **angle measure** of each sector of the graph. There are 360° in a circle, so multiply each percent by 360°.

Step 2: Use a compass to draw a large circle. Use a straightedge to draw a radius.

Step 3: Use a protractor to measure the angle of the first sector. Draw the angle.

Step 4: Use the protractor to measure and draw each of the other angles.

Step 5: Give the graph a title, and label each sector with its name and percent. Color the sectors.

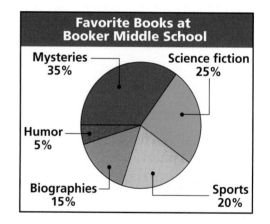

Favorite Books at Booker Middle School

Mysteries 35% · Science fiction 25% · Humor 5% · Biographies 15% · Sports 20%

PRACTICE

1. Use the given data to make a circle graph.

Alan's Leisure Time	
Activity	**Percent**
Reading	30%
Playing Sports	25%
Working on computer	40%
Watching TV	5%

Choose an Appropriate Graph

Depending on the data to be displayed, some types of graphs are more useful than others.

Common Uses of Data Displays			
	You can use a line plot to show how often each number occurs.		You can use a bar graph to display and compare data in separate categories.
	You can use a line graph to show how data change over a period of time.		You can use a circle graph to compare data that are parts of a whole.

EXAMPLE

The table shows the number of miles of coastline for states bordering the Gulf of Mexico. Which graph would be more appropriate to show the data: a bar graph or a line graph? Draw the more appropriate graph.

State	AL	FL	LA	MS	TX
Miles of coastline	33	770	397	44	367

Think: Is the information in the table describing a change over time? Is the information in the table divided into different categories?

The table shows the number of miles of coastline in different states. The data should be displayed in separate categories. So a bar graph is more appropriate than a line graph.

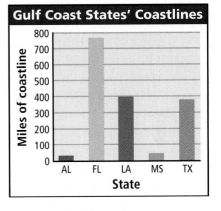

PRACTICE

1. The table shows the average high temperatures in Atlanta for six months of one year. Which graph would be more appropriate to show the data: a line plot or a line graph? Draw the more appropriate graph.

Month	Jan	Mar	May	Jul	Sep	Nov
Temp. (°F)	54	63	81	88	83	62

2. The table shows the average life span of several animals. Which graph would be more appropriate to show the data: a bar graph or a line graph? Draw the more appropriate graph.

Animal	Bear	Carp	Elephant	Tiger
Life span (yr)	40	100	70	22

Skills Bank

Selected Answers

Chapter 1

1-1 Exercises

1. Add 8 to each number to get the next number; 38, 46, 54.
3. Subtract 9 from each number to get the next number; 23, 14, 5.
5. Equilateral triangles each divided into six congruent triangles with a pair of opposite congruent triangles shaded in two different colors so that the shaded pairs rotate clockwise from each equilateral triangle to the next.
7. Figure 5 has 10 green triangles.
9. Divide each number by 4 to get the next number; 16, 4, 1.
11. Add 23 to each number to get the next number; 106, 129, 152.
13. Regular heptagons sliced into 7 triangles with one triangle shaded in each figure. In each successive figure the shaded triangle rotates clockwise 4 triangles. **15.** 7, 23, 39, 55, 71
17. 50, 48, 44, 38, 30 **19.** Multiply each number by 4 to get the next number; 48, 3,072, 12,288.
21. Add 8 to each number to get the next number; 3, 11, 43.
23. 134 beats per minute; 114 beats per minute **31.** 51
33. 12,500,000 **35.** 118 **37.** 378

1-2 Exercises

1. 32 **3.** 36 **5.** 1,000,000 **7.** 4^2
9. 10^2 **11.** 121 **13.** 512 **15.** 81
17. 5 **19.** 125 **21.** 9^2 **23.** 4^3
25. 2^5 **27.** 40^2 **29.** 10^5 **31.** 3^4 or 9^2 **33.** $8^2, 4^3,$ or 2^6 **35.** 5^4 or 25^2
37. < **39.** < **41.** > **43.** >
45. $21.87 **47.** Yuma: 688,560; Phoenix: 11,370,384
49. $4 \cdot 3^3 = 108$ stars **51.** 10^1, 33, $6^2, 4^3, 5^3$ **53.** $0, 1^8, 2, 16^1, 3^4$

55. $8^1, 9, 5^2, 3^3, 2^5$ **61.** A **63.** $84
65. Add one more than the number that was previously added; 37, 44, 52.

1-3 Exercises

1. 47 **3.** 23 **5.** 4 **7.** $280 **9.** 42
11. 15 **13.** 73 **15.** 588 **17.** $139
19. 18 **21.** 20 **23.** 1 **25.** > **27.** >
29. = **31.** $4 \cdot (8 - 3) = 20$
33. $(12 - 2)^2 \div 5 = 20$
35. $(4 + 6 - 3) \div 7 = 1$ **37.** $82
39a. $4 \cdot 15$ **39b.** $2 \cdot 30$
39c. $4 \cdot 15 + 2 \cdot 30 + 6$; $126
43. C **45.** D **47.** Multiply by 2; 160, 320, 640. **49.** 262,144
51. 1,024 **53.** 7

1-4 Exercises

1. Associative Property
3. Commutative Property
5. Associative Property **7.** 33
9. 1,100 **11.** 47 **13.** 38 **15.** 44
17. 208 **19.** Identity Property
21. Associative Property
23. Identity Property **25.** 1,600
27. 900 **29.** 163 **31.** 135 **33.** 174
35. 92 **41.** 220 ft² **43.** 9,000
45. 17,500 **47.** 15 **49.** 0 **51.** 8
53. 2 **59.** C **61.** < **63.** < **65.** 1
67. 3

1-5 Exercises

1. 36 **3.** 132 **5.** 8 **7.** 19 **9.** 4
11. 16 **13.** 11 **15.** 24 **17.** 12
19. 41 **21.** 9 **23.** 16 **25.** 26 **27.** 6
29. $4.50 **31a.** 100°C **31b.** 212°F
35. C **37.** 13 **39.** 89 **41.** 80
43. 161

1-6 Exercises

1. $7p$ **3.** $\frac{n}{12}$ **5.** $2a + 3j$; 14
7. $y - 2$ **9.** $9n$ **11.** $r - f$; 6
13. $\frac{23}{u} - t$ **15.** $2(y + 5)$
17. $35(r - 45)$ **19.** $3r + 8p + 15b$
29. $15y + 12$ **35.** $(104 + 19 \cdot 2)x$; $426 **37.** 5 **39.** 35

1-7 Exercises

1. no **3.** yes **5.** yes **7.** 53 feet is equal to 636 inches. **9.** no
11. yes **13.** no **15.** yes **17.** no
19. yes **21.** 300 m is not equal to 300,000 cm. **23.** yes **25.** no
27. no **29.** yes **31.** no **33.** yes
35. $17 \neq 350 \div 20$; no, they do not have the same amount of money.
37. 6 **39.** 2 **41.** 3 **43.** C **47.** C
49. 123 **51.** $\frac{p}{55}$

1-8 Exercises

1. $x = 36$ **3.** $n = 19$ **5.** $p = 18$
7. 6 blocks **9.** $r = 7$ **11.** $b = 25$
13. $z = 9$ **15.** $g = 16$ **17.** 6 meters
19. $n = 7$ **21.** $y = 19$ **23.** $h = 78$
25. $b = 69$ **27.** $t = 26$ **29.** $m = 22$
31. $p + 20 = 36$ **33.** 880 m **37.** B
39. 15 **41.** 87 **43.** $t - 7$
45. $12 - (x + 10)$ **47.** $24(w + 7)$

1-9 Exercises

1. $p = 17$ **3.** $a = 31$ **5.** $n = 33$
7. $y = 25$ **9.** $a = 38$ **11.** $a = 97$
13. $p = 33$ **15.** $s = 31$ **17.** $x = 36$
19. $a = 21$ **21.** $f = 14$ **23.** $r = 154$
25. $g = 143$ **27.** $m = 18$
29. 13 million **33.** D **35.** 71
37. 22 **39.** $y = 38$ **41.** $b = 56$

1-10 Exercises

1. $x = 3$ **3.** $a = 9$ **5.** $c = 11$
7. 45 feet **9.** $a = 4$ **11.** $x = 4$
13. $t = 7$ **15.** $m = 11$ **17.** 6 feet
19. $y = 9$ **21.** $y = 8$ **23.** $y = 20$
25. $z = 40$ **27.** $y = 23$ **29.** $y = 18$
31. $y = 8$ **33.** $a = 14$ **35.** $x = 3$
37. $t = 6$ **39.** 15 to 177 segments
41. 4,000 light-sensitive cells
45. C **47.** 69 **49.** $b = 42$
51. $n = 212$

1-11 Exercises

1. $y = 12$ **3.** $r = 63$ **5.** $j = 36$
7. $f = 60$ **9.** 90 min **11.** $c = 26$
13. $g = 98$ **15.** $x = 144$ **17.** $r = 81$
19. $c = 96$ **21.** $c = 165$ **23.** $c = 70$
25. $c = 60$ **27.** $\frac{w}{381} = 76$;
$w = 28{,}956$ m **33.** D **35.** $b = 13$
37. $m = 74$ **39.** $k = 16$ **41.** $q = 7$

Chapter 1 Study Guide: Review

1. exponent; base **2.** numerical
expression **3.** equation
4. algebraic expression **5.** Add 4
to each number to get the next
number; 22, 26, 30. **6.** Add 20 to
each number to get the next
number; 95, 115, 135. **7.** Add 7 to
each number to get the next
number; 35, 42, 49. **8.** Multiply
each number by 5 to get the next
number; 5,000, 25,000, 125,000.
9. Subtract 4 from each number to
get the next number; 25, 21, 17.
10. Subtract 7 from each number
to get the next number; 40, 33, 26.
11. 81 **12.** 10 **13.** 128 **14.** 1
15. 121 **16.** 27 **17.** 3 **18.** 103
19. 5 **20.** 67 **21.** Commutative
Property **22.** Distributive
Property **23.** 19 **24.** 524 **25.** 10
26. $4 \div (n + 12)$ **27.** $2(t - 11)$
28. yes **29.** no **30.** yes **31.** $x = 6$
32. $n = 14$ **33.** $c = 29$ **34.** $y = 6$
35. $p = 27$ **36.** $w = 9$ **37.** $b = 11$
38. $n = 44$ **39.** $p = 16$ **40.** $d = 57$
41. $k = 45$ **42.** $d = 9$ **43.** $p = 63$
44. $n = 67$ **45.** $r = 14$ **46.** $w = 144$
47. $h = 60$ **48.** $p = 167$ **49.** $v = 8$
50. $y = 9$ **51.** $c = 7$ **52.** $n = 2$
53. $s = 8$ **54.** $t = 10$ **55.** $a = 8$
56. $y = 8$ **57.** $r = 42$ **58.** $t = 15$
59. $y = 18$ **60.** $n = 72$ **61.** $z = 52$
62. $b = 100$ **63.** $n = 77$
64. $p = 90$

Chapter 2

2-1 Exercises

1. [number line with points at −2 and 2; marks at −5, −2, 0, 2, 5]
3. [number line with points at −1 and 3; marks at −5, −3, −1, 1, 3, 5]
5. > **7.** < **9.** −5, −3, −1, 4, 6
11. −6, −4, 0, 1, 3 **13.** 8 **15.** 10
17. [number line from −10 to 10]
19. [number line from −10 to 10]
21. > **23.** < **25.** −9, −7, −5, −2, 0
27. 16 **29.** 20 **31.** < **33.** =
35. = **37.** = **39.** Aug, Jul, Sep,
May, Jun, Apr, Mar, Oct **41.** −29
45. decreased by about 9% **51.** B
53. 112 **55.** 9

2-2 Exercises

1. 12 **3.** −2 **5.** 15 **7.** −15 **9.** −12
11. −20 **13.** −9 **15.** 13 **17.** 7
19. −17 **21.** −19 **23.** −16
25. −88 **27.** −55 **29.** −14
31. −13 **33.** −13 **35.** −26 **37.** 14
39. > **41.** > **43.** > **45.** $45 + 18 +$
$27 - 21 - 93$; −24; Cody's account
is reduced by $24. **47.** −16 **49.** 3
51. 4,150 ft **57.** A **59.** 4 **61.** 4

2-3 Exercises

1. −3 **3.** 6 **5.** −4 **7.** −10 **9.** 7
11. −14 **13.** −5 **15.** 8 **17.** 12
19. 16 **21.** −17 **23.** 8 **25.** 50
27. 18 **29.** 16 **31.** −5 **33.** −20
35. 14,787 ft **37.** −478 **39.** −2
41. 2 **43.** 16 **45.** −27 **47.** −17
51. 1,234°F **53.** 265°F **57.** $m + n$
has the least absolute value. **59.** 3
61. 19 **63.** 24

2-4 Exercises

1. −15 **3.** −15 **5.** 15 **7.** −15
9. −8 **11.** 4 **13.** 7 **15.** −7
17. −$30 **19.** −10 **21.** −12
23. 48 **25.** 35 **27.** 7 **29.** −8

31. −9 **33.** −9 **35.** −40 **37.** −3
39. 50 **41.** −3 **43.** 30 **45.** −42
47. −60 ft **49.** 2 **51.** −12
53. 1,400 **55.** 11 **57.** less; −$72
59. more; $12 **63.** C **65.** $x + 6$
67. $2d - 4$ **69.** 5 **71.** −2

2-5 Exercises

1. $w = 4$ **3.** $k = -7$ **5.** $y = -30$
7. This year's loss is $57 million.
9. $k = -3$ **11.** $v = -4$ **13.** $a = 20$
15. $t = -32$ **17.** $n = 150$
19. $l = -144$ **21.** $y = 100$
23. $j = -63$ **25.** $c = 17$
27. $y = -11$ **29.** $w = -41$
31. $x = -58$ **33.** $x = 4$ **35.** $t = 9$
37. 3 mi **39.** $-13 + p = 8$; $p = 21$
41. $t - 9 = -22$; $t = -13$
43. oceans or beaches **45.** C
49. C **51.** −15 **53.** 4 **55.** −5
57. −14

2-6 Exercises

1. III **3.** I **5.** (1, 2)
7, 9.

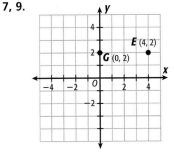

11. II **13.** I **15.** IV **17.** (−2, 4)
19. (4, 4) **21.** (−3, 0)
23, 25, 27.

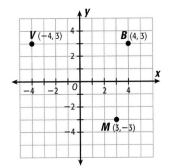

29. I **31.** III **33.** IV **35.** III
37, 39, 41, 43, 45, 47.

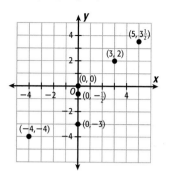

49. Gabon **55.** B **57.** 46
59. −22 **61.** $x = 34$ **63.** $m = -6$

2-7 Exercises

1. Possible answer: $y = x + 6$; 15
3. Possible answer: j = Jen's age, b = brother's age, $j = b - 6$
5. Possible answer: $y = 4x$; 28
7. Possible answer: c = cost of a case, s = cost of 1 bottle, $c = 12s - 2$ **9.** Possible answer: p = number of points, m = number of prizes, $p = 150m$
11. $y = -4x$; −56 **13.** $y = 2x$; −2; 6 **15.** Let c be the total cost and h be the number of hours. $c = \$125 + \$55h$ **17.** 9 hours
23. B **25.** 3,200 **27.** 168
29. −10 **31.** −13

2-8 Exercises

1. (1, 8); (2, 14); (3, 20); (4, 26)
3. no **5.** 2 **7.** 0
9.

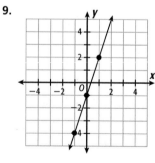

11. (1, −3); (2, −7); (3, −11); (4, −15) **13.** yes **15.** 1
17. 0 **19.** 2

21.

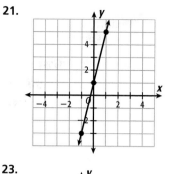

23.

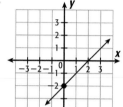

25.

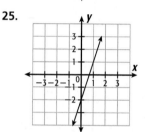

27. −3; −2; −1; 0 **29.** (1, 14)
33. 219 kelvins **39.** C
41. $y = -120$ **43.** $j = -12$

Chapter 2 Study Guide: Review

1. x-coordinate; y-coordinate
2. coordinate plane, quadrants
3. > **4.** < **5.** < **6.** >
7.
  −6 −2 0 4 5
8. −8 −3 12 8
  −10 0 10
9. 0; 0 units
  −1 0 1
10. 17; 17 units
  −18 −12 −6 0
11. 6; 6 units
  −1 0 1 2 3 4 5 6
12. −3 **13.** 1 **14.** −56 **15.** 9

16. 14 **17.** −6 **18.** 11 **19.** 15
20. 6 **21.** −9 **22.** −1 **23.** −9
24. −42 **25.** 24 **26.** −22 **27.** −5
28. −38 **29.** 23 **30.** −16 **31.** −4
32. 6 **33.** −1 **34.** −2 **35.** 11
36. −50 **37.** 3 **38.** 16 **39.** −2
40. −12 **41.** −3 **42.** −96 **43.** −4
44. 70 **45.** 16 **46.** −70 **47.** −21
48. $y = 10$ **49.** $d = 14$ **50.** $j = -26$
51. $n = 72$ **52.** $c = 13$ **53.** $m = -4$
54. $y = -105$ **55.** $g = -19$
56. $p = 21$ **57.** $f = 16$ **58.** $n = -17$
59. $x = -12$ **60.** $b = -4$
61. $d = -32$ **62.** $c = 22$ **63.** $y = 7$
64. (−2, −3) **65.** (1, 0) **66.** III
67. II **68.** Possible answer: $y = x + 6$; 14 **69.** $\ell = 4w$, ℓ = length, w = width **70.** $m = 27 + d$, m = mother's age, d = daughter's age
71. (1, −3), (2, −1), (3, 1), (4, 3)
72. (1, 8), (2, 9), (3, 10), (4, 11)
73. yes **74.** no

Chapter 3

3-1 Exercises

1. prime **3.** composite **5.** 2^4
7. 3^4 **9.** $2 \cdot 3^2$ **11.** $3^2 \cdot 5$
13. $2 \cdot 5^3$ **15.** $2^2 \cdot 5^2$ **17.** $3^2 \cdot 71$
19. $2^3 \cdot 5^3$ **21.** prime **23.** prime
25. composite **27.** composite
29. $2^2 \cdot 17$ **31.** $2^3 \cdot 3 \cdot 5$
33. $3^3 \cdot 5$ **35.** $2 \cdot 7 \cdot 11$ **37.** $2^5 \cdot 5^2$
39. 5^4 **41.** $3^2 \cdot 5 \cdot 7$ **43.** $3^3 \cdot 7$
45. $2 \cdot 11^2$ **47.** $11 \cdot 17$ **49.** $5^2 \cdot 7^2$
51. $2^3 \cdot 3^2 \cdot 5$ **53.** 3^2 **55.** 5^2
57. 2^4 **61.** 7 **63.** 4 or 8 people
67. B **69.** $2^3 \cdot 3 \cdot 5$ **71.** 0 **73.** −1
75. $y = 1$ **77.** $x = 0$

3-2 Exercises

1. 6 **3.** 12 **5.** 4 **7.** 12 kits **9.** 12
11. 11 **13.** 38 **15.** 2 **17.** 26 **19.** 3
21. 1 **23.** 2 **25.** 22 **27.** 40 **29.** 1

31. 7 **33.** 3 **35.** 13 **37.** 7 shelves
39a. 7 students **39b.** 5 carrots,
3 pizza slices, 1 can of juice, and
2 apples **45.** B **47.** 21 **49.** −7
51. −5 **53.** 2 **55.** −2 **57.** 9

3-3 Exercises
1. 28 **3.** 48 **5.** 45 **7.** 24 min
9. 24 **11.** 42 **13.** 24 **15.** 80
17. 180 **19.** 360 **21.** 60 min
23. 12 **25.** 132 **27.** 90 **29.** 12
31. 144 **33.** 210 **35.** only if the
two numbers are the same
37. no **41.** C **43.** $x = -18$
45. $x = -32$ **47.** 4 **49.** 15

3-4 Exercises
1. Possible answer: $\frac{1}{2}, \frac{42}{84}$
3. Possible answer: $\frac{5}{6}, \frac{30}{36}$ **5.** $\frac{1}{2}$
7. $\frac{4}{5}$ **9.** no **11.** yes **13.** $3\frac{3}{4}$
15. $1\frac{4}{13}$ **17.** $\frac{31}{5}$ **19.** $\frac{38}{5}$
21. Possible answer: $\frac{9}{10}, \frac{36}{40}$
23. Possible answer: $\frac{3}{5}, \frac{18}{30}$ **25.** $\frac{7}{9}$
27. $\frac{17}{24}$ **29.** yes **31.** yes **33.** yes
35. no **37.** $6\frac{1}{3}$ **39.** $7\frac{4}{11}$ **41.** $\frac{128}{5}$
43. $\frac{29}{3}$ **45.** No **57.** $\frac{12}{20}, \frac{6}{10}$
59. $\frac{9}{5}, \frac{72}{40}$ **61.** $8\frac{1}{3}$ ft **63.** $3\frac{1}{2}$ ft
65. $\frac{150}{4}$ **69.** C **71.** $\frac{4}{7}$ **73.** $y = 12$
75. $z = 80$ **77.** 45 **79.** 168

3-5 Exercises
1. 0.57 **3.** 1.83 **5.** 0.12 **7.** 0.05
9. $\frac{1}{125}$ **11.** $-2\frac{1}{20}$ **13.** 0.720
15. 6.4 **17.** 0.88 **19.** 1 **21.** 1.92
23. 0.8 **25.** 0.55 **27.** $\frac{1}{100}$ **29.** $-\frac{2}{25}$
31. $15\frac{1}{4}$ **33.** $8\frac{3}{8}$ **43.** yes **45.** no
47. yes **49.** no **51.** $18\frac{2}{20}, 18\frac{1}{25},$
$18\frac{11}{20}$ **55.** D **57.** $x = 216$
59. $t = 75$ **61.** $\frac{7}{9}$ **63.** $\frac{11}{12}$

3-6 Exercises
1. < **3.** < **5.** < **7.** < **9.** $-\frac{13}{5},$
2.05, 2.5 **11.** < **13.** > **15.** >
17. > **19.** > **21.** < **23.** < **25.** $\frac{5}{8},$
0.7, 0.755 **27.** $-2.25, 2.05, \frac{21}{10}$
29. $-2.98, -2\frac{9}{10}, 2.88$ **31.** $\frac{3}{4}$
33. $\frac{7}{8}$ **35.** 0.32 **37.** $-\frac{7}{8}$

39. Saturn (0.69), Jupiter and
Uranus (1.32), Neptune (1.64),
Mars (3.93), Venus (5.20), Mercury
(5.43), Earth (5.52) **41.** sloths
47. D **49.** $6 + 5x$ **51.** 38 **53.** −61

Chapter 3 Study Guide: Review
1. rational number; terminating
decimal **2.** improper fraction;
mixed number **3.** $2^3 \cdot 11$ **4.** 3^3
5. $2 \cdot 3^4$ **6.** $5 \cdot 13$ **7.** $2 \cdot 47$ **8.** $2 \cdot$
$5 \cdot 11$ **9.** 3^4 **10.** $3^2 \cdot 11$ **11.** $2^2 \cdot$
19 **12.** 97 **13.** $5 \cdot 11$ **14.** $2 \cdot 23$
15. 30 **16.** 3 **17.** 12 **18.** 25
19. 12 **20.** 220 **21.** 60 **22.** 32
23. 27 **24.** 90 **25.** 12 **26.** 315
27. 30 **28.** 48 **29.** 27 **30.** 60
31. 225 **32.** 660 **33.** 20 days
34. Possible answer: $\frac{2}{3}, \frac{8}{12}$
35. Possible answer: $\frac{8}{10}, \frac{12}{15}$
36. Possible answer: $\frac{1}{4}, \frac{6}{24}$
37. Possible answer: $\frac{8}{9}, \frac{24}{27}$
38. Possible answer: $\frac{42}{48}, \frac{7}{8}$
39. Possible answer: $\frac{16}{21}, \frac{96}{126}$
40. $\frac{7}{8}$ **41.** $\frac{3}{10}$ **42.** $\frac{4}{5}$ **43.** $\frac{1}{5}$ **44.** $\frac{3}{7}$
45. $\frac{2}{3}$ **46.** $\frac{21}{5}$ **47.** $\frac{19}{6}$ **48.** $\frac{43}{4}$
49. $\frac{34}{9}$ **50.** $\frac{29}{12}$ **51.** $\frac{37}{7}$ **52.** $3\frac{1}{3}$
53. $2\frac{1}{2}$ **54.** $2\frac{3}{7}$ **55.** $3\frac{5}{6}$ **56.** $3\frac{2}{5}$
57. $5\frac{1}{8}$ **58.** $\frac{1}{4}$ **59.** $-\frac{1}{250}$ **60.** $\frac{1}{20}$
61. $\frac{37}{100}$ **62.** $-\frac{12}{25}$ **63.** $\frac{2}{25}$ **64.** 3.5
65. 0.6 **66.** 0.67 **67.** 0.88
68. −0.06 **69.** 0.78 **70.** 0.93
71. < **72.** > **73.** > **74.** < **75.** >
76. > **77.** < **78.** > **79.** < **80.** >
81. $-0.55, \frac{6}{13}, \frac{1}{2}, 0.58$ **82.** $\frac{13}{10}, 1\frac{2}{5},$
1.45, 1.5 **83.** $-\frac{14}{5}, -2\frac{1}{2}, -2.09,$
-0.2 **84.** $-\frac{8}{9}, -0.7, 0.8, \frac{7}{8}$

Chapter 4

4-1 Exercises
1. about 4 feet **3.** 0 **5.** 2
7. Possible answer: 3
9. Possible answer: 48 **11.** 1

13. 3 **15.** $\frac{1}{2}$ **17.** $11\frac{1}{2}$
19. Possible answer: 6
21. Possible answer: 30
23. Possible answer: 2
25. Possible answer: 4 **27.** $\frac{1}{2}$
29. Possible answer: 24
31. Possible answer: 8
33. 4 **35.** 11 **37.** 5 **39.** $14
41. greater **43.** 2 m **47.** D
49. $x = 27$ **51.** $m = 13$ **53.** −100
55. 128

4-2 Exercises
1. $\frac{1}{3}$ **3.** $\frac{3}{7}$ **5.** $\frac{1}{2}$ **7.** $\frac{19}{24}$ **9.** $\frac{1}{12}$ **11.** $\frac{1}{2}$
13. $\frac{3}{5}$ **15.** $\frac{2}{3}$ **17.** $\frac{1}{5}$ **19.** $\frac{1}{4}$ **21.** $\frac{3}{4}$
23. $\frac{1}{6}$ **25.** $\frac{8}{15}$ **27.** $\frac{1}{6}$ mi **29.** $\frac{13}{18}$
31. $\frac{4}{5}$ **33.** $\frac{1}{12}$ **35.** $\frac{1}{2}$ **37.** $1\frac{1}{4}$
39. $\frac{14}{15}$ **41.** $\frac{41}{63}$ **43.** $\frac{41}{45}$ **45.** 0
47. $\frac{91}{120}$ **49.** $\frac{5}{6}$ hour **51.** $\frac{13}{24}$ mi
53. Cai **55.** $\frac{3}{8}$ lb of cashews **59.** B
61. 1 **63.** 6

4-3 Exercises
1. $7\frac{3}{5}$ **3.** $6\frac{1}{3}$ **5.** $1\frac{1}{3}$ **7.** $\frac{11}{12}$ **9.** $5\frac{1}{6}$ ft
11. $11\frac{2}{5}$ **13.** $6\frac{14}{15}$ **15.** $15\frac{1}{40}$
17. $10\frac{13}{20}$ **19.** $2\frac{5}{6}$ **21.** $2\frac{1}{12}$ **23.** $\frac{17}{24}$
25. $4\frac{4}{9}$ **27.** $15\frac{8}{15}$ **29.** $13\frac{5}{6}$ **31.** $6\frac{5}{24}$
33. $\frac{5}{6}$ **35.** $4\frac{1}{6}$ **37.** $10\frac{1}{24}$ **39.** <
41. > **43.** $3\frac{3}{4}$ ounces **45.** $117\frac{1}{3}$ mi
47. the waterfall trail; $\frac{1}{6}$ mi **51.** D
53. 6 **55.** −12 **57.** $\frac{3}{4}$ **59.** $1\frac{5}{36}$

4-4 Exercises
1. $2\frac{1}{2}$ h **3.** $\frac{2}{5}$ **5.** 9 **7.** $2\frac{2}{5}$
9. 20 **11.** $1\frac{2}{3}$ tsp **13.** $\frac{1}{2}$ **15.** 4
17. $\frac{1}{4}$ **19.** $\frac{5}{9}$ **21.** $44\frac{2}{5}$ **23.** $17\frac{1}{2}$
25. $2\frac{1}{3}$ **27.** $8\frac{1}{4}$ **29.** $3\frac{29}{42}$ **31.** $\frac{1}{3}$
33. $\frac{1}{6}$ **35.** $\frac{1}{12}$ **37.** $\frac{1}{5}$ **39.** $\frac{7}{10}$
41. $\frac{1}{5}$ **43.** 1 **45.** 3 **47.** 5 **49.** 6
51. 1 **53.** $2\frac{1}{12}$ lb **55.** $11\frac{1}{3}$ mi
59. B **61.** > **63.** < **65.** $1\frac{5}{12}$
67. $7\frac{11}{24}$

4-5 Exercises

1. 18 **3.** $\frac{3}{32}$ **5.** $\frac{1}{4}$ **7.** 2 **9.** 3 capes
11. 18 **13.** $4\frac{3}{8}$ **15.** $\frac{1}{27}$ **17.** 40
19. $\frac{5}{14}$ **21.** 14 **23.** $12\frac{4}{7}$ **25.** $9\frac{3}{5}$
27. 6 pieces **29.** $5\frac{2}{5}$ **31.** 2 **33.** $\frac{8}{147}$
35. $\frac{16}{25}$ **37.** $\frac{18}{25}$ **39.** $10\frac{1}{2}$ **41.** $\frac{1}{3}$
43. 1 **45.** 87 hamburger patties
47. 42 side pieces **49.** $11\frac{3}{4}$ hours
53. B **55.** 30 **57.** 36 **59.** $\frac{1}{12}$
61. $3\frac{15}{28}$

4-6 Exercises

1. $a = \frac{3}{4}$ **3.** $p = 1\frac{1}{2}$ **5.** $r = \frac{9}{10}$
7. $1\frac{1}{8}$ c **9.** $t = \frac{5}{8}$ **11.** $x = 2\frac{5}{24}$
13. $y = \frac{7}{60}$ **15.** $w = \frac{1}{2}$ **17.** $z = \frac{1}{12}$
19. $n = 1\frac{23}{25}$ **21.** $t = \frac{1}{4}$ **23.** $w = 6$
25. $x = \frac{3}{5}$ **27.** $n = 2\frac{2}{5}$ **29.** $y = \frac{1}{2}$
31. $r = \frac{1}{77}$ **33.** $h = \frac{5}{6}$ **35.** $v = \frac{3}{4}$
37. $d = 14\frac{17}{40}$ **39.** $11\frac{3}{16}$ lb
41. 15 million species
43. 48 stories **49.** B
51. 3, 3.02, $3\frac{2}{10}$, 3.25 **53.** $\frac{24}{25}$
55. $1\frac{1}{3}$

4-7 Exercises

1. 21.82 **3.** 1.98 **5.** 0.6 **7.** −0.315
9. 334.7379 mi **11.** 18.97
13. 10.132 **15.** 12.79 **17.** 4.47
19. 4.48 **21.** 2.814 **23.** −9.256
25. 6.161 **27.** 5.445 mi **29.** 4.883
31. 14.33 **33.** 1.92 **35.** 1.911
37. 0.351 **39.** 0.00864
43. 0.9 g/mL **47.** B **49.** $x = -14$
51. $z = -16$ **53.** $n = \frac{11}{14}$
55. $m = 2$

4-8 Exercises

1. 0.9 **3.** 4.6 **5.** −3.2 **7.** 2.5
9. −16 **11.** −4.8 **13.** 28 mi/gal
15. −0.12 **17.** −14 **19.** 4.2
21. 47.5 **23.** 4 **25.** −48.75
27. 2.4 min **29.** 22.5 **31.** −0.4
33. 25 **35.** 20 **37.** 18 **39.** 6.4
41. 2,500 years **43.** 11 years
45. 363.64 days **47.** A **49.** 14
51. 13

4-9 Exercises

1. kilograms **3.** centimeters
5. 12,000 g **7.** 0.07 cm **9.** Monday
11. milligrams **13.** centimeters
15. 0.0014 km **17.** 3,550 mm
19. 199.5 cm **21.** 2,050,000 L
23. 0.37 cm **25.** = **27.** < **29.** <
31. Mona Lisa; 4 cm **33.** 1,200 mm;
130 cm; 1.5 m **35.** 0.0008 kg;
1,000 mg; 9.03 g **37.** Red Bat
39. 1 kg **43.** C **45.** 4; Distributive
Property **47.** 3; Associative
Property **49** $\frac{1}{2}$ **51.** $\frac{1}{6}$

4-10 Exercises

1. $w = 7$ **3.** $k = 24.09$ **5.** $b = 5.04$
7. $t = 9$ **9.** $4.25 **11.** $c = 44.56$
13. $a = 5.08$ **15.** $p = 53.21$
17. $z = 16$ **19.** $w = 11.76$
21. $a = -74.305$ **23.** $7.50
25. $n = -4.92$ **27.** $r = 0.72$
29. $m = -0.15$ **31.** $k = 0.9$
33. $t = 0.936$ **35.** $v = 5.6$
37. $n = 12.254$ **39.** $j = 11.107$
41. $g = 0.5$ **43.** $171 **45a.** 148.1
million **45b.** between English
and Italian **49.** C **53.** 91 **55.** 1.5
57. 3 **59.** 9

Chapter 4 Study Guide: Review

1. 24 **2.** 8 **3.** 3 **4.** 1 **5.** 30 **6.** 3
7. about $5\frac{1}{2}$ laps **8.** $\frac{5}{12}$ **9.** $\frac{17}{20}$
10. $\frac{5}{11}$ **11.** $\frac{1}{9}$ **12.** $1\frac{5}{24}$ **13.** $\frac{13}{80}$
14. $6\frac{5}{24}$ **15.** $3\frac{1}{3}$ **16.** $6\frac{1}{4}$ **17.** $1\frac{5}{12}$
18. $11\frac{13}{60}$ **19.** $1\frac{2}{3}$ **20.** $\frac{1}{36}$ **21.** $\frac{5}{21}$
22. $\frac{1}{4}$ **23.** $\frac{1}{30}$ **24.** $7\frac{1}{2}$ **25.** $1\frac{21}{25}$
26. $17\frac{17}{63}$ **27.** $6\frac{1}{4}$ **28.** $1\frac{7}{9}$ **29.** $1\frac{1}{2}$
30. $\frac{1}{2}$ **31.** $1\frac{1}{2}$ **32.** $\frac{4}{75}$ **33.** $\frac{2}{15}$ **34.** 1
35. $1\frac{11}{12}$ **36.** 28 slices **37.** $1\frac{2}{3}$
38. $\frac{1}{15}$ **39.** $1\frac{5}{7}$ **40.** $\frac{13}{28}$
41. $m = 1\frac{2}{15}$ **42.** $p = \frac{1}{60}$
43. $y = 1\frac{1}{28}$ **44.** $c = 3$
45. $1\frac{3}{4}$ cups **46.** 27.88 **47.** 51.2
48. 6.22 **49.** 52.902 **50.** 14.095
51. 35.88 **52.** 3.5 **53.** −38.7
54. 40.495 **55.** 60.282 **56.** 77.348

57. −18.81 **58.** 4.5 **59.** −1.09
60. −15.4 **61.** −500 **62.** 2 **63.** 4
64. 18,000 mL **65.** 0.72 g
66. 5,300 m **67.** 6 mm
68. $x = 10.44$ **69.** $s = 107$
70. $n = 0.007$ **71.** $k = 8.64$
72. $e = 5.05$ **73.** $w = -3.08$

Chapter 5

5-1 Exercises

1. $\frac{10}{3}$, 10 to 3, 10:3 **3.** $\frac{3}{1}$ or 3 to 1
or 3:1 **5.** $\frac{25}{30}$, 25 to 30, 25:30, or $\frac{5}{6}$,
5 to 6, 5:6 **7.** $\frac{30}{15}$, 30 to 15, 30:15,
or $\frac{2}{1}$, 2 to 1, 2:1 **9.** $\frac{4}{1}$ or 4 to 1 or 4:1
11. group 1 **13.** The ratio is
greater than $\frac{1}{2}$ for all three groups.
15. 3:1, $\frac{3}{1}$, 3 to 1 **17.** 3:2, $\frac{3}{2}$, 3 to 2
19. greater than **21.** B
23. $x = 4.24$ **25.** $v = 8.5$

5-2 Exercises

1. 83.5 mL per min **3.** 458 mi/h
5. $7.75 per h **7.** about 74.63 mi/h
9. 3 runs per game **11.** $335
per mo **13.** 18.83 mi per gal
15. $5.75 per h **17.** 122 mi per trip
19. 0.04 mi per min
21. $\frac{1,026 \text{ students}}{38 \text{ classes}}$; 27 students
per class **23.** $0.06, $0.07;
$\frac{$2.52}{42 \text{ oz}}$ is the better buy
25. $27.60, $32.50; $\frac{$8.28}{0.3 \text{ m}}$ is the
better buy **27.** 287, 329, 611
(France, Poland, Germany) **31.** D
33. Julita's; by $\frac{7}{24}$ ft **35.** <

5-3 Exercises

1. yes **3.** yes **5.** yes **7.** no **13.** no
15. no **17.** no **19.** no **29.** 3, 24, 15
39a. $\frac{1 \text{ can}}{4 \text{ hours}}$ **39b.** No, 1:4 =
x:2,080; the class recycled 520 cans.
41. 1:2 = 2:4, 2:1 = 4:2, 1:1 = 2:2,
1:1 = 4:4, 2:2 = 4:4 **43a.** 8:5
43b. Mill Pond and Clear Pond
49. C **51.** −21 **53.** $\frac{1}{50}$

5-4 Exercises

1. $x = 60$ **3.** $m = 16.4$ **5.** 150 s, or 2.5 min **7.** $x = 20$ **9.** $r = 6\frac{1}{2}$
11. $x = 9$ **13.** $s = 4\frac{4}{5}$ **15.** $8.75
17. $h = 8$ **19.** $t = 117$ **21.** $y = 8.5$
23. $m = 35$ **25.** 3 hours
27a. Within the Tuesday sample of 100 fish, 4 had been part of the Monday sample. **27b.** $\frac{50}{n}$
27c. $\frac{4}{100} = \frac{50}{n}$; $n = 1{,}250$ fish
29. 3 km **35.** 27 **37.** 5
39. 64 mi/h **41.** $9.50/h

5-5 Exercises

1. Feet; the width of a sidewalk is similar to the length of several sheets of paper. **3.** Tons; the weight of a truck is similar to the weight of several buffalo. **5.** 48 qt
7. 4.5 lb **9.** 14.5 gal **11.** Inches; the wingspan of a sparrow is similar to the length of several paper clips. **13.** Feet or yards; the height of an office building is similar to the length of many sheets of paper. **15.** 3 mi
17. 75 in. **19.** > **21.** < **23.** >
25. < **27.** < **29.** 3,941 m **31.** 8 c, 5 qt, 12 pt, 2 gal **33.** 12,000 ft, 2.5 mi, 5,000 yd **35.** 9.5 yd, 380 in., 32.5 ft **37.** 46,145 yd **39.** The object that you are measuring will contain fewer of the larger units, so it makes sense to divide to get a smaller value for the measure.
43. A **45.** $1\frac{5}{12}$ cups **47.** no
49. no

5-6 Exercises

1. similar **3.** similar **5.** not similar
7. similar **9.** no **11.** similar
13. yes **15.** yes **17.** no **19.** no
23. C **25.** $10\frac{1}{2}$ **27.** $\frac{3}{2}$

5-7 Exercises

1. $a = 22.5$ cm **3.** 28 ft **5.** $x = 13.5$ in. **7.** 3.9 ft **9.** 21 m **15.** B
17. $18y$ **19.** $\frac{12}{z}$ or $12 \div z$ **21.** 3 lb

5-8 Exercises

1. $\frac{1}{14}$ **3.** 67.2 cm tall, 40 cm wide
5. $\frac{1}{15}$ **7.** 135 in. **9.** 16 in.
11. $4\frac{7}{24}$ in. **13.** 2 in.
15. about 25 mi **17.** 1 mi = 0.25 ft or 1 ft = 4 mi **19.** B **21.** 0.054, 0.41, $\frac{4}{7}$ **23.** $\frac{7}{11}$, 0.7, $\frac{7}{9}$ **25.** 0.25 kg
27. 1.36 m

Chapter 5 Study Guide: Review

1. similar **2.** ratio; rate **3.** scale factor **4.** $\frac{7}{15}$, 7 to 15, 7:15
5. red to blue **6.** 6 ft per s
7. 109 mi per h **8.** $2.24, about $2.14; $\frac{\$32.05}{15 \text{ gal}}$ **9.** 32 dollars per g, 35 dollars per g; $\frac{\$160}{5 \text{ g}}$ **10.** $\frac{9}{27} \neq \frac{6}{20}$
11. $\frac{15}{25} \neq \frac{20}{30}$ **12.** $\frac{21}{14} = \frac{18}{12}$
13. $\frac{2}{5} \neq \frac{4}{7}$ **14.** $\frac{8}{10} = \frac{20}{25}$
15. $\frac{18}{39} = \frac{24}{52}$ **16.** Possible answer: $\frac{10}{20} = \frac{30}{36}$ **17.** Possible answer: $\frac{45}{50} = \frac{90}{100}$ **18.** Possible answer: $\frac{9}{15} = \frac{27}{45}$ **19.** Possible answer: $\frac{4}{9} = \frac{8}{18}$ **20.** $n = 2$ **21.** $a = 6$
22. $b = 4$ **23.** $x = 66$ **24.** $y = 10$
25. $w = 20$ **26.** feet (or yards)
27. gallons **28.** inches **29.** 2 pints
30. 3,000 pounds **31.** 2.5 miles
32. not similar **33.** similar
34. $x = 100$ ft **35.** about 8 ft
36. 12.1 in. **37.** 163.4 mi

Chapter 6

6-1 Exercises

1. 79% **3.** 50% **5.** $\frac{41}{50}$ **7.** $\frac{19}{50}$ **9.** 0.22
11. 0.0807 **13.** 0.11 **15.** 45%
17. $\frac{11}{20}$ **19.** $\frac{83}{100}$ **21.** $\frac{81}{100}$ **23.** 0.098
25. 0.663 **27.** $\frac{27}{1{,}000}$, 0.027 **29.** $\frac{11}{25}$, 0.44 **31.** $\frac{21}{200}$, 0.105 **33.** < **35.** <
37. = **39.** > **41.** Brad
45. Sean's team **47.** $11\frac{79}{90}$ **49.** $3\frac{13}{60}$
51. $x = 13$ **53.** $m = 99$

6-2 Exercises

1. 60% **3.** 54.4% **5.** 8.7% **7.** 12%
9. 17.5% **11.** 40% **13.** 15%
15. 32.5% **17.** 42% **19.** 40%
21. 18.75% **23.** 40% **25.** > **27.** <
29. 1% **35.** 75% **37.** $2\frac{1}{4}$ **39.** $\frac{1}{9}$

6-3 Exercises

1. Possible answer: 30 **3.** Possible answer: 5 **5.** Yes; 35% of $43.99 is close to $\frac{1}{3}$ of $45, which is $15. Since $45 − $15 = $30, Darden will have enough money. **7.** Possible answer: 8 **9.** Possible answer: 7.7
11. Possible answer: 26
13. Possible answer: 70
15. Possible answer: 216
17. Possible answer: 13 **19.** Fancy Feet **21.** Possible answer: 24
23. Possible answer: 12
25. Possible answer: 12
27. Possible answer: 24 **37.** about 26 oz **39.** about 2% more
49. −56 **51.** −120

6-4 Exercises

1. 24 **3.** 20 **5.** 8 **7.** 423 **9.** $3.24
11. 11.2 **13.** 3,540 **15.** 0.04
17. 18 **19.** 13 **21.** 1.74 **23.** 39.6
25. 12.4 **27.** 6 **29.** 4.5 **31.** 11.75
33. 5,125 **35.** 80 **37.** 120 **39.** 0.6
41. 4.2 **43.** $4.80 **45.** 2.25 g
47. about 2,150 megawatts **53.** C
55. $1.75 per lb **57.** $-\frac{1}{4}$, 0.2, $\frac{1}{4}$
59. $\frac{6}{7}$, 0.87, $\frac{7}{8}$

6-5 Exercises

1. 25% **3.** 60 **5.** 18% **7.** 50 **9.** 8%
11. $33\frac{1}{3}$% **13.** 300% **15.** 225
17. 100% **19.** 30 **21.** 22 **23.** 55.6%
25. 68.8 **27.** 77.5 **29.** 158.3
31. 5% **35.** 45 pieces **41.** 75
43. $m = \frac{23}{24}$ **45.** $n = 3\frac{1}{2}$ **47.** 6.6
49. 66.64

6-6 Exercises

1. 28% **3.** 16.1% **5.** $34.39
7. 37.5% **9.** 22.2% **11.** $55.25
13. 100% **15.** 43.6% **17.** 30

19. 56.25 gal   **21.** $48.25
23a. $41,500   **23b.** $17,845
23c. 80.7%   **25.** about 8,506
trillion Btu   **27.** A   **29.** 8   **31.** 6
33. 179,520 ft   **35.** 0.082 tons

6-7 Exercises

1. $I = 24 **3.** $P = 400 **5.** just over
4 yr   **7.** $I = $3,240$ **9.** $P = $2,200$
11. $r = 11\%$ **13.** almost 9 yr
15. $5,200   **17.** $212.75   **19.** 20 yr
21. $4   **23.** high yield CD: gain
$606; Dow Jones: loss $684; a
difference of $1,290   **29.** just over
$2\frac{1}{2}$ yr   **31.** $17.91

Chapter 6 Study Guide: Review

1. interest; simple interest;
principal   **2.** percent of increase
3. percent of decrease   **4.** percent
5. $\frac{39}{50}$, 0.78   **6.** $\frac{2}{5}$, 0.40   **7.** $\frac{1}{20}$, 0.05
8. $\frac{4}{25}$, 0.16   **9.** $\frac{13}{20}$, 0.65   **10.** $\frac{89}{100}$,
0.89   **11.** 60%   **12.** 16.7%
13. 6%   **14.** 80%   **15.** 66.7%
16. 0.56%   **17.** Possible answer: 8
18. Possible answer: 90
19. Possible answer: 24
20. Possible answer: 32
21. Possible answer: 40
22. Possible answer: 3
23. Possible answer: $3   **24.** 68
25. 24   **26.** 4.41   **27.** 120   **28.** 27.3
29. 54   **30.** about 474   **31.** 125
32. 8%   **33.** 12   **34.** 37.5%   **35.** 8
36. 27.8%   **37.** 7.96%   **38.** 50%
39. 14.3%   **40.** 30%   **41.** 83.1%
42. 23.1%   **43.** 75%   **44.** $208.25
45. $7.80   **46.** $I = 15
47. $t = 3$ years   **48.** $I = 243
49. $r = 3.9\%$ **50.** $P = $2,300$
51. 7 years   **52.** 9 years, 3 months

Chapter 7

7-1 Exercises

1. mean = 22   **3.** mean = 6.5
5. mean = 57, median = 54, no

mode, range = 23   **7.** range = 19,
mean ≈ 508.2, median = 508.5,
mode = 500   **9.** 11   **11.** 4
13. 70   **15.** 6, 7, 12, 15, 15   **19.** C
21. 25   **23.** $\frac{14}{13}$; 14 to 13; 14:13
25. $\frac{27}{14}$; 27 to 14; 27:14

7-2 Exercises

1a. mean = 4.75, median = 5, no
mode, range = 7   **1b.** mean = 10,
median = 7, no mode, range = 30
3. with: mean ≈ 45.4, median =
42, no mode, range = 42; without:
mean ≈ 40.2, median = 40, no
mode, range = 11   **5.** 9
7. mean ≈ 118.29, median = 128,
no mode   **13.** 70   **15.** $n = \frac{9}{10}$
17. median: 35; no mode;
range = 45

7-3 Exercises

1. Mean: 192.5; median: 185; no;
the data set does not include an
outlier, so either the mean or the
median would be useful for
describing the typical lengths of
the books.   **3.** Mean: 17; median:
14; yes; in this case, the mean is
greater than all but one of the
ages, so the median is a better
representation of the typical age.
5. Median; the median gives the
middle score.   **7a.** blue   **7b.** no
11. B   **13.** −8   **15.** −9   **17.** 63
19. 2.56

7-4 Exercises

1. Florida   **3.** 34%   **5.** about $19
7. Yes. The maximum 24-hour
precipitation for Oklahoma is
about 15 in. Twice this maximum
is about 30 in., which is less than
the maximum of about 38 in. for
Florida.   **9.** Yes. There is not a
sector labeled "Africa," so visitors
from Africa are included in the
sector labeled "Other," which
represents 7%. This percent is less
than the 11% who came from

Central and South America.
11. No. The average ticket cost in
2005 was about $22, so a family
of four would have spent about
$88 on tickets.   **13.** no   **17.** no
19. Mean: 17; median: 14; median;
the mean is greater than all but
one of the data values.

7-5 Exercises

1. Graph A; the broken axis
exaggerates the difference in
lengths.   **3.** Possible answer: The
icons represent different numbers
of students.   **5.** Possible answer:
The icons represent different
quantities of food and are
different sizes.   **7.** The graphs do
not use the same scale, so it looks
as though September had fewer
sales than October, which is not
true; redraw the graphs using the
same scale.   **15.** $x = \frac{1}{6}$
17. $x = \frac{11}{24}$

7-6 Exercises

1. No; the population is small.
3. The percent of adults in City A
who visited a zoo (12%) is the
same as the national percent. The
percent of adults in City B who
visited a zoo (40%) is greater than
the national percent.   **5.** No; the
population is small.   **7.** The
average for Town A (5.9 h per
week) is close to the national
average. The average for Town B
(4.7 h per week) is less than the
national average.   **11.** 575   **17.** C
19. 43 mi per h

7-7 Exercises

1. random sample   **3.** Daria's
method is better; it uses a
random sample, and Nadia's
method uses a convenience
sample.   **5.** convenience sample
13. B   **15.** $x = 3$ **17.** $y = 63$

7-8 Exercises

1. The sample is not biased; it is a systematic sample that is likely to be representative of all of the company's customers.   **3.** The question is biased; it leads people to say yes because it only mentions one way of improving education.   **5.** The sample is biased; listeners who call the station may have stronger feelings about the song than other listeners would.   **7.** The question is not biased; it does not lead people to give a particular answer. **15.** B   **17.** 10   **19.** 12   **21.** $m = -5$ **23.** $p = -9$

Chapter 7 Study Guide: Review

1. population; sample   **2.** mean **3.** 302; 311.5; 233 and 324; 166 **4.** 43; 46; none; 25   **5.** 29; 29; 35; 15   **6.** 111; 110; none; 14   **7.** With outlier: mean ≈ 14.29; median = 11; mode = 12; range = 30; without outlier: mean ≈ 10.33; median = 10.5; mode = 12, range = 4   **8.** With outlier: mean = 31; median = 32; mode = 32; range = 33; without outlier: mean = 35.75; median = 33; mode = 32; range = 13   **9.** With outlier: mean ≈ 19.67; median = 14; mode = none; range = 42; without outlier: mean = 13.2; median = 13; mode = none; range = 6   **10.** Mean: 26; median: 26; no; there is no outlier. **11.** The mean; the mean is $467.20, the median is $495, and there is no mode. The mean makes the sales amounts seem greatest.   **12.** about 30   **13.** No; there are about 210 sixth graders, 180 seventh graders, and 220 eighth graders. There are about 610 students in all.   **14.** Yes; there are about 220 eighth graders and

180 seventh graders. There are about 40 more eighth graders than seventh graders.   **15.** Because the vertical axis is broken, it appears that there was a big change in temperature from day to day. The temperature changed very little. **16.** Yes; the population is large. **17.** No; the population is small. **18.** No; based on the sample, the number of defective posters will be about 200 per day.   **19.** systematic sample   **20.** convenience sample **21.** random sample   **22.** The sample may be biased; it is a convenience sample that may not be representative of all park users. **23.** The question is not biased; it does not lead people to give a certain answer.

Chapter 8

8-1 Exercises

1. unlikely   **3.** $\frac{5}{6}$ **5.** certain **7.** unlikely   **9.** $\frac{2}{5}$ **11.** as likely as not **13.** certain   **15.** not likely **17a.** It is very likely.   **17b.** It is impossible.   **23.** $\frac{7}{12}$ **25.** $0.17 per lemon   **27.** $0.55 per pair

8-2 Exercises

1. $\frac{6}{31}$; ≈ 0.194; ≈ 19.4%; Teri scored a goal on about $\frac{1}{5}$ of her tries, so the experimental probability that she will score a goal on her next try should be about $\frac{1}{5}$, or 20%. An answer of 19.4% is reasonable. **3.** $\frac{13}{30}$; ≈ 0.433; ≈ 43.3%; Jack hit the ball on about $\frac{1}{2}$ of his tries, so the experimental probability that he will hit the ball on his next try should be about $\frac{1}{2}$, or 50%. An answer of 43.3% is reasonable. **5a.** $\frac{9}{14}$ **5b.** $\frac{5}{14}$ **7.** $\frac{16}{25}$ **9a.** 9 in. **9b.** 0   **9c.** $\frac{1}{5}$ **13.** A   **15.** =   **17.** >

8-3 Exercises

1. $\frac{1}{6}$, ≈ 0.17, ≈ 17%; exactly $\frac{1}{6}$ of the marbles are red, so an answer of $\frac{1}{6}$ is reasonable.   **3.** $\frac{3}{7}$ **5.** $\frac{4}{7}$ **7.** $\frac{5}{23}$, ≈ 0.22, ≈ 22%; about $\frac{1}{4}$ of the disks are purple, so the theoretical probability of drawing a purple disk should be about $\frac{1}{4}$, or 25%. An answer of 22% is reasonable. **9.** $\frac{3}{7}$ **11.** $\frac{1}{5}$ **13.** $\frac{2}{5}$ **15.** 0   **17.** $\frac{11}{12}$ **19.** ≈ 0.41, ≈ 41%   **25.** $\frac{4}{5}$ or 0.8 **27.** 1   **29.** $1\frac{1}{2}$ lb

8-4 Exercises

1. H1, H2, T1, T2; the theoretical probability of each of the 4 outcomes is $\frac{1}{4}$.   **3.** 24   **5a.** H1, H2, H3, H4, H5, T1, T2, T3, T4, T5 **5b.** $\frac{1}{10}$ **7.** 27   **9a.** 9 outcomes **9b.** 6 outcomes   **11.** 12   **15.** D **17.** $1\frac{1}{15}$ **19.** $\frac{9}{20}$ **21.** $67.50

8-5 Exercises

1. Disjoint; you cannot roll a 5 and a number less than 3 at the same time.   **3.** 1   **5.** $\frac{5}{9}$ **7.** Not disjoint; because 20, 40, 60, 80, and 100 are multiples of both 4 and 5, it is possible to choose a multiple of 4 and a multiple of 5 at the same time.   **9.** 1   **11.** $\frac{1}{2}$ **13.** $\frac{5}{36}$ **15.** $\frac{2}{9}$ **17.** 25%   **19.** 0.26%   **25.** D **27.** 5.6 m   **29.** $\frac{3}{5}$

8-6 Exercises

1. Independent; the outcome of one coin does not affect the outcome of the other. **3.** Dependent; there are fewer students to choose from after the first student is picked.   **5.** $\frac{1}{60}$ **7.** Dependent; the choice of the first book affects the choice of the second.   **9.** Independent; the outcome of the first spin does not affect the outcome of the second spin.   **11.** $\frac{1}{4}$ **13.** independent; $\frac{1}{4}$ **15.** $\frac{1}{24}$ **17.** $\frac{1}{32}$ **21.** A   **23.** $7\frac{1}{4}$

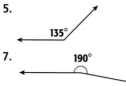

8-7 Exercises

1. about 600 **3.** about 200 tickets
5. about 32 **7.** about 129 donors
9. No; they are only surveying people who like frozen yogurt.
11. about 90 **15.** D **17.** $x = -12$
19. $x = -5$ **21.** $\frac{1}{6}$ **23.** 1

Chapter 8 Study Guide: Review

1. independent events
2. outcome **3.** unlikely
4. impossible **5.** $\frac{2}{3}$ **6.** $\frac{1}{3}$
7. $\frac{3}{7}$, ≈ 0.43, $\approx 43\%$ **8.** $\frac{1}{2}$, 0.5, 50%
9. $\frac{11}{29}$, ≈ 0.38, $\approx 38\%$ **10.** R1, R2, R3, R4, W1, W2, W3, W4, B1, B2, B3, B4 **11.** $\frac{1}{12}$ **12.** $\frac{3}{7}$ **13.** $\frac{11}{14}$
14. $\frac{1}{3}$ **15.** Independent; the outcome of tossing one coin does not affect the outcome of tossing the other coin. **16.** Dependent; removing the first book changes the number of possible outcomes when the second book is chosen.
17. $\frac{16}{121}$ **18.** 0.16% **19.** 100 items
20. 25 times **21.** 1,575 teenagers
22. 100 students

Chapter 9

9-1 Exercises

1. Possible answer: Q, R, S
3. Possible answer: plane QRS
5. Possible answer: $\overline{QU}$, $\overline{RU}$, $\overline{SU}$
7. Possible answer: D, E, F
9. Possible answer: plane DEF
11. Possible answer: $\overline{DE}$, $\overline{EF}$, $\overline{DF}$
13. Plane ABC contains points A, B, and C; lines $\overleftrightarrow{AB}$ and $\overleftrightarrow{BC}$; line segments $\overline{AB}$, $\overline{AC}$, and $\overline{BC}$; and rays $\overrightarrow{AB}$, $\overrightarrow{BA}$, $\overrightarrow{BC}$, $\overrightarrow{CB}$, and $\overrightarrow{CA}$. Plane ACD contains points A, C, and D; line segments $\overline{AC}$, $\overline{AD}$, and $\overline{CD}$; and ray $\overrightarrow{CA}$. **21.** C **23.** 16 **25.** -7
27. $67.15

9-2 Exercises

1. 90° **3.** 60°

5.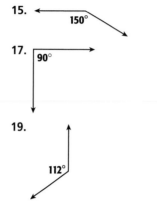

7. 190°

9. straight **11.** $\angle G$ acute; $\angle H$ obtuse; $\angle J$ right; $\angle K$ obtuse; $\angle L$ obtuse **13.** 35°

15. 150°

17. 90°

19. 112°

21. acute **23.** $\angle A$ obtuse; $\angle B$ obtuse; $\angle C$ acute; $\angle D$ obtuse; $\angle E$ obtuse; $\angle F$ acute **27.** straight
29. acute **35.** B **37.** 18 **39.** 295.2
41. Biased; the wording of the question might make people embarrassed to admit how much time they spend at the mall.

9-3 Exercises

1. adjacent **3.** neither
5. supplementary **7.** adjacent
9. complementary
11. supplementary **13.** $\angle 2$, $\angle 4$
15. $\angle 1$, $\angle 3$ **17.** Always; vertical angles have the same measure.
19. Never; the sum of the measures of a pair of angles can equal 90° or 180°, but not both.
21. True; the sum of the angles' measures is 180°. **29.** C
31. 55 mi/h **33.** $\frac{1}{6}$ **35.** $\frac{2}{3}$

9-4 Exercises

1. $a = 9°$ **3.** $c = 56°$ **5.** $a = 70°$, $b = 70°$, $c = 55°$ **7.** $d = 118°$
9. $f = 102°$ **11.** 43° **13.** 35°
15. 105° **17.** 44° **19.** $m\angle 1 = 108°$, $m\angle 3 = 108°$, $m\angle 4 = 72°$ **21.** 45°
25. C **27.** $n = 2$ **29.** $p = 0.25$

31. Dependent; after the first student is chosen, there are fewer students to select from when the second student is chosen.

9-5 Exercises

1. no; not all sides are line segments **3.** no; not a closed figure **5.** quadrilateral
7. quadrilateral; yes; all sides and all angles are congruent
9. triangle; no; all sides and all angles are not congruent
11. no; not all sides are line segments **13.** pentagon
15. heptagon **17.** pentagon; no; all sides and all angles are not congruent **21.** 16-gon **23.** A
25. 14 in. **27.** 20.3

9-6 Exercises

1. isosceles right **3.** isosceles acute
5. scalene right **7.** equilateral acute **9.** scalene **11.** isosceles
13. right **15.** 8 in., isosceles
17. isosceles acute **19.** scalene right **21.** isosceles triangle
23. D **27.** C **29.** $a = 32°$
31. $c = 135°$

9-7 Exercises

1. 77° **3.** 55° **5.** 60° **7.** 32°
9. 23°; obtuse **11.** 60°; acute
13. 60° **15.** 38° **19.** B **21.** 5.6; 6; 6; 5 **23.** 38; 38; 41; 34 **25.** $\frac{1}{2}$

9-8 Exercises

1. parallelogram **3.** parallelogram, rhombus; rhombus **5.** not possible **7.** parallelogram
9. parallelogram, rhombus; rhombus **11.** parallelogram, rectangle; rectangle

13.

15. parallelogram, rectangle, rhombus, square
17. parallelogram, rhombus, rectangle, square **19.** true **21.** true

23. false **25.** 1 triangle, 1 pentagon, and 2 trapezoids
27. parallelogram, rhombus, square, rectangle, trapezoid, right triangle **33.** 40.3; 41.5; 57; 39
35. $\frac{4}{5}$; 0.8; 80%

9-9 Exercises

1. the triangles on the game board and the holes on the game board
3. blue squares and blue rectangles **5.** no **7.** 2.5 **9.** the triangles in the kite's design
11. no **13.** 80°; 8 cm **15.** the lengths of all the sides **17.** the lengths of adjacent sides in each rectangle **19.** 40 m **21.** C
25. B **27.** $\frac{3}{8}$ **29.** $\frac{1}{6}$ **31.** 25°; obtuse **33.** 90°; right

Chapter 9 Study Guide: Review

1. acute or isosceles **2.** obtuse triangle **3.** complementary angles **4.** D, E, F **5.** $\overline{DF}$ **6.** plane DEF **7.** $\overrightarrow{ED}$, $\overrightarrow{FD}$, $\overrightarrow{DF}$ **8.** $\overline{DE}$, $\overline{DF}$, $\overline{EF}$
9. acute **10.** obtuse **11.** acute
12. straight **13.** supplementary
14. complementary **15.** neither
16. $b = 27°$ **17.** $d = 98°$ **18.** Yes; all sides are congruent and all angles are congruent. **19.** No; all sides are not congruent.
20. equilateral acute **21.** scalene right **22.** isosceles obtuse
23. scalene acute **24.** 53°
25. 110° **26.** 55° **27.** 74°
28. parallelogram, rhombus; rhombus **29.** parallelogram, rectangle; rectangle
30. parallelogram **31.** trapezoid
32. 133° **33.** 10 m

Chapter 10

10-1 Exercises

1. 2 in. **3.** 40 m **5.** 7 yd **7.** 96 in.
9. 7 cm **11.** 42 m **13.** 6 in.
15. 42 in. **17.** 36 m **23.** D

25. $95\frac{7}{8}$ **27.** $211\frac{7}{20}$ **29.** $a = 4$
31. $x = 4$

10-2 Exercises

1. circle G, diameter $\overline{EF}$, and radii $\overline{GF}$, $\overline{GE}$, and $\overline{GD}$ **3.** about 66 in.
5. 12.56 in. **7.** about 11 yd
9. 4.71 m **11.** 0.50 in. **13.** 5.75 ft, 11.5π ft **15b.** about 12.56 in.
17. 29 ft **19.** C **23.** about 840 revolutions **25.** $\frac{10}{12}$, $\frac{3}{4}$, $\frac{1}{12}$
27. $\frac{3}{4}$, $\frac{5}{8}$, $\frac{7}{16}$ **29.** 4.25 **31.** 59.25

10-3 Exercises

1. 48 in^2 **3.** 28.6 m^2 **5.** 21 m^2
7. 11 ft **9.** 6 m^2 **11.** 31.98 cm^2
13. $131\frac{3}{4}$ in^2 **15.** 15 m **17.** 8 yd
19. 14 units^2 **21a.** 320 in^2
21b. 72 in. **21c.** 621 in^2 **23.** C
27. B **29.** 159° **31.** 24°

10-4 Exercises

1. 28 units^2 **3.** 39.2 units^2 **5.** 64 m^2
7. 44,735 mi^2 **9.** 7.5 units^2
11. 330 yd^2 **13.** 22.5 cm^2
15. 4.5 cm **17.** 22 in.
19. 15 units^2 **21.** 12 units^2
23. 1,282 mi; 100,740 mi^2 **27.** A
29. 90° **31.** 49°

10-5 Exercises

1. Possible answer: formula value: 12.56 square units; estimate: 12 square units; because 12 is close to 12.56, an answer of 12.56 square units is reasonable.
3. 201.0 cm^2 **5.** 3.8 m^2
7. Possible answer: formula value: 3.14 square units; estimate: 4 square units; because 4 is close to 3.14, an answer of 3.14 square units is reasonable. **9.** 803.8 ft^2
11. 176.6 cm^2 **13.** about 15,400 mi^2
15. 14π m; 49π m^2 **17.** 24π ft; 144π ft^2 **19.** $r = 6$ cm **21.** $r = 3$ in.
23. 27,450.7 ft^2 **29.** The mega pizza is 4 times as big as the large. The area of the large is approximately 113 in^2, and the

area of the mega pizza is approximately 452 in^2.

10-6 Exercises

1. about 28 ft^2 **3.** 224 ft^2 **5.** 38 ft^2
7. about 25 ft^2 **9.** about 84.56 m^2
11. 46 cm^2 **13.** 30 ft^2; 30 ft
15. about 255.25 m^2; about 65.7 m
17. 10 **21.** D **23.** 57° **25.** 30°
27. 706.5 m^2 **29.** 254.3 in^2

10-7 Exercises

1. 5 faces, 8 edges, 5 vertices
3. 5 faces, 8 edges, 5 vertices
5. square pyramid **7.** 5 faces, 9 edges, 6 vertices **9.** 6 faces, 12 edges, 8 vertices
11. rectangular prism **13.** square pyramid, yes **15.** cone, no
17. B, C and D **19.** B **21.** true
23. true **25.** 8; octagonal pyramid
29. C **31.** < **33.** > **37.** not possible

10-8 Exercises

1. 162 cm^3 **3.** 10 ft^3 **5.** 320 ft^3
7. No; the volume of the ramp is only 2 ft^3. **9.** 79.36 in^3 **11.** 54 m^3
13. ≈ 71.72 ft^3 **15.** 3 m **17.** 6 in.
19. 8.96 g/cm^3, 19.32 g/cm^3, 5.02 g/cm^3, 0.4 g/cm^3, 10.5 g/cm^3
21. Check to see whether the egg floats in water; if it does then the egg is spoiled. **25.** A **27.** 6 **29.** 2

10-9 Exercises

1. 754 m^3 **3.** $\approx 3,140$ in^3
5. Cylinder B **7.** 314 ft^3 **9.** 31 cm^3 and 283 cm^3 **11.** 138 in^3 **13.** 4 m^3
15. 32π in^3 **17.** 618.75π ft^3
19. $4,000\pi$ mm^3 **21.** ≈ 923 ft^3
23. It cannot hold 200 cm^3 of juice because it only has a volume of about 196.25 cm^3. **25.** Gene has the largest cylinder; Gene—blue, Fran—red, Ira—yellow, Helen—green **29.** Chicken noodle; ≈ 215.875 cm^3; tomato: ≈ 376.8 cm^3; the tomato soup can

holds more soup. **31.** -25
33. 192 ft^3

10-10 Exercises
1. 94 in^2 **3.** 56 cm^2 **5.** $2{,}640 \text{ cm}^2$
7. $104\pi \text{ ft}^2$ **9.** $120\pi \text{ m}^2$
11. $16\frac{1}{2} \text{ m}^2$ **13.** 133 cm^2
15. 11 km^2 **17.** $226.98\pi \text{ m}^2$
19a. 312 in^2 **19b.** 22.8 in.
21. about 96 ft^2 **23.** about 190 cm^2
31. $y = 42$ **33.** $4\frac{5}{9}$ **35.** $\frac{1}{12}$

Chapter 10 Study Guide: Review
1. polyhedron **2.** volume
3. 33.9 in. **4.** 6 ft **5.** 31.4 ft
6. 9 m **7.** 50.24 cm **8.** 11 ft
9. 50.74 cm^2 **10.** 826.2 yd^2
11. 266 in^2 **12.** 108.75 cm^2
13. 36.3 m^2 **14.** 226.9 ft^2
15. $\approx 34.31 \text{ ft}^2$ **16.** 12 m^2
17. 5 faces, 8 edges, 5 vertices; rectangular pyramid **18.** 6 faces, 12 edges, 8 vertices; rectangular prism **19.** 384 cm^3 **20.** $6{,}300 \text{ in}^3$
21. $\approx 353 \text{ m}^3$ **22.** $\approx 2{,}308 \text{ ft}^3$
23. 125 m^2 **24.** 102 cm^2

Chapter 11

11-1 Exercises
1. $n = 7$ **3.** $x = \frac{1}{3}$ **5.** $y = 136$
7. 12 refills **9.** $p = -12$ **11.** $d = \frac{1}{7}$
13. $y = 5$ **15.** $k = 85$ **17.** $m = -80$
19. $m = -112$ **21.** 6 more than a number divided by 3 equals 18; $m = 36$. **23.** 2 equals 4 less than a number divided by 5; $n = 30$.
25. $x = 2$ **27.** $g = 20$ **29.** $w = -9$
31. $p = 2$ **33.** 120 min **35.** 1,300 calories **37.** 2 chicken sandwiches for lunch and again for dinner
39. C **41.** $57°$ **43.** $142°$

11-2 Exercises
1. $6b$ and $\frac{b}{2}$, $5x^2$ and x^2 **3.** $8x$
5. There are no like terms.
7. b^6 and $3b^6$, $2b$ and b

9. m and $2m$, 3^3 and 2
11. $8a + 2b$ **13.** $3a + 3b + 2c$
15. $3q^2 + 2q$ **17.** $2n + 3a + 3a + 2n + 5a$; $11a + 4n$ **19.** $27y$
21. $2d^2 + d$ **23.** no like terms
25. no like terms **27.** $4n + 5n + 6n = 15n$; 15, 30, 45, 60, 75
29a. $21.5d + 23d + 15.5d + 19d$; $79d$ **29b.** $750.50 **29c.** the amount Brad earned in June
31. $23x^2$; $3x + 23x^2 + 6y^2 + 2x + y^2 - 23x^2$ **35.** D **37.** 15 **39.** 87
41. 230 mm **43.** 500 mg

11-3 Exercises
1. $n = 5$ **3.** $p = 2$ **5.** $q = 2$
7. 5 books **9.** $x = \frac{7}{8}$ **11.** $n = 6$
13. $x = -2$ **15.** $n = -2$
17. $n = 1.5$ **19.** $t = -9$ **21.** $x = -1$
23. $w = 8$ **25.** $a = 8$ **27.** $b = -12$
29. $x = 3$ **31.** $6.70 **33.** $25
35. 91 **39.** A **41.** $x = -6$
43. $z = -18$ **45.** $\frac{1}{4}$

11-4 Exercises
1. $n = 32$ **3.** $12w = 32$ **5.** $a = 2$
7. 5 movies **9.** $-8 = 12p$
11. $-6 = 2c$ **13.** $6 = \frac{1}{10}a$
15. $b = -8$ **17.** $a = -0.8$
19. $c = -2$ **21.** $y = -7$ **23.** $r = 4$
25. $r = -2$ **27.** 67 members
29. $x = 6$ **31.** 20 days
37. $0.03m = 2 + 0.01m$; $m = 100$; 100 minutes makes the cost for long distance from both plans equal. **39.** $1°$ **41.** $45°$ **43.** 154 m^2
45. $346\frac{1}{2} \text{ yd}^2$

11-5 Exercises
1. number of people ≤ 18
3. water level > 45
5.
7.
9.
11. temperature < 40
13. number of tables ≤ 35

15.
17.
19.
21.
23.
25.
27.
29.
31.
33. $-2 < c < 3$ **35.** $-3 < x < 1$
37. $-200 \leq \text{depth} \leq 0$ **39.** $0 \geq$ *Manshu* depth measurement $\geq -32{,}190 \text{ ft}$; $0 \geq$ *Challenger* depth measurement $\geq -35{,}640 \text{ ft}$; $0 \geq$ *Horizon* depth measurement $\geq -34{,}884 \text{ ft}$; $0 \geq$ *Vityaz* depth measurement $\geq -36{,}200 \text{ ft}$
41. B **43.** 59 m/h **45.** $n = 42$
47. $w = 13.6$

11-6 Exercises
1. $x < 27$ **3.** $p \leq 7$ **5.** $b \leq -24$
7. no more than $42°F$ **9.** $m < 11$
11. $c \leq 11$ **13.** $x \geq 80$ **15.** $z > -12$
17. $f > -6$ **19.** $n \geq -4$ **21.** at most 24 birds **23.** $a > 3$ **25.** $m \leq -38$
27. $g < 6\frac{1}{3}$ **29.** $w \leq 15.7$
31. $t \geq -242$ **33.** $v \leq 0.6$
35. $\ell - 12 \geq 62$; $\ell \geq 74$; at least 74 in. **37.** no more than 3.1 meters
39. up to 50,000 hertz **43.** B
45. 17; 17; 20; 7 **47.** $\frac{1}{4}$

11-7 Exercises
1. $w < -32$ **3.** $p < 48$ **5.** $y > -2$
7. at least 27 candles **9.** $m > 52$
11. $c \geq -120$ **13.** $x \geq -1.1$
15. $z < \frac{3}{5}$ **17.** $f < -3$ **19.** $n \leq -10$
21. at least 46 wreaths **23.** $p > 4$
25. $y \geq 18$ **27.** $g > 0.63$ **29.** $w \leq \frac{3}{8}$
31. $t < 4$ **33.** $v \geq -2.5$ **35.** 5 hours

37. more than 480 subscriptions
43. 301 **45.** 56 **47.** 3.5

1. $x < 3$ **3.** $y \geq 6$ **5.** $p \leq -5$
7. more than \$26 each **9.** $b < 12$
11. $c \geq -3$ **13.** $x \leq -27$ **15.** $j \leq 2$
17. at most 6 bagels **19.** $x \geq -6$
21. $c < 1.8$ **23.** $w \leq 8$ **25.** $s > -24$
27. $d \leq 4$ **29.** \$14 **31.** at least 225
students **33.** at most 60% **37.** B
39. $\frac{2}{7}$ **41.** $1\frac{1}{2}$ **43.** $\frac{1}{12}$

Chapter 11 Study Guide: Review

1. inequality **2.** compound
inequality **3.** solution set
4. $y = 8$ **5.** $z = 30$ **6.** $w = 147$
7. $x = 4$ **8.** $b = 2$ **9.** $k = 18$
10. $a = 15$ **11.** $p = -4$
12. $10b^2 + 8$ **13.** $15a^2 + 2$
14. $x^4 + x^3 + 6x^2$ **15.** $6x^2 + 7x - 9$
16. $7p + 5$ **17.** $a = \frac{1}{3}$ **18.** $j = 9$
19. $b = 4$ **20.** $y = 5$ **21.** $x = 7$
22. $k = 1$ **23.** 5 mi **24.** $b = \frac{1}{2}$
25. $c = 6$ **26.** $m = \frac{8}{3}$ or $2\frac{2}{3}$
27. $x = 20$ **28.** $x = 48$ **29.** $y = 18$
30. weight limit ≤ 9 tons
31. age > 200 **32.** weight ≥ 2 tons
33. depth < 49 ft
34.

35.

36. $r > 25$ **37.** $x \leq -26$ **38.** $g < 8$
39. $t < \frac{1}{6}$ **40.** $9 > r$ **41.** $u \geq -66$
42. at least 38 points
43. $n < -55.2$ **44.** $p \leq 6$
45. $k < -130$ **46.** $p < 5$
47. $v \geq 2.76$ **48.** $c > 33$
49. $g < -7$ **50.** $x \geq \frac{1}{2}$
51. at least 16 purses **52.** $b < -2$
53. $d < -6$ **54.** $n \geq -4$
55. $y \leq 18$ **56.** $c > -54$
57. $x \leq 10$ **58.** $h \geq -156$
59. $-10 < t$ **60.** $52 > w$
61. $y \leq 35$ **62.** at most 4 T-shirts

Glossary/Glosario

A

ENGLISH	SPANISH	EXAMPLES
absolute value The distance of a number from zero on a number line; shown by | |. (p. 71)	**valor absoluto** Distancia a la que está un número de 0 en una recta numérica. El símbolo del valor absoluto es ||.	$\|5\| = 5$ $\|-5\| = 5$
acute angle An angle that measures less than 90°. (p. 433)	**ángulo agudo** Ángulo que mide menos de 90°.	
acute triangle A triangle with all angles measuring less than 90°. (p. 452)	**triángulo acutángulo** Triángulo en el que todos los ángulos miden menos de 90°.	
addend A number added to one or more other numbers to form a sum.	**sumando** Número que se suma a uno o más números para formar una suma.	In the expression 4 + 6 + 7, the numbers 4, 6, and 7 are addends.
Addition Property of Equality The property that states that if you add the same number to both sides of an equation, the new equation will have the same solution. (p. 44)	**Propiedad de igualdad de la suma** Propiedad que establece que puedes sumar el mismo número a ambos lados de una ecuación y la nueva ecuación tendrá la misma solución.	$x - 6 = 8$ $\underline{+ 6 \quad + 6}$ $x = 14$
Addition Property of Opposites The property that states that the sum of a number and its opposite equals zero. (p. 94)	**Propiedad de la suma de los opuestos** Propiedad que establece que la suma de un número y su opuesto es cero.	$12 + (-12) = 0$
additive inverse The opposite of a number. (p. 94)	**inverso aditivo** El opuesto de un número.	The additive inverse of 5 is −5.
adjacent angles Angles in the same plane that are side by side and have a common vertex and a common side. (p. 436)	**ángulos adyacentes** Ángulos en el mismo plano que están uno al lado del otro y comparten un vértice y un lado.	∠1 and ∠2 are adjacent angles.
algebraic expression An expression that contains at least one variable. (p. 24)	**expresión algebraica** Expresión que contiene al menos una variable.	$x + 8$ $4(m - b)$
algebraic inequality An inequality that contains at least one variable. (p. 572)	**desigualdad algebraica** Desigualdad que contiene al menos una variable.	$x + 3 > 10$ $5a > b + 3$

ENGLISH	SPANISH	EXAMPLES

angle A figure formed by two rays with a common endpoint called the vertex. (p. 432)

ángulo Figura formada por dos rayos con un extremo común llamado vértice.

area The number of non-overlapping unit squares needed to cover a given surface. (p. 497)

área El número de unidades cuadradas no superpuestas que se necesitan para cubrir una superficie dada.

5

2

The area is 10 square units.

Associative Property of Addition The property that states that for all real numbers a, b, and c, the sum is always the same, regardless of their grouping. (p. 20)

Propiedad asociativa de la suma Propiedad que establece que para todos los números reales a, b y c, la suma siempre es la misma sin importar cómo se agrupen.

$2 + 3 + 8 = (2 + 3) + 8 = 2 + (3 + 8)$

Associative Property of Multiplication The property that states that for all real numbers a, b, and c, their product is always the same, regardless of their grouping. (p. 20)

Propiedad asociativa de la multiplicación Propiedad que establece que, para todos los números reales a, b y c, el producto siempre es el mismo sin importar cómo se agrupen.

$2 \cdot 3 \cdot 8 = (2 \cdot 3) \cdot 8 = 2 \cdot (3 \cdot 8)$

axes The two perpendicular lines of a coordinate plane that intersect at the origin. (p. 100)

ejes Las dos rectas numéricas perpendiculares del plano cartesiano que se intersecan en el origen.

y-axis

0

x-axis

B

bar graph A graph that uses vertical or horizontal bars to display data. (p. 342)

gráfica de barras Gráfica en la que se usan barras verticales u horizontales para presentar datos.

Sunlight's Travel Time to Planets

4800

5000
4000
3000
2600
2000
1000 500 760

Time (s)

Earth Mars Jupiter Saturn

Planet

base-10 number system A number system in which all numbers are expressed using the digits 0–9. (p. 211)

sistema de base 10 Sistema de numeración en el que todos los números se expresan con los dígitos 0–9.

base (in numeration) When a number is raised to a power, the number that is used as a factor is the base. (p. 10)

base (en numeración) Cuando un número es elevado a una potencia, el número que se usa como factor es la base.

$3^5 = 3 \cdot 3 \cdot 3 \cdot 3 \cdot 3$; 3 is the base.

base (of a polygon) A side of a polygon, or the length of that side. (p. 497)

base (de un polígono) Lado de un polígono o la longitud de ese lado.

---

base (of a three-dimensional figure) A face of a three-dimensional figure by which the figure is measured or classified. (p. 518)

base (de una figura tridimensional) Cara de una figura tridimensional a partir de la cual se mide o se clasifica la figura.

Bases of a prism   Base of a pyramid

---

base (of a trapezoid) One of the two parallel sides of a trapezoid. (p. 502)

base (de un trapecio) Uno de los dos lados paralelos del trapecio.

b_1

b_2

---

biased question A question that leads people to give a certain answer. (p. 362)

pregunta tendenciosa Pregunta que lleva a las personas a dar una respuesta determinada.

---

biased sample A sample that does not fairly represent the population. (p. 362)

muestra no representativa Muestra que no representa adecuadamente la población.

---

break (graph) A zigzag on a horizontal or vertical scale of a graph that indicates that some of the numbers on the scale have been omitted. (p. 348)

discontinuidad (gráfica) Zig-zag en la escala horizontal o vertical de una gráfica que indica la omisión de algunos de los números de la escala.

65
60
55
0

C

capacity The amount a container can hold when filled. (p. 210)

capacidad Cantidad que cabe en un recipiente cuando se llena.

A large milk container has a capacity of 1 gallon.

Celsius A metric scale for measuring temperature in which 0°C is the freezing point of water and 100°C is the boiling point of water; also called *centigrade*. (p. 27)

Celsius Escala métrica para medir la temperatura, en la que 0° C es el punto de congelación del agua y 100° C es el punto de ebullición. También se llama *centígrado*.

---

center (of a circle) The point inside a circle that is the same distance from all the points on the circle. (p. 492)

centro (de un círculo) Punto interior de un círculo que se encuentra a la misma distancia de todos los puntos de la circunferencia.

A

---

certain (probability) Sure to happen; having a probability of 1. (p. 382)

seguro (probabilidad) Que con seguridad sucederá. Representa una probabilidad de 1.

Glossary/Glosario

ENGLISH	SPANISH	EXAMPLES
circle The set of all points in a plane that are the same distance from a given point called the center. (p. 492)	**círculo** Conjunto de todos los puntos en un plano que se encuentran a la misma distancia de un punto dado llamado centro.	
circle graph A graph that uses sectors of a circle to compare parts to the whole and parts to other parts. (p. 342)	**gráfica circular** Gráfica que usa secciones de un círculo para comparar partes con el todo y con otras partes.	**Residents of Mesa, AZ** 65+ 13% 45–64 19% 25–44 30% 18–24 11% Under 18 27%
circumference The distance around a circle. (p. 492)	**circunferencia** Distancia alrededor de un círculo.	Circumference
coefficient The number that is multiplied by a variable in an algebraic expression. (p. 558)	**coeficiente** Número que se multiplica por una variable en una expresión algebraica.	5 is the coefficient in $5b$.
common denominator A denominator that is the same in two or more fractions. (p. 150)	**común denominador** Denominador que es común a dos o más fracciones.	The common denominator of $\frac{5}{8}$ and $\frac{2}{8}$ is 8.
common factor A number that is a factor of two or more numbers. (p. 132)	**factor común** Número que es factor de dos o más números.	8 is a common factor of 16 and 40.
common multiple A number that is a multiple of each of two or more numbers. (p. 136)	**común múltiplo** Número que es múltiplo de dos o más números.	15 is a common multiple of 3 and 5.
Commutative Property of Addition The property that states that two or more numbers can be added in any order without changing the sum. (p. 20)	**Propiedad conmutativa de la suma** Propiedad que establece que sumar dos o más números en cualquier orden no altera la suma.	$8 + 20 = 20 + 8$
Commutative Property of Multiplication The property that states that two or more numbers can be multiplied in any order without changing the product. (p. 20)	**Propiedad conmutativa de la multiplicación** Propiedad que establece que multiplicar dos o más números en cualquier orden no altera el producto.	$6 \cdot 12 = 12 \cdot 6$
compatible numbers Numbers that are close to the given numbers that make estimation or mental calculation easier. (p. SB10)	**números compatibles** Números que están cerca de los números dados y hacen más fácil la estimación o el cálculo mental.	To estimate $29.15 \div 4.87$, use the compatible numbers 30 and 5: $30 \div 5 = 6$.
complement (of an event) The set of all outcomes that are not the event. (p. 383)	**complemento (de un suceso)** El conjunto de todos los resultados que no son el suceso.	When rolling a number cube, the complement of rolling a 3 is rolling a 1, 2, 4, 5, or 6.

Glossary/Glosario **G5**

ENGLISH	SPANISH	EXAMPLES
complementary angles Two angles whose measures add to 90°. (p. 437)	**ángulos complementarios** Dos ángulos cuyas medidas suman 90°.	37° 53° A B
composite figure A figure made up of simple geometric shapes. (p. 510)	**figura compuesta** Figura formada por figuras geométricas simples.	2 cm 5 cm 4 cm 4 cm 4 cm 3 cm 5 cm
composite number A whole number greater than 1 that has more than two positive factors. (p. 128)	**número compuesto** Número cabal mayor que 1 que tiene más de dos factores positivos.	4, 6, 8, and 9 are composite numbers.
compound event An event made up of two or more simple events. (p. 394)	**suceso compuesto** Suceso que consta de dos o más sucesos simples.	Rolling a 3 on a number cube and spinning a 2 on a spinner is a compound event.
compound inequality A combination of more than one inequality. (p. 573)	**desigualdad compuesta** Combinación de dos o más desigualdades.	$-2 \le x < 10$
cone A three-dimensional figure with a circular base lying in one plane plus a vertex not lying on that plane. The remaining surface of the cone is formed by joining the vertex to points on the circle by line segments. (p. 519)	**cono** Figura tridimensional con una base circular que está en un plano más un vértice que no está en ese plano. El resto de la superficie del cono se forma uniendo el vértice con puntos del círculo por medio de segmentos de recta.	
congruent Having the same size and shape. (p. 429)	**congruentes** Que tienen la misma forma y el mismo tamaño.	Q R P S $\overline{PQ} \cong \overline{RS}$
congruent angles Angles that have the same measure. (p. 436)	**ángulos congruentes** Ángulos que tienen la misma medida.	C D F E A B $\angle ABC \cong \angle DEF$
constant A value that does not change. (p. 24)	**constante** Valor que no cambia.	3, 0, π
convenience sample A sample based on members of the population that are readily available. (p. 358)	**muestra de conveniencia** Una muestra basada en miembros de la población que están fácilmente disponibles.	

ENGLISH	SPANISH	EXAMPLES
coordinate One of the numbers of an ordered pair that locate a point on a coordinate graph. (p. 100)	**coordenada** Uno de los números de un par ordenado que localizan un punto en una gráfica de coordenadas.	
coordinate plane (coordinate grid) A plane formed by the intersection of a horizontal number line called the x-axis and a vertical number line called the y-axis. (p. 100)	**plano cartesiano (cuadrícula de coordenadas)** Plano formado por la intersección de una recta numérica horizontal llamada eje x y otra vertical llamada eje y.	
corresponding angles (for lines) For two lines intersected by a transversal, a pair of angles that lie on the same side of the transversal and on the same sides of the other two lines. (p. 445)	**ángulos correspondientes (en líneas)** Dadas dos líneas cortadas por una transversal, el par de ángulos ubicados en el mismo lado de la transversal y en los mismos lados de las otras dos líneas.	$\angle 1$ and $\angle 3$ are corresponding angles.
corresponding angles (in polygons) Matching angles of two or more polygons. (p. 258)	**ángulos correspondientes (en polígonos)** Ángulos que se ubican en la misma posición relativa en dos o más polígonos.	$\angle A$ and $\angle D$ are corresponding angles.
corresponding sides Matching sides of two or more polygons. (p. 258)	**lados correspondientes** Lados que se ubican en la misma posición relativa en dos o más polígonos.	$\overline{AB}$ and $\overline{DE}$ are corresponding sides.
cross products In the statement $\frac{a}{b} = \frac{c}{d}$, bc and ad are the cross products. (p. 244)	**productos cruzado** En el enunciado $\frac{a}{b} = \frac{c}{d}$, bc y ad son productos cruzados.	For the proportion $\frac{2}{3} = \frac{4}{6}$, the cross products are $2 \cdot 6 = 12$ and $3 \cdot 4 = 12$.
cube (geometric figure) A rectangular prism with six congruent square faces. (p. 518)	**cubo (figura geométrica)** Prisma rectangular con seis caras cuadradas congruentes.	
customary system of measurement The measurement system often used in the United States. (p. 249)	**sistema usual de medidas** El sistema de medidas que se usa comúnmente en Estados Unidos.	inches, feet, miles, ounces, pounds, tons, cups, quarts, gallons
cylinder A three-dimensional figure with two parallel congruent circular bases. The third surface of the cylinder consists of all parallel circles of the same radius whose centers lie on the segment joining the centers of the bases. (p. 517)	**cilindro** Figura tridimensional con dos bases circulares paralelas y congruentes. La tercera superficie del cilindro consiste en todos los círculos paralelos del mismo radio cuyo centro está en el segmento que une los centros de las bases.	

D

decagon A polygon with ten sides. (p. 449)

decágono Polígono de 10 lados.

---

degree The unit of measure for angles or temperature. (p. 432)

grado Unidad de medida para ángulos y temperaturas.

---

denominator The bottom number of a fraction that tells how many equal parts are in the whole. (p. SB7)

denominador Número de abajo de una fracción que indica en cuántas partes iguales se divide el entero.

$\frac{3}{4}$ ← denominator

---

dependent events Events for which the outcome of one event affects the probability of the second event. (p. 406)

sucesos dependientes Dos sucesos son dependientes si el resultado de uno afecta la probabilidad del otro.

A bag contains 3 red marbles and 2 blue marbles. Drawing a red marble and then drawing a blue marble without replacing the first marble is an example of dependent events.

---

diameter A line segment that passes through the center of a circle and has endpoints on the circle, or the length of that segment. (p. 492)

diámetro Segmento de recta que pasa por el centro de un círculo y tiene sus extremos en la circunferencia, o bien la longitud de ese segmento.

---

difference The result when one number is subtracted from another. (p. 28)

diferencia El resultado de restar un número de otro.

In $16 - 5 = 11$, 11 is the difference.

---

dimension The length, width, or height of a figure. (p. 266)

dimensión Longitud, ancho o altura de una figura.

---

disjoint events Two events are disjoint if they cannot both occur in the same trial of an experiment. (p. 402)

sucesos desunidos Dos sucesos son desunidos si no pueden ocurrir en la misma prueba de un experimento.

Distributive Property The property that states if you multiply a sum by a number, you will get the same result if you multiply each addend by that number and then add the products. (p. 21)

Propiedad distributiva Propiedad que establece que, si multiplicas una suma por un número, obtendrás el mismo resultado que si multiplicas cada sumando por ese número y luego sumas los productos.

$5(20 + 1) = 5 \cdot 20 + 5 \cdot 1$

---

dividend The number to be divided in a division problem. (p. SB6)

dividendo Número que se divide en un problema de división.

In $8 \div 4 = 2$, 8 is the dividend.

---

divisible Can be divided by a number without leaving a remainder. (p. SB8)

divisible Que se puede dividir entre un número sin dejar residuo.

18 is divisible by 3.

ENGLISH	SPANISH	EXAMPLES
Division Property of Equality The property that states that if you divide both sides of an equation by the same nonzero number, the new equation will have the same solution. (p. 47)	**Propiedad de igualdad de la división** Propiedad que establece que puedes dividir ambos lados de una ecuación entre el mismo número distinto de cero, y la nueva ecuación tendrá la misma solución.	$4x = 12$ $\frac{4x}{4} = \frac{12}{4}$ $x = 3$
divisor The number you are dividing by in a division problem. (p. 206)	**divisor** El número entre el que se divide en un problema de división.	In $8 \div 4 = 2$, 4 is the divisor.
double-bar graph A bar graph that compares two related sets of data. (p. 342	**gráfica de doble barra** Gráfica de barras que compara dos conjuntos de datos relacionados.	

E

ENGLISH	SPANISH	EXAMPLES
edge The line segment along which two faces of a polyhedron intersect. (p. 518)	**arista** Segmento de recta donde se intersecan dos caras de un poliedro.	Edge
endpoint A point at the end of a line segment or ray. (p. 429)	**extremo** Un punto ubicado al final de un segmento de recta o rayo.	A B / D
equally likely outcomes Outcomes that have the same probability. (p. 390)	**resultados igualmente probables** Resultados que tienen la misma probabilidad de ocurrir.	
equation A mathematical sentence that shows that two expressions are equivalent. (p. 34)	**ecuación** Enunciado matemático que indica que dos expresiones son equivalentes.	$x + 4 = 7$ $6 + 1 = 10 - 3$
equilateral triangle A triangle with three congruent sides. (p. 452)	**triángulo equilátero** Triángulo con tres lados congruentes.	
equivalent Having the same value. (p. 142)	**equivalentes** Que tienen el mismo valor.	
equivalent fractions Fractions that name the same amount or part. (p. 142)	**fracciones equivalentes** Fracciones que representan la misma cantidad o parte.	$\frac{1}{2}$ and $\frac{2}{4}$ are equivalent fractions.
equivalent ratios Ratios that name the same comparison. (p. 240)	**razones equivalentes** Razones que representan la misma comparación.	$\frac{1}{2}$ and $\frac{2}{4}$ are equivalent ratios.
estimate (n) An answer that is close to the exact answer and is found by rounding, or other methods. (p. SB10)	**estimación (s)** Una solución aproximada a la respuesta exacta que se halla mediante el redondeo u otros métodos.	

ENGLISH	SPANISH	EXAMPLES
estimate (v) To find an answer close to the exact answer by rounding or other methods. (p. SB10)	**estimar (v)** Hallar una solución aproximada a la respuesta exacta mediante el redondeo u otros métodos.	
evaluate To find the value of a numerical or algebraic expression. (p. 24)	**evaluar** Hallar el valor de una expresión numérica o algebraica.	Evaluate $2x + 7$ for $x = 3$. $2x + 7$ $2(3) + 7$ $6 + 7$ 13
even number An integer that is divisible by two. (p. 379)	**número par** Número entero divisible entre 2.	2, 4, 6
event An outcome or set of outcomes of an experiment or situation. (p. 382)	**suceso** Un resultado o una serie de resultados de un experimento o una situación.	When rolling a number cube, the event "an odd number" consists of the outcomes 1, 3, and 5.
experiment In probability, any activity based on chance, such as tossing a coin. (p. 382)	**experimento** En probabilidad, cualquier actividad basada en la posibilidad, como lanzar una moneda.	Tossing a coin 10 times and noting the number of "heads"
experimental probability The ratio of the number of times an event occurs to the total number of trials, or times that the activity is performed. (p. 386)	**probabilidad experimental** Razón del número de veces que ocurre un suceso al número total de pruebas o al número de veces que se realiza el experimento.	Kendra attempted 27 free throws and made 16 of them. Her experimental probability of making a free throw is $\frac{\text{number made}}{\text{number attempted}} = \frac{16}{27} \approx 0.59.$
exponent The number that indicates how many times the base is used as a factor. (p. 10)	**exponente** Número que indica cuántas veces se usa la base como factor.	$2^3 = 2 \cdot 2 \cdot 2 = 8$; 3 is the exponent.
expression A mathematical phrase that contains operations, numbers, and/or variables. (p. 14)	**expresión** Enunciado matemático que contiene operaciones, números y/o variables.	$6x + 1$

F

ENGLISH	SPANISH	EXAMPLES
face A flat surface of a polyhedron. (p. 518)	**cara** Superficie plana de un poliedro.	
factor A number that is multiplied by another number to get a product. (p. 128)	**factor** Número que se multiplica por otro para hallar un producto.	7 is a factor of 21 since $7 \cdot 3 = 21.$
factor tree A diagram showing how a whole number breaks down into its prime factors. (p. 128)	**árbol de factores** Diagrama que muestra cómo se descompone un número cabal en sus factores primos.	12 / \\ 3 · 4 / \\ 2 · 2 $12 = 3 \cdot 2 \cdot 2$

ENGLISH	SPANISH	EXAMPLES
Fahrenheit A temperature scale in which 32°F is the freezing point of water and 212°F is the boiling point of water. (p. 27)	**Fahrenheit** Escala de temperatura en la que 32° F es el punto de congelación del agua y 212° F es el punto de ebullición.	
fair When all outcomes of an experiment are equally likely, the experiment is said to be fair. (p. 390)	**justo** Se dice de un experimento donde todos los resultados posibles son igualmente probables.	
formula A rule showing relationships among quantities. (p. SB12)	**fórmula** Regla que muestra relaciones entre cantidades.	$A = \ell w$ is the formula for the area of a rectangle.
fraction A number in the form $\frac{a}{b}$, where $b \neq 0$. (p. 142)	**fracción** Número escrito en la forma $\frac{a}{b}$, donde $b \neq 0$.	
Fundamental Counting Principle If one event has m possible outcomes and a second event has n possible outcomes after the first event has occurred, then there are $m \cdot n$ total possible outcomes for the two events. (p. 395)	**Principio fundamental de conteo** Si un suceso tiene m resultados posibles y otro suceso tiene n resultados posibles después de ocurrido el primer suceso, entonces hay $m \cdot n$ resultados posibles en total para los dos sucesos.	There are 4 colors of shirts and 3 colors of pants. There are $4 \cdot 3 = 12$ possible outfits.

G

ENGLISH	SPANISH	EXAMPLES
graph of an equation A graph of the set of ordered pairs that are solutions of the equation. (p. 109)	**gráfica de una ecuación** Gráfica del conjunto de pares ordenados que son soluciones de la ecuación.	
greatest common divisor (GCD) The largest whole number that divides evenly into two or more given numbers. (p. 132)	**máximo común divisor (MCD)** El número cabal mayor que divide exactamente dos o más números dados.	The GCD of 27 and 45 is 9.

H

ENGLISH	SPANISH	EXAMPLES
height In a triangle or parallelogram, the perpendicular distance from the line containing the base to the opposite vertex or side. (pp. 497, 502)	**altura** En un triángulo o paralelogramo, la distancia perpendicular desde la línea que contiene la base al vértice o lado opuesto.	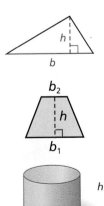
In a trapezoid, the perpendicular distance between the bases.	En un trapecio, la distancia perpendicular entre las bases.	
In a prism or cylinder, the perpendicular distance between the bases. (pp. 524, 528)	En un prisma o cilindro, la distancia perpendicular entre las bases.	

Glossary/Glosario **G11**

ENGLISH	SPANISH	EXAMPLES
heptagon A seven-sided polygon. (p. 449)	**heptágono** Polígono de siete lados.	
hexagon A six-sided polygon. (p. 449)	**hexágono** Polígono de seis lados.	
histogram A bar graph that shows the frequency of data within equal intervals. (p. SB15)	**histograma** Gráfica de barras que muestra la frecuencia de los datos en intervalos iguales.	

I

ENGLISH	SPANISH	EXAMPLES
Identity Property of One The property that states that the product of 1 and any number is that number. (p. 20)	**Propiedad de identidad del uno** Propiedad que establece que el producto de 1 y cualquier número es ese número.	$3 \cdot 1 = 3$ $-9 \cdot 1 = -9$
Identity Property of Zero The property that states that the sum of zero and any number is that number. (p. 20)	**Propiedad de identidad del cero** Propiedad que establece que la suma de cero y cualquier número es ese número.	$5 + 0 = 5$ $-4 + 0 = -4$
impossible (probability) Can never happen; having a probability of 0. (p. 382)	**imposible (en probabilidad)** Que no puede ocurrir. Suceso cuya probabilidad de ocurrir es 0.	
improper fraction A fraction in which the numerator is greater than or equal to the denominator. (p. 143)	**fracción impropia** Fracción en la que el numerador es mayor que o igual al denominador.	$\frac{5}{5}$ $\frac{7}{4}$
independent events Events for which the outcome of one event does not affect the probability of the other. (p. 406)	**sucesos independientes** Dos sucesos son independientes si el resultado de uno no afecta la probabilidad del otro.	A bag contains 3 red marbles and 2 blue marbles. Drawing a red marble, replacing it, and then drawing a blue marble is an example of independent events.
indirect measurement The technique of using similar figures and proportions to find a measure. (p. 262)	**medición indirecta** La técnica de usar figuras semejantes y proporciones para hallar una medida.	
inequality A mathematical statement that compares two expressions by using one of the following symbols: <, >, ≥, ≤, or ≠. (p. 572)	**desigualdad** Enunciado matemático que compara dos expresiones por medio de uno de los siguientes símbolos: <, >, ≥, ≤, ó ≠.	$5 < 8$ $5x + 2 \geq 12$
integers The set of whole numbers and their opposites. (p. 70)	**enteros** Conjunto de todos los números cabales y sus opuestos.	$\ldots -3, -2, -1, 0, 1, 2, 3, \ldots$

ENGLISH	SPANISH	EXAMPLES
interest The amount of money charged for borrowing or using money, or the amount of money earned by saving money. (p. 312)	**interés** Cantidad de dinero que se cobra por el préstamo o uso del dinero, o la cantidad que se gana al ahorrar dinero.	
intersecting lines Lines that cross at exactly one point. (p. 436)	**líneas secantes** Líneas que se cruzan en un solo punto.	
interval The space between marked values on a number line or the scale of a graph. (p. SB14)	**intervalo** El espacio entre los valores marcados en una recta numérica o en la escala de una gráfica.	
inverse operations Operations that undo each other: addition and subtraction, or multiplication and division. (p. 40)	**operaciones inversas** Operaciones que se cancelan mutuamente: suma y resta, o multiplicación y división.	Adding 3 and subtracting 3 are inverse operations: $5 + 3 = 8$; $8 - 3 = 5$
isolate the variable To get a variable alone on one side of an equation or inequality in order to solve the equation or inequality. (p. 94)	**despejar la variable** Dejar sola la variable en un lado de una ecuación o desigualdad para resolverla.	$\begin{aligned} x + 7 &= 22 \\ -7 \quad &\quad -7 \\ x \quad &= 15 \end{aligned}$
isosceles triangle A triangle with at least two congruent sides. (p. 452)	**triángulo isósceles** Triángulo que tiene al menos dos lados congruentes.	

L

least common denominator (LCD) The least common multiple of two or more denominators. (p. 176)	**mínimo común denominador (mcd)** El mínimo común múltiplo de dos o más denominadores.	The LCD of $\frac{3}{4}$ and $\frac{5}{6}$ is 12.
least common multiple (LCM) The least number, other than zero, that is a multiple of two or more given numbers. (p. 136)	**mínimo común múltiplo (mcm)** El menor de los números, distinto de cero, que es múltiplo de dos o más números.	The LCM of 10 and 18 is 90.
like terms Two or more terms that have the same variable raised to the same power. (p. 558)	**términos semejantes** Dos o más términos que contienen la misma variable elevada a la misma potencia.	In the expression $3a + 5b + 12a$, $3a$ and $12a$ are like terms.
line A straight path that extends without end in opposite directions. (p. 428)	**línea** Trayectoria recta que se extiende de manera indefinida en direcciones opuestas.	ℓ
line graph A graph that uses line segments to show how data changes. (p. 343)	**gráfica lineal** Gráfica que muestra cómo cambian los datos mediante segmentos de recta.	

ENGLISH	SPANISH	EXAMPLES
line plot A number line with marks or dots that show frequency. (p. 335)	**diagrama de acumulación** Recta numérica con marcas o puntos que indican la frecuencia.	 x x x x x x x x x 0 1 2 3 4 Number of pets
line segment A part of a line between two endpoints. (p. 429)	**segmento de recta** Parte de una línea con dos extremos.	A ●——————————● B
linear equation An equation whose solutions form a straight line on a coordinate plane. (p. 109)	**ecuación lineal** Ecuación cuyas soluciones forman una línea recta en un plano cartesiano.	$y = 2x + 1$

M

ENGLISH	SPANISH	EXAMPLES
mean The sum of the items in a set of data divided by the number of items in the set; also called *average*. (p. 331)	**media** La suma de todos los elementos de un conjunto de datos dividida entre el número de elementos del conjunto. También se llama *promedio*.	Data set: 4, 6, 7, 8, 10 Mean: $\frac{4 + 6 + 7 + 8 + 10}{5} = \frac{35}{5} = 7$
median The middle number, or the mean (average) of the two middle numbers, in an ordered set of data. (p. 332)	**mediana** El número intermedio, o la media (el promedio), de los dos números intermedios en un conjunto ordenado de datos.	Data set: 4, 6, 7, 8, 10 Median: 7
metric system of measurement A decimal system of weights and measures that is used universally in science and commonly throughout the world. (p. 210)	**sistema métrico de medición** Sistema decimal de pesos y medidas empleado universalmente en las ciencias y comúnmente en todo el mundo.	centimeters, meters, kilometers, grams, kilograms, milliliters, liters
mixed number A number made up of a whole number that is not zero and a fraction. (p. 143)	**número mixto** Número compuesto por un número cabal distinto de cero y una fracción.	$5\frac{1}{8}$
mode The number or numbers that occur most frequently in a set of data; when all numbers occur with the same frequency, we say there is no mode. (p. 332)	**moda** Número o números más frecuentes en un conjunto de datos; si todos los números aparecen con la misma frecuencia, no hay moda.	Data set: 3, 5, 8, 8, 10 Mode: 8
multiple The product of any number and any nonzero whole number is a multiple of that number. (p. 136)	**múltiplo** El producto de un número y cualquier número cabal distinto de cero es un múltiplo de ese número.	30, 40, and 90 are all multiples of 10.
Multiplication Property of Equality The property that states that if you multiply both sides of an equation by the same number, the new equation will have the same solution. (p. 51)	**Propiedad de igualdad de la multiplicación** Propiedad que establece que puedes multiplicar ambos lados de una ecuación por el mismo número y la nueva ecuación tendrá la misma solución.	$\frac{1}{3}x = 7$ $(3)(\frac{1}{3}x) = (3)(7)$ $x = 21$

| | ENGLISH | SPANISH | EXAMPLES |

ENGLISH	SPANISH	EXAMPLES
Multiplication Property of Zero The property that states that for all real numbers a, $a \times 0 = 0$ and $0 \times a = 0$.	**Propiedad de multiplicación del cero** Propiedad que establece que para todos los números reales a, $a \times 0 = 0$ y $0 \times a = 0$.	$6 \cdot 0 = 0$ $-5 \cdot 0 = 0$
multiplicative inverse One of two numbers whose product is 1; also called *reciprocal*. (p. 192)	**inverso multiplicativo** Uno de dos números cuyo producto es 1; también llamado *recíproco*.	The multiplicative inverse of $\frac{3}{4}$ is $\frac{4}{3}$.

N

negative integer An integer less than zero. (p. 70)	**entero negativo** Entero menor que cero.	-2 is a negative integer.
net An arrangement of two-dimensional figures that can be folded to form a three-dimensional figure. (p. 534)	**plantilla** Arreglo de figuras bidimensionales que se doblan para formar una figura tridimensional.	10 m, 6 m, 10 m, 6 m
numerator The top number of a fraction that tells how many parts of a whole are being considered. (p. SB7)	**numerador** El número de arriba de una fracción; indica cuántas partes de un entero se consideran.	$\frac{4}{5}$ ← numerator
numerical expression An expression that contains only numbers and operations. (p. 14)	**expresión numérica** Expresión que incluye sólo números y operaciones.	$(2 \cdot 3) + 1$

O

obtuse angle An angle whose measure is greater than 90° but less than 180°. (p. 433)	**ángulo obtuso** Ángulo que mide más de 90° y menos de 180°.	
obtuse triangle A triangle containing one obtuse angle. (p. 452)	**triángulo obtusángulo** Triángulo que tiene un ángulo obtuso.	
octagon An eight-sided polygon. (p. 449)	**octágono** Polígono de ocho lados.	
odd number An integer that is not divisible by two. (p. 379)	**número impar** Entero que no es divisible entre 2.	

Glossary/Glosario

ENGLISH	SPANISH	EXAMPLES
opposites Two numbers that are an equal distance from zero on a number line; also called *additive inverse*. (p. 70)	**opuestos** Dos números que están a la misma distancia de cero en una recta numérica. También se llaman *inversos aditivos*.	5 and −5 are opposites.
order of operations A rule for evaluating expressions: first perform the operations in parentheses, then compute powers, then perform all multiplication and division from left to right, and then perform all addition and subtraction from left to right. (p. 14)	**orden de las operaciones** Regla para evaluar expresiones: primero se hacen las operaciones entre paréntesis, luego se hallan las potencias, después todas las multiplicaciones y divisiones de izquierda a derecha y, por último, todas las sumas y restas de izquierda a derecha.	$3^2 - 12 \div 4$ $9 - 12 \div 4$ Evaluate the power. $9 - 3$ Divide. 6 Subtract.
ordered pair A pair of numbers that can be used to locate a point on a coordinate plane. (p. 100)	**par ordenado** Par de números que sirven para ubicar un punto en un plano cartesiano.	The coordinates of *B* are (−2, 3).
origin The point where the *x*-axis and *y*-axis intersect on the coordinate plane; (0, 0). (p. 100)	**origen** Punto de intersección entre el eje *x* y el eje *y* en un plano cartesiano: (0, 0).	
outcome A possible result of a probability experiment. (p. 382)	**resultado** Posible resultado de un experimento de probabilidad.	When rolling a number cube, the possible outcomes are 1, 2, 3, 4, 5, and 6.
outlier A value much greater or much less than the others in a data set. (p. 335)	**valor extremo** Un valor mucho mayor o menor que los demás de un conjunto de datos.	

P

ENGLISH	SPANISH	EXAMPLES
parallel lines Lines in a plane that do not intersect. (p. 444)	**líneas paralelas** Líneas que se encuentran en el mismo plano pero que nunca se intersecan.	
parallelogram A quadrilateral with two pairs of parallel sides. (p. 462)	**paralelogramo** Cuadrilátero con dos pares de lados paralelos.	
pentagon A five-sided polygon. (p. 449)	**pentágono** Polígono de cinco lados.	

G16 *Glossary/Glosario*

ENGLISH	SPANISH	EXAMPLES
percent A ratio comparing a number to 100. (p. 286)	**porcentaje** Razón que compara un número con el número 100.	$45\% = \frac{45}{100}$
percent of change The amount stated as a percent that a number increases or decreases. (p. 308)	**porcentaje de cambio** Cantidad en que un número aumenta o disminuye, expresada como un porcentaje.	
percent of decrease A percent change describing a decrease in a quantity. (p. 308)	**porcentaje de disminución** Porcentaje de cambio en que una cantidad disminuye.	An item that costs $8 is marked down to $6. The amount of the decrease is $2, and the percent of decrease is $\frac{2}{8} = 0.25 = 25\%$.
percent of increase A percent change describing an increase in a quantity. (p. 308)	**porcentaje de incremento** Porcentaje de cambio en que una cantidad aumenta.	The price of an item increases from $8 to $12. The amount of the increase is $4, and the percent of increase is $\frac{4}{8} = 0.5 = 50\%$.
perimeter The sum of the lengths of the sides of a polygon. (p. 486)	**perímetro** La suma de las longitudes de los lados de un polígono.	18 ft / 6 ft / perimeter = 18 + 6 + 18 + 6 = 48 ft
perpendicular lines Lines that intersect to form right angles. (p. SB14)	**líneas perpendiculares** Líneas que al intersecarse forman ángulos rectos.	n / m
pi (π) The ratio of the circumference of a circle to the length of its diameter; $\pi \approx 3.14$ or $\frac{22}{7}$. (p. 492)	**pi (π)** Razón de la circunferencia de un círculo a la longitud de su diámetro; $\pi \approx 3.14$ ó $\frac{22}{7}$.	
plane A flat surface that extends forever. (p. 428)	**plano** Superficie plana que se extiende de manera indefinida en todas direcciones.	A • C • / B • / plane *ABC*
point An exact location in space. (p. 428)	**punto** Ubicación exacta en el espacio.	*P* • / point *P*
polygon A closed plane figure formed by three or more line segments (sides). Each side meets exactly two other sides, one on each end, in a common endpoint (vertex). (p. 448)	**polígono** Figura plana cerrada formada por tres o más segmentos de recta (lados). Cada lado se cruza únicamente con otros dos lados, uno en cada extremo, en un extremo común (vértice).	
polyhedron A three-dimensional figure in which all the surfaces or faces are polygons. (p. 518)	**poliedro** Figura tridimensional cuyas superficies o caras tienen forma de polígonos.	

ENGLISH	SPANISH	EXAMPLES
population The entire group of objects or individuals considered for a survey. (p. 354)	**población** Grupo completo de objetos o individuos que se desea estudiar.	In a survey about the study habits of middle school students, the population is all middle school students.
positive integer An integer greater than zero. (p. 70)	**entero positivo** Entero mayor que cero.	
power A number produced by raising a base to an exponent. (p. 10)	**potencia** Número que resulta al elevar una base a un exponente.	$2^3 = 8$, so 2 to the 3rd power is 8.
prediction A guess about something that will happen in the future. (p. 410)	**predicción** Pronóstico sobre algo que puede ocurrir en el futuro.	
prime factorization A number written as the product of its prime factors. (p. 128)	**factorización prima** Un número escrito como el producto de sus factores primos.	$10 = 2 \cdot 5$ $24 = 2^3 \cdot 3$
prime number A whole number greater than 1 that has exactly two positive factors, itself and 1. (p. 128)	**número primo** Número cabal mayor que 1 que tiene dos factores positivos: 1 y él mismo.	5 is prime because its only positive factors are 5 and 1.
principal The initial amount of money borrowed or saved. (p. 312)	**capital** Cantidad inicial de dinero depositada o recibida en préstamo.	
prism A three-dimensional figure with two congruent parallel polygonal bases. The remaining edges join corresponding vertices of the bases so that the remaining faces are rectangles. (p. 516)	**prisma** Figura tridimensional con dos bases poligonales congruentes y paralelas. El resto de las aristas se unen a los vértices correspondientes de las bases de manera que el resto de las caras sean rectángulos.	
probability A number from 0 to 1 (or 0% to 100%) that describes how likely an event is to occur. (p. 382)	**probabilidad** Un número entre 0 y 1 (ó 0% y 100%) que describe qué tan probable es un suceso.	A bag contains 3 red marbles and 4 blue marbles. The probability of randomly choosing a red marble is $\frac{3}{7}$.
product The result when two or more numbers are multiplied. (p. 28)	**producto** Resultado de multiplicar dos o más números.	The product of 4 and 8 is 32.
proportion An equation that states that two ratios are equivalent. (p. 240)	**proporción** Ecuación que establece que dos razones son equivalentes.	$\frac{2}{3} = \frac{4}{6}$
protractor A tool for measuring angles. (p. 432)	**transportador** Instrumento para medir ángulos.	
pyramid A three-dimensional figure with a polygonal base lying in one plane plus one additional vertex not lying on that plane. The remaining edges of the pyramid join the additional vertex to the vertices of the base. (p. 518)	**pirámide** Figura tridimensional con una base poligonal en un plano más un vértice adicional que no está en ese plano. El resto de las aristas de la pirámide unen el vértice adicional con los vértices de la base.	

ENGLISH	SPANISH	EXAMPLES

Q

quadrant The *x*- and *y*-axes divide the coordinate plane into four regions. Each region is called a quadrant. (p. 100)

cuadrante El eje *x* y el eje *y* dividen el plano cartesiano en cuatro regiones. Cada región recibe el nombre de cuadrante.

quadrilateral A four-sided polygon. (p. 449)

cuadrilátero Polígono de cuatro lados.

quotient The result when one number is divided by another. (p. 28)

cociente Resultado de dividir un número entre otro.

In $8 \div 4 = 2$, 2 is the quotient.

R

radius A line segment with one endpoint at the center of a circle and the other endpoint on the circle, or the length of that segment. (p. 492)

radio Segmento de recta con un extremo en el centro de un círculo y el otro en la circunferencia; o bien a la longitud de ese segmento.

Radius

random sample A sample in which each individual or object in the entire population has an equal chance of being selected. (p. 354)

muestra aleatoria Muestra en la que cada individuo u objeto de la población tiene la misma oportunidad de ser elegido.

Mr. Henson chose a random sample of the class by writing each student's name on a slip of paper, mixing up the slips, and drawing five slips without looking.

range (in statistics) The difference between the greatest and least values in a data set. (p. 332)

rango (en estadística) Diferencia entre los valores máximo y mínimo de un conjunto de datos.

Data set: 3, 5, 7, 7, 12
Range: $12 - 3 = 9$

rate A ratio that compares two quantities measured in different units. (p. 236)

tasa Una razón que compara dos cantidades medidas en diferentes unidades.

The speed limit is 55 miles per hour, or 55 mi/h.

rate of interest The percent charged or earned on an amount of money; see *simple interest*. (p. 312)

tasa de interés Porcentaje que se cobra por una cantidad de dinero prestada o que se gana por una cantidad de dinero ahorrada; ver *interés simple*.

ratio A comparison of two numbers or quantities. (p. 232)

razón Comparación de dos números o cantidades.

12 to 25, 12:25, $\frac{12}{25}$

ENGLISH	SPANISH	EXAMPLES
rational number A number that can be written in the form $\frac{a}{b}$, where a and b are integers and $b \neq 0$. (p. 151)	**número racional** Número que se puede expresar como $\frac{a}{b}$, donde a y b son números enteros y $b \neq 0$.	6 can be expressed as $\frac{6}{1}$. 0.5 can be expressed as $\frac{1}{2}$.
ray A part of a line that starts at one endpoint and extends forever. (p. 429)	**rayo** Parte de una línea que comienza en un extremo y se extiende de manera indefinida.	
reciprocal One of two numbers whose product is 1; also called *multiplicative inverse.* (p. 192)	**recíproco** Uno de dos números cuyo producto es igual a 1. También se llama *inverso multiplicativo.*	The reciprocal of $\frac{2}{3}$ is $\frac{3}{2}$.
rectangle A parallelogram with four right angles. (p. 462)	**rectángulo** Paralelogramo con cuatro ángulos rectos.	
rectangular prism A three-dimensional figure that has three pairs of opposite parallel congruent faces that are rectangles. (p. 517)	**prisma rectangular** Figura tridimensional que tiene tres pares de caras opuestas, paralelas y congruentes que son rectángulos.	
regular polygon A polygon in which all angles are congruent and all sides are congruent. (p. 449)	**polígono regular** Polígono en el que todos los ángulos y todos los lados son congruentes.	
repeating decimal A rational number in decimal form in which a group of one or more digits (where all digits are not zero) repeat infinitely. (p. 146)	**decimal periódico** Número racional en forma decimal en el que un grupo de uno o más dígitos (donde todos los dígitos son distintos de cero) se repiten infinitamente.	$0.757575\ldots = 0.\overline{75}$
rhombus A parallelogram with all sides congruent. (p. 462)	**rombo** Paralelogramo en el que todos los lados son congruentes.	
right angle An angle that measures 90°. (p. 433)	**ángulo recto** Ángulo que mide exactamente 90°.	
right triangle A triangle containing a right angle. (p. 452)	**triángulo rectángulo** Triángulo que tiene un ángulo recto.	
rounding Replacing a number with an estimate of that number to a given place value. (p. SB3)	**redondear** Sustituir un número por una estimación de ese número hasta cierto valor posicional.	2,354 rounded to the nearest thousand is 2,000, and 2,354 rounded to the nearest 100 is 2,400.

S

ENGLISH	SPANISH	EXAMPLES
sales tax A percent of the cost of an item, which is charged by governments to raise money. (p. 303)	**impuesto sobre la venta** Porcentaje del costo de un artículo que los gobiernos cobran para recaudar fondos.	
sample A part of the population. (p. 354)	**muestra** Una parte de la población.	
sample space All possible outcomes of an experiment. (p. 394)	**espacio muestral** Conjunto de todos los resultados posibles de un experimento.	When rolling a number cube, the sample space is 1, 2, 3, 4, 5, 6.
scale The ratio between two sets of measurements. (p. 266)	**escala** La razón entre dos conjuntos de medidas.	1 cm:5 mi
scale drawing A drawing that uses a scale to make an object smaller than or larger than the real object. (p. 266)	**dibujo a escala** Dibujo en el que se usa una escala para que un objeto se vea mayor o menor que el objeto real al que representa.	
scale factor The ratio used to enlarge or reduce similar figures. (p. 266)	**factor de escala** Razón que se usa para agrandar o reducir figuras semejantes.	
scale model A proportional model of a three-dimensional object. (p. 266)	**modelo a escala** Modelo proporcional de un objeto tridimensional.	
scalene triangle A triangle with no congruent sides. (p. 452)	**triángulo escaleno** Triángulo que no tiene lados congruentes.	
sector (data) A section of a circle graph representing part of the data set. (p. 342)	**sector (datos)** Sección de una gráfica circular que representa una parte del conjunto de datos.	
segment A part of a line between two endpoints. (p. 429)	**segmento** Parte de una línea entre dos extremos.	
self-selected sample A sample made up of members of the population who volunteer to respond to a survey. (p. 358)	**muestra auto-seleccionada** Muestra formada por miembros de la población que se ofrecen para responder a una encuesta.	
side One of the segments that form a polygon. (p. 448)	**lado** Uno de los segmentos que forman un polígono.	

ENGLISH	SPANISH	EXAMPLES
Side-Side-Side (SSS) A rule stating that if three sides of one triangle are congruent to three sides of another triangle, then the triangles are congruent. (p. 466)	**Lado-Lado-Lado (LLL)** Regla que establece que dos triángulos son congruentes cuando sus tres lados correspondientes son congruentes.	$\triangle ABC \cong \triangle DEF$
similar Figures with the same shape but not necessarily the same size are similar. (p. 258)	**semejantes** Figuras que tienen la misma forma, pero no necesariamente el mismo tamaño.	
simple interest A fixed percent of the principal. It is found using the formula $I = Prt$, where P represents the principal, r the rate of interest, and t the time. (p. 312)	**interés simple** Un porcentaje fijo del capital. Se calcula con la fórmula $I = Cit$, donde C representa el capital, i, la tasa de interés y t, el tiempo.	\$100 is put into an account with a simple interest rate of 5%. After 2 years, the account will have earned $I = 100 \cdot 0.05 \cdot 2 = \$10$.
simplest form A fraction is in simplest form when the numerator and denominator have no common factors other than 1. (p. 142)	**mínima expresión** Una fracción está en su mínima expresión cuando el numerador y el denominador no tienen más factor común que 1.	Fraction: $\frac{8}{12}$ Simplest form: $\frac{2}{3}$
simplify To write a fraction or expression in simplest form. (p. 14)	**simplificar** Escribir una fracción o expresión numérica en su mínima expresión.	
solid figure A three-dimensional figure. (p. 518)	**cuerpo geométrico** Figura tridimensional.	
solution (of an equation) A value or values that make an equation true. (p. 34)	**solución (de una ecuación)** Valor o valores que hacen verdadera una ecuación.	Equation: $x + 2 = 6$ Solution: $x = 4$
solution (of an inequality) A value or values that make an inequality true. (p. 572)	**solución (de una desigualdad)** Valor o valores que hacen verdadera una desigualdad.	Inequality: $x + 3 \geq 10$ Solution: $x \geq 7$
solution set The set of values that make a statement true. (p. 572)	**conjunto solución** Conjunto de valores que hacen verdadero un enunciado.	Inequality: $x + 3 \geq 5$ Solution set: $x \geq 2$
solve To find an answer or a solution. (p. 38)	**resolver** Hallar una respuesta o solución.	
square (geometry) A rectangle with four congruent sides. (p. 462)	**cuadrado (en geometría)** Rectángulo con cuatro lados congruentes.	
square (numeration) A number raised to the second power. (p. 10)	**cuadrado (en numeración)** Número elevado a la segunda potencia.	In 5^2, the number 5 is squared.

ENGLISH	SPANISH	EXAMPLES
standard form (in numeration) A way to write numbers by using digits. (p. SB2)	**forma estándar (en numeración)** Una manera de escribir números por medio de dígitos.	Five thousand, two hundred ten in standard form is 5,210.
straight angle An angle that measures 180°. (p. 433)	**ángulo llano** Ángulo que mide exactamente 180°.	
substitute To replace a variable with a number or another expression in an algebraic expression. (p. 24)	**sustituir** Reemplazar una variable por un número u otra expresión en una expresión algebraica.	
Subtraction Property of Equality The property that states that if you subtract the same number from both sides of an equation, the new equation will have the same solution. (p. 40)	**Propiedad de igualdad de la resta** Propiedad que establece que puedes restar el mismo número de ambos lados de una ecuación y la nueva ecuación tendrá la misma solución.	$x + 6 = 8$ $-6 \quad -6$ $x = 2$
sum The result when two or more numbers are added. (p. 28)	**suma** Resultado de sumar dos o más números.	The sum of $6 + 7 + 1$ is 14.
supplementary angles Two angles whose measures have a sum of 180°. (p. 437)	**ángulos suplementarios** Dos ángulos cuyas medidas suman 180°.	$30°$ $150°$
surface area The sum of the areas of the faces, or surfaces, of a three-dimensional figure. (p. 534)	**área total** Suma de las áreas de las caras, o superficies, de una figura tridimensional.	
systematic sample A sample based on selecting one member of the population at random and then selecting other members by using a pattern. (p. 358)	**muestra sistemática** Muestra en la que se elige a un miembro de la población al azar y luego se elige a otros miembros mediante un patrón.	Mr. Henson chose a systematic sample of the customers visiting a grocery store in one day by selecting one of the first 10 customers at random and then selecting every tenth customer after that.

T

term (in an expression) The parts of an expression that are added or subtracted. (p. 558)	**término (en una expresión)** Las partes de una expresión que se suman o se restan.	$3x^2 + 6x - 8$ Term Term Term
terminating decimal A decimal number that ends or terminates. (p. 146)	**decimal finito** Decimal con un número determinado de posiciones decimales.	6.75
theoretical probability The ratio of the number of equally likely outcomes in an event to the total number of possible outcomes. (p. 390)	**probabilidad teórica** Razón del número de resultados igualmente probables en un suceso al número total de resultados posibles.	When rolling a number cube, the theoretical probability of rolling a 4 is $\frac{1}{6}$.

ENGLISH	SPANISH	EXAMPLES
transversal A line that intersects two or more lines. (p. 444)	**transversal** Línea que cruza dos o más líneas.	
trapezoid A quadrilateral with exactly one pair of parallel sides. (p. 462)	**trapecio** Cuadrilátero con un par de lados paralelos.	
tree diagram A branching diagram that shows all possible outcomes of an event. (p. 395)	**diagrama de árbol** Diagrama ramificado que muestra todas las posibles resultados de un suceso.	
trial In probability, a single repetition or observation of an experiment. (p. 382)	**prueba** En probabilidad, una sola repetición u observación de un experimento.	When rolling a number cube, each roll is one trial.
triangle A three-sided polygon. (p. 449)	**triángulo** Polígono de tres lados.	
Triangle Sum Theorem The theorem that states that the measures of the angles in a triangle add to 180°. (p. 459)	**Teorema de la suma del triángulo** Teorema que establece que las medidas de los ángulos de un triángulo suman 180°.	
triangular prism A three-dimensional figure with two congruent parallel triangular bases and whose other faces are rectangles. (p. 524)	**prisma triangular** Figura tridimensional con dos bases triangulares congruentes y paralelas cuyas otras caras son rectángulos.	

U

unit conversion The process of changing one unit of measure to another. (p. 211)	**conversión de unidades** Proceso que consiste en cambiar una unidad de medida por otra.	
unit price A unit rate used to compare prices. (p. 237)	**precio unitario** Tasa unitaria que sirve para comparar precios.	
unit rate A rate in which the second quantity in the comparison is one unit. (p. 236)	**tasa unitaria** Una tasa en la que la segunda cantidad de la comparación es la unidad.	10 cm per minute

V

variable A symbol used to represent a quantity that can change. (p. 24)	**variable** Símbolo que representa una cantidad que puede cambiar.	In the expression $2x + 3$, x is the variable.

ENGLISH	SPANISH	EXAMPLES
verbal expression A word or phrase. (p. 28)	**expresión verbal** Palabra o frase.	
vertex (of an angle) The common endpoint of the sides of the angle. (p. 432)	**vértice de un ángulo** Extremo común de los lados del ángulo.	A is the vertex of $\angle CAB$.
vertex (of a polygon) The intersection of two sides of the polygon. (p. 448)	**vértice (de un polígono)** La intersección de dos lados del polígono.	
vertex (of a polyhedron) A point at which three or more edges of a polyhedron intersect. (p. 518)	**vértice (de un poliedro)** Un punto en el que se intersecan tres o más aristas de un poliedro.	Vertex
vertical angles A pair of angles that are formed by two intersecting lines and are not adjacent. (p. 436)	**ángulos opuestos por el vértice** Par de ángulos no adyacentes formados por dos líneas secantes.	$\angle 1$ and $\angle 3$ are vertical angles. $\angle 2$ and $\angle 4$ are vertical angles.
volume The number of cubic units needed to fill a given space. (p. 524)	**volumen** Número de unidades cúbicas que se necesitan para llenar un espacio.	

X

x-axis The horizontal axis on a coordinate plane. (p. 100)	**eje x** El eje horizontal del plano cartesiano.	
x-coordinate The first number in an ordered pair; it tells the distance to move right or left from the origin, (0, 0). (p. 100)	**coordenada x** El primer número en un par ordenado; indica la distancia que debes avanzar hacia la izquierda o hacia la derecha desde el origen, (0, 0).	The x-coordinate of the point located at $(-2, -3)$ is -2.

Y

y-axis The vertical axis on a coordinate plane. (p. 100)	**eje y** El eje vertical del plano cartesiano.	
y-coordinate The second number in an ordered pair; it tells the distance to move up or down from the origin, (0, 0). (p. 100)	**coordenada y** El segundo número de un par ordenado; indica la distancia que debes avanzar hacia arriba o hacia abajo desde el origen, (0, 0).	The y-coordinate of the point located at $(-2, -3)$ is -3.

Index

Index (vertical tab)

Index

Credits

Staff Credits

Bruce Albrecht, Tica Chitrarachis, Lorraine Cooper, Marc Cooper, Jennifer Craycraft, Martize Cross, Nina Degollado, Julie Dervin, Michelle Dike, Lydia Doty, Sam Dudgeon, Kelli R. Flanagan, Ronald Fowler, Stephanie Friedman, Jeff Galvez, Pam Garner, Diannia Green, Liz Huckestein, Jevara Jackson, Simon Key, Jane A. Kirschman, Kadonna Knape, Cathy Kuhles, Jill M. Lawson, Liann Lech, Jessika Maier, Virginia Messler, Stacey Murray, Susan Mussey, Kim Nguyen, Manda Reid, Michael Rinella, Annette Saunders, Kay Selke, Robyn Setzen, Patricia Sinnott, Victoria Smith, Dawn Marie Spinozza, Jeannie Taylor, Karen Vigil, Kira J. Watkins, Sherri Whitmarsh, David W. Wynn

Photo Credits

All photos Sam Dudgeon/HRW unless otherwise noted.

Title Page: (Ferris wheel), Ron Niebrugge/Alamy; (turbines), Stock Connection Distribution/Alamy; (otter), Robert E. Barber/Alamy; (poppies), Macduff Everton/CORBIS; (buildings), J. A. Kraulis/Masterfile **Front Matter:** iii (border), PhotoDisc; iv (tl), Courtesy of Charlie Bialowas; iv (cl), Courtesy of Lee Haines; iv (tr), Courtesy of Robin Scarcella; iv (cr), Courtesy of Wendy Taub-Hoglund; ix (border), Photopix/Photonica/Getty Images; x (border), Gordon Wiltsie/National Geographic/Getty Images; xi (border), Craig Aurness/CORBIS; xii (border), Snark/Art Resource, NY; xiii (border), Gilles Mingasson/Liaison/Getty Images; xiv (border), Lester Lefkowitz/CORBIS; xv (border), Gary Bell/zefa/Corbis; xvi (border), Travis Lindquist/Getty Images; xvii (border), Greg Stott/Masterfile; xviii (border), Mike Dobel/Masterfile; xix (border), Tom Servais/Getty Images **Chapter One:** 2–3 (bkgd), Photopix/Photonica/Getty Images; 6 (tr), © Royalty Free/CORBIS; 11 (l), Barrie Rokeach/Alamy; 13 (all), Bruce Iverson; 17 (tr), Sam Dudgeon/HRW; 24 (child), Everett Collection; 24 (teen), Ulvis Alberts/Motion Picture & Television Photo Archive; 24 (adult), Frederic De Lafosse/Sygma/CORBIS; 28 (tr), © David Allan Brandt/Stone/Getty Images; 31 (tl), Photo Researchers, Inc.; 33 (b), PhotoDisc/Getty Images; 35 (br), Brandon D. Cole/CORBIS; 40 (tr), Franklin Jay Viola/Viola's Photo Visions; 43 (tl), Peter Yang/HRW; 44 (tl), Library of Congress; 44 (tr), AP/Wide World Photos; 44 (bkgd), © Royalty-Free/CORBIS; 46 (tl), Mark E. Gibson/CORBIS; 47 (tr), © National Geographic Image Collection/Bianca Lavies; 50 (tr), Darwin Dale/Photo Researchers, Inc.; 51 (c), Eric Kamp/Index Stock Imagery/PictureQuest/Jupiter Images; 51 (tr), Takeshi Takahara/Photo Researchers, Inc.; 55 (tl), © COMSTOCK, Inc.; 55 (b), PhotoDisc/Getty Images; 57 (br), Sam Dudgeon/HRW **Chapter Two:** 66–67 (bkgd), Gordon Wiltsie/National Geographic/Getty Images; 70 (tc), Natalie B. Forbes/National Geographic Image Collection; 70 (tr), Chuck Nicklin/Al Giddings Images, Inc.; 73 (l), © SHOTFILE/Alamy; 76 (tr), © 2008 Jay Mallin; 79 (l), © Lee Foster/Words & Pictures/PictureQuest/Jupiter Images; 85 (t), © CORBIS; 88 (tr), Steve Boyle/NewSport/Corbis; 91 (r), © Ann Purcell; Carl Purcell/Words & Pictures/PictureQuest/Jupiter Images; 99 (b), © David A. Northcott/CORBIS; 108 (tr), Ken Karp/HRW; 111 (tr), Simon Fraser/MRC Unit, Newcastle General Hospital/Science Photo Library/Photo Researchers, Inc.; 115 (tl), Copyright Dorling Kindersley; 115 (b), The Image Bank/Getty Images; 116 (br), Jenny Thomas/HRW; 117 (b), Sam Dudgeon/HRW **Chapter Three:** 124–125 (bkgd), Craig Aurness/CORBIS; 128 (tr), © Declan McCullagh; 132 (tr), Sam Dudgeon/HRW; 133 (tr, c), Victoria Smith/HRW; 135 (tl), Richard Cummins/SuperStock; 136 (tr), © Royalty Free/CORBIS; 139 (t), © D. Donne Bryant/DDB Stock Photo/All Rights Reserved; 139 (c), Erich Lessing/Art Resource, NY; 141 (b), Lisette LeBon/SuperStock; 145 (l), Michael Rosenfeld/Stone/Getty Images; 146 (tr), © Tim Johnson/Reuters/CORBIS; 149 (t), Image Copyright © Digital Vision; 149 (c), © Underwood & Underwood/CORBIS; 153 (l), © Buddy Mays/CORBIS; 156 (br), © Jenny Thomas/HRW; 157 (br), Sam Dudgeon/HRW **Chapter Four:** 166–167 (bkgd), Snark/Art Resource, NY; 170 (tr), Iconotec; 179 (l), © Gallo Images/CORBIS; 179 (r), G.K. & Vikki Hart/Getty Images; 180 (tr), Dorling Kindersley/Getty Images; 180 (tc), Botanica/Jupiter Images; 183 (l), © Michael John Kielty/CORBIS; 185 (b), © Michael T. Sedam/CORBIS; 188 (tr), © Glen Allison/Alamy Photos; 195 (tr), Victoria Smith/HRW; 195 (tc), Richard Heinzen/SuperStock; 196 (t), Peter Van Steen/HRW/Courtesy Russell Korman Fine Jewelry, Austin, TX; 199 (l), CORBIS; 201 (bl), © Tom Brakefield/CORBIS; 209 (tr), © Galen Rowell/CORBIS; 213 (l), National Geographic/Getty Images; 214 (tr), Sam Dudgeon/HRW; 217 (l), © Gail

Mooney/CORBIS; 219 (b), Jill Kelly; 220 (b), Ken Karp/HRW; 221 (br), Sam Dudgeon/HRW **Chapter Five:** 228–229 (bkgd), Gilles Mingasson/Liaison/Getty Images; 232 (tr), Darren Caroll/HRW; 235 (c), © Chris Mellor/Lonely Planet Images; 235 (t), © Gavin Anderson/Lonely Planet Images; 240 (tr), Victoria Smith/HRW; 243 (cr), © Lynda Richardson/Corbis; 245 (l), © Tim de Waele/Corbis; 249 (tr), Gerald Hoberman/The Hoberman Collection; 252 (l), AP Photo/Paul Sakuma; 255 (b), Sam Dudgeon/HRW; 262 (t), © Francis E. Caldwell/Affordable Photo Stock; 266 (t), Sam Dudgeon/HRW/Courtesy Chuck and Nan Ellis; 267 (tr), Van Gogh Museum, Amsterdam/SuperStock; 269 (tr), Library of Congress; 269 (c), Library of Congress; 269 (tc), Victoria Smith/HRW; 269 (b-frame), © 1999 Image Farm Inc.; 272 (b), Randall Hyman/HRW; 273 (br), Sam Dudgeon/HRW; 273 (br), Sam Dudgeon/HRW **Chapter Six:** 282–283 (bkgd), Lester Lefkowitz/CORBIS; 286 (tr), © Louie Psihoyos/Corbis; 292 (tr), Peter Van Steen/HRW; 299 (b), Victoria Smith/HRW; 301 (l), Lawrence Migdale/Photo Researchers, Inc.; 302 (tr), © Buddy Mays/CORBIS; 305 (l), © Ellen Senisi/The Image Works; 307 (b), © 1998 Joseph De Sciose; 308 (tr), Sam Dudgeon/HRW; 317 (tl), © Hemera Technologies/Alamy; 317 (br), Getty Images/Taxi; 318 (b), Randall Hyman/HRW; 319 (all), Sam Dudgeon/HRW **Chapter Seven:** 326–327 (bkgd), Gary Bell/zefa/Corbis; 331 (tr), Jenny Thomas Photography/HRW; 334 (r), Stockdisc Classic/Alamy; 335 (tr), © Trent Nelson/The Salt Lake Tribune/CORBIS Sygma; 336 (l), David Cardinal/San Francisco Zoo; 338 (tr), NASA/Science Photo Library/Photo Researchers, Inc.; 339 (tr), Myrleen Ferguson Cate/PhotoEdit; 353 (b), © Stephen Frink/Index Stock Imagery/PictureQuest/Jupiter Images; 354 (tr), © Randy M. Ury/CORBIS; 357 (tl), Richard Cummins/SuperStock; 358 (tr), David Young-Wolff/Alamy; 367 (br), © Richard Hutchings/PhotoEdit; 367 (tl), Sam Dudgeon/HRW; 367 (bc), © Thinkstock/Alamy; 369 (b), Sam Dudgeon/HRW **Chapter Eight:** 378–379 (bkgd), Travis Lindquist/Getty Images; 385 (tl), Richard Herrmann/Oxford Scientific/Jupiter Images; 386 (tr), © V. C. L. Tipp Howell/Getty Images/Taxi; 389 (cr), REUTERS/Gary Wiepert/NewsCom; 389 (tr), Courtesy of National Weather Service, NOAA; 394 (tr), © Royalty Free/CORBIS; 397 (tl), © Tom & Dee Ann McCarthy/Corbis; 399 (br), Sam Dudgeon/HRW; 400 (br), PhotoDisc/Getty Images; 400 (bc), Peter Van Steen/HRW; 401 (cr), © Left Lane Productions/CORBIS; 410 (tr), Jack Hollingsworth/PhotoDisc/age fotostock; 413 (tr), © Jeff Curtes/CORBIS; 413 (cl), Yvette Cardozo/Index Stock Imagery/PictureQuest; 413 (tc), © Richard T. Nowitz/CORBIS; 413 (cr), © Reuters NewMedia Inc./CORBIS; 415 (t), Stockdisc/Superstock; 415 (b), Gail Mooney/Masterfile; 416 (b), Ken Karp/HRW; 417 (b), Sam Dudgeon/HRW **Chapter Nine:** 424–425 (bkgd), Greg Stott/Masterfile; 428 (tr), The Art Archive/Private Collection/Harper Collins Publishers/© 2004 Artists Rights Society (ARS), New York/ADAGP, Paris; 430 (br), Science Kit & Boreal Laboratories; 431 (tr), Diana Ong/SuperStock; 431 (cr), Copyright Tate Gallery, London, Great Britain/Art Resource, NY/© 2004 Artist Rights Society (ARS), New York/Pro Litteris, Zurich; 432 (tr), Courtesy of Icon Health Fitness; 436 (c), © Michael Kelley/Getty Images/Stone; 436 (b), © TempSport/CORBIS; 438 (tl), Peter Van Steen/HRW; 438 (tr), Peter Van Steen/HRW; 438 (cl), Werner Forman Archive/Piers Morris Collection/Art Resource, NY; 438 (cr), P. W. Grace/Photo Researchers, Inc.; 438 (tc), Peter Van Steen/HRW; 439 (cl), John Wang/PhotoDisc/Getty Images; 439 (tr), Joseph Sohm; Visions of America/CORBIS; 440 (tr), Lawrence Migdale/Photo Researchers, Inc.; 442 (c), alwaysstock, LLC/Alamy; 447 (b), © Michael Boys/CORBIS; 448 (tr), © Gianni Dagh Orti/CORBIS; 451 (t), John Warden/SuperStock; 451 (c), © Roman Soumar/CORBIS; 451 (b), © Jacqui Hurst/CORBIS; 452 (tr), Mark Schneider/Visuals Unlimited/Getty Images; 455 (l), © Craig Aurness/CORBIS; 468 (tl), Peter Van Steen/HRW; 468 (bl), Peter Van Steen/HRW/Courtesy International Playthings, Inc.; 468 (tc), Sam Dudgeon/HRW; 468 (bc, tc), Sam Dudgeon/HRW; 468 (br), © Mark Snyder, TetraLite Kites, Seattle, WA; 473 (bl), Sam Dudgeon/HRW; 473 (br), Sam Dudgeon/HRW **Chapter Ten:** 482–483 (all), Mike Dobel/Masterfile; 486 (tr), Courtesy of Sigma Tau Pharmaceuticals, Inc.; 486 (b), Victoria Smith/HRW; 488 (br), PhotoDisc/Getty Images; 488 (cr), Artville/Getty Images; 495 (tl), Mark McKeown/The Paris News/AP/Wide World Photos; 498 (t), © Nik Wheeler/CORBIS; 500 (cr), Christian Pierre /SuperStock; 500 (frame), © 1998 Image Farm Inc.; 507 (l), © Carl & Ann Purcell; 509 (t), © Stefan Schott/Panoramic Images, Chicago 1998; 515 (bl), © Omni Photo Communications Inc./Index Stock Imagery/PictureQuest; 518 (t), With permission from the Isamu Noguchi Foundation Inc., NY © Michael S. Yamashita/CORBIS; 519 (c), Sam Dudgeon/HRW; 519 (b), Sam Dudgeon/HRW; 520 (cl), Barry L. Runk/Grant Heilman Photography; 520 (c), © Charles D. Winters/Photo Researchers, Inc.; 520 (cr), © Charles D. Winters/Photo Researchers, Inc.; 521 (cl), © Richard Cummins/CORBIS; 521 (c), © Joseph Sohm; ChromoSohm Inc./CORBIS; 521 (cr), © Hisham Ibrahim/CORBIS; 524 (c), Sam Dudgeon/HRW; 524 (t), Sam Dudgeon/HRW; 527 (tr), TEK Image/Science Photo Library/Photo Researchers, Inc.;

527 (c), Runk/Schoenberger/Grant Heilman Photography; 527 (br), Charles D. Winters/Photo Researchers, Inc.; 528 (c), U.S. Department of the Interior, National Park Service, Edison National Historic Site; 528 (t), LOC/Science Source/Photo Researchers, Inc.; 534 (tr), Courtesy of California State University, Long Beach; 537 (cr), Peter Van Steen/HRW; 539 (l), NASA; 539 (r), CORBIS; 540 (c), Tim Davis/HRW; 541 (b), Sam Dudgeon/HRW **Chapter Eleven:** 548–549 (bkgd), Tom Servais/Getty Images; 557 (cr), Sam Dudgeon/HRW; 557 (tr), ON PAGE CREDIT; 558 (tr), Digital Vision/GettyImages; 561 (tl), Courtesy of the National Grocers Association Best Bagger Contest; 566 (tr), Masterfile; 569 (l), Stock Connection/Alamy; 571 (br), Victoria Smith/HRW; 575 (t), U.S. Geological Survey Western Region Coastal and Marine Geology; 575 (c), James Wilson/Woodfin Camp & Associates; 576 (tr), Ambient Images Inc./Alamy; 579 (tl), © Al Grotell 1990; 580 (tr), Spencer Tirey/AP/Wide World Photos; 584 (tr), © Tony Freeman/Photo Edit; 587 (tr, tl, cr), Sam Dudgeon/HRW; 587 (cl), Dr. E. R. Degginger/Color-Pic, Inc.; 589 (tl), © Dinodia Images/Alamy; 589 (b), © Rolf Bruderer/Corbis; 590 (br), Randall Hyman/HRW; 591 (br), Sam Dudgeon/HRW **Back Matter:** 600 (t), Sam Dudgeon/HRW; 601 (b), Gary Russ/HRW

Table of Measures

METRIC

Length

1 kilometer (km) = 1,000 meters (m)

1 meter = 10 decimeters (dm)

1 meter = 100 centimeters (cm)

1 meter = 1,000 millimeters (mm)

1 centimeter = 10 millimeters

Capacity

1 liter (L) = 1,000 milliliters (mL)

Mass and Weight

1 kilogram (kg) = 1,000 grams (g)

1 gram = 1,000 milligrams (mg)

CUSTOMARY

Length

1 mile (mi) = 1,760 yards (yd)

1 mile = 5,280 feet (ft)

1 yard = 3 feet

1 yard = 36 inches (in.)

1 foot = 12 inches

Capacity

1 gallon (gal) = 4 quarts (qt)

1 gallon = 16 cups (c)

1 gallon = 128 fluid ounces (fl oz)

1 quart = 2 pints (pt)

1 quart = 4 cups

1 pint = 2 cups

1 cup = 8 fluid ounces

Mass and Weight

1 ton (T) = 2,000 pounds (lb)

1 pound = 16 ounces (oz)

TIME

1 year (yr) = 365 days

1 year = 12 months (mo)

1 year = 52 weeks (wk)

1 leap year = 366 days

1 week = 7 days

1 day = 24 hours (hr)

1 hour = 60 minutes (min)

1 minute = 60 seconds (s)